John Mitchell

The History of Ireland

From the treaty of Limerick to the present time

John Mitchell

The History of Ireland
From the treaty of Limerick to the present time

ISBN/EAN: 9783742837370

Manufactured in Europe, USA, Canada, Australia, Japa

Cover: Foto ©ninafisch / pixelio.de

Manufactured and distributed by brebook publishing software (www.brebook.com)

John Mitchell

The History of Ireland

THE HISTORY OF IRELAND,

FROM THE

TREATY OF LIMERICK TO THE PRESENT TIME:

BEING

A CONTINUATION

OF THE

HISTORY OF THE ABBÉ MACGEOGHEGAN.

COMPILED BY

JOHN MITCHEL.

VOL. II.

GLASGOW:
CAMERON & FERGUSON, 88 WEST NILE STREET.
LONDON: CHARLES GRIFFIN & CO.

MDCCCLXIX.

NOTE BY THE PUBLISHERS.

Mr Mitchel's Preface not having yet arrived from America, we shall be obliged to issue it with Vol. 2, or supply it afterwards separately.

We have left out, *at Mr Mitchel's request,* an incorrect Index, which is published in other Editions. Mr Mitchel says in his letter to us—"I beg you to omit the Index at the end, which was prepared by some printer, and *is a blemish to the book.* The table of contents and headings of chapters, prepared by myself, are the best and only Index."

CONTENTS.

CHAPTER I.—1798.

Rising in Ulster — Antrim — Saintfield — Ballinahinch — Insurgents Defeated — McCracken and Monro Hanged—Skirmish in Cork County—Courts-martial—Many Executions—Hanging of Father Redmond—Surrender of Fitzgerald and Aylmer—Compact between Prisoners and Government—In order to Save the Lives of Byrne and Bond—Compact Violated by Government—Byrne Hanged—Bond Dies Suddenly in Prison—Reign of Terror in Dublin—Brothers Sheares Tried—Hanged—Other State Trials—Curran in Court—"The Three Majors"—Sirr, Swan, and Sandys—The "Major's People"—John Claudius Beresford—Tortures in Dublin—Country in Wild Alarm—Spiked Heads—Fit Time to Propose Legislative Union—Marquis Cornwallis comes as Viceroy—To bring about the Union—"Impression of Horror"—Apparent Measures to End the Devastations—Offers of "Protection"—Not Efficacious—Testimony of Lord Camden himself—True Account of the "Compact"—United Irishmen sent to Fort-George 13

CHAPTER II.—1798.

Parliament—The Acts of Attainder—French Landing under Humbert—Killala—Conduct of the Little French Army—Ballina—The Races of Castlebar—Panic and Route of the British Force—French give a Ball—Lord Cornwallis Collects a Great Army—Marches to meet the French—Encounters them at Ballinamuck—Defeat and Capture of the French—Recovery of Ballina—Slaughter—Courts-martial, &c. —End of the Insurrections of 1798—New French Expedition—Commodore Bompart—T. W. Tone—Encounter British Fleet at mouth of Lough Swilly—Battle—The *Hoche* Captured—Tone a Prisoner—Recognized by Sir George Hill—Carried to Dublin in Irons—Tried by Court-martial—Condemned to be Hanged—His Address to the Court—Asks as a Favour to be Shot—Refused by Cornwallis—Suicide in Prison.. 27

CHAPTER III.—1798-1799.

Examination of O'Connor, Emmet, and M'Neven—Lord Enniskillen and his Court-martial—Project of Union—Bar Meeting—Speech from the Throne—Union Proposed—Reception in the Lords—In the Commons—Ponsonby—Fitzgerald—Sir Jonah Barrington—Castlereagh's Explanation—Speech of Plunket—First Division on the Union—Majority of One—Mr. Trench and Mr. Fox—Methods of Conversion to Unionism—First Contest a Drawn Battle—Excitement in Dublin..................... 39

CHAPTER IV.—1799.

Second Debate on Union—Sir Lawrence Parsons—Mr. Smith—Ponsonby and Plunket—Division—Majority against Government—Ponsonby's Resolution for Perpetual Independence—Defection of Fortescue and Others—Resolution Lost—"Possible Circumstances"—Tumult—Danger of Lord Clare—Second Debate in the Lords—Lord Clare Triumphant—"Loyalists' Claim Bill"—"Rebels Disqualification Bill"—"Flogging Fitzgerald"—Asks Indemnity—Regency Act—Opposed by Castlereagh... 49

CHAPTER V.—1799.

Union Proposed in British Parliament—Opposed by Sheridan—Supported by Canning—Great Speech of Mr. Pitt—Ireland to be Assured of English Protection—Of English Capital—Promises to the Catholics—Mr. Pitt's Resolutions for Union—Sheridan—Dundas—Resolutions Passed—In the House of Lords—Labours of Cornwallis and Castlereagh—Corruption—Intimidation—Onslaught of Troops in Dublin—Lord Cornwallis makes a Tour—Lord Downshire Disgraced—Handcock of Athlone—His Song and Palinode—Opposition Inorganic—The Orangemen—The Catholics—Arts to Delude them—Dublin Catholics against Union—O'Connell—System of Terror—County Meeting Dispersed by Troops—Castlereagh's Announcement of "Compensation" 55

CHAPTER VI.—1799-1800.

Progress of Union Conspiracy—Grand Scale of Bribery—Castlereagh Organizes "Fighting Men"—Dinner at his House—Last Session of the Irish Parliament—Warm Debate the First Day—Daly Attacks Bushe and Plunket—Reappearance of Grattan—His Speech—Corry Attacks Him—Division—Majority for Government—Castlereagh Proposes "Articles" of Union—His Speech—Promises Great Gain to Ireland from Union—Ireland to "Save a Million a Year"—Proposed Constitution of United Parliament—Irish Peerage—Ponsonby—Grattan—Again a Majority for the Castle—Lord Clare's Famous Speech—Duel of Grattan and Corry—Torpor and Gloom in Dublin—The Catholics—"Articles" finally Adopted—By Commons—By Lords... 64

CHAPTER VII.—1800.

The Union in English Parliament—Opposed by Lord Holland—Mr. Grey—Sheridan—Irish Act for Electors—Distribution of Seats—Castlereagh brings in Bill for the Union—Warm Debates—Union Denounced by Plunket, Bushe, Saurin, Grattan—Their Earnest Language—Last Days of the Parliament—Last Scene—Passes the Lords—The Protesting Peers—The Compensation Act—The King Congratulates the British Parliament—Lord Cornwallis—The Irish—Union to date from January 1, 1801—Irish Debt—History of it 73

CHAPTER VIII.—1800-1803.

The Catholics Duped—Resignation of Pitt—Mystery of this Resignation—First Measure of United Parliament—Suspension of *Habeas Corpus*—Report of Secret Committee—Fate of Lord Clare—Lord Hardwicke, Viceroy—Peace of Amiens—Treaty Violated by England—Malta—War again Declared by England—Mr. Pitt Resumes Office—Coalition against France... 81

CHAPTER IX.—1802-1803.

First Year of the Union—Distress in Ireland—Riot in Dublin—Irish Exiles in France—Renewed Hopes of French Aid—The two Emmets, M'Neven, and O'Connor in France—Apprehensions of Invasion in England—Robert Emmet comes from France to Ireland—His Associates—His Plans—Miles Byrne—Despard's Conspiracy in England—Emmet's Preparations—Explosion in Patrick Street—The 23d of July—Failure—Bloody Riot—Murder of Lord Kilwarden—Emmet sends Miles Byrne to France—Retires to Wicklow—Returns to Dublin—Arrested—Tried—Convicted—Hanged—Fate of Russell 87

CHAPTER X.—1803-1804.

Reason to believe that Government was all the time aware of the Conspiracy—"Striking Terror"—Martial Law—Catholic Address—Arrests—Informers—Vigorous Measures—In Cork—In Belfast—Hundreds of Men Imprisoned without Charge—Brutal Treatment of Prisoners—Special Commission—Eighteen Persons Hung—Debate in Parliament—Irish Exiles in France—First Consul Plans a New Expedition to Ireland—Formation of the "Irish Legion"—Irish Legion in Bretagne—Official Reply of the First Consul to T. A. Emmet—Designs of the French Government—Buonaparte's Mistake—French Fleet again Ordered Elsewhere—The Legion goes to the Rhine and to Walcheren—End of the Addington Ministry—Mr. Pitt Returns to Office—Condition of Ireland—Decay of Dublin—Decline of Trade—Increase of Debt—Ruinous Effects of the Union—Presbyterian Clergy Pensioned, and the Reason... 96

CHAPTER XI.—1804-1805.

Mr. Pitt in Office—Royal Speech—No Mention of Ireland—Alarm about Invasion—Martello Towers—Reliance of the Irish Catholics on Mr. Pitt—Treatment of the Prisoners—Mr. James Tandy—Mr. Pitt Raises a Storm against the Catholics—Catholic Meeting in Dublin—*Habeas Corpus* Act again Suspended—Ireland "Loyal"—Duplicity of Lord Hardwicke—Catholic Deputies go to Mr. Pitt—A "Sincere Friend"—Mr. Pitt Refuses to Present Catholic Petition—Declares he will Resist Emancipation—Lord Grenville and Mr. Fox Present it—Debate in the Lords—In the Commons—Speeches of Fox, Doctor Duigenan, Grattan, Perceval, Pitt, Sir John Newport—Emancipation Refused both by Lords and Commons—Great Majorities............ 102

CHAPTER XII.—1804-1806.

Prosecution of Judge Fox—His Offence : Enforcing Law on Orangemen—Prosecution of Judge Johnson—His Offence : Censuring the Irish Government—Decline of Pitt's Power—Castlereagh Defeated in Down County—Successes of Buonaparte—Cry for Peace—Death of Mr. Pitt—Whig Ministry—Mr. Fox—His Opinion of the Union—First Whisper of "Repeal"—Release of State Prisoners—Dismissal of Lord Redesdale as Chancellor—Duke of Bedford, Viceroy—The Catholics Cheated Again—Equivocation of the Viceroy—Ponsonby—Curran's Promotion—The Armagh Orangemen—Mr. Wilson the Magistrate............ 109

CHAPTER XIII.—1806-1807.

Revenue and Debt of Ireland—Rapid Increase of Debt—Drain of Wealth from Ireland—Character of the Imports and Exports—Rackrents, Tithes, &c.—Distress of the People—The "Threshers"—Threshers Hung—Catholic Meetings—Increase of Maynooth Grant—From Apprehension of the Irish College in France—Catholic Officers' Bill—To Promote Depopulation—Bill Abandoned—Change of Ministry—The King Demands a No-Popery Pledge—Duke of Cumberland—Perceval Administration—Camden and Castlereagh in Office—No-Popery—Recruiting in Ireland—John Keogh on Catholic Officers' Bill—O'Connell—Too Easy Gratitude of the Irish towards Whigs—Populace Draw the Duke of Bedford's Coach 117

CHAPTER XIV.—1807-1808.

Duke of Richmond, Viceroy—Sir A. Wellesley, Secretary—Their System—Depression of Catholics—Insolence of Orangemen—Government Interference in Elections—Ireland Gets a New Insurrection Act—And an Arms Act—Grattan Advocates Coercion Acts—Sheridan Opposes Them—Acts Passed—The Bishop of Quimper—Means Used to Create Exasperation against Catholics—"Shanavests" and "Caravats"—"Church in Danger"—Catholic Petition—Influence of O'Connell—Lord Fingal—Growing Liberality amongst Protestants—Maynooth Grant Curtailed—Doctor Duigenan Privy Councillor—Catholic Petition Presented—The "*Veto*" Offered—Mr. Ponsonby and Mr. Grattan—They Urge the *Veto* as a Security—Petition Rejected—Controversies on the *Veto*—Bishops' Resolutions—No Catholics in Bank of Ireland—Dublin Police 123

CHAPTER XV.—1808-1809.

The Duke of Richmond's Anti-Catholic Policy—The Orangemen Flourish—Their Outrages and Murders—Castlereagh and Perceval Charged with Selling Seats—Corruption—Sir Arthur Wellesley—Tithes—Catholic Committee Reorganized—John Keogh on Petitioning Parliament—O'Connell and the Convention Act—Orangemen also Reorganized—Orange Convention—More Murders by Orangemen—Crooked Policy of the Castle—Defection of the Bandon Orangemen—Success of the Castle Policy in Preventing Union with Irishmen 131

CHAPTER XVI.—1810-1812.

Duke of Richmond's "Conciliation"—Orange Oppression—Treatment of Catholic Soldiers—The *Veto* again—Debate on *Veto* in Parliament—Catholic Petition Presented by Grattan—Rejected—O'Connell's Leadership—New Organization of Catholics—Repeal of the Union First Agitated—Insanity of the King—Treachery of the Regent—Prosecution of the Catholic Committee—Convention Act—Suppression of the Committee—New Measures of O'Connell—Mr. Curran at Newry Election—Effects of the Union............ 137

CHAPTER XVII.—1813-1821.

Grattan's Emancipation Bill—More *Veto*—Quarantotti—Unanimity in Ireland against *Veto*—Mr. Peel and his New Police—Stipendiary Magistrates—Close of the War—Restoration of the Bourbons—Waterloo—Evil Effects on Ireland—The Irish Legion in France—Its Fate—Miles Byrne and his Friends—Effects of the Peace in Impoverishing the Irish—Cheap Ejectment Law Passed—Beginning of Extermination—"Surplus Population"—Catholic Claims Ruined by the Peace—O'Connell and Catholic Board—Board Suppressed—O'Connell in Court—His Audacity—His Scorn of the Dublin Corporation—Duel with D'Esterre—Distress in Ireland—Famine of 1817—Coercion in Ireland—"Six Acts" in England—Mr. Plunket's Emancipation Bill—Peel and the Duke of York—Royal Visit to Ireland—Catholics Cheated again.. 143

CHAPTER XVIII.—1822-1825.

Famine of 1822—Its Causes—Financial Frauds upon Ireland—Horrors of the Famine—Extermination—Suspension of *Habeas Corpus* Act—Castlereagh Cuts his Throat—Marquis Wellesley, Viceroy—Sir Harcourt Lees—The Bottle Riot—Catholic Association Formed—Dr. Doyle; "J. K. L."—Progress of Catholic Association—"Catholic Rent"—Maynooth Professors "Loyal"—Rage of the Orangemen—"O'Connell, the Pope, and the Devil"—Passiveness of the Dissenters—O'Connell's Appeals to Them—Intellectual and Literary Power of the Movement—Act to Suppress "Unlawful Associations"—First Attempt to Cheat the Catholics—A Relief Bill with "Wings"—Defeated—Catholic Deputation in London—O'Connell and the Whigs—Strong Feeling in Ireland against "Wings"......................... 152

CHAPTER XIX.—1825-1829.

Action of the Catholic Association—Waterford Election—Louth Election—Change of Ministry—Canning, Premier—Lord Anglesea, Viceroy—The "New Reformation"—Pope and Maguire—Death of Canning—Goderich Cabinet—Catholic Petition for Repeal of Test and Corporation Acts—Acts Repealed—Clare Election—O'Connell Returned—Its Results—Suppression of Catholic Association—Peel and Wellington Prepare Catholic Relief Bill—Rage of the Bigots—Reluctance of the King—O'Connell at the Bar of the House—Passage of the Emancipation Act—Disfranchisement of the Forty-Shilling Freeholders—Abstract of the Relief Act—The New Oath—Meaning and Spirit of the Relief Act.. 159

CHAPTER XX.—1829-1840.

Results of the Relief Act—O'Connell Re-elected for Clare—Drain of Agricultural Produce—Educated Class of Catholics Bought—The Tithe War—Lord Anglesea, Viceroy—O'Connell's Associations—Anglesea's Proclamations—Prosecution of O'Connell—National Education—Tithe Tragedies—Newtownbarry—Carrickshock—Change of Dynasty in France—Reform Agitation in England—What Reform meant in Ireland—Cholera—Resistance to Tithe—Lord Grey's Coercion Act—Abolition of Negro Slavery—Church Temporalities Act—Repeal Debate—Surplus Population—Surplus Produce—Tithe Carnage at Rathcormack—Queen Victoria's Accession—Three Measures against Ireland—Poor Law—Tithe Law—Municipal Reform—Castle Sheriffs... 168

CHAPTER XXI.—1840-1843.

Spirit of Legislation for Ireland—More Spying in the Post-Office—Savings Banks—"Precursor Society"—Support to the Whigs—Whigs go Out—Peel comes In—Repeal Association—Export of Food—Extermination—The Repeal Year—Corporation Debate—The Younger Nationalists—New "Arms Bill"—O'Brien Moves for Inquiry—Preparations for Coercion—All England against Repeal—Monster Meetings—Mallow—Tara—Mullaghmast—Clontarf—Proclamation........................... 179

CHAPTER XXII.—1843-1844.

Why England could not Yield—Cost to her of Repeal—Intention of Government at Clontarf—The "Projected Massacre"—Meeting Prevented—State Prosecution—O'Brien declares for Repeal—Packing of the Jury—Verdict of *Guilty*—Debate in Parliament—Russell and Macaulay on Packing of Juries—O'Connell in Parliament—Speculation of the Whigs—Sentence and Imprisonment of "Conspirators"—Effects on Repeal Association—Appeal to the House of Lords—Whig Law Lords—Reversal of the Sentence—Enthusiasm of the People—Their Patience and Self-Denial—Decline of the Association.. 190

CONTENTS.

CHAPTER XXIII.—1844.

Decadence of Repeal Association—Land Tenure Commission—Necessity of Exterminating "Surplus Population"—Report of the "Landlord and Tenant Commission"—Tenant-Right to be *Disallowed*—Farms to be Consolidated—People to be Extirpated—Methods of the Minister to Divide Repealers—Grant to Maynooth—Queen's Colleges—Secret Agents at Rome—American Slavery—Distraction in Repeal Ranks—Bill for "Compensation to Tenants"—Defeated—Death of Thomas Davis—The Famine—Commission of Chemists to gain Time—Demands of Ireland—Of the Corporations—Of O'Connell and O'Brien—Repudiation of Alms—Coercion Bill—Repeal of Corn Laws—Irish Harvests go to England—"Relief Measures"—Delays—Fraud—Havoc of the People—Peel's System of Famine Slaughter fully Established—Peel Resigns Office.. 198

CHAPTER XXIV.—1846-1847.

Progress of the Famine Carnage—Pretended Relief Measures—Imprisonment of O'Brien—Dissensions in Repeal Association—Break up of that Body—Ravages of Famine—"Labour Rate Act"—Useless Public Works—Extermination—Famine of 1847—How they lived in England—Advances from the Treasury—Attempts of Foreign Countries to relieve the Famine—Defeated by British Government—Vagrancy Act—Parish Coffins—Constant Repudiation of Alms—An Englishman's Petition for Alms to Ireland—"Ingratitude" of the Irish—Death of O'Connell—Preparations to Insure the Next Year's Famine—Emigration—British Famine Policy—New Coercion Act called for—Famine in Ireland.. 212

CHAPTER XXV.—1847-1848.

Lord Clarendon, Viceroy—His Means of Insuring the Shipment to England of the Usual Tribute—Bribes the Baser Sort of Editors—Patronage for Catholic Lawyers—Another Coercion Act—Projects for Stopping Exports of Grain—Arming—Alarm of Government—Whigs active in Coercion—French Revolution of February—Confederate Clubs—Deputation from Dublin to Paris—O'Brien's Last Appearance in Parliament—Trials of O'Brien and Meagher—Trial of Mitchel—Packing of the Jury—Reign of Terror in Dublin.. 224

CHAPTER XXVI.—1848-1849.

Reconstitution of the Irish Confederation—New National Journals Established—The *Tribune*—The *Felon*—New Suspension of *Habeas Corpus*—Numerous Arrests—O'Brien attempts Insurrection—Ballingarry—Arrest and Trial of O'Brien and others—Conquest of the Island—Destruction of the People—Encumbered Estates Act—Its Effects—No Tenant-Right—"Rate-in-Aid"—Queen's Visit to Ireland—Places given to Catholics—Catholic Judges—Their Office and Duty—Ireland "Prosperous"—Statistics of the Famine Slaughter—Destruction of Three Millions of Souls—Flying from "Prosperity"... 233

CHAPTER XXVII.—1850-1851.

Depopulation—Emigration—"Plea for the Celtic Race"—Decay of the Irish Electoral Body—Act to Amend Representation—"Papal Aggression"—Rage in England—Ecclesiastical Titles Bill—Never Enforced—And Why?—Orange Outrage in Down County—"Dolly's Brae"—Style of Orange Processions—Condition of the Country—Further Emigration—Still more Extermination—Crime and Outrage—Plenty and Prosperity in England—Conclusion... 244

APPENDIX.. 257

HISTORY OF IRELAND.

CHAPTER I.

1798.

Rising in Ulster—Antrim—Saintfield—Ballinahinch—Insurgents Defeated—McCracken and Monro Hanged—Skirmish in Cork County—Courts-Martial—Many Executions—Hanging of Father Redmond—Surrender of Fitzgerald and Aylmer—Compact between Prisoners and Government in order to Save the Lives of Byrne and Bond—Compact Violated by Government—Byrne Hanged—Bond Dies suddenly in Prison—Reign of Terror in Dublin—Brothers Sheares Tried—Hanged—Other State Trials—Curran in Court—"The Three Majors"—Sirr, Swan, and Sandys—The "Major's People"—John Claudius Beresford—Tortures in Dublin—Country in Wild Alarm—Spiked Heads—Fit Time to Propose Legislative Union—Marquis Cornwallis comes as Viceroy to bring about the Union—"Impression of Horror"—Apparent Measures to End the Devastations—Offers of "Protection"—Not Efficacious—Testimony of Lord Camden himself—True Account of the "Compact"—United Irishmen sent to Fort George.

The rising of the United Irishmen of Ulster was delayed for two weeks after the day agreed upon (May 23d), by the arrest of some of their leaders. On the 7th of June, however, a meeting of magistrates having been appointed in the town of Antrim, for the prevention of rebellion, some insurgents, with design of seizing their persons, attacked the town at two o'clock in the afternoon, and soon overpowering the troops within it, very nearly gained possession. Major-General Nugent, who commanded in that district, having received intelligence of the intended rising, had ordered a body of troops to march to Antrim, who arrived after the rebels had taken possession of the town. They then attacked the insurgents in the town, but their vanguard, consisting of cavalry, being repulsed with the loss of twenty-three men killed and wounded, of which three were officers, Colonel Durham, who commanded the troops, brought the artillery to batter the town, which obliged the insurgents to abandon it, together with a six-pounder which they had brought with them, and two curricle guns which they had taken from the King's army. They were pursued towards Shane's Castle and Randal's Town, with considerable slaughter; on this day Lord O'Neil was mortally wounded.* A small body made an unsuccessful assault on the town of Larne, and some feeble attempts were also made at Ballymena and Ballycastle. The main body of these northern insurgents retired to Donegar Hill, where, disgusted with their want of success and other circumstances, they agreed to surrender their arms, and almost all of them dispersed.

On the 8th of June another body of insurgents in the County Down, near Saintfield, under the command of a Dr. Jackson, set fire to the house of a man named Mackee, an informer against the United Irishmen. They placed themselves the next day in ambuscade, and nearly surrounded a body of troops under Colonel Stapleton, consisting of York Fencibles and yeomen cavalry, of whom they killed about sixty. The infantry, however, on whom the cavalry had been driven back in confusion, rallying with a coolness not very common in this war, succeeded in repulsing their assailants, but could not pursue, and eventually themselves retreated to Belfast. The loss of the insurgents was very small. The next day, under command of Henry Monro, a shopkeeper in Lisburn, they took possession of a strong post on Windmill Hill, above the little town of Ballinahinch, near the centre of the County Down, and at the house and in the demesne of Lord Moira. On the 12th, General Nugent, marching from Belfast, and Colonel Stewart from Downpatrick, formed with fifteen hundred men a junction near the Windmill Hill, of which they gained possession, together with the town, which before the action they wantonly set on fire. The action was maintained about three hours with artillery, with little or no execution. At length the Monaghan regiment of militia, posted with two field-pieces at Lord Moira's great gate, was attacked with such determined fury by the pikemen of the insurgents that it fell back in disorder. The

* He had ridden into the town to attend the meeting of the magistrates, not knowing that the insurgents were in possession of it. He shot one who had seized the bridle of his horse, after which he was dragged from his saddle, and so wounded with pikes that he died in a few days.

want of discipline in the insurgents lost what their valour had gained. The disordered troops found means to rally, while the Argyleshire Fencibles, entering the demesne, were making their attack on another side. The insurgents, confused and distracted, retreated up the hill, and making a stand at the top, at a kind of fortification, defended the post for some time with great courage, but at length gave way and dispersed in all directions. Their loss exceeded a hundred; that of the royal army not above half that number. The main body of these insurgents retired to the mountains of Slieve Croob, where they soon surrendered or separated, returning to their several homes; and thus terminated this short and partial, but active insurrection in the north, in the course of which some slighter actions had taken place, particularly at Portaferry, where they were repulsed by the yeomanry. They also set fire to a revenue cruiser, in which forty men perished.

The official bulletin of the affair of Ballinahinch is as follows:—

"DUBLIN CASTLE, eleven o'clock A.M., June 14, 1798.

"Intelligence is just arrived from Major-General Nugent, stating that, on the 11th instant, he had marched against a large body of rebels who were posted at Saintfield. They retired on his approach to a strong position on the Saintfield side of Ballinahinch, and there made a show of resistance, and endeavoured to turn his left flank: Lieutenant-Colonel Stewart arriving from Down with a pretty considerable force of infantry, cavalry, and yeomanry, they soon desisted, and retired to a very strong position behind Ballinahinch.

"General Nugent attacked them next morning at three o'clock, having occupied two hills on the left and right of the town, to prevent the rebels from having any other choice than the mountains in their rear for their retreat. He sent Lieutenant-Colonel Stewart to post himself, with part of the Argyle Fencibles and some yeomanry, as well as a detachment of the Twenty-second Light Dragoons, in a situation from whence he could enfilade the rebel line; whilst Colonel Leslie, with part of the Monaghan militia, some cavalry, and yeoman infantry, should make an attack upon their front. Having two howitzers and six six-pounders with the two detachments, the Major-General was enabled to annoy them very much from different parts of his position.

"The rebels attacked impetuously Colonel Leslie's detachment, and even jumped into the road from the Earl of Moira's demesne, to endeavour to take one of his guns; but they were repulsed with slaughter. Lieutenant-Colonel Stewart's detachment was attacked by them with the same activity, but he repulsed them also, and the fire from his howitzer and six-pounder soon obliged them to fly in all directions. Their force was, on the evening of the 12th, near five thousand; but, as many persons are pressed into their service, and almost entirely unarmed, the general does not suppose that on the morning of the engagement their numbers were so many.

"About four hundred rebels were killed in the attack and retreat, and the remainder were dispersed all over the country. Parts of the towns of Saintfield and Ballinahinch were burned. . . Three or four green colours were taken, and six one-pounders, not mounted, but which the rebels fired very often, and a considerable quantity of ammunition."

Of course, the failure in Ulster was attended by the usual penalty of failure. The leader of the Antrim insurgents was Henry Joy McCracken, a manufacturer of Belfast, a brave, well-educated, and highly estimable man in the prime of life. He and some others were tried and executed in Belfast. Monro was carried to Lisburn and hung at his own door, his wife and family being in the house.

An attempt at insurrection was next made in Cork County. The principal action, and the only one which Government has thought proper to communicate to the public, took place near the village of Ballynascarty, where, on the 19th of June, two hundred and twenty men of the Westmeath regiment of militia, with two six-pounders, under the command of their Lieutenant-Colonel, Sir Hugh O'Reilly, were attacked on their march from Clognakelty to Bandon, by a body of between three and four hundred men, mostly armed with pikes. The attack was made from a height on the left of the column so rapidly and fiercely that the troops had scarcely time to form. It seems plain, from Sir Hugh O'Reilly's dispatch, that at this moment there was imminent danger of his detachment being cut to pieces, when, fortunately for him, a hundred men of the "Caithness Legion," under Major Innes, came up on the flank of the insurgents, and assailed them with so sharp and well-sustained a fire of musketry that O'Reilly had time to rally his men and get his guns into position. At last the people were forced to retire, but were not pursued. Sir Hugh estimates their loss at one hundred and thirty. He does not tell his own. This action took place on the 19th of June.

There remained little to do now but to try and execute insurgent leaders by martial law. Courts-martial were instituted everywhere at the head-quarters of commanding officers. These terrible tribunals were in full action throughout Wexford County—in New Ross, Enniscorthy, Gorey, Newtownbarry, and Wexford town—and multitudes were hung or transported. Amongst the executions which caused the most horror was that of Father John Redmond, who had absolutely done nothing to favour the insurrection. "His body after death underwent the most indecent mutilations."

Those Wexford insurgents who remained with Mr. Fitzgerald, along with Mr. Aylmer, as outstanding chiefs, negotiated with General Dundas, to whom they surrendered on the 12th of July, on condition that all the other leaders who had adventured with them should be at liberty to retire whither they pleased out of the British dominions. The same terms were afterwards secured by General Moore to Mr. Garret Byrne, who was sent into confinement in the Castle of Dublin, together with Messrs. Fitzgerald and Aylmer, by which they fared much better than those who laid down their arms in Wexford, depending on the faithful fulfilment of the terms entered into with Lord Kingsborough.

The plan of proposing terms for saving the lives of Mr. Oliver Bond and Mr. Byrne was proposed through Mr. Dobbs, a member of Parliament. That gentleman went with the sheriff to the prison in which Mr. A. O'Connor was confined, on the 24th of July, with a paper† signed by seventy state prisoners, purposing to give such information as was in their power, of the arms, ammunition, schemes of warfare, internal regulations and foreign negotiations of the United Irishmen, provided the lives of Messrs. Bond and Byrne should be spared.

In consequence of this agreement, some of the insurgent chiefs, who were still in arms, among whom was Mr. Aylmer, of Kildare, surrendered themselves.* Several principals of the Union, particularly Arthur O'Connor, Thomas Addis Emmet, Dr. MacNeven, and Samuel Neilson, gave details on oath in their examinations before the secret committees of the two Houses of Parliament, in whose reports, although garbled and falsified, published by authority of Government, is contained a mass of information concerning the conspiracy. Yet certain it is, that whatever were the original terms of the contract, and by whatever subsequent events the contractors were influenced or affected, the principal prisoners (fifteen in number) were not liberated, and a power was reserved or assumed by ministers to retain them in custody, at least during the continuance of the war with France. Oliver Bond died in the meantime in prison, "of apoplexy," as was given out; but the friends of this gentleman believe to the present hour that he was murdered at night by one of the jailers or turnkeys of Newgate prison—for what cause or at whose instigation was never known. The other prisoner, Byrne—to save whose life, along with that of Bond, the contract was expressly made—was hung.

During the whole time of the insurrection the city of Dublin was held under strict military law. A large force, consisting chiefly of yeomanry, was kept

---

* Gordon's *History*. Mr. Gordon knew Mr. Redmond well, and declared that during the insurrection he was mostly hiding in Protestant houses, to avoid the "rebels," who considered him an enemy to their cause.

† The following was the agreement signed by seventy-three on the 29th of July:—

"That the undersigned state prisoners, in the three prisons of Newgate, Kilmainham, and Bridewell, engage to give every information in their power of the whole of the internal transactions of the United Irishmen, and that each of the prisoners shall give detailed information of every transaction that has passed between the United Irishmen and foreign states; but that the prisoners are not, by naming or describing, to implicate any person whatever, and that they are ready to emigrate to such country as shall be agreed on between them and Government, and give security not to return to this country without the permission of Government, and give security not to pass into an enemy's country, if on their so doing they are to be freed from prosecution, and also Mr. Oliver Bond be permitted to take the benefit of this proposal. The state prisoners also hope that the benefit of this proposal may be extended to such persons in custody, or not in custody, as may choose to benefit by it."

Signed by seventy-three persons.
29th of July, 1798.

* In a pamphlet, styled a *Letter from Arthur O'Connor to Lord Castlereagh*, dated from prison, January the 4th, 1799, that Minister is directly charged with a violation of the contract, and a misrepresentation to Parliament of the transactions between him and the prisoners of state. Other charges are made, one of which is, that the information given by these prisoners to Government was garbled, to serve the purposes of the ministry, and particularly that of a hundred pages, delivered by O'Connor himself, only one had been published in the reports of the secret committees. Since to this pamphlet, in which his lordship is peremptorily challenged to disprove any of the charges therein made, no reply has appeared, we have only the honour of his lordship for a disproof of these accusations, which *may be* a vindication to persons unacquainted with his lordship's character. The pamphlet was said to have been suppressed by Government, at least was not otherwise than clandestinely sold and circulated.

constantly in the metropolis. The grand and royal canals, which were fifty feet broad and twelve deep, were a security against a surprise; and the several bridges were strongly palisaded, and guarded both by night and by day. The trials and executions of some of the principal leaders in the rebellion tended to keep others in awe, and prevented any further attempts of individuals. Among others, an insurgent officer, a Protestant, named Bacon, having been apprehended disguised in female apparel, was executed on the 2d of June, near Carlisle bridge. On the 14th was executed, on the same scaffolding, Lieutenant Esmond. On the 12th of July, Henry and John Sheares were brought to trial, condemned, and soon after put to death. The trial of John M'Cann, who had been Secretary of the Provincial Committee of Leinster, followed on the 17th; that of Michael William Byrne, delegate from the County Committee of Wicklow, and that of Oliver Bond, on the 23d. Mr. Curran was the leading counsel on all these trials; and it was a service of danger. The Court was usually crowded with armed men; and as the undaunted advocate delivered his powerful and indignant pleadings, often at midnight, amidst a hostile and menacing audience, the lamplight glittered upon serried bayonets, and he was sometimes interrupted by a clash of arms. "What is that?" he sternly exclaimed, on the trial of Oliver Bond. "The question was occasioned by a clash of arms among the military that thronged the Court. Some of those who were nearest to the advocate appeared, from their looks and gestures, about to offer him personal violence; upon which, fixing his eye sternly upon them, he exclaimed: 'You may assassinate, but you shall not intimidate me.'" *

While the insurrection was raging in Wexford, and capital convictions and executions were very frequent all over the country, it must be supposed that the people of Dublin were in a state of profound alarm, sometimes real and genuine terror, sometimes a factitious alarm, created by the agents of Government to furnish excuse for brutal acts of severity. Then was the reign of the "three Majors," Sirr, Swan, and Sandys. These men had been officers of the militia; and all in a sufficiently decent rank of life—the last-named, indeed, was brother-in-law to Mr. Under-Secretary Cooke. This triumvirate were now really the rulers of Dublin, and the most indispensable of all the agencies of the Castle. Their services chiefly consisted in organizing and maintaining a band of wretches, who were employed at the assizes throughout the country, but especially in the vicinity of Dublin, as informers. They were known to the people by the name of the "Battalion of Testimony."

It is said, on high authority, that the employment of spies and informers tends rather to the increase than the suppression of crime, and that a good government has no need of their infamous services. One thing is certain, that their services were thought useful to a bad government; and the same circumstance that rendered their services necessary made their infamy a matter of little moment to their employers. From the year 1796 to 1800, a set of miscreants, steeped in crime, sunk in debauchery, prone to violence, and reckless of character, constituted what was called the "Major's People." A number of these people were domiciled within the gates of the Castle, where there were regular places of entertainment allotted for them contiguous to the Viceroy's palace; for another company of them a house was allotted opposite Kilmainham jail, familiarly known to the people by the name of the "Stag House;" and for one batch of them, who could not be trusted with liberty, there was one of the yards of that prison, with the surrounding cells, assigned to them, which is still called the "Stag Yard." These persons were considered under the immediate protection of Majors Sirr, Swan, and Sandys, and to interfere with them in the course of their duties as spies or witnesses was to incur the vengeance of their redoubtable patrons.

Sandys had been a captain in the Longford militia. Shortly after his marriage with the sister of the Under-Secretary's wife, he was appointed Brigade-Major to the garrison of Dublin. In 1797, '98, and '99 he presided over the Prevot Prison, in the Royal Barracks—a filthy, close, dark, and pestilential place of confinement, with a small court-yard, and some ill-constructed sheds, set up to afford increased accommodation for the multitude of persons daily sent to the depot.

Major Sandys carried on a regular trade in the official advantages of his functions in the Prevot. He sold indulgences to the state prisoners, of a little more than the ordinary scant allowances of air, light, and food. He sold exemption from the taws and triangles for money and for goods, for every marketable commodity.

The court-yard of that miserable den was ringing for ever, by day and by night, with the shrieks of wretches scourged at

* *Life of Curran.* By his Son.

the Major's triangles, to extort confessions, or to force the prisoners to make statements inculpating others. The court in the rear of the Royal Exchange was another place of torture; but perhaps the most dreadful scene of continual lacerations, pitch-cappings, and picketings, in Dublin, was in the Riding-School in Marlborough Street, where the punishments were administered under the eye and by the direction of Mr. John Claudius Beresford, a scion of the great house of Waterford.* Yet, in a debate in the English House of Commons in March, 1801, on the Irish Martial Law Bill, in reply to an observation with respect to the use of torture, made by Mr. Taylor, Lord Castlereagh had certainly the boldness to affirm that "torture never was inflicted in Ireland with the knowledge, authority, or approbation of Government." Mr. John Claudius Beresford, who was the most competent of all men to speak on that subject, observed that "it was unmanly to deny torture, as it was notoriously practised;" and in a subsequent debate in the House of Lords, on another occasion, in the Imperial Parliament, Lord Clare avowed the practice, and defended it on the grounds of its necessity.

No specific orders, undoubtedly, emanated from the Government to Mr. Beresford to convert the Riding-School into a scourging-hall—to Mr. Hepenstal to make a walking gallows of his person—to Mr. Love for the half-hanging of suspected rebels at Kilkea Castle—to Mr. Hunter Gowan for burning down the cabins of the croppies—to the High Sheriff of Tipperary for the laceration of the peasant's back, of which Sir John Moore was an eye-witness —to Captain Swaine for the picketings at Prosperous, or Sir Richard Musgrave for writing a treatise in defence of torture; or to all the other gentlemen of "discernment and fortitude" for adopting "the new expedient" for discovery of crime.

"But," observes Dr. Madden, "it is in vain, utterly futile, and fruitless, to deny the constant use of torture in 1797 and 1798, in the Riding-House, Marlborough Street, under the direction of John Claudius Beresford, and in the Prevot Prison in the Royal Barracks, then governed by Major Sandys, brother-in-law to Mr. Under-Secretary Cooke (Lord Castlereagh's chief official in the Secretary's office); occasionally, too, in the Royal Exchange, and in the small vacant space adjoining the entrance to the Upper Castle Yard,

immediately behind the offices of Lord Castlereagh, and having on the opposite side the back part of the Exchange, where, *under the very windows of Lord Castlereagh's office*, the triangles were set up for fastening the wretches to, who were flogged—tortured even to death."

There was at that time a military order enforced in Dublin, that every householder should expose a list on his front door of all the inmates of his house; but this observance being complied with by no means insured families against domiciliary visits from the military, or from the "Major's People," whenever there was any suspicion that obnoxious persons or papers might be secreted there. There are still alive many who recollect the terror and agony of households when invaded by these odious wretches, who did not generally confine themselves to their ostensible errand, but insulted women and girls, and carried off valuable plate. One instance of this is mentioned in a speech of Curran, where a silver cup was taken possession of because it had engraved upon it the words *Erin go bragh!* The accounts of pay and weekly "subsistence money" given to the "Major's People," as well as to other common swearers, are extant, and may be read in the collections of Dr. Madden. When it is remembered that scenes similar to these were passing in every town, as well as in Dublin; that many bridges and "gallows-hills" showed their blackening corpses swinging in the winds; that in front of many court-houses, and over the gateways of many jails, ghastly heads were grinning upon spikes;* while every hour gave birth to some new and fearful rumour of horrors yet unknown, some idea may be formed of the terror in Ireland.

The country was now, therefore, precisely in the frame of mind which Mr. Pitt considered favourable for facilitating his favourite measure, a Legislative Union. Divided into two bitterly hostile parties, vindictive rage on the one side, affright and despondency on the other—the United Irish Society ruined, partly by the savage extirpation of Catholic insurgents, partly

---

* On the trial of John Magee for libel, in 1813, O'Connell, in his memorable speech on that occasion, thus alludes to Toler (Lord Norbury), when employed on special commissions: "Why, in one circuit, during the administration of the cold-hearted and cruel Camden, there were one hundred individuals tried before *one judge*; of these ninety-eight were *capitally convicted*, and *ninety-seven hanged!* One escaped, but he was a soldier, who murdered a peasant—a thing of a trivial nature. *Ninety-seven victims in one circuit!!*"

Toler was Solicitor-General in 1798, but was sometimes put on the Commission, and went circuit.

---

* Dr. Madden has gone to the trouble of collecting a great many of the authentic cases of half-hangings, scourgings, and other tortures inflicted in those days.

by the defection of the Republican Presbyterians of the north, and the mutual distrust which had been carefully sown between these two sections of that organization—all hope of either Catholic emancipation or Reform (through an *Irish Parliament*) being now apparently adjourned to an indefinite futurity, it was believed that the parties would at last be led to throw themselves into the arms of England, who would know how to take care of them all. Accordingly Lord Camden, having done his office in stirring up rebellion, was recalled; and the Marquis Cornwallis, already unfavourably known in two worlds, arrived in Ireland on the 20th day of June—the very day before the battle of Vinegar Hill—to assume the reins of government, but invested, besides the vice-regal power, with the additional authority of Commander of the forces. It appeared that the instructions of this nobleman were to moderate, by degrees, the horrible rage of extermination. The estimates given of his character and conduct by contemporary Irish writers are wonderfully various. Sir Jonah Barrington says of him: "Lord Cornwallis was now selected to complete the project of a Union, and Lord Castlereagh was continued as Chief Secretary. His system was of all others the most artful and insidious; he affected impartiality while he was deceiving both parties; he encouraged the United Irishman, and he roused the Royalist; one day he destroyed, the next day he was merciful. His system, however, had not exactly the anticipated effect. Everything gave reason to expect a restoration of tranquillity; but it was through the impression of *horror* alone that a union could be effected; and he had no time to lose, lest the country might recover its reason."

Mr. Plowden, on the other hand, who was devoted to the measure of a union, and was himself already writing pamphlets in its favour, can find no terms strong enough in lauding Lord Cornwallis. He says: "This appointment, in this critical juncture, appears, under Providence, to have been the immediate salvation of Ireland, not only by putting an immediate check upon the uncontrolled ferociousness of the soldiery, by stopping military executions, suspending the sentences of courts-martial till he had himself revised the minutes, by converting the system of coercion and terrorism into that of conciliation, by gaining the affections of the people, by drawing upon himself the hatred of the Orangemen, *by bringing to bear the incorporate union with Great Britain*, as the efficient means of redressing popular grievances, and crushing the seeds of perpetual feuds and acrimony kept up chiefly by the subsistence of Orangeism."

Lord Cornwallis certainly did, not long after his arrival, begin to interpose a check upon the bloody work then going on in Wexford. On the 28th of June, after the heads of the Wexford leaders had been duly spiked in front of the jail, and the yeomanry cavalry had glutted themselves for one whole week with carnage and conflagration, picketings, and scourgings, Lord Lake was removed from command in that quarter, and it was given to General Hunter, with directions to put an end to the indiscriminate slaughter. A proclamation was issued and printed in the Dublin *Gazette*, but not till the 3d of July (thus giving the Orangemen one other week's bloody carnival), authorizing His Majesty's generals to give *protections* on certain terms. The proclamation is in these words:—

"Whereas, it is in the power of His Majesty's generals, and of the forces under their command, entirely to destroy all those who have risen in rebellion against their sovereign and his laws; yet it is nevertheless the wish of Government that those persons who, by traitorous machinations, have been seduced, or by acts of intimidation have been forced, from their allegiance, should be received into His Majesty's peace and pardon, —— commanding in the county of —— specially authorized thereto, does hereby invite all persons who may be now assembled in any part of the said county against His Majesty's peace, to surrender themselves and their arms, and to desert the leaders who have seduced them; and for the acceptance of such surrender and submission the space of fourteen days from the date hereof is allowed, and the towns of —— are hereby specified, at each of which places one of His Majesty's officers and a Justice of the Peace will attend; and upon entering their names, acknowledging their guilt, and promising good behaviour for the future, and taking the oath of allegiance, and, at the same time, abjuring all other engagements contrary thereto, they will receive a certificate which will entitle them to protection so long as they demean themselves as becomes good subjects.

"And, in order to render such acts of submission easy and secure, it is the General's pleasure that persons who are now with any portion of the rebels in arms, and willing to surrender themselves, do send to him, or to —— any number from each body of rebels not exceeding ten, with whom the General or —— will settle the manner in which they may repair to the above towns, so that no alarm may be excited, and no injury to their persons be offered.

"June 29, 1798."

Then follows the form of certificate of "protection." Next, on the 17th of July, a message from the Viceroy was read in the House of Commons, signifying the king's pleasure that an "Amnesty Act" should be passed, with certain conditions and large exceptions. Accordingly such a bill was passed in favour of all rebels who had not been leaders; who had not committed manslaughter, except in the heat of battle, and who should comply with the conditions mentioned in the proclamation. But practically there was no cessation, at least in the unhappy County of Wexford, of the horrors of military outrage, even after the proclamation. General Hunter, indeed, seems to have endeavoured to appease the minds of the people, and restore confidence and tranquillity to that distracted county.

But some principal gentlemen of the county, and others besides, attempted to interpose their authority to supersede the tenor of the general pardon held out by proclamation, pursuing the same line of arbitrary conduct which they had practiced previous to the insurrection. They even proceeded to the length of presuming to tear some of the protections which the country people had obtained; but this coming to the General's knowledge, he quieted them by threatening to have them tied to a cart's tail and whipped. Others had been rash enough to levy arbitrary contributions for the losses they had sustained during the insurrection. A curate was induced to wait on the General, with an account of an intended "massacre" of the Protestants, which he detailed with the appearance of the utmost alarm, and was patiently heard out by the General, who then addressed him with this marked appellation and strong language:—"*Mr. Massacre*, if you do not prove to me the circumstances you have related, I shall get you punished in the most exemplary manner for raising false alarms, which have already proved so destructive to this unfortunate country." The curate's alarm instantly changed its direction and became personal; and on allowing that his fears had been excited by vague report to make this representation, his piteous supplication, and apparent contrition, procured him forgiveness.

The various outrages that were committed in the country prevented numbers from coming into the quarters of the several commanding officers to obtain protections, as many of the yeomen and their supplementaries continued the system of conflagration, and shooting such of the peasantry as they met; and this necessarily deterred many from exposing themselves to their view, and prevented, of course, the humane and moderate intentions of the present Government from having their due effect. The melancholy consequence of such a system of terror, persecution, and alarm had very nearly brought on the extermination of an extensive and populous tract of the County of Wicklow, called the Macomores. The perpetration of the plan was providentially prevented by the timely and happy intervention of Brigade-Major Fitzgerald, under the directions and orders of General Hunter. Incessant applications and remonstrances had been made by different magistrates in Gorey and its vicinity, to Government, complaining that this range of country was infested with constant meetings of rebels, who committed every species of outrage, and these reports were confirmed by affidavits. They were credited by Government, to whom they were handed in by a magistracy presumed to be deliberate, grave, and respectable. The Viceroy was rendered indignant at these reiterated complaints, and orders were sent to the different generals and other commanding officers, contiguous to the devoted tract, to form a line along its extent on the western border, and at both ends, north and south, on the land side, so as to leave no resource to the wretched inhabitants, *who were to be slaughtered by the soldiery, or to be driven into the sea*, as it is bounded by the channel on the eastward. Even *women and children were to be included* in this terrific example. The execution of this severe exemplary measure was intrusted to the discretion of General Hunter, who fortunately discovered the inhuman misrepresentation that had produced those terrific orders. The devoted victims found an opportunity to implore protection from the incursions of the black mob (they thus denominated the supplementaries to the different corps of yeomanry), who wreaked their vengeance even upon those who had received protection from General Needham, at Gorey, as different parties of the soldiery and yeomanry waited their return in ambush, and slaughtered every one they could overtake. This prevented many from coming in for protection. Afterwards these sanguinary banditti made incursions into the country, fired into the houses, thus killing and wounding many unoffending peasants. Several houses after being plundered were burned, and the booty was brought into Gorey. By the frequency of these horrible excesses and depredations, such houses as remained unburned were of course crowded with several families, and this multiplied the number of victims at each succeeding incursion. At last most of the inhabitants took refuge on the hills, and armed themselves with every offensive weapon they could procure.

The false alarmists were not depressed by several discomfitures; for although General Hunter reported the country to be in a perfect state of tranquillity, they again returned to the charge, and renewed their misrepresentations. Mr. Hawtry White, Captain of the Ballaghkeen Cavalry, and a Justice of the Peace for the county, sent several informations to Government of the alarming state of the country; and the commanding officer at Gorey was so far persuaded of the intention of a general rising, that he quitted the town and encamped on a hill above it. These representations, made under the semblance of loyalty, had not, however, the wished-for weight with the Government. General Hunter was ordered to inquire into the information of Mr. Hawtry White. Major Fitzgerald was again sent out, and the result of his inquiry was that the information was unfounded. Upon this the General ordered Mr. Hawtry White to be brought to Wexford, and he was accordingly conducted thither and put under arrest; and on his still persisting in his false representations, he was conducted to the island where he asserted the rebels were encamped, and, lo! no island appeared above the water. Mr. Hawtry White was conducted back to Wexford, and General Hunter determined to bring him to a court-martial. Many gentlemen and ladies, however, interfered in the most earnest manner to prevent this investigation, representing that Mr. White's great age might have subjected him to the imposition of fabricated information; and the firmness of the General relaxed at the instance of so many respectable persons.

To show how very far the people of the country were really protected by the proclamations and protections announced by Lord Cornwallis, it will be needful only to give one or two extracts from the *Memoirs and Correspondence* of that nobleman, published many years later.

[*Extract of a letter of Lord Cornwallis to the Duke of Portland, dated the 8th of July, 1798.*]

"The Irish militia are totally without discipline, contemptible before the enemy when any serious resistance is made to them, but ferocious and cruel in the extreme when any poor wretches, either with or without arms, come within their power; in short, murder appears to be their favourite pastime." (Vol. ii., p. 357.)

[*Extract from a letter of Marquis Cornwallis to Major-General Ross.*]
"DUBLIN CASTLE, July 24, 1798.

"Except in the instances of the six state trials that are going on here, there is no law either in town or country but martial law, and you know enough of that to see all the horrors of it, even in the best administration of it. Judge, then, how it must be conducted by Irishmen, heated with passion and revenge. But all this is trifling compared to the numberless murders that are hourly committed by our people without any process or examination whatever. The yeomanry are in the style of the loyalists in America, only much more numerous and powerful, and a thousand times more ferocious. These men have saved the country; but they now take the lead in rapine and murder. The Irish militia, with few officers, and those chiefly of the worst kind, follow closely on the heels of the yeomanry in murder and every kind of atrocity, and the fencibles take a share, although much behind-hand, with the others. The feeble outrages, burnings, and murders which are still committed by the rebels serve to keep up the sanguinary disposition on our side; and as long as they furnish a pretext for our parties going in quest of them, I see no prospect of amendment.

"The conversation of the principal persons of the country all tends to encourage this system of blood; and the conversation, even at my table, where you will suppose I do all I can to prevent it, always turns on hanging, shooting, burning, &c.; and if a priest has been put to death, the greatest joy is expressed by the whole company. So much for Ireland and my wretched situation." (Vol. ii., p. 368.)

The Marquis Cornwallis issued the following "General Orders," with the view of restraining the murderous and rapacious conduct of the troops in Ireland, dated August 31, 1798:—

"It is with great concern that Lord Cornwallis finds himself obliged to call on the general officers and the commanding officers of regiments in particular, and in general on officers of the army, to assist him in putting a stop to the licentious conduct of the troops, and in saving the wretched inhabitants from being robbed, and in the most shocking manner ill-treated, by those to whom they had a right to look for safety and protection.

"Lord Cornwallis declares that if he finds that the soldiers of any regiment have had opportunities of committing those excesses from the negligence of their officers, he will make those officers answerable for their conduct; and that if any soldiers are caught either in the act of robbery, or with the articles of plunder in their possession, they shall be instantly tried, and immediate execution shall follow their conviction."

The editor of the *Cornwallis Memoirs* informs us (p. 13, vol. iii.) that between the landing of the French, in the autumn of 1798, and the month of February, 1799 (a period of four months), although there were three hundred and eighty persons tried by court-martial, one hundred and thirty-one capitally convicted, and ninety executed, yet the number of the latter fell short of what "the loyal party expected and desired;" and he adds, "Many persons in England, as well as in Ireland, who were considered mild and temperate in their views, severely censured what they termed a ruinous system of lenity; nor was the British Government free from a participation in such feelings."

At p. 90, vol. iii., we find the following observations:—

"To Dr. Duigenan's letter Lord Castlereagh replied, on the 6th of March, 1799, that, exclusive of all persons tried at the assizes, Lord Cornwallis had decided personally upon four hundred cases; that out of one hundred and thirty-one condemned to death, eighty-one had been executed; and that four hundred and eighteen persons had been transported or banished, in pursuance of the sentences of courts-martial, since Lord Cornwallis had arrived in Ireland."

[*Extract from a letter of Marquis Cornwallis to Major-General Ross, April 15, 1799.*]

"You write as if you really believed that there was any foundation for all the lies and nonsensical clamour about my lenity. On my arrival in this country I put a stop to the burning of houses and murder of the inhabitants by the yeomen, or any other persons who delighted in that amusement; to the flogging for the purpose of extorting confession; and to the free-quarters, which comprehend universal rape and robbery throughout the whole country." (Vol. iii., p. 89.)

We have seen that the clamour about Lord Cornwallis's clemency was in reality "nonsensical," as he declares; and that he is not even to be credited with the amount of lenity to which he himself lays claim. In fact, it is altogether impossible to believe that, with the immense military force then in Ireland, and of which he was absolute Commander-in-chief, he could not (if he would) have put a stop to the murders and depredations upon the now defenceless people. The only admissible theory of his conduct is, that he had instructions to keep alive what Barrington calls the "impression of horror," until the Union should be effectuated.

All this time there was nothing changed in the state of things in Dublin itself. The three majors and their "people" still predominated with absolute sway, and the state trials were proceeding, before carefully packed juries, of course. It was under this lenient and conciliatory Cornwallis that some of the best and worthiest gentlemen of Ireland were hunted to death by the basest of mankind, with the prostituted forms of law, before judges predetermined to convict, and juries of Orangemen specially brought together by perjured sheriffs, not to try, but simply to hang. The two brothers Sheares were hung and beheaded in front of Newgate prison on the 22d of July (a month after the accession of Cornwallis to the viceroyalty). Byrne and Bond were both convicted and sentenced to death. It was at this moment that the "compact" already mentioned was entered into by certain of the state prisoners with the Government, with a view of stopping, if possible, the further effusion of blood, and specifically and expressly of saving the lives of Byrne and Oliver Bond. As the Government not only violated that compact, but made it the occasion of slandering men to whom all was lost except their honour, it is necessary, in justice to those best and purest of Irish patriots, to record the actual facts. They are to be found in the collections of the laborious Dr. Madden.

The account of the compact of the state prisoners with the Irish Government, taken from the original draft of that document in the handwriting of Thomas Addis Emmet, John Sweetman, and William James MacNeven, was drawn up by them in France, on their liberation from Fort George, and remained in the possession of John Sweetman. The following part of the Statement is in the handwriting of Thomas A. Emmet:—

"We, the undersigned, until this day state prisoners and in close custody, feel that the first purpose to which we should apply our liberty is to give to the world a short account of a transaction which has been grossly misrepresented and falsified, but respecting which we have been compelled to silence for nearly the last three years. The transaction alluded to is the agreement entered into by us and other state prisoners with the Irish Government, at the close of the month of July, 1798; and we take this step without hesitation, because it can in nowise injure any of our friends and former fellow-prisoners, we being among the last victims of perfidy and breach of faith.

"From the event of the battles of Antrim and Ballinahinch, early in June, it was manifest that the northern insurrection had failed in consolidating itself. The severe battle of Vinegar Hill, on the 21st of the same month, led to its termination in Leinster; and the capitulation of Ovidstown, on the 12th of July,* may be understood as the last public appearance in the field of any body capable of serving as a rallying point. In short, the insurrection, for every useful purpose that could be expected from it, *was at an end;* but blood still continued to flow—courts-martial, special commissions, and, above all, sanguinary Orangemen, now rendered doubly malevolent and revengeful from their recent terror, desolated the country, and devoted to death the most virtuous of our countrymen. These were lost to liberty, while she was gaining nothing by the sacrifice.

"Such was the situation of affairs when the idea of entering into a compact with Government was conceived by one of the undersigned, and communicated to the rest of us conjointly with the other prisoners confined in the Dublin prisons, by the terms of which compact it was intended that as much might be saved and as little given up as possible. It was the more urgently pressed upon our minds, and the more quickly matured, by the impending fate of two worthy men. Accordingly, on the 24th of July, the state prisoners began a negotiation with Government, and an agreement was finally concluded, by the persons named by their fellow-prisoners, at the Castle of Dublin, and was finally ratified by the Lord Chancellor, Lord Castlereagh, and Mr. Cooke, three of the King's ministers. In no part of this paper were details or perfect accuracy deemed necessary, because the ministers, and particularly Lord Castlereagh, frequently and solemnly declared that it should in every part be construed by Government with the utmost liberality and good faith; and particularly the last clause was worded in this loose manner to comply with the express desire of the ministers, who insisted upon retaining to Government the entire popularity of the measure; but it was clearly and expressly understood, and positively engaged, that every leading man not guilty of deliberate murder should be included in the agreement who should choose to avail himself of it, in as full and ample a manner as the contracting parties themselves, and that there should be a general amnesty, with the same exceptions, for the body of the people.

"We entered into this agreement the more readily, because it appeared to us that by it the public cause lost nothing. We knew, from the different examinations of the state prisoners before the Privy Council, and from conversations with ministers, that Government was already in possession of all the important knowledge which they could obtain from us. From whence they derived their information was not entirely known to us, but it is now manifest that *Reynolds*, M'Ginn, and Hughes—not to speak of the minor informers—had put them in possession of every material fact respecting the internal state of the Union; and it was from particular circumstances well known to one of us, and entirely believed by the rest, that its external relations had been betrayed to the English Cabinet, through the agency of a foreigner with whom we negotiated.

"This was even so little disguised that, on the preceding 12th of March, the contents of a memoir which had been prepared by one of the undersigned at Hamburg and transmitted thence to Paris, were minutely detailed to him by Mr. Cooke. Nevertheless, those with whom we negotiated seemed extremely anxious for our communications. Their reasons for this anxiety may have been many; but two, particularly, suggested themselves to our minds. They obviously wished to give proof to the enemies of an Irish republic and of Irish independence of the facts with which they were themselves well acquainted; while, at the same time, they concealed from the world their real sources of intelligence. Nor do we believe we are uncharitable in attributing to them the hope and wish of rendering unpopular and suspected men in whom the United Irishmen had been accustomed to place an almost unbounded confidence. The injurious consequences of Government succeeding in both these objects

---

* The event preceding the massacre of the capitulated body of the United Irishmen, on the Rath of the Curragh of Kildare, by the command of Major-General Sir James Duff, executed chiefly by the yeomanry cavalry of Captain Bagot, and the *Fox-hunters' Corps*, commanded by Lord Roden.

were merely personal; and, as they were no more, though they were revolting and hateful to the last degree, we did not hesitate to devote ourselves that we might make terms for our country.

"What were these terms? That it should be rescued from civil and military execution; that a truce should be obtained for liberty, which she so much required. There was also another strongly impelling motive for entering into this agreement. If Government, on the one hand, was desirous of rousing its dependents by a display of the vigorous and well-concerted measures that were taken for subverting its authority and shaking off the English yoke; so we, on the other hand, were not less solicitous for the vindication of our cause in the eyes of the liberal, the enlightened, and patriotic. We perceived that, in making a fair and candid development of those measures, we should be enabled boldly to avow and justify the cause of Irish union, as being founded upon the purest principles of benevolence, and as aiming only at the liberation of Ireland. We felt that we could rescue our brotherhood from those foul imputations which had been industriously ascribed to it—the pursuit of the most unjust objects by means of the most flagitious crime.

"If our country has not actually benefited to the extent of our wishes and of our stipulations, let it be remembered that this has not been owing to the *compact*, but to the *breach of the compact*—the gross and flagrant breach of it, both as to the letter and spirit, in violation of every principle of plighted faith and honour.

"Having been called upon to fulfil our part of the compact, a stop being put to all further trials and executions, a memoir was drawn up and signed by two of the undersigned, together with another of the body (they being selected by Government for that purpose), and was presented to Mr. Cooke on the 4th of August. It was very hastily prepared in a prison, and, of course, not so complete and accurate as it might otherwise have been, but sufficiently so to draw from Mr. Cooke an acknowledgment that it was a complete fulfilment of the agreement; though he said the Lord-Lieutenant wished to have it so altered as not to be a justification of the United Irishmen, which he said it manifestly was.

"Upon the refusal to alter it, Government thought proper to suppress it altogether, and adopted a plan which they had already found convenient for promulgating, *not the entire truth*, but so much of the truth as accorded with their views, and whatever else they wished to have passed upon mankind under colour of authority for the truth. This was no other than examination before the secret committees of Parliament. By these committees several of us were examined; and, to our astonishment, we soon after saw in the newspapers, and have since seen in printed reports of these committees, misrepresented and garbled, and as far as relates to some of us, very untrue and fallacious statements of our testimony—even in some cases the very reverse of what was given. That no suspicion may attach to this assertion from its vagueness, such of us as were examined will, without delay, state the precise substance of our evidence on that occasion.

"The Irish Parliament thought fit, about the month of September in the same year, to pass an act to be founded expressly on this agreement. To the provisions of that law we do not think it worth while to allude, because their severity and injustice are lost in comparison with the enormous falsehood of its preamble. In answer to that, we most distinctly and formally deny that any of us did ever publicly or privately, directly or indirectly, *acknowledge crimes*, *retract opinions*, or *implore pardon*, as is therein most falsely stated. A full and explicit declaration to this effect would have been made public at the time, had it not been prevented by a message from Lord Cornwallis, delivered to one of the subscribers on the 12th of that month. Notwithstanding we had expressly stipulated, at the time of the negotiation, for the entire liberty of publication, in case we should find our conduct or motives misrepresented, yet this perfidious and inhuman message threatened that such declaration would be considered as a breach of the agreement on our part, and in that case the executions in *general should go on as formerly.*

"Thus was the truth stifled at the time; and we believe firmly that to prevent its publication has been one of the principal reasons why, in violation of the most solemn engagements, we were kept in close custody ever since, and transported from our native country against our consent.

"We conceive that to ourselves, to our cause, and to our country, and to posterity, we owe this brief statement of facts, in which we have suppressed everything that is not of a nature strictly vindicatory;

because our object in this publication is not to criminate, but to defend. As to their truth, we positively aver them, each for himself, as far as they fall within his knowledge, and we firmly believe the others to be the truth, and nothing but the truth."

The following part of the statement is in the handwriting of John Sweetman:—

"On the 12th of March, 1798, the deputies from several counties having met in Dublin, to deliberate upon some general measures for Union, were arrested in a body at Mr. Bond's, as were also many other of its principal agents, and put into a state of solitary confinement. Some of those persons were examined by the Privy Council, previous to their committal to prison; when it appeared, beyond a possibility of doubt, that the negotiations of the United Irishmen with France had been betrayed to the British Government. On the 30th, the kingdom was officially declared in a state of rebellion, and put under martial law. A proclamation from the Lord-Lieutenant had directed the military to use the most summary methods for repressing disturbances; and it was publicly notified by the commanders in some counties that, unless the people brought in their arms within ten days from the period of publication, large bodies of troops would be quartered on them, who should be licensed to live at free-quarters, and that other severities would be exercised to enforce acquiescence. In the latter end of May the united armed men of the County Kildare felt themselves obliged to take the field, and hostilities commenced between them and the King's forces on the 24th. About this time the Counties of Wexford and Wicklow were generally up, and those of Down, Derry, Antrim, Carlow, and Meath were preparing to rise. The appeal to arms in these counties was attended with various success on both sides; and the military were invested with further powers by a proclamation, issued by the Lord-Lieutenant and Council, directing the generals to punish all attacks upon the King's forces according to martial law, either by death or otherwise, as to them should seem expedient. For some time the people had the advantage in the field; but the defeat at New Ross on the 5th of June, at Antrim on the 7th, that of Arklow on the 9th, of Ballinahinch on the 12th, of Vinegar Hill on the 21st, and Kilconnell on the 26th, with the evacuation of Wexford, and some unsuccessful skirmishes which afterwards took place in the County of Wicklow, removed all hope of maintaining the contest *for the present* with any probability of success. In the interim troops were arriving from England, and several regiments of English militia had volunteered their services for Ireland. About the end of June a proclamation was issued, promising pardon and protection to all persons, except the leaders, who should return to their allegiance and deliver up their arms, which, it was said, had a very general effect. A large body of the Kildare men had already surrendered to General Dundas, and on the 21st of July another party, with its leaders, capitulated to General Wilford. The King's troops by this time were victorious in every quarter; and the park of artillery which had been employed in the south had returned to the capital.

"It was now upwards of two months since the war broke out, during which time no attempt had been made by the French to land a force upon the coast, nor was there any satisfactory account then received that such a design was in contemplation. The expedition of Buonaparte and the forces under his command were already ascertained to have some part of the Mediterranean for their object. No other diversion was made by the French to distract the British power during this period. Military tribunals, composed of officers who, in many instances, as it was publicly admitted, had not exceeded the inconsiderate age of boyhood, were everywhere instituted, and a vast number of executions had been the consequence. The yeomen and soldiery, licensed to indulge their rancour and revenge, were committing those atrocious cruelties which unfortunately distinguish the character of civil warfare. The shooting of innocent peasants at their work was occasionally resorted to by them as a species of recreation—a practice so inhuman that, unless we had incontestible evidence of the fact, we never should have given it the slightest credence. During these transactions a special commission, under an act of Parliament, passed for the occasion, was sitting in the capital; and the trials having commenced, it was declared from the bench that to be proved an United Irishman was sufficient to subject the party to the penalty of death; and that any member of a baronial or other committee was accountable for every act done by the body to which he respectively belonged in its collective capacity, whether it was done without his cognizance, in his absence, or even at the extremity of the land. As it was openly avowed that convictions would be sought for only through the medium of informers, the Government used every influence to dignify the character of this wretched class of beings in the eyes of those who were selected to decide on the lives of the accused; and they so effectually succeeded as to secure implicit respect to whatever any of them chose to swear, from juries so appointed, so prepossessed. It was made a point by the first connections of Government to flatter those wretches, and some peers of the realm were known to have hailed the arch-apostate Reynolds with the title of 'Saviour of his country.'"

The following part of the statement is in the handwriting of William James MacNeven:—

"In the case of Mr. Bond, the jury, with an indecent precipitation, returned a verdict of guilty on the 23d of July, and on the 25th he was sentenced to die. Byrne was also ordered for execution. In this situation of our affairs a negotiation was opened with Government, and proceeded in through the medium of Mr. Dobbs. An agreement was in consequence concluded and signed, which, among other things, stipulated for the lives of Byrne and Bond; but Government thought fit to annul this by the execution of Byrne. As, however, the main object, *the putting a stop to the useless effusion of blood*, was still attainable, it was deemed right to open a second negotiation. In its progress, Government having insisted on some dishonourable requisitions, which were rejected with indignation, occasioned the failure of this also. It was, however, proposed by them to renew it again, and deputies from the jails were appointed to confer with the official servants of the Crown. A meeting accordingly took place at the Castle on the 29th of July, when the final agreement was concluded and exchanged.

"In addition to the *fulfilment to the letter* of this agreement, the official servants of the Crown pledged the faith of Government for two things—one that the result and end of that measure should be the putting a stop to the effusion of blood, and that all executions should cease, except in cases of wilful murder; the other was, that the conditions of the agreement should be liberally interpreted. The agreement was, in the course of a day or two, generally signed by the prisoners.

"Having thus stated the facts, we proceed to declare our reasons for entering into and ratifying this agreement:—*First*. Because we had seen, with great affliction, that in the course of the appeal to arms, while four or five counties out of the thirty-two were making head against the whole of the King's forces, no effectual disposition was manifested to assist them, owing, as we believe, to the extreme difficulty of assembling, and the want of authentic information as to the real state of affairs. *Second*. Because the concurring or quiescent spirit of the English people enabled their Government to send not only a considerable additional regular force, but also many regiments of English militia into Ireland. *Third*. Because it was evident that in many instances the want of military knowledge in the leaders had rendered the signal valour of the people fruitless. *Fourth*. Because, notwithstanding it was well known in France that the revolution had commenced in Ireland—an event that they were previously taught to expect—no attempt whatever was made by them to land any force during the two months which the contest had lasted, nor was any account received that it was their intention even shortly to do so. *Fifth*. Because, that by the arrest of many of the deputies and chief agents of the Union, and by the absence of others, the funds necessary for the undertaking were obstructed or uncollected, and hence arose insurmountable difficulties. *Sixth*. Because, from the several defeats at New Ross and Wexford, no doubt remained on our minds that further resistance, for the present, was not only vain, but nearly abandoned. *Seventh*. Because we were well assured that the proclamation of amnesty issued on the 29th of June had caused great numbers to surrender their arms, and take the oath of allegiance. *Eighth*. Because juries were so packed, justice so perverted, and the testimony of the basest informers so respected, that trial was but a mockery, and arraignment but the tocsin for execution. *Ninth*. Because we were convinced by the official servants of the Crown, and by the evidence given on the trials, that Government was already in possession of our external and internal transactions. The former they obtained, as we believe, through the perfidy of some agents of the French Government at Hamburg; the latter through informers who had been more or less confidential in all our affairs. *Tenth*, and final. Every-day accounts of the murders of our most virtuous and energetic countrymen assailed our ears; many were perishing on the scaffold, under pretext of martial or other law, but many more the victims of individual Orange hatred and revenge. To stop this torrent of calamity, to preserve to Ireland her best blood ... we determined to make a sacrifice of no trivial value—we agreed to abandon our country, our families, and our friends.

"And now we feel ourselves further called upon to declare that an act, passed in Ireland during the autumn of 1798, reciting our names, and asserting that we had 'retracted our opinions, acknowledged our crimes, and implored pardon,' is founded upon a gross and flagrant calumny. Neither we, the undersigned, nor any of our fellow-prisoners, so far as we know or believe, having ever done either the one or the other; and we solemnly assert that we never were consulted about that act, its provisions, or preamble; and that no copy of it was ever sent to us by any servant of the Crown—though repeatedly promised by the Under-Secretary —nor by any other person. On the contrary, it had, unknown to us, passed the House of Commons, when one of us (Samuel Neilson), having seen by mere accident an abstract of it in an English newspaper, remonstrated with the servants of the Crown on the falsity of the preamble, and was silenced only by a message from the Lord-Lieutenant, that it was his positive determination to annul the agreement and *proceed with the executions*, &c., if any further notice whatever was taken of the preamble, or if one word was published on the subject. We did not conceive ourselves warranted, situated as things then were, in being instrumental to a renewal of bloodshed. We have ever since been constrained to silence; for, in violation of a solemn agreement, we have been kept *close prisoners*.

"To our country and to our posterity, we felt that we owed this declaration; and to their judgment upon our conduct and motives we bow with respectful submission."

These gentlemen were all still kept close prisoners. Three of them, Thomas Addis Emmet, Arthur O'Connor, and Dr. MacNeven, were twice, in the course of the year 1798, brought up and examined, as already described, before secret Committees of both Houses; and in April, 1799, were sent to Fort-George, a strong place near Inverness, in the Highlands of Scotland, where they were kept prisoners until the Peace of Amiens. The names of the Fort-George prisoners were:—

THOMAS ADDIS EMMET.
ARTHUR O'CONNOR.
ROGER O'CONNOR.
WILLIAM JAMES MACNEVEN.
JOHN SWEETMAN.
MATTHEW DOWLING.
JOHN CHAMBERS.
EDWARD HUDSON.
GEORGE CUMMING.
SAMUEL NEILSON.
THOMAS RUSSELL.
ROBERT SIMMS.
WILLIAM TENNENT.
ROBERT HUNTER.
HUGH WILSON.
JOHN SWEENEY.
JOSEPH CUTHBERT.
WILLIAM STEELE DIXON.
JOSEPH CORMICK.

"We were selected," says Dr. Steele Dixon, in his narrative, "from the three provinces of Ulster, Leinster, and Munster, but principally from the city of Dublin and town of Belfast. We comprehended in our body three magistrates, three barristers, two physicians, one attorney, one apothecary, one printer and bookseller, one printer and proprietor of a newspaper, one dentist, one military captain, one runner to a bank, one merchant tailor, and one Presbyterian minister, with an eminent porter brewer, two wholesale merchants, one broker, and two young gentlemen without profession, trade, or calling. . . I should have added, a clergyman of the Church of England, as Arthur O'Connor was ordained as such previous to his being called to the bar; and as Episcopal ordination impresses an indelible character, he not only then was, and now is, but ever must be, a *clergyman*. Of our circumstances, I shall only say that we *had* all been *independent*, most of us *respectable* in our professions; some possessed of large capitals in trade, and others of considerable landed property. Perhaps it may not be amiss to mention here that, as we were selected from the three principal provinces of Ireland, we were respectively members of the three principal churches in the kingdom, and which alone Government has yet acknowledged *as churches*. Nor is it unworthy of notice that the number of Catholics, Protestants, and Presbyterians in our little colony was in an *inverse ratio* of the number of each denomination in Ireland at large. Perhaps the proportion may be stated as follows, though not correctly:—

Catholics (two-thirds of the people), prisoners... 4
Presbyterians (more than one-fifth of the people), prisoners,........................ 6
Protestants (less than one-seventh of the people), prisoners,........................10

CHAPTER II.

1798.

Parliament—The Acts of Attainder—French Landing under Humbert—Killala—Conduct of the little French Army—Ballina—The Races of Castlebar—Panic and Rout of the British Force—French give a Ball—Lord Cornwallis collects a great Army—Marches to meet the French—Encounters them at Ballinamuck—Defeat and Capture of the French—Recovery of Ballina—Slaughter—Courts-Martial, &c.—End of the Insurrections of 1798—New French Expedition—Commodore Bompart—T. W. Tone—Encounter British Fleet at mouth of Lough Swilly—Battle—The *Hoche* Captured—Tone a Prisoner—Recognized by Sir George Hill—Carried to Dublin in Irons—Tried by Court-Martial—Condemned to be Hanged—His Address to the Court—Asks as a favour to be Shot—Refused by Cornwallis—Suicide in Prison.

In the midst of this reign of terror and of vengeance, Parliament continued to sit from time to time. Lord Castlereagh's majority in Parliament had its functions to discharge, as well as the "Major's People," in the general system of operations which were all to lead towards, and end in, the one grand point—a Legislative Union. On the 18th of July Lord Castlereagh, after a long speech on the rebellion in general, and its atrocities (which were all, according to him, on the part of the people), proposed that a measure should be brought in to grant compensation to such of His Majesty's *loyal* subjects as had sustained losses in their property during the insurrection. This Bill was brought in, was passed, and commissioners were appointed for carrying it into effect. On the 27th the Attorney-General brought in a Bill for the attainder of Lord Edward Fitzgerald, Cornelius Grogan, and Beauchamp Bagenal Harvey, in order that their estates might be forfeited. All efforts in opposition to this new procedure against men who were all dead, and had never been convicted of any crime, proved quite fruitless. It was the informer Reynolds, who had been implicitly trusted by the unsuspecting Lord Edward, that proved the case against him, to the satisfaction of the Committee. Curran was heard in defence, on the part of Lady Pamela Fitzgerald and her children, and made a very strong argument. On the unheard-of nature of this species of proceeding, he said—"Upon the previous and important question—namely, the guilt of Lord Edward (without the full proof of which no punishment can be just)—I have been asked by the Committee if I have any defence to go into. ... Sir, I now answer the question: I have no defensive evidence—it is impossible that I should. I have often of late gone to the dungeon of the captive, but *never have I gone to the grave of the dead*, to receive instructions for his defence; nor, in truth, have I ever before been at the trial of a dead man." It was all in vain; that Parliament was quite ready to make a new precedent, in order to starve the widows and children of dead rebels. The bills of Attainder passed.* Besides these, the Parliament was busy with its "Fugitive Bill," and its "Banishment Bill," excepting from all amnesty certain United Irishmen not then in the country, and certain others who were to be allowed to exile themselves. These two lists comprehend one hundred and forty names, including Napper Tandy, Wolfe Tone, Richard McCormick, Dean Swift, Lewins, Emmet, Neilson, O'Connor, &c.; and all the names may be found in one of the appendixes of Madden. The last-named gentlemen, indeed, before their banishment, had some years to pass in the dreary fortress of Fort-George.

The whole country was still under martial law; many were suffering the extreme penalty, and that wholesome feeling, called by Barrington "an impression of horror," was sufficiently prevalent for all the purposes of Mr. Pitt, when his policy was materially served by a new and most pitiful French invasion, which came too late to serve Ireland, but was in admirable time to help England.

Fortunately for England, and, therefore, unhappily for Ireland, the French Republic was, during the year 1798, in its most helpless and chaotic condition. Napoleon was in Egypt; and the miserable Directory, with neither money nor credit, was lamentably unequal to the exigencies of the time. Wolfe Tone was still in France. As the news of each arrest, and of each action, successively reached France, he urged the generals and Government to assist the gallant and desperate struggle of his countrymen, and pressed on them the necessity of availing themselves of the favourable opportunity

---

* A remnant of Lord Edward's property was saved for his widow by Mr. Ogilvie, Lord Edward's stepfather, who bought it when sold in Chancery to satisfy a mortgage. But what was saved was a trifle; and Lady Pamela died in poverty. As to Mr. Grogan, who possessed a large estate, Sir Jonah Barrington says:—

"This Attainder Bill was one of the most illegal and unconstitutional acts ever promoted by any government; but after much more than £10,000 costs to Crown officers, and to Lord Norbury as Attorney-General, had been extracted from the property, the estates were restored to the surviving brother."

The surviving brother had fought on the royalist side during the insurrection.

which flew so rapidly by. They began their preparations without delay; but money, arms, ammunition, and ships, all were wanting. By the close of June, the insurrection was nearly crushed, and it was not till the beginning of July that Tone was called up to Paris, to consult with the Ministers of the War and Navy Departments on the organization of a new expedition. At this period his journal closes, and the subsequent events are elsewhere recorded.

The plan of the new expedition was to dispatch small detachments from several ports, in the hope of keeping up the insurrection, and distracting the attention of the enemy, until some favourable opportunity should occur for landing the main body, under General Kilmaine. General Humbert, with about one thousand men, was quartered for this purpose at Rochelle; General Hardy, with three thousand, at Brest; and Kilmaine, with nine thousand, remained in reserve. This plan was judicious enough, if it had been taken up in time. But long before the first of these expeditions was ready to sail, the insurrection was subdued in every quarter.

The indignation of the unfortunate Irish was just and extreme against that French Government which had so repeatedly promised them aid, and now appeared to desert them in their utmost need.

A miserable expedition, at the instance of Napper Tandy, was at length fitted out, of which Tone's son thus speaks:—

"The final ruin of the expedition was hurried by the precipitancy and indiscretion of a brave but ignorant and imprudent officer. This anecdote, which is not generally known, is a striking instance of the disorder, indiscipline, and disorganization which began to prevail in the French army. Humbert, a gallant soldier of fortune, but whose heart was better than his head, impatient of the delays of his Government, and fired by the recitals of the Irish refugees, determined to begin the enterprise on his own responsibility, and thus oblige the Directory to second or to abandon him."

With three or four ships, about one thousand men, and a small force of artillery —without instructions, and without any assurance of being supported, he compelled the captains to select for the most desperate attempt which is, perhaps, recorded in history. Three Irishmen accompanied him, Matthew Tone, Bartholomew Teeling, of Lisburn, and Sullivan, nephew to Madgett, whose name is often mentioned in Tone's memoirs. On the 22d of August they made the coast of Connaught, and landing in the Bay of Killala, immediately stormed and occupied that little town.

The Protestant Bishop of Killala was then at his house, called the Castle, and there was with him a company of parsons, holding a visitation. It is from his narrative that we learn the details; and he especially bears witness to the excellent conduct of the French, both officers and men; although his testimony to this effect was "at the expense of his own translation."*

The French entered the bay under English colours; and the feint succeeded so well that two of the bishop's sons, with the Port-Surveyor, took a fishing-boat and went out with the intention of going on board one of the ships; they were presently surprised to find themselves prisoners. Between seven and eight, a terrified messenger came and told the bishop that the French were landed, and that near three hundred of them were within a mile of the town. The cavalry officers rode off directly, in full speed, with the intelligence to Ballina. The yeomanry and fencibles drew up before the castle-gate, and resolutely advanced into the main street to meet the French advance-guard.

Borne down by numbers, and seeing two of their corps fall, they were seized with a panic, and fled. Kirkwood and nineteen yeomen were taken, and ordered into close custody at the castle. All opposition being now at an end, the French General marched into the castle-yard at the head of his officers, and demanded to see the bishop, who, fortunately, was conversant with the French language. Humbert desired him to be under no apprehension for himself or his people; they should be treated with respectful attention, and nothing should be taken by the French troops but what was absolutely necessary for their support; a promise which, as long as those troops continued in Killala, was most religiously observed.

Mr. Kirkwood was examined as to the supplies that could be drawn from the town and neighbourhood to assist the progress of the invaders. The queries were interpreted by some Irish officers who came with the French, to which he answered with such an appearance of frankness and candour, that he gained the esteem of the French General, who told him he was on his parole, and should have full permission to return to his family, and attend to his private affairs. The conjugal affection of this gentleman on the next day made him forget his parole, and go to attend his sick wife,

* Sir J. Barrington. *Rise and Fall*, &c.

who, from the dread of the enemy, had secreted herself in the mountains. Enraged at this breach of parole, the French took everything they wanted out of his stores—oats, salt, and iron, to a considerable amount; nor had they been careful to prevent depredations by the rebels in his dwelling-house, as they would have done if he had not fled; so that when he returned he found it a wreck.

The bishop's castle was made the head-quarters of the French General. But such excellent discipline was constantly maintained by these invaders while they remained in Killala, that with every temptation to plunder, which the time and the number of valuable articles within their reach presented to them—a sideboard of plate and glasses, a hall filled with hats, whips, and greatcoats, as well of the guests as of the family, not one single article of private property was carried away.

On the morning after his arrival, Humbert began his military operations by pushing forward to Ballina a detachment of a hundred men, forty of whom he had mounted on the best horses he could seize. A green flag was mounted over the castle-gate, with the inscription, *Erin go Bragh*, importing to invite the country people to join the French. Their cause was to be forwarded by the immediate delivery of arms, ammunition, and clothing to the new levies of the country. Property was to be inviolable. Ready money was to come over in the ships expected every day from France. In the meantime, whatever was bought was paid for in drafts on the future Directory.

Though cash was wanting, the promise of clothing and arms to the recruits was made good to a considerable extent. The first that offered their service received complete clothing to the amount of about a thousand. The next comers, at least as many, received arms and clothing, but no shoes and stockings. To the last, arms only were given. And of arms, Colonel Charost assured the bishop, five thousand and five hundred stand were delivered.

The Right Rev. narrator thus describes the little army of invaders:—

"Intelligence, activity, temperance, patience, to a surprising degree, appeared to be combined in the soldiery that came over with Humbert, together with the exactest obedience to discipline; yet, if you except the grenadiers, they had nothing to catch the eye. Their stature, for the most part, was low, their complexion pale and sallow, their clothes much the worse for the wear; to a superficial observer they would have appeared almost incapable of enduring any hardship. These were the men, however, of whom it was presently observed that they could be well content to live on bread or potatoes, to drink water, to make the stones of the street their bed, and to sleep in their clothes, with no cover but the canopy of heaven. One half of their number had served in Italy, under Buonaparte, the rest were from the army of the Rhine."

The French, and the Irish officers who accompanied them, did not find the Connaught people so well prepared to receive them, nor so well organized as they had hoped and expected. The general insurrection which was just suppressed had not penetrated into Mayo at all; yet the bishop mentions some circumstances to show that the landing was not unexpected by the peasantry of those parts. At any rate, a French flag displayed anywhere in Ireland was sure to attract the fighting part of the population around it; as, indeed, the same phenomenon would do at this day. The bishop, whose professional prejudices may lead him to exaggerate a little, gives a curious account of the astonishment of the French when they found their Irish allies were devout Catholics—as if they had not known this before. He says:—

"The contrast with regard to religious sentiments between the French and their Irish allies was extremely curious. The atheist despised and affronted the bigot; but the wonder was how the zealous papist should come to any terms of agreement with a set of men who boasted openly in our hearing, that they had just driven Mr. Pope out of Italy, and did not expect to find him again so suddenly in Ireland. It astonished the French officers to hear the recruits, when they offered their services, declare that they were come to take arms for France and the Blessed Virgin."

Humbert left Killala with a quantity of ammunition in the possession of two hundred men and six officers, and on the 25th, about seven o'clock in the evening, took possession of Ballina, from whence the garrison fled on his approach. Here he left behind him an officer named True, with a very small part of the French and several of the Irish recruits. Humbert was sensible of the advantage of pushing forward with vigour, and a rapid progress into the interior could alone bring the natives to his standard. At Ballina many hundred peasants repaired to the French standard, and with eagerness received arms and uniforms. The French commander determined to attack the forces at Castlebar, and began his march on the morning of the 26th, with eight hundred of his own men, and less than fifteen hundred Irish.

There was then in Castlebar an army of six thousand men, under command of General Lake, including some fine militia regiments, with the Marquis of Ormond, General Lord Hutchinson, the Earls of Longford and Granard, and Lord Roden, with his boasted regiment of cavalry called the "Foxhunters," who had shown themselves capable of at least riding down flying and disarmed peasants in Meath and Kildare. It was a force with which General Lake reasonably enough thought he should give a good account of eight hundred French and some raw levies of Connaught men. The English commander expected the French to advance by the high road leading to Castlebar; but Humbert, having good guides, took the way over the pass of Barnagee westward, and so appeared, early in the morning, not precisely at the point where he was looked for.

General Lake with his staff had just arrived and taken command (as an elder officer), as Lord Hutchinson had determined to march the ensuing day and end the question, by a capture of the French detachment. The change of commanders had occasioned discontent and demoralization amongst the troops; at least, that is one of the reasons or excuses which loyalist writers have been fain to allege for the shameful conduct of the British force in the action which followed. Plowden says on this subject:—

"There is no question but that a very serious difference happened previous to the disgraceful action at Castlebar between General (now Lord) Hutchinson and General Lake; and that the army in general was strongly affected by the former's having been superseded in his command by the latter. General Hutchinson was acquainted with every inch of the country, and had prepared an able and efficient plan for stopping the progress of the enemy; he commanded alike the confidence of the army and the affections of the natives. As cruelty and cowardice are ever inseparable, it was unlikely that troops which had debased themselves by massacring the fugitive, surrendered or unoffending, by burning their houses and destroying their property, by torturing, strangling, and flogging the suspected to extort confessions, should, when left to themselves or under the command of the promoter of that savage warfare, bravely face an enemy upon whom they dared not exercise their wonted atrocities."

However that might be, on the appearance of the French and Irish deploying from the pass of Barnagee, Sir Jonah Barrington describes thus the singular action that followed:—

"The troops were moved to a position about a mile from Castlebar, which, to an unskilled person, seemed unassailable. They had scarcely been posted with nine pieces of cannon, when the French appeared on the opposite side of a small lake, descending the hill in columns, directly in front of the English. Our artillery played on them with effect. The French kept up a scattered fire of musketry, and took up the attention of our army by irregular movements. In half an hour, however, our troops were alarmed by a movement of small bodies to turn their left, which, being covered by walls, they had never apprehended. The orders given were either mistaken or misbelieved; the line wavered, and in a few minutes the whole of the royal army was completely routed; the flight of the infantry was as that of a mob, all the royal artillery was taken, our army fled to Castlebar, the heavy cavalry galloped amongst the infantry and Lord Jocelyn's Light Dragoons, and made the best of their way, through thick and thin, to Castlebar, and towards Tuam, pursued by such of the French as could get horses to carry them.

"About nine hundred French and some peasants took possession of Castlebar without resistance, except from a few Highlanders stationed in the town, who were soon destroyed."

So violent was the panic of the British that they never halted till they reached Tuam, forty miles from the field of battle. They lost the whole of their artillery—fourteen pieces—five stand of colours, and in killed, wounded, and prisoners, eighteen officers and three hundred and fifty men, but the French calculated the loss of the enemy at six hundred. The fugitives renewed their march, or rather flight, from Tuam on the same night, and proceeded to Athlone, where an officer of carbineers with sixty of his men arrived at one o'clock on Tuesday, the 29th, having performed a march of above seventy English miles—the distance of Athlone from Castlebar—in twenty-seven hours. The whole battle and rout are familiarly known to this day in Connaught as the "*Races of Castlebar.*"

The French, having thus easily possessed themselves of the county town of Mayo, immediately gave a ball and supper. Sir Jonah Barrington says:—

"The native character of the French never showed itself more strongly than after this action. When in full possession of the large town of Castlebar, they immediately set about putting their persons in the best order, and the officers advertised a ball and supper that night for the ladies of the town; this, it is said, was well attended, decorum in all points was strictly preserved, they paid ready money for everything; in fact, the French army established the French character wherever they occupied."

But they thought of something else besides amusement. With that love of order which is a distinguishing trait of their nation, they established districts, each under its own elected magistrate; they repressed any disposition which showed itself on the part of the people to maltreat the loyalist inhabitants, if indeed such disposition existed as the bishop affirms. A provincial government was at once established, with Mr. Moore, of Moore Hall, as President, and proclamations were issued in the name of the "Irish Republic."

From the terror which this handful of French troops inspired, we may form some idea of the effects which might have followed the landing of even Humbert's little force anywhere in the south of Ireland, while the Wexford men were gallantly holding their own county; or we may conjecture what might have been the result if Humbert had brought with him ten thousand men instead of one thousand, even in that month of August, crushed as the people had been by the savage suppression of their insurrection,—or if Grouchy had marched inland with his six thousand men at the moment when the people were eager to begin the rising, and the English had but three thousand regular troops in the island. It seemed as if England were destined to have all the luck, and either by favour of the elements or the miscalculations of her enemies, to escape, one after another, the deadly perils that for ever beset her empire.

As it was, this arrival of Humbert, even followed by so brilliant a victory, was really so much profit to the British Government. Barrington truly remarks:—

"The defeat of Castlebar, however, was a victory to the Viceroy; it revived all the horrors of the rebellion, which had been subsiding, and the desertion of the militia regiments tended to impress the gentry with an idea that England alone could protect the country."

The Marquis Cornwallis determined to collect a great army, and march in imposing force; but he did not hasten his movements so much as it was thought he might have done; and, in the meantime, the French and insurgents were profiting by the delay. It was said that forty thousand of the Westmeath people were preparing to assemble at the Crooked Wood, in that county, so as to join the French on their passage, and march on the metropolis.

At length the Marquis was ready; and having assured himself of the presence of twenty thousand men on his line of march, he thought himself strong enough to encounter the eight hundred audacious Frenchmen and their Irish allies. These latter were by no means increasing, but rather diminishing since the day of Castlebar; and indeed, at no time exceeded two thousand men—a circumstance which greatly surprised and disgusted the French.

The Marquis proceeded on the 30th of August on the road to Castlebar, and arrived on the 4th of September at Hollymount, fourteen miles distant from Castlebar; in the evening of that day he received intelligence, that the enemy had abandoned his post, and marched to Foxford.

The advanced guard of the French having arrived at Coloony, was opposed on the 5th by Colonel Vereker, of the city of Limerick militia, who had marched from Sligo for the purpose, with about two hundred infantry, thirty of the Twenty-fourth Regiment of Light Dragoons, and two curricle guns. After a smart action of about an hour's continuance, he was obliged to retreat, with the loss of his artillery, to Sligo.

This opposition, though attended with defeat to the opposers, is supposed to have caused the French General to relinquish his design on Sligo. He directed his march by Drumnahair towards Manorhamilton, in the County of Leitrim, leaving on the road, for the sake of expedition, three six-pounders dismounted, and throwing five pieces more of artillery over the bridge at Drumnahair into the river. In approaching Manorhamilton he suddenly wheeled to the right, taking his way by Drumkerin, perhaps with design of attempting, if possible, to reach Granard, in the County of Longford, where an insurrection had taken place. Crawford's troops hung so close on the rearguard of the French as to come to action with it on the 7th, between Drumshambo and Ballynomore, in which action they were repulsed with some loss, and admonished to observe more caution in the pursuit.

The French army, passing the Shannon at Ballintra, and halting some hours in the night at Claone, arrived at Ballinamuck,

County Longford, on the 8th of September, so closely followed by the troops of Colonel Crawford and General Lake, that its rearguard was unable to break the bridge at Ballintra, to impede the pursuit; while Lord Cornwallis, with the grand army, crossed the same river at Carrick-on-Shannon, marched by Mohill to Saint-Johnstown, in the County of Longford, in order to intercept the enemy in front, on his way to Granard; or, should he proceed, to surround him with an army of thirty thousand men. In this desperate situation, Humbert arranged his forces, with no other object, as it must be presumed, than to maintain the honour of the French arms. The rearguard having been attacked by Colonel Crawford, about two hundred of the French infantry surrendered. The rest continued to defend themselves for above half an hour, when, on the appearance of the main body of General Lake's army, they also surrendered, after they had made Lord Roden, with a body of dragoons, a prisoner. His lordship had precipitately advanced into the French lines to obtain their surrender. The Irish insurgents who had accompanied the French to this fatal field, being excluded from quarter, fled in all directions, and were pursued, with the slaughter of about five hundred men, which seems much less to exceed the truth than the returns of slain in the south-eastern parts of the island. About one thousand five hundred insurgents were with the French army at Ballinamuck, at the time of the surrender of Humbert. The loss of the King's troops was officially stated at three privates killed, twelve wounded, three missing, and one officer wounded. The troops of General Humbert were found, when prisoners, to consist of seven hundred and forty-six privates and ninety-six officers, having sustained a loss of about two hundred men since their landing at Killala on the 22d of August.

Vengeful executions began on the field of battle. It appears that, on the day of the "Races of Castlebar," a considerable part of the Louth and Kilkenny regiments, not finding it convenient to retreat, thought the next best thing they could do would be to join the victors, which they immediately did, and in one hour were completely equipped as French riflemen. About ninety of those men were hung by Lord Cornwallis at Ballinamuck. One of them defended himself by insisting "that it was the army, and not he, who were deserters; that whilst he was fighting hard, they all ran away, and left him to be murdered."

A Mr. Blake, who had been an officer in the British army, was also executed on the field. Bartholomew Teeling and Matthew Tone (brother of Theobald Wolfe Tone) were among the prisoners, and were both executed within a few days in Dublin. Mr. Moore, President of the Provincial Government, which had been instituted at Castlebar, was one of the prisoners at Ballinamuck, and was sentenced to banishment. Roger Maguire, one of the leaders of the Irish insurgents, was transported, and his father, a brewer, was hung.

The small French garrison which had been left in Killala still occupied that place, and great part of North Connaught continued in insurrection.

On the 22d of September, thirty-two days after the landing of the French army, and fifteen after its capture at Ballinamuck, a large body of troops arrived at Killala, under the command of Major-General Trench, who would have been still some days later in his arrival had he not been hastened by a message from the bishop, to announce the fearful apprehensions his lordship's family and the other loyalists were under.

The bishop's narrative of what followed indicates that the recovery of this place by the British forces was a scene rather of indiscriminate massacre than of combat. He describes how "a troop of fugitives in full race from Ballina, women and children, tumbled over one another to get into the castle, or into any house in the town where they might hope for a momentary shelter, continued for a painful length of time to give notice of the approach of an army."

There was, however, a momentary resistance.

The insurgents quitted their camp to occupy the rising ground close by the town, on the road to Ballina, and posted themselves under the low stone walls on each side, in such a manner as enabled them with great advantage to take aim at the King's troops. They had a strong guard also on the other side of the town towards Foxford, having probably received intelligence, which was true, that General Trench had divided his forces at Crosmolina, and sent one part of them by a detour of three miles, to intercept the fugitives that might take that course in their flight. This last detachment consisted chiefly of the Kerry militia, under the orders of Lieutenant-Colonel Crosbie and Maurice Fitzgerald, the Knight of Kerry, their Colonel, the Earl of Glandore, attending the General.

The two divisions of the royal army

were supposed to make up about twelve hundred men, and they had five pieces of cannon. The number of the insurgents could not be ascertained. Many ran away before the engagement, while a very considerable number flocked into the town in the very heat of it, passing under the castle windows in view of the French officers on horseback, and running upon death with as little appearance of reflection or concern as if they were hastening to a show. About four hundred of these people fell in the battle, and immediately after it. Whence it may be conjectured that their entire number scarcely exceeded eight or nine hundred.

The whole scene passed in sight of the castle, and so near it that the family could distinctly hear the balls whistling by their ears.

The attempt at resistance lasted twenty minutes, when the insurgents scattered in two directions—some into the town, where they were shot down in the streets, some along the shore of the bay, where they were enfiladed by a gun placed in position for that purpose.

The court-martial began the day after, and sat in the house of Mr. Morrison. They had to try not less than seventy-five prisoners at Killala, and a hundred and ten at Ballina, besides those who might be brought in daily. The two first persons tried at this tribunal were General Bellew and Mr. Richard Bourke. The trial of these two gentlemen was short. They were found guilty on Monday evening, and hung the next morning in the park behind the castle.

So ended the last of the series of partial insurrections in Ireland in the year 1798. Little reliance is to be placed on the official accounts of the killed, wounded, and missing, in the several engagements and encounters. According to the most probable accounts to be had from the War Office, the number of the army lost in this rebellion amounts in the whole to nineteen thousand seven hundred men; and according to the general Government accounts of the total loss of the insurgents, it exceeded fifty thousand, without including women and children, great numbers of whom were shot down by the yeomanry or burned in their own houses. The mere loss of life, too, gives but a faint idea of the sufferings endured by the poor people. Many hundreds had been put to the torture, and lacerated by cruel scourging, to extort information. Never, perhaps, was any national insurrection in the world so savagely crushed; never was insurrection so thoroughly justified by the oppression which provoked it; and never were chiefs of any insurrection more pure in their motives, more gallant, honourable, and self-sacrificing, than those whose bodies were now swinging upon gibbets, whose heads were grinning upon spikes, or who were languishing in various prisons, to expiate the crime of loving their country and hating its oppressors.

The policy of Mr. Pitt was now in full operation; and the "impression of horror" was strong and deep: indeed, the plans of the Minister were rather aided by the driftless and helpless French expeditions which the imbecile government of the Directory sent to help the insurgents, but which came too late, and arrived at the wrong places. Before narrating the measures of the Government with a view to the Legislative Union, it is necessary to tell how it fared with Theobald Wolfe Tone. The founder of the United Irish Society was not a man to evade the consequences and responsibilities of his own acts, nor to take his ease in France, where he held a high commission in the army, while his comrades were perishing on the field or on the gallows. He never for one moment relaxed his efforts to effect the great task of his life, which was to bring an adequate force of Frenchmen into Ireland, and so to stop and to punish the shocking atrocities, of which every new report tortured his soul.

The news of Humbert's attempt, as may well be imagined, threw the Directory into the greatest perplexity. They instantly determined, however, to hurry all their preparations, and send off at least the division of General Hardy, to second his efforts, as soon as possible. The report of his first advantages, which shortly reached them, augmented their ardour and accelerated their movements. But such was the state of the French navy and arsenals, that it was not until the 20th of September that this small expedition, consisting of one sail of the line and eight frigates, under Commodore Bompart, and three thousand men, under General Hardy, was ready for sailing. The news of Humbert's defeat had not yet reached France.

Paris was then crowded with Irish emigrants, eager for action. Some Irishmen embarked before Bompart, in a small and fast-sailing vessel, with Napper Tandy at their head. They reached, on the 16th of September, the Isle of Raghlin, on the north coast of Ireland, where they heard of Humbert's disaster: they merely spread some proclamations, and escaped to Norway. Three Irishmen only accompanied Tone in Hardy's flotilla; he alone was

C

embarked in the Admiral's vessel, the Hoche, the others were on board the frigates. These were Mr. T. Corbett, and MacGuire, two brave officers, who afterwards died in the French service, and a third gentleman, connected by marriage with his friend Russell.

At the period of this expedition Tone was hopeless of its success, and in the deepest despondency at the prospect of Irish affairs. Such was the wretched indiscretion of the Government that, before his departure, he read himself, in the *Bien Informé*, a Paris newspaper, a detailed account of the whole armament, where his own name was mentioned in full letters, with the circumstance of his being on board the *Hoche*. There was, therefore, no hope of secrecy. He had all along deprecated the idea of those attempts on a small scale. But he had also declared repeatedly, that if the Government sent only a corporal's guard, he felt it his duty to go along with them; he saw no chance of Kilmaine's large expedition being ready in any reasonable time, and therefore determined to accompany Hardy. His resolution was, however, deliberately taken, in case he fell into the hands of the enemy, never to suffer the indignity of a public execution. And his son, William Theobald Wolfe Tone, informs us that he had expressed himself to this effect "at dinner, in our own house, and in my mother's presence, a little before leaving Paris."*

At length, about the 20th of September, 1798, that fatal expedition set sail from the Bay de Camaret. It consisted of the *Hoche*, seventy-four; *Loire*, *Resolue*, *Bellone*, *Coquille*, *Embuscade*, *Immortalité*, *Romaine*, and *Semillante*, frigates; and *Biche*, schooner, and aviso. To avoid the British fleets, Bompart, an excellent seaman, took a large sweep to the westward, and then to the north-east, in order to bear down on the northern coast of Ireland, from the quarter whence a French force would be least expected. He met, however, with contrary winds, and it appears that his flotilla was scattered; for on the 10th of October, after twenty days' cruise, he arrived off the entry of Loch Swilly, with the *Hoche*, the *Loire*, the *Resolue*, and the *Biche*. He was instantly signalled, and on the break of day next morning, 11th of October, before he could enter the bay or land his troops, he perceived the squadron of Sir John Borlase Warren, consisting of six sail of the line, one razee of sixty guns, and two frigates, bearing down upon him. There was no chance of escape for the large and heavy man-of-war. Bompart gave instant signals to the frigates and schooner to retreat through shallow water, and prepared alone to honour the flag of his country and liberty by a desperate but hopeless defence. At that moment a boat came from the *Biche* for his last orders. That ship had the best chance to get off. The French officers all supplicated Tone to embark on board of her. "Our contest is hopeless," they observed; "we will be prisoners of war, but what will become of you?" "Shall it be said," replied he, "that I fled whilst the French were fighting the battles of my country?" He refused their offers, and determined to stand and fall with the ship. The *Biche* accomplished her escape.

The British Admiral dispatched two men-of-war, the razee and a frigate, after the *Loire* and *Resolue*; and the *Hoche* was soon surrounded by four sail of the line and a frigate, and began one of the most obstinate and desperate engagements which have ever been fought on the ocean. During six hours she sustained the fire of a whole fleet, till her masts and rigging were swept away, her scuppers flowed with blood, her wounded filled the cockpit, her shattered ribs yawned at each new stroke, and let in five feet of water in the hold; her rudder was carried off, and she floated a dismantled wreck on the waters. Her sails and cordage hung in shreds; nor could she reply with a single gun from her dismounted batteries to the unabating cannonade of the enemy. At length she struck. The *Resolue* and *Loire* were soon reached by the English fleet; the former was in a sinking condition; she made, however, an honourable defence. The *Loire* sustained three attacks, drove off the English frigates, and had almost effected her escape. At length, engaged by the *Anson*, razee of sixty guns, she struck, after an action of three hours, entirely dismasted. Of the other frigates, pursued in all directions, the *Bellone*, *Immortalité*, *Coquille*, and *Embuscade*, were taken; and the *Romaine* and *Semillante*, through a thousand dangers, reached separate ports in France.

During the action Tone commanded one of the batteries, and, according to the report of the officers who returned to France, fought with the utmost desperation, and as if he were courting death. When the ship struck, confounded with the other officers, he was not recognized for some time; for he had completely

---

* *Memoirs of Wolfe Tone.* By his son. Published in Washington. The English edition is much mutilated.

acquired the language and appearance of a Frenchman. The two fleets were dispersed in every direction; nor was it till some days later that the *Hoche* was brought into Loch Swilly, and the prisoners landed and marched to Letterkenny. Yet rumours of his being on board must have been circulated, for the fact was public at Paris. But it was thought he had been killed in the action. It was at length a gentleman, well-known in the County Derry as a leader of the Orange party, and one of the chief magistrates in that neighbourhood, Sir George Hill, who had been his fellow-student in Trinity College, and knew his person, who undertook the task of discovering him. It is known that in Spain grandees and noblemen of the first rank pride themselves in the functions of familiars, spies, and informers of the Holy Inquisition. It remained for Ireland to offer a similar example. The French officers were invited to breakfast with the Earl of Cavan, who commanded in that district. Tone sat undistinguished amongst them, when Sir George Hill entered the room, followed by police officers. Looking narrowly at the company, he singled out the object of his search, and, stepping up to him, said, "Mr. Tone, I am *very happy* to see you." Instantly rising, with the utmost composure he replied, "Sir George, I am happy to see you. How is Lady Hill and your family?"* Beckoned into the next room by the police officers, an unexpected indignity awaited him. It was filled with military, and one General Lavau, who commanded them, ordered him to be ironed, declaring that, as on leaving Ireland to enter the French service he had not renounced his oath of allegiance, he remained a subject of Britain, and should be punished as a traitor. Seized with a momentary burst of indignation at such unworthy treatment and cowardly cruelty to a prisoner of war, he flung off his uniform, and cried, "These fetters shall never degrade the revered insignia of the free nation which I have served!" Resuming then his usual calm, he offered his limbs to the irons, and when they were fixed he exclaimed, "For the cause which I have embraced, I feel prouder to wear these chains than if I were decorated with the star and garter of England."

From Letterkenny he was hurried to Dublin without delay. Contrary to usual custom, he was conveyed during the whole route, fettered and on horseback, under an escort of dragoons. The escort was composed of Cambridgeshire yeomanry cavalry, and commanded by a Captain Thackeray, afterwards a clergyman and Rector of Dundalk. He often, long afterwards, described this journey, and said that Tone was the most delightful companion he ever travelled with.

Though the reign of terror was drawing to a close, and Lord Cornwallis had restored some appearance of legal order and regular administration in the kingdom, a prisoner of such importance to the Irish Protestant Ascendancy party as the founder and leader of the United Irish Society, and the most formidable of their adversaries, was not to be trusted to the delays and common forms of law. Though the Court of King's Bench was then sitting, preparations were instantly made for trying him summarily before a court-martial. It has been erroneously stated that Tone imagined his French commission would be a protection to him, and that he pleaded it on his trial. He never, indeed, was legally condemned; for, though a subject of the Crown (not of Britain, but of Ireland), he was not a military man in that kingdom. He had taken no military oath; and of course the court-martial which tried him had no power to pronounce on his case, which belonged to the regular criminal tribunals. But his heart was sunk in despair at the total failure of his hopes, and he did not wish to survive them. To die with honour was his only wish; and his only request, to be shot like a soldier. For this purpose he preferred himself to be tried by a court-martial; and proffered his French commission, not to defend his life, but as a proof of his rank, as he stated himself on his trial.

If further proof were required that he was perfectly aware of his fate, according to the English law, his own journals, written during the Bantry Bay expedition, afford an incontestible one. (See *Journal of December* 26, 1796.) "If we are taken, my fate will not be a mild one; the best I can expect is to be shot as an *emigré rentré*, unless I have the good fortune to be killed in the action; for most assuredly, if the enemy will have us, he must fight for us. Perhaps I may be reserved for a trial, for the sake of striking terror into others, in which case I shall be hanged as a traitor, and embowelled, &c. As to the embowelling, '*Je m'en fiche.*' If ever they hang me, they are welcome to embowel me if they please. These are pleasant prospects!

---

* Dr. Madden points out that this Sir George Hill was a regular secret agent of the Government, and quotes several payments made to him, and through him to other agents, out of the Secret Service money. See accounts of Secret Service money in Madden's work.

Nothing on earth could sustain me now but the consciousness that I am engaged in a just and righteous cause."

Tone appeared before this court in the uniform of a *Chef de Brigade* (Colonel). The firmness and cool serenity of his whole deportment gave to the awe-struck assembly the measure of his soul. Nor could his bitterest enemies, whatever they deemed of his political principles, and of the necessity of striking a great example, deny him the praise of determination and magnanimity.

The members of the Court having taken the usual oath, the Judge Advocate proceeded to inform the prisoner that the court-martial before which he stood was appointed by the Lord-Lieutenant of the kingdom, to try whether he had or had not acted traitorously against His Majesty, to whom, as a natural-born subject, he owed all allegiance, from the very fact of his being born in the kingdom. And, according to the usual form, he called upon him to plead guilty or not guilty.

The prisoner admitted all the facts, "stripping the charge of its technical word *traitorously*." He would make no defence, and give no trouble, but asked leave to read an address, giving his own account of his conduct. This address is given at full length in his son's *Memoir*, and is in these words:—

"*Mr. President, and Gentlemen of the Court-martial*,—I mean not to give you the trouble of bringing judicial proof to convict me legally of having acted in hostility to the Government of His Britannic Majesty in Ireland. I admit the fact. From my earliest youth I have regarded the connection between Ireland and Great Britain as the curse of the Irish nation; and felt convinced that whilst it lasted this country could never be free nor happy. My mind has been confirmed in this opinion by the experience of every succeeding year, and the conclusions which I have drawn from every fact before my eyes. In consequence, I determined to apply all the powers which my individual efforts could move, in order to separate the two countries.

"That Ireland was not able, of herself, to throw off the yoke, I knew. I therefore sought for aid wherever it was to be found. In honourable poverty I rejected offers which, to a man in my circumstances, might be considered highly advantageous. I remained faithful to what I thought the cause of my country, and sought in the French Republic an ally to rescue three millions of my countrymen from—"

The President here interrupted the prisoner, observing that this language was neither relevant to the charge nor such as ought to be delivered in a public court. One member said, it seemed calculated only to inflame the minds of a certain description of people (the United Irishmen), many of whom might probably be present; and that, therefore, the Court ought not to suffer it. The Judge Advocate said he thought that if Mr. Tone meant this paper to be laid before His Excellency, in way of *extenuation*, it must have quite a contrary effect, if any of the foregoing part was suffered to remain.

Tone.—" I shall urge this topic no further, since it seems disagreeable to the Court; but shall proceed to read the few words which remain."

General Loftus.—" If the remainder of your address, Mr. Tone, is of the same complexion with what you have already read, will you not hesitate for a moment in proceeding, since you have learned the opinion of the Court?"

Tone.—" I believe there is nothing in what remains for me to say which can give any offence. I mean to express my feelings and gratitude towards the Catholic body, in whose cause I was engaged."

General Loftus.—" That seems to have nothing to say to the charge against you, to which only you are to speak. If you have anything to offer in defence or extenuation of that charge, the Court will hear you; but they beg that you will confine yourself to that subject."

Tone.—" I shall, then, confine myself to some points relative to my connection with the French Army. Attached to no party in the French Republic, without interest, without money, without intrigue, the openness and integrity of my views raised me to a high and confidential rank in its armies. I obtained the confidence of the Executive Directory, the approbation of my generals, and, I venture to add, the esteem and affection of my brave comrades. When I review these circumstances I feel a secret and internal consolation which no reverse of fortune, no sentence in the power of this Court to inflict, can ever deprive me of, or weaken in any degree. Under the flag of the French Republic I originally engaged, with a view to save and liberate my own country. For that purpose I have encountered the chances of war amongst strangers; for that purpose I have repeatedly braved the terrors of the ocean, covered, as I knew it to be, with the triumphant fleets of that power which it was my glory and my duty to oppose. I have sacrificed all my views in life; I have courted poverty; I have left a beloved wife unprotected, and children whom I adored, fatherless. After such sacrifices in a cause which I have always conscientiously considered as the cause of justice and freedom, it is no great effort at this day to add, 'the sacrifice of my life.'

"But I hear it said that this unfortunate country has been a prey to all sorts of horrors. I sincerely lament it. I beg, however, it may be remembered that I have been absent four years from Ireland. To me these sufferings can never be attributed. I designed, by fair and open war, to procure the separation of the two countries. For open war I was prepared; but if, instead of that, a system of private assassination has taken place, I repeat, while I deplore it, that it is not chargeable on me. Atrocities, it seems, have been committed on both sides. I do not less deplore them; I detest them from my heart; and to those who know my character and sentiments, I may safely appeal for the truth of this assertion. With them I need no justification.

"In a cause like this, success is everything. Success, in the eyes of the vulgar, fixes its merits. Washington succeeded, and Kosciusko failed.

"After a combat nobly sustained, a combat which would have excited the respect and sympathy of a generous enemy, my fate was to become a prisoner. To the eternal disgrace of those who gave the order, I was brought hither in irons, like a felon. I mention this for the sake of others; for me, I am indifferent to it; I am aware of the fate which awaits me, and scorn equally the tone of complaint and that of supplication.

"As to the connection between this country and Great Britain, I repeat it, all that has been imputed to me, words, writings, and actions, I here deliberately avow. I have spoken and acted with reflection, and on principle, and am ready to meet the consequences. Whatever be the sentence of this Court, I am prepared for it. Its members will surely discharge their duty; I shall take care not to be wanting in mine."

This speech was pronounced in a tone so magnanimous, so full of noble and calm serenity, as seemed deeply and visibly to affect all its hearers, the members of the Court not excepted. A pause ensued of some continuance, and silence reigned in the hall, till interrupted by Tone himself, who inquired whether it was not usual to assign an interval between the sentence and execution? The Judge Advocate answered that the voices of the Court would be collected without delay, and the result transmitted forthwith to the Lord-Lieutenant. If the prisoner, therefore, had any observations to make, now was the moment.

Tone.—" I wish to offer a few words relative to one single point—to the mode of punishment. In France our *emigrés*, who stand nearly in the same situation in which I suppose I now stand before you, are condemned to be shot. I ask that the Court should adjudge me the death of a soldier, and let me be shot by a platoon of grenadiers. I request this indulgence rather in consideration of the uniform which I wear—the uniform of a *Chef de Brigade* in the French army—than from any personal regard to myself. In order to evince my claim to this favour, I beg that the Court may take the trouble to peruse my commission and letters of service in the French army. It will appear from these papers that I have not received them as a mask to cover me, but that I have been long and *bonâ fide* an officer in the French service."

Judge Advocate.—" You must feel that the papers you allude to will serve as undeniable proofs against you."

Tone.—" Oh, *I know it well.* I have already admitted the facts, and I now admit the papers as full proofs of conviction."

The papers were then examined; they consisted of a brevet of *Chef de Brigade*, from the Directory, signed by the Minister of War; of a letter of service, granting him the rank of Adjutant-General; and of a passport.

General Loftus.—" In these papers you are designated as serving in the army of England."

Tone.—" I did serve in that army when it was commanded by Buonaparte, by Desaix, and by Kilmaine, who is, as I am, an Irishman. But I have served elsewhere."

General Loftus observed that the Court would undoubtedly submit to the Lord-Lieutenant the address which he had read to them, and also the subject of his last demand. In transmitting the address, he however took care to efface all that part of it which he would not allow to be read. Lord Cornwallis refused the last demand of the prisoner, and he was sentenced to die the death of a traitor, in forty-eight hours, on the 12th of November. This cruelty he had foreseen; for England, from the days of Llewellyn of Wales, and Wallace of Scotland, to those of Tone and Napoleon, has never shown mercy or generosity to a fallen enemy. He, then, in perfect coolness and self-possession, determined to execute his purpose, and anticipate their sentence.

The sentence upon Tone, pronounced by a court-martial, was obviously illegal; and so every lawyer knew it to be. But the people looked on as if in stupor. The son of Tone has truly described the condition of Dublin at that moment:—

"No man dared to trust his next neighbour, nor one of the pale citizens to betray by look or word his feelings or sympathy. The terror which prevailed in Paris under the rule of the Jacobins, or in Rome during the proscriptions of Marius, Sylla, and the Triumviri, and under the reigns of Tiberius, Nero, Caligula, and Domitian, was never deeper or more universal than that of Ireland at this fatal and shameful period. It was, in short, the feeling which made the people, soon after, passively acquiesce in the Union, and in the extinction of their name as a nation. Of the numerous friends of my father, and of those who had shared in his political principles and career, some had perished on the scaffold, others rotted in dungeons, and the remainder dreaded, by the slightest mark of recognition, to be involved in his fate."

But there was one friend of the gallant prisoner who was determined that the law of the land should at least be invoked, and one effort made to rescue this noble Irishman from the jaws of death. The friend was John Philpot Curran. He believed that by moving the Court of King's Bench to assert its jurisdiction some delay might be interposed—the French Government might threaten to retaliate upon some important prisoner of war; the case might thus become a political and not a criminal one, and in the end, either through threats of retaliation, or by an arrangement with the British Government, Tone might be saved.

On the next day, November 12th (the day fixed for his execution), the scene in the Court of King's Bench was awful and impressive to the highest degree. As soon as it opened, Curran advanced, leading the aged father of Tone, who produced his affidavit that his son had been brought before a bench of officers, calling itself a court-martial, and sentenced to death. "I do not pretend," said Curran, "that Mr. Tone is not guilty of the charges of which he is accused. I presume the officers were honourable men. But it is stated in this affidavit, as a solemn fact, that Mr. Tone had no commission under His Majesty; and, therefore, no court-martial could have cognizance of any crime imputed to him whilst the Court of King's Bench sat in the capacity of the great Criminal Court of the land. In times when war was raging, when man was opposed to man in the field, courts-martial might be endured; but every law authority is with me whilst I stand upon this sacred and immutable principle of the Constitution—that martial law and civil law are incompatible, and that the former must cease with the existence of the latter. This is not, however, the time for arguing this momentous question. My client must appear in this Court. He is cast for death this very day. He may be ordered for execution whilst I address you. I call on the Court to support the law, and move for a *habeas corpus*, to be directed to the Provost-Marshal of the barracks of Dublin and Major Sandys, to bring up the body of Tone."

Chief Justice.—"Have a writ instantly prepared."

Curran.—"My client may die whilst the writ is preparing."

Chief Justice.—"Mr. Sheriff, proceed to the barracks and acquaint the Provost-Marshal that a writ is preparing to suspend Mr. Tone's execution, and see that he be not executed."

The Court awaited, in a state of the utmost agitation and suspense, the return of the Sheriff. He speedily appeared, and said: "My lord, I have been to the barracks, in pursuance of your order. The Provost-Marshal says he must obey Major Sandys. Major Sandys says he must obey Lord Cornwallis." Mr. Curran announced at the same time that Mr. Tone (the father) was just returned, after serving the *habeas corpus*, and that General Craig would not obey it. The Chief Justice exclaimed: "Mr. Sheriff, take the body of Tone into custody; take the Provost-Marshal and Major Sandys into custody, and show the order of the Court to General Craig."

The general impression was now that the prisoner would be led out to execution, in defiance of the Court. This apprehension was legible in the countenance of Lord Kilwarden, a man who, in the worst of times, preserved a religious respect for the laws, and who, besides, I may add, felt every personal feeling of pity and respect for the prisoner, whom he had formerly contributed to shield from the vengeance of Government on an occasion almost as perilous. His agitation, according to the expression of an eye-witness, was magnificent.

The Sheriff returned at length with the fatal news. He had been refused admittance in the barracks; but was informed that Mr. Tone, who had wounded himself dangerously in the neck the night before, was not in a condition to be removed. In short, on the night before, after writing a letter to the French Directory, and a touching adieu to his wife, while the soldiers were erecting a gibbet for him in the yard before his window, he cut his throat with a knife. But it was not effectually done, and he lingered in that dungeon, stretched on his bloody pallet, in the extremity of agony, seven days and nights. No friend was allowed access to him; and nobody saw him but the prison surgeon, a French emigrant, and therefore his natural enemy. At length he died.*

The Government allowed the body to be carried away by a relative named Dunbavin, and it was buried in the little churchyard of Bodenstown, County Kildare, where Thomas Davis caused a monumental slab to be erected to his memory.

"Thus passed away," says Madden, "one of the master spirits of his time. The curse of Swift was upon this man—he was an Irishman. Had he been a native of any other European country, his noble qualities, his brilliant talents, would have raised him to the first honours in the state, and to the highest place in the esteem of his fellow-citizens. His name lives, however, and his memory is probably destined to survive as long as his country has a history. Peace be to his ashes!"

The expenses incurred in first exciting the insurrection, next in suppressing it, and afterwards in carrying out its real object—a Legislative Union, are estimated moderately by Dr. Madden, as follows:—

From 1797 to 1802, the cost of the large military force that was kept up in Ireland, estimated at £4,000,000 per annum,	£16,000,000
Purchase of the Irish Parliament,	1,500,000
Payment of claims of suffering loyalists,	1,500,000
Secret Service money, from 1797 to 1804 (from official reports),	53,547
Secret Service money, previous to August 21, 1797, date of first entry in preceding account—say from date of Jackson's mission in 1794, estimated at	20,000
Probable amount of pensions paid for services in suppression of the Rebellion and the promotion of the Union, to the present time,	1,200,000
Increased expense of legal proceedings and judicial tribunals,	500,000
Additional expenditure in public offices, consequent on increased duties in 1798, and alterations in establishments attendant on the Union, the removal of Parliamentary archives, and compensation of officers, servants, &c.,	800,000
Total,	£21,573,547

* Madden states that one friend of Tone, a Mr. Fitzpatrick, of Capel Street, was admitted to see him once. This is a matter on which Tone's son, who was then far away, might easily have been misinformed. Madden further testifies that the surgeon, a Dr. Lentaigne, was a very good and humane man.

The whole of which was, the next year, in the arrangement of the terms of "Union," carried to the account of Ireland, and made part of *her* national debt—as if it were Ireland that profited by these transactions.

The military force in Ireland, during and immediately after the insurrection, was:—

FROM PARLIAMENTARY RETURNS.

The Regulars,	52,281
The Militia,	26,634
The Yeomanry,	51,274
The English Militia,	24,201
Artillery,	1,500
Commissariat,	1,700
Total,	137,590

These figures are taken from a report of the Parliamentary proceedings of the 16th of February, 1799. They are introduced in a speech of Lord Castlereagh, prefacing a motion on military estimates. He did not think that one man could be then spared of the 137,590,—though the rebellion was completely over, and though he had to deal with a population only *one-half* of the present. We have not at hand the means of ascertaining the force of 1800, but there is ground for concluding that it was over that of 1799, though the time of the rebellion was still further off by a year.

But, in fact, Ministers had in reserve still another ordeal which our country had to pass through—the *Union;* and this immense military force was still thought needful, "as good lookers-on"—to use Lord Strafford's phrase of a century and a half earlier.

CHAPTER III.

1798—1799.

Examination of O'Connor, Emmet, and MacNeven—Lord Enniskillen and his Court-Martial—Project of Union—Bar Meeting—Speech from the Throne—Union Proposed—Reception in the Lords—In the Commons—Ponsonby—Fitzgerald—Sir Jonah Barrington—Castlereagh's Explanation—Speech of Plunket—First Division on the Union—Majority of One—Mr. Trench and Mr. Fox—Methods of Conversion to Unionism—First Contest a Drawn Battle—Excitement in Dublin.

PARLIAMENT continued sitting. In August and September, 1798, the examination of Thomas Addis Emmet, Arthur O'Connor, and Dr. MacNeven, proceeded before the secret committees. While the report of these examinations was still secret, the Dublin newspapers under the control of the Government published some very garbled and falsified accounts of them, calculated not only to criminate and degrade those gentlemen themselves, but to hold them forth as betraying their comrades and associates. The object of this was very plain. They thought it necessary to protest against it by a published card. Thereupon they were examined again; were asked whether they meant to retract anything; were shown the minutes of their evidence as taken down, and interrogated as to its correctness and fidelity. They answered that they found it correct, so far as it went; but Emmet declared that very much of their evidence was *omitted*. On the whole, they admitted that the report *shown to them* was substantially correct (except the omissions), and that they had only meant to protest against the false newspaper accounts. Their new examination was triumphantly paraded as a complete exculpation of the committees from all charge of garbling; but, in fact, the newspapers could not have come by even their partial and carefully distorted accounts of this evidence, except through some one connected with the Government or secret committees; and so the intended effect was in part produced without the Government seeming to be a party to it. This affair is obscure; but, in justice to the unfortunate gentlemen then in the hands of most unscrupulous enemies, it is right to throw all the light possible upon it. Arthur O'Connor, in a letter to Lord Castlereagh, gives this account of the misunderstanding:—

"At the instance of Government, Emmet, MacNeven, and I, drew up a memoir containing thirty-six pages, giving an account of the origin, principles, conduct, and views of the Union, which we signed and delivered to you on the 4th of August last. On the 6th, Mr. Cook came to our prison, and after acknowledging that the memoir was a perfect performance of our agreement, he told us that Lord Cornwallis had read it; but, as it was a vindication of the Union, and a condemnation of the Ministers, the Government, and Legislature of Ireland, he could not receive it; and, therefore, he wished we would alter it. We declared we would not change one letter—it was all true, and it was the truth we stood pledged to deliver. He then asked us, if Government should publish such parts only as might suit them, whether we would refrain from publishing the memoir entire. We answered that, having stipulated for the liberty of publication, we would use that right when and as we should feel ourselves called on. To which he added that, if we published, he would have to hire persons to answer us; that then he supposed we would reply, by which a paper war would be carried on without end between us and the Government. Finding that we would not suffer the memoir to be garbled, and that the literary contest between us and these hirelings was not likely to turn out to your credit, it was determined to examine us before the secret committees, whereby a more complete selection might be made out of the memoir, and all the objectionable truths—with which it was observed it abounded—might be suppressed. For the present I shall only remark that, of one hundred pages, to which the whole of the information I gave to the Government and to the secret committees amounts, only one page has been published."

On the 6th of October, Parliament was prorogued with a highly congratulatory speech from the Throne, on the suppression of the "dangerous and wicked rebellion," and on the glorious victory obtained by "Sir Horatio Nelson over the French fleet in the Mediterranean."

About the same time occurred a certain sham court-martial, under the presidency of the Earl of Enniskillen, a Colonel in the army—a great favourite with the Orangemen, and probably an Orangeman himself. A man named Wollaghan, a yeoman, had brutally shot a poor peaceable man in his own house. The affair is not otherwise deserving of notice than that the evidence on this trial shows the horrid state of the country. A corporal of the corps deposed that a certain Captain Armstrong, who commanded at Mount Kennedy before and after the murder, had given orders "that any body of yeomanry going out (he would not wish them less than nine or ten for their own safety), and if they should meet with any rebels, whom they knew or suspected to be such, they need not be at the trouble of bringing them in, but were to shoot them on the spot; that he (the witness) communicated this to the corps, and is very certain in the hearing of the prisoner Wollaghan, who was a sober, faithful, and loyal yeoman, and not degrading the rest of the corps—one of the best in it; that it was the practice of the corps to go out upon scouring parties without orders," &c.

The affair, however, made a noise—became notorious; and Lord Cornwallis thought himself obliged to disapprove the judgment of the court-martial (which acquitted Wollaghan), and to rebuke Lord Enniskillen. The murderer, however, was only dismissed the service. The Orangemen were highly disgusted with Lord Cornwallis, and called him "Croppy

Corny." But the cases of local tyranny and brutality exercised upon the people were very seldom indeed brought into any court. Seldomer still were they punished. The juryman who should have ventured to hesitate about acquitting an Orangeman would have been himself hunted down as a "croppy." The moment was come to propose the *Union*, as the only way of putting a stop to these horrors and to all the other woes of Ireland.

Even before the fury of rebellion had subsided, had the British Ministry recommended preparatory steps to enable the Irish Government to introduce the proposal of a Legislative Union with plausibility and effect upon the first favourable opening. In pursuance of this recommendation a pamphlet was written, or procured to be written, by Mr. Edward Cooke, the Under-Secretary of the Civil Department. It was published anonymously, but was well understood to speak the sentiments of the British Administration, and the Chief Governor, and those of the Irish Administration who went with his Excellency upon the question of union. It was circulated with incredible industry and profusion throughout every part of the nation, and certainly was productive of many conversations on the question under the then existing circumstances of that nation; the most prominent of which were,—the still unallayed horrors of blood and carnage, the excessive cruelty and vindictive ferocity of the Irish yeomanry towards their countrymen, compared with the pacific, orderly, and humane conduct of the English militia, of which about eighteen regiments were still in the country, and, above all, the confidence which the conciliatory conduct of the Chief Governor inspired. This pamphlet was considered as a kind of official proclamation of the sentiments of Government upon the question, and had no sooner appeared than it produced a general warfare of the press, and threw the whole nation into a new division of parties.

No sooner was the intention of Government unequivocally known, than most of the leading characters took their ranks according to their respective views and sentiments,—the Earl of Clare at the head of the Unionists, and the Right Honourable Mr. Foster, his late zealous colleague in the extorted system of coercion and terror, put himself at the head of the Anti-Unionists. Amongst the first dismissals for opposing the Union were those of Sir John Parnell, the Chancellor of the Exchequer, and Mr. Fitzgerald, the Prime-Sergeant. The most interesting public meeting upon the subject of the Union was that of the gentlemen of the Irish bar. It has before been observed, that in Ireland the bar was the great road that led to preferment, and few were the families in the nation which looked up to it that did not furnish one member or more to that profession. The bar, consequently, commanded a very powerful influence over the public mind, even independently of the weight of respectability attending the opinions of that learned body. In pursuance of a requisition signed by twenty-seven lawyers of the first respectability and character in the profession, a meeting of the Irish bar took place on the 9th of December, at the Exhibition House in William Street, to deliberate on the question of Legislative Union. The meeting was very numerous. It must be observed that the bar of Ireland was the only great body in the state or in society that Lords Clare and Castlereagh feared, as a serious obstruction to their plans. In its ranks were the most accomplished statesmen and most formidable debaters of the country; and the most earnest opponents of Union to the last were barristers. Lord Clare, therefore, had taken measures to corrupt the bar by creating a great many new legal offices, which they were expected to solicit, and for which they would sell themselves to the Castle. He doubled the number of the Bankrupt Commissioners; he revived some offices, created others; and, under pretence of furnishing each county with a local judge, in two months he established thirty-two new offices of about six or seven hundred pounds per annum each. His arrogance in court intimidated many whom his patronage could not corrupt; and he had no doubt of overpowering the whole profession.

There was much interest, therefore, felt in the result of this preliminary meeting of the bar. Among those who had called the meeting were fourteen of the King's counsel: E. Mayne, W. Saurin, W. C. Plunket, C. Bushe, W. Sankey, B. Burton, J. Barrington, A. M'Cartney, G. O'Farrell, J. O'Driscoll, J. Lloyd, P. Burrowes, R. Jebb, and H. Joy, Esquires —a very distinguished list of names; some of which will be met with again and again, before the final catastrophe of the nation. Saurin spoke against the Union project. "He was a moderate Huguenot," says Sir Jonah Barrington, "and grandson of the great preacher at the Hague— an excellent lawyer and a steadfast and pious Christian." Sir Jonah goes on to describe this important meeting:—

"Mr. Saint George Daly, a briefless barrister, was the first supporter of the Union. Of all men he was the least thought of for preferment; but it was wittily observed, 'that the Union was the first brief Mr. Daly had spoken from.' He moved an adjournment.

"Mr. Thomas Grady was the Fitzgibbon spokesman—a gentleman of independent property, a tolerable lawyer, an amatory poet, a severe satirist, and an indefatigable quality-hunter. He had written the *Flesh Brush*, for Lady Clare; the *West Briton*, for the Union; the *Barrister*, for the bar; and the *Nosegay*, for a banker at Limerick—who sued him successfully for a libel.

"'The Irish,' said Mr. Grady, 'are only the *rump of an aristocracy*. Shall I visit posterity with a system of *war, pestilence*, and *famine?** No, no! give me a Union. Unite me to that country where all is peace, and order, and prosperity. Without a Union we shall see embryo chief judges, attorney-generals in perspective, and *animalcula sergeants*. All the cities of the south and west are on the *Atlantic Ocean*, between the rest of the world and Great Britain; *they* are all for *it*—they must all become warehouses; the people are Catholics, and they are all for it,' &c., &c., &c. Such an oration as Mr. Grady's had never before been heard at a meeting of lawyers in Europe.

"Mr. John Beresford, Lord Clare's nephew and purse-bearer, followed, as if for the charitable purpose of taking the laugh from Mr. Grady, in which he perfectly succeeded, by turning it on himself. Mr. Beresford afterwards became a parson, and is now Lord Decies.

"Mr. Goold said: 'There are forty thousand British troops in Ireland, and with forty thousand bayonets at my breast the Minister shall not plant another Sicily in the bosom of the Atlantic. I want not the assistance of divine inspiration to foretell, for I am enabled by the visible and unerring demonstrations of nature to assert, that Ireland was destined to be a free and independent nation. Our patent to be a state, not a shire, comes direct from heaven. The Almighty has, in majestic characters, signed the great charter of our independence. The great Creator of the world has given our beloved country the gigantic outlines of a kingdom. The God of nature never intended that Ireland should be a province, and, *by G——, she never shall!*'

"The assembly burst into a tumult of applause. A repetition of the words came from many mouths, and many an able lawyer swore hard upon the subject. The division was—

Against the Union, . . . 166
In favour of it, ... 32

Majority, ... 134

"Thirty-two," continues Sir Jonah Barrington, "was the precise number of the county judges, and of this minority the following persons were afterwards rewarded for their adherence to Lord Clare:—

"*List of Barristers who Supported the Union, and their Respective Rewards.*

Per Annum.
1. Charles Osborn, appointed a Judge of the King's Bench, . . . £3,900
2. Saint John Daly, appointed a Judge of the King's Bench, . . . 3,000
3. William Smith, appointed Baron of the Exchequer, . . . 2,300
4. Mr. M'Cleland, appointed Baron of the Exchequer, . . . 2,300
5. Robert Johnson, appointed Judge of the Common Pleas, . . . 3,300
6. William Johnson, appointed Judge of the Common Pleas, . . . 3,300
7. Mr. Torrens, appointed Judge of the Common Pleas, . . . 3,300
8. Mr. Vandeleur, appointed a Judge of the King's Bench, . . . 3,300
9. Thomas Maunsell, a County Judge, . 600
10. William Turner, a County Judge, . 600
11. John Scholes, a County Judge, . . 600
12. Thomas Vickers, a County Judge, . 600
13. J. Homan, a County Judge, . . . 600
14. Thomas Grady, a County Judge, . . 600
15. John Dwyer, a County Judge, . . 600
16. George Leslie, a County Judge, . . 600
17. Thomas Scott, a County Judge, . . 600
18. Henry Brook, a County Judge, . . 600
19. James Geraghty, a County Judge, . 600
20. Richard Sharkey, a County Judge, . 600
21. William Stokes, a County Judge, . 600
22. William Roper, a County Judge, . 600
23. C. Garnet, a County Judge, . . . 600
24. Mr. Jenison, a Commissioner for the distribution of one million and a half Union compensation, . . . 1,200
25. Mr. Fitzgibbon Henchy, Commissioner of Bankrupts, ... 400
26. J. Keller, Officer in the Court of Chancery, 500
27. P. W. Fortescue, M.P., *a secret pension*, . 400
28. W. Longfield, an officer in the Custom House, ... 500
29. Arthur Brown, Commission of Inspector, 800
30. Edmund Stanley, Commission of Inspector, ... 800
31. Charles Ormsby, Counsel to Commissioners, Value, . . . 5,000
32. William Knott, M.P., Commission of Appeals, ... 800
33. Henry Deane Grady, Counsel to Commissioners, Value, . . . 5,000
34. John Beresford, his father a title."

It was already so notorious, during this winter, that a Union was to be imme-

---

* Nothing could be more unfortunate than this crude observation of Mr. Grady, as the very three evils—war, pestilence, and famine—which he declared a union would avert, have since visited, and are still visiting, the unioned country; which has, since the connection with England, been depopulated by the *famine* which that Union caused; and, inoculated with the late plague from Great Britain, they are now declared in a state of *war* by the British Legislature.

diately proposed, that the measure was already warmly discussed, in anticipation of the approaching meeting of Parliament. Mr. Cooke's pamphlet called forth scores of other pamphlets, for and against. Before the end of December, no less than thirty appeared, of which Plowden records the titles.

The city of Dublin, which it was natural to suppose would be more prejudiced by the Union than any other part of the kingdom, inasmuch as it would lose much of the advantages of a metropolis by the abolition of the Parliament, was also prominently forward in its opposition to that measure. A post-assembly of the Lord Mayor, sheriffs, commons, and citizens of the city of Dublin was convened on the 17th of December; who, referring to a variety of rumours that were then in circulation, of an intended union of Ireland with Great Britain, came to resolutions strongly denouncing any such project; which certainly, whatever it might be supposed to do for other parts of the kingdom, was sure to ruin Dublin at all events.

Next came a very numerous and respectable meeting of the merchants and bankers of the city, who resolved—"That they looked with abhorrence on any attempt to deprive the people of Ireland of their Parliament, and thereby of their constitutional right, and immediate power to legislate for themselves. That, impressed with every sentiment of loyalty to their King, and affectionate attachment to British connection, they conceived that to agitate in Parliament a question of the Legislative Union between that kingdom and Great Britain would be highly dangerous and impolitic."

Even the fellows and scholars of Trinity College held their meeting, and passed a resolution calling on their representatives in Parliament to oppose the Union. Similar resolutions of county and borough meetings appeared nearly every day; so that when Lord Cornwallis, on the 22d of January, 1799, came down, along with his trusty counsellors, Lords Clare and Castlereagh, to open the session of Parliament, it was very evident that there was a considerable mass of opposition to be broken down.

On that day there was a great concourse in Dublin streets, and College Green was filled with anxious multitudes, not gay and jubilant as they had been when once before they had crowded those avenues to witness the parade of the volunteers, but with a gloomy feeling of the miseries then actually upon the country, and foreboding of something worse to come. The Viceroy came from the Castle to the House with a strong guard, and duly delivered his speech from the throne; of which these two portentous paragraphs were listened to with breathless attention:—

"The zeal of His Majesty's regular and militia forces, the gallantry of the yeomanry, the honourable co-operation of the British fencibles and militia, and the activity, skill, and valour of His Majesty's fleets, will, I doubt not, defeat every future effort of the enemy. But the more I have reflected on the situation and circumstances of this kingdom, considering on the one hand the strength and stability of Great Britain, and on the other those divisions which have shaken Ireland to its foundations, the more anxious I am for some permanent adjustment which may extend the advantages enjoyed by our sister kingdom to every part of this island.

"The unremitting industry with which our enemies persevere in their avowed design of endeavouring to effect a separation of this kingdom from Great Britain, must have engaged your particular attention, and His Majesty commands me to express his anxious hope that this consideration, joined to the sentiment of mutual affection and common interest, may dispose the Parliaments in both kingdoms to provide the most effectual means of maintaining and improving a connection essential to their common security, and of consolidating, as far as possible, into one firm and lasting fabric, the strength, the power, and the resources of the British empire."

Here, then, was the dreaded *Union* distinctly enough raised up before Parliament and the country, and avowed as the policy of the Administration. At once began the tumult of debate on the address. In the Lords, an address was proposed which was almost an echo of the speech, promising to "give the fullest attention to measures of such importance."

Upon which it was proposed by Lord Powerscourt to amend the said motion, by inserting after the word importance the following words:—"That it is our most earnest desire to strengthen the connection between the two countries by every possible means, but the measure of a Legislative Union we apprehend is not within the limit of our power; we beg leave, also, to represent to your Majesty that, although this House were competent to adopt such a measure, we conceive that it would be highly impolitic so to do, as it would tend, in our opinion, more than any other cause, ultimately to a separation of this kingdom from that of Great Britain."

A motion was then made for leave to withdraw the amendment. A debate arose thereupon, and the question being put, the House divided, and the Earl of Glandore reported that the contents below the bar were nineteen, and the non-contents in the House were forty-six.

A motion was then made that after the word "security," in the same paragraph, the following words be expunged, "and of consolidating, as far as possible, into one firm and lasting fabric, the strength, the power, and the resources of the British empire," which also passed in the negative. Another motion was then made by the Earl of Bellamont, that after the said word "importance" the following words be inserted: "So far as may be consistent with the permanent enjoyment, exercise, and tutelary vigilance, of our resident and independent Parliament, as established, acknowledged, and recognized." This motion was also negatived by a division of forty-nine against sixteen. Fourteen of the lords in the minority protested.*

In the House of Commons were many anxious faces and gloomy brows. It had already been sufficiently indicated that Government, to carry this measure, would stop at nothing. Immediately after the bar meeting the Right Honourable James Fitzgerald, Prime-Sergeant, was dismissed from office, and deprived of his precedency at the bar. It was known, also, that unlimited funds would be used by Government, without scruple, both in buying up boroughs (which were then treated as the private property of their patrons), and in direct bribery to pay for votes. The innumerable methods which a powerful government has at its disposal both to reward and to punish, all these considerations rose up before the anxious minds of the members occupying those benches. It must be confessed, too, that the previous history of the Irish Parliament, as recorded in these pages, was not calculated to make the country expect any exhibition of stern patriotism. "I have now seen," said Theobald Wolfe Tone, "the Parliament of Ireland, the Parliament of England, the Congress of the United States of America, the Corps Legislatif of France, and the Convention of Batavia; I have likewise seen our shabby Volunteer Convention in 1783, and the General Committee of the Catholics in 1793, so that I have seen, in the way of deliberate bodies, as many I believe as most men, and of all those I have mentioned, beyond all comparison, the most shamelessly profligate and abandoned by all sense of virtue, principle, or even common decency, was the Legislature of my own unfortunate country—the scoundrels!"

But when we read so harsh a judgment upon the Legislature of our country, it must not be forgotten that it did not represent the country, did not even represent the Protestant minority of the country, represented nothing (as to its vast majority) save a few noble families, great proprietors, and the enormous "interest" of place and pension. Considering all this, it is rather surprising, and was indeed very surprising to Lord Castlereagh, that on the present vital occasion the policy of the Castle met with so hearty an opposition.

The address in the Commons was moved by Lord Tyrone, eldest son of the Marquis of Waterford. The address, he said, did not pledge him in any manner to support the measure of an union; let that question of policy stand upon its own merits, let it be adopted or rejected as the interests of Ireland and the prosperity of the empire should dictate.

Colonel Fitzgerald (member for the County of Cork) seconded the address, expressing a zealous desire that any step likely to cement and strengthen the connection between the two countries should be adopted.

After several speeches opposing the measure of an union in a vague and hypothetical sort of way, as if there were really no such question before the House, Lord Castlereagh, whose fault was certainly not lack of boldness, rose to say that although there were not in the address any specific pledge to a measure of union, yet it was clearly implied in the wish to strengthen the resources of the empire; for he had no difficulty in saying that he thought the only means of settling that unhappy country in permanent tranquillity and connection with Britain were to be found in a Legislative Union, and on that subject he did intend, at an early day, to submit a specific motion to the House.*

Mr. G. Ponsonby entered on an able attack and exposure of the general prin-

* Viz., Leinster.
Granard.
Belvidere.
Arran.
Charlemont.
Bellamont.
Mountcashel.
Kilkenny.
Belmore.
Powerscourt.
De Vesci.
Dunsany.
Lismore.
Wm. Down and Connor.

* On occasion of this first and most remarkable of the debates on the Union it has been judged expedient to go somewhat further into detail than usual. It was now that Members of Parliament took their positions on that great question, from which positions many of them afterwards retreated and changed sides, from motives, unhappily, too well known, as will soon appear.

ciple of an union, by boldly avowing the principle that neither the Legislature nor any power on earth had a right or authority to annihilate the Irish Parliament, and deprive people for ever of their rights to the benefits of the Constitution and civil liberty.

The Minister had told them they ought to discuss this measure with coolness; but when the Minister himself would not leave men to the free exercise of their understanding, but turned out of office the best and oldest servants of the Crown, because they would not prostitute their conscience; when the terror of dismissal was thus holden out to deter men in office from a fair exercise of their private judgment, how could he talk of cool discussion? He concluded by moving an amendment, which would give every gentleman, who did not wish to pledge himself to a surrender of the rights of the country, an opportunity of speaking his mind. The amendment was, —that after the passage which declared the willingness of the House to enter on a consideration of what measures might best tend to confirm the common strength of the empire, should be inserted, "maintaining, however, the undoubted birthright of the people of Ireland to have a resident and independent legislature, such as was recognized by the British Legislature in 1782, and was finally settled at the adjustment of all differences between the two countries."

Sir L. Parsons seconded the amendment.

Many gentlemen warmly supported Ponsonby's amendment; amongst others, Mr. Fitzgerald, ex-Prime-Sergeant, who raised the vital Constitutional question,— "It was not, in his opinion, within the moral competence of Parliament to destroy and extinguish itself, and with it the rights and liberties of those who created it. The constituent parts of a state are obliged to hold their public faith with each other, and with all those who derive any serious interest under their engagements; such a compact may, with respect to Great Britain, be an union; but with respect to Ireland, it will be a revolution, and a revolution of a most alarming nature."

Mr. Fitzgerald also quoted Dr. Johnson's remark to an Irishman, on the subject of an union: "Don't unite with us," said he, "we shall unite with you only to rob you; we should have robbed the Scots if they had anything to be robbed of."

The debate proceeded, warming as it went. Sir Boyle Roche, in his blundering way, stumbled upon a most accurate description of the real Castle policy. He said "he was for an union to put an end to uniting between Presbyterians, Protestants, and Catholics, to overturn the Constitution."

One of the most patriotic speeches made in the course of this historic argument was by Sir Jonah Barrington, then a Judge of the Admiralty Court. He strongly deprecated this plan to subject irrevocably one independent country to the will of another, and both to the will of a Minister already stronger than the Crown, and more powerful than the people; and this great and important usurpation, stolen into Parliament through the fulsome paragraphs of an echoing congratulation, pledging the House to the discussion of a principle subversive of their liberties, and in the hour of convalescence calling on it to commit suicide. Ireland (he said) had not fair play: her Parliament had not fair play. The foulest and most unconstitutional means, he believed, had been used to intimidate and corrupt it, and either to force or to seduce a suffrage, when nothing but general, independent, uninfluenced opinion could warrant for a moment the most distant view of so ruinous a subject. He had good reason to believe that corrupt and unconstitutional means had been used by the noble lord to individuals of the Irish Parliament. Some of those means were open and avowed. Two of the oldest, most respectable, and most beloved officers of the Crown had been displaced, because they presumed to hint an opinion adverse to the stripling's dictates, on a subject where their country was at stake; their removals crowned them with glory, and the Minister with contempt. He asserted that other gentlemen in office, whose opinions were decidedly adverse to the measure, but whose circumstances could not bear similar sacrifices, were dragged to the altar of pollution, and forced against their will to vote against their country. He had good reason to believe that unconstitutional interference had been used by the executive power with the legislative body. One gentleman refused the instructions of his constituents, and had been promoted. Peerages (as was rumoured) were bartered for the rights of minors, and every effort used to destroy the free agency of Parliament. If this were true, it encroached on the constitution; and if the executive power overstepped its bounds, the people were warranted to do the same on their part; and between both it might be annihilated, and leave a wondering world in amazement how the same people could have been wise enough to frame the best constitution on earth, and foolish enough to destroy it. One king and two kingdoms was the cry of the people of Ireland.

Sir John Blaquiere, on the side of the Government, remonstrated against "the charges of undue influence and corruption;" and then proceeded to use an argument in behalf of the Union, which may serve as a sample of the means by which so many of the Catholics were induced to favour that measure. Sir John said, "the honourable member who proposed the amendment, with a flow of such transcendent eloquence as had seldom been heard in that House, had expressly stated that the Roman Catholics must oppose the Union. He knew not the mind of Catholics upon the subject; but he should speak his own, that the Roman Catholics under the present order of things *could never be accommodated, as he feared, with what they asked*, without imminent danger to the Protestant establishment, both in Church and State; but *if once an union should be adopted, all those difficulties would vanish, and he should see none in granting them everything they desired.*"

Mr. Knox and Mr. Hans Hamilton made violent attacks upon the Union and upon the Government.

Mr. Knox (member for Philipstown) lamented that that accursed measure had long been the favourite object of that Minister of England, whose wild ambition had already led to the destruction of empires, and which then sought to annihilate that nation. In order to forward that wicked scheme, great pains had been taken by those who managed the affairs of Government under his guidance, to promote and keep alive among the people every distinction of party and religion; all differences of opinion, whether in politics or religion, had been industriously fomented and encouraged, and every means taken to distract and divide the inhabitants of that land. If that fatal measure should ever be carried, henceforth that insulted, degraded, debased country would be made a barrack, a depôt from whence to draw the means of enslaving Great Britain, and no resource left to save either country but a revolution.

Mr. Hans Hamilton declared that an union was a measure he should very firmly oppose within those walls with his vote, without them with his life. But he foresaw that the hour was at hand which would prove this to be the most glorious day that Ireland had ever beheld, and enable the members to go forth to their constituents, and assure them they were represented by an Irish Parliament, and never would betray their independence.

Lord Castlereagh felt that the day was going against him. He rose to state his reasons for favouring the measure of a Legislative Union, and spoke, as he well knew how, with a noble air of candour. It is almost incredible, however, that in the abstract of his speech which has come down to us, actually appear the following words:—

"His lordship trusted that no man would decide on a measure of such importance as that in part before the House, *on private or personal motives;* for if a decision were thus to be influenced, it would be the most unfortunate that could ever affect the country."

His reasons for supporting the measure were of course of the purest description. If the means he used to support it had been as free from taint as his personal conduct, his lordship's name and fame would now be much higher than they are. "Dissensions" and "divisions" unhappily existing in Ireland (which Mr. Knox said the Government had "industriously fomented"), formed the chief motive, in his mind, for our country to fling itself into the arms of the English, who had carefully created and kept alive those dissensions and divisions in Ireland for centuries! One passage in his lordship's argument reads strangely in the light of subsequent history:—

"Absentees (he said) formed another objection. They would be somewhat increased, no doubt, by an union; but the evil would be compensated by other advantages, and among them by the growth of *an intermediate class of men between the landlord and the peasant; a class of men whose loss was felt in Ireland,* to train *the mind of the lower class.* These an union would bring over *from England.* They would also have *capital from thence.* At all events, these inconveniences would be but a grain of sand compared with the advantages which would be derived from internal security, and their growing together in habits of amity and affection."

The next powerful speech on the debate was that of William Conyngham Plunket, then in the prime of life. He had been the warm friend of Tone and of Emmet, and was now fast rising into high eminence, both as a barrister and a member of Parliament. It is his famous *Hamilcar* speech in which he assails the Government, as he had promised to do, more daringly than Sir Jonah Barrington. He spoke of the apparently bluff, downright old soldier (Cornwallis) "who, as an additional evidence of the directness and purity of his views, had chosen for his secretary a simple and modest youth *(Puer ingenui vultûs ingenuique pudoris)*, whose inexperience was the voucher of his innocence; yet, was he bold to say, that during the Vice-royalty of that unspotted veteran, and during the administration of that unassuming stripling, within the last six weeks, a system of black corruption had been carried on within the walls of the Castle, which would disgrace the annals of the worst period of the history of either country. Did they choose to take down his words? He needed to call no witnesses to their bar to prove them. He saw two right honourable gentlemen sitting within those walls who had long and faithfully served the Crown, and who had been dismissed, because they dared to express a sentiment in favour of the freedom of their country. He saw another honourable gentleman who had been forced to resign his place as Commissioner of the Revenue, because he refused to co-operate in that dirty job of a dirty Administration. Did they dare to deny this? I say," he continued, "that at this moment the threat of dismissal from office is suspended over the heads of the members who now sit around me, in order to influence their votes on the question of this night, involving everything that can be sacred or dear to man. Do you desire to take down my words? Utter the desire, and I will prove the truth of them at your bar. Sir, I would warn you against the consequences of carrying this measure by such means as this, but that I see the necessary defeat of it in the honest and universal indignation which the adoption of such means excites; I see the protection against the wickedness of the plan in the imbecility of its execution, and I congratulate my country that, when a design was formed against their liberties, the prosecution of it was entrusted to such hands as it is now placed in."

Mr. Plunket then dealt with the Constitutional grounds of opposition to an union, and especially to the *time* of its being proposed. It is impossible, within our limits, to give more than a mere abstract of such a speech :—

"At a moment," he said, "when Ireland was filled with British troops, when the loyal men were fatigued and exhausted by their efforts to subdue rebellion—efforts in which they had succeeded before those troops arrived; whilst their *Habeas Corpus* Act was suspended, whilst trials by court-martial were carrying on in many parts of the kingdom, whilst the people were taught to think that they had no right to meet or to deliberate, and whilst the great body of them were so palsied by their fears and worn down by their exertions that even the vital question was scarcely able to rouse them from their lethargy; at a moment when they were distracted by domestic dissensions —dissensions artfully kept alive, as the pretext for their present subjugation and the instrument of their future thraldom. He thanked Administration for the measure. They were, without intending it, putting an end to Irish dissensions. Through that black cloud, which they had collected over them, he saw the light breaking in upon their unfortunate country. They had composed dissensions, not by fomenting the embers of a lingering and subdued rebellion; not by hallooing the Protestant against the Catholic, and the Catholic against the Protestant; not by committing the North against the South; not by inconsistent appeals to local or party prejudices. No! but by the avowal of that atrocious conspiracy against the liberties of Ireland they had subdued every petty feeling and subordinate distinction. They had united every rank and description of men by the pressure of that grand and momentous subject; and he told them that they would see every honest and independent man in Ireland rally round her Constitution, and merge every other consideration in his opposition to that ungenerous and odious measure. For his own part he would resist it to the last gasp of his existence, and with the last drop of his blood; and when he felt the hour of his dissolution approaching, he would, like the father of Hannibal, take his children to the altar, *and swear them to eternal hostility against the invaders of their country's freedom.*"

This gallant speech was often cited afterwards against Plunket; and it was remarked that Hamilcar, after that swearing scene, never helped the Romans to govern Carthage as a province.

Strange to say, of all the Beresfords, John Claudius Beresford, of the Riding-House and the pitch-caps, opposed the Government measure, and supported Mr. Ponsonby's amendment. Some of the strongest Irish nationalists of that day were Orangemen, and bitter persecutors of Catholics.

At length, after twenty-two hours' debate, at ten o'clock on the morning of the 24th, the House divided, and the vote stood—for Mr. Ponsonby's amendment,

105; against it, 106. Majority for the Government, 1.

It was held by both sides of the House to be substantially a defeat for the Government, and the multitudes who had been thronging the corridors, the porticos, and the streets all around, burst into acclamations of joy. The mob waited for members as they came out, and hooted or cheered, as they heard each member had voted for the Castle or the Nation.

As to the method by which Castlereagh had gained even that apparent and most unsatisfactory victory, Sir Jonah Barrington, an eye-witness, gives us this detail, which illustrates the whole mode and machinery whereby the Union was finally carried:—

"A very remarkable incident," says Sir Jonah, "during the first night's debate, occurred in the conduct of Mr Luke Fox and Mr. Trench, of Woodlawn, afterwards created Lord Ashtown. These were the most palpable, undisguised acts of public tergiversation and seduction ever exhibited in a popular assembly. They afterwards became the subject of many speeches and of many publications; and their consequences turned the majority of one in favour of the Minister.

"It was suspected that Mr. Trench had been long in negotiation with Lord Castlereagh; but it did not, in the early part of that night, appear to have been brought to any conclusion—his conditions were *supposed* to be too extravagant. Mr. Trench, after some preliminary observations, declared, in a speech, that he would vote against the Minister, and support Mr. Ponsonby's amendment. This appeared a stunning blow to Mr. Cooke, who had been previously in conversation with Mr. Trench. He was immediately observed sidling from his seat nearer to Lord Castlereagh. They whispered earnestly, and, as if restless and undecided, both looked wistfully towards Mr. Trench. At length the matter seemed to be determined on. Mr. Cooke retired to a back seat, and was obviously endeavouring to count the House, probably to guess if they could that night dispense with Mr. Trench's services. He returned to Lord Castlereagh—they whispered, again looked most affectionately at Mr. Trench, who seemed unconscious that he was the subject of their consideration. But there was no time to lose—the question was approaching—all shame was banished—they decided on the terms; and a significant and certain glance, obvious to everybody, convinced Mr. Trench that his conditions were agreed to. Mr. Cooke then went and sat down by his side; an earnest but very short conversation took place; a parting smile completely told the House that Mr. Trench was that moment satisfied. These surmises were soon verified. Mr. Cooke went back to Lord Castlereagh; a congratulatory nod announced his satisfaction. But could any man for one moment suppose that a member of Parliament, a man of very large fortune, of respectable family, and good character, could be publicly, and without shame or compunction, actually seduced by Lord Castlereagh in the very body of the House, and under the eye of two hundred and twenty gentlemen? Yet this was the fact. In a few minutes Mr. Trench rose, to apologize for having indiscreetly declared he would support the amendment. He added, that he had thought better of the subject since he had *unguardedly* expressed himself; that he had been *convinced* he was wrong, and would support the Minister.

"Scarcely was there a member of any party who was not disgusted. It had, however, the effect intended by the desperate purchaser, of proving that ministers would stop at *nothing* to effect their objects, however shameless or corrupt. This purchase of Mr. Trench had a much more fatal effect upon the destinies of Ireland. His change of sides, and the majority of *one* to which it contributed, were probably the remote causes of persevering in an Union. Mr. Trench's venality excited indignation in every friend of Ireland.*

"Another circumstance, that night, proved by what means Lord Castlereagh's majority of even *one* was acquired.

"The Place Bill, so long and so pertinaciously sought for, and so indiscreetly framed by Mr. Grattan and the Whigs of Ireland, now, for the first time, proved the very engine by which the Minister upset the opposition, and annihilated the Constitution.

"That bill enacted, that members accepting offices, places, or pensions, during the pleasure of the Crown, should not sit in Parliament unless re-elected; but, unfortunately, the bill made no distinction between valuable offices which might influence, and nominal offices which might job; and the Chiltern Hundreds of England were, under the title of the Escheatorships of Munster, Leinster, Connaught, &c., transferred to Ireland, with salaries of forty shillings, to be used at pleasure by the Secretary. Occasional and temporary seats were thus bartered for by Government, and, by the ensuing session,

* No fewer than three Trenches are found in the "Black List," as voting for the Union. They were all appointed to valuable offices for it, and one was made a peer and an ambassador.

made the complete and fatal instrument of packing the Parliament, and effecting an union.

"Mr. Luke Fox, a barrister of very humble origin, of vulgar manners, and of a coarse, harsh appearance, was endued with a clear, strong, and acute mind, and was possessed of much cunning. He had acquired very considerable legal information, and was an obstinate and persevering advocate. He had been the usher of a school, and a sizer in Dublin University; but neither politics nor the *belles-lettres* were his pursuit. On acquiring eminence at the bar he married an obscure niece of the Earl of Ely's. He had originally professed what was called Whiggism, merely, as people supposed, because his name was Fox. His progress was impeded by no political principles; but he kept his own secrets well, and, being a man of no importance, it was perfectly indifferent to everybody what side he took. Lord Ely, perceiving he was manageable, returned him to Parliament as one of his automata; and Mr. Fox played his part very much to the satisfaction of his manager.

"When the Union was announced, Lord Ely had not made his terms, and remained long in abeyance;* and, as his lordship had not issued his orders to Mr. Fox, he was very unwilling to commit himself until he could dive deeper into probabilities; but rather believing the Opposition would have the majority, he remained in the body of the House, with the Anti-Unionists, when the division took place. The doors were scarcely locked when he became alarmed, and slunk, unperceived, into one of the dark corridors, where he concealed himself. He was, however, discovered, and the Sergeant-at-Arms was ordered to bring him forth, to be counted amongst the Anti-Unionists. His confusion was very great, and he seemed at his wit's end. At length he declared he had taken advantage of the Place Bill, had *actually accepted the Escheatorship of Munster*, and had thereby vacated his seat, and could not vote.

"The fact was doubted; but after much discussion, his excuse, *upon his honour*, was admitted, and he was allowed to return into the corridor. On the numbers being counted, there was a majority of ONE for Lord Castlereagh, and exclusive of Mr. Trench's conduct; but for that of Mr. Fox the numbers would have been equal. The measure would have been negatived by the Speaker's vote, and the renewal of it the next day would have been prevented. This would have been a most important victory.

"The mischief of the Place Bill now stared its framers in the face, and gave the Secretary a code of instruction how to arrange a Parliament against the ensuing session.

"To render the circumstance still more extraordinary and unfortunate for Mr. Fox's reputation, it was subsequently discovered by the public records that Mr. Fox's assertion was false. But the following day Lord Castlereagh purchased him outright; and then, *and not before*, appointed him to the nominal office of Escheator of Munster, and left the seat of Lord Ely for another of his creatures.* This is mentioned not only as one of the most reprehensible public acts committed during the discussion, but because it was the primary cause of the measure being persisted in."

Thus the preliminary contest on the very threshold of the Union question may be said to have ended in a drawn battle. It was known, however, that it was to be renewed on that very evening. It was an exciting day for the people of Dublin; and to those who know into what a dismal condition the Union has since dragged down the once proud metropolis of our island, there is something pathetic in the passionate anxiety with which its thronging people then crowded round their Parliament House, hanging on the momentous vote, watching with beating hearts the progress of a struggle which was to decide the destinies of their city and their nation.

CHAPTER IV.

1799.

Second Debate on Union—Sir Lawrence Parsons—Mr. Smith—Ponsonby and Plunket—Division—Majority against Government—Ponsonby's Resolution for Perpetual Independence—Defection of Fortescue and others—Resolution Lost—"Possible Circumstances"—Tumult—Danger of Lord Clare—Second Debate in the Lords—Lord Clare triumphant—"Loyalists' Claim Bill"—"Rebels Disqualification Bill"—"Flogging Fitzgerald"—Asks Indemnity—Regency Act—Opposed by Castlereagh.

IT was naturally supposed that if the Minister was left in a minority on the

---

* He "made his terms," however, in due time. We afterwards find him in receipt of a sum of £45,000, the price of his three boroughs, which he sold to Government, that it might put its own creatures into the representation.

* This did not conclude the remarkable acts of Mr. Fox. After his seat had been so vacated, he got himself re-elected for a borough, under the influence of the Earl of Granard, a zealous Anti-Unionist. Here he once more betrayed the country, and was appointed a Judge when the subject was decided.

second debate upon the reception of the address, he would, according to all precedents, resign his situation; whilst an increased majority, however small, in favour of his measure, might give plausible grounds for pressing it forward at all hazards. No wonder, then, that the excitement and anxiety were intense on that day. Sir Jonah Barrington describes the scene:—

"The people collected in vast multitudes around the House; a strong sensation was everywhere perceptible. Immense numbers of ladies of distinction crowded at an early hour into the galleries, and by their presence and their gestures animated that patriotic spirit, upon the prompt energy of which alone depended the fate of Ireland.

"Secret messengers were dispatched in every direction to bring in loitering or reluctant members. Every emissary that Government could rely upon was busily employed the entire morning; and five and thirty minutes after four o'clock in the afternoon of the 24th of January, 1799, the House met to decide—by the adoption or rejection of the address—the question of national independence or annihilation. Within the corridors of the House, a shameless and unprecedented alacrity appeared among the friends of the Government.

"Mr. Cooke, the Under-Secretary, who, throughout all the subsequent stages of the question, was the private and efficient actuary of the Parliamentary seduction, on this night exceeded even himself, both in his public and private exertions to gain over the wavering members. Admiral Pakenham, a naturally friendly and good-natured gentleman, that night acted like the captain of a pressgang, and actually *hauled* in some members who were desirous of retiring. He had declared that he would act in *any* capacity, according to the exigencies of his party; and he did not shrink from his task.

"This debate, in point of warmth, much exceeded the former. Lord Castlereagh sat long silent; his eye ran round the assembly, as if to ascertain his situation, and was often withdrawn with a look of uncertainty and disappointment. The members had a little increased since the last division, principally by members who had not declared themselves, and of whose opinions the Secretary was ignorant."

When the address was reported, on the reading of that part of it which related to the Union, Sir Lawrence Parsons offered an amendment, objecting to the paragraph which "pledged the House, under a metaphorical expression ('maintaining and imploring a connection,' &c.), to admit the principle of the Legislative Union." Two short passages of his long speech are enough to show its spirit:—

"Were the Union ever so good a measure, why bring it forward at that time? Was it not evidently to take advantage of England's strength there, and their own internal weakness? It was always in times of division and disaster that a nation availed itself of the infirmities of its neighbour, to obtain an unjust dominion. That Great Britain should desire to do so he did not much wonder; for what nation did not desire to rule another? Nor was he surprised that there should be some among them base enough to conspire with her in doing so; for no country could expect to be so fortunate as not to have betrayers and parricides among its citizens."

"Annihilate the Parliament of Ireland! that is the cry that came across the water. Now is the time: Ireland is weak—Ireland is divided—Ireland is appalled by civil war—Ireland is covered with troops—martial law brandishes its sword throughout the land; now is the time to put down Ireland for ever—now strike the blow! *Who?* Is it you? Will you obey that voice? Will you betray your country?"

On the second debate, the most important speech in favour of union (though Castlereagh spoke strongly) was that of Mr. William Smith, a barrister—afterwards rewarded with the place of a Baron of the Exchequer. He addressed himself principally to the refutation of the main constitutional objection to an union decreed by Parliament—namely, the objection that Parliament had been "elected to make laws, and not legislatures,"—that it had no powers to divest itself of its legislative capacity to give itself away to another people, still less to sell itself, and sell its constituents along with itself. Mr. Smith said:—

"Of the competency of Parliament to the enactment of such reform, he had never heard any doubts expressed; and the arguments which he thought might be offered against the alleged right were inconclusive, yet, perhaps, as plausible as any that could be urged against the competency of the Legislature to a decree of union. That the authority of the Parliament had this extent, he had not the slightest doubt. His opinion," he said, "was founded on precedent, on the mischiefs which would result from a contrary doctrine, on the express authority of constitutional writers, and on the genuine principles of the Constitution itself. By enacting an union, Parliament would do no more than change (it would not surrender or subvert) the Constitution. Ireland, after a Legislative incorporation, would still be governed by three estates; and her inhabitants would enjoy all their privileges unimpaired. If the Legislature could new-model the succession of the Crown, or change the established religion, it might certainly ordain those alterations which an union would involve. To controvert its right would be to deny the validity of the act for the incorporation of Scotland with England and Wales. But," he added, "that if he conceived that the measure would be a surrender of national independence, he would by no means agree to it; but it would merely be an incorporation of national distinctions; nor would he promote the scheme if he thought that it would not ensure an identity or community of interests."

Between Lord Castlereagh and Mr. Ponsonby the debate took a very bitter personal turn. The Secretary was provoked out of his usual cool indifference. To the bar he applied the term "pettifoggers;" to the Opposition, "cabal—combinators—desperate faction;" and to the nation itself, "barbarism—ignorance," and "insensibility to *protection and paternal regards* she had ever experienced from the British nation." His speech was severe beyond anything he had ever uttered within the walls of Parliament, and far exceeded the powers he was supposed to possess.

After many speeches on each side, Mr. Plunket arose; and, in what Sir Jonah Barrington calls "the ablest speech ever heard from any member in that Parliament," went at once to the grand and decisive point,—the incompetence of Parliament. He could go no farther in principle than Mr. Ponsonby, but his language was irresistible, and he left nothing to be urged. It was perfect in eloquence, and unanswerable in reasoning. Its effect was indescribable; and for the first time Lord Castlereagh, whom he personally assailed, seemed to shrink from the encounter. That speech was of great weight, and it proved the eloquence and the fortitude of the speaker.

But a short speech on that night, which gave a new sensation and excited novel observations, was a maiden speech by Colonel O'Donnell, of Mayo County, the eldest son of Sir Neil O'Donnell, a man of very large fortune in that County. He was Colonel of a Mayo regiment. He was a brave officer, and a well-bred gentleman; and in all the situations of life he showed excellent qualities. On this night, roused by Lord Castlereagh's invectives, he could not contain his indignation; and by anticipation, "disclaimed all future allegiance, if an union were effected; he held it as a vicious revolution, and avowed that he would take the field at the head of his regiment to oppose its execution, and would resist rebels in rich clothes as he had done the rebels in rags." And for this speech in Parliament he was dismissed his regiment without further notice.

On a division being called for, there appeared a majority of *six* against the Union. The gratification of the Anti-Unionists was unbounded; and as they walked in one by one to be counted, "the eager spectators," says Sir Jonah, "ladies as well as gentlemen, leaning over the galleries, ignorant of the result, were panting with expectation. Lady Castlereagh, then one of the finest women of the Court, appeared in the Sergeant's box, palpitating for her husband's fate. The desponding appearance and fallen crests of the Ministerial benches, and the exulting air of the Opposition members as they entered, were intelligible. Mr. Egan, Chairman of Dublin County, a large, bluff, red-faced gentleman, was the last who entered. As No. 110 was announced, he stopped a moment at the bar, flourished a stick which he held in his hand over his head, and, with the voice of a stentor, cried out, '*And I'm a hundred and eleven!*'"

The same writer has thus analyzed for us this celebrated division :—

For Mr. Ponsonby's amendment,	111
For Lord Tyrone's address,	105
Majority against Government,	6

On this debate the members who voted were circumstanced as follows:—

Members holding offices during pleasure,	69
Members rewarded by offices for their votes,	19
Member openly seduced in the body of the House,	1
Commoners created peers, or their wives peeresses, for their votes,	18
Total,	102
Supposed to be uninfluenced,	3
The House composed of	300
Voted that night,	216
Absent members,	84

Of these eighty-four absent members, twenty-four were kept away by absolute necessity, and of the residue there can be no doubt they were not friends to the Union, from this plain reason, that the Government had the power of enforcing the attendance of all dependent members.

Thus the moral effect of this victory—to those who knew the composition of the House—was much greater than was indicated by the mere numerical majority. It was hoped that "Union" was defeated for ever.

But now, in the very moment of triumph, and even by the means taken to make that triumph definitive and irreversible, the tide was turned.

The members assembled in the lobby were preparing to separate, when Mr. Ponsonby requested they would return into the House and continue a very few minutes, as he had business of the utmost importance for their consideration. This produced a profound silence. Mr. Ponsonby then, in a few words, "congratulated the House and the country on the honest and patriotic assertion of their liberties; but declared that he considered there would be no security against future attempts to overthrow their independence but by a direct and absolute declaration of the rights of Irishmen, recorded upon their journals, as the decided sense of the people through their Parliament; and he therefore without further preface moved, '*That this House will ever maintain the undoubted birthright of Irishmen, by preserving an independent Parliament of Lords and Commons residing in this kingdom, as stated and approved by His Majesty and the British Parliament in 1782.*'"

Lord Castlereagh, conceiving that further resistance was unavailing, only said, "that he considered such a motion of the most dangerous tendency; however, if the House were determined on it, he begged to declare his entire dissent, and on their own heads be the consequences of so wrong and inconsiderate a measure." No further opposition was made by Government, and, the Speaker putting the question, a loud cry of approbation followed, with but two negatives, those of Lord Castlereagh and Mr. Toler (Lord Norbury); the motion was carried, and the members were rising to withdraw, when the Speaker, wishing to be strictly correct, called to Mr. Ponsonby to *write down* his motion accurately. He accordingly walked to the table to write it down.

During this short delay the Ministerialists and Opposition regarded one another in silence. Some members who had voted with Mr. Ponsonby did not wish the Government to be finally defeated. They had heard of the determination of the Castle to buy a majority, and that at very high prices; and these patriots, though they would not give themselves away, desired to sell themselves. Accordingly, when Mr. Ponsonby's absolute resolution was put in writing, and the Speaker had read it and put the question, and a loud cry of "*Aye*" burst forth, Mr. Chichester Fortescue, of Louth County, desired to be heard before the resolution should finally pass. He said he was "adverse to the Union—had voted against it—but did not wish to bind himself *for ever; possible* circumstances might occur which should render that measure expedient for the empire," &c. This was caught at by some moderate and hesitating members of Parliament—by some from honest, and by others from dishonest motives—amongst others, by John Claudius Beresford (of the Riding-House); and the motion was not pressed by Mr. Ponsonby, for fear of a defeat.*

This created great despondency and alarm amongst the honest Anti-Unionists. But for this incident Cornwallis and Castlereagh must probably have resigned; but now chagrin and disappointment had changed sides, and the friends of the Union who, a moment before, had considered their measure as nearly extinguished, rose upon their success, retorted in their turn, and opposed its being withdrawn. It was, however, too tender a ground for either party to insist upon a division; a debate was equally to be avoided, and the motion was suffered to be withdrawn. Sir Henry Cavendish keenly and sarcastically remarked that "it was a retreat after a victory." After a day and a night's debate, without intermission, the House adjourned at eleven o'clock the ensuing morning.

Upon the rising of the House the populace became tumultuous, and a violent disposition against those who had supported the Union was manifest, not only amongst the common people, but amongst those of a much higher class, who had been mingling with them.

On the Speaker's coming out of the House the horses were taken from his carriage, and he was drawn in triumph through the streets by the people, who conceived the whimsical idea of tackling the Lord Chancellor to the coach, and (as a captive general in a Roman triumph) forcing him to tug at the chariot of his conqueror.

The populace closely pursued his lordship for that extraordinary purpose; he escaped with great difficulty, and fled, with a pistol in his hand, to a receding

---

* Those "possible circumstances" did occur, and very soon. Both Mr. Fortescue and others who had voted with Ponsonby voted for the Union on its passage in the next session.

doorway in Clarendon Street. But the people, who pursued him in sport, set up a loud laugh at him as he stood terrified against the door. They offered him no personal violence, and returned in high glee to their more innocent amusement of drawing the Speaker.

Formally, however, and for the moment, the division of that day was a triumph. A scene of joy and triumph appeared universal; every countenance had a smile, throughout all ranks and classes of the people; men shook their neighbours heartily by the hand, as if the Minister's defeat was an event of individual good fortune; the mob seemed as well disposed to joy as mischief, and that was saying much for a Dublin assemblage. But a view of their enemies, as they came skulking from behind the corridors, occasionally roused them to no very tranquil temperature. Some members had to try their speed, and others their intrepidity.

Sir Jonah Barrington, who looked on at all these proceedings with the eye rather of a humourist than of a statesman, tells us that Mr. Richard Martin, unable to get clear, turned on his hunters, and boldly faced a mob of many thousands with a small pocket pistol in his hand. He swore most vehemently that, if they advanced six inches on him, he would immediately "shoot *every mother's babe* of them as dead as that paving stone" (kicking one). The united spirit and fun of his declaration, and his little pocket pistol aimed at ten thousand men, women, and children, were so entirely to the taste of our Irish populace that all symptoms of hostility ceased. They gave him three cheers, and he regained his home without further molestation.

In the House of Lords, on the same question, upon the reception of this address, Lord Clare carried everything with a high hand. The same handful of spirited peers who had voted against union on the former division again opposed it; and it is remarked that Dr. Dickson, Bishop of Down, and Marlay, Bishop of Limerick, were the only two spiritual peers who ventured to stand up against the stern and haughty Chancellor. The Bishop of Limerick was Grattan's uncle, and the Bishop of Down was an intimate friend of Mr. Fox. That degraded assemblage, the Irish House of Peers, many of whom had bought their titles within the past few years for money, or for the Castle votes of their borough members, and others of whom were promised a noble price for those boroughs to promote the Union, lay helplessly prostrate at the feet of Government, and the low-born but audacious Chancellor cracked his whip over the coroneted slaves.

Not much business of great national importance was transacted in the remainder of that session; the Government had resolved to employ all its resources in favour of union during the recess. The Loyalist Claim Bill, however, was passed, under which bill the country was afterwards charged more than a million sterling to compensate "loyalists" who had suffered loss by the insurrection. An attempt was made to pass also a "Rebel Disqualification Bill;" the title was "A Bill for preventing Persons who have ever taken the Oath of the United Irishmen from voting for Members to serve in Parliament." On the second reading, this bill of disfranchisement was opposed by Sir Hercules Langrishe, supported vehemently, of course, by Dr. Duigenan, John Claudius Beresford, and Mr. Ogle, but was defeated.

A very singular discussion took place in the House of Commons this session, on the presentation of a petition from Mr. Thomas Judkin Fitzgerald, known as the "flogging sheriff" of Tipperary. It seems that he had been so wanton and indiscriminate in his flagellations that he thought even the "Indemnity Act" not sufficient to screen him from the legal consequences of such a raging loyalty, and this petition was to ask a special indemnity for himself. "Many actions," the petition said, "had been brought, and many more threatened." Several members of Parliament from Munster bore the warmest testimony to the zeal and activity of this monster in dealing with rebels. The Attorney-General "bore testimony, from official information as well as from local knowledge, to the very spirited and meritorious conduct of Mr. Fitzgerald, and he trusted the House would cheerfully accede to the prayer of the petition." Mr. Yelverton then read to the House the sworn testimony of witnesses in one case—that of Mr. Wright, which has been already mentioned.

"The action," he said, "brought by Mr. Wright was for assault and battery. It appeared that Mr. Wright was a teacher of the French language, of which he was employed as professor by two eminent boarding schools at Clonmel, and in the families of several respectable gentlemen in the town and neighbourhood.

"Mr Wright had heard that Mr. Fitzgerald had received some charges of a seditious nature against him, and with a promptitude not very characteristic of conscious guilt he immediately went to the house of Mr. Fitzgerald, whom he did not find at home, and afterwards to that of another magistrate, who was also out, for the purpose of surrendering himself for trial. He went again the same day, accompanied by a gentleman, to the house of Mr. Fitzgerald, and being shown into his presence, explained the purpose of his coming, when Mr. Fitzgerald, drawing his sword, said, 'Down on your knees, you rebellious scoundrel, and receive your sentence!' In vain did the poor man protest his innocence; in vain did he implore trial, on his knees. Mr. Fitzgerald sentenced him first to be flogged, and then shot. The unfortunate man surrendered his keys to have his papers searched, and expressed his readiness to suffer any punishment the proof of guilt could justify. But no—this was not agreeable to Mr. Fitzgerald's principles of jurisdiction; his mode was first to sentence, then punish, and afterwards investigate. His answer to the unfortunate man was, 'What, you Carmelite rascal! do you dare to speak after sentence?' and then struck him, and ordered him to prison.

"Next day this unhappy man was dragged to a ladder in Clonmel Street, to undergo his sentence. He knelt down in prayer with his hat before his face. Mr. Fitzgerald came up, dragged his hat from him and trampled on it, seized the man by the hair, dragged him to the earth, kicked him, and cut him across the forehead with his sword, and then had him stripped naked, tied up to the ladder, and ordered him fifty lashes.

"Major Rial, an officer in the town, came up as the fifty lashes were completed, and asked Mr. F. the cause. Mr. F. handed the major a note written in French, saying he did not himself understand French, though he understood Irish, but he (Major Rial) would find in that letter what would justify him in flogging the scoundrel to death.

"Major Rial read the letter. He found it to be a note addressed for the victim, translated in these words:—

"'SIR,—I am extremely sorry I cannot wait on you at the hour appointed, being unavoidably obliged to attend Sir Lawrence Parsons. Yours, BARON DE CLUES.'

"Notwithstanding this translation, which Major Rial read to Mr. Fitzgerald, he ordered fifty lashes more to be inflicted, and with such peculiar severity, that, horrid to relate, the bowels of the bleeding victim could be perceived to be convulsed and working through his wounds! Mr. Fitzgerald, finding he could not continue the application of his cat-o'-nine-tails on that part without cutting his way into his body, ordered the waistband of his breeches to be cut open, and fifty more lashes to be inflicted there. He then left the unfortunate man bleeding and suspended, while he went to the barrack to demand a file of men to come and shoot him; but, being refused by the commanding officer, he came back and sought for a rope to hang him, but could not get one. He then ordered him to be cut down and sent back to prison, where he was confined in a dark, small room, with no other furniture than a wretched pallet of straw, without covering, and there he remained six or seven days, without medical assistance!*

The Attorney-General, in reply, said: "The petitioner, whose exertions had been productive of the happiest consequences, only complained of the persecutions to which he was exposed. His property, and what was of infinitely more importance to an honourable man, his character, was at stake." He also censured Mr. Yelverton, and said that gentleman would have acted more becomingly by awaiting in discreet patience the testimony offered by the petitioner, &c. The petition was at length referred to a committee, then to a *secret* committee. Nothing seems to have been done upon it; but Mr. Judkin Fitzgerald afterwards received a considerable pension "for his active services in quelling the rebellion."†

Before the adjournment of Parliament, the Anti-Unionists conceived they might preclude the possibility of any conflict between the two Parliaments—and thus take one main argument away from the Unionists—by the simple measure of a *Regency Act*, enacting that the Regency in Ireland should for ever be exercised by the same person who should be Regent of England. Lord Castlereagh opposed the

---

* Mr. Plowden records another case, almost precisely alike, in which Fitzgerald's victim was a young man named Doyle, a respectable tradesman of Carrick. The action was tried at Clonmel Spring Assizes, in 1801. Mr. Plowden says: "The plaintiff, who was a young man of excellent character and untainted loyalty, was seized in the street by the defendant, in order to be flagellated. In vain did he protest his innocence, which was also supported by some of the most respectable inhabitants of the place. He begged to have Captain Jephson sent for, the commander of the yeomanry, of which he was a member; that was refused. He offered to go to instant execution if the least trace of guilt appeared against him on inquiry; that was also refused. Bail was offered to any amount for his appearance. 'No,' says the sheriff, 'I know by his face that he is a traitor—a Carmelite scoundrel.' The plaintiff was tied to the whipping-post; he received one hundred lashes, till his ribs appeared. The young man's innocence was afterwards fully established. He applied to a court of law for redress; the action was tried at Clonmel Assizes; these facts fully proved; an Orange jury acquitted the defendant."

† Plowden's *Hist. Review*, 5th vol.

measure, being unwilling to lose any of his arguments, and maintained that such an Act would not meet the difficulty.

His lordship's opinion was, that it would not prove a remedy for the inconvenience complained of. It went, in his mind, only to a part of the evil, namely, the effect—but left the cause of the evil untouched. Thus the great malady still remained, and the connection between both countries would in no instance be better secured. Two Parliaments, perfectly equal in point of rights, might at any future period differ respecting their choice of a regent; and, therefore, the bill could not effect that unity of the executive which the measure proposed to establish.

Circumstanced as the countries were, the questions of peace and war, of treaties with foreign powers, of different religions, might at some future period lead to a difference of decision between their Parliaments; and such an occurrence would shake the connection, and, in consequence, the empire, to its foundations.

If questions of comparative advantage between countries might arise, how could a Regency Bill operate as a remedy for the evil?

His lordship wished to be informed how a bill, which went to establish the unity of the regal powers, could identify the necessary powers of a regent for other countries? Might not the particular circumstances of one country differ so materially from the other that the Regency for both kingdoms could not conveniently be exercised by the same person? Or, did not the bill go to oblige the monarch to appoint one and the same regent, which, in fact, went to restrict the regal authority? Thus, either the regal powers were curtailed, or the Regency Bill was inefficient to remove the inconvenience it went to remedy. The Regent was, to all intents and purposes, a deputy; and could a Regent in that case appoint a Lord-Lieutenant? Could a deputy appoint a deputy? He presumed he could not; and should a Regent send over a Lord-Lieutenant to that country, he was satisfied that the Council could object to his authority.

His lordship read part of a speech of Mr. Fox, to show that the adjustment of 1782 was not considered as a final one; that it went merely to quiet the political struggle which then existed; and that it was indispensably necessary to give up something for that imperial purpose.

His lordship concluded by saying that the measure was inefficient to the purpose it held forth, calculated to blind the country, and disgrace the Legislature.

It must be acknowledged that these arguments of Lord Castlereagh have considerable weight, and that the only possibility of Ireland's real and effective independence lies in complete separation from England. It was on the discussion of the Regency Bill that Mr. Foster, the Speaker, took occasion to express his sentiments with great weight and earnestness against the project of Union, contending that the Settlement of 1782 was a final settlement, and that the pending Regency Bill would remove the last remaining difficulty in the way of harmonious action between the two independent countries. The Regency Bill, however, was not acted upon. That, with all other legislation having reference to the Union, was thrown over till the next session, by which time Lord Castlereagh hoped to have his votes ready to carry his grand measure. He violently opposed the Regency Bill, and got rid of it by moving an adjournment of the House, which was carried.

In the meantime, the English Lords and Commons were also busy upon the Union; and we must now turn from College Green to Westminster for a time.

CHAPTER V.

1799.

Union proposed in British Parliament—Opposed by Sheridan—Supported by Canning—Great Speech of Mr. Pitt—Ireland to be Assured of English Protection—Of English Capital—Promises to the Catholics—Mr. Pitt's Resolutions for Union—Sheridan—Dundas—Resolutions Passed—In the House of Lords—Labours of Cornwallis and Castlereagh—Corruption—Intimidation—Onslaught of Troops in Dublin—Lord Cornwallis makes a Tour—Lord Downshire Disgraced—Hancock of Athlone—His Song and Palinode—Opposition Inorganic—The Orangemen—The Catholics—Arts to delude them—Dublin Catholics against Union—O'Connell—System of Terror—County Meeting dispersed by Troops—Castlereagh's Announcement of "Compensation."

On the same day (January 22, 1799) on which the Union was proposed to the Irish Parliament in the speech of Lord Cornwallis, the same business was brought before both Houses in England. Mr. Pitt was so confident of his power to carry that measure, that he did not think it advisable to await the result of the deliberations of the Irish Senate upon it; but presuming on his strength in the Irish, as much as in the British Houses of Parliament, he opened his plan of operations in both on the same day. Accordingly, on the 22d of January,

1799, a message from the Sovereign was delivered to the British Peers by Lord Granville, recommending an Union in the following terms:—

"His Majesty is persuaded that the unremitting industry with which our enemies persevere in their avowed design of effecting the separation of Ireland from this kingdom cannot fail to engage the particular attention of Parliament. And His Majesty recommends it to this House to consider of the most effectual means of counteracting and finally defeating this design; and he trusts that a review of all the circumstances which have recently occurred (joined to the sentiments of mutual affection and common interests) will dispose the Parliaments of both kingdoms to provide, in the manner which they shall judge most expedient, for settling such a complete and final adjustment as may best tend to improve and perpetuate a connection."

The same day a similar message was presented to the Commons by Mr. Dundas, who moved that it should be taken into consideration on the morrow. Richard Brinsley Sheridan, though a member for an English borough, did not forget that he was an Irishman. He immediately rose; and while he declared his concurrence in the general sentiments which the message conveyed, he thought it but fair thus to give early notice that he viewed the bringing forward of that question at that time as a measure replete with so much mischief, that he held it his duty to take the first opportunity to do everything in his power to arrest the further progress of it.

Mr. Pitt, in reply, said he was at a loss to guess on what grounds the honourable gentleman would attempt to satisfy the House. They ought not to proceed to the consideration of the important measure which His Majesty, from his paternal regard to the interests of the empire, had thought proper to recommend to their consideration. At the same time he informed the House that his intention was only to propose an address to His Majesty on the next day; and then, after a sufficient interval (about ten days), to proceed to the further discussion of the subject.

When the address, accordingly, was proposed the next day, Mr. Sheridan made a long and able speech against the whole project. "He thought it incumbent," he said, "upon Ministers to offer some explanations with regard to the failure of the last solemn adjustment between the countries, which had been generally deemed final. There was the stronger reason to expect this mode of proceeding, when the declaration of the Irish Parliament in 1782* was recollected. The British Legislature having acquiesced in this declaration, no other basis of connection ought to be adopted."

He then spoke of the injustice of attempting to consummate this union by intimidation and corruption. He contended that the adjustment proposed would only unite two wretched bodies—that the minds would still be distinct, and that eventually it might lead to separation.

"Let no suspicion," he continued, "be entertained that we gained our object by intimidation or corruption. Let our Union be an union of affection and attachment, of plain-dealing and free-will. Let it be an union of mind and spirit, as well as of interest and power. Let it not resemble those Irish marriages which commenced in fraud and were consummated by force. Let us not commit a brutal rape on the independence of Ireland, when, by tenderness of behaviour, we may have her the willing partner of our fate. The state of Ireland did not admit such a marriage. Her bans ought not to be published to the sound of the trumpet, with an army of forty thousand men. She was not qualified for hymeneal rites, when the grave and the prison held so large a share of her population."

Sheridan was answered by George Canning, who spoke earnestly in favour of an Union. Canning is sometimes claimed as an Irishman; but he was born in London, and never in all his life allowed the claim, no more than Swift, who said it was too hard if he was to be considered an Irishman, although he had the misfortune to be "dropped" in that island. At any rate, Mr. Canning never in his whole career showed the slightest Irish feeling; and on this occasion he viewed the question wholly as an Englishman, as he was. Here is an extract from his speech:—

"It had been said that for the space of three hundred years we had oppressed

* "We beg leave to represent to His Majesty that the subjects of Ireland are entitled to a free Constitution; that the Imperial Crown of Ireland is inseparably annexed to the Crown of Great Britain, on which connection the happiness of both nations essentially depends; but that the kingdom of Ireland is a distinct dominion, having a Parliament of her own, the sole Legislature thereof; that there is no power whatsoever competent to make laws to bind this nation, except the King, Lords, and Commons of Ireland. Upon which exclusive right of legislation we consider the very essence of our liberties to depend—a right which we claim as the birthright of the people of Ireland, and which we are determined, in every situation of life, to assert and maintain."

Ireland; but for the last twenty years the conduct of England had been a *series of concessions.* The Irish wanted an octennial Parliament; it was granted. They wished for an independent Legislature; they had their wish. They desired a free trade; it was given to them. A very large body of the people of Ireland desired a repeal of a part of the Penal Code, which they deemed oppressive; the repeal was granted. The honourable gentleman had spoken as if nothing had been done for Ireland but what she extorted, and what she had a right to demand. He seemed to think that past favours were no proofs of kindness. It was undoubtedly expedient that these advantages should be given to Ireland, because her prosperity was the prosperity of England; but *they were not privileges which she could claim as matters of right."*

It was on the 31st, after the message had been again read, that Mr. Pitt made his great speech, fully developing the view which the British Ministry desired to be received on the question of Union. In justice to the Unionists, it is necessary to give an abstract of what this able statesman urged on his own part:—

"The nature of the existing connection," he said, "evidently did not afford that degree of security which, even in times less dangerous and less critical, was necessary to enable the empire to avail itself of its strength and resources.

"The Settlement of 1782, far from deserving the name of a final adjustment, was one that left the connection between Great Britain and Ireland exposed to all the attacks of party and all the effects of accident. That settlement consisted in the demolition of the system which before held the two countries together— a system unworthy of the liberality of Great Britain, and injurious to the interests of Ireland. But to call that a system in itself—to call that a glorious fabric of human wisdom, which was no more than the mere demolition of another system—was a perversion of terms."

Mr. Pitt then quoted the Parliamentary journals, to prove that the repeal of the Declaratory Act was not considered by the Minister of the day as precluding endeavours for the formation of an ulterior settlement between the kingdoms.

Mr. Pitt was good enough to add, that Great Britain had always felt a common interest in the *safety* of Ireland; but that interest was never so obvious and urgent as when the common enemy made her attack upon Britain through the medium of Ireland, and when the attack upon Ireland tended to deprive her of her connection with Britain, and to substitute in lieu of it the new government of the French Republic. When that danger threatened Ireland, the purse of Great Britain was opened for the wants of Ireland, as for the necessities of England.

To those who know how Ireland has been drained of her wealth and crushed in her industry since the Union, and by the Union, the following paragraph of Mr. Pitt's speech will seem strange:—

"Among the great and known defects of Ireland, one of the most prominent features was its want of industry and of capital. How were those wants to be supplied but by blending more closely with Ireland the industry and capital of Great Britain?"

The Minister enlarged very much upon the benefit which Ireland would derive from the certainty of being defended by England against foreign enemies, and upon her inability to protect herself. Of course, he did not advert to the fact (which he well knew) that the great majority of the Irish people, Protestants as well as Catholics, knew of no other foreign enemy than England; that in resisting French invasions of Ireland, England was defending not Ireland but herself; and that in capturing Frenchmen at Ballinamuck, or in Lough Swilly, the English forces were not capturing Ireland's enemies but Ireland's friends. He drew a glowing picture of the great advantages which the lesser country would draw from her union with the greater; the protection which she would secure to herself in the hour of danger; the most effectual means of increasing her commerce and improving her agriculture; the command of English capital; the infusion of English manners and English industry; necessarily tending to meliorate her condition, to accelerate the progress of internal civilization, and to terminate those feuds and dissensions which distracted the country, and which she did not possess within herself the power either to control or to extinguish. She would see the avenue to honours, to distinctions, and exalted situations in the general seat of empire, opened to all those whose abilities and talents enabled them to indulge an honourable and laudable ambition.

He did not forget to make his bid for the Catholics; and without giving in this speech any distinct pledge of emancipation by the Imperial Parliament, he intimated very clearly that the principal difficulty in the way of that measure would be removed by the Union. "No man could say," he remarked, "that, in the present state of things, and while Ireland remained a separate kingdom, full concessions could be made to the Catholics, without endangering the State, and shaking the Constitution of Ireland to its centre. On the other hand, when the conduct of the Catholics should be such as to make it safe for the Government to admit them to the participation of the privileges granted to those of the established religion, and when the temper of the times should be favourable to such a measure, it was obvious that this question might be agitated in an United Imperial Parliament with much greater safety than it could be in a separate Legislature."

The minister dwelt much upon the weakness of Ireland, which was not, he said, able to protect herself — he had not said so in the days of the volunteers; upon the confusions and atrocities which prevailed at that moment throughout the country — but he did not say that it was he who had ordered and organized those horrors; upon "the hostile division of sects in Ireland, and the animosities between ancient settlers and original inhabitants" — but without saying that English policy had created and perpetuated those evils; upon the "ignorance and want of civilization which," he was pleased to say, "marked that country more than any in Europe" — but he forgot to say that for a century it had been a penal offence for any Catholic to go to school, or to teach a school. For all this, he insisted there was no cure but in the formation of a general Imperial Legislature, free alike from terror and from resentment, removed from the danger and agitation, uninfluenced by the prejudices, and uninflamed by the passions, of that distracted country.

Ireland, Mr. Pitt admitted, might suffer somewhat "by the absence of the chief nobility and gentry who would flock to the imperial metropolis;" but this disadvantage would be far more than counterbalanced by the beneficial results of the system in other respects. And as to the idea that the project of union with England meant subjecting Ireland to a foreign yoke, Mr. Pitt met that with a quotation from Virgil —

"——— Nec Teucris Italos parere jubebo,
Nec nova regna peto: paribus se legibus ambæ
Invictæ gentes æterna in fœdera mittant."

All this looks to-day like cruel and deadly irony. It was with the most severe gravity, however, that Mr. Pitt enumerated all the great blessings which would flow from the Union to Ireland. If England was to benefit by it, he did not seem to be aware of that circumstance, did not think of it apparently at all, — so much absorbed was he by the generous thought of binding up the bleeding wounds of Ireland, and whispering peace to her distracted spirit. He ended by moving his eight resolutions, to serve as a basis for the proposed Union. As these preliminary resolutions were greatly enlarged in the subsequent "Articles" and "Act of Union," they need not be here given at length. They were to the effect that it was fit to propose an Union of the two kingdoms of Great Britain and Ireland. That the succession to the Crown should remain settled as it was. That the United Kingdom should be represented in one Parliament, in proportions afterwards to be agreed upon. That the two Churches of England and Ireland should be preserved. That the people of the two kingdoms should stand on the same footing as to trade and navigation, and no duties should be imposed on export or import between the two islands. That the charge for the debts of the two kingdoms should be separately defrayed; the proportions of future expenses to be settled by the two Parliaments previous to the Union. That all laws and courts should remain as they were then established, subject to future modifications by the United Parliament. Mr. Sheridan opposed these resolutions from first to last.

"If the condition of Ireland," he said, "were really as deplorable as it was stated to be, the House ought to be informed from what misconceptions such evils had arisen, amidst the advantages which God and nature had bestowed upon her. It might be concluded, indeed, that her poverty was chiefly occasioned by the narrow, unwise policy of Britain, a policy which, he was glad to find, the Minister now disapproved. Her weakness, perhaps, was not so great as it was supposed to be; and, if it were, it was ungenerous to insult her. Such an insult would not have been offered to her while her volunteers were in arms."

In the course of the several debates which took place, Sheridan was supported by several eminent members of the House; by Mr. Grey (afterwards Lord Grey), by General Fitzpatrick (who had been Irish Secretary under Lord Portland), Mr. Tierney, the Honourable Mr. St. John, Mr. Hobhouse, and others; most of whom opposed the measure on account of the time being improper for its discussion. Of those who supported it may be named Sir John Mitford, Mr. Perceval, Mr. Dudley Ryder; Mr. Secretary Dundas, afterwards Lord Melville (a Scotchman), spoke warmly for the Union, and in his speech took occasion to throw out again the bait which was to catch the Catholics; and as he was a member of the Administration, his words were supposed to have weight. He said, "that, after union, the Protestants would lay aside their jealousies and distrust, being certain that against any attempt to endanger their Establishment the whole strength of the united Legislature would be exerted; and, on the other hand, the Catholics would expect that their cause would be candidly and impartially considered by a general Parliament, the great body of which would be relieved from the apprehensions and animosities interwoven with the constitution of the existing Legislature."

Mr. Dundas further vaunted the excellent effects which, he said, had followed the union of Scotland with England, and referred to a letter of Queen Anne to the Northern Parliament, predicting the various blessings, with respect to religion, liberty, and property, which would result from the scheme of incorporation; and, he said, that not one syllable of her predictions had failed.

It is observable that, throughout the whole of these debates in the English Parliament, not one of the advocates of union ever seems to have thought of the interest or honour of his own country. It was for Ireland they were all concerned. At length, on the 12th of February, came the division on bringing up the report. The *ayes* were 120; *nays*, 16. This was followed by a conference between the Lords and Commons; and the House of Peers ordered a month's interval before entering upon the discussion in their House.

On the 19th of March, the matter was brought before the British House of Peers by Lord Grenville. He went through all the common arguments for the Union, and repeated the usual carefully calculated phrases intended to win the Irish Catholics, without any distinct ministerial pledge for emancipation. He said:—

"The good consequence of union would quickly appear, in the progress of civilization, the prevalence of order, the increase of industry and wealth, and the improvement of moral habits. The Hibernian Protestants would feel themselves secure under the protection of a Protestant Imperial Parliament; and the anxiety of the Catholics would be allayed by the hope of a more candid examination of their claims from a Parliament not influenced by the prejudices of a local Legislature.'

The Union was opposed by Earl Fitzwilliam, advocated by the Marquis of Townshend, Lord Clifton, Lord Minto, the Bishop of Llandaff, and many others. Lord Moira opposed it. Lord Camden (the rebellion Viceroy) supported it. This nobleman took occasion to enter on a defence of his own administration in Ireland, which seemed indeed to need defence. He denied that the recall of Earl Fitzwilliam was productive of disorder or disaffection, and affirmed that the rigorous proceedings of the Government were rendered necessary by that seditious spirit which existed independently of the Catholic question. He declared that all the severities imputed to his administration were *preceded* by acts of outrage, of insurrection, or of rebellion. He allowed that his conduct, in adopting active and vigorous measures, and apprehending some of the leaders, did accelerate the rebellion; but, as the same steps facilitated its suppression, he did not think that he could justly be blamed.

Lord Minto advised the insertion of a distinct clause in the Articles or Act of Union, providing for the "just claims of the Catholic Irish;" but he did not insist on this, and Ministers took care that no such clause should be inserted. Their policy at that moment, with regard to Catholics, was only to whisper hopes and private promises into the ear of bishops and peers of that persuasion, as will be seen more fully hereafter. At the end of a long debate the address was finally adopted, embracing Mr. Pitt's proposals; and so the matter rested until the next session.

The remainder of the year 1799 was a busy time for Lord Cornwallis, Lord Clare, Lord Castlereagh, and Under-Secretary Cooke. They were all excessively mortified at the temporary failure of this measure; but if certain too credulous and generous Irishmen fondly imagined that the danger was over, they were signally mistaken. Neither Clare nor Castlereagh was the man to be so easily discouraged at a crisis on which their own future political honours and existence depended. They had it in command from London to carry the Union through. Mr. Pitt, by a *private* dispatch to Lord Cornwallis, desired that the measure should not be pressed unless he could be *certain* of a majority of fifty;* and his lordship knew what that meant, coming from Mr. Pitt. Lord Cornwallis seems to have been quite a willing agent in the system of corruption and intimida-

* "This original dispatch I saw and read."—*Sir J. Barrington.*

tion now to be inaugurated on a grander scale than ever before; and, indeed, to an extent never witnessed, either before or since, in any country of the globe. And never had a government two more efficient officers for such a purpose than Clare, the Lord Chancellor, and Castlereagh, the Secretary. The Chancellor, in fact, was too violent and arrogant to be politic. He called that a pusillanimous idea; and could have been well content for his part to carry the Union with a majority of one, and then dragoon the island into submission. In his rage at the first check in Parliament, and at the somewhat tumultuous rejoicings of the Dublin mob (who, however, hurt nobody), he hastily had the Privy Council called together, and urged the necessity of making what in Ireland is called a salutary example. Accordingly, about nine at night, a party of the military stationed in the old Custom House, near Essex Bridge, silently sallied out, with trailed arms, without any civil magistrate, and only a sergeant to command them; arriving at Capel Street, the populace were in the act of violently huzzaing for their friends, and, of course, with equal vehemence execrating their enemies; but no Riot Act was read, no magistrate appeared, and no disturbance or tumult existed to warrant military interference.

The soldiers, however, having taken a position a short way down the street, without being in any way assailed, fired a volley of balls amongst the people. Of course, a few were killed and some wounded; amongst the former were a woman and a boy. A man fell dead at the feet of Mr. P. Hamilton, the King's Proctor of the Admiralty, who, as a mere spectator, was viewing the illumination. This is only mentioned to evince the violent spirit which guided the Government of that day, and the tyrannic means which were employed to terrify the people from testifying their joy at their deliverance, as they fancied, from the proposed annexation.*

Lord Castlereagh, however, knew a better way of going to work. The session had scarcely closed when his lordship recommenced his warfare against his country. The treasury was in his hands, patronage in his note-book, and all the influence which the scourge or the pardon, reward or punishment, could possibly produce on the trembling rebels, was openly resorted to. Lord Cornwallis determined to put Irish honesty to the test, and set out upon an experimental

* Sir J. Barrington.

tour through those parts of the country where the nobility and gentry were most likely to entertain him. He artfully selected those places where he could best make his way with corporations at public dinners, and with the aristocracy, country gentlemen, and farmers, by visiting their mansions and cottages. Ireland was thus canvassed, and every jail was converted to a hustings, at which prisoners of various grades of crime were asked to sign petitions for the Union, by the promise of pardon.* Lord Castlereagh's ulterior efforts were extensive and indefatigable; his spirit revived, and every hour gained ground on his opponents. He clearly perceived that the ranks of the Opposition were too open to be strong, and too mixed to be unanimous. The extraordinary fate of Mr. Ponsonby's declaration of rights, and the debate on a similar motion by Lord Corry, which so shortly afterwards met a more serious negative, proved the truth of these observations, and identified the persons through whom that truth was to be afterwards exemplified.

It was soon perceived by the Anti-Unionists that Government was recruiting and marshalling its forces to carry its measure with a high hand in the next session; and that they also must do somewhat on their side to maintain the high national spirit in resistance to the hated measure. The Marquis of Downshire, the Earl of Charlemont, and William Brabazon Ponsonby, member for the County of Kilkenny, sent circular letters to the Irish gentry and yeomanry, to the following effect. They were authorized, they said, by a number of gentleman of both houses of Parliament—thirty-eight of whom were representatives of counties—to intimate their opinion that petitions to Parliament, declaring the real sense of the freeholders on the subject of a Legislative Union, would at that time be highly expedient.

The Marquis of Dowshire was at once dismissed from the government of his county, the colonelcy of the Royal Downshire regiment of twelve hundred men, and his name was erased from the list of Privy Councillors.† All the resources of Government, either for reward or punishment, were to be used, and that without reserve. The management of Mr. Handcock, member for Athlone, is an example of the system of treatment opposite to that pursued towards Lord Downshire. Immediately after the close of the session

* This fact, that felons in the jails were thus induced to sign Union petitions, was mentioned in Parliamentary debate, and not contradicted.—Sir J. Barrington.
† Plowden.

of 1799 a public dinner of the patriotic members was had in Dublin, to commemorate the rescue of their country from so imminent a danger. One hundred and ten members of Parliament sat down to that splendid and triumphant entertainment.

Never was a more cordial, happy assemblage of men of rank, consideration, and *proven* integrity collected in one chamber, than upon that remarkable occasion. Every man's tried and avowed principles were supposed to be untaintable, and pledged to his own honour and his country's safety; and, amongst others, Mr. Handcock, member for Athlone, appeared to be conspicuous. He spoke strongly, gave numerous Anti-Union toasts, vowed his eternal hostility to so infamous a measure, pledged himself to God and man to resist it to the utmost, and, to finish and record his sentiments, he had composed an Anti-Union song of many stanzas, which he sung himself, with a general chorus. In short, he was the life of the party. Lord Castlereagh marked him as a man to be won upon any terms. Before Parliament assembled in the next session, Mr. Handcock was composing and singing *Union* songs. He received a large bribe in money. "But," says Sir Jonah Barrington, "still he held out until title was added to the bribe; his own conscience was not strong enough to resist the charge; the vanity of his family lusted for nobility. He wavered, but he yielded; his vows, his declaration, his song, all vanished before vanity, and the year 1800 saw Mr. Handcock, of Athlone, Lord Castlemaine." It is unnecessary to say that he voted for the Union.

The very heterogeneous nature of the Opposition which had rejected the Union in the last session gave Lord Castlereagh great facilities in breaking it down. In that fortuitous concourse of members were to be found old reformers and those who had always opposed reform, Catholic Emancipators as well as the most violent and bitter of the Orangemen. Indeed, the most fatal cause of division amongst them was their radical difference of opinion on the Catholic question. Those who had determined to support the Catholic cause, as the surest mode of preventing any future attempts to attain an union, were obliged to dissemble their intentions of proposing emancipation, lest they should disgust the ascendancy party who acted with them solely against the Union. Those who were enemies to Catholic relaxation were also obliged to conceal their wishes, lest their determination to resist that measure should disgust the advocates of emancipation, who had united with them on the present occasion.

The *talent* of Parliament principally existed amongst the members who had formed the general opposition to the Union. Some habitual friends of administration, therefore, who had on this single question seceded from the Court, and who wished to resume their old habits on the Union being disposed of, obviously felt a portion of narrow jealousy at being *led* by those they had been accustomed to *oppose*, and reluctantly joined in any *liberal* opposition to a Court which they had been in the habit of supporting. They desired to vote against the Union in the abstract, but to commit themselves no further against the Minister. Many, upon this temporizing and ineffective principle, cautiously avoided any discussion save upon the *direct* proposition; and this was remarkable, and felt to be ruinous in the succeeding session.

In the meetings and discussions which took place during that anxious interval between the two sessions and in the first days of the new one, the Orange body held aloof from the question *as* Orangemen; and in the first days of the new session a circular was issued, signed by the "Grand Master" and "Graud Secretary," and dated "Grand Orange Lodge," exhorting Orangemen "to avoid, as injurious to the institution, all controversy upon subjects not connected with their principles." There is no doubt, however, that most of the Orangemen were for the Union, and both the Grand Master and Grand Secretary, being members of Parliament, voted for it in 1800.

To the countless petitions which were poured in, almost all *against* the Union, were signed the names of Catholics and Protestants indiscriminately; but the Catholic Bishops certainly used their influence, in many cases, to dissuade the people of their flocks from coming forward against the measure. "It may indeed be said with truth," says Mr. Plowden, "that a very great preponderancy in favour of the Union existed in the Catholic body, particularly in their nobility, gentry, and clergy." The same authority accounts for this by "the severities and indignities practised upon them after the rebellion by many of the Orange party, and the offensive affected confusion in the use of the terms papist and rebel, producing fresh soreness in the minds of many." But this is not a satisfactory account of the indifferent or hostile position assumed at that time of peril by many leading Catholics towards the Legislature of their country. If they did see some Orangemen sitting upon the Opposition benches, they also saw there *all* their own old and tried friends and advocates; and their attitude is rather to be ascribed to the impression produced by the underhand half-promises made by people connected with the Government. Sir Jonah Barrington says:—

"'The Viceroy knew mankind too well to dismiss the Catholics without a comfortable conviction of their certain emancipation; he turned to them the honest side of his countenance; the priests bowed before the soldierly condescensions of a starred veteran. The titular archbishop was led to believe he would instantly become a real prelate, and before the negotiation concluded, Dr. Troy was consecrated a decided Unionist, and was directed to send pastoral letters to his colleagues to promote it."

Sir Jonah tells us, further, that "some of the persons, assuming to themselves the title of *Catholic leaders*, sought an audience in order to inquire from Marquis Cornwallis, 'What would be the advantage to the Catholics if an union should happen to be effected in Ireland?'

"Mr. Bellew (brother to Sir Patrick Bellew), Mr. Lynch, and some others, had several audiences with the Viceroy; the Catholic Bishops were generally deceived into the most disgusting subservience; rewards were not withheld; Mr. Bellew was to be appointed a County Judge, but that being found impracticable, he got a secret pension, which he has now enjoyed for thirty-two years."

But, undoubtedly, the main motive of the anti-national conduct of leading Catholics is to be sought in those uniform declarations of Ministers, both in England and in Ireland, that the Union, and the Union alone, would remove all impediments to a fair settlement of the demands of the Catholics.

There were, however, some Catholics not to be so easily deluded. The trading and commercial class of Catholics in Dublin was vehemently opposed to union; and, immediately before the opening of the session, a meeting of these people was held at the Royal Exchange to deliver their opinions upon it. It was proposed to prevent this meeting from assembling by military force—such was always Lord Clare's first thought; but better counsels prevailed, and the meeting was held, Mr. Ambrose Moore in the chair.

No less a person than *Daniel O'Connell*, then a rising young barrister, took the leading part at this meeting, and it is interesting to see with what patriotic earnestness he then protested against the perpetration of that Union which, near half a century later, he laid down his life in the effort to repeal. He said:—

"'That under the circumstances of the present day, and the systematic calumnies flung at the Catholic character, it was more than once determined by the Roman Catholics of Dublin to stand entirely aloof, as a mere sect, from all political discussion; at the same time that they were ready, as forming generally a part of the people of Ireland, to confer with and express their opinions in conjunction with their Protestant fellow-subjects. This resolution which they had entered into gave rise to an extensive and injurious misrepresentation, and it was asserted by the advocates of Union—daringly and insolently asserted—that the Roman Catholics of Ireland were friends to the measure of Union, and silent allies to that conspiracy formed against the name, the interests, and the liberties of Ireland. This libel on the Catholic character was strengthened by the partial declarations of some mean and degenerate members of the communion, wrought upon by corruption or by fear, and, unfortunately, it was received with a too general credulity. Every Union pamphlet, every Union speech, imprudently put forth the Catholic name as sanctioning a measure which would annihilate the name of the country, and there was none to refute the calumny. In the speeches and pamphlets of Anti-Unionists it was rather admitted than denied, and, at length, the Catholics themselves were obliged to break through a resolution which they had formed, in order to guard against misrepresentation, for the purpose of repelling this worst of misrepresentations. To refute a calumny directed against them, as a sect, they were obliged to come forward as a sect, and in the face of their country to disavow the base conduct imputed to them, and to declare that the assertion of their being favourably inclined to the measure of a legislative incorporation with Great Britain was a slander the most vile—a libel the most false, scandalous, and wicked—that ever was directed against the character of an individual or a people.

"Sir," continued Mr. O'Connell, "it is my sentiment, and I am satisfied it is the sentiment, not only of every gentleman who now hears me, but of the Catholic people of Ireland, that if our opposition to this injurious, insulting, and hated measure of Union were to draw upon us the revival of the penal laws, we would boldly meet a proscription and oppression which would be the testimonies of our virtue, and sooner throw ourselves once more on the mercy of our Protestant brethren, than give our assent to the political murder of our country. Yes, I know—I do know, that although exclusive advantages *may be ambiguously held forth to the Irish Catholic,* to seduce him from the sacred duty which he owes his country; I know that the Catholics of Ireland still remember that they have a country, and that they will never accept of any advantages, as a *sect,* which would debase and destroy them as a *people.*"

After which Mr. O'Connell moved certain resolutions, which were unanimously agreed to.

The first of these resolutions was—

"*Resolved,* That we are of opinion that the proposed incorporate Union of the Legislature of Great Britain and Ireland is, in fact, an extinction of the liberty of this country, which would be reduced to the abject condition of a province, surrendered to the mercy of the Minister and Legislature of another country, to be bound by their absolute will, and taxed at their pleasure by laws, in the making of which this country could have no efficient participation whatever."

As the decisive moment approached for the trial of this great issue, men's minds became more and more excited on both sides of the question. The patriotic leaders did what was possible to evoke a respectable body of public opinion, by way of meetings, petitions, and resolutions; but this was a service of danger, as Lord Downshire had found. A far more extraordinary example of the determination of Government to crush down all legitimate expression of public feeling occurred at a proposed county meeting in King's County. The circumstances were thus related by Sir Lawrence Parsons, in his place in Parliament, and were never denied:—

"Some time ago Major Rogers, who commands at Birr, having been told that there was an intention of assembling the freeholders and inhabitants to deliberate on the propriety of petitioning against a Legislative Union, the Major replied that he would disperse them by force if they attempted any such thing; that the Major, however, applied to Government for directions. What answer or directions he received could only be judged of by his immediate conduct. On Sunday last, several magistrates and respectable inhabitants assembled in the session-house, when the High-Sheriff (Mr. Derby) went to them and ordered them to disperse, or he would compel them. They were about to depart, when a gentleman came and told them the army was approaching. The Assembly had but just time to vote the resolutions, but not to sign them. They broke up, and as they went out of the session-house they saw moving towards it a column of troops with four pieces of cannon in front, matches lighted, and every disposition for an attack upon the session-house—a building so constructed that, if a cannon had been fired, it must have fallen on the magistrates and the people, and buried them in its ruins. A gentleman spoke to Major Rogers on the subject of his approaching in that hostile manner. His answer was, that he waited but for one word from the Sheriff that he might blow them to atoms! These were the dreadful measures, Sir Lawrence said, by which Government endeavoured to force the Union upon the people of Ireland, by stifling their sentiments and dragooning them into submission."

Sir Jonah Barrington states positively that many other meetings throughout the counties were thus prevented by simple "dread of grape-shot." English generals then quartered in various parts of the island, at a moment when either martial law still existed or the horrible memory of it was fresh, could not fail to have their own influence over proclaimed districts and a bleeding peasantry. To them nothing could be easier than to prevent any political meetings, under pretence that they might endanger the public peace.

The Anti-Union addresses, innumerable and ardent, in their very nature voluntary, and with signatures of high consideration, were stigmatized by Government journals as seditious and disloyal; "while those of the compelled, the bribed, and the culprit, were printed and circulated by every means that the Treasury or the influence of the Government could effect."*

There were a good many new elections held this summer; because members were persuaded to resign their seats "upon terms," says Mr. Plowden; but he does not tell us what those terms were. In fact, they simply accepted one of the "Escheatorships," a species of "Chiltern Hundreds," to vacate their seats, that those seats might be filled by creatures of the Castle. In this way a small majority had already been secured before the opening of the session.

Lords Cornwallis and Castlereagh, having made so good progress during the recess, now discarded all secrecy and reserve. Many of the peers and several of the com-

* Sir Jonah Barrington. He states, and O'Connell has affirmed the same, that, notwithstanding all obstacles and intimidations, seven hundred thousand persons petitioned against union; and, notwithstanding all inducements, only three thousand petitioned for it—the most of these being Government officials and prisoners in the jails.

moners had the patronage of boroughs, the control of which was essential to the success of the Minister's project. These patrons Lord Castlereagh assailed by every means which his power and situation afforded. Lord Cornwallis was the remote, Lord Castlereagh the intermediate, and Mr. Secretary Cooke the immediate, agents on many of these bargains. Lord Shannon, the Marquis of Ely, and several other peers commanding votes, after much coquetry had been secured during the first session; but the defeat of Government rendered their future support uncertain. The Parliamentary patrons had breathing time after the preceding session, and began to tremble for their patronage and importance; and some desperate step became necessary to Government, to insure a continuance of the support of these personages.

Accordingly, Lord Castlereagh boldly announced his intention to turn the scale, by bribes to all who would accept them, under the name of *compensation* for the loss of patronage and interest. He publicly declared, *first*, that every nobleman who returned members to Parliament should be paid, in cash, £15,000 for every member so returned; *secondly*, that every member who had *purchased* a seat in Parliament should have his purchase-money repaid to him out of the Treasury of Ireland; *thirdly*, that all members of Parliament, or others, who were *losers* by the Union should be fully recompensed for their losses, and that £1,500,000 should be devoted to this service. In other words, all who should affectionately support his measure were, under some pretext or other, to share in this "bank of corruption."

A declaration so desperately and recklessly flagitious was never made in any country on earth by the Minister of any Sovereign. It was treating the elective franchise of the country as the private property of those proprietors who returned the members by means of their unconstitutional influence. It was acknowledging and consecrating the practice of those members themselves in treating their seats also as a property, from which, during their tenure, they drew profit in bribes, or place, or some substantial Court favour. And it was charging the whole expense of this nefarious transaction to the Irish tax-payers themselves, the very people who were thus to be sold by their representatives, and purchased with their own money by their enemies.

But the declaration had a powerful effect in favour of the Castle; and before the meeting of Parliament in January he found, through the infallible information of the Under-Secretary, Mr. Cooke, that he could count upon a small majority of about eight. This he hoped to increase.

CHAPTER VI.

1799—1800.

Progress of Union Conspiracy—Grand Scale of Bribery—Castlereagh Organizes "Fighting Men" —Dinner at his House—Last Session of the Irish Parliament—Warm Debate the First Day—Daly Attacks Bushe and Plunket—Reappearance of Grattan—His Speech—Corry Attacks Him—Division—Majority for Government—Castlereagh Proposes "Articles" of Union—His Speech—Promises Great Gain to Ireland from Union—Ireland to "Save a Million a Year"—Proposed Constitution of United Parliament—Irish Peerage—Ponsonby—Grattan—Again a Majority for the Castle—Lord Clare's Famous Speech—Duel of Grattan and Corry—Torpor and Gloom in Dublin — The Catholics — "Articles" finally Adopted by Commons—By Lords.

In the cool calculating head of the Irish Secretary the whole project was now matured, and its accomplishment provided for. Things were, he thought, in a good train. County meetings of freeholders were prevented by "dread of grape-shot;" the Catholic Bishops and gentry were lulled asleep by what Mr. O'Connell had well described as "hopes of advantage ambiguously held forth;" the people were crushed, disarmed, bleeding; there were one hundred and fifty thousand armed men in the country, one-third regular troops, the other two-thirds officered and controlled by Government; and above all, and beyond all, Mr. Cooke was successfully driving his bargains with the Lords Spiritual and Temporal and Commons of the Parliament of Ireland. Yet his lordship evidently dreaded the meeting of Parliament. He loved not that inevitable encounter with so many honest, ardent, and able men, who all knew and would proclaim the villanies he was practising. In fact, he felt, with uneasiness, that the genius and eloquence of the land, as well as its integrity, were full against him; and no legislative body ever yet sitting in one house has possessed so large a proportion of grand orators, learned lawyers, and accomplished gentlemen. It may be fearlessly added, that no Parliament has ever had so large a proportion of honourable men. Had it not been so, the splendid bribes then ready to be thrust into every man's hand would have insured to the Castle a much greater majority, and we should not have seen the noble ranks of unpurchasable patriots thronging so thick on the Opposition benches to the last. What Parliament or Congress has ever been tempted so?* There is no need to make invidious or disparaging reflections; but Englishmen, and Frenchmen, and Americans, should pray that their respective Legislatures may never be subjected to such an ordeal.

But still, Castlereagh disliked this meeting with the Irish Parliament; and, as his party fell so far short of their opponents in point of talent and oratory, he bethought him of a singular expedient to make sure of an effective corps of fighting men amongst his supporters in the House. He was himself a man of most reckless courage; but he saw the necessity of infusing a little of that spirit into his party. Sir Jonah Barrington describes his system of procedure in this matter, which is too characteristic of the time and of the country to be here omitted:—

"He invited to dinner, at his house in Merrion Square, about twenty of his most staunch supporters, consisting of 'tried men,' and men of 'fighting families,' who might feel an individual pride in resenting every personality of the Opposition, and in identifying their own honour with the cause of Government. This dinner was sumptuous; the champagne and Madeira had their full effect; no man could be more condescending than the noble host. After due preparation, the point was skilfully introduced by Sir John Blaquiere (since created Lord de Blaquiere), who, of all men, was best calculated to promote a gentlemanly, convivial, fighting conspiracy; he was of the old school, an able diplomatist, and with the most polished manners and imposing address, he combined a friendly heart and decided spirit; in polite conviviality he was unrivalled.

"Having sent round many loyal, mingled with joyous and exhilarating, toasts, he stated that he understood the Opposition were disposed to personal unkindness, or even incivilities, towards His Majesty's best friends—the Unionists of Ireland. He was determined that no man should advance upon him by degrading the party he had adopted, and the measures he was pledged to support. A full bumper proved his sincerity, the subject was discussed with great glee, and some of the company began to feel a zeal for '*actual service.*'

"Lord Castlereagh affected some coquetry, lest this idea should appear to have originated with him; but, when he perceived that many had made up their minds to act even on the offensive, he calmly observed that some mode should, at all events, be taken to secure the constant presence of a sufficient number of the Government friends during the discussion, as subjects of the utmost importance were often totally lost for want of due attendance. Never did a sleight-of-hand man juggle more expertly.

"One of his lordship's prepared accessories (as if it were a new thought) proposed, humorously, to have a dinner for twenty or thirty, every day, in one of the committee-chambers, where they could be always at hand to make up a House, or for any *emergency* which should call for an unexpected reinforcement during any part of the discussion.

"The novel idea of such a detachment of legislators was considered whimsical and humorous, and, of course, was not rejected. Wit and puns began to accompany the bottle. Mr. Cooke, the Secretary, then, with significant nods and snirking inuendoes, began to circulate his official rewards to the company. The hints and the claret united to raise visions of the most gratifying nature, every man became in a prosperous state of official pregnancy—embryo judges, counsel to boards, envoys to foreign courts, compensation pensioners, placemen and commissioners in assortments, all revelled in the anticipation of something *substantial* to be given to every member who would do the Secretary the honour of accepting it.

"The scheme was unanimously adopted, Sir John Blaquiere pleasantly observed that, at all events, they would be sure of a good *cook* at their dinners. After much wit, and many flashes of convivial bravery, the meeting separated after midnight, fully resolved to eat, drink, speak, and *fight* for Lord Castlereagh."

It was not long before one of these gentlemen found an opportunity of proving his mettle.

On the 15th of January the last session of the Parliament of Ireland assembled.

---

* It must be remembered that the *compensation* fund of £1,500,000 represents a small part of the bribery. Vast sums were also paid for votes out of the Secret Service money. O'Connell, in his Corporation Speech, estimates these latter bribes at "more than a million." Then there were about forty new peerages created, and conferred as bribes. The tariff of prices for Union votes was familiarly known—£8,000, or an office worth £2,000 a year if the member did not like to touch the ready-money. Ten bishoprics, one chief-justiceship, six puisne-judgeships, besides regiments and ships given to officers of the army and navy. On the whole, the amount of all this in money must have been, at least, *five millions* sterling—£25,000,000. If bribery upon the same scale, say $100,000,000, were now judiciously administered in the English Parliament, a majority could be obtained which would annex the Three Kingdoms to the United States.

Every member expected that the speech from the Throne would have again introduced the subject of an Union, the basis for which was now firmly laid by the action of the British Parliament in adopting the *Articles of Union*. There was deep and expectant attention, as the Viceroy congratulated Parliament upon "victories of the combined imperial armies" over France; upon good understanding with Naples; upon the failure of the plans of "the enemy" in India; upon the check given to Buonaparte's Egyptian successes; and he went on to demand supplies as usual, and to promise economy;—and earnestly recommended to their care and patronage agriculture, manufactures, and the "Protestant Charter Schools;" but he ended without saying one word of *Union*.

Lord Viscount Loftus (afterwards Marquis of Ely) moved the address, which was as vague as the speech was empty. It was this gentleman's father, Marquis of Ely, who had been promised £45,000 for his three boroughs. Sir Jonah Barrington says this young nobleman "had been christened *Lee-boo* by the humorous party of the House, and was only selected to show the Commons that his father had been purchased,"—in other words, *pour encourager les autres*.

There was not a point in the Viceroy's speech intended to be debated. Lord Castlereagh, having judiciously collected his flock, was better enabled to decide on numbers, and to count with sufficient certainty on the result of his labours since the preceding session, without any hasty or premature disclosure of his definitive measure.

This negative and insidious mode of proceeding, however, could not be permitted by the Opposition, and Sir Lawrence Parsons, after one of the most able and luminous speeches he had ever uttered, moved an amendment, declaratory of the resolution of Parliament to preserve the constitution as established in 1782, and to support the freedom and independence of the nation. This motion occasioned a warm debate on the very first day of the session. Lord Castlereagh, in pursuance of the bullying policy which had been agreed upon, spoke contemptuously of the arguments of Sir Lawrence. The silence of the Lord-Lieutenant on the subject did not arise from any conviction of the impolicy of prosecuting the scheme. The question had been withdrawn when the House of Commons seemed unwilling to entertain it, but, *as a great majority of the people now approved the measure*, and as there was reason to believe that many of its late Parliamentary opponents had renounced their ideas of its demerits, his Majesty's counsellors had resolved to give it a new chance of regular investigation. The reason of its not having been mentioned in the Viceroy's speech was merely that it was to be made a subject of distinct communication to Parliament.

There ensued a vehement debate on the whole question of Union. Many members now ventured to show their hands. After Mr. Ponsonby had spoken strongly and earnestly in favour of Sir L. Parsons' amendment, up rose Dr. Brown, member for the University, who had voted against the Union in the preceding session. He said "he had become more inclined to the Union than he had been in the preceding session, because he thought it more necessary, from *intermediate circumstances*." Unhappily, we know what those circumstances were. He had been promised the place of Prime-Sergeant, and got it for his vote, and for that alone, as he had no other merit.*

Charles Kendal Bushe made a vigorous speech in this debate. He said:—

"You are called upon to give up your independence, and to whom are you to give it up? To a nation which for six hundred years has treated you with uniform oppression and injustice. The Treasury Bench startles at the assertion —*Non meus hic sermo est*. If the Treasury Bench scold me, Mr. Pitt will scold them; it is his assertion, in so many words, in his speech. *Ireland*, says he, *has always been treated with injustice and illiberality*. Ireland, says Junius, has been uniformly plundered and oppressed. This is not the slander of Junius, or the candour of Mr. Pitt; it is history. For centuries has the British nation and Parliament kept you down, shackled your commerce, paralyzed your exertions, despised your character, and ridiculed your pretensions to any privileges, commercial or constitutional. She never conceded a point to you which she could avoid, or granted a favour which was not reluctantly distilled. They have been all wrung from her like drops of her heart's blood, and you are not in possession of a single blessing, except those which you derive from God, that has not been either purchased or extorted by the virtue of your own Parliament from the illiberality of England."

Mr. Plunket also had spoken with his usual force against the project of Union, when Mr. St. George Daly, a very third-rate barrister, who had been appointed Prime-Sergeant on the dismissal of Mr. Fitzgerald, rose and began to put in

* This gentleman was by birth an American.

practice the bullying policy which had been settled upon at Lord Castlereagh's. "He was a gentleman," says Sir Jonah Barrington, "of excellent family, and, what was formerly highly esteemed in Ireland, of a 'fighting family.' He was proud enough for his pretensions, and sufficiently conceited for his capacities, and a private gentleman he would have remained had not Lord Castlereagh and the Union placed him in public situations where he had himself too much sense not to feel that he certainly was over-elevated." This Mr. Daly ventured upon the system of personal insolence. Barrington describes the scene:—"Mr. Daly's attack on Mr. Bushe was of a clever description, and had Mr. Bushe had one vulnerable point, his assailant might have prevailed. He next attacked Mr. Plunket, who sat immediately before him; but the materials of his vocabulary had been nearly exhausted: however, he was making some progress, when the keen visage of Mr. Plunket was seen to assume a curled sneer, which, like a legion offensive and defensive, was prepared for an enemy. No speech could equal his glance of contempt and ridicule. Mr. Daly received it like an arrow, it pierced him, he faltered like a wounded man, his vocal infirmity became more manifest, and after an embarrassed pause, he yielded, changed his ground, and attacked by wholesale every member of his own profession who had opposed an union, and termed them a disaffected and dangerous faction."

But the House had nearly wearied itself out, and exhausted the subject, when, about seven o'clock in the morning, a sudden apparition broke upon the House, which caused men to hold their breath for a time. It was the entrance of Henry Grattan. Since his "secession" from Parliament more than two years before, along with Curran, Fitzgerald, and others, Grattan had been an invalid, trying to recruit his shattered constitution by change of scene and climate. He had spent some time in the mild air of the Isle of Wight, then among the mountains of Wales, and had but lately returned to his house of Tinnehinch, near Bray, when this momentous session of Parliament opened.

At that time Mr. Tighe returned the members for the close borough of Wicklow, and a vacancy having occurred, it was tendered to Mr. Grattan, who would willingly have declined it but for the importunities of his friends.

The Lord-Lieutenant and Lord Castlereagh, justly appreciating the effect his presence might have on the first debate, had withheld the writ of election till the last moment the law allowed, and till they conceived it might be too late to return Mr. Grattan in time for the discussion. It was not until the day of the meeting of Parliament that the writ was delivered to the returning officer. By extraordinary exertions, and perhaps by following the example of Government in overstraining the law, the election was held immediately on the arrival of the writ, a sufficient number of voters were collected to return Mr. Grattan before midnight. By one o'clock the return was on its road to Dublin; it arrived by five; a party of Mr. Grattan's friends repaired to the private house of the proper officer, and making him get out of bed, compelled him to present the writ to Parliament before seven in the morning, when the House was in warm debate on the Union. A whisper ran through every party that Mr. Grattan was elected, and would immediately take his seat. The Ministerialists smiled with incredulous derision, and the Opposition thought the news too good to be true.

Mr. Egan was speaking strongly against the measure, when Mr. George Ponsonby and Mr. Arthur Moore (afterwards Judge of the Common Pleas) walked out, and immediately returned leading, or rather helping, Mr. Grattan, in a state of total feebleness and debility. The effect was electric. Mr. Grattan's illness and deep chagrin had reduced a form, never symmetrical, and a visage at all times thin, nearly to the appearance of a spectre. As he feebly tottered into the House every member simultaneously rose from his seat. He moved slowly to the table; his languid countenance seemed to revive as he took those oaths that restored him to his pre-eminent station; the smile of inward satisfaction obviously illuminated his features, and reanimation and energy seemed to kindle by the labour of his mind. The House was silent, Mr. Egan did not resume his speech, Mr. Grattan, almost breathless, attempted to rise, but found himself unable at first to stand, and asked permission to address the House from his seat. Never was a finer illustration of the sovereignty of mind over matter. Grattan spoke two hours with all his usual vehemence and fire, against the Union, and in favour of the amendment of Sir Lawrence Parsons. The Treasury Bench was at first disquieted, then became savage; and it was resolved to bully or to kill Mr. Grattan. Sir Jonah Barrington describes the scene:—

"He had concluded, and the question was loudly called for, when Lord Castlereagh was perceived earnestly to whisper to Mr. Corry. They for an instant looked round the House, whispered again, Mr. Corry nodded assent, and amidst the cries of 'question,' began a speech which, as far as it regarded Mr. Grattan, few persons in the House could have prevailed upon themselves to utter. Lord Castlereagh was not clear what impression Mr. Grattan's speech might have made upon a few hesitating members; he had, in the course of the debate, moved the question of adjournment; he did not like to meet Sir Lawrence Parsons on his motion; and Mr. Corry commenced certainly an able, but, towards Mr. Grattan, an ungenerous and unfeeling personal assault."

For that time the Castle bravo carried the matter with a high hand; the exhausted invalid was too feeble to attend to him—perhaps, did not even hear him. At ten o'clock in the morning a division was called for. Ninety-six voted for the amendment of Sir Lawrence Parsons; one hundred and thirty-eight against it—a majority of forty-two for the Castle. This majority of forty-two exceeded the warmest expectations of Government; and the Viceroy hoped to increase it by allowing an interval of some weeks to pass before he sent to either House a copy of the resolutions of the Parliament of Great Britain.

The defeat of the Anti-Unionists by a majority of forty-two, flushed the Minister with confidence. The members were now so far marshalled into their ranks, that considerable changes or conversions were not to be expected on either side. Some solitary instances of conversions did appear. A hot and open canvass was carried on in the House itself by the friends of Government, wherever an uncertain or reluctant member was observed, or his convictions, interests, and aspirations could be discovered. What effect attended this canvass is seen in the subsequent divisions, and in the Black List.

It was on the 15th of February that Lord Castlereagh, for the first time, formally brought the project of Union before the House, by reading a message from Lord Cornwallis, recommending that measure to the earnest attention of Parliament. His lordship then delivered a long speech, setting forth the several articles of Union, as agreed upon by the British Houses. He affirmed, without scruple, that public opinion was now favourable to Union. With regard to the multitudinously-signed petitions which had poured in against it, he remarked:—

"That had also been the case in the Scottish Union. The table of the Parliament was, day after day, for the space of three months, covered with such petitions; but the Scottish legislators acted as, he trusted, the Irish Parliament would act; they considered only the public advantage; and, steadily pursuing that object, neither misled by artifices nor intimidated by tumult, they received, in the gratitude of their country, that reward which amply compensated their arduous labours in the great work so happily accomplished."*

As to the principle of the measure—the competency of the Parliament of Ireland to extinguish itself—his lordship affirmed that this had been so firmly established by a speech, that of Mr. Smith, which had been published, "that he considered it as placed beyond question or doubt." He then described the articles in succession. He attempted to show that the contemplated financial arrangement, making the two countries bear separately the charge of their respective debts, and requiring Ireland to pay in the proportion of one to seven and a half, towards the general expenses of the United Kingdom, for twenty years—the proportions to be afterwards modified according to the respective abilities of the two countries—was an arrangement by which Ireland would *save a million per annum*. The proposed commercial regulations also he discussed, most elaborately, and showed to the satisfaction of his friends, that in this article also, Ireland would be the gainer. His lordship then spoke of the article to consolidate the Church of England and Church of Ireland. In this place he took care to introduce the regular ministerial phrase, intended to comfort the Catholics:—

"The cause of distrust must vanish with the removal of weakness; strength and confidence would produce liberality; and the claims of the Catholics *might be temperately discussed and impartially decided* before an Imperial Parliament, divested of those local circumstances which would ever produce irritation and jealousy."

With respect to the composition of the United Parliament, his lordship observed that, while the population of Great Britain exceeded ten millions, that of Ireland was only three million five hundred thousand or four millions;† and while Ireland's

* The reader will recollect that the Scottish Union also was accomplished by purchasing a majority with money and office.
† It was at least five millions. Mr. Plowden, though he does not like to contradict Lord Castlereagh, says, "there are many strong reasons for believing that it amounted to near five millions. Six years later, it was five million three hundred and ninety-five thousand four hundred and fifty-six, according to the estimate for that year (1805), given in the official Irish Directory. But as there was then no census, Lord Castlereagh felt himself at liberty to give his own estimate."

share in the general expenses of the empire was to be only one, against Great Britain's seven and a half, she was to have a hundred members in the Imperial Parliament.

Lord Castlereagh next approached the delicate question—What was to be done with the Irish Peerages? According to the Articles of Union, Irish Peers were not to sit in any House of Lords by their own right; yet they were not to be altogether degraded to Commoners, which would have been republican, and savouring of "French principles." So the awkward compromise which was adopted caused his lordship some trouble to explain, in a plausible manner. They were to be *represented* in the Imperial House of Lords by four spiritual Peers, elected by their order, and twenty-eight temporal Peers, elected by theirs, and holding their seats for life. Peers of Ireland were to be capable of holding seats in the House of Commons, but not for an Irish constituency; only for a county or borough in England.

In describing the apportionment of the representation between counties and boroughs, giving sixty-four to the former and thirty-six to the latter, his lordship said this would necessarily disfranchise many boroughs; and here he took occasion formally to promise "compensation," not to the disfranchised electors, but to the landed proprietors who were the "patrons" of those boroughs, and were supposed to own the franchise of those electors. This intended purchase of the "pocket boroughs," and the immense prices to be paid for them, had been known before; but this was the first time the stupendous bribe had been mentioned in Parliament. Lord Castlereagh coolly said:—

"As the disfranchisement of many boroughs would diminish the influence and privileges of those gentlemen whose property was connected with such places of election, he endeavoured to obviate their complaints by promising that, if the plan submitted to the House should be finally approved, he would offer some measure of compensation to those individuals whose peculiar interests should suffer in the arrangement.

"Much and deep objection might be stated to such a measure; but it surely was consonant with the privileges of private justice; it was calculated to meet the feelings of the moderate; and it was better to resort to such a measure, however objectionable, than adhere to the present system, and keep afloat for ever the dangerous question of Parliamentary reform. If this were a measure of purchase, it should be recollected that it would be the purchase of peace, and the expense of it would be redeemed *by one year's saving of the Union.*"

Lord Castlereagh did not feel it necessary to mention any of the other classes of bribes which were to reward those patriots who would consent to enrich Ireland by all these gains and savings. He knew that the faithful Mr. Cooke was arranging these matters of business in the lobbies, in the corridors, on the very floor of the House.

Mr. George Ponsonby made a violent attack upon the Minister and his whole scheme. He treated as visionary all the proffered advantages of Union. In the ecclesiastical establishment Union would produce but one solid effect, which would be to translate the Irish into English bishops.

He then summed up the effects of the Union in these terms:—"Your peerage is to be disgraced, your Commons purchased; no additional advantage in commerce; for twenty years a little saving in contributions, but if the Cabinet of England think that we contribute more than we should, why not correct that extravagance now? If anything should be conceded in the way of trade, why is it not conceded now? Are any of those benefits incompatible with our present state? No! but the Minister wants to carry his union; and no favour, however trifling, can be yielded to us, unless we are willing to purchase it with the existence of Parliament and the liberties of the country."

Sir John Parnell, Mr. Dobbs, Mr. Saurin, Mr. Peter Burrowes, all attacked the measure, and exposed the fallacies of Lord Castlereagh; and amongst the opponents of the Minister, we still find the name of John Claudius Beresford, of the "Riding-House," Grand Secretary of the Orangemen. His time for being converted had not yet come.

Mr. Grattan spoke at considerable length. He said, "In this proposition, the Minister had gigantic difficulties to encounter. It was incumbent upon him to explain away the tyrannical acts of a century; to apologize for the lawless and oppressive proceedings of England, for a system which had counteracted the kindness of Providence towards Ireland, and had kept her in a state of thraldom and misery; to prove that the British Parliament had undergone a great change of disposition; to disprove two consequences which were portended by the odium of the Union, and the increased expenses of the empire—namely, a military government for a considerable time, and at no very distant period an augmentation of taxes; to deny or dispute the growth of the prosperity of Ireland under the maternal wing of her own Parliament; to controvert the sufficiency of that Legislature for imperial purposes or commercial objects, though facts were against him; and to explode or recall his repeated declarations in its favour. In short, he had to prove many points which he could by no means demonstrate, and to disprove many which might be forcibly maintained against him. It was, moreover, singular to behold the man who denied the right of France to alter her government, maintaining the omnipotence of the Parliament of Ireland to annul her Constitution."

He then urged the very serious importance of the question. It was not such as had formerly occupied their attention; not old Poynings, not peculation, nor an embargo, not a Catholic Bill—not a Reform Bill. It was their being; it was more, it was their life to come, whether they would go to the tomb of Charlemont and the volunteers, and erase his epitaph, or whether their children should go to their graves, saying, "A venal, a military court attacked the liberties of the Irish, and here lie the bones of the honourable men who saved their country." Such an epitaph was a nobility which the king could not give to his slaves—it was a glory which the Crown could not give to the king.

On a division there appeared for the printing of the Articles one hundred and fifty-eight; against it, one hundred and fifteen; giving the Minister a majority of forty-three.*

Even the staunch Unionist, Mr. Plowden, is honest enough to say on this occasion:—

"When the number of the placemen, pensioners, and other influenced members who had voted on the late division is considered, the Minister had but slender grounds for triumphing in his majority of forty-three, if from them were to be collected the genuine sense of the independent part of that House, and of the people of Ireland, whom they represented."

And he adds in a note:—

"Many, it is to be feared, in both Houses, sacrificed their convictions. Twenty-seven new titles were added to the Peerage; promotions, grants, concessions, arrangements, promises, were lavished with a profusion never before known in that country. Pity for both sides that so great and important a political measure should owe any part of its success to other than the means of temperate reason and persuasion."

Triumphantly Lord Castlereagh sent up his Articles to the Lords, where Lord Clare was ready for his part of the work. It was on this occasion that he made that long and able discourse which has been so often reprinted, and from which many extracts have been already given in these pages. Great part of it consists of a historical disquisition upon the whole career of the English colony: its connection on one hand with the mass of the Irish nation, and on the other with the English Crown and Parliament; and whilst it contains many truths powerfully expressed, the general effect of the whole is to traduce all the classes, sects, and parties of Ireland for several centuries. Grattan afterwards wrote an answer to this speech, charging the Chancellor with many deliberate misrepresentations and falsehoods. "His idea," said Mr. Grattan, "was to make the Irish history a calumny against their ancestors, in order to disfranchise their posterity."

The measure was opposed in the House of Peers by the Earl of Charlemont, the Marquis of Downshire, the Earl of Bellamont, Lord Powerscourt, Lord Dillon, and others, supported by Lord Glentworth, Lord Glendore, and the Archbishop of Cashel. However, on the first division there was a large majority for the Government—seventy-five for, and twenty-six against. The general principles of the Union were thus propounded and accepted in both Houses of the Irish Legislature.

In the next debate in the House of Commons the Honourable Isaac Corry, who seemed to have taken special charge of replying to Mr. Grattan, again made a coarse personal attack on that gentleman. Grattan replied with such studied and contemptuous insult as to throw upon Mr. Corry the *onus* of resentment.

The House saw the inevitable consequences. The Speaker (the House was in Committee) sent for Mr. Grattan into his chamber, and pressed his interposition for an amicable adjustment, which Mr. Grattan positively refused, saying, he saw, and had been for some time aware of, a set made at him, to *pistol him off* on that question; therefore it was as well that the experiment were tried then as at any other time. Both parties instantly left the House upon Mr. Grattan's finish-

* For the Articles of Union at full length, see Appendix No. 1.

ing his philippic. They met without delay in a field on the Ball's Bridge Road, and after an exchange of two shots, Mr. Corry received a wound in the hand. So the affair ended. The populace, amongst whom the certainty of a duel was noised abroad, followed the parties to the ground; and there was reason to fear that if Mr. Grattan had fallen, his antagonist would have been sacrificed on the spot.

On the 21st of February Lord Castlereagh took his next step. This was to move the adoption in the Commons of the Articles, one by one. It is unnecessary to analyze the speeches made at the various debates which intervened before the final scene of the Irish Parliament. They generally dealt with the same facts and the same principles; but on one of these occasions there were two efforts to obtain at least some delay in the remorseless progress of the Minister. On the 4th of March Mr. G. Ponsonby, alleging that the Sovereign would not have persisted in recommending the present measure unless he had firmly believed that the sentiments of the public on the subject had undergone a great change, urged the House to remove so injurious a delusion by an intimation of the truth. A knowledge of the number of Anti-Union petitions would, he said, correct that error; and he therefore proposed an address, stating that, in conformity with the constitutional rights of the people, petitions against a Legislative Union had been presented to the Parliament from twenty-six counties, and from various cities and towns.

The reply of Lord Castlereagh to this moderate proposal was highly characteristic. He contented himself with *affirming* that the public opinion had really undergone a change friendly to the measure, and that seventy-four declarations, nineteen of which were those of counties, had been presented in its favour. *Even if this were not the case*, he would oppose a motion which derogated from the deliberative power of Parliament, and *tended to encourage a popular interference* pregnant in these critical times with danger and alarm.

In another debate Mr. Speaker Foster took occasion to point out and denounce the manifest object of the Government in their Article relating to the Irish peerage. He said it created a sort of mongrel peer, half lord, half commoner, neither the one nor the other complete, and yet enough of each to remind you of the motley mixture. It would depress the spirit and enervate the exertions of all the rising nobility of the land. Further, by a strange sort of absurdity, the measure, in suffering a peer, as a commoner, to take a British seat, and refusing to allow him an Irish one, admitted this monstrous position, that in the country where his property, his connections, and residence were, he should not be chosen a legislator, but where he was wholly a stranger he might. The certain consequence of which was that it would induce a residence of the Irish nobility in Britain, where they might be elected commoners, and must, of course, solicit interest; thereby increasing the number of Irish absentees, and gradually weaning the men of largest fortune from an acquaintance or a connection with their native country.

Mr. Saurin and Sir John Parnell then severally proposed an appeal to the people, by a dissolution of Parliament; but this project was scouted by the triumphant Castle party. If that present Parliament, they argued, had no power to do the deed, neither would any other. Besides, that very Parliament was already bought up by the Castle; and the Castle would have value for its money, or rather the nation's money—for the peculiar and exquisite villany of this transaction was, that the people of Ireland were to pay the purchase-money of their own sale to their enemies.

While these last struggles of a perishing nation were taking place within the walls of Parliament, there was deep gloom hanging over Dublin and the country. The Houses were now always surrounded by military, judiciously posted in College Green, Dame and Westmoreland Streets, ostensibly to keep the peace, but really to strike terror, and prevent any manifestation of popular feeling by the fear of a sudden onslaught. Lord Castlereagh also threatened to remove the Parliament to Cork, if its proceedings were at all troubled by the populace. Unfortunately, the Anti-Unionists had no efficient organization, and no acknowledged leader. "Conversions" to Unionism were every day taking place, through the earnest persuasions of Mr. Cooke. Some of the cheated and deluded Catholic Bishops began to send addresses to the Castle favourable to the Union. Bishop Lanigan, of Kilkenny, and his clergy, addressed Lord Cornwallis in this sense: a proceeding which bitterly hurt and grieved the mass of the Catholic laity, although in the address itself occurred a ludicrous application of a phrase, which made the people laugh, as they are at all times willing to do. One of his Excellency's eyes, by some natural defect, appeared considerably diminished, and, like the pendulum of a clock, was generally in a state of *motion*. The Right Reverend Bishop and clergy having never before seen the Marquis, unfortunately commenced their address with the most *mal à propos* exordium of—"Your Excellency has always kept a *steady eye* on the interests of Ireland." The address was presented at levee. His Excellency, however, was graciously pleased not to return any answer to that part of their compliment.

It must be admitted, in justice to the Catholic Bishops, that they were really deceived by the continual representations of Ministers; and, indeed, we may be sure that in private conference with Archbishop Troy, Lord Cornwallis did not confine himself to the stereotyped formula always repeated in Parliament, with regard to the claims of the Catholics, but plainly promised that Catholic Emancipation would be immediately made a Cabinet question.* However that may

* Mr. Plowden, who could not think of supposing that British Ministers did not mean what they said, gives what he considers a clear proof of their sincerity and devotion to the cause of the Catholics:—

"That the British Ministers were *sincere in their intentions* of bringing forward, and confident in their expectations of carrying, the question of Catholic Emancipation in an Imperial Parliament, is manifest from certain written communications made by them to some of the leading persons of the Catholic body, about the time of their retiring from office, which were to the following effect:—

"The leading part of His Majesty's Ministers, finding insurmountable obstacles to the bringing forward measures of concession to the Catholic body, whilst in office, have felt it impossible to continue in administration under the inability to propose it with the circumstances necessary to carrying the measure with all its advantages, and they have retired from His Majesty's service, considering this line of conduct as most likely to contribute to its ultimate success. The Catholic body will therefore see how much their future hopes must depend upon strengthening their cause by good conduct in the meantime. They will prudently consider their prospects as arising from the persons who now espouse their interests, and compare them with those which they could look to from any other quarter. They may with confidence rely on the zealous support of all those who retire, and of many who remain in office, when it can be given with a prospect of success. They may be assured that Mr. Pitt will do his utmost to establish their cause in the public favour, and prepare the way for their finally attaining their objects; and the Catholics will feel that, as Mr. Pitt could not concur in a hopeless attempt to force it now, he must at all times repress, with the same decision as if he held an adverse opinion, any unconstitutional conduct in the Catholic body.

"Under these circumstances, it cannot be doubted that the Catholics will take the most loyal, dutiful, and patient line of conduct; that they will not suffer themselves to be led into measures which can, by any construction, give a handle to the opposers of their wishes, either to misinterpret their principles or to raise an argument for resisting their claims; but that by their prudent and exemplary demeanour they will afford additional grounds to the growing number of their advocates to enforce their claims on proper occa-

be, it is certain that the friends of independence, while they were struggling against the Union in Parliament, were discouraged on finding their efforts not only not appreciated, but actually thwarted by certain of the Catholic prelates who exercised necessarily so large an influence in the country.

Thus all was gloom and despondency, while the several "Articles" were separately argued and assented to. This was finished on the 22d of March.

A message was then sent to the House of Lords, importing that the Commons had agreed to the Articles of the Union; and on the 27th the Peers intimated to the other House, that they had adopted them with some alterations and additions. Two amendments had been proposed by the Earl of Clare, and adopted, importing that on the extinction of three Irish peerages, one might be created, till the number should be reduced to one hundred, and afterwards one for every failure; and that the qualifications of the Irish for the Imperial Parliament should be the same in point of property with those of the British members. These amendments were readily approved by the Commons; and Lord Castlereagh immediately proposed an address to His Majesty, in which both Houses concurred. In this address they declared that they cordially embraced the principle of incorporating Great Britain and Ireland into one kingdom, by a complete and entire union of their Legislatures; that they considered the resolutions of the British Parliament

sions, until their objects can be finally and advantageously attained.

"*The Sentiments of a Sincere Friend* (i. e., *Marquis Cornwallis*) *to the Catholic Claims.*

"'If the Catholics should now proceed to violence, or entertain any ideas of gaining their object by convulsive measures, or forming associations with men of Jacobinical principles, they must, of course, lose the support and aid of those who have sacrificed their own situations in their cause, but who would, at the same time, feel it to be their indispensable duty to oppose everything tending to confusion.

"'On the other hand, should the Catholics be sensible of the benefit they possess by having so many characters of eminence pledged not to embark in the service of Government, except on the terms of the Catholic privileges being obtained, it is to be hoped that, on balancing the advantages and disadvantages of their situation, they would prefer a quiet and peaceable demeanour to any line of conduct of an opposite description.'

"The originals of these two declarations were handed to Dr. Troy, and afterwards to Lord Fingall on the same day, by Marquis Cornwallis, in the presence of Lieutenant-Colonel Littlehales, in the beginning of May, 1801, shortly before his departure from the Government of Ireland, and before the arrival of Lord Hardwicke, his successor. His Excellency desired they should be *discreetly communicated to the Bishops and principal Catholics, but not inserted in the newspapers.*"

as wisely calculated to form the basis of such a settlement; that by those propositions they had been guided in their proceedings; and that the resolutions now offered were those Articles which, if approved by the Lords and Commons of Great Britain, they were ready to confirm and ratify, in order that the same might be established for ever by the mutual consent of both Parliaments.

At this stage of the business, the matter rested in Ireland; and the British Parliament had next to do its part—a matter which might be supposed somewhat doubtful, if all the advantages of the proposed Union were to be, as Lord Castlereagh said, on the side of Ireland; but we shall find that this consideration did not act upon the Lords and Commons of England.

CHAPTER VII.

1800.

The Union in English Parliament—Opposed by Lord Holland—Mr. Grey—Sheridan—Irish Act for Electors—Distribution of Seats—Castlereagh brings in Bill for the Union—Warm Debates—Union denounced by Plunket, Bushe, Saurin, Grattan—Their Earnest Language—Last Days of the Parliament—Last Scene—Passes the Lords—The Protesting Peers—The Compensation Act—The King Congratulates the British Parliament—Lord Cornwallis—The Irish—Union to date from January 1, 1801—Irish Debt—History of it.

In the Parliament of England there was no danger that any time would be lost. The Articles of Union passed through the Irish Parliament as they had been originally framed by the British Ministry, having received no other alterations in their progress than such as were dictated by the Court. They were now brought forward as terms proposed by the Lords and Commons of Ireland, in the form of resolutions; and on April 2, 1800, the Duke of Portland communicated to the House of Lords a message from the King, and at the same time presented to them, as documents, a copy of the Irish address, with the resolutions.

Lord Holland in vain opposed the appointment of a committee; he objected to the whole project of Union. "It was evidently offensive to the great body of the Irish; and, if it should be carried into effect against the sense of the people, it would endanger the connection between the countries, and might produce irreparable mischief. He should oppose the motion for a committee."

All remonstrance was useless. Ministers felt that their arrangements were perfect, and the result sure; they would never, perhaps, hold Ireland so thoroughly in hand as they held her now—thanks to Lord Castlereagh.

On a division, only three Peers (the Earl of Derby, and the Lords Holland and King) voted against, and eighty-two supported the motion for going into a committee. The first three Articles were then proposed to the committee, and received the assent of the Peers.

The motion for a committee was made in the House of Commons by Mr. Pitt. On the House resolving itself into a committee, Mr. Pitt entered at great length into the whole question, going in general over the same well-beaten ground. In closing his speech, this Minister (knowing well the system of management of the Irish Parliament—and knowing, also, that everybody else knew it) was not ashamed to say:—

"The ample discussion which every part of this subject has met with (so ample that nothing like its deliberation was ever known before in any Legislature) has silenced clamour, has rooted out prejudice, has *overruled objections*, has *answered all argument*, has *refuted all cavils*, and *caused the plan to be entirely esteemed*. Both branches of the Legislature, after long discussion, mature deliberation, and laborious inquiry, have expressed themselves clearly and decidedly in its favour. The opinion of the people, who, from their means of information, were most likely, because best enabled to form a correct judgment, is decidedly in its favour."

Mr. Grey (afterwards Lord Grey) still opposed the Union. Referring to Mr. Pitt's last assertions, he permitted himself to doubt their accuracy:—

"It was said that the public voice was in its favour, after a fair appeal to the unbiassed sense of the nation. Nineteen counties were said to have signified a wish for its adoption; and he believed that addresses had really been presented from that number of shires; but by whom they were signed he did not exactly know, though it had been understood they were procured at meetings not regularly convened, and promoted by the personal exertions of a governor who, to the powerful influence of the Crown, added the terrors of martial law. To speak of the uncontrolled opinion of the community in such a case, reminded him of the Duke of Buckingham's account to Richard III. of the manner in which the citizens of London had agreed to his claim of the Crown—

'Some followers of mine own
At lowest end o' the hall hurl'd up their caps,
And some ten voices cried, God save King
 Richard!
And thus I took the 'vantage of those few—
Thanks, gentle citizens and friends, quoth I;
This general applause and cheerful shout
Argues your wisdom and your love to Richard.'"

Mr. Grey proceeded further. He indignantly exposed a portion of the infamies then perpetrated in Ireland; and in such a manner as to show that he had fully informed himself. He said:—

"He did not mean to speak disrespectfully of the Irish Parliament. But the facts were notorious. There are three hundred members in all, and one hundred and twenty of these strenuously opposed the measure; among whom were two-thirds of the county members, the representatives of the city of Dublin, and almost all the towns which it is proposed shall send members to the Imperial Parliament. One hundred and sixty-two voted in favour of the Union—of those, one hundred and sixteen were placemen, some of them were English Generals on the Staff, without one foot of ground in Ireland, and completely dependent upon Government. Is there any ground, then, to presume that even the Parliament of Ireland thinks as the right honourable gentleman supposes; or that, acting only from a regard to the good of their country, the members would not have reprobated the measure as strongly and unanimously as the rest of the people? But this is not all. Let us reflect upon the arts which have been used since the last session of the Irish Parliament, to pack a majority in the House of Commons. All holding offices under Government, even the most intimate friends of the Minister, who had uniformly supported his administration till the present occasion, if they hesitated to vote as directed, were dismissed from office, and stripped of their employments. Even this step was found ineffectual, and other arts were had recourse to, *which I cannot name in this place;* all will easily conjecture. A bill for preserving the purity of Parliament was likewise abused, and no less than sixty-three seats were vacated by their holders having received nominal offices. I will not press this subject further upon the attention of the committee. I defy any man to lay his hand upon his heart and say, that he believes the Parliament of Ireland was sincerely in favour of the measure." Mr. Grey then moved an address to His Majesty, praying him to direct his Ministers to suspend all proceedings of the Union till the sentiments of the people of Ireland respecting that measure should have been ascertained.

Mr. Sheridan, of course, was at his post, and supported the motion of Mr. Grey. He deprecated the prosecution of a measure which, if it should be carried into effect by corruption or violence, would become the fatal source of discontent and rebellion. That the Union had the general approbation and independent assent of the Irish nation, a number of addresses and declarations were mentioned as a proof; *but where were these addresses?* The addresses against it were easy to be found. Twenty-seven of the counties had openly declared against it; and with these would have united Antrim and Sligo, if martial law had not been proclaimed, and prevented the intended meetings. If the measure were thus to be carried, he had no hesitation in saying that it would be an act of tyranny and oppression, and must become the fatal source of new discontents and future rebellions; and the only standard round which the pride, the passions, and the prejudices of Irishmen would rally, would be that which would lead them to the recovery of a constitution that would have been thus foully and oppressively wrested from them. *No attempt had been made to deny the notorious fact,* that sixty-five seats had been vacated to make places for men whose obsequiousness would not permit them to oppose the measure; and it was equally notorious that no art or influence which the policy of corruption and intimidation could put in play had been left untried to gain over partizans to the Union.

It is, indeed, singular that in the course of these debates no Minister was hardy enough to deny the system of intimidation and bribery. Mr. Secretary Dundas contented himself on this occasion with saying "he would not admit" that the Irish in general dissented from the scheme. Lord Carysford boldly propounded a strange argument; he affirmed, that the Unionists in the Irish Parliament had a much greater extent of property than their adversaries, in the Lords ten to one, and that the judging portion of the people approved the project. Mr. Pitt, however, indignantly scouted the idea of appealing to a community so influenced by factious leaders; he was satisfied with the constitutional assent of Parliament.

In short, Mr. Grey's motion, to "suspend proceedings on the Union till the sentiments of the people of Ireland should be ascertained," was negatived by a vote of two hundred and thirty-six, against thirty.

And the first three Articles were adopted by the committee.

Other debates upon various parts of the Articles had uniformly the same result—vast majorities for the Minister. Two incidents only of these discussions merit notice.

On the 30th of April, a debate arose upon a motion of Lord Holland, tending to give the Catholics a pledge or prospect of the abolition of the disabilities to which they were still subject both in Ireland and Great Britain. This was opposed on the part of Government as "unseasonable." Ministers, in fact, intended that the Catholic bishops and influential leaders should content themselves with the vague promises already so often mentioned. The Government was practically receiving support for their measure from many of those prelates and gentlemen, on the faith of the treacherous promises of Lord Cornwallis and his underlings; and had no idea of pledging the British Parliament to emancipation. Lord Grenville "was of opinion that these questions would be best determined by an United Parliament." So the subject dropped.

The other incident arose from the alarm of the woollen manufacturers. It will be remembered how this class of manufacturers, in the reign of William III., had been able to procure express Acts of the English Parliament for the destruction of that kind of industry in Ireland, and to ensure to themselves the full monopoly of Irish wool in fleece. They were now very naturally of opinion that the commercial "Article" in the Articles of Union, permitting the free mutual import and export between the two islands, was a gross infringement upon their vested rights. They, accordingly, petitioned the House of Commons against the "Article." Their demand was too monstrous, but it was sustained in the House by Mr. Peel and Mr. Wilberforce. Mr. Pitt, however, who knew that the English monopoly of the woollen manufacture was now practically safe enough, maintained that, if any transfer of manufacture should result from the permission of exporting wool, it would be gradual and inconsiderable; that any void which it might occasion would be much more than filled up by the great increase of our trade in this article; that we had no reason to apprehend a scarcity of the commodity, nor dread the rivalry of the Irish in the manufacture; and that his friend's proposal would be an unnecessary deviation from that liberal principle of a free intercourse which was the intended basis of the Union. The Article, therefore, was adopted as it stood, to the deep indignation of the good people of Leeds and all Yorkshire.

All the Articles had been adopted before the 9th of May. A joint address was on that day presented to the King, importing that they were now ready to conclude an Union with the Irish Parliament upon the basis of the Articles. This address, in a tone which resembles a cold and solemn sneer, expresses the "unspeakable satisfaction" of Parliament at "the general conformity of the Articles transmitted from Ireland with those which they had voted in the preceding year."

The next thing in order was that each Parliament was to frame the Articles into a bill, and so pass the *Act of Union*.

As an Irish Act for regulating elections was to be incorporated in the general bill of Union, Lord Castlereagh at once, in the Irish House of Commons, brought in that parliamentary measure. It passed the House of Commons on the 20th of May. This measure arranged the representation as it remained from the Union until the "Reform Act." It gave one member of Parliament to each of the following towns:—

Waterford, Limerick, Belfast, Drogheda, Carrickfergus, Newry, Kilkenny, Londonderry, Galway, Clonmell, Wexford, Armagh, Youghall, Bandon, Dundalk, Kinsale, Lisburne, Sligo, Catherlogh, Ennis, Dungarvan, Down-Patrick, Coleraine, Mallow, Athlone, New-Ross, Tralee, Cashel, Dungannon, Portarlington, and Enniskillen. One member for each of these towns, with four for Dublin and Cork, one for the University, and sixty-four representatives of the thirty-two counties.

The Act then made its singular provision to allow present Irish members of Parliament to sit in a Parliament they had never been elected to serve in. It provided that, if the King should authorize the present Lords and Commons of Great Britain to form a part of the first Imperial Legislature, the sitting members for Dublin and Cork, and for the thirty-two counties of Ireland, should represent the same cities and shires in that Parliament; that the written names of the members for the college of the Holy Trinity, for the cities of Waterford and Limerick, and the other towns before mentioned, should be put into a glass, and successively drawn out by the clerk of the Crown, and that, of the two representatives of each of those places, the individual whose name should be first drawn should serve for the same place in the first

United Legislature; and that, when a new Parliament should be convoked, writs should be sent to the Irish counties, to the University, and to the cities and boroughs above specified, for the election of members in the usual mode, according to the number then adjusted.

The Act also arranged the rotation in which the four Irish bishops should sit in the House of Peers, and also the election of the twenty-eight Irish Peers by their own order.

On the very next day—for Ministers were in hot haste—Castlereagh moved for leave to bring in his bill for the Legislative Union. Leave was given by a vote of one hundred and sixty against one hundred. It was at once presented, read, and ordered to be printed. On the 25th it was read again. The uncorrupted members of the House looked on with impotent indignation. Mr. Grattan proposed a delay until the 1st of August, to allow the measure to be more fully canvassed. He proceeded also to argue very warmly against the whole principle of it. He said it was "a breach of a solemn covenant, an innovation promoted by martial law, an unauthorized assumption of a competency to destroy the independence of the realm, an unjustifiable attempt to injure the prosperity of the country. The bill would be, *quoad* the constitution, equivalent to a murder, and, *quoad* the Government, to a separation. If it should be carried into effect, he foretold its want of permanence, and intimated his apprehensions that popular discontent, perhaps dangerous commotions, might result from its enforcement."

Lord Castlereagh defended the bill, and censured the inflammatory language of Mr. Grattan. "But he defied," he said, "their incentives to treason, and had no doubt of the energy of the Government in defending the Constitution against every attack." Such was the insolent and half-menacing tone adopted upon system by the Administration.

Several earnest debates followed. The faithful representatives of the people, whom money, and place, and title could not buy, did their sad duty to the end. The ablest lawyers in the country, and some of the purest patriots of whom history makes mention, could at least protest against this parricide and suicide, and their solemn and well-weighed words of warning and expostulation, if they could not save the country for that time, remain on record as a protest, as a continual claim, and perpetual muniment of title, on behalf of the independence of the Irish nation. As several passages of these Anti-Union pleadings have been often cited by Mr. O'Connell, and others, who have never ceased to demand the repeal of that evil Act, they have become classical, and must always be held an essential part of any history of Ireland.

William Conyngham Plunket, afterwards Lord Chancellor, said:—

"Sir, I, in the most express terms, deny the competency of Parliament to do this act. I warn you, do not dare to lay your hands upon the Constitution. I tell you that if, circumstanced as you are, you pass this Act, it will be a mere nullity, and no man in Ireland will be bound to obey it. I make the assertion deliberately. I repeat it. I call on any man who hears me to take down my words. You have not been elected for this purpose. You are appointed to make laws, and not legislatures. You are appointed to exercise the function of legislators, and not to transfer them.

"You are appointed to act under the Constitution, and not to alter it; and if you do so, your act is a dissolution of the Government—you resolve society into its original elements, and no man in the land is bound to obey you. Sir, I state doctrines that are not merely founded on the immutable laws of truth and reason. I state not merely the opinions of the ablest and wisest men who have written on the science of government, but I state the practice of our Constitution, as settled at the era of the Revolution; and I state the doctrine under which the House of Hanover derives its title to the Throne.

"For me, I do not hesitate to declare, that if the madness of the revolutionists were to tell me, 'You must sacrifice British connection,' I would adhere to that connection in preference to the independence of my country. *But I have as little hesitation in saying that, if the wanton ambition of a Minister should assail the freedom of Ireland, and compel me to the alternative, I would fling the connection to the winds, and clasp the independence of my country to my heart.*"

Mr. Bushe (subsequently Chief-Justice of Ireland), spoke these words:—

"I strip this formidable measure of all its pretensions and all its aggravations; I look on it nakedly and abstractedly, and I see nothing in it but one question, Will you give up the country? I forget for a moment the unprincipled means by which it has been promoted. I pass by for a moment the unseasonable time at which it has been introduced, and the contempt of Parliament upon which it is bottomed, and I look upon it simply as England reclaiming in a moment of your weakness that dominion which you extorted from her in a moment of your virtue—a dominion which she uniformly abused, which invariably oppressed and impoverished you, and from the cessation of which *you date all your prosperity*. . . .

"Odious as this measure is in my eyes, and disgusting to my feelings, if I see it is carried by the free and uninfluenced sense of the Irish Parliament, I shall not only defer and submit, but I will cheerfully obey. It will be the first duty of every good subject. *But fraud, and oppression, and unconstitutional practice, may possibly be another question.* If this be factious language, Lord Somers was factious, the founders of the Revolution were factious, William III. was an usurper, and the Revolution was a rebellion."

Mr. Saurin (subsequently a Privy Councillor and an Attorney-General) spoke these words:—

"You make the Union binding as a law, but you cannot make it obligatory on conscience. It will be obeyed so long as England is strong; but resistance to it will be in the abstract a duty; and the exhibition of that resistance will be a mere question of prudence."

Mr. Grattan, who was afterwards deemed worthy of a resting-place in Westminster Abbey, spoke these words in the Irish House of Commons, in one of the debates on Union:—

"Many honourable gentlemen thought differently from me. I respect their opinions, but I keep my own; and I think now as I thought then, *that the treason of the Minister against the liberties of the people was infinitely worse than the rebellion of the people against the Minister*. . . .

"The cry of the connection (the Union measure) will not in the end avail against the principles of liberty. . . .

"The cry of disaffection will not in the end avail against the principle of liberty.

"Yet I do not give up the country. I see her in a swoon; but she is not dead. Though in her tomb she lies helpless and motionless, still there is on her lips a spirit of life, and on her cheek a glow of beauty.

"Thou art not conquered; beauty's ensign yet is crimson on thy lips and in thy cheek, and death's pale flag is not advanced there." *

Eloquence and constitutional law-learning were alike vain. The bill was hurried to its third reading; and when it was seen that the evil deed was inevitable, most of the Anti-Unionists rose and left the House, that they might not witness the division by which it was to be carried. This was on the 7th of June. There was, if we are to credit Sir Jonah Barrington, a certain theatrical solemnity in some of these last scenes of our national life. For example:—

"Before the third reading of the bill, when it was about to be reported, Mr. Charles Ball, member for Clogher, rose, and without speaking one word, looked round impressively—every eye was directed to him—he only pointed his hand significantly to the bar, and immediately walked forth, casting a parting look behind him, and turning his eyes to heaven, as if to invoke vengeance on the enemies of his country. His example was contagious. Those Anti-Unionists who were in the House immediately followed his example, and never returned into that Senate, which had been the glory, the guardian, and the protection of their country. There was but one scene more, and the curtain was to drop for ever."

On these last days of the Irish Parliament there was an ostentatious display of military force. Troops were drawn up under the Ionic colonnades of the superb Parliament House; and the citizens of Dublin knew that batteries of field artillery were ready at convenient spots to sweep their streets at a moment's notice —an arrangement to which they have been long accustomed. Sir Jonah, who was present and saw all, and who, though not in all respects an estimable man, at least stood by his country in this crisis to the last, describes the scene for us:—

"The day of extinguishing the liberties of Ireland had now arrived, and the sun took his last view of independent Ireland; he rose no more over a proud and prosperous nation. She was now condemned by the British Minister to renounce her rank amongst the States of Europe. She was sentenced to cancel her Constitution, to disband her Commons, and disfranchise her nobility, to proclaim her incapacity, and register her corruption in the records of the empire.

"The Commons House of Parliament, on the last evening, afforded the most melancholy example of a fine, indepen-

---

* It is true that several of these Anti-Union orators subsequently acted as if they had not been altogether sincere in so strongly denouncing the Union, pronouncing it a nullity, and proclaiming, as Lord Plunket and Mr. Saurin did, that no man would be bound to obey it—that is, to obey laws enacted in the Imperial Parliament. Yet the speakers were sincere at the time; and even if their own personal position afterwards seem inconsistent with the principles then laid down, yet the principles are not to suffer, nor is the law less sound on that account.

dent people, betrayed, divided, sold, and, as a State, annihilated. British clerks and officers were smuggled into her Parliament to vote away the Constitution of a country to which they were strangers, and in which they had neither interest nor connection. They were employed to cancel the royal charter of the Irish nation, guaranteed by the British Government, sanctioned by the British Legislature, and unequivocally confirmed by the words, the signature, and the great seal of their monarch.

"The situation of the Speaker on that night was of the most distressing nature. A sincere and ardent enemy of the measure, he headed its opponents; he resisted it with all the power of his mind, the resources of his experience, his influence, and his eloquence.

"It was, however, through his voice that it was to be proclaimed and consummated. His only alternative (resignation) would have been unavailing, and could have added nothing to his character. His expressive countenance bespoke the inquietude of his feeling; solicitude was perceptible in every glance, and his embarrassment was obvious in every word he uttered.

"The galleries were full; but the change was lamentable. They were no longer crowded with those who had been accustomed to witness the eloquence and to animate the debates of that devoted assembly. A monotonous and melancholy murmur ran through the benches; scarcely a word was exchanged amongst the members. Nobody seemed at ease; no cheerfulness was apparent, and the ordinary business for a short time proceeded in the usual manner.

"At length the expected moment arrived. The order of the day—for the third reading of the bill for a 'Legislative Union between Great Britain and Ireland'—was moved by Lord Castlereagh. Unvaried, tame, cold-blooded,—the words seemed frozen as they issued from his lips; and, as if a simple citizen of the world, he seemed to have no sensation on the subject.

"The Speaker, Mr. Foster, who was one of the most vehement opponents of the Union from first to last, would have risen and left the House with his friends, if he could. But this would have availed nothing. With grave dignity he presided over 'the last agony of the expiring Parliament.' He held up the bill for a moment in silence, then asked the usual question, to which the response, '*Aye*,' was languid, but unmistakeable. Another momentary pause ensued. Again his lips seemed to decline their office. At length, with an eye averted from the object which he hated, he proclaimed, with a subdued voice, '*The ayes have it.*' For an instant he stood statue-like; then, indignantly and in disgust, flung the bill upon the table, and sunk into his chair with an exhausted spirit."*

So far, the picturesque historian of the *Rise and Fall of the Irish Nation;* and, doubtless, to many readers this closing performance will appear somewhat histrionic and melodramatic. Yet, in sad and bitter earnest, that scene was deep tragedy; and its catastrophe is here with us at this day—in thousands upon thousands of ruined cabins, and pining prisoners, and outlawed rebels, and the poverty and hunger that move and scandalize the world. A few details will fitly close up this subject.

The bill was carried up to the House of Peers by Lord Castlereagh, but the consideration of it was postponed. On its second reading, the Earls of Farnham and Bellamont offered some clauses, which were negatived, and the bill was committed. It passed the committee without amendment, was reported in due form, and, after an uninteresting debate, was read a third time on the 13th of June. A protest was entered by the Duke of Leinster and the other dissenting Peers. This protest is given at full length in the Lords' journals; but it will be enough in this place to record its last paragraph and summing up, with the names of the dissentient Peers. It concludes in these words:—

"Because the argument made use of in favour of the Union, namely, that the sense of the people of Ireland is in its favour, we know to be untrue; and as the Ministers have declared that they would not press the measure against the

---

* It is well to preserve the record of those Irishmen who voted against the extinction of their country. As for the names of those persons, placemen, pensioners, and bribe-takers, who voted on the other side, it were better to forget them. But their names and crime are also a portion of history; and many readers may be interested to know the manner in which some great families in Ireland obtained their titles and laid the foundation of their fortunes. Candour also requires it to be stated that some few members did vote for the Union without either bribe or pension, without being influenced either by interest or intimidation; and, therefore, it is presumable, from a sincere conviction that this measure would benefit the two countries. There was published soon after the Union a "Red List" and a "Black List," giving the names of those who were for and against the measure. The lists have often been reprinted. They may be found in Plowden's Appendix and in Sir Jonah Barrington's *Rise and Fall.* But as the latter has added some observations to many of the names, either from his own personal knowledge or from common notoriety at the time, we adopt his edition of the lists.—*See Appendix*, No. II.

sense of the people, and as the people have pronounced decidedly, and under all difficulties, their judgment against it, we have, together with the sense of the country, the authority of the Minister to enter our protest against the project of Union, against the yoke which it imposes, the dishonour which it inflicts, the disqualification passed upon the peerage, the stigma thereby branded on the realm, the disproportionate principle of expense it introduces, the means employed to effect it, the discontents it has excited and must continue to excite. Against all these, and the fatal consequences they may produce, we have endeavoured to interpose our votes, and failing, we transmit to after-times our names in solemn protest, on behalf of the Parliamentary Constitution of this realm, the liberty which it secured, the trade which it protected, the connection which it preserved, and the Constitution which it supplied and fortified. This we feel ourselves called upon to do in support of our characters, our honour, and whatever is left to us worthy to be transmitted to our posterity.

"LEINSTER.
ARRAN.
MOUNTCASHEL.
FARNHAM.
BELMORE, by proxy.
MASSY, by proxy.
STRANGFORD.
GRANARD.
LUDLOW, by proxy.
MOIRA, by proxy.
REV. WATERFORD and LISMORE.
POWERSCOURT.
DE VESCI.
CHARLEMONT.
KINGSTON, by proxy.
RIVERSDALE, by proxy.
MEATH.
LISMORE, by proxy.
SUNDERLIN."

No part of the plan now remained for the Secretary to bring forward but the scheme of compensation. This he plausibly ushered in upon a principle of justice. He proposed a grant of £1,260,000 for those who should suffer a loss of patronage, and be deprived of a source of wealth, by the disfranchisement of eighty-four boroughs—at the rate of £15,000 to each. Mr. Saurin, Mr. J. Claudius Beresford, and Mr. Dawson, maintained that the grant of compensation to those who had no right to hold such a species of property would be an insult to the public, and an infringement of the Constitution. Mr. Prendergast defended the proposition, alleging, that though such possessions might have been vicious in their origin, yet, from prescriptive usage, and from having been the subject of contracts and family settlements, they could not be confiscated without a breach of honour and propriety. In the House of Peers, this bill was chiefly opposed by the Earl of Farnham; but it passed into law with little opposition in either House, the Anti-Unionists having now given up the question as lost.*

Soon after the Union bill had passed through both Houses of the Irish Parliament, Mr. Pitt brought a bill in the same form into the British House of Commons. It proceeded through the usual stages without occasioning any important debate; and was sent, on the 24th of June, to the Peers. On the 30th, Lord Granville moved for its third reading, declaring that he rose for that purpose with greater pleasure than he had ever felt before in making any proposition to their lordships. The Marquis of Downshire merely said that his opinion of the measure remained unaltered, and that he would, therefore, give the bill his decided negative. It passed without a division; and, on the 2d of July, it received the royal assent.

On the 29th of July, in proroguing the last separate Parliament of Great Britain, the King felicitated his Parliament, as he well might:—

"With peculiar satisfaction I congratulate you on the success of the steps which you have taken for effecting an entire Union between my kingdoms. This great measure, on which my wishes have been long earnestly bent, I shall ever consider as the happiest event of my reign."

The royal assent was given in Ireland to the Union Bill on the 1st of August, the anniversary of the accession of the

* When the Compensation Statute had received the royal assent, the Viceroy appointed four commissioners to carry its provisions into execution. Three were members of Parliament, whose salaries of £1,200 a year each (with probable advantages) were a tolerable consideration for their former services. The Honourable Mr. Annesley, Secretary Hamilton, and Dr. Duigenan, were the principal commissioners of that extraordinary distribution. Unfortunately, we have not full details and accounts of this scandalous pecuniary transaction. Sir Jonah Barrington says:—

"It is to be lamented that the records of the proceedings have been *unaccountably disposed of*. A voluminous copy of claims, accepted and rejected, was published, and partially circulated; but the great and important grants, the *private* pensions, and *occult* compensations, have never been made public, further than by those who received them. It is known that—

"Lord Shannon received for his patronage in the Commons, . . £45,000
The Marquis of Ely, . . 45,000
Lord Clanmorris (besides a peerage), . 23,000
Lord Belvidere (besides his *douceur*), . 15,000
Sir Hercules Langrishe, . . . 15,000 "

House of Brunswick to the thrones of these realms. The next day the Lord-Lieutenant put an end to the session with an appropriate speech from the Throne. Lord Cornwallis said, amongst other fine things,—speaking to the legislators whom he had bribed:—

"The whole business of this important session being at length happily concluded, it is with the most sincere satisfaction that I communicate to you, by his Majesty's express command, his warmest acknowledgments for that ardent zeal and unshaken perseverance which you have so conspicuously manifested in maturing and completing the great measure of Legislative Union between this kingdom and Great Britain.

"The proofs you have given on this occasion of your uniform attachment to the real welfare of your country, inseparably connected with the security and prosperity of the empire at large, not only entitle you to the full approbation of your Sovereign, and to the applause of your fellow-subjects, but must afford you the surest claim to the gratitude of posterity.

"You will regret, with His Majesty, the reverse which His Majesty's allies have experienced on the Continent; but His Majesty is persuaded that the firmness and public spirit of his subjects will enable him to persevere in the line of conduct which will best provide for the honour and the essential interests of his dominions, whose means and resources have now, by your wisdom, been more closely and intimately combined."

Immediately after passing the English Act of Union, early in July, the British Parliament was prorogued; and the "Union," in so far as parchment can make an union, was complete. It was to take effect from the 1st of January, 1801. Pursuant to proclamation, a new Imperial Standard was on that day displayed on the Tower of London, and on the Castles of Edinburgh and Dublin. It was the same Royal Standard now in use; being "quartered, first and fourth, England; second, Scotland; third, Ireland." So, since that day, the Harp of Ireland has its place in the corner of the great Banner of England.

The "Union Jack" was also ordained and described by the same proclamation— "And it is our will and pleasure that the Union flag shall be azure, the crosses, saltires of St. Andrew and St. Patrick, quarterly per saltire, counterchanged, argent and gulas; the latter imbrated of the second, surmounted by the Cross of St. George of the third, as the saltire."

As for the Public Debt of Ireland, which was to remain a separate charge on the revenues of that country, that debt had been less than four millions just before the insurrection. At the Union that debt was declared to be £26,841,219, being increased nearly *seven-fold* in three years. That is to say, the whole of the expenses incurred in provoking that insurrection—then in maintaining a great army to crush it—the cost of keeping English and Scotch militia regiments in the country—the pay of the Hessians—the bribes and pensions to spies, informers, and members of Parliament—the compensation fund to owners of boroughs—all was charged to Irish account.

O'Connell said, "It was strange that Ireland was not afterwards made to pay for the knife with which Lord Castlereagh, twenty-two years later, cut his own throat!"

This enormous debt was to remain separate from the English Debt, according to the Act of Union,* until these two conditions should occur: *First.* That the two debts should come to bear to each other the proportion of fifteen parts for Great Britain to two parts for Ireland; and, *Second.* That the respective circumstances of the two countries should admit of uniform taxation.

After that, they were to be consolidated. Since that day, an English Chancellor of the Exchequer has "kept the books" of the two islands; so that while the debt of England went on increasing rapidly, owing to the war, and subsidies to all enemies of France, the debt of Ireland was somehow found to increase more than twice as fast as that of England —as if Ireland had a *double* interest in crushing France.

"Woe to the land on whose judgment-seats a stranger sits—at whose gates a stranger watches!" We may add, "whose books a stranger keeps!" †

* See the Act in the Appendix, No. III.
† Mr. O'Neill Daunt, in his excellent paper entitled, *Financial Grievances of Ireland*, extracts from *Parliamentary Paper No. 35, of 1819*, this table:—

YEAR.	BRITISH DEBT.	AN. CHARGE.	IRISH DEBT.	AN. CHARGE.
	£	£	£	£
5th Jan. 1801.	450,504,984	17,718,851	28,545,134	1,244,463
5th Jan. 1817.	734,522,104	28,238,416	112,704,773	4,104,514

The difference between the statement of the Irish Debt given in this table, and that given in the text (from another Parliamentary paper of the same year), is made up by adding a small amount of *unfunded* debt.

Thus, while the Imperial Government less than doubled the British Debt, they quadrupled the Irish Debt. By this management the Irish Debt,

The two debts were consolidated in 1817. According to Lord Castlereagh's report to Parliament, the military force in Ireland at the time of the Union amounted to one hundred and twenty-six thousand five hundred men—viz., forty-five thousand eight hundred and thirty-nine regulars, twenty-seven thousand one hundred and four militia, and fifty-three thousand five hundred and fifty-seven yeomanry.

CHAPTER VIII.

1800—1803.

The Catholics Duped—Resignation of Pitt—Mystery of this Resignation—First Measure of United Parliament—Suspension of *Habeas Corpus*—Report of Secret Committee—Fate of Lord Clare—Lord Hardwicke Viceroy—Peace of Amiens—Treaty Violated by England—Malta—War again Declared by England—Mr. Pitt resumes Office—Coalition against France.

The Union had scarcely been accomplished, when those Irish Catholics who had supported the measure found they had been cheated, as usual, by the British Government. They had been told that Catholic Emancipation would at once be made a Ministerial measure; and in so far as the distinct pledges of Mr. Pitt and of Lord Cornwallis could avail them, they were assured of their liberties.

The first United Parliament met on the 22d of January. It immediately began to be rumoured that Mr. Pitt and his Ministry were about to resign. The reason falsely alleged for the resignation was that King George III. would not tolerate the idea of Catholic Emancipation, which he imagined to be contrary to his Coronation Oath; and as Mr. Pitt pretended to be pledged to that measure, he made this difference the pretext for a temporary resignation, which he found expedient at this time for other reasons.

Mr. Pitt had been the all-powerful Minister who had governed England for seventeen years. It was he who had recalled Lord Fitzwilliam from the Irish Viceroyalty, because that nobleman favoured Catholic Emancipation. It was he who had sent over Lord Camden which in 1801 had been to the British as one to sixteen and a half, was forced up to bear to the British Debt the ratio of one to seven and a half. This was the proportion required by the Act of Union, as a condition of subjecting Ireland to indiscriminate taxation with Great Britain. Ireland was to be loaded with inordinate debt; and then this debt was to be made the pretext for raising her taxation to the high British standard, and thereby rendering her liable to the pre-union debt of Great Britain!

with express instructions to prevent such emancipation by the Irish Parliament; and in desiring Lord Cornwallis and Lord Castlereagh to promise Catholic relief after the Union, he intended to delude the Catholics into a support of his measure, and to deceive them afterwards. He knew the King's opinion upon that question—if anything that passed in the mind of George III. can be called an opinion—and that the obstinate and stupid old man would *never* suffer any project of Catholic Emancipation to be made a Ministerial measure.

No human being acquainted with public affairs ever believed that Mr. Pitt resigned office at that time on account of the Catholic question, or any other Irish question whatever. The truth was, simply, that Mr. Pitt's continental policy had failed, and that the English people, devoured by taxes, and wearied out with the still unfulfilled predictions of the total ruin of their French enemy, were crying aloud for peace. Mr. Pitt saw that peace must be made, at least for a little while; but his sullen pride could not submit to negotiate that peace himself. Mr. Plowden * says:—

"The only transaction which furnished him with a plausible or popular pretext for resignation was the *Catholic question*, which that crafty Minister and his followers have so frequently used as a most powerful engine for the worst of political purposes. Within very few days after the meeting of Parliament, he made no secret of his resignation. Great were the surprise and consternation which attended the report. Few, indeed, gave credit to the alleged cause of resignation—namely, his inability *to carry* the Catholic question, which was imperiously necessary for the safety of the state. He was too fond of power, his influence in the country was too imposing, Ireland was too insignificant to have caused such an important change in all the departments of the state. Abstracting from the merits and justice of the question, and from the expediency or necessity of its being then propounded and carried, neither Mr. Pitt's friends nor opponents could bring their minds to believe that an administration which had established itself in spite of the House of Commons; which had baffled, and at last subdued, a most formidable opposition; which had main-

* Worthy Mr. Plowden, who had rather supported the Union, as many other leading Catholics had done, when he wrote, ten years later, the second series of his *Historical Collections*, says, in its first page: "They (the Catholics) now beheld the baleful measure of Union in its full deformity." But they beheld it too late.

F

tained itself upon new courtly principles for seventeen years, and still commanded a decided majority in the Cabinet and Senate, should have been thus broken up from the Premier's inability to carry so simple and just a measure as that of an equal participation of Constitutional rights amongst all the King's subjects."

"Simple and just a measure" as this naturally appeared to the Catholic historian, it was steadily refused and resisted, both by Mr. Pitt and by his whole party, for twenty-nine years longer, and then only carried on account of the imminent danger of civil war, as its Ministerial supporters alleged.

There was an air of mystery about the retirement of Ministers at this crisis. Nobody gave credit to the ostensible motives of it; and several distinct reasons were alleged and discussed. In fact, every conceivable reason, except the true one, was assigned by the friends of Mr. Pitt. One was a serious difference which had sprung up between the Minister and the Duke of York,* partly with respect to military arrangements and operations; partly because certain "unconstitutional influence in a high quarter counteracted and embarrassed the important duties of His Majesty's official and responsible advisers;" and partly, it was also alleged, because the Duke of York, as the special patron of the Orange Society, was resolutely opposed to the project of Catholic Emancipation. His Royal Highness might have spared his uneasiness. No Grand Master of Orangemen was ever more violently opposed to all claims and rights of Catholics than Mr. Pitt himself.

Innocent Catholics had been expecting that the King's speech, on opening this session, would have recommended a measure for their emancipation. The subject was not once alluded to. The address was moved in the House of Commons by Sir Watkin William Wynne (commander of the Ancient Britons). Mr. Grey moved an amendment, and made some pointed observations upon Ireland and the Union. "If any good effect," he said, "could result from a measure so brought forward and so supported, he hoped it would be the extension of the British Constitution to the Catholics of Ireland, and their restoration to all the rights of British subjects. This they had been taught to expect, and this was the least they were entitled to in return for that measure having been forced upon them by England." Mr. Pitt, in replying to Mr. Grey, studiously avoided even remote reference to Ireland. Ireland had served his turn; she was now safe under British law and government; and he desired to hear of her no more. But he had much to say in denunciation of "Jacobinism," which was the name then given to any assertion of any kind of right or liberty, concluding his speech with a warm appeal to the majority of the House, whether all the public calamities of this, and all the nations of the Continent, were not occasioned by those principles which the gentleman opposite to him had uniformly supported, and which he and the gentlemen on his side of the House had as uniformly combated.

Before quitting the subject of Mr. Pitt's deliberate deception upon the Irish Catholics, it must be mentioned that the paper which had been delivered by Lord Cornwallis to Doctor Troy, Catholic Archbishop of Dublin, and Lord Fingal, soon became public; although Lord Cornwallis had prudently stipulated that it should be "*discreetly* communicated to the Bishops, and should not find its way into the newspapers."* When Mr. Grey, on the 25th of March, moved the House of Commons to resolve itself into a Committee of the whole House, to take into consideration the state of the nation, he referred to these written pledges, and roundly charged them with having been given without sincerity and without authority. "If Catholic freedom were offered to the Irish as the price of their support of the Union, if the faith of the Government were pledged on that occasion, it forms the highest species of criminality in Ministers; because I am confident," said he, "if such were the case, it was so pledged without the authority of the King; for I know His Majesty is superior to the idea of swerving in the slightest degree from the observance of his word. This, then, was a crime of the

---

* From the year 1797, the Orange Societies were so tenderly cherished and zealously promoted by the Duke of York, that almost every regiment, even of militia, in Ireland, received from the office of the Commander-in-chief encouragement, authority, or orders for establishing Orange Lodges in their respective regiments. The person delegated for this mission was generally the Sergeant-major, or some other non-commissioned officer, signalized for his zeal against the Catholics. In some instances, the institution of Orange Lodges, under this high and official sanction, has produced ferment and dissension, which compelled the commanding officer to investigate and punish both those who gave rise to, and those who perpetrated, the consequent outrages; when often, to the astonishment of the corps, and in defiance of military discipline and subordination, the conduct of the Sergeant has been justified by the production of the official document or warrant, most irregularly superseding that immediate authority upon which alone the subordination and union of a regiment depend.

* This is the document which is printed in a note to the preceding chapter.

highest denomination in Ministers, and calls for inquiry. I ask, if such promise were made, was Lord Clare and the Protestant Ascendancy Party made acquainted with it? If so, they were a party to the delusion that was intended to be practised on the unhappy Catholic."

Mr. Pitt, though no longer in office, sat on the Ministerial side of the House—in fact, he was virtually Prime Minister all the while. He replied to Mr. Grey, and touched as lightly as possible upon that part of his speech which referred to Ireland. Concerning the famous written pledge, he said, "he had no part in the *wording* of that paper. It was drawn up *by Lord Castlereagh*. To the sentiments it contained, *when properly interpreted*, he, however, subscribed: further, he would neither avow nor explain." He added: "As to the particular expressions in the paper, he knew nothing of them, having never seen it before it was published. He denied that any pledge had been given to the Catholics, either by himself, Lord Cornwallis, or the noble lord near him (Castlereagh). The Catholics might very naturally have conceived a hope, and he himself had always thought that in time that measure would be a consequence of the Union, because the difficulties would be fewer than before."

Mr. Plowden wrote to Lord Cornwallis upon the subject; and his lordship, in his reply, stated that *the paper* (which has been called the pledge to the Catholics) "was hastily given by him to Dr. Troy, to be circulated amongst his friends, with the view of preventing any immediate disturbances, or other bad effects."

In short, the Catholics very soon perceived that they had been deluded, and understood very well that their cause had been turned into a convenient pretext by Mr. Pitt for abandoning office, in order to throw upon other men the business of making the Peace of Amiens.*

Thus, within six weeks after carrying the Union, Mr. Pitt, Lord Grenville, Mr. Dundas (Lord Melville), Lord Cornwallis, and Lord Castlereagh, all went out of office. Mr. Addington, Speaker of the House of Commons, was the new Prime Minister; and Lord Hardwicke was sent over as Lord-Lieutenant of Ireland. Mr. Pitt and his colleagues resigned, pledging themselves to support their successors (who declined to accept office without that support), in an administration avowedly placed on implacable hostility to that identical measure which he scrupled not to declare essential to the safety of the empire.

The first measure which the Imperial Parliament bestowed upon Ireland was not an Act of Emancipation, but an Act for suspending the writ of *Habeas Corpus*, and establishing martial law. Lord Castlereagh had for some time been preparing the materials for the fabrication of a report of a secret committee, to prove (contrary to the fact) that rebellion still existed in Ireland, and, therefore, that there was a necessity for renewing the Act for suspending the *Habeas Corpus*, which was about to expire on the 25th of March. Accordingly, he had fixed the 20th of February for moving for a bill to enable the Lord-Lieutenant of Ireland to put martial law in force in such parts of Ireland as he should think proper.

The first Act for this purpose was passed in the beginning of April, and was to expire in three months. Shortly after its passage, the Chancellor of the Exchequer, by command of His Majesty, laid before the House of Commons copies and extracts of papers, containing secret information received by His Majesty's Government relative to the state of Ireland, and proceedings of certain disaffected persons in both parts of the United Kingdom, which, upon his motion, were referred to a committee. This was a preconcerted plan for representing Ireland, and collaterally the whole United Kingdom, as overrun with the spirit of Jacobinism. On no occasion was Mr. Pitt more vehement in his declamation against Jacobinism, apparently with a view of drawing off the public attention from the real authors of the national disasters, by directing its indignation against the Jacobins, whose cause they essentially tended to strengthen. "It was," said he, "the inherent spirit of Jacobinism to ally itself with every disaster, to press into its service every evil of the state, to wed itself to every misfortune of the country it inhabits, and to make them forerunners of its ruin."

The report of this secret committee was well got up to effect Mr. Pitt's favourite policy—that of "exciting alarm." It represented the three kingdoms as infested with the spirit of rebellion, French principles, or "Jacobinism." It recited with great emphasis certain songs and toasts, which were alleged to be favourites with the seditious rabble.

* It has always been considered by English statesmen a small and easy matter to cheat the Irish. More than two hundred years before, Sir Francis Bacon (afterwards Lord Bacon), in his "Considerations Touching the Queen's Service in Ireland," said: "Nothing can be more fit than a treaty, or a shadow of a treaty, of a peace with Spain, which, methinks, should be in our power to fasten, at least *rumore tenus*, to the deluding of as wise a people as the Irish."

It reported the formation of new societies of Millenarians, New Jerusalemites, Spensonians, and other fanatics, whom it traced from London into Yorkshire, Lancashire, Nottingham, Scotland, and other neighbouring places, but it extended them not to Ireland. Yet Ireland was not to be wholly omitted where the report was, incidentally at least, calculated to justify the coercive measures intended for that part of the United Kingdom; and the committee added to their own surmises of the workings of these fanatics, *that they borrowed their ideas from the Irish rebellion.* "They saw *in Ireland* the example of such a rebellion as they wished to promote here." They further produced a printed address, signed *Hybernicus,* directed to Britons and fellow-citizens. The committee said : "They had thus detailed the proceedings of the disaffected, carried on in the metropolis, and as directed principally to its disturbance, but these would afford a very inadequate representation of the extent of the confederacy; yet, in proceeding to advert to the state of the other parts of the country, *and even of Ireland,* they omitted to notice the concert which, in some measure, pervaded the whole." In other parts of the report they lay stress upon the exaggerated statements of some men of the number of the confederates, all trained to military exercise, which, including Ireland, amounted to one hundred and fifty thousand. They added that the principal of these emissaries were represented as delegated from London, York, Birmingham, Bristol, Sheffield, and other considerable towns, *as well as from Ireland.*

The committee added that a new Revolutionary Association had been formed in Ireland; that a "Committee of Rebellion," composed of certain Irishmen, existed in Paris, and was negotiating with the French Government on the best mode of abolishing the British Constitution.

This astounding report was received by Parliament as ample proof of all that it affirmed.

When Lord Hobart, as Secretary of State for Ireland, introduced to the Lords the bill for continuing martial law in Ireland, he observed that he had not attempted to use any arguments to prove the necessity for passing the bill, because "the report on the face of it proved the necessity, and he thought their lordships would be more impressed with the arguments contained in the report than by any he could add." All the restrictive and coercive bills touching Ireland were passed under the still prevailing influence of Mr. Pitt and Lord Grenville; the opposition to them was numerically insignificant. During the first session of the Imperial Parliament, no question respecting Ireland caused any difference between the seceders and their successors. They both equally deprecated the very mention of Catholic Emancipation, and emulated each other in zeal for curbing and coercing the Irish people.

The bill passed both Houses by immense majorities; and the British Constitution was suspended, so far as respected Ireland. The Lord-Lieutenant was empowered to proclaim any part, or the whole, of the island under martial law; the Act professed to be only temporary, as these coercion laws for Ireland are always said to be, but they are almost always renewed before they expire; and thus, under one name or another, "Insurrection Act," "Crime and Outrage Act," and the like, this coercive code has been substantially the law of Ireland from that day to the present.

Another Irish measure, passed about the same time, was an Act to regulate the office of Master of the Rolls in Ireland. Before the Union this office was a mere sinecure, holden at the pleasure of the Crown by two Peers (Lords Glandore and Carysfort), with considerable salaries. These had been promised a large compensation for the loss of their places in case the Union should be carried. Henceforward it was to be an efficient legal office, to be holden for life, with a suitable salary, in order to give the Irish Chancellor an opportunity of attending his legislative duties in the House of Peers. It was warmly contended that, as the Commissioners for the Rolls were removable at pleasure from the sinecures, they were entitled to no compensation, as the Chancellor of the Exchequer and Prime-Sergeant had been. Mr. Pitt and Lord Castlereagh justified the compensation, because it had been promised by the Irish Parliament, and they were bounden in honour to make it good.

"In fact," as Mr. Plowden bitterly observes, "none but the *Catholic* supporters of the Union had to complain of Ministerial infidelity in the observance of previous stipulations and promises."

There was one other who thought he had reason to complain. This was Lord Clare. The Irish Chancellor had for many years made himself the instrument, and a most able and thorough-going instrument, of Mr. Pitt's policy in Ireland. Scarcely had Lord Castlereagh himself been more efficient in accomplishing the Union; and his lordship, who was naturally arrogant and presumptuous, evidently imagined that he was only promoting himself from a narrow provincial stage to the wide imperial theatre, where his audacity and powerful will would soon enable him to predominate in London as he had done in Dublin. In the discussion of this bill to complete the great job of the Rolls Court, Mr. Pitt said, "It was highly desirable that the House of Lords should enjoy the benefit of that great luminary of the law who had rendered such eminent services to his country." Mr. Grey replied that much had been said that night in praise of the Irish Chancellor. "He only knew his politics, and those he highly disapproved of. It had been already shown that night that the noble lord vindicated the use of torture to extort confessions." Lord Clare, from his first arrival in England, put himself at the head of the opponents of the Catholic claims. Foreseeing that the new administration was to consist of men assuming the arrogant appellation of the *King's friends*, he attempted, by decrying his own country in the Imperial Parliament, to secure, as one of the *King's friends*, an influence in the councils of Great Britain.

He failed in this unworthy ambition. He was reminded, in the House of Lords, that he was not now predominating over an assembly of Irish Peers. He was not at all consulted in the arrangements for the new Addington Administration. He returned to Ireland consumed by disappointment, and did not scruple to express his bitter regret at the part he had taken in carrying the Union. If he did regret that act it was for his own sake alone, not for the sake of his country.

He remained some time in London in order to negotiate for some more efficient influence in the British Cabinet than the Great Seal of Ireland was ever likely to give him. Mr. Pitt, who well knew that nobleman's insatiable ambition, cautioned Mr. Addington against admitting him to a situation in which, in case of resumption (of which Mr. Pitt never lost sight), he might meet a rival in the colleague. Lord Clare, foiled in his projects of British ambition, his pride wounded by the speeches of the late Duke of Bedford and some other of the Whig Lords in Parliament, who freely reminded him that Union had not transferred his dictatorial powers to the Imperial Parliament, had, in disgust, formed the resolution of withdrawing from scenes which he neither directed nor controlled. He had determined to return to his official situation in Ireland; but, by the Union, the Irish Seal had been shorn of its lustre and all political consequence.

Lord Clare soon fell into bad health; and he died within the year and day after that Act of Union which was to have crowned him with triumph. He died in January, 1802. His remains were interred with great pomp, in St. Peter's Churchyard, in Dublin. Some of the populace attempted at the funeral to express their horror of the deceased by offering indignities to his corpse.

It is singular that the only two eminent men who were within the present century borne to their graves amidst the hootings of the people, were the Earl of Clare and the Marquis of Londonderry (Castlereagh), the two able tools of British policy in ruining the independence of their country.

The Earl of Hardwicke arrived in Dublin, to assume his government, on the 25th of May. Lord Cornwallis proceeded to England in June; and we next hear of him as the negotiator of the Peace of Amiens.

The English and French people both eagerly desired peace. The First Consul, Buonaparte, was also sincerely desirous of giving repose to his countrymen, after so many years of bloody warfare. As Mr. Pitt and his high Anti-Jacobin friends were notoriously the party of war, it was believed in France that the change of Ministry betokened a disposition towards peace in the councils of England. The First Consul was not aware that Mr. Pitt still continued really to govern the country; and that he had made this new arrangement because he desired that other men than himself should make that treaty and afterwards violate it. It is manifest that Napoleon Buonaparte did not at that time fully know how incompatible, how mutually destructive, were a French Government—the product of the revolution—and an English oligarchy. He not only truly desired peace, but could see no reason why it might not be attained; while Mr. Pitt and the Court were fully resolved that, while England had a ship afloat and a guinea to hire allies, the struggle must go on. The momentary Peace of Amiens was intended to delude the French; and Mr. Pitt ceased for awhile to be the ostensible Minister, adroitly availing himself of his pretended zeal for the Catholic question, by which he had deluded the Irish.

The preliminaries of peace were signed at London, the 1st of October, in this year, 1801. The treaty itself was signed at the city of Amiens, the 27th of March, 1802, between France, Great Britain,

Spain, and the Batavian Republic. France and England were represented by Joseph Buonaparte and Lord Cornwallis. England was to preserve, of her maritime conquests, the two islands of Ceylon and Trinidad. France was to repossess all her colonies. The Republic of the Seven Islands was to be recognized. Malta was to be restored to the Order of the Knights. Spain and the Batavian Republic were to have back all their colonies, except Ceylon and Trinidad; and the French were to evacuate Rome, Naples, and the Isle of Elba. A cessation of hostilities, by land and sea, had been already proclaimed; and on the signature of the treaty, the people really began to taste the luxury of peace.

The popular outcry for peace was now satisfied; but as it had been resolved upon from the first that this repose should be of very short duration, pretexts began to be immediately sought for breaking the treaty. The French Government was making active naval preparations in the port of Brest, intended ostensibly for St. Domingo; but it was assumed that the armament was really for Ireland.

Similar naval preparations and military movements were on foot in England in the winter of 1802. In the spring of 1803, volunteering in England, and the raising of yeomanry corps in Ireland, were matters of public notoriety.

In fact, the English Government was resolved never to give up the island of St. Malta; and as this was a vital article of the treaty in the eyes of Buonaparte, it was evident that war must again break out. Lord Whitworth was sent over as Minister to France; and from his dispatches to London, and those of Lord Hawkesbury in reply, it is easy to discover what were the true obstacles to the real establishment of peace.

Buonaparte, in a conference with Lord Whitworth, communicated to the British Government, 21st February, 1803, reiterated his complaints against the British Government in reference to the retention of Malta, in direct violation of the terms of the treaty. He said: "Of the two, he would rather see us (the English) in possession of the Faubourg St. Antoine than of Malta." . . . He complained of the protection given in England to the assassin Georges, handsomely pensioned, and of his plans being permitted to be carried into effect in France, and of two of his fellow-agents being sent into France by the *emigrés* to assassinate him (Buonaparte), and being then in custody. The two men he referred to were subsequently tried, and convicted of the crime they were charged with on their own confessions.

In regard to the abuse launched on Buonaparte in the English papers, and French emigrant journals published in London, he (the First Consul) said to Lord Whitworth: "The irritation he felt against England increased daily, because every wind which blew from England brought nothing but enmity and hatred against him." Lord Hawkesbury, in reply to Lord Whitworth's communication, 18th February, 1803, made the following admission, for the first time explicitly and plainly expressed: "With regard to that article of the treaty which relates to Malta, the stipulations contained in it, owing to circumstances which it was not in the power of His Majesty to control, had not been found capable of execution."

In Lord Whitworth's communication (dated February 21, 1803) to Lord Hawkesbury, an account is given of an interview with Buonaparte, when the latter, in reference to the proofs he had given of a desire to maintain peace, said he wished to know what he had to gain by going to war with England. A descent was the only means of offence he had, and if determined to attempt one, it must be made by putting himself at the head of an expedition. But how could it be supposed that, after having gained the height on which he stood, he would risk his life and reputation in such a hazardous attempt, unless forced to it by necessity, when the chances were, that he and the *greatest part of the expedition would go to the bottom of the sea*. He talked much on the subject, but never affected to diminish the danger. He acknowledged there were a hundred chances to one against him; but still he was determined to attempt it, if war should be the consequence of the present discussion; and, such was the disposition of the troops, that army after army would be found for the enterprise. He concluded by stating that France, with an army of four hundred and eighty thousand men, to be immediately completed, was ready for the most desperate enterprise; that England, with her fleet, was mistress of the seas, which he did not think he should be able to equal in ten years. Two such countries, by a proper understanding, might govern the world, but by their strifes might overturn it.

On the 9th of March, 1803, a message from the King was delivered to the Parliament, wherein His Majesty "thinks it necessary to acquaint the House of Commons that, as very considerable military preparations were carrying on in the ports of France and Holland, he had judged it expedient to adopt additional measures of precaution for the security of his dominions."

Lord Whitworth, in March, by the instructions of his Government, demanded an explanation of the motives and objects of the warlike preparations in the French ports, and the reply (not official) of M. Talleyrand was said to have been short and not satisfactory—" It was the will of the First Consul." Buonaparte, on the other hand, on the 11th of March, at a levee at the Tuilleries, attended by the different ambassadors and a great number of distinguished persons, on entering the grand saloon seemed violently agitated, and appeared to be conversing with his attendants, or rather thinking aloud, for the following words, pronounced in a very audible voice, were heard by all the persons in the audience chamber:—" Vengeance will fall on that power which will be the cause of the war." He approached the British Ambassador, Lord Whitworth, and said: " You know, my lord, that a terrible storm has arisen between England and France." Lord Whitworth said it was to be hoped that this storm would be dissipated without any serious consequences. Buonaparte replied: " It will be dissipated when England shall have evacuated Malta; if not, the cloud would burst and the bolt must fall. The King of England had promised by treaty to evacuate that place; and who was to violate the faith of treaties?"

All this while, Mr. Pitt was out of office; and it was given out that his health was so shattered as to render him quite incapable of the cares and labours of public business; yet, in reality, while the London *Chronicle* was officially announcing his great sufferings, Mr. Pitt had never been so intensely and indefatigably occupied with state affairs as he was at the very time of these negotiations.* There can be no reasonable doubt that he directed and governed them from point to point.

On the 10th of May, the Court of London presented certain new projects plainly inadmissible; making further demands on France, and saying nothing of the surrender of Malta. The new conditions being rejected, Lord Whitworth demanded his passports, in order to quit the country.

On the 15th of May, 1803, His Britannic Majesty sent a message to Parliament announcing the recall of the British Ambassador from Paris, and the departure of the French Ambassador from London. The declaration of hostilities with France was published in *The Gazette* of 18th May, 1803.

Mr. Pitt's health was immediately restored. On the 23d of May there was an animated debate in the House on an address to the King, pledging the House to support him in the vigorous prosecution of the war. On that night, the night of the debate of the 23d of May, Mr. Pitt was found in his place in Parliament, and it is hardly necessary to add that his "voice was still for war." Perhaps greater vigour of mind or body was never exhibited by him than on that occasion. The ex-Minister was himself again. War was about to be let loose on the world, and all the principles of evil seemed concentrated in the unholy exultation with which the prospect of war was hailed on that occasion. In the heat of his passion, he reviled Buonaparte in the most vehement terms of invective; he spoke of the First Consul as "a sea of liquid fire, which destroyed everything which was unfortunate enough to come in contact with it." It then only remained for honourable members to express a hope that "the only man in the empire qualified to conduct the war to a successful issue" should be recalled to the councils of his Sovereign.

Mr. Pitt resumed in May, 1804, the supreme direction of public affairs as Prime Minister. He made no stipulation with the King concerning the Catholic claims; nor did he ever again offend his Sovereign's ear upon this subject, nor urge him to "violate his coronation oath" by emancipating four millions of his subjects.

Mr. Pitt's first great task now was to form that gigantic coalition of European Powers against France; and, occupied by these mighty projects, he thought no more of Ireland, unless when she seemed to need more coercion.

CHAPTER IX.

1802—1803.

First Year of the Union—Distress in Ireland—Riot in Dublin—Irish Exiles in France—Renewed Hopes of French Aid—The two Emmets, MacNeven, and O'Connor in France—Apprehensions of Invasion in England—Robert Emmet comes from France to Ireland—His Associates—His Plans—Miles Byrne—Despard's Conspiracy in England—Emmet's Preparations—Explosion in Patrick Street—The 23d of July—Failure—Bloody Riot—Murder of Lord Kilwarden—Emmet sends Miles Byrne to France—Retires to Wicklow—Returns to Dublin—Arrested—Tried—Convicted—Hanged—Fate of Russell.

---

* Doctor Madden (*U. I. Third Series*, p. 310), makes this statement on the authority of Lady Hester Stanhope, Mr. Pitt's niece and private secretary.

THE first year of the Union was, for Ireland, a year of severe distress. The crops of 1801 had in great measure failed; and as the people then depended for subsistance chiefly upon agriculture, as they do still, the usual results ensued. Hunger and hardship produced discontent, and in some places disorder also. The fair promises of immediate prosperity which was to have followed the Union, were not realized. Even trade and commerce were languishing. Mr. Foster, late Speaker, stated, in his place in the Imperial Parliament, that in 1801 the decrease of exported linen was five million yards. The taxes were increasing as the means of paying them diminished; for Ireland had now to provide for the charges of that immense debt which had been contracted for slaughtering her people and purchasing her Parliament. Mr. Foster, in the same speech, mentioned that, although it had been acknowledged that the expenses of the current year would be considerably less than they had been in the preceding year, yet a million more was borrowed for the present than for the last year. The inference to be drawn from that measure, for various Union purposes, was too obvious to mention. The revenue was then collected at a much lighter rate of expense than it had been in 1782, when it was at £11, 12s. 4d. per cent. The revenues of the Post Office were, at the time he was speaking, collected at the enormous expenditure of £224 per cent. In 1800, the amount of grants, pensions, &c., on that score, was £34,000; in 1802, £51,000; and this is what he called "a falling year." Then the Catholics, whose eyes were at length opened to the gross deception of which they had been victims, felt sore and disappointed; especially as the persecuting Orange Societies were now greatly multiplied, and became each day, by direct encouragement of the Government and of a Royal Duke, more insolent and aggressive. A serious riot took place in Dublin. The anniversary commemoration of the battle of Aughrim, on the 12th of July, was in 1802 solemnized with more than ordinary pomp. The statue of King William, in College Green, was most superbly decorated with Orange colours, and several corps of yeomanry paraded round it in the course of the day. In the evening, the conduct of the yeomanry, and the spirit of this ill-judged and mischievous commemoration, so worked on the popular feelings, that the most serious consequences were apprehended. Mr. Alderman Stamer failed in his endeavours to prevent outrages; some yeomen were beaten to the ground. Major Swan was knocked down and severely wounded: nor was the mob dispersed until Alderman Darley arrived with a large party of the Castle guard. Some of the populace were taken and severely punished. Attempts were made to raise this expression of popular soreness into a general spirit of disaffection, and a renovation of rebellion. Nothing, however, could be certainly traced beyond the temporary and local outrage upon the popular feeling, from this senseless annual ovation of the Ascendancy, lately rendered more poignantly provoking by the ferocity and growing power of the Orange societies.

On the whole, therefore, when the insidious negotiations of the English Government, preparatory to the violation of the treaty of Amiens, were going forward in London and Paris, the mass of the Irish people was still thoroughly disaffected; and persons connected with the Government were of opinion that, immediately on the fresh outbreak of war with France, a new French expedition, and on a larger scale than that of Hoche, would be dispatched to Ireland; in which case there was no doubt of a general rising in the island.

The two Emmets, O'Connor, and many other Irish exiles, were then on the Continent; and were in communication with the First Consul, provisionally, with a view to future operations in case of the renewal of the war, which then seemed highly probable. Robert Emmet was then about twenty-four years of age. He had seen the atrocities of '98, the frauds and villanies by which the Union was accomplished; he saw his unhappy country still groaning under martial law, the great majority of his compatriots shut out from the Constitution, and, by means of packed juries and Orange magistrates, effectually deprived of the protection of law. His ardent spirit burned to redress these wrongs, and to do at least what one man might, to rouse the people for one more manly effort. The purity and elevation of his motives have never been questioned even by his enemies. What he desired and longed for with all the intensity of his passionate nature, was simply to see his people invested with the ordinary civil right of human beings, leading peaceful and honourable lives under the protecting shelter of a native Legislature, and having a law over them which they might reverence and obey, not curse and abhor.*

* Lord Castlereagh, a young man like Robert Emmet, but more "prudent," thus describes Emmet and his insurrection, after the danger was over, in a speech in Parliament:—"In place of a formidable conspiracy fraught with danger to the existing Gov-

Robert Emmet passed several months of the years 1800 and 1801 on the Continent and Peninsula—the greater part of that time on the tour in which he visited the south of France, Switzerland, and some parts of Spain. On his return from this tour, he visited Amsterdam and Brussels, where his brother, T. A. Emmet, had been sojourning since his liberation from Fort George, and banishment, in June, 1802.

It was impossible for Irishmen to be in France or Belgium in that year without perceiving the evident symptoms of a new and formidable struggle approaching. The English Minister had already refused to give up Malta; and formidable military and naval preparations were rapidly advancing both in France and in England. Equally impossible was it for the exiled United Irishmen not to turn with anxious hope to this new conjuncture of affairs. Doctor MacNeven was then in France, as well as Tone's friend, Thomas Russell. With whom the idea originated of entering upon a negotiation with the French Government does not seem clear; but certain it is that Robert Emmet, in the summer of 1802, had interviews both with Buonaparte and Talleyrand.

His design was, then, based on the expectation of a speedy rupture of the amicable relations between Great Britain and France, on a knowledge of extensive naval preparations in the northern seaports of France, and the impression left on his mind, by his interview with Buonaparte, and his frequent communications with Talleyrand, that those preparations were for an invasion of England, which was likely to be attempted in August, 1803; on the knowledge, communicated to him by Dowdall, of a movement being determined on by the Secret Society of England, with which Colonel Despard was connected; on the assurance of support and pecuniary assistance from very influential persons in Ireland; and, lastly, on the concurrence of several of the Irish leaders in Paris.

The late Lord Cloncurry informed Doc-

ernment, it was only the wild and contemptible project of Mr. Emmet a young man of a heated and enthusiastic imagination, who, inheriting a property of £3,000 from his father, which was entirely at his own disposal, thought he could not dispose of it to more advantage than in an attempt to overturn the Government of his country."

What a contrast between these two Irishmen! Castlereagh certainly was not of "a heated and enthusiastic imagination." He did not invest his patrimony in pikes. The one sold his country to her enemies, and was laden with riches and honours. The other, who spent all he possessed in an effort to redeem that country, perished on a gibbet, and the dogs of Thomas Street lapped his blood.

tor Madden that he dined in company with Robert Emmet and Surgeon Lawless, the day before the departure of the former for Ireland. "Emmet spoke of his plans with extreme enthusiasm; his features glowed with excitement, the perspiration burst through the pores, and ran down his forehead." Lawless was thoroughly acquainted with his intentions, and thought favourably of them; but Lord Cloncurry considered the plans impracticable, and was opposed to them. Doctor MacNeven, Hugh Wilson, Russell, Byrne, William and Thomas Corbett, Hamilton, and Sweeney, were intimate and confidential friends of Robert Emmet, as well as of his brother—several of them, there is positive proof, concurred in the attempt. All of them, it may be supposed, were cognisant of it. All their surviving friends are agreed on one point, that the project did not originate with Robert Emmet.

The letters of T. A. Emmet, at this period, establish the fact that, in the autumn and winter of 1802, the leading United Irishmen then on the Continent, in the event of a rupture between France and England, were bent on renewing their efforts, and that they looked upon the struggle in Ireland as suspended, but not relinquished.

That this also was the opinion of the English Government is equally certain. After the declaration of war, a number of intercepted letters, found on board the East Indiaman, Admiral Aplin, captured by the French, and published in the *Moniteur* by the Government, afford abundant proof of the panic which prevailed in England, and of the expectation of invasion that was general at that period. Very serious apprehensions were expressed in these letters of the results of an invasion in Ireland. It was stated, in a letter of Lord Charles Bentinck to his brother, Lord William Bentinck, Governor of Madras: "If Ireland be not attended to, it will be lost; these rascals (an endearing, familiar, gentleman-like way of describing the people of Ireland) are as ripe as ever for rebellion."

In an extract of a letter to General Clinton, of the 2d of June, we find the following passage: "I have learned from them (Irish people in England), with regret, that the lower classes of the men in Ireland were more disaffected than ever, even more than during the last rebellion, and that if the French could escape from our fleet, and land their troops in the north of Ireland, they would be received with satisfaction, and joined by a great number."

In a letter of Lord Grenville to the Marquis of Wellesley, dated the 12th of July, 1803, we find the following passage: "I am not certain whether the event of the war, which our wise Ministers have at last declared, may not have induced them to beg you to continue your stay in India some time longer. I hope nothing, however, will prevent me from having the pleasure of seeing you next year, *supposing at that period that you have still a country to revisit.*"

Letter from Mr. Finers to General Lake, July 14th: "The invasion, which has been so long the favourite project of the First Consul, will certainly take place."

Letter from one of the Directors of the East India Company, Thomas Faulder, to Mr. J. Ferguson Smith, Calcutta, August 3d: "I have heard from the first authority, that if the French can land in Ireland with some troops, they will be immediately joined by one hundred thousand Irish."*

Robert Emmet set out for Ireland in the beginning of October, 1802, and arrived in Dublin in the course of the same month. His brother, Thomas Addis, was then in Brussels. His father, the worthy Doctor Emmet, and his mother, were then residing at Casino, near Milltown; and here Robert remained some weeks in seclusion. Gradually and cautiously he put himself in communication with those whom he knew to be favourable to his enterprise—especially the old United Irishmen of '98. The principal persons concerned with him were—Thomas Russell, formerly Lieutenant of the Sixty-fourth Regiment of Foot; John Allen, of the firm of Allen and Hickson, woollen-drapers, Dame Street, Dublin; Philip Long, a general merchant, residing at No. 4 Crow Street; Henry William Hamilton (married to Russell's niece), of Enniskillen, barrister-at-law; William Dowdall, of Mullingar (natural son of Hussey Burgh, formerly Secretary to the Dublin Whig Club); Miles Byrne, of Wexford; Colonel Lumm, of the County Kildare; ——— Carthy, a gentleman farmer, of Kildare; Malachy Delany, the son of a lauded proprietor, County Wicklow; the Messrs. Perrot, farmers, County Kildare; Thomas Wylde, cotton manufacturer, Cork Street; Thomas Lenahan, a farmer, of Crew Hill, County Kildare; John Hevey, a tobacconist, of Thomas Street; Denis Lambert Redmond, a coal factor, of Dublin; ——— Branagan, of Irishtown, timber merchant; Joseph Aliburn, of Kilmacud, Windy Harbour, a small landholder;

Thomas Frayne, a farmer, of Boven, County of Kildare; Nicholas Gray, of Wexford.*

Some other persons of more humble rank, tradesmen, whose services would be required in the preparations, are enumerated by Doctor Madden:—James Hope, of County Antrim; Michael Quigley, a master bricklayer, of Rathcoffy, in the County Kildare; Henry Howley, a master carpenter, who had been engaged in the former rebellion; Felix Rourke, of Rathcoole, a clerk in a brewery in Dublin, who had been engaged in the former rebellion; Nicholas Stafford, a baker, of James Street; Bernard Duggan, a working cotton manufacturer, of the County Tyrone, who had been engaged in the former rebellion; Michael Dwyer, the well-known Wicklow insurgent, who, along with Holt and Miles Byrne, had kept up their resistance amidst the glens and mountains of Wicklow.

The plan of Robert Emmet's insurrection was, while agents were quietly organizing both the city and county, to make secret preparations in the city of Dublin itself;—then, when all was ready, to make one spring at the Castle, to seize upon the authorities, and give the signal for a general insurrection from Dublin Castle. There is good military authority for approving this plan of a rising in Ireland; and it certainly might have well succeeded but for one fatal accident. The gallant Miles Byrne, after many a campaign as a French officer, in every quarter of Europe, deliberately, in his latter days, avowed his preference for Emmet's scheme to every other that could be devised in the circumstances of Ireland. He says, in closing his own narrative of that part of his career :—

"I shall ever feel proud of the part I took with the lamented Robert Emmet. I have often asked myself, How could I have acted otherwise, seeing all his views and plans for the independence of my country so much superior to anything ever imagined before on the subject? They were only frustrated by accident, and the explosion of a depôt; and, as I have always said, whenever Irishmen think of obtaining freedom, Robert Emmet's plans will be their best guide. First, to take the capital, and then the provinces will burst out and raise the same standard immediately."†

Myles Byrne himself, after being much sought after by the Government, on

* The above extracts are given by Doctor Madden.—*C. I. Third Series*, p. 315.

* Dr. Madden adds the names of Lord Wycombe and John Keogh, as favourable to the enterprise, not actually concerned in it.
† *Memoirs of Miles Byrne.* Paris.

account of his part in the Wexford insurrection, and after many escapes, was, in 1802, under a feigned name, employing himself as a measurer of timber in the timber-yard of his stepbrother, Kennedy; but still keeping up his connections with the remnant of Wexford rebels, and hoping for better times. Here, while he was one day measuring logs, news came of the Peace of Amiens. "I felt," he says, "unnerved and disappointed at the news of the peace. I had been living in hopes that, ere the war terminated, something good would be done for poor Ireland."

Soon after the arrival of Robert Emmet, we find him in close communication with Mr. Byrne.

In reporting their first conversation, Mr. Byrne gives his unimpeachable testimony with regard to the real views of Emmet, and his motives for engaging in the enterprise, and his anxious care to avoid French domination as well as to abolish that of England. The *Memoir* says:—

"Mr. Emmet soon told me his plans. He said he wished to be acquainted with all those who had escaped in the war of '98, and who continued still to enjoy the confidence of the people; that he had been inquiring since his return, and even at Paris. He was pleased to add that he had heard my name mentioned amongst them, &c. He entered into many details of what Ireland had to expect from France in the way of assistance, now that that country was so energetically governed by the First Consul, Buonaparte, who feared (he, Buonaparte) that the Irish people might be changed, and careless about their independence, in consequence of the union with England. It became obvious, therefore, that this impression should be removed as soon as possible. Robert Emmet told me the station his brother held in Paris, and that the different members of the Government there frequently consulted him. All of them were of opinion that a demonstration should be made by the Irish patriots to prove that they were as ready as ever to shake off the English yoke. To which Mr. Thomas Addis Emmet replied, it would be cruel to commit the poor Irish people again, and to drive them into another rebellion before they received assistance from France; but at the same time he could assure the French Government that a secret organization was then going on throughout Ireland, but more particularly in the city of Dublin, where large depôts of arms and of every kind of ammunition were preparing with the greatest secrecy, as none but the tried men of 1798 were intrusted with the management of those stores and depôts.

"After giving me this explanation, Mr. Robert Emmet added: 'If the brave and unfortunate Lord Edward Fitzgerald and his associates felt themselves justified in seeking to redress Ireland's grievances by taking the field, what must not be our justification, now that not a vestige of self-government exists, in consequence of the accursed Union; that, until this most barbarous, fraudulent transaction took place, from time to time, in spite of corruption, useful local laws were enacted for Ireland? Now, seven-eighths of the population have no right to send a member of their body to represent them, even in a foreign Parliament; and the other eighth part of the population are the tools and taskmasters, acting for the cruel English Government and its Irish Ascendancy—a monster still worse, if possible, than foreign tyranny.'

"Mr. Emmet mentioned again the promises obtained from the chief of the French Government, given to himself, his brother, and other leaders, that in the event of a French army landing in Ireland, it should be considered as an auxiliary one, and received on the same principle as General Rochambeau and his army were received by the American people, when fighting for their independence. He added: 'That though no one could abhor more than he did the means by which the First Consul came to be at the head of the French nation, still he was convinced that this great military chief would find it his interest to deal fairly by the Irish nation, as the best and surest way to obtain his ends with England. He therefore thought the country should be organized and prepared for those great events, which were now inevitable. That as for himself, he was resolved to risk his life, and to stake the little fortune he possessed, for the accomplishment of those preparations so necessary for the redemption of our unfortunate country from the hands of a cruel enemy.'"

It was while Mr. Emmet was making his preparations in Dublin that an English revolutionary conspiracy was detected and broken up in London. A certain Colonel Despard and thirty other persons were arrested, on a charge of high treason, at a public-house in Lambeth, the 15th of November, 1802. By some of the witnesses it appeared that Government was cognizant of the treasonable proceedings of Despard and his associates six months previous to their arrest; that spies were set on them, and suggested acts in some cases to them, which were adopted; that they had printed pages to the following effect: "Constitution, the independence of Great Britain and Ireland; an equalization of civil, political, and religious rights; an ample provision for the families of the heroes who shall fall in the contest; a liberal reward for distinguished merit. These are the objects for which we contend. We swear to be united, in the awful presence of God."

February 7, 1803, Colonel Despard was tried at the Surrey Assizes, before Lord Ellenborough, on a charge of high treason, conspiring to *assassinate the King*, &c. Of this last charge there was no evidence; but it plainly appeared that Despard, as well as Robert Emmet, had been encouraged to make his attempt by the French Government, which very naturally desired to create for the English Government as much embarrassment as possible at home. Despard was convicted and hung.

In the meantime Emmet was quietly collecting arms and forming depôts of them at several points in Dublin. In January, 1803, his good father, Doctor Robert Emmet, died, and was buried in the churchyard of St. Peter's, Aungier Street. Robert could not even attend his father's funeral; because his presence in Dublin was intended to be a secret, and he knew there was a warrant for his apprehension in the hands of Major Sirr, since early in the year 1800.* He was proceeding actively with his preparations. Miles Byrne and others were busy in getting pikes, pistols, and blunderbusses manufactured, and ammunition laid in. Emmet invented a species of explosive machines, consisting of beams of wood bored by a pump augur, and filled with powder and small stones, intended to be exploded in the face of advancing troops at the moment of action. Large quantities of pikes were forged and mounted, and carried from their places of manufacture to the depôts in hollow logs prepared for their reception, and which were drawn through the streets like ordinary lumber.

It is not a little strange that the Irish Government, usually so vigilant and suspicious, seems to have had no knowledge of these formidable arrangements. This was not for want of warnings, and report of spies; but the Government did not believe them. And it is no wonder that the executive was so incredulous, because there had not probably been one week for the past half century, when the Government had not received some alarming intelligence of this nature. Plainly also the information was not so precise as to indicate persons and places, so that no interruption was given to the arrangements; and the 23d of July, 1803, was fixed for the outbreak.

Before that day arrived, a circumstance occurred which threatened to ruin all.

On the Saturday night week previous to the turn-out, an explosion of some combustibles took place in the depôt of Patrick Street, which gave some alarm in the neighbourhood. Major Sirr came to examine the house: previous to his coming, some one removed the remaining powder, arms, &c., and all the matters which were moveable in the place, notwithstanding some obstruction given by the watchman. Other arms were secreted on the premises, and were not discovered until some time afterwards. It was concluded that the affair was only some chemical process, which had accidentally caused the explosion.

The accident does not seem to have placed any serious obstacle in the way of the enterprise. Miles Byrne says:—

"Now, the final plan to be executed consisted principally in taking the Castle, whilst the Pigeon House, Island Bridge, the Royal Barracks, and the old Custom House Barracks were to be attacked, and if not surprised and taken, they were to be blockaded, and intrenchments thrown up before them. Obstacles of every kind to be created through the streets, to prevent the English cavalry from charging. The Castle once taken, undaunted men, materials, implements of every description, would be easily found in all the streets in the city, not only to impede the cavalry, but to prevent infantry from passing through them.

"As I was to be one of these persons designed to co-operate with Robert Emmet in taking the Castle of Dublin, I shall here relate precisely the part which was allotted to me in this daring enterprise. I was to have assembled early in the evening of Saturday, the 23d of July, 1803, at the house of Dennis Lambert Redmond, on the Coal Quay, the Wexford and Wicklow men, to whom I was to distribute pikes, arms, and ammunition; and then, a little before dusk, I was to send one of the men, well known to Mr. Emmet, to tell him that we were at our post, armed and ready to follow him; men were placed in the house in Ship Street, ready to seize on the entrance to the Castle on that side, at the same moment the principal gate would be taken.

---

*Madden discovers this fact in *Sirr's Papers*, deposited in Trinity College Library.

"Mr. Emmet was to leave the depôt at Thomas Street at dusk, with six hackney coaches, in each of which six men were to be placed, armed with jointed pikes and blunderbusses concealed under their coats. The moment the last of these coaches had passed Redmond's house, where we were to be assembled, we were to sally forth and follow them quickly into the Castle Courtyard, and there to seize and disarm all the sentries, and to replace them instantly with our own men, &c.

"Emmet, after the explosion in Patrick Street, took up his abode in the depôt in Marshalsea Lane. There he lay at night on a mattress, surrounded by all the implements of death, devising plans, turning over in his mind all the fearful chances of the intended struggle, well knowing that his life was at the mercy of upwards of forty individuals, who had been, or still were employed in the depôts; yet confident of success, exaggerating its prospects, extenuating the difficulties which beset him, judging of others by himself, thinking associates honest who seemed to be so, confiding in their promises, and animated, or rather inflamed, by a burning sense of the wrongs of his country, and an enthusiasm in his devotion to what he considered its rightful cause.

"The morning of the 23d of July found Emmet and the leaders in whom he confided not of one mind; there was division in their councils, confusion in the depôts, consternation among the citizens who were cognizant of what was going on, and treachery tracking Robert Emmet's footsteps, dogging him from place to place, unseen, unsuspected, but perfidy nevertheless, embodied in the form of patriotism, employed in deluding its victim, making the most of its foul means of betraying its unwary victims, and counting already on the ultimate rewards of its treachery. Portion after portion of each plan of Robert Emmet was defeated, as he imagined, by accident, or ignorance, or neglect on the part of his agents. 'But it never occurred to him,' says Madden, 'that he was betrayed, that every design of his was frustrated, every project neutralized, as effectually as if an enemy had stolen into the camp.'

There is, however, no satisfactory evidence of treason on the part of any of those whom he trusted. The rest of this sad tale is soon told:—

Various consultations were held on the 23d, at the depôt in Thomas Street, at Mr. Long's, in Crow Street, and Mr. Allen's, in College Green, and great diversity of opinion prevailed with respect to the propriety of an immediate rising, or a postponement of the attempt. Emmet and Allen were in favour of the former, and, indeed, in the posture of their affairs, no other course was left, except the total abandonment of their project, which it is only surprising had not been determined on. The Wicklow men, under Dwyer, on whom great dependence was placed, had not arrived; the man who bore the order to him from Emmet neglected his duty, and remained at Rathfarnham. The Kildare men came in, and were informed, evidently by a traitor, that Emmet had postponed his attempt, and they went back at five o'clock in the afternoon. The Wexford men came in, and, to the number of two or three hundred, remained in town the early part of the night to take the part assigned to them, but they received no orders. A large body of men were assembled at the Broadstone, ready to act when the rocket signal agreed upon should be given, but no such signal was made.

It was evident that Emmet, to the last, counted on large bodies of men at his disposal, and that he was deceived. At eight o'clock in the evening he had eighty men nominally under his command, collected in the depôt in Marshalsea Lane.

A man rushed in to announce that troops were at that moment marching upon them, which was not true; yet it seems to have been believed by Emmet and the rest. It was then he resolved to sally out, with such poor following as he had, march upon the Castle, and, if necessary, meet death by the way. Even this happiness—of dying with arms in his hands—was not reserved for the unfortunate gentleman.

The motley assembly of armed men, some of them intoxicated, marched along Thomas Street, with their unhappy leader at their head, who was endeavouring to maintain some order, with the assistance of Stafford, a man who remained close by him throughout this scene, and faithful to the last. It was now about half-past nine, and quite dark. The sequel is painful to tell; yet it must be told. Doctor Madden says:—

"The stragglers in the rear soon commenced acts of pillage and assassination. The first murderous attack committed in Thomas Street was not that made on Lord Kilwarden, as we find by the following account in a newspaper of the day.

"'A Mr. Leech, of the Custom House, was passing through Thomas Street in a hackney coach, when he was stopped by the rabble; they dragged him out of the coach without any inquiry; it seemed enough that he was a respectable man; he fell on his knees, implored their mercy, but all in vain; they began the work of blood, and gave him a frightful pike wound in the groin. Their attention was then diverted from their humbler victim by the approach of Lord Kilwarden's coach. Mr. Leech then succeeded in creeping to Vicar Street watch-house, where he lay a considerable time apparently dead from loss of blood, but happily recovered from his wound.'"

Now, of all the judges, and other high official persons in Ireland in those days, not one was so estimable, so good and humane, as Lord Kilwarden, Chief Justice of the King's Bench. He had often stood between an innocent prisoner and the death to which his enemies had already doomed him. Most unfortunately, just as the mad mob of rioters had got beyond the control of their leader, and had already dipped their hands in blood, a private carriage was seen moving along that part of Thomas Street which leads to Vicar Street. It was stopped and attacked; Lord Kilwarden, who was inside, with his daughter and his nephew, the Rev. Richard Wolfe, cried out: "It is I, Kilwarden, Chief Justice of the King's Bench." A man, whose name is said to have been Shannon, rushed forward, plunged his pike into his lordship, crying out: "You are the man I want." A portmanteau was then taken out of the carriage, broken open and rifled of its contents; then his lordship, mortally wounded, was dragged out of the carriage, and several additional wounds inflicted on him. His nephew endeavoured to make his escape, but was taken, and put to death. The unfortunate young lady remained in the carriage, till one of the leaders rushed forward, took her from the carriage, and led her through the rabble to an adjoining house; and it is worthy of observation, that in the midst of this scene of sanguinary tumult, no injury or insult was offered to her, or attempted to be offered to her, by the infuriated rabble. Mr. Fitzgerald states that the person who rescued her from her dreadful situation was Robert Emmet.

Miss Wolfe, after remaining some time in the place of refuge she was placed in, proceeded on foot to the Castle, and entered the Secretary's office in a distracted state, and is said to have been the first bearer of the intelligence of her father's murder. Lord Kilwarden was found lying on the pavement dreadfully and mortally wounded. When the street was cleared of the insurgents, he was carried almost lifeless to the watch-house in Vicar Street.

This foul murder was an atrocity really horrible. Reasons have been assigned or suggested for it, as that the man who first attacked him had had a relative sentenced to death by him; that he was mistaken for Lord Carleton, a very different kind of judge, &c.; but the odious deed stands out in all its bloody horror; no better—but also no worse—than many of the outrages done upon the people in '98, by Orange yeomanry and Ascendancy magistrates.

Doctor Madden thus narrates the close of this dreadful affair:—

"Emmet halted his party at the market-house, with the view of restoring order, but tumult and insubordination prevailed. During his ineffectual efforts, word was brought that Lord Kilwarden was murdered; he retraced his steps, proceeded towards the scene of the barbarous outrage, and in the course of a few minutes returned to his party. From that moment he gave up all hope of effecting any national object. He saw that his attempt had merged into a work of pillage and murder. He, and a few of the leaders who were about him, abandoned their project and their followers. A detachment of the military made its appearance at the corner of Cutpurse Row, and commenced firing on the insurgents, who immediately fled in all directions. The rout was general in less than an hour from the time they sallied forth from the depôt. The only place where anything like resistance was made was on the Coombe, where Colonel Brown was killed, and two members of the Liberty Rangers, Messrs. Edmonston and Parker. The guard-house of the Coombe had been unsuccessfully attacked, though with great determination: a great many dead bodies were found there."

The whole affair was now over, and all was lost; yet during this night, Miles Byrne, with his two hundred picked Wexford men, was in the house on Coal Quay, anxiously awaiting the orders that had been agreed upon. Dwyer was ready with another party; and the Kildare men were expecting to be summoned by a messenger. They were all left without orders.

The next day was, of course, a time of arrests, discoveries, and domiciliary visits in Dublin. The several depôts were examined, and quantities of uniforms, firearms, and several thousand pikes, were found; together with eight thousand copies of two proclamations intended for distribution on the day of the rising.

These documents declare that the object of the movement is an Irish Republic, separation from England, and freedom and justice for all. (See Appendix, No. IV.) Emmet went out to a private house at Rathfarnham. Within a week before his sad failure, he had sent Russell and James Hope to the north, upon whose people he placed great reliance, and he requested Miles Byrne to go to France with dispatches for his brother, Thomas Addis Emmet, which Byrne, after many adventures, accomplished. Emmet himself proceeded from Rathfarnham to the Wicklow mountains, where he found the Wicklow insurgents bent on prosecuting their plans, and making an immediate attack on some of the principal towns in that county. Emmet, to his credit, being then convinced of the hopelessness of the struggle, had determined to withhold his sanction from any further effort; convinced, as he then was, that it could only lead to the effusion of blood, but to no successful issue. His friends pressed him to take immediate measures for effecting his escape, but unfortunately he resisted their solicitations. He had resolved on seeing one person before he could make up his mind to leave the country, and that person was dearer to him than life—Sarah Curran, the youngest daughter of the celebrated advocate, John Philpot Curran. With the hope of obtaining an interview with her, if possible, before his intended departure—of corresponding with her—and of seeing her pass by Harold's Cross, which was the road from her father's country-house, near Rathfarnham, to Dublin, he returned to his old lodgings at Mrs. Palmer's, Harold's Cross. Here, on the 25th of August, he was arrested, at about seven o'clock in the evening, by Major Sirr, who, according to the newspaper accounts, "did not know his person till he was brought to the Castle, *where he was identified by a gentleman of the College.*"*

On Monday, September 19, 1803, at a special commission, before Lord Norbury, Mr. Baron George, and Mr. Baron Daly, Robert Emmet was put on his trial, on a charge of high treason, under 25th Edward III. The counsel assigned him were Messrs. Ball, Burrowes, and M'Nally.

The counsel for the prosecution were Mr. Standish O'Grady, Attorney-General, and William Conyngham Plunket, King's Counsel. There is nothing specially worthy of remark on the trial, except the very bitter and superfluous speech of Mr. Plunket. Mr. Plunket had been the friend of Emmet's father. It was the political doctrine so loudly announced by Mr. Plunket in his Anti-Union speeches—that the Union would leave Ireland without any constitution or law which men would be bound to obey—it was this, and other eloquent denunciations, which had so deeply sunk into Emmet's mind, that he at length resolved to put those doctrines in practice, at the risk of his life. This could only be done by expelling the British authorities from his country.

It is true that Mr. Plunket, if he practised his profession at all, was bound to take the brief for the Crown; but he was not bound to display a furious and vindictive zeal in prosecuting his friend's son, especially as the prisoner made no defence. When the witnesses for the prosecution had all been examined, Mr. M'Nally said, as Mr. Emmet did not intend to call any witness, or to take up the time of the Court by his counsel stating any case or making any observations on the evidence, he presumed the trial was now closed on both sides.

Mr. Plunket declined following the example of the prisoner's counsel, and launched into a most violent and needless philippic, ending with this passionate imprecation:—

"They imbrue their hands in the most sacred blood of the country, and yet they call upon God to prosper their cause as it is just! But as it is atrocious, wicked, and abominable, I must devoutly invoke that God to confound and overwhelm it."

How nobly Emmet asserted himself and his cause, in his last speech, is known to all who read our language. There exist at least ten editions of that speech, some of them varying materially from others. The latest, and probably most correct version of it, is that contained in Doctor Madden's *Memoir of Emmet*, in the third series of his Collections. Thomas Moore, in his Diary, February 15, 1831, mentions Burrowes having remarked to him, on the subject of Plunket's conduct in Emmet's case: "Plunket could not have refused the brief of Government, *though he might have avoided, perhaps, speaking to evidence*. It was not true, I think he said, that Plunket had been acquainted with young Emmet. The passage in a printed speech of Emmet, where he is made to call Plunket '*that viper,*' &c., was never spoken by Emmet."

On the 20th of September he was executed. The same morning the death of his mother was announced to him in his prison. Early in the afternoon he was

---
* Madden says this was Doctor Elrington, Provost of the College.

removed, attended by a strong guard, both of cavalry and infantry, to Thomas Street, where a scaffold and gibbet had been erected. He died with the utmost calmness and fortitude.

It is said that Robert Emmet had been made acquainted with a design that was in contemplation to effect his escape at the time and place appointed for execution. Of that design Government appears to have had information, and had taken precautionary measures, which had probably led to its being abandoned. The avowed object of Thomas Russell's going to Dublin, after his failure in the north, was to adopt plans for this purpose.

Russell, the close friend and associate both of Tone and Emmet, was himself soon after arrested, and executed at Downpatrick; and this was the end of the United Irishmen,—at least for that generation. Russell's burial slab is to be seen in a churchyard of Downpatrick, with no word on it but the simple name "Thomas Russell." Robert Emmet's tomb is still uninscribed.

CHAPTER X.

1803—1804.

Reason to believe that Government was all the time aware of the Conspiracy—"Striking Terror"—Martial Law—Catholic Address—Arrests—Informers—Vigorous Measures—In Cork—In Belfast—Hundreds of Men Imprisoned without Charge—Brutal Treatment of Prisoners—Special Commission—Eighteen Persons Hung—Debate in Parliament—Irish Exiles in France—First Consul plans a New Expedition to Ireland—Formation of the "Irish Legion"—Irish Legion in Bretagne—Official Reply of the First Consul to T. A. Emmet—Designs of the French Government—Buonaparte's Mistake—French Fleet again ordered Elsewhere—The Legion goes to the Rhine, and to Walcheren—End of the Addington Ministry—Mr. Pitt returns to Office—Condition of Ireland—Decay of Dublin—Decline of Trade—Increase of Debt—Ruinous Effects of the Union—Presbyterian Clergy Pensioned, and the Reason.

A LARGE number of the bravest and purest men whom Ireland ever produced having now, within three or four years, been either hung or banished, it was hoped that the Protestant Ascendancy and British connection, the tithes, the Oligarchical Government, the packed juries—in short, our Constitution in Church and State—were at last secure against "Jacobins," and all manner of French principles.

Although the government of Lord Hardwicke had *seemed* to shut its eyes and see nothing of the preparations for Emmet's insurrection, there is reason to believe that most of its details were well known at the Castle.

In the collection of papers of Major Sirr, in the volume for 1803, and a succeeding volume containing miscellaneous letters, of dates from 1798 to 1803, are found various letters of spies and informers, of the old battalion of testimony of 1798, giving information to the Major of treasonable proceedings, meetings, preparing pikes, &c., being in existence in the three months preceding the outbreak of the insurrection of July 23, 1803. In the latter volume are many similar letters from a Roman Catholic gentleman in Monasterevan, suggesting arrests to the Major, and, amongst others, the arrest of a gentleman of some standing in society, a Brigadier-Major Fitzgerald.

It is also plain that Government knew of Emmet's having come from France to Dublin, and knew his errand, and at least some of his movements; for in October, 1802, Robert Emmet dined at Mr. John Keogh's, of Mount Jerome, shortly after his arrival in Dublin, in the company of John Philpot Curran. The conversation turned on the political state of the country—on the disposition of the people with respect to a renewal of the struggle. Robert Emmet spoke with great vehemence and energy in favour of the probability of success, in the event of another effort being made. John Keogh asked, in case it were, how many counties did he think would rise? The question was one of facts and figures. Robert Emmet replied that nineteen counties could be relied on. This dinner party was immediately known to Government; and, next day, a well-known magistrate, with two attendants, waited on Mr Keogh, demanded and carried off his papers.*

Mr. Plowden does not hesitate to speak of the Government on this occasion as having "made the full experiment of their favourite tactic of *not urging the rebels to postpone their attempts by any appearance of too much precaution and preparation of inviting rebellion,* in order to ascertain its extent, and of forcing premature explosion for the purpose of *radical cure.*"

After the danger was past, however, and after it was known how very wretched and impotent the whole attempt had turned out, superabundant precautions were taken, with the usual objects of "creating alarm" and striking terror. A Privy Council sat for several hours, and a proclamation was prepared and issued immediately, ordering the army to disperse all assemblies of armed rebels, and to do

* Madden. *Memoir of Emmet.* Third Series.

military execution upon all such found in arms. Barriers were erected in Dublin, and strong detachments stationed with cannon upon the bridges, and in the most frequented avenues and passes in the city.

On the 28th of July, the King sent a message to both Houses of Parliament, asking for additional powers in Ireland— that is, a renewed suspension of the writ of *Habeas Corpus*. The Act was passed at once. In Ireland, the judges went circuit that summer with strong escorts of troops.

We now again find the Catholics of rank and title coming forward to profess their loyalty; and, indeed, the brutal murder of the excellent Kilwarden, and others, on that ill-omened night, appeared but too well to justify good citizens in treating the whole movement as a mere riot for pillage and assassination. On the 4th of August, an address, signed by the most respectable Roman Catholics in and about Dublin, was presented to the Lord-Lieutenant, by a deputation consisting of the Earl of Fingal and Lord Viscount Gormanstown, and the Catholic Archbishops of Armagh and Dublin. It expressed their utmost horror and detestation of the late atrocious proceedings, their attachment to the King, and admiration of the Constitution. It contained a special declaration, that, however ardent their wish might be to participate in the full enjoyment of its benefits, they never should be brought to seek for such participation through any other medium than that of the free, unbiassed determination of the Legislature.

In Lord Hardwicke's reply he made not the slightest allusion to the wish those gentlemen had expressed, that they might be admitted within the pale of that Constitution they so much admired.

A system of suspicious repression was now once more enforced. Even before the suspension of the *Habeas Corpus* Act, many persons, who had been obnoxious to Government, or to the agents or favourites of the Castle, were apprehended, without any charge or ostensible cause of detention.* And, as it usually happens, when strong measures are resorted to by a weak government, the subalterns, who advised against reason, executed these measures without discretion. On this occasion, most of those who, upon the Secretary's warrants, were thrown into jail under colour of the suspension of the *Habeas Corpus*, were treated with a rigorous inhumanity which the law neither intended nor warranted. The system of espionage was extended, and the wages of information raised.

Not only rewards of £1,000 were offered for the information of any of the murderers of Lord Kilwarden, or his nephew, Mr. Wolfe, and for the apprehension of Mr. Russell, but a reward of £50 for each of the first one hundred rebels who might be discovered, that were of the number who appeared under arms in Thomas Street, on Saturday night, the 23d of July.

The whole of the yeomanry of Ireland was put upon permanent duty, at the enormous expense of £100,000 per month. In Cork, too, precautionary measures were adopted—viz., that no one should quit the country without a passport, and that every householder should affix a list of the family and inmates on their doors, by order of General Myers, who commanded in that district. The Sovereign of Belfast issued an order for the inhabitants to remain within their houses after eight o'clock in the evening, and for several other regulations of strict observance. In Dublin, the magistrates convened a meeting, at the suggestion of Government, at which they determined that the city should be divided into forty-eight sections, each section to be divided by a *chevaux de frise*, to prevent a surprise from the pikemen, which would not at the same time prevent the fire of, the musketry of the troops and yeomanry.

From the moment of the passage of martial law, the arrests became much more numerous; and any one pointed out as *suspicious*, generally by a personal enemy, was at once thrown into a dungeon. The horrors of these Irish dungeons came out, years afterwards, on an inquiry before Parliament. Mr. Plowden cautiously and timidly alludes to them in this manner:—*

"Sensible that general charge and invective come not within the province of the historian, the author felt it his duty to inform the reader that at this time commenced a new system of gradual inquisitorial torture in prison. Suffice it here to observe that there are many surviving victims of these inhuman and unwarrantable confinements who, without having been charged with any crime or tried for any offence, have from this period undergone years of confinement and incredible afflictions and sufferings, under the full conviction that they were inflicted from motives of personal resentment, and for the purpose of depriving them of life."

* Plowden. *History of Ireland since the Union*.

---

* Some of these were William Todd Jones, at Cork, who was arrested on the 29th of July, and after him Messrs. Drennan, Donovan, and others; Mr. Ross M'Cann, Bernard Coile, Mr. James Tandy, and others, at Dublin.

In fact, although only eighty men had turned out with Robert Emmet, and very few of these were ever found, the jails were, in the autumn of this year, crowded with many hundreds of persons, and all the horrors of the Prevot prison were repeated upon their unfortunate victims. This was the more unaccountable as Emmet never allowed any of his followers to be *sworn in;* there was no pretext, as in '98, for charging suspected persons with having taken "unlawful oaths," nor for torturing men in order to wring out information of such an offence having been committed. The system of Government, then, has no assignable motive save one—to strike terror and wreak vengeance. Every house in the city and neighbourhood of Dublin was searched for arms, and the names of the inmates of each house were once more required to be posted on the outer door.

Thus the entire system of Irish coercion, to which our country is so well accustomed, was in full operation within a few days after Emmet's attempt.

On the 11th of August, the day before Parliament was prorogued, Mr. Hutchinson made one effort to draw attention to these atrocities. He moved an address to the King praying to have papers laid before the House preparatory to an inquiry into the state of Ireland. The motion was opposed by Ministers on the ground that it was more than useless to demand information from Government upon the state of Ireland without having proposed any specific measure to be based upon such information when received, and that on the very eve of a prorogation. They roundly asserted that the Irish Government had not been surprised on the 23d of July, and that the *prevention* of what did happen would have taught wisdom and given strength to the rebel cause. The motion was negatived without a division.

At the "special commission" which tried Emmet, twenty persons were tried for their lives. Of these one was acquitted and one respited; the rest were hung.

Parliament met again on the 22d of November. Charles James Fox originated a short debate on the state of Ireland. He charged the Government with want of candour in endeavouring to convey an idea that it was the intention of the rebels in Ireland to put that country into the hands of France, when such a design had been so strongly disavowed by their leaders. "It was not," he added, "to be hoped or expected that as long as grievances existed Ireland could become loyal, and he sincerely hoped that the House would not, by confiding in words, leave her exposed to a repetition of those scenes that had lately occurred."

Mr. Addington insisted that some leaders of the United Irishmen "were really disposed to subserve the purposes of France. From the close intercourse now carried on between the two countries, he concluded that the people of Ireland would be led to compare the different principles of the two governments, by which they would learn to appreciate *the blessings of their own Constitution,* and to foresee the miseries which *any change* would bring upon them." Further, Mr. Addington and Mr. Yorke vehemently urged the House to give them credit in assuring them that though the leaders of the late insurrection were not immediately connected with the French Government, they were yet connected with Irish traitors abroad, who held immediate intercourse with that Government.

This last statement was true at any rate — omitting the word "traitors." Thomas Addis Emmet, Doctor MacNeven, and Arthur O'Connor, were then in close communication with the French Government, and eagerly awaiting the determinations of Buonaparte with regard to a descent upon Ireland. Miles Byrne had safely arrived at Paris and communicated with Thomas Addis Emmet; but, almost immediately, news came of Robert's capture, of the certainty of his execution, and of the total prostration of Ireland under the iron heel of military power. There was then in France a large number of Irish exiles, and Mr. Emmet informed the First Consul that they were ready to go as volunteers in any expedition which had for its object the emancipation of their country. It was in the month of November, 1803, that the decree was issued for the formation of the *Irish Legion.*

Miles Byrne, who was himself afterwards a distinguished officer of the Legion, gives this account of its origin:—"The First Consul eagerly entered into all the details related in the report on the state of Ireland, given to him by Mr. Thomas Addis Emmet, on the arrival at Paris of the confidential agent sent from Dublin in August, 1803; and, in consequence, it was stipulated that a French army should be sent to assist the Irish to get rid of the English yoke; the First Consul, understanding from Mr. Emmet that Augereau was a favourite with the Irish nation, had him appointed General-in-Chief to command the expedition, and immediately ordered the formation of an Irish Legion in the service of France. He gave to all those who volunteered to enter the Irish Legion commission as French officers, so that, in the event of their falling into the hands of the English, they should be protected; or, should any violence be offered them, he should have the right to retaliate on the English prisoners in France.

"The decree of the First Consul for the formation of this Irish Legion was dated November, 1803; by it the officers were all to be Irishmen, or Irishmen's sons born in France. The pay was to be the same as that given to officers and soldiers of the line of the French army. No rank was to be given higher than captain till they should land with the expedition in Ireland.

"It was, however, stipulated that on leaving Brest a certain number of captains were to get the rank of colonel, and also a certain number of lieutenants that of lieutenant-colonel; which rank was to be confirmed to them even in the event of the expedition failing, and their getting back to France. In naming these captains and lieutenants, the preference was to be given to those who had been obliged to expatriate themselves for their exertions in Ireland to effect its independence."

Adjutant-General MacSheehy, an Irishman by birth, but in the French service, was charged with the organization of the Legion; and for that purpose was commanded to repair to Morlaix, where the Irish exiles were assembled.

Adjutant-General MacSheehy received unlimited powers at Morlaix to propose officers for advancement up to the rank of captain; all he named were confirmed by the Minister of War, General Berthier.

The greatest exertions were made to have the officers splendidly equipped and ready for sailing. They received the same outfit given to French officers entering on campaign, no expense being spared by the French Government.

Three months later, General Augreau was at Brest, having attached to his staff Arthur O'Connor, then made a General of Division in the service of France.

Morlaix is a seaport town in Bretagne, not far from Brest, but more to the north, and looking straight over towards Cork and Waterford harbours. It was here that a large number of gallant and generous young Irishmen, many of them of good position in society and great accomplishments, were flocking together in those days, full of spirit and hardihood, and eagerly gazing over the blue water, as if they could already see the crests of the Cummeragh mountains. Amongst these men we find many names of officers who afterwards distinguished themselves in Germany, in Holland, and in Spain. O'Reilly, Allen, Corbet, Burgess, O'Morin, O'Mara, Ware, Barker, Fitzhenry, Masterson, St. Leger, Murray, and MacMahon. "We were happy and united," says Miles Byrne.

"The Legion assembled at Morlaix was marched to Quimper in March, 1804, where all those officers who had been proposed for advancement by Adjutant-General MacSheehy received their brevets. From Quimper the Legion was ordered to Carhaix, in Finistère, a small town (the native place of Latour d'Auvergne, premier grenadier de France), which, from being more inland and less frequented, was better suited for manœuvring, and where the best results were obtained. Two officers, Captain Tennant and Captain William Corbet, were deputed from thence by the Legion to go to Paris, to be present at the coronation of the Emperor (May, 1804), who on that occasion presented it, as well as the French regiments, with colours and an eagle. On one side of the colours was written, 'Napoléon I., Empereur des François, à la Legion Irlandaise;' on the reverse was a harp (without a crown) with the inscription: 'L'indépendence d'Irlande.'

The Irish Legion was the only foreign corps in the French service to which Napoleon ever intrusted an eagle.

Rejoicings took place at Carhaix, as in the other towns of France, in honour of the coronation, by order of the authorities.

It was while the legion was yet at Morlaix, that Thomas Addis Emmet, who had remained in Paris, obtained from the First Consul what seemed a definitive and positive assurance, both as to the certainty of the expedition parting for Ireland, and as to the fair terms to be observed with that country in leaving to it its cherished independence. In this document Buonaparte (not yet Emperor) assures the Irish Envoy that his intention is to assure the independence of Ireland, and to give sufficient protection to such as may join the French army; that in case of being joined by a considerable corps of Irish, he will never make a peace with England without stipulating for Ireland's independence; that Ireland shall be treated in all respects as America was in the last war; that every one embarking with the French army shall be considered a French soldier; and if any of these be arrested and not treated as a prisoner of war, retaliation shall follow; that every corps of United Irishmen shall be considered a part of the French army; and that in case of the expedition being unsuccessful, France will keep on foot a number of Irish Brigades on the same footing as French troops. The First Consul suggests the formation of a committee to frame proclamations and to prepare narratives of English oppressions in Ireland, to be published in the *Moniteur*.* This official paper not only proves what excellent foundation then existed for the sanguine hope of the exiles that something effectual was at last to be done for Ireland, but proves also how carefully those exiles stipulated always that the interposition of a French army should be only on the footing of auxiliaries, like that of Rochambeau in America. It is a sufficient answer to those constant accusations made in England, that Irish revolutionists sought to throw their country under the dominion of France. And it must be said, once for all, in the negotiations and projects for French aid, whether with Tone, Lewis, or Emmet, there was no reason to doubt that the single object of the successive French Governments was to aid Ireland, in good faith, to win a real independence—not, perhaps, so much from a love and sympathy for Ireland, as from a desire to weaken England, whose intrigues and subsidies were stirring up the whole continent to effect the ruin of France.

Yet, after all, those enthusiastic Irishmen of the Legion were not destined to see Ireland. Other urgent necessities arose; and most of the fleet at Brest was withdrawn for different destinations. It was the greatest mistake that Buonaparte ever made, and the noblest opportunity lost. The Legion was ordered to the Rhine, and from thence to Holland, where they had at least the satisfaction of meeting their enemies at Walcheren, and aiding in the destruction of that imposing armament of England. Thomas Addis Emmet, despairing of effecting anything through French agency, emigrated at last to America, where he took the first rank at the bar of New York, and lived long honoured and beloved.

Meanwhile, the imbecile administration of Mr. Addington came to an end. Mr. Pitt had put him into office to serve a temporary purpose, and was now ready to resume the reins himself. It has already been stated, by anticipation, that on returning to power this treacherous Minister made no condition in favour of Catholic relief, which is in itself a sufficient proof that his former resignation, ostensibly on that question, had been made on a false pretext. In the new Administration (gazetted May 14, 1804), he was Chancellor of the Exchequer and First Lord of the Treasury. The Secretary of War was Lord Camden—a name associated in Ireland with torture and "free quarters." The President of the Board of Control was Lord Castlereagh. No Government more hostile to Ireland ever ruled in the three Kingdoms. The King's mental malady had grown more alarming about the time of Mr. Pitt's return; and his advisers could by no means think of troubling the conscience of the invalid by any suggestion tending to emancipation of Catholics and "breach of his coronation oath."

Ireland had now had more than three years' experience of Legislative Union; and already began to experience the wasting and draining effects of that odious and fatal transaction. Trade was declining, debt and taxes increasing; but the debt much faster than the produce of the

---

* Here is the original, which was instantly communicated by Emmett to MacNeven, then at Morlaix:—
"COPY OF THE FIRST CONSUL'S ANSWER TO MY MEMOIRE OF 13TH NIVOSE, DELIVERED TO ME 27TH NIVOSE:—
"Le Premier Consul a lu avec la plus grande attention, la memoire qui lui a été addressée par M. Emmet le 13 Nivose.
"Il desire que les Irlandais Unis soyent bien convaincus que son intention est d'assurer l'indépendence de l'Irlande, et de donner protection entière et efficace à tous ceux d'entre eux, qui prendront part à l'expedition, ou qui se joindront aux armées Françaises.
"Le Gouvernement Français ne peut faire aucune proclamation avant d'avoir touché le territoire Irlandais. Mais le général qui commandera l'expedition sera muni de lettres scellées, par lesquelles le Premier Consul declarera qu'il ne fera point la paix avec l'Angleterre, sans stipuler pour l'indépendence de l'Irlande, dans le cas, cependant, où l'armée aurait été jointe par un corps considerable d'Irlandais Unis.
"L'Irlande sera en tout traitée, comme l'a été l'Amérique, dans la guerre passée.
"Tout individu qui s'embarquera avec l'armée Française destinée pour l'expedition sera commissioné comme Français: s'il était arrêté, et qu'il ne fut pas traité comme prisonnier de guerre la represaille s'exercera sur les prisonniers Anglais.
"Tout corps formé au nom des Irlandais Unis sera consideré comme faisant partie de l'armée Française Enfin, si l'expedition ne réussissait pas et que les Irlandais fussent obligés de revenir en France, la France entretiendra un certain nombre de Brigades Irlandaises, et fera des pensions, à tout individu qui aurait fait partie du gouvernement ou des autorités du pays.
"Les pensions pourraient été assimilées à celles qui sont accordées en France aux titulaires de grade ou d'emploi correspondant, qui ne sont pas en activité.
"Le Premier Consul desire qu'il se forme un comité d'Irlandais Unis. Il ne voit pas d'inconvenant à se que les membres de ce comité fassent des proclamations, et instruisent leurs compatriotes de l'état de choses.
"Ces proclamations seront inserées dans L'Argus et dans les differens journaux de l'Europe, à fin d'eclairer les Irlandais, sur la parti qu'ils ont à suivre, et sur les esperances qu'ils doivent concevoir. Si la comité veut faire une relation des actes de tyrannie exercées contre l'Irlande par le Gouvernement Anglais, on l'insorera dans Le Moniteur."

taxes. The absenteeism of proprietors, as had been expected, and indeed intended, occasioned year by year a greater and greater depletion of wealth. The fine country-seats of wealthy proprietors were generally deserted, and their estates were managed by agents. Dublin, which in the eighteen years of independence (even such partial independence as it was) had grown to the rank of a fine metropolitan city, had been adorned by many sumptuous palaces of a resident nobility, and enriched by the expenditure of a luxurious society, was now sunk into a provincial town. The centre of political interest, of intellectual activity, and of fashionable life, had been transferred to London. The fine mansions of Irish Peers and wealthy Commoners, after lying long vacant, were gradually turned to other uses.* It is true that Ireland might well afford to do without those great Peers and feudal proprietors, as France has done; but the difference is, that in Ireland's case they still draw away in rent the produce of the land: they are sponges, which are filled in Ireland to be squeezed in England: they are clouds, formed by sucking up all the juices of our island, and which then float off, "to rain down in London or dissipate at Cheltenham." Thus it was found, very soon after union, that the exports of Ireland greatly increased; but they were exports of corn, cattle, and raw material for manufactures, to pay the absentee rent; while our imports were chiefly of manufactured articles and colonial produce from England—England thus deriving the profit both from our exports and from our imports. Then there was the enormous cost of the war in Europe, to put down French principles, to which expense Ireland was made to contribute in a much greater ratio than England. Mr. Foster, in a speech in Parliament on the Irish budget, immediately after Pitt's return to office, said he lamented to find the predictions, which he had ventured to urge on the probable state of Ireland, during the discussions upon the Union, but too forcibly verified by the then deplorable state of her finances, as compared with her public debt and expenditure. Within the last ten years, the public debt of Ireland had made an alarming progress. It stood in 1793 at £2,400,000, in 1800, at £25,400,000.

On January 5, 1804, at £43,000,000, and in that year there had been added to it no less a sum than £9,500,000. This formed a quota far exceeding the *ratio* established by the Union compact to be paid by Ireland. This ruinous race, in which Ireland was so far exceeding her means by her expenditure, would shortly equalize her debt in proportion to that of England, and entitle England to call for a Parliamentary decision, and consolidation of accounts and equalization of taxes. He then stated to the House the corresponding produce of the Irish revenue. In the year 1800, which immediately preceded the Union, the net produce of the revenue was £2,800,000, when she owed £25,000,000: in the last year it was only £2,789,000, whilst the debt amounted to £53,000,000. There was every reason to believe, that for the running year the produce of the Irish revenue would not yield one shilling towards Ireland's quota in the common expenditure of the empire. Such was the situation of Ireland in the summer of 1804, as depicted by Mr. Foster, with an enormous and growing increase of debt, a rapid falling off of revenue, and a decay in commerce and manufactures.

It may, of course, be alleged, that as the Act of Union places, or purports to place, the two countries on a footing of perfect equality and reciprocity, in respect to trade and commerce, there has been nothing to prevent Ireland, if its inhabitants had energy and enterprise like Englishmen, to manufacture for themselves, and so keep at home a great portion of the wealth which is annually drained from them. The fallacy of this suggestion is now well understood. It is true, the laws regulating trade are the same in the two islands; Ireland *may* export even woollen cloth to England; she *may* import, in her own ships, tea from China, and sugar from Barbadoes; the laws which made those acts penal offences no longer exist, they are no longer needed; England is fully in possession; and by the operation of those old laws Ireland was utterly ruined. England has the commercial marine—Ireland has it to create. England has the manufacturing machinery and skill, of which Ireland was deprived, by express laws for that purpose. England has the current of trade established, setting strongly in her own channel, while Ireland is left dry. To create or recover at this day these great industrial and commercial resources, and that in the face of wealthy rivals already in full possession, is manifestly impossible, without one or other of these two conditions—

---

* The Duke of Leinster's palace accommodates a Museum of Natural History; Powerscourt House is a warehouse of linen-drapers. The mansion of the Earls of Tyrone is a school-house; Belvedere House is a convent; Aldborough House is a barrack, &c.

either immense command of capital or effectual protective duties. But by the Union our capital is drained away to England; and by the Union we are deprived of the power of imposing protective duties. It was to this very end that the Union was forced upon Ireland, through "intolerance of Irish prosperity." "Do not unite with us, sir," said Samuel Johnson, "*we shall rob you.*"

It was in the year 1803 that the British Government bethought itself of making the Presbyterians of Ulster more "loyal," and weaning them the better from "French principles," by largely increasing the scanty means of the Dissenting clergy. The Ministers had been previously aided, in a very grudging and shabby manner, by a sort of bribe, the *Regium Donum*, or royal gift, first granted in 1672 by Charles II., who gave £600 of "Secret Service money" to be distributed in equal portions among them annually. The grant was discontinued towards the close of his reign and during that of James II., but was renewed by William III., who augmented it to £1,200 a-year. In 1784, the amount was increased to £2,200; in 1792, to £5,000. Still, this was a most paltry pittance for so large a body of clergymen, and rather degraded than enriched those who received it; while the Anglican Church, with a smaller proportion of the population, was so munificently endowed with lands and tithes.

The Government took alarm on finding that the Presbyterians of Ulster, both clergy and laity, had been generally Republicans and United Irishmen in 1798. Overtures were soon after made to them through their most influential pastors,—especially Doctor Black of Londonderry,—giving them a prospect of great increase to their grant if they would not oppose the Union. This Doctor Black had been a delegate to the Dungannon Convention, in 1772, and had appeared amongst the other delegates in his uniform as a volunteer officer.

These overtures had the desired success; and therefore, in 1803, the *Regium Donum* was quintupled. The total yearly grant to Nonconforming Ministers in Ireland amounted, in 1852, to £38,561. (*Thom's Official Directory.*)

Doctor Black had a good place; he was agent and distributor of this disgraceful *Donum*; and some years afterwards he very naturally (like Castlereagh) committed suicide, by throwing himself off the bridge of Derry into the River Foyle.

CHAPTER XI.

1804—1805.

Mr. Pitt in Office—Royal Speech—No Mention of Ireland—Alarm about Invasion—Martello Towers—Reliance of the Irish Catholics on Mr. Pitt—Treatment of the Prisoners—Mr. James Tandy—Mr. Pitt raises a Storm against the Catholics—Catholic Meeting in Dublin—*Habeas Corpus* Act again Suspended—Ireland "Loyal"—Duplicity of Lord Hardwicke — Catholic Deputies go to Mr. Pitt—A "Sincere Friend"—Mr. Pitt refuses to present Catholic Petition—Declares he will resist Emancipation—Lord Grenville and Mr. Fox present it—Debate in the Lords—In the Commons—Speeches of Fox, Doctor Duigenan, Grattan, Perceval, Pitt, Sir John Newport—Emancipation refused, both by Lords and Commons—Great Majorities.

WHEN Mr. Pitt returned to office in 1804, he did not find himself so omnipotent in the country as he had been during his former administration, or even during that of his *locum tenens*. Although Mr. Addington had affected not to control the late elections by any treasury influence, he now exerted his personal influence upon all the members who owed their seats to his patronage or favour, to join him in opposing Mr. Pitt. Though he could brook the injury of being displaced, in order to re-admit Mr. Pitt to power, he could neither forgive nor forget the insult of being expelled for incapacity and weakness. Mr. Pitt expected to regain more of his lost power by negotiation during the recess than by his oratory in the Senate; but was reluctantly constrained to prolong the session to the 31st of July. Under the combination of great external and internal difficulties, it became an object of peculiar anxiety with the Minister to give the nation some open and unequivocal proof of the complete recovery of His Majesty's health. When the King went to prorogue the Parliament, the House of Peers was attended by an unusual crowd, and particularly by the few foreign Ministers then resident in London. In no part of the speech was there even an indirect reference to Ireland.

Ireland, indeed, was completely removed into the background by the Union; and while the Government felt it had her safe under the coercion of a great army, and the exhaustion and terrorism which now formed the single British policy for that island, Ministers evidently thought the less said about Ireland the better.

The apparent alarm about invasion was carefully kept up during the whole summer. The Government prints sedulously warned the public against the machinations of the French party, which then prevailed throughout the country. Upon this assumption they inveighed against French tyranny and injustice, and decried the loyalty of the native Irish. Thus they justified the expense of their public measures of defence, and affected to sanction the necessity of internal coercion. The encampment of fifteen thousand men, near the Curragh of Kildare, consisted of regular militia, artillery, British horse artillery, and a vast commissariat and drivers' corps. Everything bore the appearance of active service. The Martello Towers, and other defensive works on the coast, were forwarded with unusual energy. Many additional persons were taken into custody under the suspension of the *Habeas Corpus*, and the rigorous treatment of the state prisoners, who had been for several months in confinement, was sharpened, without any visible or known cause.*

The Catholics, whom Pitt had insidiously deluded by prospects of emancipation, were now so simple as to anticipate, on his return to place, some efficient steps for carrying that object, for which he professed to have abandoned his official situation. They now publicly rejoiced "*in the benefit of having so many characters of eminence pledged not to embark in the service of Government, except on the terms of Catholic privileges being obtained.*" Frequent Catholic meetings were holden in Dublin, in which the general sense of the body to petition Parliament for their total emancipation was unanimously resolved. Mr. Pitt dreaded nothing so much as to have the sincerity of his pledges brought under discussion. As Lord Fingal, from his rank in life, and more from the amiable qualities of his mind, was known to possess the confidence of many of his Catholic countrymen, Sir Evan Nepean was directed to attempt through his lordship every means to hold back the petition. He was invited to dinner, frequently closeted at the Castle, and more sedulously courted than on any former occasion. However his lordship may have been personally disposed to hold back, few or none of the body could be induced to postpone their petition.

In proportion to the failure of the Minister's Continental plans, did the Catholic body of Ireland feel their own weight in the Imperial scale. The aggrandizement of Napoleon had been the unvarying result of Mr. Pitt's vehement exertions to crush him. He was quietly and solemnly crowned Emperor of the French at Paris by Pope Pius VII.; a circumstance which Mr. Pitt, with his usual craft, attempted to convert into an engine of obloquy on the Catholic body, and an opportune and plausible objection to their petition, which in spite of his secret manœuvres, through Sir Evan Nepean, he now foresaw would be brought forward. The Government papers industriously published and severely commented upon a memorial, said to have been written by MacNeven at Paris, addressed to the Irish officers of the several Continental powers, particularly to those in the Austrian service, encouraging them to join in the then intended attempts to liberate Ireland from the thraldom of England; and promising to give them timely notice of the sailing of the expedition.

These Ministerial journals vied also with one another in republishing and commenting on the Papal allocution, addressed by His Holiness to a secret consistory at Rome, on October 28, 1804, immediately before his departure for Paris to perform the ceremony of the Imperial coronation. It referred to the gratitude due to Napoleon for having re-established the Catholic religion in France by the *concordat;* since which he had put forth all his authority to cause it to be freely professed and publicly exercised throughout that renowned nation, and had again recently shown himself most anxious for the prosperity of that religion. It also contained confident assurance that a personal interview with the Emperor would be for the good of the Catholic Church, which *is the only ark of salvation.*

* Mr. James Tandy, and thirteen other of the principal state prisoners of the first class, as they were styled at the Castle, petitioned the Lord-Lieutenant, July 11, 1804; and after having specified many of the acts of barbarous cruelty inflicted upon them, as sworn to in the King's Bench, they conclude in these words: In short, we experience a treatment rather calculated for untamed beasts than men. They assured his Excellency that, to the pressing and repeated remonstrances which they had presented to Doctor Trevor (the inspector of the prisons) against the harshness of their treatment, they had received a formal answer,— that it had not only the sanction, but its origin in the express directions of Lord Hardwicke's Government. The first petition not having been attended to, was followed by a second on August 12th, which again complained that Doctor Trevor executed his office in a manner at once mean and malicious, and pleaded orders from Government for their rigorous treatment. They complained that they were so reduced by their sufferings (not merited by them, nor necessary for safe custody), that their lives were become of no value, and literally a burden to them; and that there was not one of the petitioners, who from many concurring circumstances could not on oath declare a firm belief of an intention to deprive them of life by underhand means.

These appeals received not the smallest attention; and great numbers of the prisoners, without a charge against them, were kept in various prisons for years. Mr. J. Tandy, indeed, was liberated before the end of the year; having first promised not to flog Mr. Secretary Marsden, as he says he had threatened to do.

Here was a dreadful thing! they exclaimed; as if all the world had not known before that Catholics believed their Church to be the only ark of salvation. Editors, preachers, and pamphleteers shrieked out, in all the tones of alarm and horror, that this meant burning heretics. Here was extreme danger, they insisted, to a "Protestant State," in this ominous reconciliation of the Emperor with the Church; as it would give him greater influence in Ireland, when he should land there to overthrow Church and State, throne and altar. These topics were enlarged on with so much apparent sincerity of terror, that an enlightened public really began to fancy the dungeons of the Inquisition were already yawning before them. Those scribes, indeed, did not mention the fact, that along with the Catholic Church the Emperor had also re-established the Protestant Church in France. They forgot to state that in France the Protestants had long been *emancipated*; and stood, then and thenceforth, on a footing of perfect equality with their Catholic neighbours.

The Irish Catholics did not yet know the meaning of this new outbreak of foaming rage against them and their religion; and at any rate thought Mr. Pitt must be above all the storm of stupid malice which they saw raging,—as, in fact, he was, but he was not above exciting it and directing it to his own ends.

The leading part of the Irish Catholics, most of whom had supported the Union in plenary confidence of the professions made by Mr. Pitt and Lord Cornwallis that emancipation would immediately follow it, held frequent meetings in Dublin, in order to concert the most efficient means of rendering available Mr. Pitt's disposition to favour their cause, which they fondly assumed had returned with him into power. The general precipitancy of the body to bring the ministerial sincerity to the test, was with difficulty repressed by those who were considered to be most directly under the influence of the Castle. An adjournment was carried from December 31st to February 16th.

Parliament met again, January 15, 1805; and again His Majesty's speech contained not one word in reference to Ireland. It mentioned the prompt and decisive steps which he had been obliged to take in order to guard against the effects of hostility from Spain.* The speech also denounced the "violence and outrage" of the French Government, and spoke vaguely of the European coalition against France which Mr. Pitt was engaged in negotiating.

Several interesting debates passed in the Commons upon Sir Evan Nepean's motion for suspending the *Habeas Corpus* Act in Ireland, which he proposed to extend to six weeks after the commencement of the next session of Parliament. He and Mr. Pitt urged, as the grounds for that harsh measure, that there were then at Paris committees of United Irishmen, who communicated with traitors in Ireland upon the most efficient means of effecting the invasion of that country; and when the House considered the *humane and just character of Lord Hardwicke*, they would with plenitude of confidence deposit that extraordinary power in his hands. Mr. Fox, on the other hand, warmly replied that the character of the Lord-Lieutenant was immaterial. The Constitution taught him to be jealous of granting extraordinary powers to any man; and if there were a possibility of their being abused, the mild character of the man in whom they were to be vested was the worst of arguments. If the powers were not necessary, they ought not to be granted; and if necessary, and the Lord-Lieutenant were not fit to be entrusted with them, he ought to be removed. Mr. Fox added that it was universally admitted that Ireland was at that moment as tranquil as any county in England; why not as well, then, propose to suspend the Constitution in England? But the bill passed: out of two hundred and thirteen members, only fifty-four voted against it.

A respectable Catholic writer,* speaking of this debate, says: "Ireland in the meantime was loyal and tranquil, in spite of the aspersions and calumnies of the hired writers, and the unsupported charges of some of the Ministerialists in Parliament." Now Ireland was, indeed, "tranquil," at that moment, but not "loyal," if loyalty means attachment to the King of England. Irish Catholics of that day who could be loyal, must have been something more, or a good deal less, than men. Tranquil they were, but had never been better disposed to rise around the standards of a French army; and, indeed, the English Government knew then, as they know now, that tranquillity is a bad omen for loyalty, and that the Irish people are never so eager to shake off the British yoke as when sheriffs present judges with white gloves.

---

* This meant the sudden attack upon a Spanish fleet in harbour, previous to a declaration of war; one of those feats of arms (like the seizure of the Danish fleet under similar circumstances) by which Great Britain at length was enabled to boast that she "ruled the seas."

* Plowden's *Post-Union History*.

On the 16th of February, pursuant to adjournment, a numerous meeting of Catholic noblemen, gentlemen, and merchants, was held in Dublin, at which they unanimously entered into the following resolutions: *First.* That the Earl of Fingal, the Honourable Sir Thomas (now Lord) French, Sir Edward Bellew, Councillor Denys Scully, and Mr. Ryan, should be appointed as a deputation, to carry into effect the under-mentioned instructions; and that the other Roman Catholic Peers (of whom Lords Gormanstown and Southwell were then present) should be requested to accede to the deputation. *Second.* That the petition prepared by the Catholic Committee, and reported by Lord Fingal to that meeting, should be then signed by Lord Fingal and the other Catholic gentlemen, and that the above-mentioned deputies should present it to Mr. Pitt, with a request that he would bring it into Parliament.

Now was seen the excessive duplicity of Lord Hardwicke. He had been selected from the mass of the peerage as the best qualified to resist the emancipation of Ireland, under the insidious mission of reconciling her to thraldom. The ordinary manœuvres of the Castle upon Lord Fingal and other leading men of the Catholic body, to induce them to hold back their petition, had failed. His lordship could not, consistently with his duty to his employers, back, countenance, or recommend their petition, however just the claims, however worthy the claimants. But now, under the British Minister's assurance of a decided majority against the question, the Irish Viceroy affected to favour the Catholics' application by discountenancing counter petitions, as encroaching upon the freedom of Parliamentary debate. He even did one act which was intended as a proof of his sincerity. He dismissed the notorious Mr. John Giffard from a lucrative post for having proposed and carried, in the Dublin Corporation, some violent resolutions *against* Catholic Emancipation. He thought the sacrifice of one man was a trifle, and so punished Giffard for opposing a measure which he himself was doubly pledged to resist.

The Catholic deputies proceeded to London, and had their conference with Mr. Pitt on the 12th of March. Eight deputies attended the conference—viz., the Earl of Shrewsbury (Waterford and Wexford in Ireland), Earl of Fingal, Viscount Gormanstown, Lord Southwell, Lord Trimblestown, Sir Edward Bellew, Councillor Denys Scully, and Mr. Ryan. They told Mr. Pitt they regarded him as their "sincere friend;" that they hoped everything from his liberality and justice, and so urged him to present their petition to Parliament.

Mr. Pitt declared "that the confidence of so very respectable a body as the Catholics of Ireland was highly gratifying to him;" but he added, that the time had not come; there were obstacles—that, in short, he would not present their petition at all. After many arguments and much urgency, they at last intreated him only to lay it on the table of the House of Commons. They would authorize him to state to the House that *they did not press the immediate adoption of the measure prayed for.*

Mr. Plowden, who had the best means of knowing what passed at this conference, says, with asperity, that Mr. Pitt "drily repeated his negative;" and then adds, "He neither threw out a suggestion for their applying to any other channel, nor gave any ground for presuming that the introduction of the petition through any Ministerial member would be likely to soften his opposition, for he very explicitly declared that *he should feel it his duty to resist it.* The only advice he condescended to offer was to withdraw their petition altogether, or at all events to postpone it."*

The "leading Catholics" found themselves now completely in the position of dupes; and they richly deserved it, for having assented to the destruction of their country's national independence, seduced by the professions of an English Minister. At all events the time was not yet come, nor the man. But a more vigorous race of Catholics was growing up; and in especial one bold, blue-eyed young man, who was then carrying his bag in the hall of the Four Courts— destined one day to hold the great leading brief in the mighty cause of six millions of his countrymen. O'Connell was not yet a leading Catholic, but was fast becoming well known in his own profession; and an Orange judge in a party case preferred to see any other advocate pleading before him.

The Catholic delegates next applied to Mr. Fox and Lord Grenville, who agreed to present the petition—one in the Lords, the other in the Commons. This was done on the 25th of March. When Lord

---

* Mr. Pitt might on this occasion have candidly acknowledged what Lord Hawkesbury publicly and officially declared in the House of Lords, March 26, 1807, in debating the grounds of the Grenville Administration's retiring from office, that although Mr. Pitt had in 1801 gone out of office on that question, yet on his return *he voluntarily engaged that he never would again bring the subject under the consideration of His Majesty.*

Grenville moved in the House of Lords that it should lie on the table, Lord Auckland rose with precipitancy, and observed with some warmth, that as far as his ears could catch the tenor of it, it went to overthrow the whole system of Church and State; and if the prayer of it were to be granted, he should soon see a Protestant Church without a Protestant congregation, and a Protestant King with a Popish Legislature. He expressed great anxiety that the question should be calmly and fully discussed, summoned the Reverend Bench to arm themselves for the combat, &c. The venerable Lord Eldon objected even to the formal motion that the petition should be printed. After Mr. Fox presented it in the House of Commons, the matter stood over for early days in May in both Houses of Parliament. Petitions against it were presented from the Universities of Oxford and Cambridge, from the cities of London and Dublin, the County Fermanagh, and other Corporations and public bodies.

Lord Fitzwilliam, who was still a friend to the Catholics, and well remembered how Mr. Pitt had cheated *him* also upon that question, conceived the idea of bringing Mr. Grattan into the debate; and accordingly induced the Honourable C. L. Dundas to vacate his seat for the borough of Malton, and Mr. Grattan was returned for it.

On the appointed day the discussion in the Lords arose, on motion to commit the bill. After some other Peers had been heard, His Royal Highness the Duke of Cumberland (an Orangeman) gave his decided opposition to the motion before the House, and urged every resistance in his power to a "measure subversive of all the principles which placed the House of Brunswick upon the throne of these realms."

Lord Camden found full reason for opposing the motion on the grounds upon which the Irish Parliament had negatived the question, whilst he had the honour of being placed at the head of the Irish Government.

The Bishop of Durham, the wealthiest prelate in Europe, and who naturally valued that constitution in Church and State which had made him so, urged that the motion could not be acceded to without danger to the Church and State. It would be a direct surrender of the security of the best constitution in the world.

Lord Redesdale made a very violent speech against the motion. He said: "To pass such a measure would be to take the titles and lands from the Protestant hierarchy and give them to the Catholic bishops." He said, further: "If the Catholic hierarchy were abolished, something might be done to conciliate the Catholic body; and to the generality of that body he was confident the abolition of the hierarchy would be extremely grateful."

Lord Carleton, an Irish Judge, ran over all the usual Protestant phrases about the faithlessness and cruelty of Catholics. He laid much stress upon certain "maps of the forfeited estates," which, he said, had been prepared, in order to guide the proceedings of *resumption.** Lord Carleton added a singular legal opinion: "That the spiritual supremacy of the Church was by the law of this country vested in the Crown; and surely it was a piece of the highest contumacy in a sect of His Majesty's subjects to deny that supremacy, and to vest the control in a foreign potentate."

Lord Buckinghamshire, like all other opposers of the motion, spoke much of his own disposition to liberality and conciliation; denied that any such pledge for emancipation, as had been alluded to, was or could have been given, and deemed it most inflammatory to allege that the Catholics would be sore or irritated at the refusal of the prayer of the petition.

After an astonishing mass of benighted spite and bigotry had been vented all night, at six in the morning a division was had. The motion to commit was rejected by a majority of one hundred and twenty-nine; and so ended Emancipation in the Lords for that time.

In the Commons, Mr. Fox introduced the same subject in a long and able speech. He gave a history of the Penal Code, and of its successive relaxations; pointed out how useless, and at the same time how irritating, were the remaining links in the chain which it was then proposed to strike off; proved that the Catholics had received assurances, on the part of Mr. Pitt, which induced them as a body to remain passive at the time of the Union, and that now those pledges ought to be redeemed. Mr. Fox concluded an excellent address by saying, "He relied on the affection and loyalty of the Roman Catholics of Ireland, but he would not press them too far—he would not draw the cord too tight. It was surely too much to expect that they would always fight for a constitution in the benefits of which they were assured they never should participate

---

* His lordship thus described a map of Ireland prepared by the antiquary, Mr. Charles O'Conor, of Belanagare, showing the situation of the tribelands of the ancient clans before the reign of Elizabeth.

equally with their fellow-subjects. Whatever was to be the fate of the petition, he rejoiced at having had an opportunity of bringing it under their consideration, and moved to refer it to a committee of the whole House."

The famous Doctor Duigenan had the courage to reply to Mr. Fox, although he saw Grattan opposite, who already threatened him with his eye. He opposed the motion in a long speech, which lasted above three hours, the general spirit and substance of which was to prove that by the ancient councils of the Catholic Church and her invariable doctrine, no Catholic could take an oath from the obligations of which he could not, at the will of the priest, be released; that the Catholics maintained no faith was to be kept with heretics, and such they considered every denomination of Christians but themselves; and that it was impossible for a Catholic to be truly loyal to a Protestant King. He contended that the ninety-one persons who had signed the Catholic petition did not, by any means, represent the body of the Irish Catholics; he assumed that none of the clergy had signed, because they still maintained the obnoxious doctrines which the best-informed of the laity wished to renounce.

He contended that the oath of supremacy (swearing that the King is head of the Church) was a mere *simple oath of allegiance*, and that it imported neither exclusion nor restriction to any but traitors. He commented largely upon the oath of canonical obedience to the Pope taken by the Catholic bishops; inveighed fiercely against Doctor Hussey, the late Catholic Bishop of Waterford, for forbidding his flock to send their children to Protestant schools for education; and he drew the conclusion from Doctor Hussey's remark—that the loss or abandonment of his religion by the Catholic soldier might be felt in the day of battle—that, *in plain English, the Romish soldier might then turn upon and assassinate his officer or desert to the enemy.* This measure would let in a universal deluge of atheism, infidelity, and anarchy. It would admit the Pope's supremacy over the Church of these realms; it would violate the conditions of both Unions, with Scotland and with Ireland; and to tender to His Majesty a bill of that import for his royal signature would be to insult him, by supposing him capable of violating his coronation oath.

Mr. Grattan rose, and his rising was greeted with breathless attention. He had never appeared in that House before; and his fame, as a noble orator and incorruptible patriot, impressed the English legislators more than they would have liked to own to themselves.

Mr. Grattan said he rose to defend the Catholics from Doctor Duigenan's attack, and the Protestants from his defence. The question for their consideration was not, as the learned member had stated, whether they should now qualify or still keep disqualified some few Roman Catholic gentlemen for seats in Parliament, or certain officers in the State; but whether they would impart to a fifth portion of the population of their European empire a community in that which was their vital principle and strength, and thus confirm the integrity and augment the power of the Empire. That learned member had emphatically said that the people of Ireland, to be good Catholics, must be bad subjects; that the Irish Catholic is not, never was, and never can be, a faithful subject to a Protestant English King. Thus has he pronounced against his countrymen three curses—eternal war with each other, eternal war with England, eternal peace with France. He fully answered the doctrinal parts of Doctor Duigenan's speech, and concluded that as the Catholic religion was professed by above two-thirds of all Christendom, it would follow that Christianity was in general a curse; but of his own countrymen he had added that they were depraved by religion, and rendered perverse by nativity; that is to say, according to him, blasted by their Creator, and damned by their Redeemer. Mr. Grattan closed an animated detail of the evils of the prospective system with observing that, if they wished to strip rebellion of its hopes, and France of her expectations, they should reform their policy; they would gain a conquest over their enemies when they had gained a victory over themselves.

The speaker entered into long detail of all the dealings of the Irish Government with the Catholics on this question; but it would be in vain, with our limits, to attempt even a full abstract of this remarkable speech. When the Parliament of Ireland, he said, rejected the Catholic petition, and assented to the calumnies uttered against the Catholic body, on that day she voted the Union, and should they adopt a similar conduct on that day they would vote the separation. He was surprised to see them running about like grown-up children in search of old prejudices, preferring to buy foreign allies by subsidies rather than to subsidize fellow-subjects by privileges. He figured them then drawn up, sixteen against thirty-six millions, and paralyzing one-fifth of their own numbers by excluding them from some of the principal benefits of their constitution at the very time they said all their numbers were inadequate unless inspired by those very privileges. Such a system could not last; if the two islands renounced all national prejudices, they would form a strong empire in the west to check, and ultimately to confound, the ambition of the enemy.

Mr. Perceval, a pious man, and one of the first of the race of "saints" (he was then Attorney-General), opposed the motion, for the sort of reasons, and in the precise style, of some conventicle preacher. "But," he said, "he remarked the indisposition of the house to listen to him; which he was not surprised at; for he was conscious that, after the blaze of Mr. Grattan's eloquence, everything that fell from him must appear vapid and uninteresting. Had he been in the Irish Parliament, he never would have consented to grant the elective franchise, nor the establishment of Maynooth for educating the Catholic."

Mr. Perceval knew that he could safely pay a tribute to Mr. Grattan's eloquence, and disparage himself with all the humility of a "saint." He felt that the grand cause of Ascendancy was safe in that House, and that though Grattan spoke with the tongue of men and angels, he could not prevent or reverse the inevitable decision.

The motion was supported by some liberal Englishmen (for there is always a small minority of liberal Englishmen), and warmly advocated by George Ponsonby; when the Chancellor of the Exchequer, Mr. Pitt, arose. His speech was highly characteristic. He said:—

"He was favourably disposed to the *general principle* of the question; but, differing in many points from those who had introduced or supported the motion, he thought fit to observe that he had never considered the question as involving any claim of right. *Right* was totally independent of circumstances; *expediency* included the consideration of circumstances, and was wholly dependent upon them. Upon the principle of expediency he felt that, entertaining as he did a wish for the repeal of the whole Penal Code, and a regret that it had not been abolished, he felt that in no possible case before the Union could those privileges have been granted to the Catholics with safety to the existing Protestant establishment in Church and State. After that measure, he saw the matter in a different light; though certainly no pledge was ever given to the Catholics that their claims should be granted. [Nobody had ever said such a pledge had been given; the pledge *he* had given was, that he, Mr. Pitt, would support the measure, and would never hold office without making it a Ministerial question.] But he said there were *irresistible obstacles* [which he had taken care to raise up]; and should the question not be carried, and he saw no probability that it would, the only effect of agitating it would be to excite hopes that would never be gratified, and to give rise to expectations which were sure to terminate in disappointment."

He next took another line of argument. "They were anxious to conciliate the Catholics; but let them not, in so doing, irritate a much larger portion of their fellow-subjects. Whilst they drew together the bonds which united one class of the population, let them not give offence to another part of it, whose loyalty and attachment [to their own interests] had long been undoubted. He should disguise the truth if he did not say the prevailing opinion against the petition was strong and rooted. He should, therefore, act contrary to all sense of his duty, and inconsistently with the original line he had marked for his conduct, were he to countenance that petition in any shape, or to withhold giving his negative to the proposition for going into the committee."

Sir John Newport, of Waterford, rose with the special object of rebutting the assertions contained in the petition from the ignorant Orange Corporation of Dublin. The corporators had asserted (in utter ignorance) that the Irish Catholics were placed on a footing of political power not enjoyed by any other dissenters from an Established Church in Europe. Sir John Newport said he would give one instance to the contrary—he might have given many:—

"The States of Hungary," he said, "resembled our Constitution more closely than any other Continental establishment. They formed a population of above seven millions, and had for centuries suffered all the evils of being divided by religion, distracted by the difference of their tenets, and restrictions on account of them. At length, in 1791, at the most violent crisis of disturbance, a Diet was convened, at which a decree was passed by which full freedom of religious faith, worship, and education, was secured to every sect without exception. The tests and oaths were rendered unobjectionable to any native Hungarian, be his religion what it would; and then came the clause which gave them precisely what these petitioners have in contemplation,—That 'the public offices and honours, whether high or low, great or small, should be given to natural-born Hungarians who had deserved well of their country, and possessed the other requisite qualifications, *without any respect to their religion.*' The Diet consisted of nearly four hundred members, with a splendid civil establishment for the Roman Catholic religion. The measure was adopted in a most critical moment, and it had successfully passed an ordeal of fourteen revolutionary years—equal, in fact, to the trial of a century less disturbed and agitated."

Mr. Maurice Fitzgerald supported the motion; and solemnly declared that when he voted for Union in the Irish Parliament, it was in view and contemplation of that measure, for no man could deny that the impression then made on the Catholic mind was that Ministers, as well as Opposition, were in favour of their claims. They expected, of course, that much more attention would be paid to them now.

Colonel Archdall (a North of Ireland Orangeman) asserted, that the bulk of the Roman Catholics were not anxious about the result of the question; if the cause were a good one, it had been very ill-conducted: and he gave the motion his decided negative.

Sir John Cox Hippesley supported the motion to commit the bill; and in order, as he said, to obviate the objections of those who apprehended the supremacy of the Pope over Irish Catholics, he suggested that the Catholic Church in Ireland should be put upon the footing of the Gallican Church; in other words, that the Crown should have a *veto* upon the appointment of bishops by the Pope. This was the first distinct mention of the *veto* in Parliament — a question which afterwards led to much grave dissension in Ireland.*

* But this was not the origin of the *veto*. It had been a favourite scheme of Mr. Pitt's since 1799. In that year an insidious proposal had been made to give a State endowment to Catholic bishops in Ireland, on certain conditions, amounting in principle to the *veto*. Mr. Plowden relates that the prelates did not then fully appreciate the object of this proposal; which was no less than to buy them up, and make them a species of ecclesiastical police. Plowden tells us :—
"It was admitted by a number of the prelates, then convened in Dublin, that it ought to be thankfully accepted.
"They went a step further, and signed the following resolution: 'That in the appointment of the prelates of the Roman Catholic religion to vacant sees within the kingdom, such interference by the Government, as may enable it to be satisfied with the loyalty of the person appointed, is just, and ought to be agreed to.' And for the purpose of giving it effect, they further resolved: 'That after the usual canonical election, the president should transmit the name of the elected to Government, which in one month after such transmission

Honourable H. Augustus Dillon denied that the question involved a party measure. It affected the safety of Ireland, and the vitality of the empire. The hearts of the Irish people had been alienated by martial law, and the suspension of the *Habeas Corpus* Act, and by other severities and oppressions. Were that measure allowed to pass, such expedients would cease to be necessary, and the mass of brave and grateful people would present a firm, an iron bulwark for the protection of the country against the designs of the enemy.

On the whole, it was apparent in this famous debate that all the lofty intellect, and all the honest principles, in the British Parliament were in favour of the measure of Catholic Emancipation. But that was a contemptible minority. The question upon the motion of Mr. Fox was negatived—ayes, 124; nays, 336; majority, 212.

So Catholic Emancipation was set at rest in both Houses of the British Parliament; and the "Protestant Interest," and the Constitution in Church and State, were saved, it was hoped, for ever.

CHAPTER XII.

1804—1806.

Prosecution of Judge Fox—His Offence, Enforcing Law on Orangemen—Prosecution of Judge Johnson—His Offence, Censuring the Irish Government — Decline of Pitt's Power—Castlereagh Defeated in Down County—Successes of Buonaparte—Cry for Peace—Death of Mr. Pitt—Whig Ministry—Mr. Fox—His Opinion of the Union—First Whisper of "Repeal"—Release of State Prisoners — Dismissal of Lord Redesdale as Chancellor — Duke of Bedford Viceroy — The Catholics Cheated Again—Equivocation of the Viceroy—Ponsonby—Curran's Promotion—The Armagh Orangemen—Mr. Wilson the Magistrate.

SOME very extraordinary proceedings took place in this and subsequent sessions of Parliament, with respect to two of the most irreproachable of the Irish judges—Mr. Justice Fox and Mr. Justice Johnson.

In the summer of 1803 Judge Fox had gone the North-west Circuit, a region

should return the name of the elected (if unobjectionable), that he might be confirmed by the Holy See. If he should be objected to by Government, the president on such communication should, after the month, convene the electors in order to choose some other candidate.' Mr. Pitt never lost sight of this insidious negotiation, into which he had seduced a certain number of the unsuspecting prelates. This was the foundation-stone of that deep-laid plan of Mr. Pitt and his associates, to seduce or force the Irish Catholics into the same state of schism from the Church of Rome as that which took place in England in the reign of Henry VIII. This was the origin of that vital question of *veto*."

which was then predominated over by a few great Orange magnates, and magistrates who were their very humble servants, and the savage tyrants of the poor country people, who were principally Catholics. As senior judge it was Judge Fox's duty to charge the Grand Juries; and in Longford, at Enniskillen, and Lifford, he made them very paternal and loyal addresses; intended, as usual, for the whole of the people of those counties. Endeavouring to awaken them to a high sense of the dangers which hovered over them from external and internal foes, he called upon the exertion of their best energies. He reminded them of the recent horrors of the 23d of July, and warned them of the dangers of the leaders of that rebellion still remaining at large. He strongly commented on the nature and extent of that insurrection, and on the origin and motives of the persons engaged in it. He exhorted them to *union amongst themselves—to forget their religious animosities, by which the country had been so long weakened and divided*, and to join in presenting a dutiful and loyal address to the throne, praying his Majesty to strengthen the executive government of the country, &c.

Now, if Judge Fox had done nothing more than utter in the ears of an Orange Grand Jury the words above printed in italics, he could never have been forgiven. But he did worse. When he came to Enniskillen, and proceeded, as his duty was, to deliver the jail there, the names of two prisoners were returned to him by the jailer, who had been committed by the Earl of Enniskillen, as a magistrate, but without any offence being charged against them. Their names were Breslin and Maguire. The committals were called for and produced—they specified no offence; but in one of them was an order to keep poor Breslin in solitary confinement. The judge thereupon ordered the prisoners to be brought to the bar in order to inquire of them the facts alleged against them. The jailer then informed the judge that those two prisoners were taken out of his custody on the 18th of August (that is, during the assizes), by a military guard sent for the purpose.* The judge felt this to be a high indignity offered to His Majesty's commission, and inquired if Lord Enniskillen were in town. On learning that he was at his country seat (Florence Court), he desired a friend of his lordship's to go over to him, with full instructions to relate the whole faithfully, make his compliments, and intreat his lordship's attendance in court on the next day, which was the last day of the assizes. The judge having waited in court to as late an hour as he could for the appearance of Lord Enniskillen, and having repeatedly inquired for him, he found it his duty, upon his lordship's non-appearance, to fine him in each of those cases £100—£200 in all. But the audacity of the judge in looking into the doings of Orange magistrates did not stop here. In the same county, Fermanagh, Mr. Stewart was fined £50 for committing one Neale Ford to the jail of Enniskillen without any charge on oath having been made against him, and releasing him on the eve of the assizes without taking bail for his appearance. Mr. Pallas was fined £20, as well as Mr. Webster, for releasing without bail a prisoner charged with *a capital offence*. But the prisoner was of the religion of Mr. Pallas.

When the judge came to Lifford, in Donegal, amongst the presentments tendered by the Grand Jury to the judge for his *fiat*, was one for a very large sum to be levied upon occupiers of land, under pretence of repaying Government for money advanced to pay bounties to three hundred and fifty men, the quota of that county, under the "Army of Reserve Act." But not one man of that force had been recruited; although it was the duty of the Marquis of Abercorn, as Governor of the county, to have caused that recruiting to be effected. The presentment of the Grand Jury, then, was a fraud upon the public. Judge Johnson refused to put his *fiat* on it, and publicly censured Lord Abercorn for neglect of duty—Lord Abercorn! the great patron and favourite of the Orange Society of that region. Such a judge as this, it was evident, was somehow to be got rid of.

Many months after the occurrences above-mentioned, the Marquis of Abercorn, in a most malignant and vindictive speech in the House of Lords, brought the conduct of Judge Fox before their lordships. He said, "that he had grave and serious matters of complaint to bring before their lordships against one of His Majesty's judges, in which the administration of justice was deeply concerned."

There ensued one of the most extraordinary State prosecutions ever seen in any country—the House of Lords, which had no original jurisdiction, undertaking to make itself a court to try a judge on a

---

* Maguire never was heard of more. Breslin was hurried off by soldiers to a military prison, where he was kept a long time; then tried by court-martial on the charge of trying to seduce a soldier to desert, convicted, and sentenced to be hung. He cut his throat to avoid the execution of the sentence, but the wound was not mortal; and he was hung near Enniskillen, with the rope forced into the bleeding gash.

criminal charge. The distinct charges were numerous, including many cases of "unjust fines," "excessive" fines, partiality, seeking to bring Lord Abercorn into contempt, casting censure on Lord Enniskillen, impeding the course of justice, and the like; and the Protestant interest of the North of Ireland was filled with anxiety for the result. Lord Abercorn pressed these prosecutions with wonderful virulence; Lord Hardwicke and the Irish Government aided it.* The public purse was opened to pay for it. A great mass of evidence (all *ex parte*) was produced. The proceedings lasted three years; and the excellent judge was ruined in health and fortune. At last, on the motion of Lord Grenville, the House of Lords voted, by a small majority, that the proceedings *should be quashed*. The cost to the public in the prosecution of this case amounted to £30,000.

On the division in the House of Lords, the old Lord Thurlow voted for getting rid of the whole matter, as unconstitutional and vexatious. He said it was a proceeding "to gratify the malignant resentments of individuals who fancied themselves insulted and exposed by any instance of virtuous independence upon the Bench."

Lord Eldon voted for continuing the prosecution to the end; and the Duke of Cumberland (Queen Victoria's uncle), an Orangeman, and special friend of Lord Abercorn, strongly opposed Lord Grenville's motion. "He trusted," he said, "and *expected*, that the matter would not be put off *sine die*." His Royal Highness was naturally of opinion that no justice could be done in Ireland if there were to be judges going round checking the wholesome severities of the very masters of lodges.

It is but justice towards the British House of Lords to admit, that after spending the public time and the public money for three years in prosecuting a virtuous judge, *because* he was a virtuous judge, did at last grow ashamed of the foul transaction, and by a small majority thrust it out of Court.

The case of Mr. Justice Johnson, one of the Justices of the Common Pleas, was even more extraordinary. Some anonymous Irishman, signing himself "*Juverna*," had, in November of 1803, immediately after Robert Emmet was executed, published a series of letters in Cobbett's *Political Register*, containing severe animadversions upon Lord Redesdale, Lord Hardwicke and his government, upon the public proceedings of Secretaries Wickham and Marsden, upon a charge delivered by Mr. Justice Osborne, and other matters. No government in Ireland ever before had the press so thoroughly corrupted or intimidated as that of Lord Hardwicke; and the first of the "*Juverna*" letters was sent to Mr. Cobbett avowedly because every printer in Dublin had refused to publish it. The sturdy William Cobbett (who was then, and for many years after, a sharp thorn in the side of Pitt and Castlereagh) admitted the letter at once to his *Register;* and then several others. These letters excited much attention, and extremely exasperated the Government, because they were evidently the production of some personage highly placed, who knew the secret machinations of the Irish officials against the people.

Great efforts were made to discover the audacious "*Juverna;*" but in the meantime, as the next best thing, the Attorney-General prosecuted Cobbett himself for publishing the "libels." His trial took place on May 24, 1804.

Cobbett had an interval of repose from persecution of *two days* allowed him, when, at the suit of the Right Honourable W. C. Plunket, Solicitor-General of Ireland, he was again called on to sustain an action for libels contained in letters signed "*Juverna*," published in the *Register*, reflecting on Mr. Plunket's conduct on the occasion of Robert Emmet's trial. Cobbett was again convicted, and damages were awarded to the plaintiff to the amount of £500.

It was believed, by the Irish Government, that the letters in question had been written by Judge Johnson. On the second trial of Mr. Cobbett, the manuscript of the letter relating to Lord Plunket was produced; and witnesses were easily found to swear that it was in the handwriting of the judge. The Government, therefore, determined to prosecute him also, and to bring him over to London for trial, as the publication had been in the County of Middlesex. But there was a difficulty in the way. There was no law then—no law in existence—giving power to remove offenders from Ireland to England, or *vice versa*, for trial. But Parliament was in session, and a new law was quickly procured, the two principal persons on the committee which framed it being Mr. Perceval, brother-in-law of Lord Redesdale, and Mr. Yorke, brother of Lord Hardwicke, who were

---

* The Marquis read, as a part of his speech before the Lords, a letter from the Lord-Lieutenant of Ireland to the British Minister, in which the judicial conduct of Mr. Justice Fox, on the North-west Circuit, was arraigned in terms of marked reprobation.

two of the persons complaining of being libelled.

A warrant was issued to bring the judge to London, and he was arrested at his house near Dublin. Thus he was taken under an *ex post facto* Act, which his counsel contended could not operate retrospectively.

The matter was discussed during six days, in the King's Bench in Ireland, in January, 1805. The legality of the warrant was confirmed. In the meantime, the *persecuted* judge procured a writ of *Habeas Corpus* from the Court of Exchequer, where the case was argued, February 4th and 7th, and, subsequently, in the Court of Common Pleas; and in both courts the arrest was held good. The judge was then brought over to London, and put on his trial before Lord Ellenborough, November 23, 1805.

Lord Ellenborough, staunch and consistent—always ready to lend the weight of his judicial character and position to the Government on any seditious libel case prosecution—unjustly on this occasion threw discredit on the respectable witnesses produced by Judge Johnson, to prove that the MSS. of the libel prosecuted was not in the handwriting of the defendant. But the jury, misdirected by Lord Ellenborough, brought in a verdict of "guilty;" the Attorney-General, however, never applied for judgment.

It was true, indeed, that Judge Johnson was the author of the letters of "*Juverna*," which were a very just, necessary, and well-merited castigation of the Irish Government; yet he was found guilty on bad evidence, for the manuscript was not his.*

The matter, however, was pressed no further. It was judged sufficient to disgrace a judge of the land by a criminal conviction, to ruin him by heavy expenses incurred in his defence, and to render the justice of Westminster Hall auxiliary to the police of Dublin. But the prosecution had caused great scandal by its unusual features; and in order to put as quiet a close to the matter as possible, the Attorney-General was directed, and he, accordingly, did enter a *nolle prosequi* on the record, as of Trinity Term, 1806. The learned judge, whose health was much on the decline, was allowed to retire upon a pension for his life.†

The treatment of these two honest judges was a significant warning to the judges of Ireland—first, that they were not to embarrass Orange justice with *their* justice; and second, that they were not to presume to say that a Lord-Lieutenant, or Chancellor, or Secretary, could do wrong.

In this year, Mr. Pitt's political power began to decline; and many of his partizans fell from him. Lord Sidmouth deserted him on the occasion of the impeachment of Lord Melville. Mr. Foster, the Irish Chancellor of the Exchequer, had tendered his resignation; and it was known that Lord Hardwicke was resolved to tender his. The star of the great Minister was growing pale; his Continental combinations against Buonaparte were all failures; and men were already beginning to speculate upon their chances under Mr. Pitt's successor, about the time when Parliament was suddenly prorogued on July 12th.

The defection of Lord Sidmouth, the impeachment of Lord Melville, and consequent shiftings in the Cabinet, created the necessity of Lord Castlereagh's vacating his seat for the County Down, in order to accept the office of Secretary of State for the Colonies and War Department. He sought a re-election for Down; but in that county there was a very strong feeling against him on account of the outrage put upon the Marquis of Downshire, by the Irish Government (when Castlereagh was Secretary), in dismissing him from the command of his regiment, and from the rank of Lord-Lieutenant of the county, because he had recommended petitions against the Union. Lord Castlereagh, most unexpectedly, found himself at the foot of the polls through the Downshire influence; and had to return to London and accept a seat for one of the "pocket boroughs" of the Government. This defeat by Castlereagh is said to have been felt as a severe blow by Mr. Pitt in his already failing fortunes. Mr. Plowden says it was a "triumph over political profligacy which was hailed by the nation at large;" but, in truth, the event had a much narrower significance: it was simply a triumph of the Downshire interest over the rival Stewart interest in the County Down. Political profligacy remained as before. But what really broke down Mr. Pitt was the success of the French armies in Germany.

The total failure of all his plans on the Continent, and the vast ascendancy which

---

* "The libel above-mentioned, I know (on the authority of Lord Cloncurry), though the production of Judge Johnson, was sent to Cobbett in the handwriting of the judge's daughter."—*Madden.*

† This excellent judge afterwards, in his retirement in France, wrote a very excellent treatise on the *Military Defence of Ireland*, under the name of Captain Philip Roche Fermo'. This work has specially in view a defence of the country by the inhabitants of it against the English, and has been much studied since that time.

Napoleon had acquired by his late conquest and treaty, had filled the unbiassed part of the British nation with dissatisfaction and dismay.

The campaign was only opened in September, and Napoleon, with the velocity of the eagle, marched into the heart of Germany, and took an Austrian army, under General Mack, prisoners at Ulm. On the 2d of December, he gained the renowned victory of Austerlitz, which was followed by the treaty of Presburg, signed on the 26th of the same month. This dissolved the new confederacy, and blasted Mr. Pitt's last hopes on the Continent.

All England cried out for peace, and for an administration which would give her peace. Austria was dismembered, Russia debilitated, Prussia neutralized, if not treacherously gone over to the enemy, Hanover lost to the King of England, and the British forces were too late in the field even to make any important diversion against the triumphant legions of France. Lord Melville (the former Secretary Dundas) was pleading to an impeachment before the House of Lords; Lord Castlereagh had returned from his own country, baffled and discredited. All these things together preyed on Mr. Pitt's mind, and ruined his already frail health. Parliament met on the 20th of January, 1806; and three days after, William Pitt died. His last words were: "*Oh! my country!*" —meaning England alone; to Ireland he had ever been a bitter, and at last a mortal enemy.

Lord Hawkesbury was at first named First Lord of the Treasury, merely to supply the vacancy, without any change of Ministry. His lordship held that office only long enough to hurry through the necessary forms of office to grant to himself the lucrative place of Warden of the Cinque Ports, and then resigned. At last, after some days' delay, and much reluctance on the part of the King, was formed the new Grenville-Fox Ministry,—Lord Grenville being First Lord of the Treasury, and Mr. Fox Secretary for Foreign Affairs. The Duke of Bedford was to be Lord-Lieutenant of Ireland, with the Right Honourable William Elliott as Chief Secretary; Right Honourable George Ponsonby as Lord-Chancellor; Mr. Plunket as Attorney-General; and Mr. Bushe as Solicitor-General. In short, it was not only a Whig, but was supposed to be also an *Anti-Union* administration. Reform, Emancipation, Repeal of the Union even—anything in satisfaction of Ireland's just claims—was at first imagined to be possible under such a government.

Amongst the earliest Parliamentary proceedings on the change of the Ministry, which in any way related to Ireland, must be noticed Mr. O'Hara's spirited objection to Lord Castlereagh's vote for monumental honours to Marquis Cornwallis, who died in India. He opposed the motion, because he could not with consistency vote funeral honours to a man who had brought about the Union between Great Britain and Ireland; with regard to which he trusted that, some time or other, it would come under the consideration of that House; and if it were not, as he hoped it would be, utterly rescinded, it would, at all events, be considerably modified, and, if possible, ameliorated. Upon this interesting subject Mr. Fox declared that he concurred with the motion; for that the words in which it was expressed did not, in imitation of a late precedent, assert that the object of it was *an excellent statesman*. Although, however, he supported the motion, yet he agreed with Mr. O'Hara in characterizing the Union as *one of the most disgraceful transactions in which the Government of any country had been involved.*

In consonance with this marked reprobation of that fatal measure of Union by the most enlightened and irreproachable member of the new administration, several of the Corporations of Dublin formed meetings to prepare petitions to the Legislature for the Repeal of the Union. Of these, the Company of Stationers, at their hall in Capel Street, gave the example, by appointing a respectable committee of nine to draw up a petition. At a subsequent meeting, however, they resolved not at that moment to embarrass Ministers with their claims.

A few days later, Mr. Fox was called upon in Parliament, by Mr. Alexander, for an explanation of his words relative to the Union.

Mr. Fox conceived he had spoken very intelligibly; but he never refused explanation. He adhered to every syllable he had uttered relative to the Union, upon the motion for funeral honours to Lord Cornwallis. But when he had reprobated a thing done, he said nothing prospectively. However bad the measure had been, an attempt to repeal it without the most urgent solicitation from the parties interested should not be made, and hitherto none such had come within his knowledge.

"The parties interested" are the English, the Scottish, and the Irish people; so that in the apparently explicit reply of Mr. Fox there is a breadth of application sufficient to enable a prudent statesman to do as he pleases afterwards. Even so early did it become apparent that neither English Tory nor English Whig would ever listen to any proposal for the undoing of that shameful deed. Gradually, as time has worn on, men of all parties in England have become willing to admit that the Union was a foul act, foully accomplished; yet no British Minister, of any party, would dare, for his head, to propose that it be undone. It was thus, in 1806, on the accession of Mr. Fox to office, that the first whisper was heard of that demand which afterwards rang so loud—the Repeal of the Union.

Two or three agreeable incidents at the same time happened in Ireland. The Act for suspending the *Habeas Corpus* had been permitted to expire without any attempt by Government to continue or revive it. Thereupon the several jails in Ireland were cleared of all those State prisoners who could bear the expenses of *Habeas Corpus*, and who had been confined there for two or three years. The restoration to society of many respectable and popular characters, dignified by unmerited sufferings, spread a sympathetic glow of exultation through the people, which broke out into an eagerness to hail the new Governor as their deliverer, and stifled all efforts to procure valedictory addresses to the departing Viceroy, who had so long kept them in bondage. The instantaneous removal of Lord Redesdale from his situation, even before his successor had arrived in Ireland, created much satisfaction throughout every rank of the Catholic population, which he had so coarsely and unfoundedly insulted and traduced. This early and marked removal of Lord Redesdale was a seasonable atonement to the insulted feelings of the Irish Catholics, and was received by them as an earnest of the new Ministers' adopting a new system of measures calculated to secure the internal peace, welfare, and prosperity of Ireland.

As for Lord Hardwicke, after his five years' administration, not even the efforts of his paid press could succeed in procuring him those customary addresses of courtesy which are given to departing Viceroys. The attendance even of his favoured yeomanry of Dublin was solicited to perform the last honour to the ex-Governor, and was refused in the first instance. Out of all Ireland, addresses on his departure came only from Dublin, the County Mayo, and the loyal Crossmolina Cavalry. He sailed from the Pigeon House on the 31st of March, 1806; and many a curse went after him.

The Duke of Bedford came to Ireland, as was firmly and fondly believed, to carry out the liberal principles which Mr. Fox had always supported for the government of the country. But Mr. Fox had more important business to attend to, in his own estimation, than the affairs of Ireland, which were, as usual, placed in the background. He had upon his hands the difficult business of negotiating a peace with France; and his fast-failing health did not permit him to go into the details of Irish appointments and Irish grievances.

Yet Charles James Fox was of a character noble, open, and generous; as opposite to Mr. Pitt in personal qualities as he was in his place in the House of Commons. If he had, at this juncture, accepted the position of Viceroy—if he had seen with his own eyes the insolent and audacious cruelty of the Orange magistracy, which was now strong enough to brave both law and Government—the too patient suffering of the great mass of the people, and the decaying trade and industry of the towns—it would have been impossible to repress indignation in such a nature as his. But he had been specially brought into power for the purpose of negotiating a peace with France; and this was enough for his diminished energies. Lord Grenville, the Premier Minister, who had been an active agent in carrying the Union, was by no means so favourable to Ireland as the Foreign Secretary. Lord Sidmouth was the boasted and pledged opponent to Catholic concession, under every possible variation of political occurrence. The friends and co-operators of Lord Redesdale, the Attorney and Solicitor-General, retained their situations and confidence. Mr. Alexander Marsden, the secret adviser and machinist of the late administrations, was not displaced. The whole of the Orange magistracy remained undisturbed in the commission of the peace. Even Major Sirr was still seen as the tutelary guardian of the Castle-yard. No floating patronage was removed from any promoter of the late, to countenance or encourage the supporters of the new, system. The name of Grattan, the friend and father of Irish liberty, was not seen on the list of changes; and Mr. Curran, the unwavering asserter of Ireland's rights and freedom, remained nearly five months unpromoted.

As for the Catholics, they were deluded again. They soon found that there was no disposition to disquiet the United Kingdom with an importunate insistance upon any claims of theirs. But at the first moment of the change of Viceroys they were so confident of their affairs being now in good hands, that they resolved not to press the matter too keenly. A newly constituted Catholic Committee met in March, before the Duke of Bedford had yet arrived at Mr. M'Donnell's house, in Allen Court, and there resolved, with the exception of two dissenting voices, that it was inexpedient to press a discussion of the Catholic question during the present session of Parliament; and that it would be proper to present an address, on behalf of the Catholics, to the Duke of Bedford, congratulating him on his appointment to the chief government of Ireland, and expressing their confidence in the wisdom and abilities of the illustrious personages who composed the present administration.

Indeed, nothing can well be conceived more helpless than the management of the Catholic cause during the whole of the Bedford administration. A Mr. Ryan, a merchant, who had a large house in Marlborough Street, threw his house open to informal meetings of active members of the Committee, and entered into correspondence with Mr. Fox as an authorized agent, or rather leader, amongst the Catholics. This produced jealousies and discontents; other meetings were held in various places, where considerable diversity of opinion made itself manifest, chiefly on this question,— Should they press for emancipation at once, or await a more convenient season? Many gatherings of Catholic gentlemen and merchants took place in some of the counties, and strong resolutions were passed. It was manifest that a good share of public spirit had been roused amongst them, but they lacked organization, and sage and bold counsel. The new Viceroy received their ultra-loyal and rather mealy-mouthed addresses with courtesy; but answered them with equivocation. For example, one address, from the Catholics of Dublin, signed by Lords Fingal, Southwell, Kenmare, Gormanstown, &c., was presented at the Castle on the 29th of April, 1806. It closes in this humble style:—

"May your Grace permit us to conclude with the expression of those sentiments in which all Irish Catholics can have but one voice. Bound as we are to the fortunes of the empire, *by a remembrance of what is past* and the hope of future benefits, by our preference and by our oaths, should the wise generosity of our lawgivers vouchsafe to crown that hope which their justice inspires, it would no longer be our duty alone, but our pride, to appear the foremost against approaching danger; and, if necessary, to remunerate our benefactors by the sacrifice of our lives."

And the gracious reply ends with these words — an admirable sample of the phraseology with which the Catholics were entertained for many years :—

"In the high situation in which His Majesty has been graciously pleased to place me, it is my first wish, as it is my first duty, to secure to all classes and descriptions of His Majesty's subjects in this part of the United Kingdom, the advantages of a *mild and beneficent administration of the law.* With this important object in view, I entertain no doubt that the Roman Catholic inhabitants of the city of Dublin will, by their loyalty to the King, their attachment to the Constitution, and their affection for their fellow-subjects, afford the strongest recommendation to a favourable consideration of *their interests.*"

His Grace takes care to say their "interests;" but it was not their interests they were pleading for, it was their rights; and of rights he said not a word.

But while rival aspirants for leadership of the Catholics were addressing excited meetings, their dissensions were suddenly somewhat allayed by ostentatious warnings contained in the Government newspapers, that they were in danger of bringing themselves within the penalties of the Convention Act. It was a sore and embarrassing suggestion for the struggling Catholics.

The Convention Act, which passed in 1793, was one of the baleful measures of the Pitt system, to muzzle the victim before the infliction of torture; to render the voice of the subject equally powerless for prevention and redress; and, in truth, this formidable Act has remained ever since one of the surest safeguards of British domination in Ireland, as well as one of the conspicuous badges of provincialism, for there is no such law in England.

Lord Chancellor Ponsonby, in whose hands was most of the patronage of Ireland, was not found to exercise that patronage as had been expected by his friends; nor is it interesting, at this time, to enter into those personal and political claims which were either admitted or rejected. Yet there is one case which interests every reader, even at this late day, because it is the case of the illustrious John Philpot Curran. He had been promised, and did expect, on a change of Ministry, a legal position commensurate with his service and standing at the bar.

The new Lord Chancellor neglected him for five months, and then offered him the place of Master of the Rolls, the second Judge in Equity. It was not satisfactory to Curran for several reasons: his practice had been more in law than in equity; and, besides, this place carried with it no political influence. In his letter to Grattan on this subject, he says: "When the party with which I had acted so fairly had, after so long a proscription, come at last to their natural place, I did not expect to have been stuck up into a window, a spectator of the procession." He took the place, however, for the sake of unanimity in the party. A singular demonstration of party malignity was made on this occasion by some of Mr. Curran's professional brethren, at a very numerous bar meeting, convened to take into consideration an address to his honour on his late promotion. His talents were too transcendent, his spirit too independent, his principles too Irish, not to have enemies, who would openly oppose this just tribute to his splendid genius and unrivaled fame. The notice of the intended meeting had no sooner been published, than the prominent supporters of the Ascendancy set every engine to work to prevent, embarrass, and defeat so critical an appeal to the virtue and independence of the Irish bar upon the brightest ornament of their profession, and the staunch and incorruptible friend of their country. On the 7th of July the meeting took place, consisting of two hundred and fifty gentlemen of the bar, of whom one hundred and eighty only chose to divide. Of these, one hundred and forty-six voted for the address; thirty-four opposed it. The question was warmly debated for several hours. In opposition to, and defiance of, the professional powers and political influence of Messrs. Saurin and Bushe, the spirited independence of the bar was honourably asserted, and the talent, integrity, and virtue of the country triumphed over the jealousies and intrigues of the system and its abettors.

While the Catholics found themselves once more thrust back from the threshold of that Constitution which they so much longed to enter, the Northern Orangemen, on their side (who had been a little nervous at first about the advent of these Whigs), soon found that they had no cause for alarm. A very singular correspondence passed this summer between Secretary Elliot and Mr. Wilson, a Tyrone magistrate, touching certain outrages perpetrated on Catholics in his neighbourhood, and particularly the burning down of the house of a man named O'Neill, a hatter. This outrage was done by night, without any provocation; and was alleged to have been perpetrated in mere wantonness, by a mob of Orangemen coming out of a lodge, and headed by two sons of Mr. Verner, a magistrate, and himself a famous Orangeman. Mr. Wilson's representations were so earnest, demanding inquiry and redress, that Mr. Sergeant Moore was sent down to the neighbourhood, accompanied by a Crown Solicitor, to investigate the facts. Mr. Plowden affirms, on the authority of Mr. Wilson probably, that Sergeant Moore, on his arrival, put himself in communication with the Messrs. Verner, the accused house-burners, to procure him evidence of what took place. "The evidences were brought forward by the young Messrs. Verner; but he could not get anything out of them (after the most strict examination) which could tend towards the crimination of these gentlemen. The house certainly was burned; but the incendiaries could not be identified. It was true the two young Messrs. Verner were there, but only as spectators, after the house was destroyed; but nothing appeared to justify an opinion that either of those gentlemen was concerned in the outrage." Of course, the learned Sergeant returned as wise as he came.

Some days after, Mr. Wilson was summoned to Dublin, and had an interview with Lord Chancellor Ponsonby, who questioned him as to the outrage, and as to the inquiry. Mr. Wilson attempted to make some comment upon the way which the Sergeant had taken for arriving at the facts: the Chancellor twice interrupted him with great energy to declare *that Mr. Sergeant Moore's conduct entitled him to, and possessed the warmest approbation of Government.* Mr. Wilson made some observations on the state of the magistracy in his part of the country, and the Chancellor asked how he proposed to remedy the evil? Mr. Wilson replied that the only effectual mode would be by issuing a general new commission. This would not give any partial offence; and care afterwards should be taken not to admit any improper persons into it. His lordship replied by a smile. This ended his personal communications with Government; but not his correspondence. He wrote several times again on the subject; but without effect. He applied to have his own commission, as a magistrate, extended from Tyrone into Armagh (as he dwelt on the border), in order that he might have some power to protect the poor Catholics, who lived in daily and nightly terror under the shadow of the original Orange Lodge, and in that very neighbourhood which had been the scene of the "Hell-or-Counaught" exterminations, ten years earlier; but Mr. Wilson's application was refused. This affair would be in itself too trifling to occupy space in a general narrative like the present, but that it is, unfortunately, only one example of very many of the same kind, of wanton oppression and official connivance, which made the North of Ireland itself a hell for the Catholic people during many a year since, and which is by no means over at this day.

Poor Mr. Wilson, who was so Quixotic as to interest himself for the oppressed Catholics of Tyrone and Armagh, after the refusal of an Armagh commission to that gentleman came to be known, was himself subjected to the outrages of the Protestant "wreckers." His range of offices, filled with hay, was burned down one night; and as he still continued to importune the Secretary and the Chancellor with applications on behalf, not of himself, but of his persecuted neighbours, he was finally (3d of July, 1807) deprived of the commission of the peace for Tyrone, by a regular writ of *Supersedeas*.

CHAPTER XIII.

1806—1807.

Revenue and Debt of Ireland—Rapid Increase of Debt—Drain of Wealth from Ireland—Character of the Imports and Exports—Rackrents, Tithes, &c.—Distress of the People—The "Threshers"—Threshers Hung—Catholic Meetings—Increase of Maynooth Grant—From Apprehension of the Irish College in France—Catholic Officers Bill—To Promote Depopulation—Bill Abandoned—Change of Ministry—The King demands a No-Popery Pledge—Duke of Cumberland—Perceval Administration—Camden and Castlereagh in Office—No Popery—Recruiting in Ireland—John Keogh on Catholic Officers' Bill—O'Connell—Too Easy Gratitude of the Irish towards Whigs—Populace draw the Duke of Bedford's Coach.

IRELAND, until the period of the consolidation of the National Debts, had a separate Chancellor of the Exchequer; and the actual Chancellor, Sir John Newport, in bringing forward his Irish Budget, in this session of 1806, made as favourable a representation of the finances of the country as possible, according to the usual custom of Finance Ministers. Everything, according to him, "afforded proofs of the increase of prosperity and *confidence in the Government.*" The revenue of Ireland for the year he proposed to increase from £3,360,000 to £3,800,000, by means of several new taxes; but later in the session Sir John Newport brought in a bill for "Relief of the Irish Poor." On his financial statement, Mr. Parnell drew the attention of the House to the general financial situation of the country, as represented by the Chancellor of the Exchequer himself. He calculated that were the debt of Ireland to increase with the same rapidity as at present for fifteen years, it would at that period amount to £120,000,000. He therefore called upon Ministers to adopt some efficient measures for restraining the progress of so alarming an evil.

Mr. Parnell either did not know, or pretended not to know, that Ministers did not regard this as an alarming evil at all, and that it was precisely for this, amongst other great objects, the Union had been effectuated. Mr. Parnell also fell short in his estimate of the rate of future increase of our debt:—"So well have British book-keepers worked our account, that within *eleven* years (in 1817) our debt was found to amount, not to £120,000,000, but to £130,561,037, and so brought Ireland up to the condition of indebtedness which entitled her to share equally in all the public liabilities of England."

The truth is, that although from the increase of population, and therefore of consumption, the actual amount of taxes now ground out of the Irish people was increasing year by year, those taxes were becoming more and more difficult to pay, and were reducing great numbers of people continually to abject poverty; so that at the very moment when the Chancellor of the Exchequer was felicitating Parliament upon Ireland's financial prosperity, he had also to bring in a bill for relief of the poor. The system of drainage of Ireland for imperial purposes was even then in full operation, although not so highly developed as we have seen it since that day. There were some circumstances then existing which in part counteracted that imperial policy: in the first place, the enfranchisement of Catholics as voters, in 1793, had considerably promoted and increased the practice of giving *leases* of small farms, so as to create freeholders to support their landlords' interests at county elections; and next, the war in Europe, though occasionally interrupted by short seasons of armed peace, maintained a good price for all kinds of agricultural produce, because the British Government was constantly obliged to victual great fleets and garrisons in all quarters of the world. And as such large numbers of the cultivators of the land had leases, their increased profits could not be immediately appropriated by their landlords in the shape of increased rents, and so carried off to England to be spent—an inconvenience and loss to the "sister kingdom" which was afterwards fully repaired by the abolition of the "Forty-shilling Freeholders," as will be seen further on.

In the meantime, however, the war certainly enhanced the profits of Irish agriculture ; and although that increase was not altogether for behoof of the people themselves (for much of it could be carried off by taxation, as we have seen, to pay the charges of an unjust debt), yet they were not then by any means so cunningly plundered, so scientifically stripped bare (for want of the requisite machinery), as they have been since, and are now. Population, therefore, was rapidly increasing during all these years of war, although thousands of young Irishmen were each year recruited for the British army, to fight against Jacobinism, French principles, and the rights of man.

The imports and exports of Ireland continued to increase after the Union in proportion to the increasing population, but by no means at so rapid a rate as during the eighteen years of national independence, when the country had the fostering care of a native Legislature, bad and corrupt as that Legislature was. But it is very material to observe the character of those imports and exports. The imports consisted more and more of British manufactures, and of foreign and colonial produce purchased in England and imported *thence*—the exports more and more of cattle, meat, and grain, raw agricultural produce, and of spirits made from grain. There is an exception in the single article of linen cloth ; yet the increase in that trade did not keep pace with the increase of population. In the

ARTICLES IMPORTED INTO IRELAND FOR TEN YEARS PREVIOUS, AND TEN YEARS SUBSEQUENT, TO THE UNION.				ARTICLES EXPORTED FROM IRELAND FOR TEN YEARS PREVIOUS, AND TEN YEARS SUBSEQUENT, TO THE UNION.			
Imports.		Years 1781 to 1800.	Years 1802 to 1821.	Exports.		Years 1781 to 1800.	Years 1802 to 1821.
Drapery,	yds.	23,833,381	49,692,058	Linen Cloth,	yds.	673,798,721	832,403,860
Sugar, Raw,	cwts.	3,796,285	6,089,175	Butter,	lbs.	5,777,566	7,915,949
Do , Refined,	cwts.	149,513	490,315	Pork,	barrels.	2,164,608	2,565,403
Tea,	lbs.	22,711,224	66,847,251	Wheat,	bushels.	1,334,567	4,223,782
Coals,	tons.	6,413,557	10,897,970	Barley,	bushels.	1,027,323	1,842,993
Iron,	cwts.	3,917,882	5,530,682	Meal and Flour,	cwts	747,674	1,686,948
Flax-seed,	hhds.	837,746	931,049	Candles,	cwts.	117,276	205,958
Cotton Wool,	cwts.	199,751	538,542	Pigs,	No.	70,272	687,569
Tobacco,	lbs.	99,402,762	116,112,836	Oats,	barrels.	7,650,359	16,112,142
Cotton Yarn,	lbs.	4,551,336	19,995,350	Bacon,	flitches.	1,013,552	6,248,527
Timber,	tons.	298,981	490,245	Horned Cattle,	No.	302,287	747,815
Hats,	No.	152,366	1,387,209	Spirits,	galls.	79,892	10,349,752
Hides, Undressed,	No.	84,287	450,031	Lard,	cwts.	80,974	313,867
Hops,	cwts.	295,234	400,701	Soap,	cwts.	92,616	219,506
Hosiery,	pieces.	3,606,074	7,995,640	Copper Ore,	tons.	9,923	30,243
Oak Bark,	bales.	2,224,655	2,550,853	Feathers,	cwts.	28,167	106,307
Barilla,	cwts.	2,122,932	2,182,060	Kelp,	tons.	31,224	64,731

accompanying table of the official returns of the exports and imports for ten years before, and ten years after, the Union (assuming those official returns to be correct), this very material difference may be studied and appreciated ; but Mr. Marmion, in his *History of the Maritime Ports of Ireland*, observes of this table: "These returns were no doubt furnished to support the opinions of certain advocates for the Legislative Union, as *wine*, the consumption of which was likely to show the means of the country, if progressing, as correctly as any other article, has been excluded altogether. The import of wine in 1799 was one million two hundred and thirty-eight thousand five hundred and twelve gallons; and it has gradually decreased since then to five hundred and twelve thousand three hundred and nineteen gallons in 1848, about which quantity still continues to be consumed annually."

The high "war prices," then, for agricultural produce, helped to establish a strong current of exportation, in all that species of commodities, out of Ireland into England; while at the same time the increasing absenteeism of Peers and landed proprietors (who now preferred to drink their wine in England) carried off also to that country more and more of the *prices* received in Ireland for those commodities. Thus England was already gaining every way by the Union, and Ireland losing every way.

Yet the system was not yet by any means perfect. So long as voters for counties had to be created by small freeholds, there were large and increasing numbers of working farmers not wholly at the mercy of their landlords, nor liable to be turned out at the end of any six months. These people could live, and could even employ labour in improvements; so that there was a certain comparative prosperity, although manufactures (except linen) still continued to decline, and the market was flooded with English fabrics. It was not till the peace brought low prices that the series of Irish famines recommenced; and after that, the abolition of the "Forty-shilling Freeholders," then the systematic refusal of leases, then the universal "tenancy at will," and finally the Poor law, rendered the British system as nearly perfect as any system of human invention can be, for reaping the full fruits of the Legislative Union.

It was under great difficulties and oppressions that Irish farmers, at the period we have now arrived at, made out life even so well as they did. Their chief troubles arose from middlemen, rackrents, tithes, church rates, and the monstrous Grand Jury jobs by which gentlemen accommodated one another, at the expense of the county, with roads and bridges, which were not useful to the county, but were convenient or ornamental to the demesnes of those gentlemen themselves. Those who knew Ireland in the early years of this century can well remember the many cases of exasperating oppression, the scenes of misery and despair, which were caused by *each* one of the plagues above enumerated. In some counties during this very year, 1806, the too long suffering country people were goaded into secret combinations and violent local resistance.

In consequence of recent exactions by the tithe proctors, in the counties of Mayo, Sligo, Leitrim, and parts of Roscommon, formerly notable for their pacific and orderly demeanour, a body of people, styling themselves *Threshers* (i. e., of tithe proctors' corn), had appeared in a sort of public confederacy. Up to that time, they had punctiliously confined their outrages and depredations to the collectors of tithes and their underlings. They frankly averred their reasons for their conduct—viz., that from the late unprecedented rise in the tithes, beyond what had before been insisted upon, the profits of their crops centred almost entirely in the tithe proctor. They sent letters, signed *Captain Thresher*, to the growers of flax and oats, warning them, under severe pains, to leave their tithes in kind on the fields, but on no account to pay any monied composition to their rectors and vicars, or their lessees or proctors. Had the managers of the Bedford administration *in all things* minutely followed the example of their predecessors, those counties would have been proclaimed, and probably a more general insurrection have existed in Ireland than in the year 1798. Many of the task-drivers under the former Government (all found in place were retained, except Lord Redesdale and Mr. Foster, discharged by Mr. Fox) urged the Government to proclaim the disturbed counties, and recommence the discipline and goadings of 1798.

But there was then no motive for resorting to the system of Camden and Carhampton; there was no need now of provoking an insurrection, because the Union had been carried, and all was safe. Accordingly, it was resolved to meet the case of the poor "Threshers" by the usual Constitutional measures, assizes, special commissions, packed juries, and the gallows. During the whole of the Bedford administration, not a single measure was adopted nor attempted for the redress or abatement of this curse of tithes; the people were left at the mercy of the grinding proctors and rectors,* and if they committed "outrage" they were hung. Twelve Threshers were executed in the autumn of this year in Mayo County alone; and others suffered death in Galway, Roscommon, and Longford. There was not the smallest evidence that they had any political views or French principles. They were simply White Boys under another name.

During this summer, the anxious negotiations for peace with France, conducted by Lord Lauderdale, failed, and his lordship returned to London. This was the

---

* *Grinding* was not the worst of it. Rectors discovered a practice of swindling farmers in the following manner. In order to encourage the labour and industry of husbandmen in improving their lands, many clergymen granted *leases of tithes* to the tenants during their incumbencies. The lessee, speculating upon the *life* of the incumbent, would make expenditures in the improvement of his lands proportionate to the probability of his own enjoyment of the fruits of his improvements. When the improved lands began to yield increased crops, in order that the church should not lose the advantage of them (*decimæ ubcriores*), the incumbent would effectuate an exchange of livings (often preconcerted) with some other lessee of *his* tithes for his incumbency; thus letting each other *gratis* into the full benefit of the tenant's labour and expenditure, upon the speculation of a life interest, at least, in his improvements. In some instances, this fructifying process has been known in two or three years to have doubled, and in others to have trebled the value of the living.

death of Charles James Fox—he died on the 13th of September, and relieved the administration of the embarrassment of the presence of one honest man. The death of Mr. Fox caused no alteration in the Irish Government. In England, Lord Howick quitted the Admiralty, and went to the Foreign Office.

Catholic meetings were held from time to time during the winter of 1806-7, mostly at the Star and Garter in Essex Street. At one of these a committee of twenty-one was appointed to prepare a petition for Catholic Relief; and amongst the twenty-one we find the names of John Keogh, the old and faithful leader of the Catholics, Daniel O'Connell, the young and ultimately victorious leader, Purcell O'Gorman, Doctor Dromgoole, Thomas Wyse, and others, whose names were afterwards household words in every Catholic home during the long struggle for emancipation. A petition was framed, adopted, and committed to Henry Grattan for presentation.

On the 4th of March, 1807, on the report of the Committee of Supply being brought up in Parliament, it appeared that the Committee estimated the grant to Maynooth College at £13,000 instead of £8,000. This increase was, of course, opposed by Mr. Perceval, who always showed himself the most zealous Protestant in Parliament. The increased grant, however, was carried, not through any feeling of liberality towards the Catholics, but for the reasons set forth by Lord Howick in supporting the grant. He said he did so on the large principle of connecting the Irish Catholic with the State. It was then particularly necessary to promote the domestic education of the Catholic clergy, as an institution of great extent had been formed at Paris, at the head of which was a Dr. Walsh, a person of considerable notoriety, with a view to re-establish the practice of Irish Catholic education at that place, and to make that education the channel of introducing and extending the political influence of the French Government in Ireland.*

English governments, after having so long prohibited by penal laws the education of Catholic youths at home, and having thus driven them abroad for education, were now almost willing to bribe them to stay at home and receive that education, which within the memory of men then living would have merited transportation or death. Yet there was nothing inconsistent in these two modes of treatment. A century before, the great object of law and government had been to get and keep possession of Catholic lands and goods— and for that purpose to debase Catholics to the condition of brutes for want of education—but in 1807, the great need and absorbing passion of the Government was to crush France, and keep out French principles; and it was desirable to keep young divinity students away from Paris, where they might learn matters not expedient to be known in Ireland;—might learn, for instance, that it is not so very miserable a case for each man to be his own landlord; that country people can be pretty comfortable even without paying tithes; that people of all religions, in France, are equal before the law; that the French are not a race of creatures altogether abandoned to crime, debauchery, and atheism, for want of noble landlords; and many other things of this nature. Therefore, when the Government at one time drove young Irishmen abroad for education, and at another time induced them to stay at home for education, it knew very well each time what it was doing, and acted in both cases upon the invariable principle that all Irish life, activity, and industry, physical and intellectual, lay and clerical, belong to England, and are to be regulated and disposed of, displaced, transferred, encouraged, and prohibited, as British policy and interest shall from time to time require.

Upon the very same invariable principle, the Government in this session introduced what was called the "Catholic Officers' Bill," to enable Catholics to hold commissions in the army or navy. This measure was intended by Ministers for two purposes: first, to stop, by a small concession, the threatening agitation of the Catholics for their complete relief; and secondly, by commissioning some Catholic officers, to make the British service more popular with the people, and thus promote enlistment. On this latter point, the words of

---

* "In the latter end of autumn, 1806, some printed copies of an *arrêt*, or decree, signed 'Napoléon, Hugh B. Maret, Champagny, and Walsh, Administrateur Général,' dated Milan, 28th Floreal. An. xiii., uniting the English, Irish, and Scotch Ecclesiastical Establishment, in the French dominions, under the general administration of the Reverend Dr. Walsh, late Superior of the Irish College at Paris, were sent from thence, *via* Hamburg, to England and Ireland. At the same time Dr. Walsh invited the students of St Patrick's Irish College at Lisbon to repair to Paris, to prosecute their studies, and encouraged them to undertake the journey, by promising that the expenses of it would be defrayed. The Roman Catholic archbishops and other prelates, Trustees of Maynooth College, having met in Dublin on business concerning it in January, 1807, availed themselves of the occasion to express their disapprobation of the invitation from Paris, in a letter to the Rev. Doctor Crotty, Rector of the Irish College at Lisbon, a copy of which was sent to Mr. Secretary Elliot, and also to Lord Howick.

Lord Howick, who introduced the bill, are worth preserving:—

"On the commonalty of Ireland the measure must have a powerful effect, by affording *a salutary check to the increasing superabundant population* of that country, as it would induce numbers to enter into the service of His Majesty, even of those who, by their own discontents, and by the artifices of others, had so lately been urged into insurrection and rebellion."

It is needless to say that this measure also was resisted by the model Protestant, Perceval. "He greatly feared," he said, "that this was but the beginning of a system which would, in its consequences, when fully disclosed, be highly dangerous to the Constitution and Protestant establishment. He perceived that, step by step, and from day to day, they were bringing forward measures, which he thought must end in the TOTAL REPEAL OF THE TEST ACT." Mr. Perceval was himself, he declared, "as great a friend to toleration as any man," but he could not see how the Constitution in Church and State was to stand, if persons were allowed to command the King's troops who believed in seven sacraments. The bill was read a first time; and immediately arose a violent ferment, both in England and amongst the "Ascendancy" in Ireland. The University of Oxford petitioned against the measure; so did the Corporation of Dublin. The Dukes of York and Cumberland, Lord Eldon and Lord Hawkesbury, had frequent access to the King, whose mental disorder was then, indeed, so much aggravated, that he had need of advisers, if those advisers had been honest. George III. was at that time an idiot—sometimes a helpless and moping idiot, sometimes a talking and busy idiot; and, unfortunately, he was in the latter species of paroxysm. Mr. Perceval advertised in the public papers that "the Church was in danger;" and a great cry of "No-Popery!" arose over all England. The events that followed are clearly set forth in the explanations given by Lord Grenville and Lord Howick in the two Houses, of the causes which led to the sudden change of Ministry. It appears that the Ministers had had several interviews with the King, who seemed at first satisfied with their statements of the expediency of the measure proposed; but the unhappy patient had evidently not understood their statements. He asked Lord Howick one day, "What was going on in the House of Commons?" On being told that the Catholic Officers' Bill was to come on, he expressed his general dislike.

"The next day (said Lord Howick) His Majesty, in the same gracious manner that we have been accustomed to experience from him, informed us that he must look out for new servants. Two days afterwards, I was authorized to state this circumstance to the House, and on Tuesday last His Majesty signified his pleasure that we should resign our offices next day." Ministers then proposed to drop the bill altogether; but this was not enough for the King, in the condition of nervous irritation to which he had been worked up by Lord Eldon, and their Royal Highnesses his two sons, the Dukes of York and Cumberland. He required from them a pledge that they would never more bring forward any measure whatever respecting Papists—in other words, would never advise His Majesty to do any act of justice towards one-fourth part of his subjects. This was too much. The Ministers had no idea of *emancipating* the Catholics; it was to stave off that question of emancipation that they had proposed the trifling concession in question; but to give such a pledge as he required (a pledge which *had*, however, been given him by Mr. Pitt), would have been contrary to their duty as Ministers of State, and to their oath as Privy-Councillors, who swear "faithfully and truly to declare their mind and opinion, according to their hearts and consciences, in all things to be moved, treated, and debated in council." Before the resignation, however, several debates took place. In one of these, Mr. Plunket, making his first speech in an united Parliament, brought under the notice of the House the singular proceedings of the Duke of Cumberland. He said:—

"Not satisfied with their placards, &c., an attempt has been made by the Chancellor of the University of Dublin (the Duke of Cumberland) to disturb the peace of that University, by endeavouring to procure a petition against the Catholic bill. Finding (to the honour of that learned body) the first application unsuccessful, a second had been sent, in which it was intimated, that the only way to preserve the favour of the royal Duke was by signing such a petition. He was not aware whether the latter application took place after the measure had been abandoned in Parliament or before. If after, it was a political scheme to support the new administration; if while the bill was pending, it was an unconstitutional and unwarrantable interference."

The matter ended with the resignation of Ministers, and the installation of the famous "No-Popery" Cabinet, with the pious Perceval at its head as Chancellor of the Exchequer. Lord Castlereagh, who had become indispensable to the councils of his sovereign, was Secretary for the Colonies and the War Department; Lord Camden was President of the Privy-Council; and George Canning, Secretary for Foreign Affairs. Lord Eldon was Lord Chancellor of England; the Duke of Richmond, Lord-Lieutenant of Ireland; and the Chief Secretary of that country was to be the victor of Assaye, and conqueror of the Mahrattas, who had just returned after his brilliant campaign in India. The Baron Sutton was created Lord Manners, and appointed Chancellor of Ireland.

The occasion or pretext for this change of Ministry was so absurd, and gave such an impression of craziness, that many members of both Houses of Parliament were unwilling to resign themselves and the country to be governed by the fitful caprices of an idiot; and several efforts were made by offering resolutions against the principle of the required *pledge* to keep Ministers in their places. Of the Parliamentary debates on these resolutions, it is only material in this place to notice such passages as throw any light on Irish affairs. Mr. Tighe, an Irish member, said the tranquillity of Ireland would, he feared, be affected by the removal of the Duke of Bedford. He did not, however, see any ground for apprehending any alarming disturbance, because the people of Ireland had been accustomed to view with cold, determined apathy all changes in administration here, as none of those changes were attended with any benefit to them. Few recruits were to be had in the South, or in the West, because there was no security for the free exercise of religion. Some years ago, a gentleman had got some men in his neighbourhood, upon his own pledge, and the pledge of a magistrate, that they should always be allowed the free exercise of their religion; but when they arrived at their quarters in the Isle of Wight, they were compelled to attend the Protestant worship, and forbidden ever to attend a neighbouring chapel of their own, under pain of military punishment. Consequently, the recruiting proceeded but slowly in Ireland, though the country was poor, and the bounties offered extravagantly high. Since the Union, Ireland had felt no community of rights, no community of commerce; the only community it felt was that of having one hundred assessors in the British Parliament, who were to give *ineffectual votes for the interest of their country, as he might do that night*.

Mr. Tighe's estimate of the value of Irish representation at Westminster remains true at this day.

Sir John Newport (as he and his friends were going out, and were not to be responsible for pledges) showed in his speech a sacred regard for "pledges." He said: "Ireland would force itself upon the consideration of the House and of the empire, of which it was a vital part; it was in vain to overlook the wants and interests, the expectations and the rights of Ireland; it was in vain to trifle with the pledges given; Ireland must have its weight, for it must be felt that the common enemy could not be resisted without Ireland. The pledge, given under the authority of the noble lord opposite, could not be evaded, though the noble lord may not act as it required him. The noble duke at the head of the present government had given a still stronger pledge. He had written two letters to two officers of the Irish Brigades, inviting them to enter into the service of this country, on the promise of making the Irish Act of 1793 general, and further, of opening the whole military career to them."

In Ireland, these Ministerial changes caused a great commotion among the Catholics. Their committee had drawn up their petition for complete Emancipation, and had sent it to Mr. Grattan for presentation. He had consulted with the friends of their cause in London, particularly with Sheridan, and wrote to the committee that they had better withhold it. A Catholic meeting was then held, at which the venerable John Keogh moved the postponement—not abandonment—of further proceedings upon their petition. As to the paltry measure of conciliation which had been proposed by Government, and which the Catholics had not petitioned for at all, Mr. Keogh thus truly described it: "The English Ministers resolved to encourage our Catholic gentlemen to enter into the army and navy, and through their influence to induce our peasantry to enter the service in great numbers. One of their objects they admit to be *to lessen our population*, and, on the whole, to change disorder and weakness into subordination and strength. But candour must compel us to allow that this bill would not have given them any great claim for gratitude from the Catholics; *to relieve them was not the object of the bill;* it did not profess to admit them to the privileges of their country. It has been called a boon to the Catholics; but, in truth, had it been carried into effect, it would have been a boon given by the Catholics; the boon of their blood, to defend a constitution from which they, and they only, were cautiously excluded."

Yet Mr. Keogh praised warmly the Ministry who had attempted to grant even this "boon;" and proposed that, from respect to them, and in deference to the advice of Mr. Grattan and other friends, their petition for Emancipation should not then be presented. This motion was opposed by Mr. O'Gorman, but sustained by the potent voice of Daniel O'Connell, who spoke on this occasion with a warm and filial regard of the veteran Catholic agitator, John Keogh, and his long services to the cause. The resolution to postpone was carried; the committee was dissolved; and Lord Fingal was deputed to present a respectful address to the Duke of Bedford; although how His Grace merited any confidence or gratitude from the Irish Catholics it would now be difficult to explain. The whole policy of his administration had been directed to keep back their claim for Emancipation, and to preserve the Orange Ascendancy in its oppressive domination.

Yet the Duke *seemed* to be removed from office upon a question which touched the Catholics, though ever so little. The Orangemen were excited against him; party spirit had been roused; and such zealous partizans are the Irish populace, and so grateful for any presumed kind intention, that the Dublin mob absolutely took out the horses from the Duke's carriage and from the Duchess's carriage, yoked some of themselves to the carriages, and drew them to the water side, where they embarked for England on the 21st of April, 1807.

CHAPTER XIV.

1807—1808.

Duke of Richmond Viceroy—Sir A. Wellesley, Secretary—Their System—Depression of Catholics—Insolence of Orangemen—Government Interference in Elections—Ireland gets a New Insurrection Act—And an Arms Act—Grattan Advocates Coercion Acts—Sheridan Opposes them—Acts Passed—The Bishop of Quimper—Means used to Create Exasperation Against Catholics—"Shanavests" and "Caravats"—"Church in Danger"—Catholic Petition—Influence of O'Connell—Lord Fingal—Growing Liberality amongst Protestants—Maynooth Grant Curtailed—Doctor Duigenan Privy Councillor—Catholic Petition Presented—The "Veto" Offered—Mr. Ponsonby and Mr. Grattan—They Urge the *Veto* as a Security—Petition Rejected—Controversies on the *Veto*—Bishops' Resolutions—No Catholics in Bank of Ireland—Dublin Police.

THE Duke of Richmond had arrived in Dublin, as Lord-Lieutenant, a few days before his predecessor left it.

As the new administration had accepted office immediately after the King had required a pledge from his Ministers that no Catholic claims or rights or wrongs should *ever* be mentioned to him again, this acceptance of office was itself a pledge to that effect by the new advisers of the Crown; and, so far as they were concerned, they certainly redeemed the pledge. They were professedly a "No-Popery" Cabinet; and the first principle of their policy was resistance to all reform, and especially to all concession to Catholics. Such being their merits, the Viceroy and his Secretary, Sir Arthur Wellesley, were at once presented by the Dublin Corporation with the freedom of the city in a gold and in a silver box respectively. The vote was accompanied by an enthusiastic speech of the notorious Mr. John Giffard, who said, this was not the mere compliment of custom, but a special recognition of their known determination "to maintain the Constitution in Church and State"—that is, the Protestant Ascendancy, and the exclusion and debasement of Catholics.

It may well be understood that this event aggravated the insolence of Orange magistrates and squires all over the island, making the lot of the Catholic country people still more bitter than before; and that it caused despondency, irritation, and some degree of disorganization amongst the Catholic leaders, who were striving in such hopeless circumstances for the civil rights of their countrymen. It would be difficult to conceive any political prospect more gloomy than that of the Catholic body at that moment; dreading the rigour of the new administration, with its ferocious Orange supporters, and reduced to be thankful to the outgoing Ministers for attempting a paltry army reform, avowedly intended to diminish the Catholic population. This is the first time—seven years after the Union—that we first find British Ministers urging the depopulation of the island; a policy which has since been prosecuted with such eminent success.

The new Parliament opened in June. In the elections which preceded it the Government made unusual exertions to secure a large majority. Of the nature of the influences employed in Ireland for this purpose one example may suffice. Soon after the House met, Mr. Whitbread stated, from a paper which he produced to the House, that Mr. Ormsby, the Solicitor for the Forfeited Estates in Ireland, went down to the election for Wexford County, and personally waited on Mr. James Grogan, for the purpose of influencing him to support the Ministerial candidates, by a promise of a restoration to the family of all the estates of his late brother, Cornelius Grogan, which had been forfeited. Ministers neither denied nor blamed, nor offered to investigate the fact, or punish the delinquent. Mr. Perceval assured Lord Howick that he had never before heard of it; and Sir Arthur Wellesley declared that the Government of Ireland had given *no instructions* to Mr. Ormsby on the subject; and any improper use of such influence was unknown to Government. The actual abuse of the Government influence, the overt negotiation of their confidential servant, and his subsequent impunity, tell the whole story plainly enough.

The first Act passed for Ireland in this Parliament was a new "Insurrection Act." The second was an "Arms Act." They were brought in by Sir Arthur Wellesley; and it appeared on the debates that they had been actually framed by the late Grenville administration, but there had not been time to pass them. The Duke of Bedford and Mr. Secretary Elliott had recommended, and now supported them—yet the Dublin people had harnessed themselves to Lord Bedford's carriage! So easily won, by even pretended kindness, are our generous hearted countrymen; and so minute is the difference between Whigs and Tories!

The "Insurrection Act" renewed the power of the Lord-Lieutenant to proclaim disturbed counties, and the authority of the magistrates to arrest persons who should be found out of their dwellings between sunsetting and sunrising. There was a clause enacting "that magistrates might have the power to enter any houses, *or authorize any persons*, by warrant, to do so, at any time from —— after sunset to sunrise, from which they should suspect the inhabitants, or any of them, to be then absent, and cause absent persons to be apprehended, and deemed idle and disorderly, unless they could prove they were absent upon their lawful occupations."

Many persons thought it singular to find Mr. Grattan, then member for Dublin, supporting this coercion law; but, in truth, it was quite consistent with his former course; he had supported the former Insurrection Act, and Gunpowder Act, in the Irish Parliament. Nobody could have a greater horror of revolutionary movements, and of French principles, than Grattan; and Mr. Elliott, the late Secretary, assured him that the poor "Threshers" were at bottom no other than *Jacobins*. He said on this occasion:—

"He understood from his Right Honourable friend beside him (Mr. Elliott) *that there were secret meetings of a dark and dangerous description in Ireland.* This formed a ground for the bill. He was afraid of a French interest in Ireland, and he wished that Government should be furnished with the means, not merely of resisting, but of extirpating that interest, wherever and whenever it should appear."

But his support of so cruel a measure greatly alienated his friends in Ireland. To do him justice, he vehemently objected to the clause authorizing magistrates to enter houses by night, on suspicion, or to give a warrant for that purpose to *any one* who might say he had a suspicion. "But who," he exclaimed, "were the persons to be vested with the power? Perhaps some lawless miscreant—some vagabond. Perhaps the discretion of that reasonable time was to be lodged in the bosom of some convenient menial, some postilion, coachman, ostler, or ploughboy, who, under the sanction of the law, was to judge when it would be a reasonable time for him to rush into the apartment of a female, while she was hastily throwing on her clothes, to open the door to this midnight visitor. This would give a wound that would be felt long."

Richard Brinsley Sheridan, to his honour be it said, went against his friend and most of his party upon this question. "His Right Honourable friend had said that the measure could only be justified by an imperious necessity. Now, it was that necessity which he wished to have clearly made out to exist, before the measure was resorted to. It was no answer to him that the measure had been prepared by his friends. If it had, the Threshers were then engaged in their disturbances, and administering unlawful oaths. Ireland was now as loyally tranquil as any part of the empire. Would they state in the preamble of the bill, 'Whereas a very small part of Ireland was some time ago disturbed by the Threshers, and whereas that disturbance has been completely put down by the ordinary course of the law, and Ireland is now completely tranquil, be it therefore enacted, &c., That most extraordinary powers, &c.'?"

The bill passed into law, however, with all its clauses; and by continual renewals (for it is always *temporary*, like the Mutiny Act), it has been substantially the law of Ireland even to this day.

Next came the Arms Bill. It was the needful complement of the other; for if the people were not very carefully deprived of arms, it was known that they would not submit to the daily and nightly outrages which were intended to be perpetrated upon them under the "Insurrection Act." But while the latter was to be contingent upon the Viceroy's proclamation, the Arms Act was universal, and was to operate at once.

Mr. Sheridan opposed this measure also. He said that if the former bill seemed odious in its form and substance, this was ten thousand times more so; it was really abominable. But at the same time, as if it were meant to make the measure both odious and ridiculous, it was so constructed as that it would plunder the people of their arms, and put down the trade of a blacksmith. Nothing like a blacksmith was to exist in Ireland, lest he might possibly form something like a pike. If ever there was an instance in which the liberties of a loyal people were taken from them, and they were thereby tempted to become disloyal, it was the present. Indeed, from the general spirit in which the bill was framed, he thought there only wanted a clause to make it high treason for any man to communicate either of these bills to Napoleon Buonaparte, Emperor of the French, lest he should conceive them to be direct invitations to him to visit that part of His Majesty's empire.

On the 14th of August, Mr. Sheridan moved for a serious Parliamentary inquiry into the state of Ireland. Mr. Perceval eagerly opposed the motion; earnestly deprecated "the *time* and the spirit " of Mr. Sheridan's motion; and got rid of it by the "previous question."

Thus, at the moment when Catholics were told to despair of ever being admitted to the privileges of the Constitution, they were to be disarmed and coerced on suspicion and hearsay; and all inquiry into the causes of their discontent was refused, because the right time had not come. And, in fact, it has never come. We have said the *Catholics* were to be disarmed and coerced; for although no religious distinction is made in the Acts, yet every one knew then, as now, that such laws are never enforced against a Protestant, unless it be, perhaps, some Protestant like Mr. Wilson, the Tyrone magistrate, who makes himself obnoxious by standing up for his Catholic neighbours.

The stern and eternal negative put upon Catholic claims soon reached France. A certain Bishop of Quimper, in a pastoral to his flock, very naturally drew a striking contrast between the intolerance of England and the regard for religion and absolute toleration shown by the Emperor's Government.* These remarks were, in the eyes of the English Government, a development of the most infamous French principles, or rather a proof of a Franco-Irish conspiracy. Indeed, nothing ever has so bitterly provoked the British public and its Government, as when the eloquent tongue of some illustrious French prelate proclaims aloud the shocking truth about Irish rule, and pours forth the hot torrent of sacred indignation upon the deliberate, cold-blooded atrocities of England.†

Upon the slender foundation of the Bishop of Quimper's pastoral, Government underlings engrafted a most base fabrication, for the double purpose of raising indignation against the French, and of throwing *odium* upon the body of the Irish Catholics. The Government prints gave out that a very important document, pregnant with danger to this country, signed by Napoleon and Talleyrand, had fallen into the hands of his Majesty's Ministers, together with a document of still more importance to the Catholic cause in Ireland, asserted to have been

---

* The good Bishop of Quimper says, amongst other things: "He (the Emperor) shall hear the acclamations of your gratitude and your love. They will prove to the eternal enemy of the glory and prosperity of France that all her perfidious intrigues will never be able to alienate from him your religious and faithful hearts. For a moment she had seduced you—at that unhappy epoch when anarchy ravaged this desolated land, and when its impious furies overturned your temples and profaned your altars. She only affected concern for the re-establishment of your holy religion in order to rend and ravage your country. See the sufferings which England inflicts upon Ireland, which is Catholic like you, and subject to her dominion! The three last ages present only the affecting picture of a people robbed of all their religious and civil rights. In vain the most enlightened men of that nation have protested against the tyrannical oppression. A new persecution has ravished from them even the hope of seeing an end to their calamities. An inflamed and misled (the English) people dares applaud such injustice. It insults with sectarian fanaticism the Catholic religion, and its venerable chief; and it is that Government, which knows not how to be just towards its own subjects, and dares to calumniate this, which has given us security and honour. Whilst the Irish Catholics groan beneath laws so oppressive, our august Emperor does not confine himself to the protection and establishment of that religion in his own states. He demanded, in his treaty with Saxony, that it should there enjoy the same liberty as other modes of worship."

† It is but a very few years since Monsieur Dupanloup, the eloquent Bishop of Orleans, having given out that he was about to preach a charity sermon for the relief of the exterminated Irish, Lord Plunket, Bishop of Tuam, wrote to Monsieur d'Orleans that he knew he was going to libel *him*, and fling foul slanders upon him. Efforts were even made through the English Embassy to induce the Emperor to forbid the sermon. It was preached, however, to a vast assemblage, and though his grace of Tuam was not slandered nor named in the discourse, yet it was a most scathing and touching *exposé* of the whole course of British policy in Ireland. The English press was bitterly indignant.

solemnly issued from the Vatican. It was falsely asserted that the Pope had lately issued a bull, addressed to the titular bishops of Ireland, exhorting them in the most forcible terms to excite in the minds of all people of the Roman Catholic persuasion under their influence and direction, an ardent devotion to the views and objects of Buonaparte, and an expectation that by his assistance and protection they might eventually obtain an uncontrolled exercise of their rights, religious and political. It was also stated that this address from the Roman Pontiff was accompanied by another paper, containing a solemn declaration on the part of the French ruler, that it was his firm determination to give the Roman Catholic religion the ascendancy in Ireland.

By foul means such as these the "No-Popery" cry was stimulated to its most savage pitch of bloodthirsty ferocity. Even the rural organizations, calling themselves "Shanavests" and "Caravats," which arose this year in Tipperary, and who were nothing in the world but White Boys and Threshers, under local names, were carefully given out to be secret political societies, which were going to bring in the French. In truth, those unhappy people had their thoughts much more occupied about the tithe-proctor than about the Emperor Napoleon; and knew more about county-cess than about French principles. Unfortunately, however, the Shanavests and Caravats were not *one* agrarian faction, but two; and sometimes, when they ought to have been threshing the tithe-corn, they threshed each other at fair and market. Mr. Plowden says:—

"Both parties seemed to be indiscriminately sore at the payment of tithes; both complained of the exorbitancy of the advanced demands of rack-rents for lands out of lease. Both manifested symptoms of a natural and interested attachment to the soil they had occupied, by their undisguised hostility to every competitor for the farms of the old occupiers. They had not then begun (as they were afterwards charged) to fix a general rate of tithe and rent, and to enforce the observance of it by threats of visiting those who should dare to exceed it. They assumed no appellation expressive of, or appropriate to, any of those objects which they have since pursued to the disgrace and disturbance of the country. When the Insurrection and Arms bills passed into law, it is no less true than singular that in all the counties then said to be disturbed, *not a single charge* was to be found on the calendar *of sedition or insurgency* at the preceding assizes. Widely as the Threshers had extended their outrages, they had been completely put down and tranquillized by the arm of the common law, without recourse to the violent measure of suspending the Constitution. The objects of their outrages had been ascertained by the judges who had gone into the disturbed parts on the late special commission; and not even a spurious whisper had reached their ears that there was amongst them anything describable as an *existing French party*."

These miserable writhings of a crushed peasantry under the heel of local tyrants, were, however, eagerly seized and dwelt upon, as both justifying the coercion bills, and exhibiting the unchangeable, ineradicable wickedness of Papists; so that when Parliament met, on the 21st of January, 1808, *No Popery!* and *Church in Danger!* rung fiercely through the three kingdoms.

Two days before Parliament assembled, there was a large meeting of Catholics in Dublin, Lord Fingal in the chair. On motion of Count Dalton, it was resolved to petition Parliament for the repeal of the remaining Penal laws. Some gentlemen, as Mr. O'Connor, of Belanagare, moved an adjournment of the meeting, as they despaired of any success under the existing *regime;* but O'Connell, who now constantly attended these meetings, and took a leading part in them, had already adopted his well-known maxim—*Agitate! agitate!* He supported the resolution to petition; so did John Byrne, of Mullinahack. The resolution of adjournment was withdrawn, and that for a petition unanimously passed. O'Connell's influence was, even thus early, very powerful in softening down irritation, soothing jealousies, and inspiring self-abnegation for the sake of the common cause. It was this great quality, not less than his commanding ability, which made him soon afterwards the acknowledged head of the Catholic cause.

The petition was intrusted to Lord Fingal, who went to London and asked Lord Grenville and Mr. Grattan to present it, after the Duke of Portland, to whom it was first offered, had coldly refused to have anything to do with it. And humiliating enough it must have been to that peer of ancient race to be obliged to hawk round among "Liberal" members of both Houses the humble petition of himself and his countrymen to be admitted to the common civil rights of human beings, and to see the representative of one of King William's Dutchmen turn his back upon the importunity of the Irish Papist.

Nothing came of this petition. It was laid on the table of the Lords; but when Mr. Grattan offered it in the Commons, the sharp eyes of Canning and Perceval detected an informality—several of the names appeared to be written in the same handwriting—a fatal objection, as they insisted, and the petition was not received. Evidently the right way had not yet been discovered to command the attention of that House to Catholic claims; and it was not till twenty-one years later that the right way was suddenly found out by O'Connell.

It is agreeable to have here to record that the furious bigotry of the Ministry, and the studied excitations to religious animosity, were not responded to by the Irish Protestants altogether as had been expected. The Duke of Cumberland had entirely failed to induce or intimidate the University of Dublin into petitioning against the Catholic claims, as Oxford had done. The Protestant inhabitants of many of the counties in Ireland presented petitions in favour of the claims of the Catholics. There were nine counties that had shown the noble example of liberality and sound policy. The Counties of Clare and Galway had, at meetings convened by the sheriff, expressed their ardent wish for admitting their Catholic brethren to the benefits of the Constitution. In the Counties of Tipperary, Kilkenny, Roscommon, Waterford, and Meath, and in the town of Newry, resolutions to the same effect were entered into, as well by the Protestant gentry and inhabitants as by the great bulk of Protestant proprietors of land. That recommendation was owing partly to the growing influence of liberality and confidence, partly to the absence of all suspicion of any real intention to invade the landed property of the county on a convenient occasion; but more particularly to the strong and immediate feeling of danger which a divided country would have to encounter in case of hostile invasion. On that principle did wise Protestants deprecate the terrible privilege of an exclusive monopoly of Constitutional right and political power.

The Duke of Cumberland, indeed, had the gratification of presenting to the House of Lords one petition from the Orange Corporation of Dublin against the Catholics; but the example was not generally followed. One reflection arises upon these facts:—That the most potent and unrelenting enemy to the Irish Catholics, *at all times*, was not the Irish Protestants, but the British imperial system. It was the English Parliament, in King William's time, then assuming to bind Ireland by its own acts, which first violated the Treaty of Limerick, by excluding Catholic Peers and Commoners from Parliament. It was while the English Parliament completely controlled the action of that of Ireland (by requiring the heads of bills to be sent over), that the dreadful Penal Code was successively elaborated and maintained in force. But it was Ireland's *free* Parliament which, in 1793, gave the grand shock to that infamous code, admitting Catholics to the bar, to the corporations, to the juries, allowing them to go to school, and to teach school, to bear arms, to own horses, to hold lands in fee, to take degrees in the university;—in short, it was the Irish Protestant Parliament, once free, that swept away in one day five-sixths of the oppressions, penalties, and disabilities accumulated and piled upon the Catholics during a whole century, by the unappeasable hate of England.

This accounts for O'Connell's frequent declaration that, rather than remain in the Union, he would gladly take back the Irish Protestant Parliament, consent to repeal of Catholic Emancipation, and take his chance with his Irish fellow-countrymen. And O'Connell was right.

Two of the first things recommended for Ireland by the Duke of Richmond were, the curtailment of the Maynooth Grant, and the appointment of Doctor Duigenan to a seat on the Irish Privy-Council. The whole spirit of the Perceval administration is apparent in these two examples. Doctor Duigenan had devoted his life to raking up all the vile, forgotten slanders that had ever been heaped upon Catholics since the days of Calvin; and was never so much in his element as when pouring forth his foul collection by the hour in a full-foaming stream of ribald abuse. The appointment of such a man to such a place was a public affront and a significant warning to Catholics, showing them in what estimation they and their claims were held by the new Government.

The other pitiful manifestation of No-Popery spite was cutting down the appropriation for Maynooth College. This was evidently a subject of difference and discussion in the Cabinet. Mr. Foster, Chancellor of the Irish Exchequer, in Committee on the Supplies, stated that additional buildings were in progress at Maynooth; that the establishment was capable of accommodating two hundred and fifty students; and that it was his intention to move that the sum of £9,250 should be granted to that Institution for the current year. Sir John Newport moved that it should be £13,000, which was the annual grant fixed by the late administration, as will be remembered, in their alarm lest the Irish College of Paris should again attract Irish pupils. A warm debate ensued. Mr. Perceval, as a matter of course, opposed the larger grant upon strictly evangelical principles; so did William Wilberforce (a gentleman whose sympathies were strongly excited by the degradation of oppressed people, provided they were of a black colour). General Mathew, a good and generous Irishman, earnestly supported the proposal to grant the larger sum.

He had been, within the last ten days, at Maynooth, and he could assure the House that, unless the whole of the last year's grant should be voted, the buildings upon which former grants had been expended would fall. There was no lead on the roofs, and the rain penetrated through them. He alluded to the offer made by order of Napoleon, to induce Irish students to go for education to France from Lisbon and Ireland, upon a promise of the restoration of all the Irish *Bourses;* and read an extract from the answer of the Irish Catholic bishops, stating their gratitude to the Government for the liberal support of Maynooth, and denouncing suspension against any functionaries, and exclusion from preferment in Ireland against any students, who should accept the offers of the enemy of their own country. Would any one say after that that the Catholics were not to be confided in? If they were not to be trusted, why not dismiss them from the army and navy? Why allow them to vote at elections?

But this was not the act of Ministers. He was sorry to be obliged to allude to the conduct of any of the Royal family. But, however, it was rumoured that even Ministers were disposed to agree to the grant, till they went to St. James's Palace, and were closeted for several hours with a royal Duke, after which they resorted to the present reduction. That royal Duke was the Chancellor of the University of Dublin; he was Chancellor of a Protestant school, and might wish to put down the education of the Catholics: but no man who knew or valued Ireland as he did himself, could countenance such a project.

Ministers, however, had a sure majority, and succeeded in cutting down the proposed grant to Maynooth. One can only wonder that the Catholic body, clergy and laity, persisted in such an obstinate "loyalty" to the British Government, and did not turn to France, and hearken to the liberal invitation of the Emperor Napoleon.

Amongst the bitter opponents of the Maynooth Grant was Dr. Duigenan, the new Privy-Councillor, who was member for an Irish borough. He vented some of the venom, of which he had plenty, upon his Catholic countrymen; said they were always traitors in theory, and wanted but the opportunity to be traitors in action. This gave rise to some sharp debating.

Mr. Barham could not contain his execration of such scandalous and wicked sentiments. This drew from Mr. Tierney the question to Mr. Perceval, Whether the official order for making Doctor Duigenan a Privy-Councillor had been sent over to Ireland? On a negative answer from the Chancellor of the Exchequer, Sir A. Wellesley apprised the House that the Right Honourable and learned gentleman had been specially recommended by the Lord-Lieutenant to be a Privy-Councillor, as from his knowledge of ecclesiastical business he could be of great service in Ireland in that situation. This induced Mr. Barham on a subsequent day to move the House, That a humble address be presented to His Majesty, praying that he would order to be laid before the House copies of the extracts of the correspondence which passed between the Lord-Lieutenant of Ireland and the Government of England, as to the appointment of Doctor Patrick Duigenan to a seat in the Privy-Council of Ireland. The question being put, Mr. W. Wynne said he was anxious to hear a vindication of so extraordinary an appointment, and one which was so much lamented. He then alluded to the dismissal and subsequent advancement of Mr. Giffard, and considered the present only as a fresh endeavour to irritate the feelings of the Catholics of Ireland. Sir A. Wellesley repeated that applications had been made to Government here to grant to the learned Doctor, as Judge of the Prerogative Court, the office of member of the Privy-Council. Till the time of his predecessor this had been the uniform custom, and it was now resorted to again as a matter of convenience. He believed that the present session was the first time it had been attempted to be argued, that because a man was friendly to the Church he ought not to be trusted. If the honourable and learned Doctor had been indiscreet in his language, why was it not taken down at that time, and complaint made to that House? *He did not care of what religion a man was.* If he could be useful in any line, in that line, he was of opinion, he ought to be employed.

There is no doubt that Sir Arthur Wellesley was quite sincere in these declarations. He did not care of what religion a man was; he was always a practical person; he desired, in a privy-councillor, as in a staff-officer or a commissary, precisely such qualities as were serviceable for the business in hand; and as the business in hand at that moment was to trample down and humiliate the Catholics, he approved of Dr. Duigenan for Privy-Councillor.

The Catholic petition, which had been rejected by the House of Commons on a point of form, had been sent back to Ireland to be signed anew. In the meantime Lord Fingal remained in London, and had frequent interviews with the friends of the Catholics, particularly with Mr. Ponsonby. It was now that the delicate subject of the *veto* first took a tangible shape. Lord Fingal was an amiable, high-minded, and unsuspicious man; but a weak one. The success of the petition, he was assured by the friends of the Catholic cause, would be greatly forwarded by an admission of the royal *veto* in the nomination of the Irish prelacy. This negotiation, which has since produced effects of great national importance, though then unforeseen, was of a private nature; and the particulars of it would not have reached the public had not subsequent events induced the parties to it to make them public. Never was a point of *politico-theological* controversy so fiercely contested, and, consequently, so misconceived and misrepresented, as this question of *veto*. Lord Fingal had certainly received no specific instruction concerning it from the Catholic meeting, which voted him the sole delegate, guardian, and manager of their petition; and the subject of a *veto* was not in contemplation at that meeting.

The history of this affair proves, in a most striking manner, how dangerous it is for any national Church, in matters affecting its discipline, government, and independence, to take counsel of any one outside of itself. In the present case Lord Fingal, only anxious for the emancipation of his countrymen, and credulous enough to believe that the English Parliament would grant it upon fair terms, without the strongest coercion, acted by the advice of Doctor Milner, an English Vicar-Apostolic, and author of a learned controversial work; and as Doctor Milner was a kind of agent in England for the Irish bishops, though not with any such purpose as this, the two together took it upon them to authorize Mr. Ponsonby and Mr Grattan (as both those gentlemen affirmed) to reinforce the prayer of the Catholic petition by offering the *veto* power to the Crown.

The petition having returned from Ireland duly signed, was presented by Mr. Grattan on the 25th of May. The only remarkable passage in his speech is that in which he proposes the *veto*. He said:—

"The influence of the Pope, so far, was purely spiritual, and did not extend even to the appointment of the members of his Catholic hierarchy. They nominated themselves, and looked to the Pope but for his spiritual sanction of such nomination. But if it should be supposed that there was the smallest danger in this course, he had a proposition to suggest, which he had authority to state, which indeed he was instructed to make—namely, that His Majesty may interfere upon any such occasion with his negative. This would have the effect of preventing any Catholic ecclesiastic being advanced to the government of that Church in Ireland, who was not politically approved of by the Government of that country."

Mr. Ponsonby, in supporting the petition, made the same proposal; and said he did so upon the authority of Doctor Milner, who was a Catholic bishop in England, and who was authorized by the Catholic bishops of Ireland to make the proposition, in case the measure of Catholic Emancipation should be acceded to. The proposition, he said, was this: That the person to be nominated to a vacant bishopric should be submitted to the King's approbation; and that, if the approbation were refused, another person should be proposed, and so on, in succession, until His Majesty's approbation should be obtained, so that the appointment should finally rest with the King.

Mr. Perceval, as might have been expected, earnestly and prayerfully opposed Mr. Grattan's motion, and all other possible concession to Papists, whether on the condition of *veto* or any other condition. Not that he would be averse, he said, from giving contentment to his Catholic brethren, whom he loved, as a Christian, as much as any man; and "should not conceive himself precluded from supporting their claims under different circumstances, in the event, for instance, *of a change taking place in the Catholic religion itself.*" On the division upon Mr. Grattan's motion, the Minister had a majority of one hundred and fifty-three—one hundred and twenty-eight having voted for going into committee, and two hundred and eighty-one against it.

Lord Grenville presented the same petition in the Lords, made the same offer of the *veto*, and the petition met the same fate as in the Commons.

These debates at once raised an immense controversy, both in England and in Ireland, which lasted many years; and produced innumerable books and pamphlets, discussing the limits between spiritual and temporal power, the meaning of loyalty, and of the oath of supremacy, and the "liberties of the Gallican Church"—which ought rather to be termed the "Slavery of the Gallican Church," because it means the subordination of the government of that Church to the civil power. *That* civil power, indeed, is native and not foreign; but when it comes to be a question of subordinating the government of the Catholic Church in Ireland to a Protestant King of England, one must only wonder that even the eagerness for civil emancipation could ever have made any Irish Catholic entertain such an idea for a moment. Into the merits of the question we do not here enter; but it is matter of history that when Mr. Pitt and Lord Castlereagh were intriguing for support to the Union, in 1799, they had deluded certain Irish bishops into accepting the principle of the *veto*, by holding out to them the bait of immediate Emancipation after the Union.*

* The Rev. Mr. Brenan, in his *Ecclesiastical History of Ireland*, narrates the circumstances thus:—
"During the course of that year, ten of the Irish bishops, constituting the Board of Maynooth College, happened to be convened in Dublin, on the arrangement of some ecclesiastical business, when Lord Castlereagh, then Secretary for Ireland, availed himself of their presence, and submitted for their adoption two vitally momentous measures, originating from the British Ministry.†

"By the first of these it was proposed, that His Majesty should be invested with the power of a veto in all future ecclesiastical promotions within this kingdom; and agreeably to the second, the Catholic clergy of Ireland were to receive a pension out of the treasury; at the same time, assurances were solemnly pledged by Government that, on the acquiescence of the Irish hierarchy in these State measures, the fate of that great national question, Catholic Emancipation, entirely depended. Thus beset by the proffers of the Minister on the one hand, and by the alarming posture of the country on the other, the bishops already alluded to agreed, 'That in the appointment of Roman Catholic prelates to vacant sees within the kingdom, such interference of Government as may enable it to be satisfied of the loyalty of the person appointed is just, and ought to be agreed to.' This statement was accompanied with an admission, 'That a provision, through Government, for the Roman Catholic clergy of this kingdom, competent and secured, ought to be thankfully accepted.'"

This transaction remained a secret for many years. Mr. Plowden speaks of "the long and mys-

† The prelates composing the board were as follows:—Richard O'Reilly, R.C.A.B., Armagh; J. T. Troy, R.C.A.B., Dublin; Edward Dillon, R.C.A.B., Tuam; Thomas Bray, R.C.A.B., Cashel; P. J. Plunkett, R.C.B., Meath; F. Moylan, R.C.B., Cork; Daniel Delaney, R.C.B., Kildare; Edmund French, R.C.B., Elphin; James Caulfield, R.C.B., Ferns; John Cruise, R.C.B., Ardagh.

The alarm and indignation excited in Ireland, both amongst clergy and laity, by the *veto* project, were quite vehement. The conscientious Catholic historian, Plowden, says:—

"The prospective view of a national religion, preserved with a virtuous hierarchy, without any *civil* establishment or State interference, through three centuries of oppression and persecution, produced alarm in every reflecting mind. The proposed innovation of introducing *Royal and Protestant* connection, influence, and power into the constitution and perpetuation of a Catholic hierarchy, to the utter exclusion of which the Irish Catholics ascribed that almost miraculous preservation, threw the public mind into unusual agitation. The laity abhorred the idea of the ministers of their religion becoming open to Court influence and intrigue, and shuddered at the prospect of prostituting the sacred function of that apostolic mission and jurisdiction, to which they had hitherto submitted as of divine institution, to its revilers, persecutors, and sworn enemies. At the same time, the whole Catholic clergy of Ireland were driven by a common electric impulse into more than ordinary reflection upon the stupendous efficacy of that evangelical purity and independence by which the spiritual pastors had so long, and under such temptations and difficulties, preserved their flocks in the religion of their Christian ancestors.

"The general voice of the people crying out against religious reform, was an awful warning to the clergy, and although the insidious concordat of 1799 was still clothed in darkness, the Irish Catholic prelates met in regular National Synod on the 14th and 15th of September, 1808, in Dublin, and came to the following resolutions:—

"It is the decided opinion of the Roman Catholic prelates of Ireland, that it is inexpedient to introduce any alteration in

terious suppression from the knowledge of the Catholic body of the resolutions of the Clerical Trustees of Maynooth College in 1799, which never came fully to light till 1810. It is not surprising," he adds, "that respectable prelates should wish to conceal them from the eyes of the public, and particularly of such of their friends as they wished to engage in their cause, and whose esteem and confidence they subsequently courted. They were the base offspring of their unguarded connection with Mr. Pitt, whilst he was meditating the Union; which they have been sorely lamenting from the hour they found themselves swindled out of the stipulated price of their seduction."

It should be stated, in justice to Doctor Milner, that, after the use of his name in Parliament, as authorizing the offer of a *veto*, he published a statement that he had no authority to sanction such an offer; and that he had been misquoted. After the Irish bishops passed their synodical resolutions, there was no more ardent opponent of the *v. to* than Doctor Milner.

the canonical mode hitherto observed in the nomination of the Irish Roman Catholic bishops, which mode long experience has proved to be unexceptionable, wise, and salutary.

"That the Roman Catholic prelates pledge themselves to adhere to the rules by which they have been hitherto uniformly guided; namely, to recommend to His Holiness only such persons as are of unimpeachable loyalty and peaceable conduct." These Synodical resolutions were signed by twenty-three prelates. Three only (they were three of those who had signed the resolutions of 1799) dissented.*

Immediately were held many meetings of Catholics throughout Ireland, who, by their resolutions and addresses, protested vehemently against the whole project of *veto*, and thanked the bishops for their firm resolutions. When the real nature of the proposal was explained and fully known, the Catholics of Ireland indignantly resolved rather to remain unemancipated than suffer their Church to be enthralled. O'Connell was a strong opponent of the *veto* from the first; the more active and educated of the laity repulsed the plan with scorn; the press teemed with pamphlets, of which none made so much impression as the republication of Burke's *Letter to a Peer* in Ireland, in which he treats of a similar project, of giving the Crown a voice in the nomination of Catholic bishops.†

The project of enslaving the Irish Catholic Church to the English Protestant State was for that time defeated, but it was brought forward again and again during the struggle for Emancipation, and for many years greatly agitated the Catholic public.

In the course of this session Lord Grenville made his motion to make Catholic merchants admissible as Governor and Directors of the Bank of Ireland. Lord Westmoreland opposed the motion on the general ground that *no further concessions whatever should, under the present circumstances, be granted to the Catholics.* But to this not very intelligent argument his lordship added a sensible observation. He said "he was surprised to see such motions so often brought forward by those who, when they were themselves in power, employed every exertion to deprecate and prevent such discussions." This was true. Ireland and her grievances, the Catholics and their wrongs, had become, in the Imperial Parliament, a stock-in-trade for Whigs out of place, and have so remained ever since. When these politicians are in power they still "deprecate such discussions." Lord Redesdale, late Chancellor of Ireland, was alarmed at the danger to the Protestant interest which would arise from allowing Catholics to be Bank Directors. He said he had only to repeat his former objections to such claims. "The more you were ready to grant them, the more power and pretensions you gave to the Catholics to come forward with *fresh claims*, and *perhaps to insist* upon them." His lordship then launched out into a general invective against the Catholics, and particularly the priests.

This debate about the Bank of Ireland is not, by any means, worth recording (for the motion was rejected, as its mover knew it would be), save to illustrate the party tactics of the Whigs, and the cool and stupid insolence of the "Ascendancy."

The Dublin Police Bill was carried, creating eighteen new places for police magistrates; and Parliament was prorogued on the 8th of July, 1808.

---

* Plowden. *Post-Union History*, p. 395, *et seq.*
† Edmund Burke, who was as warm a friend to his Catholic countrymen as Grattan, and a much wiser friend, says, in his *Letter to a Peer*:—"Never were the members of one religious sect fit to appoint pastors to another. Those who have no regard for their welfare, reputation, or internal quiet, will not appoint such as are proper. The Seraglio of Constantinople is as equitable as we are, whether Catholics or Protestant; and where their own sect is concerned, full as religious; but the sport which they make of the miserable dignities of the Greek Church, the factions of the Harem, to which they make them subservient, the continual sale to which they expose and re-expose the same dignity, and by which they squeeze all the inferior orders of the clergy, is nearly equal to all the other oppressions together exercised by Mussulmen over the unhappy members of the Oriental Church. It is a great deal to suppose that the present Castle would nominate bishops for the Roman Church of Ireland with a religious regard for its welfare. Perhaps they cannot, perhaps dare not, do it." And in another Letter to Doctor Hussey, the Catholic Bishop of Waterford, he said:—"If you (the Catholic bishops) have not wisdom enough to make common cause, they will cut you off one by one. I am sure that the constant meddling of your bishops and clergy *with the Castle, and the Castle with them*, will infallibly set them ill with their own body. All the weight which the clergy have hitherto had to keep the people quiet will be wholly lost if this once should happen. At best you will have a marked schism, and more than one kind, and I am greatly mistaken if this is not intended, and diligently and systematically pursued."

CHAPTER XV.
1808—1809.

The Duke of Richmond's Anti-Catholic Policy—The Orangemen Flourish—Their Outrages and Murders—Castlereagh and Perceval Charged with Selling Seats—Corruption—Sir Arthur Wellesley—Tithes—Catholic Committee Reorganized—John Keogh on Petitioning Parliament—O'Connell and the Convention Act—Orangemen also Re-organized—Orange Convention—More Murders by Orangemen—Crooked Policy of the Castle—Defection of the Bandon Orangemen—Success of the Castle Policy in preventing Union with Irishmen.

The administration of the Duke of Richmond showed a venomous determination to keep down the Catholic people, and to rule the island most strictly through the Orange Ascendancy, and for its profit.

The legislative rejection of the Catholic petition had been aggravated by the restoration of a certain Mr. Jacob, a notorious Orangeman, to the magistracy, the appointment of Mr. Giffard to a more valuable situation than that from which he had been displaced, the admission of Doctor Duigenan to the Privy-Council, and the curtailed grant to Maynooth College. A fostering countenance was given to the Orangemen that tended more to foment and encourage, than to put down or punish, their atrocities.

It is certainly not an agreeable part of our duty to narrate and to dwell upon these Orange outrages, because this helps, more or less, to keep alive the religious animosities between the two religious sects, which was the very object of the English Government in encouraging those outrages. Much more pleasing would it be to draw a veil of oblivion over them, and to think of them no more. But for two reasons this cannot be: first, the modern history of Ireland would be almost a blank page without the villanies of Orange persecution, the complicity of Government in those villanies, and their consequences upon the general well-being of the island; next, because however well inclined to forget those horrors, we have not been permitted to do so for a moment down to the present day. It was as late as 1848 that Lord Clarendon secretly supplied the Orange Lodges with arms; as late as '49 that a magistrate of Down County led a band of Orangemen and policemen to the wrecking and slaughter of a Catholic townland.* Later still, the records of assizes in the northern circuits show us the frequent picture of an Orange murderer shielded from justice by his twelve brethren, who have been carefully packed into the jury-box by a sheriff who is an officer of the Crown. All this odious condition of society being a direct product of British policy, and now flourishing and still bearing its poisonous fruit, a student of Irish history is bound to look at, and to study the wretched details.

On the evening of the 23d of June, 1808, a considerable number of men, women, and children were assembled round a bonfire at Corinshiga, within one mile and a half of the town of Newry. They had a garland, and were amusing themselves, some dancing, others sitting at the fire, perfectly unapprehensive of danger, when, in the midst of their mirth, eighteen *yeomen*, fully armed and accoutred, approached the place, where they were drawn up by their sergeant, who gave them the word of command to "present and fire," which they did, several times leveling at the crowd. One person was killed, many were grievously wounded. The magistrates of Newry, although far from being friendly to the Catholic people, were scandalized at this atrocity. They offered a reward for the discovery of the perpetrators, inclosed a copy of their publication to the Duke of Richmond, and prayed him to take some measures for the protection of the Catholics, who, they said, were all unarmed, while the very lowest class of Protestants were well provided with fire-arms. The Duke made a civil but unmeaning reply, expressing his "regret" at the sad circumstance. Some weeks elapsed, and still no measures were adopted. In the meantime one of the persons concerned in the outrage was apprehended, but was allowed to escape by the yeomen to whose custody Lord Gosford had intrusted him; and a number of the same corps to which the murderers belonged, so far from showing any shame or regret at the conduct of their comrades, one day returning from parade, fired a volley (by way of *bravado*) over the house of M'Keown (father of the deceased), the report of which threw his wife into convulsions.

Several inhabitants of the townland of Corinshiga came to the magistrates and made depositions as to the continual terror and danger of themselves and their families, and the atrocious threats of the Orange yeomen who lived near them. Mr. Waring, one of the magistrates, who appears to have exerted himself earnestly in this affair, sent to the Castle copies of these depositions, and intreated the Government to issue a proclamation, offering a reward for the assassins, and to take some measures of repressing open outrage.

Mr. Secretary Traill replied coldly that the Government declined to do anything in the matter. Mr. Waring again wrote, still more earnestly, "that the magistrates had expected that Government would have issued a proclamation offering a reward for prosecution, and pardon to some concerned for evidence against the others; that if this had not the desired effect, still much good might be expected to arise from the marked disapprobation of Government of an outrage of so dangerous and alarming a tendency; that it

---

* It is true that the magistrate was dismissed from the Commission. He had somewhat exceeded the intentions of the Castle in getting up a "loyal demonstration." Yet the arms of that banditti had been furnished out of the Castle vaults.

might appear not unworthy the consideration of his Grace whether such a measure might not even then (the 3d of August, 1808) be adopted with propriety; and that this procedure, so far from having a tendency to supersede the exertions of the local magistracy, could not but prove an efficient aid to them." This last letter was not answered, and so the business dropped.* The advertisement or proclamation of the Newry magistrates was sent to the *Hue and Cry*, but was not inserted. Not the least notice was taken of it or the letter accompanying it. Such was the unblushing tenderness of the Duke of Richmond for the band of eighteen Orangemen, each and every one of whom was guilty of open murder. Not one of them was ever brought to justice, and to this day the inhabitants of that and many another Catholic neighbourhood in Ulster, when the anniversaries of the 1st and 12th of July come round, either bar themselves up in their houses and put out all lights, or else prepare for defensive battle.

The foregoing incident is related in detail, because it is a characteristic example of many similar cases; save indeed that the local magistrates, instead of seeking to bring offenders to justice, as in this case, have generally sought to screen them. If an atrocity like this had been at any time done by Catholics, troops would immediately have been sent down to quarter themselves upon their houses, and a special commission would have been issued to hang at least eighteen, guilty or innocent.

It was not merely in the way of direct encouragement to lawless Orangeism that Lord Richmond's administration showed its settled design of trampling down the Catholics. We have seen that in Dublin the wealthiest and most respectable merchants were insultingly kept out of the Bank Direction because they were Catholics. In the counties, Catholic gentlemen, whose property and position entitled them to be called upon the Grand Juries, were studiously excluded. If any High Sheriff of a county was not a supporter of the Ministerial policy, or was known to be favourable to his Catholic neighbours, his name was carefully excluded from the next list. And in all these measures, Sir Arthur Wellesley was unusually active and rigorous. The time, indeed, had almost come when his services would be required in the Spanish Peninsula: and his native country could well spare him.

During this year (1808) corruption seems to have been almost as rife in Ireland as it had been immediately before the Union; and seats in Parliament were bought and sold. Early in the session of 1809 Mr. Maddox brought forward a specific charge of this sort of corruption, criminating Lord Castlereagh and Mr. Spencer Perceval, stating, amongst other things, that at the last general election a sum of money was paid by Mr. Quintin Dick to Lord Castlereagh, through means of the Honourable Henry Wellesley, and that gentleman (Mr. Dick) was thereby returned member for Cashel; and Mr. Spencer Perceval was also a party to the transaction. Upon occasion of the late investigation as to the Duke of York, Mr. Quintin Dick waited upon Lord Castlereagh, and informed him of the vote he meant to give; and the noble lord, not approving of that mode of voting, suggested to him the propriety of relinquishing his seat in Parliament.

Mr. Perceval, indeed, refused to plead to the charge; said it was an insidious plan to lay the foundation for a measure of Parliamentary reform—which it certainly was—and so bowed to the Speaker, and went out. Lord Castlereagh followed his example; but it is quite evident the charge must have been true, otherwise there would not have been, in a House of six hundred and fifteen, in the teeth of all Ministerial influence, the large minority of three hundred and ten for a motion to inquire. There is every reason to believe that Sir Arthur Wellesley, during his Secretaryship, took the largest share in all this traffic for seats and votes and influence. He had a mind of the character usually termed "eminently practical;" and thought he had a right, as he declared long after, speaking of his administration in Ireland, "to turn the moral weakness of individuals to *good* account;" that is, to the account of his party.

In the session of Parliament, in 1809, little or no attention was given to the affairs of Ireland. An attempt was made by Mr. Parnell to carry a motion for inquiry into the mode of collecting tithes in this country. The grievances and oppressions connected with the Church Establishment, and the irritating spoliation of the people, for support of clergymen whose ministrations were of no use to them, were but too well known already, and needed no committee of inquiry at all. On this very ground the motion was opposed by Ministers, who, having no idea whatever of giving any relief or redress, naturally enough refused the empty formality of an inquiry. The Chancellor of the Exchequer "did not think that the House was in ignorance with respect to the subject of

---

* See abstract of the whole correspondence in Plowden's (Volume III.) *Post-Union History.*

tithes in Ireland; but that the difficulty was, how to find out a practical mode of securing the property of the Church. He could not be persuaded that any inquiry, either by commission or committee, would do any good; for they did not *want information.*"

In the short debate on this motion, Sir John Newport observed, that he thought Lord Castlereagh bound, by his former professions at the Union, to find out some modifications to lighten the burdens of the poor oppressed people of Ireland. Instead of doing so, that noble Lord appeared to forget all his pledges for the public good, and merely to attend to those that went to provide for individuals, whom he had taken care to seduce to his own standard. Lord Castlereagh arrogantly asserted that he knew of no pledge made, either by Mr. Pitt or himself, upon the subject of tithes, *or the Catholic question.* He most distinctly denied *that he had ever made any pledge whatever* as to Ireland. Mr. C. Hutchinson deprecated the conduct of Lord Castlereagh as to Ireland. He was the parent of the Union, and in order to effect it he had made many promises; but, whenever any question as to the amelioration of the situation of Ireland came to be agitated, he either put a negative upon it, or moved the previous question. And, in fact, by the "previous question," the whole question was put aside upon this occasion also.

On the 24th of May was held, in Dublin, a numerous meeting of the Catholics, to consider what step they should take to further their claims. The requisition convening the meeting was signed by Lord Netterville, Sir Francis Goold, Daniel O'Connell, Richard O'Gorman, Edward Hay, Denis Scully, Doctor Dromgoole, and many others whose names have since been familiar in connection with the Catholic cause. Mr. O'Gorman opened the proceedings with a speech, in which he proposed to petition Parliament. This was opposed by the veteran John Keogh, who spoke with great bitterness of the treachery practised towards the Catholics in the matter of the Union, and deprecated petitioning altogether, at least while the existing Ministry remained in power. Mr. Keogh observed that, with respect to the existence and oppressiveness of their grievances, they were unanimous, and differed only as to the means most likely to remove them. He was ready, on his part, to sacrifice, to burn with his own hands the resolution which he was about to propose to the meeting, if any man could show him what was likely to be more effectual to promote the object of all their wishes. A petition at the present moment must, if presented, be presented to decided enemies or lukewarm friends, upon neither of whom could be placed any reliance for success. Mr. Perceval and his colleagues were admitted into office upon the express condition of excluding the Catholic claims from the relief of the Legislature; and their predecessors had very willingly consented to give up a bill, nominally only in favour of the Catholics, rather than resign their places. Mr. Keogh adverted in strong and pointed terms to the double imposition practised upon the Catholics at the time of the Union. He insisted that the proposals for their support from the Unionists and the Anti-Unionists were equally hollow and equally insidious. Had it been otherwise, had the Catholics been liberally treated by their Parliament, they would have raised a cry in its defence that would have been heard, and would have shaken the plan of Union to atoms. No man had a right to suppose that he wished to relinquish the Catholic claims. With his dying breath, with his last words, as a testamentary bequest to his countrymen, he would recommend to them never to relinquish, never even to relax, in the pursuit of their undoubted rights. No man could expect success to the petition. Without that expectation, he saw nothing likely to accrue from the measure but mischievous and injurious consequences. He resisted the measure, not for the purpose of retarding, but of forwarding the Catholic claims.

Mr. Keogh, therefore, moved a resolution in accordance with these views, which was passed; but the meeting then proceeded to organize a new Catholic committee, consisting of the Catholic peers, and the survivors of the Catholic delegates of 1793, together with certain gentlemen who had been lately appointed by the Catholics of Dublin to prepare an address. It was resolved that these persons "do possess the confidence of the Catholic body."

This new committee was to be permanent; and was to consider the expediency of preparing a petition, not to the then sitting, but to the next session of Parliament. The committee, undoubtedly, was capable of being regarded as a virtual representation of the Irish Catholics, and, therefore, as coming under the penalties of the "Convention Act;" for which reason Mr. O'Connell, who knew that the Government was watching their proceedings with a jealous eye, endeavoured to guard against this legal peril by introducing a resolution which was carried unanimously:—"That the noblemen and gentlemen aforesaid are not representatives of the Catholic body, or any portion thereof; nor shall they assume or pretend to be representatives of the Catholic body, or any portion thereof."

We thus find Mr. O'Connell, from the first of his long series of agitations, always anxiously steering clear of the rocks and shoals of law; and find, also, that the most dangerous of those rocks and shoals was always the same "Convention Act." It embarrassed the Catholic Committee in 1809; it stopped the "Council of Three Hundred" in 1845; and, in fact, it had been passed for the very purpose of preventing all organized deliberation, and all effectual action by Catholics for the attainment of their rights. There is no doubt that the Government might at any time have prosecuted to conviction the members of this Catholic committee as *delegates* (notwithstanding their disclaimer) by means of a well-packed Castle jury; but, in the meantime, the affairs of the Catholics seemed to acquire some consistency and strength from the permanent organization of the committee and the respectability of its members. Of course this circumstance alarmed and infuriated the Orangemen, who are generally believed to have at the same time remodelled and improved their societies. It is not easy to arrive at the exact truth regarding all the secret tests, and oaths, and "degrees" of this mischievous body—the precise forms have been from time to time altered; and their "Grand Masters" and their organs of the press have boldly denied what is alleged against the society, although such allegation had been true very shortly before, and was substantially true when denied, even if some trifling form may have been altered, to justify the denial.

Mr. Plowden, writing in 1810, says very distinctly that "a renovation of the system (of Orangeism) actually prevailed in the year 1809," and that new oaths were introduced. He says, further:—

"It was reported, believed, and not contradicted, that about the time at which the Catholic bishops of Ireland were assembled in National Synod to oppose the *veto*, the Orange associations met by deputation in Dawson Street, Dublin, in order, as may be naturally presumed, to counteract the presumed resolutions of that Episcopal Synod, and to make head generally against the alarming growth of Popery. A deputy from the seventy-two English (almost all Lancastrian) Lodges came over in unusual pomp of accredited diplomacy to the Irish societies. Through the gloom of Orange darkness it would be presumption to ascertain the points of debate within their strictly guarded sanctuary in Dawson Street." The same writer observes:—

"So much undeniable truth has lately been brought before the public concerning the Orange institution—so glaringly has the illegality and mischief of the system been exposed—such weighty and fatal objections urged against it—that it has become fashionable with many Orangemen of education and fortune to affect to disclaim everything objectionable in the system, and to throw it exclusively upon the incorrigible ignorance and bigotry of the rabble, who are alike in every country, and of every persuasion. This was base artifice to disguise or conceal the countenance and support which the Orange societies have uniformly and unceasingly received from Government. If the obligations and oaths of Orangemen were of a virtuous and beneficial tendency, why not proclaim them aloud? If illegal and dangerous, why criminally conceal them? Whilst the Orange aristocracy thus affects to disclaim their own institute in detail, their activity in keeping the evil on foot is supereminently criminal. Nor can they redeem their guilt without revealing in detail the whole mischief of the system, by enabling others, or co-operating effectually themselves (as far as they possess power), to expose and effectually extinguish it."

Upon the subject of the new and alarming development of the Orange system which took place at this date, we may further cite the language of O'Connell at an aggregate meeting in May, 1811. He said:—

"From most respectable authority I have it that Orange lodges are increasing in different parts of the country, with the knowledge of those whose duty it is to suppress them. If I have been misinformed, I would wish that what I now say may be replied to by any one able to show that I am wrong. I hold in my hand the certificate of an Orange purple man (which he produced), who was advanced to that degree as lately as the 24th of April, 1811, in a lodge in Dublin. I have adduced this fact to show you that this dreadful and abominable conspiracy is still in existence; and I am well informed, and believe it to be the fact, that the King's Ministry are well acquainted with this circumstance. I have been also assured that the associations in the North are re-organized, and that a committee of these delegates in Belfast have printed and distributed five hundred copies of their new constitution. This I have heard from excellent authority; and I should not be surprised if the Attorney-General knows it. Yet there has been no attempt to disturb these conspirators; no attempt to visit them with magisterial authority; no attempt to rout this infamous banditti."

In truth, the "banditti" were so useful and indispensable an agency of British domination in Ireland, that they were perfectly safe from the law and the Attorney-General; and that functionary was not in the least obliged to O'Connell for his information. It was against Catholics only that penal statutes were made. Thus, although the Convention Act makes no distinctions between Catholic and Protestant, the Orange lodges were never at all embarrassed about sending delegates to a meeting in Dublin. And, although the Acts against administering secret oaths especially apply to the oaths of Orangemen, no Orangeman was ever prosecuted by the Crown under those laws. The oath which Government punished was not an oath to extirpate one's neighbours, but an oath to promote the union of Irishmen.

It would be easy to accumulate examples of Orange outrages at this time in many parts of the country; but these incidents have a wearisome sameness. On the 12th of August, 1808, fifty unarmed men of the King's County Militia, who had volunteered into the line, marched from Strabane into Omagh, in Tyrone County, where fifty of their comrades occupied the barracks. As they came into the town, it happened that three hundred Orange yeomen had assembled, and were celebrating the battle of Aughrim. A yeoman began operations by knocking off and trampling upon the cap of one of the militiamen because it was bound with *green*, which, though regimental, was not considered "loyal" enough for that occasion. The militiaman resented the outrage by a blow. A general assault was made by the whole body of yeomanry upon the fifty unarmed men; they retreated in good order to the barrack, where they were attacked again; but as they were now supplied with arms, they defended themselves to some purpose, and killed four of their assailants. Thomas Hogan, a corporal of the King's County Militia, was tried for the *murder* of those four men, and was actually found guilty of manslaughter.

Again, at Mountrath, the annual return of the Orange festival, in July, 1808, had been disgraced by the most atrocious murder of the Rev. Mr. Duane, the Catholic priest of that parish; and it was followed up in the succeeding year by the no less barbarous murder of a Catholic of the name of Kavanagh, into whose house the armed yeomen rushed, and barbarously fractured his skull in the presence of his wife and four infant children. On the first day of this same July, at Bailieborough, in the County Cavan, the Orange armed yeomen went in a body to the house of the parish priest, at whom they fired several shots, and left him for dead. They then wrecked the chapel, and wounded and insulted every Catholic they met.

None of the persons guilty of these outrages, either at Mountrath or Bailieborough, was ever punished, or even questioned.

But while the Government of the Duke of Richmond thus encouraged Orange outrage, and screened the perpetrators, his Grace sometimes affected to deprecate violent demonstrations of the society, at least in his own presence. For example, he made a tour through Munster in the summer of this year, 1809; and as the object of his excursion was chiefly to conciliate the Catholics of that province (many of whom were wealthy and influential), and so to prevent them from joining in the agitation for their own rights, he issued orders that no distinctively Orange displays should take place on his line of route. The town of Bandon was in those days a great stronghold of Orangeism in the South, and possessed a "legion" of six hundred yeomanry, all brethren of the Order. On the 1st of July, the yeomanry being assembled according to custom, to celebrate the battle of the Boyne, and to flaunt before the eyes of the oppressed Catholics the emblems of their defeat, they were astonished at being addressed by their Commander and Grand-Master, Lord Bandon, in a very unusual strain. He said: "Those Orange emblems were calculated to keep up animosities, and his Grace the Lord-Lieutenant did not wish anything of the sort *on the present occasion.*" The men suddenly dispersed in high indignation. The next parade day was the 6th, and they again assembled; but to show how they valued the homily of Lord Bandon, every man of them appeared decorated with Orange lilies.

The Earl of Bandon and Colonel Oriel, the inspecting officer of the district, observed that if they wished to be considered really obedient and loyal, they would attend to the orders of their officers, as Government seemed particularly anxious to prevent the further wearing of any emblem of this kind. They then ordered them either to take these marks of distinction down, or else to ground their arms. The corps for some time remained undecisive, when at length, with the exception of twenty-five, they indignantly threw down their arms and accoutrements, sooner than obey the command of Government delivered through their officer. The whole yeomanry of Bandon amounted to about six hundred men. On the 24th of July, 1809, the members composing the Boyne, Union, and True Blue corps of yeomanry, under the denomination of the Loyal Bandon Legion, openly declared the cause for which they laid down their arms.*

This "defection of the Bandon Orangemen," as it was called, made the Government very cautious for long afterwards how it showed the least displeasure against these "loyal" displays, or the outrages which nearly always attended them. Indeed, Grand-Masters and Ascendancy journals often coolly reminded the successive Chief-Governors of Ireland that English dominion could not be maintained one day in Ireland without the lodges, which was true; so that Lords-Lieutenant and Ministers, while feeling themselves bound in common decency to affect, at least, to deprecate violence, and hypocritically to advise concord and good feeling, have been exceedingly tender of wounding the sensibilities of those people, who were, and are, their only support in the country.

So well had the Castle succeeded during the administration of the Duke of Richmond in undoing all that the Volunteers and United Irishmen had done, and in making impossible that *union* of Irishmen, which was the only thing the Castle feared in the world.

CHAPTER XVI.

1810—1812.

Duke of Richmond's "Conciliation"—Orange Oppression—Treatment of Catholic Soldiers—The *Veto* again—Debate on *Veto* in Parliament—Catholic Petition presented by Grattan—Rejected —O'Connell's Leadership—New Organization of Catholics—Repeal of the Union first Agitated— Insanity of the King—Treachery of the Regent —Prosecution of the Catholic Committee—Convention Act—Suppression of the Committee— New Measures of O'Connell—Mr. Curran at Newry Election—Effects of the Union.

THE Duke of Richmond was one of our "conciliatory" Viceroys. In his tour through the South he rendered himself

* For a fuller account of these transactions at Bandon, see Plowden, Vol. III. of *Post-Union History.*

more than usually affable and urbane; and, having a frank and gracious manner, he was not without some success in soothing the Catholics, whom long oppression had rendered too credulously impressible by a few words of hollow and hypocritical kindness. At a moment when it was notorious that he was acting as the zealous agent of a *No-Popery* Administration, that he was excluding Catholic gentlemen from the Grand Juries, Catholic merchants from the Bank, that Catholic soldiers were regularly punished by their officers for going to mass, and that his Grace's Orange banditti were killing and maiming their Catholic neighbours with a perfect certainty of impunity, we find that at the entertainment given by the Corporation of Waterford to the Lord-Lieutenant, his Grace's affability and attention to all were conspicuous. He took an opportunity of addressing Doctor Power, the Catholic Bishop of Waterford, whom in a gracious and cordial style he thanked for his and his flock's conduct in putting down the disturbances in their county. He openly and distinctly assured him that he had it in special instructions from His Majesty to make no distinction between Protestant and Catholic, which injunction he emphatically declared he had punctiliously complied with ever since he had undertaken the government of the country, as far as the laws would allow of. Those laws, he lamented, it was not in his power to deviate from. Such was the travelling style of the Vice-regal Court. At the dinner given to his Grace by the Mayor and Corporation of Cork at the Mansion House, amongst the regular Corporation toasts was announced, in its order, the *Protestant Ascendancy of Ireland,* on which his Grace arose and declared he wished to see no ascendancy in Ireland but that of loyalty, and strongly recommended the same line of conduct to be pursued by all good subjects.

At another dinner in Cork, given by the merchants, traders, and bankers, his Excellency had even the sanctimonious audacity to express his wonder that religion, being only occupied with a great object of eternal concern, men should be excited to rancorous enmity because they sought the same great end by paths somewhat different. This kind of language, which has been the common style of Irish Viceroys ever since, was first brought into vogue by the *No-Popery* Duke of Richmond; and what is very remarkable, it so far imposed upon many simple-minded Catholics that they were afterwards but slow and reluctant in even coming forward to petition for their withheld rights and franchises.

In the meantime, the daily and continual oppressions and humiliations which were inflicted upon the Catholics, not only by Orange magistrates and yeomen, but by the Government itself, were too notorious and too galling to be soothed away by the fair words of a conciliatory Viceroy. The treatment of Catholic soldiers in the army (of which they already constituted nearly one-half) excited the strongest and bitterest feelings of discontent. At Enniskillen, a Lieutenant Walsh turned a soldier's coat, in order to disgrace him, for refusing to attend the Protestant service; others were effectually prevented from attending the service of their own Church, by an order not to quit the barracks till two o'clock on the Sunday, when the Catholic service was over, as at Newry. The case which acquired the most publicity, and produced the strongest effect upon Ireland, was that of Patrick Spence, a private in the County Dublin Militia, who had been required (though known to be a Catholic) to attend the Divine service of the Established Church, and upon refusal, was thrown into the Black Hole. During his imprisonment he wrote a letter to Major White, his commanding officer, urging that in obeying the paramount dictates of conscience he had in no manner broken in upon military discipline. He was shortly after brought to a court-martial, upon a charge that his letter was disrespectful, and had a mutinous tendency. He was convicted, and sentenced to receive nine hundred and ninety-nine lashes. Upon being brought out to undergo that punishment, an offer was made to him to commute it for an engagement to enlist in a corps constantly serving abroad; this he accepted, and was transmitted to the Isle of Wight, in order to be sent out of the kingdom. The case having been represented to the Lord-Lieutenant by Doctor Troy, the titular Archbishop of Dublin, Mr. W. Pole wrote him a letter, which stated that the sentence had been passed upon Spence for writing the disrespectful letter; not denying, therefore admitting, that the committal to the "Black Hole" was for the refusal to attend the Protestant Church; but that, under all the circumstances, the Commander-in-Chief had considered the punishment excessive, and had ordered the man to be liberated, and to join his regiment. When Spence arrived in Dublin, he was confined several days, and then discharged altogether from the army. The copy of Spence's letter, which he vouched to be authentic, contained nothing in it either disrespectful or mutinous. The original letter was often called for, and always refused by those who had it in their possession, and might, consequently, by its production determine the justice of the sentence of nine hundred and ninety-nine lashes.

Many other examples of this kind of petty tyranny occurred about the same time; and as no officer was ever punished or reprimanded for any of them, they are sufficient to indicate the real feelings of the Government, and how much sincerity there was in the after-dinner liberality of the Duke of Richmond. In short, it was the settled design of the British Government, not only to break the promises made for carrying the Union (as it had formerly broken the treaty of Limerick), but also to make the Catholics feel in their daily life the whole bitterness of their degradation.

They had, of course, no representative in the British Parliament; and it appeared, in the course of the year 1810, that such Protestant friends and advocates as they possessed in that assembly—Mr. Grattan and Mr. Ponsonby, for example—desired to effect their emancipation only on the terms of enslaving the Catholic Church to the State by means of the *veto*. The subject of *veto* was now revived, both in Parliament and in the country. The English Catholics, in *their* petitions for relief, offered to accept emancipation on such terms; that is, on the terms of giving to a Protestant State a discretion as to the appointment of their bishops. In Ireland, that idea was now universally repulsed by the clergy and laity; although, as before stated, it had once been favourably received by a few of the higher clergy.

Late in January, 1810, was held a large meeting of the Catholics of Dublin. The Secretary, Mr. Hay, stated, that the most Rev. Doctor Troy had received from an English member of Parliament (Sir John Cox Hippesley) a letter, accompanied by an explanatory printed copy of a sketch of proposed regulations, concurrent with the establishment of a State provision, for the Roman Catholic clergy of Ireland.*

* The Catholic historian, Plowden, says: "This deep-laid plan, suggested by Sir John Cox Hippesley, fathered by Mr. Pitt, adopted by Lord Grenville, palmed by Lord Castlereagh upon the duped or intimidated Trustees of Maynooth College, in contemplation of the Union, was now brought forward with the privity and approbation of several of the leading members of the Board of British Catholics. The concluding sentence speaks in full its primary intent. "Al confirm the principle, that the sovereign power in every State, of whatever religious communion, has considered itself armed with legitimate authority in all matters of ecclesiastical arrangement within its dominion."

It was the project of *veto* in all its nakedness, but recommended both by the prospect of civil emancipation and by a State provision for the clergy. To the credit of the whole Catholic body (for it must be admitted that the bribe was high), all proposals of this nature were rejected, and rejected with indignation. A petition was prepared for presentation to Parliament asking for unconditional emancipation, intrusted to Lord Fingal, who carried it to London, and presented by Mr. Grattan. But, although he presented it, he said that it was merely in order to have the claims of the Catholics put on record; that he had hoped the Irish Catholics would be willing to allow, on the appointment of their bishops, a *veto* to the Crown; "he was sorry to see that at present no such sentiment appeared to prevail." Mr. Grattan had still the same violent horror of "French influence," which had formerly prevented him from joining the United Irishmen. "The Pope," he said, "was almost certain now to be a subject of France; and a subject of France, or French citizen, could never be permitted to nominate the spiritual magistrates of the people of Ireland." In short, Mr. Grattan, in both the speeches which he made in this session, spoke *against* the petition which he had presented. It would be tedious to make even an abstract of the debate; and it will be sufficient to say that on the motion for going into committee with the Catholic petition, Mr. Ponsonby, Mr. Grattan, and Sir John Cox Hippesley, were in favour of the motion *subject to veto;* Mr. Hutcheson, Mr. Parnell, and Sir John Newport, in favour of it *without veto;* Lord Castlereagh wholly against it in every shape; so, of course, were Mr. Perceval, and all other members of the No-Popery Administration; and the motion was lost by a majority against the Catholic claims of one hundred and four.

In June, the petition was presented by Lord Donoughmore to the Lords, in a very fair and just speech. He said, speaking of the Catholic Church: "No man was so ignorant as not to know that its professed unity in doctrine and in discipline, under one and the same declared head, was the essential distinguishing characteristic of the Catholic Church, and yet they were told that the Irish Catholics were the most unreasonable of men, because they would not renounce upon oath this first tenet of their religion, and consent to recognize a new head of their Church in the person of a Protestant King. The Irish Catholic, under the existing tests, solemnly abjures the authority of the Pope in all temporal matters, pledges himself to be a faithful subject of the King, and to defend the succession of the Crown, and the arrangement of property as now established by law, and that he will not exercise any privilege to which he is, or may become, entitled to disturb the Protestant religion, or Protestant government. What possible ground of apprehension could there be which was not effectually provided against by the terms of this oath? With respect to that ill-fated *veto*, the introduction of which into the Catholic vocabulary he witnessed with sincere regret, he could only say for himself, that he wanted no additional security; but he was equally ready to acknowledge that it was the bounden duty of the Catholic, whenever the happy moment of conciliation should arrive, to go the full length his religion would permit him, to quiet the scruples, however groundless and imaginary, of the Protestant Legislature."

After a short debate—in which we find Lord Holland, Lord Erskine, the Duke of Norfolk, and Lord Grey, speaking in favour of going into committee on the petition; against it, Lord Liverpool, Lord Clancarty, Lord Redesdale, and the Lord Chancellor—there appeared on a division, for the motion, sixty-eight; non-contents, one hundred and fifty-four; majority against the Catholics, eighty-six.

It was now at last tolerably evident that there was no use in petitioning that Parliament to acknowledge the rights of Catholics; that the insidious promises made by Lord Cornwallis and Lord Castlereagh, for the purpose of carrying the Union, were to be deliberately disregarded; and that the Catholic cause must be either abandoned altogether, or must be taken up by some more potent hand than any of those which had guided it up to that time. Daniel O'Connell was to be the new leader of the Irish Catholic cause, and may be said to date the commencement of his wonderful career of agitation from the Parliamentary defeat sustained by the petition of 1810. In a month after the rejection of that petition, the general committee of the Catholics, after passing a vote of thanks to the worthy old John Keogh "for his long and faithful services to the cause of Catholic Emancipation," issued an address to all the Catholics of Ireland, urging upon them a new and more combined form of political action, and bearing the signature of "Daniel O'Connell, Chairman." The programme of action presented in this address is substantially the same which was followed up by Mr. O'Connell, under several successive names, throughout all his agitations—local organizations holding frequent meetings, and corresponding with a central committee in Dublin. All proceedings were to be peaceful and legal; yet there was the *hint* of a possibility that millions of people, steadily denied their rights, might in the end be driven to extort them with the strong hand. Here is an extract:—

"Still, *whilst time and opportunity yet remain for peaceful counsels*, the virtuous Catholic will deeply revolve in his mind the wisest course for his redemption. He will prefer that success which promises the greatest permanent enjoyment to himself and his family; the most salutary to his country; the most conformable to the best laws and dearest precepts of civil society. He will prefer to opposite courses those of peace, of reason, and of temperate, but firm perseverance in well-regulated efforts.

"The committee, sir, consulting not merely local, but general feelings, entertain every wish and hope of calling into fair and free exercise the unbiased judgment and independent opinions of the Catholics of Ireland, thinking and acting for themselves throughout their respective counties, districts, cities, and towns, and deciding upon such measures as shall appear to them most eligible.

"They hope that the Catholics will take frequent opportunities, and as early as possible, of holding local meetings for these purposes; and there, unfettered by external authority, and unaffected by dictation, apply their most serious consideration to subjects of common and weighty concern, with the candour and directness of mind which appertain to the national character.

"The establishment of permanent boards, holding communication with the General Committee in Dublin, has been deemed in several counties highly useful to the interests of the Catholic cause.

"Nothing is more necessary amongst us than self-agency. It will produce that system of coherence of conduct which must insure success.

"In the exercise of the elective franchise, for instance, what infinite good might not result from Catholic coherence? What painful examples are annually exhibited of the mischief flowing from the want of this coherence?

"The Catholic Committee have, therefore, every reason to expect the most beneficial effects to the general cause, from local and frequent meetings."

During this same summer was heard the first loud cry for a *Repeal of the Union.* In the Corporation of Dublin—then, of course, an exclusively Protestant body—Mr. Hutton, pursuant to notice, made an impressive speech, in which he powerfully depicted the ruin, bankruptcy, despair, and famine, that were apparent in every street of Dublin; pointed out that the debt of the nation was then *above ninety millions;* that two millions sterling, wrung from the sweat of Irish peasants, were squandered in a foreign country by absentees,* and that £2,500,000 more was drained away to pay the interest on that insupportable debt. He proposed resolutions to the effect, that the cure for all these evils was the Repeal of the Union. Of course, he was vehemently opposed by Giffard and his party; but the resolutions were carried by a majority of thirty.

The next step was a requisition from the Grand Jurors of Dublin to the two High Sheriffs, Sir Edward Stanley and Sir James Riddall, to call a meeting of the freemen and freeholders, to consider "*the necessity that exists* of presenting a petition to His Majesty and the Imperial Parliament, for a Repeal of the Act of Union." Stanley declined to call such a meeting; he said it "would agitate the public mind." But Riddall called the meeting. On the 18th of September, at the Royal Exchange, was held this memorable meeting, at which both Protestants and Catholics were unanimous, not only in affirming the universal misery and beggary of the country, but in attributing the whole to that fatal and fraudulent measure called the Act of Union. O'Connell delivered, on this occasion, a speech of the most concentrated power and passion, which deeply impressed his audience and the entire nation. It was at once printed on a broadside, surmounted with a portrait of the orator; and O'Connell was from that moment the leader to whom all Catholics turned with pride and hope. The resolutions for the preparation of a petition for repeal of the Union were adopted unanimously.

What we have to remark is, that in those first movements favouring repeal of the Union, all speakers concurred in representing the material and financial effects of that measure as disastrous in the extreme to Ireland; yet those speakers do not appear to have bethought them that the impoverishment of Ireland was the exact measure of the profit to England; that this was the specific object

---

* Dean Swift estimated the absentee rents in his time at half a million sterling, and thought that same a great grievance. In 1848, Mr. Smith O'Brien, always moderate in his statements, said the drain through this single channel amounted to five millions.

for which England had demanded, contrived, and accomplished the Union; and that the existing relation between the two countries was the accurate fulfilment of the prediction made by that honest Englishman, Samuel Johnson, to an Irish acquaintance—"Sir, we shall rob you."

The Catholics of Ireland were by this time quite unanimous in favour of repealing that Union, the perpetration of which they had been induced to regard with indifference, or almost with complacency. At least, they knew how treacherously they had been dealt with on this occasion by the English Government and its agents, Cornwallis and Castlereagh; and the natural soreness which they felt at being duped, aggravated the sufferings which fell upon them, as well as upon the Protestants, in consequence of depressed trade and ruined manufactures.

"Repeal" was, therefore, fairly before the country; but it was too late for any peaceful redress. When the shark has once made his *union* with his prey, he does not easily disgorge; for this there needs, either a miracle, as in the case of Jonah's fish, or else that the shark be killed and cut up. *Petitioning* for restitution of that rich prey is, perhaps, the most imbecile idea that ever possessed any public man since the beginning of the world.

Catholic Emancipation, however, was another kind of question, and one quite susceptible of a peaceful solution; because to emancipate Catholics would cost England nothing, but, on the contrary, would probably win over many of the leading, educated, and professional Catholics, who might be induced, by the prospect of honours and emoluments for themselves, to abandon their people to plunder and extirpation, and to sell the cause of their country to its enemies—an anticipation which we have unhappily seen realized on a large scale.

Catholic Emancipation, then, although a minor question, was the immediately practical one for an Irish agitator; and O'Connell saw that it was so, and devoted himself to it accordingly.

In October, King George III. fell into his final and irremediable insanity, and the Prince again became Regent: this time with almost full regal powers. It was a matter of no interest whatsoever to Ireland; save that many Catholics were simple enough to believe that it removed the only real obstacle to their emancipation—namely, the stupid scruples of the idiot King as to his coronation oath. The Prince had made many professions— even distinct promises and pledges, afterwards minutely specified by O'Connell—that, so soon as he should enjoy actual power, he would do all that in him lay to bring about Catholic Emancipation. In 1806, he had made such a pledge through the Duke of Bedford, then Viceroy, in order to induce the Catholics to withhold their petitions; his good friends, the Catholics, were to trust all to *him*, the Prince. Mr. Ponsonby, then Chancellor, had, in the same year, promulgated a similar promise in the Prince's name. He had himself given such a pledge to Lord Kenmare, at Cheltenham. Finally, he had given a formal verbal pledge to Lord Fingal, in presence of Lord Petre and Lord Clifford, which was reduced to writing by those three noblemen, and signed by them soon after the interview ended. The Prince had now uncontrolled power; and, as usual, the Catholics found themselves cheated. He retained as his Prime Minister the *No-Popery* Perceval, and was surrounded by advisers intensely hostile to the Catholic cause. His mistress at that time was the wife of the Marquis of Hertford; and the conscience of that lady could not reconcile itself to the thought of conceding any right to persons who believed in seven sacraments. Even the two Protestant sacraments were one too many for her ladyship.*

Almost the first act of any consequence done in Ireland, after the Prince became Regent, was a State prosecution instituted against the Catholic Committee, in the persons of two of its members, Mr. Kirwan and Doctor Sheridan, who were charged to have been elected as delegates, in breach of the Convention Act. The Government had been long watching for this chance, and now the Castle strained every nerve to insure a conviction. Mr. Saurin, Attorney-General, commenced his speech thus: "My Lords, and Gentlemen of the Jury, I cannot but congratulate you and the public *that the day of justice has at last arrived;*"—surely a most extraordinary expression under the circumstances, seeing that these Catholics were but peacefully claiming their manifest right; and seeing that the crime of which

* Certain resolutions passed in the Catholic Committee but too plainly referred to this woman, when they spoke of the "fatal witchery" which had led the Regent to form a Ministry hostile to liberty of conscience in Ireland. The enchantress was over fifty years of age; and her husband and her son were the closest boon-companions of the lover of the father's wife and of the son's mother. These famous "witchery" resolutions were supposed to have so strongly aroused the Protestant feelings of the Prince as to adjourn all thought of Catholic Emancipation for many years, and to have been the cause of the exceedingly bad grace with which King George IV. at last assented to that measure.

they were now accused was unknown to the law of England. Mr. Bushe, then Solicitor-General, afterwards Chief-Justice, speaking of the committee, constituted as it was, thus concluded his speech upon that trial: "Compare such a constitution with the established authorities of the land, all controlled, confined to their respective spheres, balancing and gravitating to each other—all symmetry, all order, all harmony. Behold, on the other hand, this prodigy in the political hemisphere, with eccentric course and portentous glare, bound by no attraction, disdaining any orbit, disturbing the system, and affrighting the world!" The remedy for this horrible comet was a packed jury, which is one of those "established authorities, all symmetry and harmony," spoken of by Mr. Bushe. A conviction was obtained; and the Catholic Committee, in that form, ceased to exist. Mr. Shiel says: "A great blow had been struck at the cause, and a considerable time elapsed before Ireland recovered from it."

But although that organization was at an end, many angry meetings were held; and the Catholic press assumed a tone of aggression and defiance which had not been usual with it. Mr. O'Connell, in conjunction with Mr. Scully, a gentleman of large property and high talent, established a newspaper; and both in the press and in public assemblies, there was manifested by the popular leaders so much boldness and activity, as assured all men that the cause of the nation was now in a fresh and vigorous hand.

Mr. Wellesley Pole had been appointed Irish Secretary of State, as successor to his brother, Lord Wellington; and his administration was chiefly noted for his circular letter against meeting in conventions, with a view to the suppression of the Catholic Committee. Mr. Wellesley Pole was soon after succeeded by Mr. Robert Peel, who proved himself during many years after the most deadly, and, indeed, most fatal foe the Irish nation ever encountered. He was but twenty-four years of age; and continued Chief Secretary for six years, during which time he closely studied the character and wants of the people; so that of all English statesmen in modern times, Sir Robert Peel may be said to have understood Ireland best,—to Ireland's bitter cost.

In 1812, Mr. Perceval, the "No-Popery" Prime Minister, was assassinated by a maniac, in the lobby of the House of Commons; and a change of administration became necessary. But the new arrangements had little interest for Irishmen, and presented no hope of any approach to justice in the treatment of that country. Lord Liverpool was Prime Minister, and both Canning and Castlereagh were members of the Cabinet. A dissolution of Parliament and general election followed, at which several additional "Liberals" were returned from places in Ireland. Mr. Curran was persuaded by his friends, and invited by the Liberal electors of Newry, to permit himself to be placed in nomination for that borough. He had never, since the Union, sought to enter the British Parliament; and it was with no sanguine hope of being able to effect any good there for his country that he now essayed to enter public life once more. He was defeated at Newry—defeated by General Needham, one of the military tyrants who had dragooned the people into insurrection in 1798. But in Mr. Curran's speech on that occasion, to the electors of Newry, though imperfectly reported, is found a passage most vividly depicting the condition of Ireland twelve years after the Union, and Curran's estimate of the nature and effects of that measure. He said: "The whole history of mankind records no instance of any hostile Cabinet, perhaps even of any Cabinet, actuated by the principles of honour or of shame. The Irish Catholic was, therefore, taught to believe that if he surrendered his country he would cease to be a slave. The Irish Protestant was cajoled into the belief that, if he concurred in the surrender, he would be placed upon the neck of a hostile faction. Wretched dupe! you might as well persuade the jailor that he is less a prisoner than the captives he locks up, merely because he carries the key in his pocket. By that reciprocal animosity, however, Ireland was surrendered. The guilt of the surrender was most atrocious; the consequences of the crime most tremendous and exemplary. We put ourselves into a condition of the most unqualified servitude; we sold our country, and we levied upon ourselves the price of the purchase; we gave up the right of disposing of our own property; we yielded to a foreign legislature to decide whether the funds necessary to their projects, or their profligacy, should be extracted from us or be furnished by themselves. The consequence has been that our scanty means have been squandered in her internal corruption as profusely as our best blood has been wasted in the madness of her aggressions, or the feeble folly of her resistance. Our debt has, accordingly, been increased *more than ten-fold;* the common comforts of life have been vanishing; we are sinking into beggary; our poor people have been worried by cruel and unprincipled prosecutions; and the instruments of our Government have been almost simplified into the tax-gatherer and the hangman." This dismal picture of the condition of his country could not have been made in so public a manner, and by a man of Curran's character, unless it had been true. He could not have ventured to tell a large assembly of his countrymen that they were ground down by taxes and sinking into beggary, if they could all have risen up and contradicted him on the spot. Besides, the evidence from other quarters is too clear and strong to allow us to doubt of the accuracy of any one feature in the sombre scene he depicts. The country was, during all those years, as usual, disturbed now and then by a vindictive murder of some bailiff, or agent, who had turned poor families adrift, and pulled down their houses; or some tithe-proctor, who had seized on a widow's stack-yard. And all these acts of vengeance or despair were uniformly treated as seditious "insurrections." Ireland, therefore, remained under an almost uninterrupted *Insurrection Act*. The Act of *Habeas Corpus* had been suspended in 1800 by the Act *for the Suppression of the Rebellion;* that Act had been continued in 1801, and again in 1804, and had been replaced in 1807 by another martial law (substantially the same law), called the Insurrection Act, which was maintained until 1810. It will be seen hereafter how steadily the same exceptional coercion laws, but with ingenious variations of name, have been continued down to this day.

When Mr. Curran mentioned that the people were "worried by cruel and unprincipled prosecutions," he had in his thoughts the long series of "special commissions" sent down in state to the country, to hang up some scores of haggard wretches, and to terrify the rest; he was thinking of the many fathers of poor families, who were often dragged to jail without a charge against them, and without the right to demand a trial; he was thinking of the free course which suspension of the *Habeas Corpus* gave to the vindictive outrages of Orange magistrates, and to the fanatical rage of packed juries.

So uniform has been the long passion of Ireland—generation after generation wasting and withering under the very same atrocity which calls itself "Government;" the children losing heart and hope, as their fathers had done, and begetting a progeny to pine away under the same miseries still—until they are tempted to doubt whether a just God reigns over the earth.

CHAPTER XVII.

1813—1821.

Grattan's Emancipation Bill—More *Veto*—Quarantotti—Unanimity in Ireland against *Veto*—Mr. Peel and his New Police—Stipendiary Magistrates—Close of the War—Restoration of the Bourbons—Waterloo—Evil Effects on Ireland—The Irish Legion in France—Its Fate—Miles Byrne and his Friends—Effects of the Peace in Impoverishing the Irish—Cheap Ejectment Law passed—Beginning of Extermination—"Surplus Population"—Catholic Claims Ruined by the Peace—O'Connell and Catholic Board—Board Suppressed—O'Connell in Court—His Audacity—His Scorn of the Dublin Corporation—Duel with D'Esterre—Distress in Ireland—Famine of 1817—Coercion in Ireland—"Six Acts" in England—Mr. Plunket's Emancipation Bill—Peel and the Duke of York—Royal Visit to Ireland—Catholics Cheated Again.

MR. GRATTAN made his final effort to effect the Emancipation of the Catholics in the first session of the new Parliament, in 1813. The bill which he proposed was a very imperfect and restricted one; but it provided that Catholics should sit in Parliament, and hold certain offices, excepting those of Lord-Chancellor, either in England or in Ireland, and that of Lord-Lieutenant, or Lord-Deputy, in Ireland. It did not include a provision for the Royal *veto* upon Catholic bishops. The debate which ensued is scarce worth recording, inasmuch as, after several amendments providing for *veto*, and at last an amendment striking out the clause enabling Catholics to sit and vote in Parliament, the bill was withdrawn, and finally lost.

The *veto* amendments proposed by Castlereagh and Canning were the work of Sir John Hippesley, that indefatigable patron of *veto*. They proposed to constitute a Board of Commissioners to examine into the *loyalty* of those proposed for episcopal functions, and to exercise a *surveillance* and control over their official correspondence with Rome. But the Irish Catholics were now fully alive to the insidious nature of this proposal; and both clergy and people, with great unanimity, rejected all idea of Emancipation upon any such terms. But the English Catholics, not having any *national* interest at stake in the matter, were quite favourable to the project, and used their utmost endeavours to have it accepted at Rome, and recommended from thence. English influence was then very strong at Rome. The Pope was a prisoner in France; and it was to the coalition of European sovereigns against Buonaparte that the Court of Rome looked for its re-establishment. A certain Monsignor Quarantotti exercised in the year 1814 the official authority of the Pope, and was induced, under English influence, to recommend submission to the *veto* in a letter or rescript to "the Right Rev. William Poynter," Vicar-Apostolic of the London district. As the question of *veto* at that period occupied so large a share of public attention both in England and in Ireland, it may be but just to let this Monsignor Quarantotti state, in his own way, the view which was taken of it at Rome; and therefore we give an extract from the most material passage of his rescript:—

"As to the desire of the Government to be informed of the loyalty of those who are promoted to the dignity of bishop or dean, and to be assured that they possess those qualifications which belong to a faithful subject; as to the intention also, of forming a board for the ascertainment of those points, by inquiring into the character of those who shall be presented, and reporting thereon to the King, according to the tenor of your lordship's letter; and, finally, as to the determination of Government to have none admitted to those dignities who either are not natural-born subjects, or who have not been residents in the kingdom for four years preceding. As all these provisions regard matters that are merely political, they are entitled to all indulgence. It is better, indeed, that the prelates of our Church should be acceptable to the King, in order that they may exercise their ministry with his full concurrence, and also that there may be no doubts of their integrity, even with those who are not in the bosom of the Church. For 'it behoveth a bishop (as the Apostle teaches, 1 Tim. iii. 7) even to have a good witness from those who are not of the Church.' Upon these principles we, in virtue of the authority intrusted to us, grant permission that those who are elected to and proposed for bishoprics and deaneries by the clergy, may be admitted or rejected by the King, according to the law proposed. When therefore the clergy shall have, according to the usual custom, elected those whom they shall judge most worthy in the Lord to possess those dignities, the Metropolitan of the province, in Ireland, or the senior Vicar-Apostolic of England and Scotland, shall give notice of the election, that the King's approbation or dissent may be had thereupon. If the candidates be rejected, others shall be proposed who may be acceptable to the King; but if approved of, the Metropolitan or Vicar-Apostolic, as above, shall send the documents to the Sacred Congregation here, the members whereof, having duly weighed the merits of each, shall take measures for the obtainment of canonical institution from His Holiness. I perceive also that another duty is assigned to the Board above-mentioned —namely, that they are charged to inspect all letters written by the ecclesiastical power to any of the British clergy, and examine carefully whether they contain anything which may be injurious to the Government, or anywise disturb the public tranquillity. Inasmuch as a communication on ecclesiastical or spiritual affairs with the head of the Church is not forbidden, and as the inspection of the Board relates to political subjects only, this also must be submitted to. It is right that the Government should not have cause to entertain any suspicion with regard to the communication between us. What we write will bear the eyes of the world, for we intermeddle not with matters of a political nature, but are occupied about those things which the Divine and the ecclesiastical law, and the good order of the Church, appear to require. Those matters only are to be kept under the seal of silence which pertain to the jurisdiction of conscience within us; and of this it appears to me sufficient care has been taken in the clauses of the law alluded to. We are perfectly convinced that so wise a Government as that of Great Britain, while it studies to provide for the public security, does not on that account wish to compel the Catholics to desert their religion; but would rather be pleased that they should be careful observers of it. For our holy and truly Divine religion is most favourable to public authority, is the best support of thrones, and the most powerful teacher both of loyalty and patriotism."

This did by no means suit the views of the Irish Catholics, or their idea of "loyalty and patriotism." As they did not themselves "possess those qualifications which belong to a faithful subject," they naturally thought that their clergy should not. They believed, indeed, and not without reason, that loyalty and faithful attachment, on the part of the Irish Catholic clergy, towards a foreign and hostile Government, meant neither more nor less than a formal abandonment of the people to the mercy of their enemies, and a desertion of the cause of those faithful and devoted Catholics who had stood by their clergy in the worst of times, when a price was set upon a priest's head. In fact, the sequel proved that the Irish clergy of that day were not so base as it was hoped they would be. The bishops sent a strong remonstrance to

Rome by the hands of Dr. Murray, coadjutor to the Archbishop of Dublin, which, however, was not regarded in the least, so powerful was the political influence of England in the councils of the Holy See. Doctor Murray returned to Ireland. At a meeting of the prelates very energetic resolutions were adopted, one of which ran in these terms:— "Though we sincerely venerate the Supreme Pontiff as visible Head of the Church, we do not conceive that our apprehensions for the safety of the Roman Catholic Church in Ireland can or ought to be removed by any determination of His Holiness, adopted, or intended to be adopted, not only without our concurrence, but in direct opposition to our repeated resolutions, and the very energetic memorial presented on our behalf, and so ably supported by our deputy, the most Rev. Doctor Murray, who, in that quality, was more competent to inform His Holiness of the real state and interests of the Roman Catholic Church in Ireland *than any other with whom he is said to have consulted.*"

This last phrase meant the emissaries of the English Catholics, then busy at Rome; and the English Catholics have been at all times as zealous and resolute to keep Ireland subject to English domination in all respects, as any "No-Popery" Briton or Orange Grand-Master could be. The resolutions were signed by all the Catholic bishops in Ireland, and transmitted to Rome by the same Doctor Murray, accompanied by the Bishop of Cork. A vehement agitation was aroused in Ireland, which extended to the laity as well as the clergy; and, under the potent impulse of O'Connell, a resolute spirit of resistance manifested itself in the whole Catholic population, against any orders or recommendations coming even from Rome itself, tending to enchain their national Church.

While this *veto* commotion agitated the Catholics, Mr. Robert Peel, the Irish Secretary, was engaged in re-organizing and greatly increasing the Constabulary force, with a view to render it a more efficient instrument in the hands of the English Government for the coercion of the country, and the detection of seditious proceedings. With the same view, Mr. Peel invented and established the class of stipendiary or police magistrates, who were to take their instructions from the Castle, and whose business was to control and direct, as far as possible, the proceedings of justices of the peace at petty sessions and quarter sessions, and to guard against any movement of independent feeling on the part of country gentlemen who were in the commission of the peace. The men chosen for this office of stipendiary magistrate have been usually briefless barristers, or broken-down politicians in a small way, to whom the salary was a desirable livelihood; and as they have at least legal phrases at their command, a supposed acquaintance with the views of the Castle, and great self-importance of manner, it has been found in practice that these paid officials have really, to a great extent, controlled and managed the local administration of justice; which, in all conscience, had been bad enough before. Mr. Peel's police arrangements were extremely unpopular; and his new constables and stipendiaries were popularly termed *Peelers*. But although the Irish, by an infallible instinct, abhorred the new system, they were yet far from suspecting to what a deadly use Mr. Peel would eventually put his new force.

In the meantime, the grand war of coalized Europe against the French Empire drew to a close. The French armies were driven out of Spain by the patriotic efforts of the Spanish people, aided by a British force under Lord Wellington—for the English Government, with the great object of crushing the French, was willing, in a distant country, to ally itself even with patriotism. The Emperor Napoleon, after the tremendous slaughter at Leipsic (in which he fought all Europe), had been obliged gradually to withdraw his forces into France. But though he made a most brilliant and fierce resistance to the advance of the allies, they surrounded Paris in overwhelming numbers; and the great Emperor was forced, in an evil hour, to abdicate at Fontainbleau. The coalized kings and oligarchies of Europe triumphed; and the expelled Bourbons came back to sit on the throne of France for awhile. The "Congress of Vienna" was called, to settle Europe upon the basis of a distinct denial of every human right and every national aspiration; and the fitting representative of England in that Congress was no other than Lord Castlereagh, the artizan of the Irish Union.

It does not enter within the compass of this narrative to detail the wonderful series of events which followed—the escape of Buonaparte from Elba, the enthusiastic uprising of France in his favour, the tricolour flying from steeple to steeple, the reign of a Hundred Days, the renewed concentration of the forces of the allies, and the sad disaster of Waterloo. Waterloo, like every other triumph of the arms and policy of England, was, of course, a fatal misfortune to Ireland. It confirmed the

K

odious rule of an insolent oligarchy both in England and in Ireland, and placed it high, as was hoped and believed, above all apprehension of revolution and democracy. Waterloo put an end at once to all interest in Catholic claims on the part even of the "Liberals," and adjourned for fourteen years all thought either of Emancipation or of Reform. The defeat of Waterloo was not, indeed, so much a defeat for France, as for other oppressed countries of Europe; for in France the great revolution had been accomplished, and its work could not be undone. In France, all religious sects were equal, and remained equal before the law; all feudal privilege was, and remained, abolished; and all men, like all religions, were on an equal footing; in France, the people were in possession, and remained in possession, of the great confiscated estates, each one of which made hundreds or thousands of farms for free peasants; in France, tithes were, and remained, abolished; the highest dignity of the State was open to the meanest mechanic; the highest grade in the army to the humblest private. It was earnestly hoped, indeed, by the coalized allies of the Bourbons, that the forcible restoration of that family would speedily reverse and abolish all these dangerous privileges of the French people—but that was impossible. The sentiment and practice of justice and equality had entered too deeply into the life and soul of France to be eradicated even by foreign bayonets. But for Ireland, the case was very different. The apprehension of a triumph of "French principles"—that is, principles of equality and justice—which had been for twenty-five years a dreadful bugbear to the British oligarchy—was now at an end; and *privilege*, and Church and State, and the "Ascendancy," reigned supreme.

Of the armies which triumphed on the field of Waterloo, about one-fourth consisted of British troops; and of these "British" troops, nearly one-half were Irish. It is a shame to be obliged to confess it. Their country can take no pride in those Irishmen; Irish history refuses to know their names. They fought under a commander who always opposed and denied their right to rank on an equality with his other soldiers; they fought to perpetuate a domination which oppressed and despised them; fought against their own enfranchisement, and their own right to land and life on their own soil; and to establish, on an immovable basis, that odious British system which has since degraded, impoverished, and almost depopulated their country. While a vestige of genuine Irish feeling remains amongst our people, Irishmen will speak with pride of the Irish Brigade at Fontenoy, and with shame and repugnance of the Irish regiments at Waterloo.

There were, indeed, some true Irishmen in the service of France at that period. The Irish Legion, the relics of '98, as the old brigades were the relics of Limerick. In this Legion and its gallant officers, Ware, Allen, Byrne, Corbet, Lawless, MacSheehy, centred the genuine military renown of the Irish race at that day. But the Legion was not present at Waterloo; it had fought through the Peninsular campaign, and had taken part in some of the last battles of the campaign of 1814. It had thus been sadly reduced in numbers; and during the first Restoration, (before the Hundred Days), it had been entirely re-organized, and reduced to a regiment. At the time of the final struggle on the plains of Belgium, the regiment was stationed at Montreuil, on the shore of the British Channel; and after the calamity of Waterloo, and the treacherous capture of Napoleon, the Irish regiment, as well as all the rest of the army, was disbanded; and the officers were allowed at first to retire upon their half-pay to any town they might select in France, where, says the venerable Miles Byrne, "they hoped at least to enjoy their pittance and the protection of the law." But it is mortifying to learn that through the paramount influence of Castlereagh with the new Government, and through the base compliance of Clarke, Duc de Feltre (himself the son of an Irishman), these forlorn exiles were persecuted with a mean malignity, which only the spite of Lord Castlereagh could have suggested. Before quitting Montreuil to be disbanded, orders had been given to deface and destroy all their insignia and memorials of service—a bitter ordeal for the veteran heroes. Colonel Byrne, in his lately published memoirs, gives some account of the affair. He says:—

"Two beautiful standards were sent to Spain by the Emperor in 1810, for the second and third battalions of the Irish regiment, but they were left at Valadolid, as those battalions were then in Portugal. These standards were brought to the depot of the regiment, and were destroyed by Lieutenant Montague at Montreuil. They were green, with a large harp in the centre. On one side, in gold letters, 'Napoleon I. to the second Irish Battalion.' And on the other, 'The Independence of Ireland.' The third the same. The Eagle was carried by the first battalion, which, of course, had its colours like the others."

"The officers of the council left at Montreuil received two-thirds of their pay until the February following, and when all was finished, they retired on half-pay like the other officers, hoping at least to remain unmolested. But soon after the battle of Waterloo, the brave regiment was disbanded by Louis XVIII., and the Irish officers were made to feel that Lord Castlereagh and English influence prevailed in the French councils.

"Commandant Allen, who had retired to Melun, was ordered from that town to Rouen; and, passing by Paris, was there arrested by order of the Duke of Feltre, and informed he must quit the French territory without delay. Thus, without trial or judgment, one of those officers whose gallant actions had gained such renown for the Irish regiment, both in Spain and Silesia, was to be banished from his adopted country, by the orders of General Clarke, the son of an Irishman."

Many others of the officers, including Miles Byrne himself, were in like manner ordered in the harshest manner to quit France; but long afterwards we find most of them again upon active duty in the French service. Scarcely one was base enough to offer his services to England; and nothing could irritate these gentlemen so much as any suggestion of seeking a British pardon, or accepting a British favour.*

Poor Curran, when near his last, and in great misery of body and mind, had made a visit to Paris in August, 1814, and had met there some of the Irish officers. In a letter to a friend, which afterwards was made public, he had spoken of his wish to see *mercy and compassion* shown them by the English Government. Miles Byrne tells us in his memoirs:—

"I recollect a coincidence. In August, 1814, whilst at Avesnes, Inspector-General Burke was preparing his report to the Minister of War on the merits and claims of the brave Irish officers returning from the Russian prisons of Siberia, as well as those officers who escaped from Flushing, and from the English pontons, Curran's very ill-timed and most silly letters from Paris, in August, 1814, to his friend, Councillor Denis Lube, were published in the Dublin newspapers. The following extract is from one of them on the Irish exiles:—

"'I had hopes that England might let them back. The season and the power of mischief is long past; the number is almost too small to do credit to the mercy that casts a look upon them. But they are destined to give their last recollection of the green fields they are never to behold, on a foreign deathbed, and to lose the sad delight of fancied visits to them in a distant grave.'

"It caused no little indignation amongst the Irish officers who had read it, and several of them met at dinner at the Trois Frères, in the Palais Royal, to talk it over. These were General Lawless, who came in from Saint Germains for the meeting, Commandant O'Reilly, Captain Luke Lawless, Edward Lewens, and John Sweetman, &c. We were a mixture of civil and military at dinner.

"General Lawless asked Arthur Barker, as the youngest (for he was still a student at the Irish College), to read those famous letters. When read, General Lawless, turning to Lewens, said: 'You must have told Curran that our number was not worth the commiseration of Castlereagh.' 'Me, Sir!' cried Lewens, in a great passion; 'how could you think me capable of any such thing?' General Lawless rejoined: 'Of the exiles at Paris, Curran only saw you and Corbet.' It would have been better had he vented his spleen and ill-humour on something else. He might have let the brave Irish officers who have escaped the dangers of their various campaigns be again placed on active service."

Indeed, to the very last, we find the survivors of these noble Irish exiles looking forward with anxious hope to a renewal of war between France and England, that they might have one other chance of striking a mortal blow at the enemy of their country. We may be excused for giving one other characteristic extract from the Byrne memoir. Speaking of Corbet (who died a French Major-General), Colonel Byrne says:

"General Corbet was officer of the Legion of Honour, Knight of Saint Louis, and Commander of the Order of the Saviour in Greece. He valued those distinctions as highly honourable, no doubt, but he would sometimes say: 'How much the more valuable would they have been, had they been gained in the cause of my native country!' And to his last moment he lamented that her independence was not obtained; and he seemed ever anxious for something to arise between the governments of France and England which might prove beneficial to his own country.

---

* The officers of the Legion were almost all restored afterwards to active service in the armies of their adopted country. Corbet became a Major-General, and for some time commanded at Caen. Miles Byrne was commandant of Patras, in the war of Greece, and died in 1862; his rank was that of *Chef de Bataillon* in the Fifty-sixth Regiment of the Line.

"In 1840, we frequently consulted about the way we could be best employed to serve Ireland, in the event of a war between France and England, which was then on the point of being declared. I remember one day, after an audience he had had with the Minister of War, on the situation of Ireland, he told me that the Minister, General Schneider, was very desirous to have a conversation with me, respecting the reliance which could be placed on the then leader of the Irish, when a French army should land in Ireland. When he saw that there was to be no war with England, he would speak to me of going to the United States of America, being sure, he said, that from that country, one day or other, Ireland would receive ultimate assistance."

So the wholesome tradition is handed down unbroken; any and every foe of England is the Irish exile's friend; and the power of Britain must be, indeed, broadly and deeply based, if it for ever withstand the long-gathering tempest of just wrath which has been laid up against the day of wrath.

The close of the great war on the Continent had certain direct effects upon Ireland. The immense demand for agricultural produce, for victualling of armies and fortresses, had maintained high prices; and as large numbers of the small farmers then possessed leases—granted by landlords in order to manufacture voting freeholders—the people generally lived with some approach to comparative comfort. Immense contracts for the provisioning of the English navy were also made at Cork; and thus the war prices, one way and another, brought money into the country, which was not all immediately sent out again, but actually circulated to some extent amongst the people. It is true that landlords, wherever they had tenants from year to year, steadily raised the rents as prices advanced, but still the good-natured and kindly people helped one another; and, on the whole, there was not very much of either extermination or emigration. In 1815, however, and the few following years, prices of grain, cattle, and other produce, fell very low, and rents were not reduced in proportion. The increase of population—for there were now six millions of people in Ireland—produced that deadly competition for small farms which has enabled Irish landlords to wring the vitals out of a helpless peasantry, who had been left no other resource but labour on the land. Extermination may properly be said to have begun in good earnest just after "French principles" were crushed at Waterloo; and, to facilitate this process for the landlords, by recommendation of Mr. Robert Peel, the first of the series of cheap ejectment laws was passed in this very year, 1815. It provided that, in all cases of holdings, the rent of which was under £20—which included the whole class of small farms—the assistant-barrister, at sessions, could make a decree, at the cost of a few shillings, to eject a man from house and farm. Two years after, the proceedings in ejectment were still further simplified and facilitated by an Act making the sole evidence of a landlord or his agent sufficient testimony for ascertaining the amount of rent due. By these two Acts it was rendered very easy to sweep out on the highways the whole population of a village or a townland; and this was very often done towards tenants at will—a race of beings which exists in no country of Europe save Ireland. As for the possessors of a forty-shilling freehold, their leases and their voting capacity protected them for a time. It is about this date that we first meet with the expression, "surplus population in Ireland;" although, indeed, the idea itself had been common enough nearly a hundred years earlier, when Swift published his "*Modest Proposal.*" At all events, it is evident that from this moment, and for many years after, every English statesman, publicist, and political economist, held it as the grand fundamental maxim in treating of Irish affairs, that there was a surplus population in that island, and the steadiest and most earnest aim of every administration, of every party, has been to devise and execute some sure method of removing—that is, extirpating or killing—the said surplus. The young Irish Secretary, Mr. Peel, who was destined to become one of England's greatest statesmen, had, of course, turned his attention to this momentous object, and had commenced operations, as we have seen, by laws providing for cheap and easy ejectment; but he had yet other methods in his mind which were not then matured, or for which the time was not yet come.

The effect of the peace upon the prospects and claims of Catholics was altogether adverse and discouraging. England felt not only secure but triumphant, and, according to the invariable rule, it fared ill with Ireland. The English oligarchy and its dependent, the Irish Ascendancy, were absolutely drunken with an insolent and malignant pride. *Concession* of anything was no longer to be thought of; and if any person presumed to hint that there existed such a thing as human rights, he was set down as a Jacobin. A "Catholic Board" had maintained its struggling existence until the middle of summer, 1814. But whenever the news of the capitulation of Paris and imprisonment of Napoleon arrived in England, orders were at once sent to Lord Whitworth, the Lord-Lieutenant of Ireland, to suppress the board summarily by proclamation, which was accordingly done upon the 3d of June, in that year. The board met no more; but, under O'Connell's direction, the agitation took the form of "Aggregate Meetings"—thus avoiding all possibility of incurring the penalties of the Convention Act, while the meetings were even more useful than the board in arousing the people, diffusing sound information as to their rights and their wrongs, and keeping up a continual public commentary upon current events. There ensued, however, differences and dissensions amongst the Catholic leaders as to the most expedient policy to be pursued. The *veto* question had not yet entirely subsided, and something of the old jealousy between the aristocratic Catholics and the mass of the people revived. Lord Fingal, in fact, together with some other Catholic gentlemen of rank, and others who courted rank and position, retired from all participation in public affairs for some years. On the other hand, O'Connell led and stirred the democracy. But it must be confessed that it was a most arduous and difficult enterprise for him, although then in the full vigour of his vast powers, to keep alive the cause of Catholic Emancipation at all in those days of triumphant bigotry and tyranny. Richard Lalor Shiel, speaking of this gloomy period, scruples not to say: "*The hopes of the Catholics fell with the peace.* A long interval elapsed in which nothing very important or deserving of record took place. A political lethargy spread itself over the great body of the people; the assemblies of the Catholics became more unfrequent, and their language more despondent and hopeless than it had ever been."* And never before, for half a century, had the "Protestant interest" shown itself so aggressive and so spiteful towards the Catholic people. O'Connell, by his activity and audacity, concentrated upon himself the greater part of this Protestant wrath. For he made no scruple, whether in a public harangue to the people or in a speech to a jury (where the trial had anything of a political character), to denounce, with a rough and rasping tongue, all kinds of injustice and bigotry,

* Notice of "Catholic Leaders and Associations," in *Sketches of the Irish Bar.*

packed juries, church rates—in short, the most cherished principles and practices of "our glorious Constitution in Church and State." In the celebrated speech for John Magee, proprietor of the *Evening Post*, who was prosecuted for a seditious libel upon the Government, O'Connell had not only adopted and repeated the "libel," but aggravated it a thousandfold. With a fierce and vindictive energy he laid bare the whole atrocious system which in Ireland passes for Government. He thundered into the ears of the judge that he had first advised this prosecution which he was now pretending to try; and as for the twelve pious Protestants in the jury box (all "saints," and members of the "Society for the Suppression of Vice"), he told them, with cruel taunts, that they knew they were fraudulently *packed*, that they should find a man guilty (so help them God!) for stating what they knew to be true.

Mr. Shiel, in his admirable sketch of O'Connell, says: "The admirers of King William have no mercy for a man who, in his seditious moods, is so provoking as to tell the world that their idol was 'a Dutch adventurer.' Then his intolerable success in a profession where many a staunch Protestant is condemned to starve—and his fashionable house in Merrion Square—and, a greater eyesore still, his dashing revolutionary equipage, green carriage, green liveries, and turbulent, Popish steeds, prancing over a Protestant pavement, to the terror of Protestant passengers—these, and other provocations of equal publicity, have exposed this learned culprit to the deep detestation of a numerous class of His Majesty's hating subjects in Ireland. And the feeling is duly communicated to the public: the loyal press of Dublin teems with the most astounding imputations upon his character and motives." The provocation of the "Popish horses prancing over a Protestant pavement" was more serious than it may now appear, for the pavement was strictly Protestant, and so were the street lamps. No Catholic, though he might drive a coach-and-four, could be admitted on any paving or lighting board in that sacred stronghold of the Ascendancy, the Corporation of Dublin.* O'Connell was in the habit of speaking with supreme contempt of the

* It was at the height of the Catholic agitation that a Town Councillor, who was a tailor, said at a Corporation dinner: "My lord, these Papists may get their Emancipation, they may sit in Parliament, they may preside upon the Bench, a Papist may become Lord-Chancellor or Privy-Councillor; but never, *never* shall one of them set foot in the ancient and loyal Guild of Tailors."

little municipal close borough, and in one of his speeches of this year, 1815, he termed it "a beggarly corporation." "One of its most needy members," says Shiel, "was Mr. D'Esterre," and he, thinking the epithet "beggarly" too scurrilous, and too closely personal, at once sent a challenge to the speaker. O'Connell committed his conduct as to the reception of the challenge to the decision of his friends. The parties met, fought with pistols, and D'Esterre was killed, to the very great and lasting sorrow of his slayer. Mr. Shiel does not say expressly, but says "it is understood," that D'Esterre was induced to attempt O'Connell's life by the expectation that if he should rid the Government of so formidable an agitator he would be rewarded with a place; and he adds, "His claims would probably not have been overlooked by the patrons of the time." On what precise evidence Mr. D'Esterre was charged with undertaking the base job of a mercenary assassin, we have not been able to satisfy ourselves. At any rate, no dishonourable practice in the conduct of the affair was ever imputed.

In the year 1816, Sir John Newport moved in Parliament for a committee to inquire into the state of Ireland, which was then suffering greatly from scarcity of food. Sir Robert Peel steadily and successfully resisted the proposed inquiry. That prudent statesman had not been several years Chief Secretary of Ireland for nothing. He had no need of inquiry, being quite well aware of what was passing in Ireland, where he knew that things were falling out exactly according to his calculations. If there was some extermination of starving wretches, it was because his cheap ejectment laws were working well. If there was some disturbance and "agrarian crime," he had his new police ready to repress it. Better than all, he had procured the renewal of the "Insurrection Act" in 1814, had caused it to be continued in 1815, and it was now (1816) in full vigour, filling the jails with persons who could not give a good account of themselves, and transporting men for possessing a fowling-piece. He felt that an assiduous Irish Secretary could do no more, and naturally resisted Sir John Newport's meddling motion for inquiry.

But, in truth, the low price of produce had made thousands of farmers unable to pay the rent; then they had been ejected; and then that lowness of price could not enable them to procure food, because they had no money. Then there was an occasional murder, or attempt at murder. Magistrates would meet, and write to the Castle for immediate proclamation of the county under the Insurrection Act. It is useless to go through the unvarying detail of torturing oppression which has continued and repeated itself year after year, and will never end while the British Empire stands. But, in sad earnest, this year (1817) was a season of dreadful famine and suffering; and, of course, the Coercion Act of the year before was carefully renewed. The potato crop had failed; and although Ireland was then largely exporting grain and cattle to England,* yet this good food was not supposed to be sent by Providence for the nourishment of those who sowed and reaped it on their own soil. It is instructive to remark the constant similarity of the circumstances attending the series of Irish famines—the wholesale export of the Irish crops to England, the wholesale disappearance, also, of the money received as the price of those crops in the shape of absentee rents, of "surplus revenue," &c., and the never-failing Coercion Acts. If in the famine of 1847-48 there was a much greater destruction of the people, and, at the same time, a much larger export of their food and their money to England, it is only because the British system was then more fully perfected in all its details than in 1817.

In that year, however, the suffering from famine and typhus fever was already dreadful enough; and in the most fertile counties of Ireland, multitudes of people fed upon weeds of various sorts—some boiled nettles, others subsisted upon the wild kail, called in Irish *prashayh*. All political movement was suspended for several years, both in Ireland and in England; and in 1819, Lord Sidmouth introduced and carried his celebrated "Six Acts," principally to quell the "seditious" aspirations of the English people. These Acts imposed heavy penalties upon the possession of arms, and upon "blasphemous and seditious libels"—meaning all plain and truthful comments upon the proceedings of Government. A horrible military massacre was perpetrated this year at Peterloo, near Manchester, by the onslaught of a body of troops upon a perfectly peaceable meeting of the people to demand reform. This bloody day was the 16th of August, 1819; and one of the "Six Acts," passed immediately after, prohibited under cruel penalties the as-

* In this year (1817) the export to England, of grain alone, was 695,651 *quarters*.—Thom's *Official Tables in Directory*.

sembling of more than fifty persons together, unless at a meeting called by the magistrates. In short, it was the British "Reign of Terror," not inaugurated, as in France, by the people, to rid themselves of their oppressors, but by the oppressors to crush the people and their French principles into the earth.

On the 28th of February, 1821, Mr. Plunket brought up in Parliament a bill for Catholic Emancipation. It was at an unfavourable time; all the governing and controlling opinion of England was averse to any kind of claim for *rights*. The bill was vehemently opposed by the Tory party, and especially by Sir Robert Peel. In the House of Lords, the Duke of York, heir presumptive to the throne, made a furious speech against it; saying, amongst other things, that "there is a great difference between *allowing* the free exercise of religion, and the *granting* of political power"—as if there could be any freedom without political power, or as if freedom and political power were things to be allowed and granted by persons who might lawfully withhold them. It was in the same year, in the month of August, that King George IV. condescended to make a triumphal visit to Ireland; and that Mr. O'Connell, with certain views of "policy" which will not be universally appreciated, testified an enthusiastic loyalty to that individual, and drank at a public dinner the "Orange Charter toast." Overpowered by the cordiality of his reception, the King quitted the soil of Ireland with tears of emotion in his eyes. On the spot where he embarked stands a granite monument, surmounted by a crown; and Dunleary changed its name to Kingstown. It would be agreeable not to record these incidents; but they form, unhappily, part of the history of Ireland.

Touching this royal visit—not to insist in this place upon the savage comment of Lord Byron—we may give the more moderate prose of Richard Lalor Shiel: "Sir Benjamin Bloomfield arrived in Dublin before his master, and intimated the royal anxiety *that all differences and animosities should be laid aside*. Accordingly, it was agreed that a public dinner should be held at Morrison's, where the leaders of both parties should pledge each other in libations of everlasting amity. This national festivity took place; and, from the vehement protestations on both sides, it was believed by many that a lasting reconciliation had been effected. Master Ellis and Mr. O'Connell almost embraced each other. The King arrived; the Catholics determined *not to obtrude their grievances upon him*. Accordingly, our gracious Sovereign passed rather an agreeable time in Dublin. He was hailed with tumultuous hurrahs wherever he passed; and in return for the enthusiastic reception which he had found, he directed Lord Sidmouth to write a letter recommending it to the people *to be united*. His Majesty shortly afterwards set sail with tears in his eyes from Kingstown. For a little while the Catholics continued under the miserable deception under which they had laboured during the royal sojourn; but when they found that no intention existed to introduce a change of system into Ireland—that the King's visit seemed an artifice, and Lord Sidmouth's epistle meant nothing—and that while men were changed, measures continued substantially unaltered, they began to perceive that some course more effective than a loyal solicitude not to disturb the repose of His Majesty should be adopted."

In short, the Irish Catholics were once more cheated; and it is not saying much for their perspicuity—for they were twice cheated by the same cheat. Neither can we ever look back with pleasure on the scenes of "loyal" servility enacted at that period by leading Irishmen—O'Connell toasting the glorious, pious, and immortal memory of the "Dutch adventurer," and presenting a huge bunch of shamrocks to the discreditable being who then represented the desolating British domination. Doubtless these hypocritical demonstrations of "loyalty" to an enemy were transacted with an idea that it was a cunning policy to conciliate tyrants in England, and to disarm animosities at home. In these views they failed utterly, and have their place in history only as a signal example of gratuitous crouching and crawling.

The senseless gala of 1821 passed away; the horrible famine of 1822 immediately followed.*

---

* John Philpot Curran died in 1817, on the 14th of October. His remains were buried first in London; afterwards removed to the cemetery of Glasnevin. Grattan died three years after, and had the very doubtful honour of a tomb in Westminster Abbey. These two great Irishmen left the country they loved in one of the gloomiest periods of her gloomy story.

CHAPTER XVIII.

1822—1825.

Famine of 1822—Its Causes—Financial Frauds upon Ireland—Horrors of the Famine—Extermination—Suspension of *Habeas Corpus* Act—Castlereagh Cuts his Throat—Marquis Wellesley Viceroy—Sir Harcourt Lees—The Bottle Riot—Catholic Association Formed—Dr. Boyle, "J.K.L."—Progress of Catholic Association—"Catholic Rent"—Maynooth Professors "Loyal"—Rage of the Orangemen—"O'Connell, the Pope, and the Devil"—Passiveness of the Dissenters—O'Connell's Appeals to them—Intellectual and Literary Power of the Movement—Act to Suppress "Unlawful Associations"—First Attempt to Cheat the Catholics—A Relief Bill with "Wings"—Defeated Catholic Deputation in London—O'Connell and the Whigs—Strong Feeling in Ireland against "Wings."

BEFORE proceeding to the details of this dreadful famine of 1822, it is needful to consider the financial relations of the two islands since the period of the "Union."

In 1816 was passed the Act for consolidating the British and Irish Exchequers—it is the 56th George III., cap. 98. It became operative on the 1st January, 1817.

The meaning of this consolidation was—charging Ireland with the whole debt of England, pre-union and post-union; and in like manner charging England with the whole Irish debt.

Now, the enormous English national debt, both before and after the Union, was contracted for purposes which Ireland had not only no interest in promoting, but a direct and vital interest in contravening and resisting; that is, it had been contracted to crush American and French liberty, and to destroy those very powers which were the natural allies of Ireland.

But this is not all. We have next to see the proportions which the two debts bore to each other. It will be remembered that, by the terms of the so-called "Union,"

I. Ireland was to be protected from any liability on account of the British national debt contracted prior to the Union.

II. The separate debt of each country being first provided for by a separate charge, Ireland was then to contribute two-seventeenths towards the joint or common expenditure of the United Kingdom for twenty years; after which her contribution was to be made proportionate to her ability, as ascertained at stated periods of revision by certain tests specified in the Act.

III. Ireland was not only promised that she never should have any concern with the then existing British debt, but she was also assured that her taxation should not be raised to the standard of Great Britain until the following conditions should occur:—

1. That the two debts should come to bear to each other the proportion of fifteen parts for Great Britain to two parts for Ireland; and,
2. That the respective circumstances of the two countries should admit of uniform taxation.

It must be further borne in mind that, previous to the Union, the national debt of Ireland was a mere trifle. It had been enormously increased by charging to Ireland's special account, first, the expenses of getting up the rebellion; next, the expenses of suppressing it; and, lastly, the expenses of bribing Irish noble lords and gentlemen to sell their country at this Union. Thus the Irish debt, which before the Union had been less than three millions sterling, was set down by the Act of Union at nearly twenty-seven millions.

On the 20th of June, 1804 (four years after the Union had passed), Mr. Foster, Chancellor of the Irish Exchequer, observed, that whereas in 1794 the Irish debt did not exceed two millions and a half, it had in 1803 risen to forty-three millions; and that during the current year it was increased to nearly fifty-three millions.

During the long and costly war against France, and the second American war, it happened, by some very extraordinary species of book-keeping, that while the English debt was not quite doubled, the Irish debt was more than quadrupled; as if Ireland had twice the interest which England had in forcing the Bourbons back upon France, and in destroying the commerce of America.

Thus, in 1816, when the Consolidation Act was passed, the whole funded debt of Ireland was found to be £130,561,037. By this management, the Irish debt, which in 1801 had been to the British as one to sixteen and a half, was forced up to bear to the British debt the ratio of one to seven and a half. This was the proportion required by the Act of Union as a condition of subjecting Ireland to indiscriminate taxation with Great Britain—a condition equally impudent and iniquitous. Ireland was to be loaded with inordinate debt; and then this debt was to be made the pretext for raising her taxation to the high British standard, and thereby rendering her liable to the pre-union debt of Great Britain!

By way of softening down the glaring injustice of such a proposition, Lord Castlereagh said that the two debts might be brought to bear to each other the prescribed proportions, partly by the increase of the Irish debt, but partly also by the decrease of the British. To which Mr. Foster thus answered, on the 15th of March, 1800:—"The monstrous absurdity you would force down our throats is, that Ireland's increase of poverty, as shown by her increase of debt, and England's increase of wealth, as shown by diminution of debt, are to bring them to an equality of condition, so as to be able to bear an equality of taxation."

But bad as this was, the former and worse alternative was what really befell. The given ratio was reached solely by the increase of the Irish debt, without any decrease of the British.

We take from the excellent pamphlet of Mr. O'Neill Daunt,* already quoted in a former chapter, a passage presenting a summary of the financial dealings of England with Ireland:—

"The following facts stand unshaken, and should become familiarly known to every man in Ireland:—

"1. The British debt in 1801 was about sixteen and a half times as large as the Irish debt.

"2. It was promised by the authors of the Union, and the promise was embodied in the seventh Article, that as Ireland had no part in contracting that debt, so she should be for ever preserved from all concern with the payment of its principal or interest.

"3. In order to give effect to this promise, Great Britain was to be separately taxed to the extent of her separate pre-union debt charge. But Great Britain is *not* thus separately taxed; and Ireland is consequently made to contribute to the payment of a purely British liability, from which she was promised perpetual exemption.

"4. Ireland has never received from Great Britain one farthing, by way of compensation or equivalent, for being thus subjected to the pre-union British debt.

"5. By the fifth clause of the seventh Article of the Union, Ireland was guaranteed the benefit of her own surplus taxes. She has never, during the sixty-four years of Union, received one farthing in virtue of that clause. Her taxes, after defraying her public domestic expenses, have been uniformly abstracted by England; and the clause that professes to secure to Ireland the use of them has been rendered a dead letter by the Parliamentary management I have described.

* *Financial Grievances of Ireland.* Publications of the Irish National League.

"6. The amount of Irish taxes annually drawn from this kingdom is a very large item in the general pecuniary drain. Mr. Dillon, in his able and carefully compiled report to the Dublin Corporation, shows that the Irish taxes expended out of Ireland in the year 1860 amounted to £4,095,453; and that in 1861 they amounted to £3,970,715."

But even this direct drain of Irish money into England, under pretence of paying interest on a debt, represents a very small part of the systematic plunder of the country. When to this is added the absentee rental, the interest paid out of encumbered estates to Jews in London, and the cost of manufactured articles and colonial produce which Ireland ought to manufacture or import for herself, we may begin to understand why the mass of the Irish people is always on the verge of starvation, and why the failure of the meanest kind of food throws them at once into the pangs of famine.

This is what befell in 1822. Alison, the Scotch historian of modern times, attributes the dreadful havoc of the Irish famine in this year entirely to "the contraction of the currency, and consequent fall of the prices of agricultural produce fifty per cent." But the Scotch historian does not mention that the grain crop of 1821 had been carried off to England, to the amount of nearly two million quarters (1,822,816), and that of 1822 to the amount of more than one million quarters,* not to speak of countless herds of cattle, sheep, and swine. No wonder, then, if we see in Ireland perennial misery and beggary, with occasional paroxysms of murderous famine.

On the 27th of June, in this year, Sir John Newport, of Waterford, in his place in the House of Commons, endeavouring to awaken that assembly to some sense of the horrors which were to be seen in Ireland, described one parish in his neighbourhood, where fifteen persons had already died of hunger; twenty-eight more, he said, were past all hope of recovery, and one hundred and twenty (still in the same parish) were prostrated by famine fever;—and the same speaker mentioned another parish where the priest had gone round and administered extreme unction to every man, woman, and child, *all in articulo mortis* by mere starvation.†

* Thom's *Official Directory* for 1853.
† In Cobbett's *Register* we find that writer's contemporary comment upon the debate in the House. He says: "Money, it seems, is wanted in Ireland. Now, people do not eat money. No, but the money will buy them something to eat. What? The food is *there*, then. Pray observe this, and let the parties get out of the concern if they can. *The food is there;* but those who have it in their

A certain Colonel Patrickson was quartered that season in Galway with his regiment. He reports to his superior officer: "Hundreds of half-famished wretches arrive almost daily from a distance of fifty miles, many of them so exhausted by want of food that the means taken to restore them fail of effect, from the weakness of the digestive organs occasioned by long fasting."* Official statistics were not then so much attended to as they have since been; but certain returns, such as they were, stated, that in the month of June there were, in Clare County alone, 99,639 persons subsisting on daily charity, and in Cork, 122,000.† We have no record of the estimated number of deaths in this hideous famine; and if we had any such estimate, compiled as it would be under the direction of the Irish authorities, by aid of their police, it would not be trustworthy. Neither are there any census-tables, showing the decrease of the population. In Thom's *Official Directory*, the population of the island in 1821 is given at 6,801,827; and there is no statement of the population afterwards for ten years.

Of course, there was again a good deal of extermination of tenantry; and some desperate men did certainly kill here and there an ejecting landlord or agent. It appears, also, that there were "nocturnal outrages;" men with faces blackened, and wearing shirts more or less white, did come to some houses in search of arms, to defend their lives or to avenge their wrongs; but in all this there was no trace or tittle of political, seditious, or revolutionary movement. Nevertheless, the first thing that occurred to the British Government, to meet this great calamity, was a new and improved *Insurrection Act*. This new Act, together with another for the suspension of the writ of *Habeas Corpus*, was introduced and at once carried by Lord Castlereagh, then Marquis of Londonderry. It was almost the last public act of his evil life. On the 12th of August, in that same year, he executed justice upon himself by cutting his own throat with a knife. Never lived a more deadly foe of the human race, and especially of the country which gave him birth. He was almost as much hated in England as in Ireland; for he had been a warm supporter of the "Six Acts," and of every measure of despotism. The body of the suicide, instead of being staked at cross roads, was borne in solemn pomp to Westminster Abbey (where the bones of Henry Grattan must have shrunk aside), and the Duke of Wellington and the proudest peers in England were his pall-bearers; but, as the coffin was removed from the hearse to be carried into the Abbey, the multitudes around could not repress a hoot of execration, a long, loud, and hideous yell of horror and hatred. The Tory historian, Alison, reluctantly records that "savage miscreants raised a horrid shout;" but future ages will probably pronounce, that in all the mob of London was no such dreadful miscreant as the man then borne to his grave.

It must not be omitted to state that the Parliament of 1822—in addition to a Coercion Act and *Habeas Corpus* Suspension Act—voted an appropriation of £500,000 for relief of Irish distress, by employing destitute people on public works. It by no means amounted to one-tenth part of the Irish money annually drained from Ireland into England, and applied to English purposes; and even this appropriation was, as usual, corruptly and absurdly expended by English officials, principally upon useless and unproductive works, like the unmeaning obelisk upon Killiney Hill. The British press, and speakers in Parliament at that period, as at a later date, spoke of this appropriation out of the Consolidated Exchequer as so much alms given by England, and assumed immense credit for the generosity of the gift. Under this form and colour the transaction has passed into history. Sir Archibald Alison, of course, glorifies the magnanimity of England upon this occasion: "England no longer remembered the crimes of Ireland—thought only of her sorrows," and so forth. The Marquis Wellesley was Lord-Lieutenant this year; but although invested with terrible powers for the suppression of outrage and insurrection, he is not charged with exercising too savagely the extra legal authority with which the British Parliament was so prompt to clothe him. Indeed, the Marquis, from the conciliatory and mild way in which he spared the suffering people, and from his courtesy towards the Catholic leaders, some of whom he entertained at the Castle, soon became unpopular with the Orange faction. The most

---

possession will not give it without the money. And we know that the food is there; for since this famine has been declared in Parliament, thousands of quarters of corn have been imported every week from Ireland to England."—*Register*, July, 1822. Mr. Cobbett, however, was not placing "the parties" in so embarrassing a position as he imagined, when he defied them to get out of it if they could. It has always been a matter of congratulation with English ministers that, whether the Irish be starving or not, England can still draw from the country her full tribute of grain and cattle. In reading of all these transactions of 1822, one might almost imagine that he is reading of what befell twenty-five years later.

* Letter of Sir D. Baird to Sir H. Taylor, *Memoirs of Lord Wellesley*. VIII.
† Alison's *History of Europe since 1815.*

prominent Orange agitator was then a certain Sir Harcourt Lees. He was a clergyman by profession, and held preferment in the Church; but occupied himself chiefly in discovering Popish plots for the massacre of Protestants, denouncing, in the newspapers, "O'Connell, the Pope, and the Devil," and sending petitions to Parliament, praying to "put down Popery," and send O'Connell to the Tower. Sir Harcourt was slightly insane; but his morbid visions of Jesuit conspiracies, and wild stories from Fox's *Book of Martyrs*, were well enough suited to excite the ignorant Orangemen of Dublin. These pestilent people soon began to suspect that Lord Wellesley was in league with "O'Connell, the Pope, and the Devil;" and the city resounded with their imprecations. At length, on the night of the 14th of December, their rage broke out in the form of a riot at the theatre. Some ruffians threw a bottle and a piece of wood at the Vice-regal box, but failed to strike the Marquis. Three Dublin tradesmen were arrested, charged with participating in the riot, and indicted. The Grand Jury of Dublin (all Orangemen) ignored the bill. The Attorney-General, Mr. Plunket, then proceeded *ex officio*, and sent them up for trial. As might have been anticipated, the jury would not convict; and, in short, no person was ever punished for the "bottle riot."

The year 1823 is notable for the formation of the "Catholic Association." Its foundations were laid by Mr. O'Connell, in conjunction with Mr. Shiel, then a very young barrister, but already remarkable for a certain kind of polished, figurative, and antithetical rhetoric. These two gentlemen met at the house of a common friend in the Wicklow mountains; "and after exchanging their opinions," says Mr. Shiel, "on the deplorable state to which the Catholic mind had been reduced, and the utter want of organization in the body, it was agreed that they should both sign an address to the Irish Catholics," and inclose it to the principal people of that religion. The result of this procedure was for a time not very encouraging. "A very thin meeting," says Mr. Shiel, "which did not consist of more than twenty individuals, was held at a tavern in Sackville Street; and it was there determined that something should be done." The work, in truth, was difficult. The old alienation between the Catholic peers and the democratic masses still subsisted. Old Lord Fingal, Lord Gormanstown, and others of the highest rank and influence, who would have been glad to accept Emancipation even on the terms of the *veto*, were somewhat scandalized at the violence with which O'Connell and the famous Dr. Dromgoole repudiated that project of enslaving the Church. Yet a combination of all the sections and elements of the Catholic community, however difficult, was precisely the indispensable condition of effecting any very notable good to the cause. To this, then, O'Connell bent all the energies and resources of his mind. Happily the Earl of Fingal had a son, Lord Killeen, who not only did not share all the prejudices or apprehensions of his father, but longed to throw himself heart and soul into the movement by the side of O'Connell. Lord Killeen had good abilities, and was free from those habits of submission which the Catholic aristocracy had contracted at the period of their extreme depression. His example was soon followed by Lord Gormanstown, a peer of ancient descent, and hitherto of retiring habits, so far as political agitation was concerned. He conceived that the course of the aggressive agitators had the effect only of irritating enmity; and, therefore, had very much secluded himself amongst his woods near Balbriggan. Next came in the Earl of Kinmare; who, though he did not formally join the association (having an aversion to public appearance), sent in the authority of his name and his pecuniary contribution. From this time the union of the aristocracy with the rest of their countrymen was assured. Another and still more powerful element in the confederacy was the Catholic priesthood. The celebrated and very able and energetic Doctor Doyle, Bishop of Kildare and Leighlin, was the first prelate who openly joined the association; his potent pen was devoted to its service; and the whole world was long familiar with the signature "J. K. L." (the initials of his episcopal office), signed to many a vigorous pamphlet and letter. Other bishops and the great body of the clergy soon became members of the association, and the movement which had begun so humbly swelled into a puissant and apparently irresistible torrent of public opinion. O'Connell was at last in his element; and, ably supported by Shiel and Wyse, laboured continually to give a practical character to the meetings, and to bring under calm and well-considered discussion all great questions arising in the State.

In structure, the Catholic Association much resembled all the other political societies instituted by Mr. O'Connell. It consisted of members paying a guinea each year, and of associates paying one shilling. The executive consisted of a standing committee. The regular meetings were weekly, each Saturday; and the proceedings consisted in the reading of correspondence, perfecting organization, the discussion of public questions which bore any relation to the cause, and deciding on petitions. There was little or no oratorical display at these weekly meetings, the members rather applying themselves to treat subjects of discussion with a moderate and business-like calmness, so as to develop facts and diffuse sound information. Still, the proceedings attracted little attention during the first year. Indeed, Mr. Shiel informs us that "the association in its origin was treated with contempt, not only by its open adversaries, but Catholics themselves spoke of it with derision, and spurned at the walls of mud which their brethren had rapidly thrown up, which were afterwards to become *altæ mænia Romæ*." It was only in the course of the following year that Mr. O'Connell instituted the new system of monthly subscriptions of one penny (which he called "Catholic Rent"), when it became evident both to friends and enemies how deep a hold the cause had upon the hearts of the Catholic masses, and how wide-spread was their determination to achieve their liberties. The Ministry began to take some alarm. The Cabinet at that time was extremely Anti-Catholic, Lord Liverpool being still First Lord of the Treasury and Premier; the Duke of Wellington, Master-General of the Ordnance; Lord Eldon (an extreme example of the narrowest bigotry) was Lord-Chancellor; and Mr. Peel (not yet Sir Robert) was the Home Secretary. It is true that Canning, well understood to be a friend of the Catholic claims, was in the Ministry, but his place was that of Foreign Secretary, so that he could have little special influence upon that great question which was now agitating the three kingdoms, and at length disquieting seriously His Majesty's advisers; for, in truth, no phenomenon like this had ever been seen in Ireland before. Within two years after its origin, the penny subscriptions to the rent averaged £500 a week, which represented half-a-million of enrolled associates, and produced a fund quite sufficient to pay the expenses of defending men unjustly accused, to prosecute Orange violators of the law (but this was generally a hopeless enterprise), to pay the expenses of Parliamentary and election agents, and even to afford considerable appropriations for the support of Catholic schools for the poor.

But not even these evidences of imposing numbers and close organization so much alarmed the Government, as the determined attitude taken by some of the clergy, and the bold writings of Dr. Doyle. He broached doctrines which not only startled the "Protestant Ascendancy," but even affected the nerves of some of the Maynooth professors. In his letter to Mr. Robertson, after speaking of the possibility of a rebellion and a French invasion, he says: "The Minister of England cannot look to the exertions of the Catholic priesthood. They have been ill-treated, and they may yield for a moment to the influence of nature, though it be opposed to grace. The clergy, with a few exceptions, are from the ranks of the people; they inherit their feelings; they are not, as formerly, brought up under despotic governments; and they have imbibed the doctrines of Locke and Paley more deeply than those of Bellarmine, or even of Bossuet, on the Divine right of Kings. They know much more of the principles of the Constitution than they do of passive obedience. *If a rebellion were raging from Carrickfergus to Cape Clear, no sentence of excommunication would ever be fulminated by a Catholic prelate.*"

This announcement produced some consternation; and to counteract the effect of such perilous declarations from a bishop, Lord Wellesley, it was said, applied to Maynooth; and from Maynooth (which receives money from the Treasury) was, in fact, issued a protest,—from which, it was known, the students and Dr. Crotty, the President, dissented altogether. It bore, however, the names of five professors of theology; and the persons who were chiefly instrumental in getting it up were two old French doctors of the Sorbonne, who had belonged, in their own country, to the old *régime*, "and, with a good deal of learning, imported into Ireland a very strong relish for submission."* The publication of the five professors produced no effect whatever. The people and clergy now saw the most eminent of their prelates in the ranks of the association; and Dr. Murray, Archbishop of Dublin, not only joined that body, but sometimes used very energetic language tending to excite his people to be zealous in the cause. "The contemplation of the wrongs of my country," he exclaimed, in his stately cathedral in Marlborough Street—"The contemplation of the wrongs of my country makes my soul burn within me."

It is needless to say that the progress

* Shiel's Sketches: *Catholic Leaders.* Mr. Shiel gives at full length what he calls "the Sorbonne manifesto;" and adds, that "it was laughed at by the Irish priesthood."

and power of the Catholic Association excited the Orangemen of Ireland to frenzy. Sir Harcourt Lees saw visions and dreamed dreams; and many petitions were sent to Parliament "to put down Popery," and save the Protestant State from O'Connell, the Pope, and the Devil. Ministers, indeed, began to perceive that they must yield; and that Emancipation could not be far off. It had in its favour not only the entire Catholic population of Ireland, but also, in England, a small but very wealthy and influential group of nobles and gentry of that ancient faith, who, of course, expected their own restoration to civil rights from the success of the movement then in such rapid progress. The Dissenting population of the North of Ireland, it must be said to their credit, were favourable to the claims of the Catholics, although their grandfathers had gladly submitted to the Test and Corporation Acts, which excluded Nonconformists from most offices, rather than make common cause with their fellow-sufferers, the Catholics, to shake off the yoke of the Ascendancy. O'Connell had often appealed to them to give him their moral aid in his struggle; representing to them that the great reform he sought was a breaking down of *all* barriers of exclusion under pretext of men's religious belief; that if the last penal laws which oppressed the Catholics were dashed to the earth, the last penal laws which injured and insulted Dissenters must come down along with them; and if the Catholics and Nonconformists of Ireland were once united in the assertion of their rights, there would soon be an end of tithes, and church-rates, and ministers' money, and every other paltry imposition which bolstered up the "Ascendancy." Language like this had its effect. A large proportion—and that the most educated and enlightened—of the Presbyterians gave their entire sympathy to the Catholic movement; and if but few amongst them aided it actively, they at least remained passive, and left all the fanatical howling—all the pious imprecations, and vaticinations of wrath to come—to the Orange Grand-Masters, and raving rectors and curates.

But amongst the forces which were now giving impetus to the Catholic cause must also be classed the English Reformers, and their powerful organs of the press. Indeed, during this whole controversy, nothing was more observable than the great literary superiority of the advocates of the Catholics, and the utter nullity of anything which was attempted on the other side, in the shape either of argument or satire. Most of the wisest and wittiest pens of the two islands were wielded in favour of Emancipation. Trenchant reasoning from Jeffrey, in the *Edinburgh Review*— the *piquant* humour of Sidney Smith, in "Peter Plymley's Letters" —the brawny might of William Cobbett, who, wherever tyranny and intolerance showed their head, smote it amain with his knotted club—the exquisite satire of Moore, like a rapier of the finest edge, that cut clean and drew blood, and often with the lightest and most graceful movement, as if in play, searched the very vitals of some villain in high places, and made him howl—Shiel's brilliant shafts of wit, shot from the *New Monthly Magazine*;—all these were aimed at the monster called Protestant Ascendancy in Church and State, and there was nothing of the kind to oppose them; nothing but the raving letters of Sir Harcourt Lees and his friends, or the bitter spite of the Tories in *Blackwood*, and *Fraser*, and the *Quarterly*.

However, if the Government had but little to say for itself in the literary way, it could still produce Acts of Parliament and compose indictments. Early in 1825, Mr. Goulburn, then Secretary for Ireland, brought into Parliament and carried through both Houses a bill for suppression of "Unlawful Associations in Ireland." This law was of course aimed against the existing Catholic Association, which was not at all "unlawful." Immediately when it passed, the association, under the legal advice of O'Connell, dissolved itself. It was no longer in existence. The law was satisfied; and then immediately constituted itself again, under the title of the New Catholic Association. This was a usual expedient of O'Connell through his long series of agitations, in avoiding the penalties of penal enactments. He boasted that he could "drive a coach-and-six through an Act of Parliament;" and the practice of evading or practically annulling such tyrannous laws cannot certainly be condemned, seeing that the Irish people would at any time have been justified (if they had the needful force) in openly breaking, defying, and resisting them. This law against the Catholic Association was never, in fact, enforced, nor any enforcement attempted: and it continued its proceedings precisely as before, until Emancipation was secure.

But while the Government thus made a show of coercion on the one hand, they had on the other prepared a bill for granting the Catholic claims in a certain stinted and very guarded manner. And the bill for this purpose, which happily never became law, is, indeed, an instructive sample of British statesmanship with respect to Irish affairs. It proposed to admit Catholics both in England and in Ireland to Parliament, and to Municipal Corporations, but provided for Ireland two very important safeguards for the perpetuation of English supremacy in that island. In the first place, the entire class of county voters having freeholds worth forty shillings were to be disfranchised. These made the great bulk of the rural voters. The other measure was to pension the Catholic clergy. The bill was prepared under the inspiration of Sir Robert Peel. This shrewd statesman had perceived when in Ireland that the large increase of the *Regium Donum* to Presbyterian ministers had had the effect of quieting down the republican aspirations and quelling the "French principles" which had made those clergymen nearly all rebels in 1798; and that whatever influence they exercised over their flocks was now exerted in favour of "loyalty"—that is, of British dominion. And as for the Catholic clergy, we have in fact seen that the only members of that body who came to the rescue of British loyalty, against Dr. Doyle's audacious declaration, were five professors of an institution endowed by the State. He prudently calculated that to salary them all would buy them away from their people, and give England an efficient corps of clerical detectives in the interests of the British Government. Accordingly, this bill provided that they were to be paid out of the Treasury at the rate of £1,000 to each bishop, £300 to a dean, £200 to a parish priest, and £60 to a curate. It was a scale somewhat in proportion to the tariff of rewards which had been offered for the *discovery* of Catholic clergymen, and which had kept the "priest-hunters" in good business for many years. It may be thought that times had greatly altered for the better; yet the *intention* in the latter case was quite as deadly hostile to the Irish people and their clergy as it had been in the former. And so they felt it; for both priests and people were resolutely opposed to this bribe, and most desirous for the defeat of the bill. It was defeated. After passing the Lower House it encountered most infuriated opposition in the Lords; and the Duke of York made a speech of the intensest malignity, which had the more serious effect, as he was heir presumptive to the Crown of England. He declared in the most solemn manner that he never would consent to allow the claims of the Catholics—"*never, so help him God!*" On the second reading in the House of Lords the bill was defeated.

There was at this time in London a very imposing deputation of Irish Catholics. O'Connell and Shiel had been requested by the Catholic Association to go over and demand to be heard at the bar of the House of Commons against the bill for suppression of the "Unlawful Associations in Ireland." The motion that they should be heard was made by Mr. Brougham, but was rejected, and that part of their mission failed. Several distinguished gentlemen had been associated with the deputation—amongst others, Mr. O'Gorman and Sir Thomas Esmonde. They were very warmly welcomed and courteously entertained by many leading Whigs: Brougham, Burdett, the Duke of Norfolk, and the Duke of Sussex, the "Liberal" member of the Royal family.

An incident occurred during the discussion upon Mr. Brougham's motion to hear O'Connell and Shiel at the bar, which gave occasion to one of the very few imprudent things which Peel committed in his Parliamentary life. He was opposing the motion with much vehemence, and denouncing the association as a treasonable body. Alluding to a friendly address which it had presented to the venerable patriot Archibald Hamilton Rowan, "he became heated with victory," says Mr. Shiel, "and, cheered as he was repeatedly by his multitudinous partizans, turned suddenly towards the part of the House where the deputies were seated, and looking triumphantly at Mr. O'Connell, with whom he forgot for a moment that he had been once engaged in a personal quarrel, shook his hand with scornful exultation, and asked whether the House required any better evidence than the address of the association '*to an attainted traitor!*'" This language was held to be in very bad taste; and Mr. Brougham made a fierce and damaging reply. The incident, however, showed in very strong light the bitter feeling of Sir Robert Peel towards the Catholics.

Before the deputation quitted London, the other bill for Emancipation, with payment of the clergy and disfranchisement of forty-shilling freeholders, was pending. These two conditions were called the "wings" of the bill; and the deputies, especially Mr. O'Connell, had much conversation with leading Whig politicians upon the terms of the proposed measure, and upon the way in which it might probably be received in Ireland as a final settlement. Those Whig politicians were naturally desirous that the measure should pass, wings and all, for they cared nothing about the independence of the Church or the rights of electors. What they thought of was that some Irish Catholic members coming into Parliament would be an accession of force to their party, and might carry them into office. Mr. O'Connell did not then probably so fully know, as he afterwards came to know, that British Whigs regard all Irish questions solely with a view to the interests of the Whig party. The courtesies also, and the persuasive phraseology of those courtly "Liberals," and of the English Catholics, who were all for the bill, certainly imposed somewhat upon O'Connell's mind, insomuch that he is known to have signified to some principal Whig statesmen his willingness to take the bill as it stood, with the two offensive "wings." The fortunate loss of the measure in the House of Lords prevented any evil consequences arising from this unaccountable weakness; and when the deputation returned to Ireland, and found what was the state of feeling amongst the Catholics; and when O'Connell found that his complying disposition was very likely to injure his popularity and his power for good, he very promptly and frankly retracted, and took his position again with his countrymen. It had been well, indeed, if he had firmly held his ground against both those wings to the last.

CHAPTER XIX.

1825—1829.

Action of the Catholic Association—Waterford Election—Louth Election—Change of Ministry—Canning Premier—Lord Anglesea Viceroy—The "New Reformation"—Pope and Maguire—Death of Canning—Goderich Cabinet—Catholic Petition for Repeal of Test and Corporation Acts—Acts Repealed—Clare Election—O'Connell Returned—Its Results—Suppression of Catholic Association—Peel and Wellington Prepare Catholic Relief Bill—Rage of the Bigots—Reluctance of the King—O'Connell at the Bar of the House—Passage of the Emancipation Act—Disfranchisement of the Forty-Shilling Freeholders—Abstract of the Relief Act—The New Oath—Meaning and Spirit of the Relief Act.

THE Catholic Association continued its operations and extended its organization with even greater vigour and success than before. It had a machinery which extended not only into every county, but into every parish. Its funds were given to employ lawyers to protect the people in cases of extreme oppression; and in such cases as the wrecking of a chapel, or an Orange riot in the North—cases which the magistrates at petty and quarter-sessions had been in the habit of treating upon the general principle that Papists had no rights which Protestants were bound to respect—their worships were now sometimes thunderstruck by the apparition of clever barristers or attorneys from Dublin, who not only knew more law than the whole bench of justices, but were attended by newspaper reporters, sure to publish abroad to the world any too outrageous instance of magisterial partizanship. But the machinery of the Association, both central and provincial, was capable of being employed with more striking effect in the elections of representatives in Parliament, and its efficiency began to be proved in the general election of 1826. It was resolved in the Association that all its efforts should be concentrated upon favouring the return of certain liberal Protestants (seeing that Catholics were not eligible) for some counties which had been up to that time controlled absolutely by a few great families of the old colonial aristocracy. The Beresfords, for example, had long represented Waterford in person of some member of their family. The idea of opposing the Beresford interest in that county seemed the wildest dream; and the Beresford, who was Marquis of Waterford, naturally thought that he did not more clearly own the demesne of Curraghmore than he owned the representation of his county. At the election of 1826, Lord George Beresford was boldly opposed by Mr. Villiers Stuart, another large proprietor of the county, and a friend to the Catholic claims. The latter was supported by the parochial organizers and by the Catholic clergy, and won his election, to the intense mortification of the house of Curraghmore, and perfect consternation of the whole Protestant interest.

While society in Dublin was much agitated by the progress of this contest in the South, news arrived in that city of a still more stirring nature. Louth County was, in like manner, held to be an appanage of the two noble houses of Foster and Jocelyn. Their titles were Oriel and Roden. Lord Oriel was that John Foster, Speaker of the Irish House of Commons at the time of the Union, with whom this history has already had much to do—all his life a high place-holder, and bitter opponent of the Catholics. The politician of the family was now John Leslie Foster, who had long sat in Parliament as one of the members for the county, and consistently on every occasion resisted the slightest concession to the Catholics. The Jocelyns had as their nominee for the other seat Mr. Fortescue, a politician of the same deep Orange hue. At the election in 1826 there presented himself to the people to ask their suffrages a Mr. Dawson, a retired barrister of some fortune, who was favourable to the enfranchisement of six millions of his countrymen. He was attended to the polls by immense multitudes of the worthy forty-shilling freeholders, who marched with him into Dundalk with green banners flying in the wind. The contest was close; for the influence of the great landlords was nearly irresistible, unless at mortal peril. It needed all the energy of the local managers of the Association to bring up the voters and get them to defy those potent despots. Mr. Shiel went down from Dublin as counsel for Dawson. In short, at the close of the poll, Dawson was declared duly elected; Mr. Foster was the second member; and Fortescue, nominee of Lord Roden, stood defeated.

Some few other successes of a similar character showed what the Association could do. The effect of such events upon the public mind in England was very great. As for the "Ascendancy" faction in Ireland, it was as usual in a foam of rage. The great family interests—the mighty Orange houses which had been long a rock and strong tower to Protestant monopoly and religion—were now, as it seemed, to be assailed, not by sap or mine, but by open storm and escalade.

The Protestant mind of that day could not help believing that there was some Jesuit conspiracy at work in this matter, and that the Waterford election was won virtually by the Pope of Rome. Sir Harcourt Lees demanded of Parliament whether his vaticinations would be at length listened to—Popery "put down," and O'Connell sent to the Tower.

Early in the first session of the new Parliament Lord Liverpool, the Premier, was struck with paralysis. He was a helpless and timorous creature, afraid to read his letters in the morning, lest they should bring news of an insurrection in some part of the country; and his only idea of government was to disturb nothing, to reform nothing (sufficient unto the day being the evil thereof), and only praying that all mankind might remain precisely as it was for his day. In short, he was a "Conservative" of the stupidest sort.*

On his death, which followed very soon, Mr. Canning, who had been Foreign Secretary in his Administration, was sent for by the King, and received his commands to form a Cabinet. But Mr. Canning, only a month before, had made a powerful speech in favour of Catholic Emancipation; the King, therefore, must have known that in making this statesman his Prime Minister, he was taking an almost irrevocable step towards that clearly inevitable consummation. Accordingly, Sir Robert Peel, the Duke of Wellington, Lord Eldon, and other Tory members of the outgoing Cabinet, refused to serve with Mr. Canning, who thereupon formed a Ministry which was generally in favour of concession. Lord Wellesley was succeeded in the Viceroyalty of Ireland by the Marquis of Anglesea, formerly Earl of Uxbridge—a very brilliant cavalry officer, but not much of a statesman. The Chief Secretary was Lord Francis Leveson Gower.

When Lord Anglesea arrived in Ireland he found the Ascendancy faction in high excitement. The very Orangemen began to perceive the ominous signs of the times. They were making preparations to celebrate with great pomp the grand Orange anniversary of the 12th of July, being resolved, if they could not much longer trample on their fellow-countrymen, to insult them to the last. As the time approached, however, Lord Anglesea prohibited by proclamation the customary procession in Dublin, and the garlanding with Orange lilies the statue of King William in College Green. In Ulster, however, the anniversary was celebrated with even more than the usual show of insolent triumph. In every town and village the brethren assembled in great numbers, marched from town to town, all flaunting with purple and orange sashes, generally halting in the midst of districts inhabited by Catholics, firing a volley over their houses, and playing "The Protestant Boys," and "Croppies Lie Down."

The prohibition of the Dublin procession, and other alarming signs of an approaching compromise with Jezebel—for such was held to be the meaning of the threatened admission of Papists to Parliament and the Corporations—aroused all the "No-Popery" animosities of their hereditary oppressors, and the clerical agitators projected a "New Reformation." If the Catholics could but be convinced of their idolatry and superstition (which seemed so manifest to those clerical persons), it was thought that they could no longer persist in their audacious pretensions. In gene-

---

* His order of Conservatism is admirably characterized by Paul Louis Courier, who, speaking of one of Lord Liverpool's character, said: "If he had been present on the morning of the creation, he would have cried: '*Mon Dieu! conservons le chaos!*'"

ral, this new scheme of proselytism was carried on by mere ribald abuse of everything held sacred in the ancient religion, and by repeating the old stories out of Fox's *Martyrs;* but certain of the new reformers challenged public discussion with the most learned Catholic theologians in every diocese, and at first some of these challenges were promptly met by Catholic clergymen, who thought on their side that their religion could lose nothing, and might gain much by public exposition and defence of its tenets. Several oral discussions took place accordingly, of which the most notable was that between a Rev. Mr. Pope, an English clergyman, and Father Maguire, a parish priest of Leitrim County. The bold acceptance of the challenge by "Father Tom" was thought by his own partizans rather unfortunate, as he had never debated in public, though known to be a learned theologian, while Mr. Pope was a practised controversialist. The discussion was to take place in Dublin, each champion to defend three articles of his own, and assail three of his adversary's faith. The occasion excited intense interest. Not only the public room where the meeting took place, but all Sackville Street, was thronged with eager sympathizers. As the two disputants argued within the building, thousands of minor "oral discussions" were taking place on the streets, and the talk of Dublin carmen was of two sacraments and of seven. This scene lasted many days. The debate was carried on with sufficient courtesy. Father Maguire proved himself a master of theological learning, and Mr. Pope of controversial declamation; and the affair ended as might have been expected—that is, Catholics were convinced that Mr. Maguire had demolished the Protestant religion, and Protestants were satisfied that Mr. Pope had not left Popery a leg to stand on. Nobody was converted on either side.

Many other similar discussions, in which laymen sometimes bore a part, raged in each province of the island, and generally rather inflamed intolerance than advanced any good cause. The Right Rev. Dr. Doyle disapproved of them, and soon interdicted the clergy of his diocese from engaging in them. So did the Archbishop of Armagh, and then the other bishops. Soon not a priest could be found to accept a challenge, and their opponents took this as a plain proof that the Catholic religion was afraid of the light of day. They eagerly pressed their invitations, but in vain. They urgently offered to their Catholic friends to prove the mass a plain sacrifice to idols, and purgatory a lamentable infringement on the prerogatives of hell. The Catholic priests would no longer strip for this polemical prize-ring, although still ready and willing to expound their faith by the old methods of theological argument.

The year 1827 was remarkable for the first great example of the emigrant Irish in every foreign country, and in every colony, taking an active part in the struggle for liberty of their friends at home. And the sympathy and substantial aid were not confined to Irishmen alone, nor even to Catholics alone. The bold attitude of O'Connell; the mighty power he had created and directed; the vigour and wisdom of that agitation now so evidently shaking the deep-rooted and broad-based structure of the British Empire, attracted the admiration of the world. The powerful French press occupied itself warmly in the struggle; and from French Catholics, as well as from Americans of all religions, came addresses and subscriptions to the Catholic Association. Multitudinous meetings of "Friends of Ireland" were held in all considerable American cities; and a large part of the business of the Association began to be reading foreign correspondence, and receiving addresses from not only France and America, but from various German States, from Italy, from Spain, even from British India. All these things, while they violently irritated the national pride of the English, suggested to them at the same time the impossibility of continued resistance in so very bad a cause.

Mr. Canning died in August, after a very short tenure of office. He had to contend with a compact and very acrimonious opposition, consisting not only of the Tories, but of the aristocratic party of the old Whigs, headed by Lord Grey—a party which was jealous of Canning, because it sincerely believed him an interloper upon the prescriptive right of a few great families to govern the country.*

But the head and the heart of this

---

* Canning was a man of strong passions and high spirit, with great talent for satire, and of course had made many enemies—and without enemies no man is entitled to have friends. He had been a Tory, too, and had written pungent squibs in the *Anti-Jacobin* against "French principles." For example, the very clever satire of the *Needy Knife-Grinder.* In one of these *jeux d'esprit,* he had contrasted the statesman-like qualities of certain Tory lords with

"—— The temper of Grey,
And Treasurer Sheridan's promise to pay."

It was generally believed that Lord Grey did not forget this, and that it contributed very much to envenom his opposition to Canning's Ministry.

venomous opposition was Sir Robert Peel, who saw that Canning was destined, if his Government lasted, to carry the great measure of Catholic Emancipation, and who was determined, if possible, to supersede him, and carry that inevitable measure himself—a policy not unfamiliar to this prudent statesman, which he afterwards pursued in the other signal case of the Repeal of the Corn Laws. Mr. Canning, too, was in failing health, and had lost most of the original energy of his nature. Peel therefore "hounded him to death," as Lord George Bentinck long afterwards bitterly declared in Parliament.

Mr. Canning was succeeded by Lord Goderich, a statesman of little talent or influence, who did not succeed in forming a ministry which could hold together; and in January, 1828, this feeble administration gave place to the Duke of Wellington as Premier Minister, and Sir Robert Peel as Secretary for the Home Department—both of them avowed and inveterate enemies of the liberties of Catholics. The Duke, also, was still sincerely and consistently resolute to refuse all concession; while his prudent colleague had already determined to be converted at the right moment, and to have the credit of effecting a revolution which he saw to be inevitable. In this new Cabinet was Lord Palmerston—a man who never cared for Whig or Tory, Catholic or Protestant, or the rights or wrongs of any class, sect, or nation, but was always ready to bear a hand, and that efficiently, in the current events which were for the time being the order of the day.

On the opening of the session of 1828, the Catholic Association was prepared with a petition, signed by 800,000 Catholics, praying, not for any rights of their own, or relief for themselves, but for repeal of the Test and Corporation Act, which had excluded Protestant Dissenters from office for a century and a half. This idea was O'Connell's; but the petition, as he long afterwards delighted to proclaim, was drawn up by the hand of Father L'Estrange, a Carmelite friar. This was an incident well calculated to produce a fine dramatic effect—the proscribed and oppressed Catholics petitioning for the rights of the much *less* proscribed and oppressed Nonconformists! But it is fair to add that many petitions poured in this session from Protestants of all sects in favour of the Catholic claims, so that there was at least an appearance of mutual good-will, and a universal aspiration towards liberty, equality, and fraternity. The picture was somewhat marred, however, by multitudes of petitions vehemently deprecating all concession to Catholics; and these latter came from the most influential quarters in the three kingdoms of Ireland, England, and Scotland. The British Universities were especially stirred by apprehension and alarm for the Protestant interest; and the Corporations, particularly that of Dublin, felt that all was lost if a man of seven sacraments became alderman or town councillor.

In that session the Test Act and Corporation Act were in fact repealed. The measure was introduced by Lord John Russell, a statesmen who then and always professed "Liberal" principles, and aspired to lead the party of what is called "Progress;" but being essentially narrow-minded, has often shown himself actuated by the blindest bigotry and intolerance. His measure was carried, chiefly on account of the languid opposition made to it by Sir Robert Peel, who was then in a *transition* state, and was making up his mind to be converted himself to Liberal principles, and even to snatch from Lord John Russell and the Whigs the credit of carrying the grand Whig measure of that age. The Act repealing the Test and Corporation Acts became law in April; and a few weeks after, on the secession of several members from the Cabinet, Mr. Vesey Fitzgerald, then member for Clare County, was brought in to fill a vacancy in the administration as President of the Board of Trade. This vacated his seat for Clare until he should be re-elected; and he immediately issued his address to the Clare electors, nothing doubting that he would be at once replaced in his seat, having large influence in the county, and most of the larger landed proprietors being his political and personal friends. Mr. Fitzgerald was a highly honourable and liberal gentleman, and a warm friend to Catholic Emancipation. He was, moreover, the son of that steady Anti-Union patriot, Mr. Prime-Sergeant Fitzgerald, who had spoken at the bar meeting against the Union, and had been thereupon degraded from his office by the Government. He was, therefore, in some sort, a martyr to patriotism; and his son had good reason to count not only on his own possessions and influence in his county, but also on his personal merit and the traditions of his family, for a warm support in Clare.

The celebrated Clare election followed—one of the most momentous transactions in the modern history of Ireland, and, indeed, of the other island also. It was no merely local contest for one seat in Parliament; it was the making up of a decisive issue between the millions of oppressed Catholics and that potent and insolent "Ascendancy," which had so long trampled upon them in their own land.

At first, however, it was not foreseen what a sharp turning-point this Clare election was destined to prove in history. The Catholics had passed a resolution at one of their aggregate meetings to oppose the election of every candidate who should not pledge himself against the Duke of Wellington's administration. Now, here was a proven friend to those Catholics, who had always voted in their favour, actually a member of that administration, and seeking election at the hands of an Irish constituency. The question was, Should that worthy gentleman be opposed by the whole power of the Association? And whom could they hope to put in his place who would be a better friend to them than Vesey Fitzgerald? An incident now occurred which gave much additional importance to this question. Lord John Russell, charmed with his own success in repealing the Test and Corporation Acts, swelling with self-confidence, as usual, and never doubting that he was about to be the great "Liberal" leader, wrote a letter to Mr. O'Connell, suggesting that the conduct of the Duke of Wellington in the case of the repeal of the Test and Corporation Acts, had been so fair and noble as to entitle his Grace to the gratitude of "Liberals;" and that they, the said Liberals, "would consider the reversal of the resolution which had been passed against his Government as evidence of the interest which the Irish people felt, not only in the great question peculiarly applicable to that country, but in the assertion of religious freedom throughout the *empire*." * That is to say, the Whig party of the "empire" would take it very kind if Mr. O'Connell and the Catholic Association would put aside the consideration of their own country and their own rights, and use their power so as to benefit that *party*. This resembles extremely the many other occasions on which the Whigs of the "empire" have endeavoured to stifle Irish questions, and turn Irish organizations for national purposes to the service of an English faction, which always courted the Catholics when out of office, and always spurned and oppressed them when in power.

And Mr. O'Connell's greatest weakness (as we have seen in the last chapter), both then and since, was his too credulous

* See Shiel's *Sketches*—"The Clare Election."

reliance upon the fair professions of that treacherous party, which he had so often occasion to describe as "the base, brutal, and bloody Whigs." On the present occasion, Mr. O'Connell can scarcely be censured for lending an ear to the suggestion of the Whig—that Mr. Fitzgerald's election should go unopposed; for O'Connell himself did not yet foresee what a potent engine this Clare election would become in his hands. Therefore he proposed, in the Association, that the resolution should be suspended.

But O'Connell did not fully appreciate how deeply his countrymen abhorred both Wellington and Peel, of both of whom, in the capacity of Chief Secretary, Ireland had bitter experience. His motion was vehemently and successfully opposed. After some debate, the original resolution was left standing; and the Association remained committed to oppose the return of Mr. Vesey Fitzgerald. Mr. O'Connell had reason to rejoice in his failure to rescind that resolution.

Clare, then, was to be contested; and the next question was, Who was to be put forward against Fitzgerald? The Association pitched upon Major MacNamara, one of the proprietors of the county—a Protestant, of course, but descended of ancient Irish stock, very friendly to the Catholics; a man of but little weight of character, whose principal care and ambition seem to have been to dress and wig himself after the pattern of George IV., whom he personally resembled; for the rest, a good landlord, an excellent magistrate, and protector of the poor and oppressed. But this personage, though a friend to his Catholic countrymen, was still more a friend, as it turned out, to his neighbour Vesey Fitzgerald. He allowed many days to elapse without sending an answer to the Association; and as Clare was at a great distance from Dublin, in those days of slow travelling, much anxious delay was thus created. Doubts and rumours began to prevail, not only as to the acceptance of the candidacy, but as to the disposition of the priests of Clare to act warmly with the Association against so estimable and popular a gentleman. Mr. O'Gorman Mahon and Mr. Steele were sent post to Clare, to inquire into the dispositions of priests and people, and to bring an answer, if possible, from Major MacNamara. O'Gorman Mahon came back in two days. The Major's family lay under such obligations to Mr. Fitzgerald that he could not think of opposing him. Meanwhile the "Ascendancy" party, as well as the Liberal Protestants of Clare, were actively engaged in working for the candidate already in the field; and boasting that no gentleman in the county would stoop so low as to accept the patronage of the Catholic Association. Those gentlemen of the county were soon to receive a lesson.

There was earnest consultation one night at O'Connell's house in Merrion Square. Next day Dublin City was startled, and soon all Ireland was aroused, by an address from *O'Connell himself* to the electors of Clare, soliciting their suffrages, affirming that he was qualified to be elected and to serve them in Parliament, although he would never take the oath (that the mass is idolatrous), "for," continued he, "the authority which created those oaths (the Parliament) can abrogate them; and I entertain *a confident hope* that if you elect me, the most bigoted of our enemies *will see the necessity* of removing from the chosen representative of the people an obstacle which would prevent him from doing his duty to his King and to his country." At last all the world, friends and foes, saw in one moment what was to be the meaning of the Clare election.

Several members of the Association were at once sent down to Clare in order to excite the people, and prepare them for the great event; also to arouse the spirit of the priests, and induce them to use their influence with the tenantry. The great family "interests"—the O'Briens, the Vandeleurs, the Fitzgeralds, the MacNamaras—had, as they thought, organized and drilled their numerous tenantry into proper discipline. They considered the people who lived on their estates almost in the light of serfs; and it was a principle then in Ireland, that if any gentleman interfered with another's tenants, by canvassing them, in order to induce them to vote against their landlords, the interference was to be resented as a personal affront. But a power was now moving these masses on which those respectable gentlemen had not calculated—the profound and sweeping passion of a highly impulsive and imaginative people, thoroughly aroused by every feeling that could appeal either to their manhood or their religious enthusiasm—stimulated by the exhortations of priests whom they loved, and inspired by the name and renown of the redoubtable champion who promised to deliver them. All this together made up such a mass of concentrated power, as was sure to test severely the discipline of the great estates, and the traditional deference paid by tenants to their landlords.

Mr. Steele and O'Gorman Mahon undertook to canvas the county; and Steele intimated beforehand his readiness to fight any landlord who should feel himself aggrieved by interference with his tenants. Then they traversed the county, making the most earnest and impetuous appeals to the people; addressing them at all hours and in all places—in the chapels after mass, on the hill-sides, in the village markets, by day and by night, until it was clear that the generous and gallant people were fully resolved to brave, this one good time, the utmost vengeance of landlord wrath, and carry the "Man of the People" triumphantly to the door of Parliament.

The famous Father Maguire travelled all the way from Leitrim that he might help to swell the excitement. John Lawless (or, as he was usually named, Honest Jack Lawless) was then editor of a newspaper in Belfast, called the *Irishman*. He left his newspaper to other hands, and hurried to Clare, to put his fiery leading articles into the form of fiery speeches. The town of Ennis, which had a population of eight thousand, contained thirty thousand human beings on the day when O'Connell's green carriage was expected in that place. Green flags waved from the windows; priests and agitators addressed multitudes from a balcony or a flight of steps; and the excitement of expectation was at its highest. Yet there was not the slightest appearance of turbulence or disorder. On the contrary, throughout all the exciting canvas, and still more exciting days of the actual poll, old family feuds were suspended, or terminated for ever. There was no drunkenness, no angry language, and no man ventured (so strong was public opinion) to raise a hand against another upon any provocation. O'Connell at length appeared, with two or three friends; and there was one continuous shout from thirty thousand throats. Women cried and laughed; strangers, who had never seen one another, wrung each other's hands; and from every window ladies (Mr. Shiel says, "of great beauty") waved hands and handkerchiefs. No wonder that such a tempest of patriotic zeal whirled away Mr. Fitzgerald's own tenants out of the hands of their marshalling bailiffs; nor that one wave of O'Connell's arm left Mr. Vandeleur deserted by his whole army of freeholders. Sir Edward O'Brien's feudal pride was mortally hurt by the defection of his people, and he shed tears of vexation; but his son, William Smith O'Brien, then member for Ennis, though his family pride may have been hurt by such a result, was not inconsolable, being indeed a contributor to the "Catholic Rent," and one who, at all times, valued justice and fair dealing more highly than the broad acres and high towers of Drumoland.

The details of an election contest, even that of Clare in 1828, need not be related at length. Sir Edward O'Brien proposed Mr. Fitzgerald, who was seconded by Sir Augustus Fitzgerald. O'Connell was proposed by O'Gorman Mahon and Mr. Steele, both proprietors in the county. The speeches were made; the poll proceeded; and at its close the numbers stood, for O'Connell, two thousand and fifty-seven; for Fitzgerald, one thousand and seventy-five. After an argument before the assessor, Mr. Keating, in which it was contended that a Catholic could not be legally returned, the objection was overruled on the ground that it rested with the Parliament itself, on the oath being tendered and refused, to exclude a representative, and O'Connell was proclaimed duly elected.

It is somewhat difficult at this day fully to comprehend the profound impression which this event produced throughout Ireland, as well as in the other island. Mr. Vesey Fitzgerald, though deeply mortified, took his defeat with a gentlemanlike calmness; but the great proprietors of Clare County, who had supported him, could not conceal their ominous apprehensions. "Where is all this to end?" was a question frequently put in his presence; to which he replied only by looks of gloom and sorrow. In fact, the worthy Protestant "Liberals," disciples and followers of Grattan and Ponsonby, had accustomed themselves to regard the Catholic claims as their affair—*they* were the Parliamentary patrons of the Irish Catholics, and had never dreamed of the possibility of their clients taking the case into their own hands; not only throwing off all dependence upon them, but even flinging aside so decisively one of the most distinguished of their advocates, and coming in their proper person to thunder at the doors of Parliament. Still more fearful and terrible to them was the example of independence now set by the voting tenantry; the hereditary family "interests" were no longer omnipotent; and the end of the world seemed at hand. The exultation of the Catholic people of Ireland was unbounded. O'Connell travelled back to Dublin in the midst of one continued triumphal procession. Mr. Lawless, the Belfast editor, was escorted on his return to Belfast by enormous multitudes of the peasantry. Through the plains of Meath they passed in peaceable triumph, and through the southern part of Monaghan; but in this region the Orangemen were strong, armed, resolute, and infuriated; and a vast concourse of armed Protestants, excited by the harangues of their preachers, and prayerfully determined to resist this triumph of "Jezebel," at least in *their* county, were assembled at Ballybay, and showed a stern purpose of opposing the passage of Mr. Lawless and his followers. It needed all the exertions of the Catholic clergy, and the friendly expostulations of General Thornton, military commandant of the district, to prevent a collision, and induce the multitudinous escort of Mr. Lawless to disperse and go to their homes. For a week or two there were serious apprehensions of collision, and of civil war; and large numbers of troops were hastily sent over from England. It was even formally proposed in the Catholic Association that a run should be made on the banks, with a view of disorganizing society and opening the way for armed revolution; but these counsels were rejected.

The actual results of this election are well known, and may be shortly summarized. The Duke of Wellington, who had a few months before declared that "he could not comprehend the possibility of placing Roman Catholics in a *Protestant* Legislature with any kind of safety, as his personal knowledge told him that no King, however Catholic, could govern his Catholic subjects without the aid of the Pope;" this Duke, the consistent and conscientious opponent of Catholic liberties, and who had taken office expressly to defeat their claims, became suddenly converted, and felt that the choice lay between Catholic Emancipation and civil war. As for Sir Robert Peel, he had already divined the course of events—his policy was clear; and his conscience presented no serious difficulty. Lord Anglesea, the Lord-Lieutenant, though he had come over to Ireland with no friendly feeling towards the Catholics, had greatly altered his views, and now made no secret of his opinion that the time was come to settle the vexed question in the only way it could be settled—for which expression of opinion he was summarily removed from his government.

The Parliament met in February, 1829. The King's speech, prepared no doubt by Peel, recommended the suppression of the Catholic Association, *and* the subsequent consideration of Catholic disabilities, with a view to their adjustment and removal. As for the Catholic Association, there could be no difficulty about that. It had done its work; and, not waiting for the law to suppress it, dissolved itself at once—that is, nominally, for substantially the organization still subsisted, and could easily resume its usual business in case of necessity.

It was Sir Robert Peel who, on the 5th of March, moved for a Committee of the whole House, "for consideration of the civil disabilities of His Majesty's Roman Catholic subjects;" and the motion was carried, after a warm debate, by a large majority.

And now arose the most tremendous clamour of alarmed Protestantism that had been heard in the three kingdoms since the days of James II.—the last King who had ever dreamed of placing Catholics and Protestants on something like an approach to equality. Multitudinous petitions—not only from Irish Protestants but from Scottish Presbyteries, from English Universities, from corporations of British towns, from private individuals—came pouring into Parliament, praying that the great and noble Protestant State of England should not be handed over as a prey to the Jesuits, the Inquisitors, and the *Propaganda*. Never was such a jumble of various topics, sacred and profane, as in those petitions; vested interests—idolatry of the mass—principles of the Hanoverian succession—the Inquisition—eternal privileges of Protestant tailors or Protestant lightermen—our holy religion—French principles—tithes—and the beast of the Apocalypse—all were urged with vehement eloquence upon the enlightened legislators of Britain.

What may seem strange, one has to admit that a great number of these frightened petitioners were truly sincere and conscientious. The amiable Dr. Jebb, Protestant Bishop of Limerick, for example, writes an earnest letter to Sir Robert Peel, on the 11th of February, 1829 (so soon as he saw the course that matters were taking), and says to him:—"Infinitely more difficulties and dangers will attach to concession than to uncompromising resistance. . . . In defence of all that is dear to British Protestants, I am cheerfully prepared, if necessary, as many of my order have formerly done, to lay down life itself." On the other hand, the good Dr. Doyle, Catholic Bishop of Kildare and Leighlin, had uttered this prayer for O'Connell when he started for the contest in Clare:—"May the God of truth and justice protect and prosper you!" What very different, what very opposite ideas of truth and justice had these two excellent prelates!

Sir Robert Peel, however, had taken his part—the Catholics were to be emancipated; and by *him*. But the King would not yield, save at the last extremity. To assent to an act of justice seemed to George IV. like the loss of his dearest heart's blood. He endeavoured even to get rid of the Wellington Cabinet, and to form a new Ministry which would pledge itself *not* to do justice. But in this he failed. Sir Robert Peel tells us:—"At a late hour on the evening of the 4th of March, the King wrote a letter to the Duke of Wellington, informing him that His Majesty anticipated so much difficulty in the attempt to form another admistration, that he could not dispense with our services; that he must, therefore, desire us to withdraw our resignation; and that we were at liberty to proceed with the measures of which notice had been given in Parliament."*

Mr. O'Connell, who had arrived in London to claim his seat for Clare, *as a Catholic*, finding that there was now a Government pledged to Emancipation, having *carte blanche* for that purpose, decided not to present himself for the present, lest it should embarrass the administration.

The Emancipation Act was forthwith introduced. It was prepared by Sir Robert Peel. It contained neither the provision for *veto* nor that for bribing the priests; but it was accompanied by a certain other Act, as fatal, perhaps, as either of those—namely, for disfranchisement of all the forty-shilling freeholders in Ireland. Sir Robert was determined at least not to yield this point. It was the forty-shilling freeholders who had humbled the Beresford domination in Waterford, and destroyed the Foster monopoly in Louth; it was the forty-shilling freeholders who had carried O'Connell triumphantly to the head of the poll in Clare; and, by destroying that whole class of voters, Peel hoped very reasonably, not only to render the remaining voters more amenable to corrupt influences, but also to take away the motive, which had heretofore existed, for granting leases to small farmers, and thus, in good time, to turn those independent farmers into tenants at will. He had his own profound reasons for this—which will fully appear hereafter.

The debates on the Relief Bill were, as might have been expected, very violent and bitter. The fanatical section of English and Irish Protestantism was deeply moved. In the mind of those people all was lost; and Sir Robert Peel

* *Memoirs:* by the Right Honourable Sir Robert Peel, Bart. Published by the trustees of his papers—Lord Mahon, and Right Honourable Ed. Cardwell, M.P. London, 1856.

and the Duke were almost directly charged with being agents of the Pope of Rome. However, the bill passed through its two first readings in the Commons; and the third reading was passed on the 30th of March by a majority of thirty-six. Next day it was carried to the House of Lords; and on the 2d of April its second reading was moved by the Duke of Wellington, who made no scruple to urge its necessity in order "to prevent civil war." Sir Robert Peel, in his argument for the law, had been less explicit and straightforward than the Duke—he had only said the measure was needful to prevent great dangers and "public calamity." *

After violent debates in the House of Lords, lasting several days, the bill was passed a third time, and passed by a majority of one hundred and four. It then received the royal assent; and what is called Catholic Emancipation was an accomplished fact.

O'Connell, in the meantime, presented himself at the bar of the House of Commons, claiming to take his seat as member for Clare. This was before the passing of the bill into a law. But an election petition was pending, sent forward by certain electors of Clare, against the validity of his return. The investigation of this petition consumed time; but at length the committee reported Mr. O'Connell duly elected. The Emancipation Act was now passed, and was the law of the land. O'Connell, thereupon, held himself entitled to go in and take his seat, subject only to the new oaths. For this purpose he repaired to the House on the 15th of May, was introduced in the usual form by Lords Ebrington and Duncannon, and walked to the table to be sworn by the Clerk. But Sir Robert Peel had prudently provided against this in the new law, which admitted only those who should, "*after the commencement of that Act*, be returned as members of the House of Commons," to take their seats under the new oaths. It was a mean piece of spite; and its special object was to give Sir Robert an opportunity of snubbing O'Connell one last time, before yielding finally to his imperious demand.

Accordingly, the Clerk of the House tendered to the new member the now-abrogated oaths—one being the oath of Supremacy (namely, that the King of England is head of the Church), and the other, "that the sacrifice of the mass is impious and idolatrous," and so forth. He refused to take these oaths. He was then heard at the bar of the House, where he claimed his right to sit and vote: his claim was disallowed by a vote. The old oaths were once more tendered to him. He read over the stupid trash in an audible voice; then said, raising his head, that he declined to take that oath, because "one part of it he knew to be false, and another he did not believe to be true." A new writ was then issued, to hold an election for the County Clare.

The series of measures called "Emancipation" consisted of three Acts of Parliament. The first, an Act for suppression of the Catholic Association as an illegal and dangerous society; the second, an Act for the disfranchisement of the forty-shilling freeholders *in Ireland* (not in England, where that qualification was retained); and third, the Relief Act proper, abolishing the old oaths against transubstantiation, &c., and substituting another very long and ingenious oath (for Catholics only) testifying allegiance to the Crown; promising to maintain the Hanoverian settlement and succession; declaring that it is no article of the Catholic faith "that Princes excommunicated by the Pope may be deposed or murdered by their subjects; that neither the Pope nor any other foreign prince has any temporal or civil jurisdiction within the realm; promising to defend the settlement of property as established by law; solemnly disclaiming, disavowing, and abjuring 'any intention to subvert the present Church Establishment as settled by law;' and engaging never to exercise any privilege conferred by that Act 'to disturb or weaken the Protestant religion or Protestant government.'"

The Act admitted Catholics, on taking this oath, to be members of any lay body corporate, and to do corporate acts, and vote at corporate elections; but not to join in a vote for presentation to a benefice in the gift of any corporation.

The Act further most formally affirmed and preserved the great principle of Protestant Ascendancy, by specially excluding Catholics from the high offices of Lord-Lieutenant and Lord Chancellor; the former being the officer who makes nearly all appointments in Ireland, and exercises the royal power to pardon—or *not* to pardon; the latter being the person who decides on the guardianship of minors, and orders in what religion they are to be brought up, in the absence of *express* directions from their parents. The Lord Chancellor also has control over the

---

* Sir Robert Peel, in his letter to Doctor Jebb, Bishop of Limerick, in February, said:—"It is easy to blame the concessions that were made in 1782 and in 1793; but they were not made without an intimate conviction of their absolute necessity in order to prevent *greater dangers.*" Sir Robert says again:—"I can with truth affirm, that in advising and promoting the measures of 1829, I was swayed by *no fear*, except the fear of public calamity."—*Memoirs*: by Sir Robert Peel.

commissions of magistrates, and cancels them at his pleasure, thus controlling, in a very great degree, the administration of justice.

Bearing in mind these important provisions and exceptions—and further, that the Anglican Church still continued the established religion of the land, and still devoured the Catholic people by its exactions—it is tolerably clear that by the Relief Bill Catholics were not quite half emancipated.

But the most fatal blow to the liberties of the Irish people was the contemporaneous Act for disfranchisement of the forty-shilling freeholders, and for raising the county qualification to £10 a-year—five times the qualification required in England. Only seventeen members of the House of Commons voted against this grievous injustice. It was introduced by Sir Robert Peel, on the ostensible ground that there was too great a disposition on the part of Irish landlords to divide their land into minute portions; that the franchise was a mere instrument with which the landed aristocracy exercised power and control over the elections; and that this control had lately passed into the hands of the priests (which was worse); and he cited as an example what had lately taken place in Louth and Monaghan and Waterford. In other words, he would disfranchise those small farmers *because* they had shown themselves capable of defying landlord control and acting independently. Amongst those who opposed this measure were Lord Duncannon, Lord Palmerston, and Mr. Huskisson. Their argument was: "If the forty-shilling freeholders had been corrupt, *like those of Penrhyn*, their disfranchisement might be defended; but the only offence of the persons against whom the bill was directed had been that they exercised their privilege honestly and independently, according to their conscience."*

It is singular that O'Connell said not a word at any meeting, nor wrote any letter, protesting against this wholesale abolition of the civil and political rights of those to whom he owed his election for Clare. He thus consented by his silence to see cut away from under his own feet the very groundwork and material of all effective political action in Ireland; and often afterwards had occasion, as Ireland also had to lament the impotence and futility of all patriotic effort for the real advancement of their country, in consequence of the destruction of the forty-shilling freeholders. Many thousands of these freeholders, and of their children, are now working on canals and railroads in Ame-

* Account of Debate in *Annual Register* for 1829.

rica. The new and cheap ejectment laws were in full force; and were soon to act with fatal effect.

We can now appreciate in some measure the true *spirit* in which "Catholic Emancipation" was effected. It was "to avert civil war," said the Duke of Wellington; it was "to avoid greater dangers," said Sir Robert Peel. It was emphatically *not* to do justice, nor to repair a wrong. In the words of an eminent French writer on Irish affairs,* nothing is more certain than that neither the King nor his Ministers intended to do an act of justice and reparation towards the Catholics. The bill of 1829 was nothing else than a concession wrested from them by *circumstances;* which the King would never have consented to, if he had found Ministers decided, even at the cost of a civil war, to perpetuate an iniquity of three centuries; and which his Ministers would never have proposed if they had not apprehended that civil war, in the interest of the Protestant establishment itself. Now, when a concession has been extorted by force, and is not a spontaneous homage to truth and justice, those who grant it may, perhaps, respect it as to its mere letter; but certainly they will not loyally comply with its spirit. When we see their practical application of it, it is evident that they desire to hold back with one hand what they have been obliged to bestow with the other; and that, deeply regretting the necessity they have had to obey, when that necessity becomes less urgent, they observe only so much of their engagement as is needful to save them from the charge of perjury. Hence comes it also that there is so little gratitude manifested for this concession—and in truth, those may dispense with gratitude who owe only to fear "*a little justice and a little freedom.*"

CHAPTER XX.

1829—1840.

Results of the Relief Act—O'Connell re-elected for Clare—Drain of Agricultural Produce—Educated Class of Catholics Bought—The Tithe War—Lord Anglesea's Victory—O'Connell's Associations—Anglesea's Proclamations—Prosecution of O'Connell—National Education—Tithe Tragedies—Newtownbarry—Carrickshock—Change of Dynasty in France—Reform Agitation in England—What Reform meant in Ireland—Cholera—Resistance to Tithe—Lord Grey's Coercion Act—Abolition of Negro Slavery—Church Temporalities Act—Repeal Debate—Surplus Population—Surplus Produce—Tithe Carnage at Rathcormack—Queen Victoria's Accession—Three Measures against Ireland—Poor Law—Tithe Law—Municipal Reform—Castle Sheriffs.

* Le Père Perraud. *Etudes sur l'Irlande contemporaine.*

IMPERFECT and stinted and guarded as the Catholic Emancipation Act was, it was nevertheless felt in Ireland to be a great triumph and noble achievement of O'Connell, who at once rose to the highest pinnacle of popular favour. The Catholics almost worshipped him as their Heaven-sent deliverer; and the partizans of the good old traditionary Protestant Ascendancy thought the end of the world was at hand. The sword brandished in the hand of Walker's statue, standing upon a lofty column on a bastion of Derry walls, fell down with a crash, and was shivered to pieces, upon the very day when His Majesty, George 1V., placed his signature on the Emancipation Act; which he did not do, however, without having first broken and trampled upon a pen which was handed to him for that purpose, in a highly dramatic manner, and with the most perfect mimicry of deep feeling. Sir Harcourt Lees, for his part, thought the time was now at last surely come to "put down Popery" by Act of Parliament, and to send the "Arch-agitator" to the Tower.

As for O'Connell himself, and the more thoughtful amongst his friends and supporters of the Catholic Association, they saw too well that little or nothing was gained. Not only was their civil and political inferiority maintained and formally re-asserted; but the great body of brave farmers, who had frightened the "empire" by their independence, was swept out of civil existence at a blow. It at once became evident to O'Connell that there was no salvation for Ireland but in a repeal of the odious and fraudulent Union. On his return to Ireland, as if sensible that what had been already effected for his country was rather apparent than real, he declared openly that the next victory to be achieved must be the repeal of the Union. Both at Ennis and at Youghal he made speeches enforcing the necessity of this great measure, and promising never to rest until it should be accomplished—a pledge which, indeed, he laboured all his life to redeem.

On the passage of the law disfranchising the forty-shilling freeholders, orders had been at once sent to Ireland to commence a "registration" of those who still retained the franchise, possessing a freehold of £10 yearly value. This haste was for the purpose of acting as soon as practicable upon Irish elections, and, if possible, defeating O'Connell when he should again present himself in Clare under the new writ. He was not opposed, however, on his second election at Clare, and was again sent back to Parliament, with all the qualifications required even by the new law. He did not at once take his seat, as Parliament was prorogued on the 24th of June.

This year, Ireland was said to be in an "alarming" state—there was "crime and outrage" in several counties, and especially in Tipperary. In fact, the old exaction of tithes not only continued to be enforced, but was pressed with even increased rigour, seeing that Papists had become so insolent. The consequence was the most natural in the world—some tithe-proctors were forced to eat their processes, and also had their ears cut off. The Tipperary magistrates assembled in great alarm, and demanded the immediate application of the "Insurrection Act," for they could not understand how people should thus resist payment of their lawful tithes, unless there were a conspiracy to subvert the Protestant government and bring in the Pope.

In truth, there was throughout the island a very unsettled and uneasy condition of the popular mind. Men were told that they were "relieved" and "emancipated," but they felt no advantage from it whatsoever. They tried to feel pride in the victory which they were assured they had won over a British Ministry; but in the meantime they found themselves very generally disfranchised; and what was worse—landlords were refusing to make new leases of farms, and were breaking the existing leases where they could, having no longer the motive to rear up a small freehold population for the hustings. The chairmen of quarter-sessions, and the sheriffs and bailiffs, were busy with their ejectments; and pauperism began extensively to prevail. The seasons, indeed, had been for some time rather favourable, and grain and cattle were abundant; but the British system had now been so well established in our island, that all this wealth of bounteous nature flowed off instantly to England, and the price of it also. All went the same way. The export of agricultural produce to England out of Ireland had grown so enormous within the past few years, that it had been judged expedient in 1826 to place that trade "on the footing of a *coasting trade.*" In other words, no custom-house accounts were to be kept of it; and the amount of it was thus concealed for many years. In that year, 1826, however, the exports to England had been to the value of almost eight millions in corn and cattle. It was but small benefit to the Irish people to have favourable seasons and plenteous harvests. Their wealth not only made itself wings and flew to England; but as tenancy at will now became *the fashion*, landlords increased rents in proportion to increased produce, and then went to England—the centre of political action and fashionable life—to spend those improved rents. For all this there was no remedy in Emancipation.

It soon became evident, also, that the effects of the Relief Act would be disastrous in another respect. Parliament and the Judicial Bench being now opened (always with the exception of the place of Lord-Chancellor) to aspiring Catholics of the educated class, *their* interests and sympathies became separated from those of their countrymen. Undoubtedly, this result had been calculated by the prudent statesman who accomplished the Relief measure; and his plan succeeded but too well. That plan may be described, in general terms, as a plan for corrupting the higher classes and extirpating the lower; and Emancipation, disfranchising the latter and offering bribes to the former, was admirably calculated to buy over to the British interests such as aspired to the offices and emoluments dispensed by England, and to make them forget the duty they owed to their own countrymen, and the honour and welfare of their native land. Since that day, therefore, we have seen constantly more and more of the higher class of Catholics, in various positions, *helping England* to govern—that is, to pillage and depopulate—this ill-fated island. Since that day have been many Catholic members of Parliament—they have solicited places for useful constituents. Catholic attorney-generals — they have packed juries to "do the King's business." Catholic judges—they have sat complacently on the bench, and permitted those juries to be packed, and pretended to try their fellow-countrymen before those packed juries, to glut the vengeance of a Government which cannot bear to be disquieted while clearing off its "surplus population." In other words, those members of Parliament, attorney-generals, and judges, have sold themselves for money and station, to a Government which they know to be the mortal enemy of their countrymen and kinsmen, and have abandoned those countrymen and kinsmen to certain slaughter and extermination.

Such have been the substantial results of the "Relief Measures" of 1829; and O'Connell had good reason for his conclusion,—that no effectual service could be rendered to the country, short of annulling the Union with England.

The discontent and disappointment of the people (who found that Emancipation did not save them from starvation) found vent in occasional deeds of violence; and always for the old reasons — ruthless seizures for tithe, and wholesale ejectment of tenants. Many thousands of farmers now found themselves emancipated, but disfranchised, and in imminent danger of being ejected and thrown out on the highways. They were capable by law of holding high office; but exposed, in fact, to see their children perishing by hunger and hardship. The crimes committed in Ireland have nearly always one specific character, and one obvious motive and provocation. Their victims have been almost uniformly tithe-proctors, who seized upon the small store of the poor—or landlords or agents, who cleared estates—or incoming tenants, who rented farms from which others had been ejected. Murders for money, from jealousy, or in personal quarrel, have been at all times much more rare in Ireland than in England; and, indeed, the lamentable acts of violence which did occur were generally perpetrated by men who had not previously known the doomed victim, and in obedience to the decree of a secret society. The hapless people of the country had long felt and experienced that the laws were made not for them but against them; they had long been accustomed to see law at one side, and justice at the other; they could not perceive why there should be any law compelling them to pay clergymen whom they never saw, and at whose services they would shudder to assist; nor why there should be a law to fling them out from the little farm which they had improved and rendered fertile by the sweat of their brows. Hence the series of secret combinations, with their own judicial sentences and desperate executions. These proceedings, however, always drew down upon the peasantry of the neighbourhood a most ferocious and disproportionate vengeance, and formed the excuse for keeping Arms Acts and Insurrection Acts almost in permanence.

The grievance of tithes, and the whole of that monstrous iniquity called the Established Church, seemed to be felt by the people with even more intensity of irritation, since they were told that they were now "Emancipated," and that there was an end of Protestant Ascendancy. What this Emancipation might be, they did not well understand; they knew no other result from it than that they were deprived of their franchise, and could therefore get no more leases. And they thought that they saw Protestant Ascendancy all around them as rampant as ever. Protestant Ascendancy was always at their doors. It entered their cabins, and carried off their pans and pots, their calves and pigs, to satisfy a Protestant rector. Protestant magistrates (who were in the great majority) were always ready to browbeat them from the bench, and to send policemen to search their beds for concealed arms. Protestant jurors always met them in the courts of justice, and proved to them that the laws of the land were not for them. If sometimes, therefore, these people desperately took the law into their own hands, or even associated together to be a kind of law unto themselves, and executive also—dismal as such a state of society certainly is—the whole blame of it rests upon that unjust and savage system of dealing with Ireland which was called "Government," and of which a faint outline only has been traced in these pages.

King George IV. died in 1830; and was succeeded by his brother King William IV.; an event of little or no interest to Ireland.

The next year was occupied in England by a most energetic agitation for a Reform in Parliament,—an affair which also concerned Ireland extremely little. The Reform was to consist chiefly in disfranchising old boroughs which had become ruinous and almost uninhabited, and giving the franchise to large centres of population which had never returned members of Parliament before. Excitement on this question ran very high throughout the other island, but did not extend in any great measure to Ireland, whose proportions of representation had been fixed by the Act of Union. O'Connell, and the other Catholic and Liberal Irish members, all supported the "Reform" Ministry, and helped to carry the measure in 1832, imagining, probably, that Ireland would thereby establish a claim upon the popular party in England for support and friendly sympathy in asserting her own rights—an expectation which was signally disappointed.

On the 4th of February, 1830, Parliament opened, but was soon dissolved, and a new election took place. This time O'Connell abandoned Clare, and achieved another brilliant victory over the Beresford interest at Waterford. A considerable number of Catholics now entered Parliament for the first time; O'Gorman Mahon for Clare, Richard More O'Ferrall for Kildare, Lord Killeen for Meath, &c. Mr. Smith O'Brien continued to represent Ennis, and was a most attentive and industrious member of Parliament, acting on most questions with the Whig party, and sincerely cherishing the delusion (which he afterwards had to give up) that Whigs were more friendly to right and justice in Ireland than Tories.

In the beginning of 1830 the Duke of Northumberland was Lord-Lieutenant. On the change of Ministry the Marquis of Anglesea was again sent over as Viceroy, and Lord Plunket was made Lord-Chancellor—an office which he discharged with great ability for many years. He had by this time forgotten that the Union was a nullity and a fraud, which his sons were to be sworn to resist and annul. One of his sons became a bishop, by the gracious appointment of the King. Yet Mr. Plunket was right in denouncing the Union as a nullity and a fraud; and if he had been thoroughly honest, he would now have been found by O'Connell's side, demanding the restoration of an independent Irish Legislature.

During the course of this year there was established a "Society of the Friends of Ireland." It was nothing but the Catholic Association under another name; and its object was to agitate the repeal of the Union. But the course pursued by Mr. O'Connell, since the Relief Act, had occasioned violent irritation in England amongst both Whigs and Tories. That after so generous and noble a concession as Emancipation was represented to be— which was to have fully satisfied the Irish people, and filled them with rejoicing "loyalty"—that, instead of gratitude and loyal contentment, there should immediately spring up a new and acrimonious agitation, openly aiming at the "dismemberment of the empire," seemed to those Whigs and Tories an example of the basest ingratitude. O'Connell, too, whose deportment in Parliament was perfectly dignified and business-like, when he came to Ireland, and found himself the centre of a great meeting of his countrymen, often used violent and denunciatory language concerning political opponents, and even sometimes turned into ridicule some grave and reverend Tory, or some sneaking and intriguing Whig.

In short, it was decided by the administration, all Liberal as it was, to put a stop to the "Arch-agitator's" exciting proceedings; and as the "Friends of Ireland" fell undoubtedly under the former Act for suppressing illegal associations, the Viceroy was instructed to "proclaim it under that Act, and threaten prosecution." The society was, as usual, at once dissolved, and was at once succeeded by the "Anti-Union Association." O'Connell omitted no opportunity of insisting upon a restoration of the Irish Parliament, and demonstrating the necessity of that measure, which made him more popular and powerful in Dublin than he had ever been before; for it was in Dublin chiefly that the repeal spirit then existed. The country people and the provincial towns were not yet aroused on that question; but the metropolis appreciated it at once. There was to be held on the 27th of December a great assembly and procession of the trades of Dublin, with the express object of complimenting Mr. O'Connell for his advocacy of an Irish Parliament. The bands were to form at Phibsborough, in the suburbs of Dublin, and march with their banners and *insignia* into the city, to O'Connell's house, where they were to present him with an address. This procession of peaceful and unarmed men appeared to Lord Anglesea too perilous a thing to be permitted, with due regard to the peace of the city; and he issued a proclamation absolutely forbidding the assembly. This of course implied an intention of dispersing it by force. By O'Connell's advice, therefore, the meeting was not held.

This was but the beginning of a long contest between the Arch-agitator and the Marquis of Anglesea, the former using every legal device and contrivance to make for the people some occasion of meeting and expressing their sentiments, and the Marquis regularly laying on the heavy hand of power, and menacing unarmed citizens with military violence. Mr. O'Connell was unmeasured enough in the terms of very natural resentment, which he applied to Lord Anglesea, and the whole Whig Government, whom he characterized as "base, brutal, and bloody Whigs." But while he could use indignant language, the Lord-Lieutenant had all the practical advantages in such a contest. He had his sheriffs and juries at hand, and the Court of King's Bench always open; so that anything was an "illegal and dangerous association" which he might choose to prosecute. He had the garrison of Dublin constantly ready for action. And besides these things, the noble Marquis opened O'Connell's letters in the post-office, as well as letters addressed to him, in order that he might know who were his correspondents, what were his designs, and what were his resources. The Marquis had the letters always re-sealed with the utmost care with counterfeited seals, so that the persons receiving the letters should not suspect they had been opened, and so be put on their guard.*

The next name under which Mr. O'Connell made his Association appear was the Irish Volunteers for Repeal of the Union; but this had no better fate than the rest. When it was "proclaimed," however, and commanded not to meet, Mr. O'Connell for once did not submit. He said, and this was true, that a proclamation could not make law; and pledged himself as a lawyer that his organization was perfectly legal as it was. He, therefore, and many of his usual attendants, went and held the meeting. Thereupon O'Connell, together with Mr. Lawless, Mr. Steele, Mr. Barrett, Mr. Redmond, Mr. Clooney, and two or three others, were forthwith arrested, and brought before magistrates, where they were required to give bail. On issuing from the magistrates' office the Arch-agitator found a great crowd in the streets, and made them a great speech, of course:—"Yesterday," he exclaimed, "I was only half an agitator, to-day I am a whole one! Day and night will I now strive to fling off despotism, to redeem my country, to repeal the Union."

The prosecution proceeded; and as Mr. O'Connell knew perfectly well that he could have no chance before a Castle jury properly arranged, which would be sure to find him at once guilty of whatever he should be charged withal, he dexterously delayed the striking of the jury, and gained time. The Orange party was in vehement excitement; and it need scarcely be added that in England all parties were charmed with the idea of having the loud-tongued agitator locked up in a jail for a misdemeanour. After some ingenuity in pleading, O'Connell allowed judgment to go by default upon several of the counts; that is, substantially pleaded guilty on those counts. He knew he might as well do so, as he would be arraigned before a sure jury; and all the world waited till he should be called up for sentence. But he was never called up for sentence. It happened just then that the Whig Minis-

---

* The Marquis of Anglesea is first on the list of letter-spies which was laid before Parliament in 1844. But that list extends over a period of only eleven years. It was avowed by ministers that the post-office *espionage* had existed long before Lord Anglesea's time, as it certainly existed long after that of Earl de Grey, in 1843. Earl de Grey is the last of the letter-spies mentioned in the return. That return, however, has taken care not to inform us *whose* letters were thus opened and copied. It only gives a list of the Viceroys, Chancellors, Archbishops, and Lord-Justices who did order such manipulations of letters, and the years in which they so ordered it. It appears that such warrants were constantly in existence for ten years out of the eleven; but we are not informed as to the numbers of the persons whose correspondence was thus investigated, nor any of their names. O'Connell was, of course, one; and it was in the very height of the contest waged with O'Connell, to put down his several associations, that the Marquis of Anglesea is first returned as a letter-spy.

try was straining every nerve to secure a good majority for their Reform; and O'Connell and those others whom he could influence, or who would be revolted by any severity exercised towards him, were not allies to be thrown away for the sake of gratifying the Orangemen. For that time, therefore, legal proceedings against the agitator went no further.

The year 1831 was marked by the establishment of the national system of education in Ireland, in pursuance of a bill introduced by Lord Stanley. Two years after (1833) the grants of public money for the education of the poor, which had previously been enjoyed by the Kildare Place School Society and other proselytizing institutions, were intrusted to the Lord-Lieutenant, to be expended on the instruction of children of all sects, under the superintendence of commissioners appointed by the Crown, and called "Commissioners of National Education." Two years afterwards (1835), these commissioners were incorporated with power to hold lands. The ostensible principles of this new establishment were "Liberal;" there was to be no interference with the religious creed of any pupil; and clergymen of each denomination were to be allowed the opportunity of giving religious instructions to the children of their respective faiths.

But practically the Government took good care that, both on the first establishment of the board and ever since, the great majority of the commissioners should be Protestants. The scheme was intended to take into the hands of the British Government the formation of the minds of young Irishmen, and the moulding of their first impressions in such a way that they might forget they were Irish, and feel and think as like English children as possible. Their reading lessons have been carefully edited to this end; most of them by Dr. Wheatley, an Englishman, and others by Mr. Carlisle, a Scotchman. The intention was not so much to convert Catholic children as to denationalize them.

It had been for long ages prohibited to the Irish Catholics to be educated at all, under heavy penalties. When these penal laws had disappeared, and the British Government found that the Irish were very desirous to educate their children, that Government resolved, if they must be taught, to teach them itself, and especially to keep them as much as possible ignorant of the history of their own country—a very prudent and politic design, if it could only have been accomplished.

For the rest, these national schools have been tolerably well conducted; but in districts where the population is of mixed religious, Catholic children, for the most part, have received no benefit from them, on account of the objections of the Catholic clergy against mixed education. In other districts, where Catholics form the whole population, these objections did not practically apply.

In 1850 there were nearly five thousand schools under this board, and five hundred and eleven thousand two hundred and thirty-nine scholars.

The tithe war raged violently this year. The people were becoming more and more indisposed to pay Protestant rectors, especially in the South of Ireland, where those rectors often have no flocks. On the banks of the Slaney, on the very border between Wexford and Carlow County, and at the foot of the stately Mount Leinster, stands the little town of Newtownbarry. On the 18th of June, 1831, this usually quiet village was the scene of a bloody tithe tragedy. The Rev. Mr. M'Clintock would have his tithe; and by aid of the police and yeomanry, he had seized the crops and goods of several persons in the neighbourhood. These things were to be auctioned in Newtownbarry market place on the market day. Before that day anonymous written notices were sent to many persons in the country, requesting them to come in and *attend* the sale of their neighbours' pigs, beds, and kettles. Considerable numbers of people attended in consequence, but not armed—their object being only to keep all persons back from bidding at this auction. It was known that large crowds had come in, and that the forced sale must almost certainly produce a collision. But the Rev. Mr. M'Clintock would have his rights. The property seized was brought into town guarded by a large force of constabulary, who were to be supported, if needful, by another large force of yeomanry. The sale opened. The people pressed forward, and kept away, by a show of intimidation, the few who might have been disposed to purchase. At last, the police attacked the unarmed multitudes; were seconded with great alacrity by the yeomanry; and very soon thirteen slain men and twenty wounded were lying in their blood on the street of Newtownbarry. No person was ever brought to punishment for this slaughter. Indeed, it was felt by the Orange party that the Rev. Mr. M'Clintock had only shown proper spirit in vindicating his right; that this course of intimidation had gone too far; and that it was time an example should be made. More moderate persons, however, even of the Established Church, could not but think it unfortunate that ministers of religion should so often have to wring their blood-stained dues out of the very vitals of parishioners who hate them and all their works.

Six months after the affair of Newtownbarry, befell the other tithe slaughter of Carrickshock. Certain moneys were due for tithe to the Rev. Hans Hamilton, rector of Knocktopher, in the County Kilkenny. A process-server was sent out to serve the needful documents, and this functionary was protected by a large force of armed police. The people assembled in considerable and still-increasing numbers, their object being to get hold of the bailiff and force him to "eat the latitats" —papers of that nature being supposed in those parts to be the natural food of process-servers. Menacing crowds of country people gathered around the line of march of the officer and his escort; and when they arrived at a bare and desolate tract called the Common of Carrickshock, traversed by a lane which is bordered by a low wall, in most places broken down, the demands of the people to have the process-server delivered up to them became pressing and loud. At length a young man sprang into the lane, seized the process-server, and endeavoured to carry him off, out of the hands of his protectors. He was instantly shot dead. Then there was a general onslaught. The people had armed themselves with a species of short pikes, and they fell upon the police with fury. Eleven of the constables were killed, and a good many of the people also; but the legal documents were not served that day. It was fast becoming evident that some measures must be adopted to prevent these sanguinary collisions.

In England the resistance of the Irish to levies for tithes was, as usual, represented as the evidence of a deep Popish conspiracy to overturn the Protestant Church; and the Whigs were almost as much excited by this idea as the Tories. The voluminous Tory historian, Alison, discovered indeed, for once, that "the Pope's influence in Ireland" was on the present occasion beneficial: inasmuch as "the Vatican threw off the mask, and measures were commenced evidently intended to destroy the Protestant Establishment in Ireland, and open the door to the replacing of the Catholic faith in these realms." Thus, English Whigs drew off in some measure from their association with the Irish Catholics; and this weakened the party of Reform. The cholera also raged all through the summer of 1832; and this, according to the same historian, was another beneficial event, as it sensibly abated the Reform mania.

The King, however, in a speech from the Throne, recommended attention to the question of tithes; and a committee of the Lords was appointed to investigate and report upon it. They reported in favour of commuting the tithe to a charge upon land. In the debate on reception of this report, it was stated that the arrears of tithes due but not recoverable in the four dioceses of Ossory, Leighlin, Cashel, and Ferns, was computed at £84,954. A law was in the meantime proposed and carried by Government, authorizing an issue from the consolidated fund of a large sum of money for relief of those clergymen who could not collect their tithes. A part of the County Tipperary was also proclaimed under the Coercion Act then pending; and Lord Grey was preparing a still more stringent Coercion Act for the next year.

Mr. O'Connell vehemently opposed the grant from the consolidated fund, which was accompanied by an authority to *levy* the amount due, in order to repay the advance. This was in fact the Government assuming upon itself the function of the tithe-proctor and the bailiff, with the aid of all the troops and police; and it was plainly intended to make a few salutary examples of slaughter. Throughout the Parliamentary discussions on these questions there does not appear to have been the slightest intention on the part of either party to relieve Ireland from the burden of the Established Church; all their anxiety was how to insure to the clergy their income out of the pockets of the people in some way which it would be impossible to resist or evade. On the other hand, O'Connell declared in Parliament—"The Irish people are determined to get rid of tithes, and get rid of them they will."

But the resistance of the farmers was carried on peacefully; and generally consisted in deterring purchasers at tithe-sales by the demonstration of a resolute public opinion. The same force operated to prevent neighbours from aiding to remove crops or other things, even in case they should have been nominally sold. It cannot be denied that this was nothing but a very manifest intimidation, and would have been quite unjustifiable if the claim for tithe had been just.

The next year Lord Grey brought forward his Coercion Bill, and the Tories not only supported it with alacrity, but hailed it with joy, as a proof that the most "Liberal" of English reformers had come round to *their* policy for the government of Ireland; and, in fact, since that day English Tories and English Whigs have generally been in the most gratifying accord upon Coercion Bills for Ireland. However they may differ upon other matters, they are an unit whenever it is a question of dragooning the Irish.

The Coercion Acts are all very like one another; but this one contained the new provision that the Viceroy might suppress and disperse *any meeting* which he should deem dangerous to the public peace. The bill contained the usual powers and penalties. The Lord-Lieutenant might "proclaim" any district: all persons in proclaimed districts to remain within doors from one hour after sunset until sunrise, and also to abstain from attending any meeting whatsoever. No meeting was to be held, even to petition Parliament, without ten days' previous notice to the Lord-Lieutenant, and his sanction to hold such meeting. The proclaimed districts were to be subject to martial law; every offender was to be tried before a court-martial; and all officers of justice and military on duty were (in such proclaimed district) to have authority to enter houses at any hour, and search for arms. The writ of *Habeas Corpus* was to be suspended for three months after the arrest of any person, as respected that person.

These atrocious provisions for torturing the people, and for repressing even all open and peaceful expressions of opinion, continued to be the law of the land for five years. This law was then succeeded by another law of the same kind; and that by another and another. It might be supposed that the British Parliament might as well pass a perpetual Coercion Act for Ireland at once, and take away altogether the writ of *Habeas Corpus;* but such a measure as this would be supposed to be too abhorrent to the spirit of the British Constitution. The Coercion Acts, therefore, are all proposed for a limited time, and a hope is regularly expressed by the member of the Government who introduces one of them, that the time is approaching when these "exceptional" measures will be no longer needful to the good government and well-being of Ireland.

In the same session, Parliament passed the Act for abolishing negro slavery in the British West Indies, and appropriated twenty millions sterling to compensate the planters. Of course, the money was borrowed, and added to the national debt; and England and Ireland have been paying the interest on it ever since.

"The Church Temporalities Act" for Ireland was passed in the year 1833. It was introduced by Lord Althorpe, and became law on the 30th of July. His lordship stated the entire revenue of the Irish Church at £732,000 sterling. The new Act abolished ten bishoprics, by consolidating their sees with sees adjoining. The consolidation was to take place gradually, on the death of bishops. "Church rates" were abolished. The revenues of the sees which were to remain in existence were diminished; and the Church property of the suppressed sees, together with the saving by diminished revenues, were estimated as creating a fund of £3,000,000, to be vested in a board of "Ecclesiastical Commissioners," to be expended for strictly ecclesiastical purposes; the principle being that no Church property could be alienated from its legal owners, and that the country was not to be relieved of any part of the burden of this enormous Establishment. Accordingly, the people were not at all benefited by this Act. Even the abolition of "Church rates" was only a boon to the landlords, who immediately raised the rents of their tenants at will.

Next was introduced and passed another bill, appropriating one million sterling to the parsons, in compensation for the tithes due and unpaid for three years.

In 1834 O'Connell commenced seriously the work of repeal of the Union in Parliament. His first move was a proposal to appoint a committee to inquire into the conduct of Baron Smith, one of the Irish judges, whom he accused of introducing politics into his charges from the bench. The committee was refused, because it was held that an Irish judge could not avoid the subject of politics in his judicial addresses, seeing that Irish "crimes" were almost wholly of a political character. On the 23d of April, O'Connell formally brought forward in Parliament the question of repealing the Union. There followed a debate of four days. His chief opponent was Mr. Spring Rice (afterwards Lord Monteagle), who laboured to prove that Ireland had largely profited by the Union, and was at that moment enjoying exemption from several specific taxes which pressed upon Great Britain. In truth, according to his statistics, Ireland was growing rich, or at least ought to be, in consequence of the generous forbearance of the English people and Government, in burdening the other parts of the empire with imposts which she had not to pay.

But, notwithstanding statistics, the notorious truth was, that England was becoming always richer, and her people more luxurious in their style of living, while Ireland was fast sinking into destitution. The Irish rents spent by absentee proprietors now amounted to more than four millions. Manufacturers in Ireland (with the single exception of linen) no longer existed. Extermination of tenantry (or, as the people were now always termed, "surplus population") had increased to a dreadful extent; and those who had means to emigrate were flying from the country in wild terror. A writer in *Blackwood's Magazine* for January, 1833—the writer being no other than Sir Archibald Alison—states that the emigration in 1831 from Ireland amounted to eighteen thousand. The writer adds: "No reason can be assigned why it should not be one hundred and eighty thousand." From this time the leading idea of English statesmen and economists was, to devise some way of getting rid of the "surplus" people.

Yet while the people were said to be surplus, the island in which they lived was steadily and rapidly increasing her export of provisions. The export of grain and cattle into England, which had amounted in 1826 to nearly eight millions sterling, had now been augmented by about one-half; and this wasting process —shipping off men in one direction, and the food they had raised in another—went on developing itself, as we shall see, until the export of the surplus people reached three hundred thousand a year, and the export of the surplus food amounted to at least twenty millions sterling; Ireland being the only country known in ancient or in modern times, which had these two kinds of "surplus" for export at one time. It was so plainly demonstrated, however, in Parliament, by Mr. Spring Rice and other speakers, that the country was prospering under the Union, that O'Connell's motion was at once voted down. On the same occasion, the House of Peers not only rejected the proposition unanimously, but addressed the King, declaring their firm resolution to maintain the "integrity of the empire."

Various efforts were made in this and the following year to force upon Parliament some just measure for the reduction of the Irish Church Establishment. Mr. Ward, an English member, was especially zealous in this cause; but as these proposals were steadily resisted, and came to nothing whatever for several years, we need not occupy ourselves with them here. The Church bill of Mr. Ward contained what was called the "Appropriation Clause," for devoting to State purposes, and the general improvement of the country, the funds to be curtailed from the wealth of the Church. This was the great stumbling-block to the Tories, and to the House of Lords; and the measure was abandoned,

The last scene of tithe carnage was enacted at Rathcormack, a village in Waterford County. It was on the 18th of December, 1834. Seizure had been made upon the stackyard of a poor widow, to pay the Protestant rector. Her neighbours became strongly excited, and assembled in crowds, with the apparent purpose of resisting the abstraction of the property. A narrow lane, or *boreen*, led up from the highroad to the widow's place. In this lane, the people had overturned a waggon to block up the way, and seemed resolved to defend their barricade. The officers of the law approached, well supported by armed men, both police and military. There was some parley; stones were thrown; the Riot Act was read; and then orders were given to fire. A destructive volley was poured in upon the unarmed crowd; many of them fell, killed and wounded; and his reverence carried off, over the bleeding corpses, his tithe of the widow's sheaves. The excitement and indignation aroused by this "Rathcormack massacre" were profound and wide-spread. The combinations amongst the peasantry to resist tithe sales, and to prevent all persons from purchasing, at their own proper peril, became more organized and formidable. Doctor MacHale, Archbishop of Tuam, writing a public letter at this date to the Duke of Wellington, thus expresses himself: "All the united authorities, and the Senate, can never annex the conscientious obligations of law to enactments that are contrary to right, reason, and justice. And hence the stubborn and unconquerable resistance of the people of Ireland to those odious Acts—I will not call them *laws*— which have forced them to pay tribute to the teachers of an adverse creed. I shall freely declare my own resolve. I have leased a small farm, just sufficient to qualify me for the exercise of the franchise. After paying the landlord his rent, neither to parson, proctor, nor agent shall I consent to pay, in the shape of tithe or any other tax, a penny which shall go to the support of the greatest nuisance in this or any other country." It may be well supposed that such a declaration as this coming from a reverend dignitary of the Catholic Church—affirming that the Church laws were no laws, and that he himself would deny and defy them—greatly aggravated and encouraged the organized resistance of the people. If an attempt had been made to levy tithe from the archbishop's farm, no man in the diocese would have dared to bid for his corn-sheaves.

King William IV. died in June, 1837, and Queen Victoria reigned in his stead; a disastrous reign to Ireland.

Within the first three years of this Queen's reign, three measures of great importance were passed for Ireland; all brought forward under pretext of Concession and Liberalism; but all marked in reality with the invariable, inevitable stamp of mortal enmity towards the people of our country. These were, the *Poor Law*, the *Tithe Law*, and the *Law for Municipal Reform*.

Poor laws had become at once necessary in England, on the suppression of the monasteries in the reign of Henry VIII. In Catholic times, and according to Catholic ideas, alms-giving was a Christian duty; from that moment it had to become a tax. Those monasteries had been endowed by charitable and religious people mainly for the relief of the poor; but when their lands came into possession of King Henry's courtiers, the poor immediately began to be regarded as public enemies to be suppressed. The poor man had been a brother, whom it was a privilege and duty to console; he became one of the "dangerous classes," to be well watched, to be often punished, and to be for ever degraded and disgraced. The first English Poor law (27 Henry VIII.) prohibited almsgiving under heavy penalties; and as for "sturdy beggars"—"a sturdy beggar is to be whipped the first time, and if he again offend, he shall suffer death as a felon and an enemy of the commonwealth." The fourteenth of Elizabeth provided that these terrible sturdy beggars "should, for the first offence, be grievously whipped, and burned through the gristle of the right ear with a hot iron of the compass of an inch about; for the second, be deemed as felons; and for the third, suffer death as felons, without the benefit of clergy." Innumerable amendments and alterations have been made since those days in the English system of Poor laws, by which, although these ferocious punishments were mitigated, the principle was maintained, of treating the poor as enemies, and making charity a compulsory tax.

All this system had been hitherto unknown in Ireland, as it is still unknown in France and Spain. Poor men had been always with us, and that in plenty; but no "able-bodied paupers" by profession. If a third of the population was sometimes in a half-starving condition for half the year, the others, who had more comforts around them, shared generously with their suffering neighbours, and thought they were doing God service. Christian charity was not yet worked by machinery, nor exacted by sheriffs' officers. In short, poor as the Irish were—and they were only poor because the English ate them out of house and home—their whole nature and habits were totally abhorrent to the idea of Poor laws. But it was now the settled design of the British Government to fasten upon them this plague; and for two principal reasons—first, to obtain absolute control, through their own officials, of the great mass of the poor, who might otherwise be turned into elements of revolutionary disturbance; second, to aid and encourage the extermination of the "surplus population;" thus coming in aid of the new code of cheap and easy ejectment; for when there should be great poor houses in every district to receive the homeless people, landlords would have the less hesitation in turning out upon the highways the population of whole townlands at once. Besides, the immense patronage which the new system would place in the hands of the Government—a patronage to be chiefly exercised amongst the class a stage or two removed above the very poor themselves, would give to that Government, in every "Poor Law Union," a very extensive control over the interests and whole way of life of the farming class.

A person named Nicholl, a Scotchman, was sent to make a tour in Ireland, and to report on the distresses of the poor. After a journey of a few weeks, in a country quite unknown to him, this man made a report. He saw much suffering and privation; and reported that during half the year there were five hundred and eighty-five thousand persons, with two millions three hundred thousand *more* depending on them, in a state of utter destitution. He took care to report nothing of the reason of this destitution—namely, the drain of Irish produce to England. Upon the report of this Scotchman, a measure was prepared and introduced by Lord John Russell to establish a universal system of Poor laws, a board of commissioners, and distribution of the island into "Unions." It was in vain that O'Connell, many Catholic bishops, many Protestant Irishmen even, opposed this dreadful law.

It was carried by large majorities, and became law in July, 1838. Two years later there were one hundred and twenty-seven Unions marked out and constituted; fourteen immense Poor Houses, built like prisons, had been built, and the others were in rapid progress. Ireland has been blistering and festering under this British pestilence ever since that day. One of the first consequences of it was a large increase

M

in the number of ejectments. The ejected people, when they had no money to emigrate, could only take refuge in these Poor law jails, bid adieu to all decency and independence, and become paupers for ever, cursing the cruel "charity" that prolonged their miserable existence.

The second of these measures was the Tithe Bill, passed in May, 1838. It *abolished* Church tithes in Ireland; that is to say, it converted them into a charge upon the land; called tithe rent-charge, payable in the first place to the parsons by the landlords, and then leviable on the tenants by distress, along with the rent. Thus, the parsons were relieved from the necessity of coming into immediate collision with the farmers, and raising bloody riots to come at their tenth sheaf and tenth potato. The tithe, was, in fact, confounded with the rent, and put into a form impossible to be resisted or evaded. In return for the additional security and tranquillity thus assured to the clergymen, and for the saving of their heavy expenses to proctors and tithe-farmers, they were made to submit to a deduction of twenty-five per cent. upon the amount claimed by them. On the whole it was a profitable change for the parsons, who have been better paid since that time than they had been for many years before. The people were assured that they were relieved from the "tithe;" and the Church was supposed to have escaped the *odium* of this shocking imposition; but, at the same time, many a poor family saw its last bed carried off by the landlord's bailiffs to pay "tithe rent-charge." Nothing can demonstrate in a more offensive manner the savage resolution of the British Government and people to make us pay for support of that alien Church, or die.

The third great measure which signalized the first years of Queen Victoria was the Municipal Reform Act. The Emancipation Act had been quite inoperative in giving to Catholics their rightful place in the corporations. A Municipal Reform Bill had been introduced into Parliament, in 1836, by O'Loghlen, then Attorney-General. He had stated in his speech, that "although the whole number of corporators in Ireland were thirteen thousand, and although since 1792 the corporations had been nominally open to Catholics, not more than two hundred had been admitted." The municipal bodies also, being quite free from popular control, and all other control, had become quite as conspicuous for corruption as for Protestantism; and, independently of the claims of the Catholics, some cleansing process was absolutely needful amongst those dens of iniquity. The principle of the new bill was to give to the inhabitants of the towns (subject to a qualification according to rating) the power to elect town councillors, and thus infuse a popular element into the little close boroughs of municipal jurisdiction.

A Municipal Reform Bill had been within a few years enacted for England; and another object of the Government was to assimilate, as far as was prudent, the Irish institutions of this kind with the English. One great difficulty, however, at once presented itself. Some of the functions of municipal officers were connected with the administration of justice. The mayor is a magistrate. What is of still graver importance, the sheriff of a corporate city is the officer who has charge of the list of qualified *jurors* in that city, and who summons a certain number of them to serve at each assize or commission. If such sheriff should be a Catholic, there was reason to fear that he might not exercise due vigilance in keeping Catholics off those juries which might have to try "political offences"—a large and essential department of what is called "government" in Ireland.

Violent opposition was made to the bill on this and other grounds; and it was thrown out by the House of Lords. The agitation, however, was quite vehement on the subject in Ireland; and the demand for corporate reform grew loud. While the Marquis of Normanby was Lord-Lieutenant of Ireland, he did not prevent and repress political meetings, as he was invested with power to do; and the Whig Ministry soon found they could not calculate on Catholic support (which they needed) without some measure of this character. During the three years, 1837-8-9, the bill underwent several modifications, and was several times passed by the Commons and thrown out by the Peers. At last it took its final shape, and was introduced by Lord Morpeth, on the 14th of February, 1840. In his bill, the amount of *rating* fixed as the qualification for voters was £8. When it was sent up to the Lords, they insisted upon the qualification of a £10 rating; and with this change it was accepted by the Commons, and became law.[*]

The Municipal Reform Act would have been indeed an invaluable concession of right and equity to Ireland; and we should here be called upon to greatly modify or retract very much of the bitter reflections which have been made upon the deadly hostility shown by all British

[* 3 and 4 Victoria, cap. 118.]

Governments against the Irish people, but for one circumstance. A clause of the new Act not only renders all the rest comparatively worthless, but provides with deliberate malignity for the subversion of all law and justice in Ireland. It enacts that the Sheriff shall not be elected by the Town Councils, as in England, but appointed by the Lord-Lieutenant; that is to say, the Town Councils were to be allowed to submit certain names to that functionary, amongst whom they should pray him to appoint their Sheriff; and if none of the names pleased him, the nomination was to rest with him; that is to say, the officer who had charge of the jury lists, and whose special duty it is to take care that his fellow citizens are fairly represented in the jury box, was to be not an elected servant of the people, but a creature of the Castle and the Crown. There is no occasion for hesitation or delicacy in affirming that the intention of this clause was to enable the Crown to pack its juries with the utmost certainty, and to destroy a political opponent at any time, under a false pretence of law. To what deadly use this provision has been turned will be but too evident throughout the later history of the country. In the meantime, however, the Catholic townsmen of Ireland took their place in the municipal bodies, and in such municipal business as had no reference to the administration of justice. O'Connell was elected first Catholic Lord Mayor of Dublin, and took much state in his scarlet cloak and gold chain; but at the same moment was nominated a Sheriff, whose business it was to secure a jury that would send this Lord Mayor to jail on the first occasion when the Castle might desire to imprison him as a criminal.

These three measures were the first-fruits of Whig legislation for Ireland, in the first three years of Queen Victoria.

CHAPTER XXI.

1840—1843.

Spirit of Legislation for Ireland—More Spying in the Post-Office—Savings Banks—"Precursor's Society" support to the Whigs—Whigs go out—Peel comes in—Repeal Association—Export of Food—Extermination—The Repeal Year—Corporation Debate—The Younger Nationalists—New "Arms Bill"—O'Brien moves for Inquiry—Preparations for Coercion—All England against Repeal—Monster Meetings—Mallow—Tarra—Mullaghmast—Clontarf—Proclamation.

WE can now appreciate in some measure the spirit and motive of all the legislation for Ireland after "Emancipation." Catholics having been admitted into Parliament and into the Corporations, it became necessary, in the interest of British domination, to take securities against the employment of the new franchises for any Irish purpose. By the "National Education" system, provision was made for stifling all national sentiment in the young. By the Poor law, the life or death of certain millions of the people was placed at the disposal of British officials. By the Tithe law the impositions of the Established Church were rendered inevitable. By the Municipal law the perpetual packing of juries was made certain. Every enactment of the British Parliament was expressly designed and admirably calculated to nullify altogether the sentiments and aspirations of the Irish people, and to subject their whole way of life to the will and the interests of England. The police force had been gradually converted into a standing army, under the absolute control of the Castle. The post-office *espionage* had been systematized and perfected. Government officers were trained to open letters and re-seal them, without showing any trace of their manipulation; and Her Majesty's Lords-Lieutenant read the correspondence of all suspected persons. In 1834 it was Mr. Secretary Littleton (afterwards Lord Hatherton) who inspected men's letters. In 1835 it was Lord Mulgrave (afterwards Marquis of Normanby) who discharged this needful office. The next year it was the same noble Marquis, and the Irish Secretary, Mr. Drummond—the man who scandalized the whole British interest in Ireland by a casual observation of his (which, however, he did not mean), that "property had its duties as well as its rights." It was this Mr. Drummond who was the spy upon our correspondence both in 1836 and 1837. In the same year (1837) it appears that both Lord-Chancellor Plunket, one of the Lords-Justices, and Doctor Whately, Archbishop of Dublin, a member of the Privy-Council, had a curiosity to know what Mr. O'Connell and others might be writing about to their friends. They therefore gave directions that the letters to and from that gentleman, and all the other gentlemen named in their orders (we are not told who they were), should be opened in the post-office, softening the seals or envelopes by a cunning application of steam, then copied for the study of those functionaries, and then sealed up again with great skill. In 1838 Lord Morpeth (afterwards Lord Carlisle) had the opening of our letters. In 1839 the Marquis of Normanby, Lord Ebrington, and General Sir T. Blakeney, one of the Lords-Justices. In 1840 Lord Ebrington again freely indulged his curiosity.*

When to all these methods of inspection and control we add the immense police force—about thirteen thousand men, well armed and scientifically distributed over the whole island—with their complete code of signals for communicating from station to station, with blue lights, red lights, and other apparatus. When we add the numerous corps of *detectives* (a sort of institution in which Great Britain is unmatched in all the world), and when we remember the Disarming Acts and Coercion Acts always in force,† it is easy to understand how the unfortunate Irish nation, bound hand and foot, muzzled, disarmed, and half starved, could but writhe helplessly under the lash of its greedy tyrant. Yet the picture of these engines of subjugation is not complete without an account of the *savings banks*. These institutions were the only means left to industrious and frugal people by which they could safely invest their savings. Manufacturing industry was out of the question; land in small lots was not to be had; even leases for lives or years were no longer obtained (for there was now no use for small freeholders at the hustings), and those who could save a little money could do no better than deposit it in the savings bank of the nearest town. The system of savings banks had been introduced from Scotland into Ireland in 1810. Soon after, it had been made a Government institution, and the rate of interest was fixed by law. The depositors were allowed £3, 0s. 10d. per cent.; and the savings bank was bound to invest the whole of the money deposited with it in the *Government funds.* Thus the small savings of every industrious artizan, and of every prudent maid-servant, were in the hands of the Government; and their value depended upon the value of the Government funds—that is, on the credit and stability of the existing British system. This was a substantial security against revolution, because every depositor felt that his little all depended on the tranquillity of the State: in other words, on the peaceful perpetuation of the hateful system which was really making beggars of them all.

It must be admitted that, in so very helpless a condition of the country, it was a difficult task for even the most powerful and popular agitator to produce any move-

* Parliamentary Return. Session of 1845. Papers relating to Mazzini.
† Lord Grey's Coercion Act remained in force till 1839. It was soon succeeded by another Coercion Act.

ment that would be really formidable to the enemy's government, or would exert any serious pressure upon their action. O'Connell was, for several years, in a state of manifest perplexity and indecision. He always knew and felt, it is true, that the repeal of the Union—the destruction of the British empire—was the only salvation for his country. But that British empire was now on its guard at all points. Besides, the governing faction at that moment was Whig; full of fine, liberal professions, always employed in some fraudulent pretence of friendly legislation for Ireland, and even courting him and his influence for its own party purposes. It is not to be wondered at, then, that when the Liberal Lord Melbourne was Prime Minister, and the more than Liberal Lord Normanby and Lord Ebrington were Viceroys of Ireland, who were willing to distribute a large share of the Government patronage on his recommendation (whilst they inspected his letters in the postoffice), it cannot be thought strange that he held in abeyance for a time the real and rightful claims of Irish nationhood, and gave a certain qualified support to the "Liberal" administration which bestowed profitable offices on his friends. It was at this period that the Tories accused the Government of truckling to O'Connell, and that the thoroughgoing nationalists of Ireland accused O'Connell of trafficking with the Whigs; and, in fact, this was the most questionable part of his whole political career.

Yet O'Connell was too much devoted to the cause of his country to sell it to any English party. He insisted no longer on the restoration of a native legislature, but loudly claimed "justice to Ireland," and affected to believe that these Whig statesmen would consent to such justice. Thereupon he established a new agitating association, which he called by the peculiar name of "Precursor Society," in the beginning of 1839. The meaning of the name was, that Ireland was now making a last appeal for "justice," and that if this were still denied, the existing Society was but the precursor of a new and universal agitation for repeal of the Union. In the meantime, all the influence of the organization was to be used in support of the Whig administration. "What am I here for?" exclaimed O'Connell, at a meeting on the 6th of March, 1839, "What am I here for? To call on all Ireland *to rally round the Ministry;* to call for my two millions of enrolled Precursors."

Lord Normanby, while in secret he pried into everybody's letters, omitted in public none of the usual arts of popularity. He procured places for Catholic lawyers; he dismissed from the commission of the peace Colonel Verner, and other outrageous Orange magistrates, for publicly celebrating that ruffianly slaughter called Battle of the Diamond; he received Catholic notabilities at the Castle with distinguished courtesy; he made excursions through the provinces, and liberated from the jails great numbers of prisoners who were either unjustly confined or undergoing punishment for trifling offences. At length English opinion became inflamed against him; and Lord Brougham (who had entirely abandoned all pretence to Liberalism when Ireland was in question) moved a vote of censure against Lord Normanby in the House of Lords, on the express ground of an abuse of patronage and of the pardoning power. It appeared in the debate that his lordship had, between November, 1837, and the 31st January, 1839, released eight hundred and twenty-two prisoners—but not without inquiry into their cases, and not without rejecting appeals for clemency amounting to nearly as large a number. The vote of censure passed, however. Lord Normanby retired from the Viceroyalty, and was succeeded in 1839 by Lord Ebrington, another Liberal, who lost no time in commencing his duties as post-office spy,—which, indeed, he continued faithfully to discharge during the whole period of his government.

The "Precursor" Association continued its meetings at the Corn Exchange, on Burgh Quay, and Mr. O'Connell regularly, once a week, while he demanded justice to Ireland, called on the people to sustain the Whig Government.

This anomalous political situation ended in November, 1841. The Whig administration went out; and Sir Robert Peel, the proved and inveterate enemy of Ireland and of the Catholics, became Prime Minister. There was to be no more patronage at the disposal of the Corn Exchange; no more pretext for affecting to expect justice for Ireland at the hands of an English Government; and the Precursor Society merged into the *Repeal Association.*

For the next two years this new organization attracted but little attention in England, or even at home. The country had become so much accustomed to Mr. O'Connell's successive forms of agitation, that it would have surprised nobody if the Repeal Association had been upon any morning "proclaimed" out of existence, or if its versatile author had again changed its name and character, and called it the "Liberal Association," or "Justice to Ireland Association." But, in truth, no person could be more fully sensible than Mr. O'Connell that there was no justice for Ireland save in national independence. For full thirty years he had constantly avowed this creed; and if he had waived the claim for awhile, it was only to aid and encourage the Whigs in granting what he called "instalments" of justice, which might strengthen the nation to demand and enforce all that was due; or in putting "good men" into office, who, he said, were certainly better than bad men. Now, at last, he felt himself standing upon the only plain and honest principle, engaged in the only agitation by which his countrymen would be really stirred and fired to the very heart's core.

Nothing important took place during these two years. Mr. O'Connell was now Lord Mayor of Dublin, and held his *levées* in state at the Mansion House, while the Lord-Lieutenant was studying his private letters to find matter of accusation against him. The people were pleased to see their chosen chief adorned with the splendid corporate *insignia,* so long appropriated by the "Ascendancy," and did not yet perceive how firmly, instead of that old "Ascendancy," British domination was fastened upon them.

In 1843, more than three million quarters of grain were exported out of Ireland into England; besides almost a million head of live stock, including horned cattle, sheep, and swine.*

In 1843 extermination of tenantry was sweeping and destructive; and the emigration of "surplus population" from Ireland reached nearly one hundred thousand.

From a Londonderry newspaper of this year we extract an advertisement, signed by one M'Mullin, "Emigration Agent," which will show what was going on throughout Ireland better than particular details could do:—

NOTICE.—A favourable opportunity presents itself, in the course of the present month, for Quebec, to gentlemen residing in the Counties of Londonderry, Donegal, Tyrone, or Fermanagh, who wish to send out to the Canadas the *overstock tenantry* belonging to their estates—as a moderate rate of passage will be taken, and six months' credit given for a lump sum to any gentleman requiring such accommodation, &c.

The mode in which the overstock tenantry are persuaded in Ireland to embark for America is ejecting them, and pulling down their houses. And in 1843, and many years before, and every year since, this process has been going on so extensively and notoriously that there will be

* Thom's *Official Directory.* This is quite an under estimate.

no further occasion to refer to it, until we arrive at what the British call the "Famine."

In 1843, the rental of Ireland, carried off to be spent abroad, amounted (according to Mr. Smith O'Brien's estimate) to five millions sterling; and the peasantry, whose industry created all the wealth of the country, were proverbially known throughout the earth as "the worst fed, the worst clothed, and the worst housed peasantry in Europe."

The poor houses, which had been built under the new law, were all full. The farmers were paying their tithes to the landlords, with no possibility of escape—for the bailiffs were always at the door—and the tithe was levied along with the rent. The "national schools" were teaching Irish children that there is no such thing as nationality, and that it is a blessed privilege to be born "a happy English child." Thus, the mature and highly elaborated policy of the enemy towards Ireland was in full and successful operation at every point, when, in the spring of 1843, O'Connell announced that it was the *repeal year*, and proceeded to infuse into that movement an energy and power greater than any of his organizations had ever possessed, even in the days of the old Catholic Association.

First, he asked for three millions of enrolled repealers in the Repeal Association; and confidently promised, and perhaps fully believed, that no English Administration would venture to resist that great measure so enforced. The more thoroughly to arouse the people, he declined to go over to London to take his seat in Parliament (many other members following his example), and resolved to hold multitudinous meetings in every corner of the island.

First, he moved, in the Dublin Corporation, a resolution for the adoption of a petition to Parliament demanding a Repeal of the Union with England—that is to say, demanding back the Irish Parliament, which had been extinguished in 1800,—so that Ireland should once more have her own House of Peers and House of Commons; the Sovereign of England to be also Sovereign of Ireland. His speech was masterly, and covered the whole case. He cited the ablest jurists to show that the so-called Union was in law a nullity; reminded his audience of what was at any rate notorious and never denied, that—supposing the two Parliaments competent to pass such an Act—it had been obtained by fraud and open bribery; an open market of bribery, of which the accounts are extant — viz., £1,275,000 paid to proprietors for the purchase of nomination boroughs, at £15,000 per borough (which seats were immediately filled by English officers and clerks); more than one million sterling expended on mere bribes, the tariff being quite familiar, £8,000 for an Union vote, or an office worth £2,000 a year, if the member did not like to touch the ready money; twenty Peerages, ten Bishoprics, one Chief-Justiceship, six Puisne Judgeships—not to count regiments and ships given to officers in the army and navy, all dispensed as direct payment for the vote. He reminded them that the right of holding public meetings to protest against all this was taken away during the time the Union was in agitation; that county meetings, convened by High Sheriffs of counties, as in Tipperary and Queen's County, were dispersed by troops; martial law was in force, and the *Habeas Corpus* Act suspended; that, in 1800, the number of soldiers concentrated in that small island was one hundred and twenty-nine thousand, as "good lookerson;" that notwithstanding all intimidation, seven hundred thousand persons had petitioned against the measure; and notwithstanding all enticements, only three thousand had petitioned for it—most of these being Government officials and prisoners in the jails. If he had stopped here, most persons would think it enough: *that* was a deed which at the earliest possible moment must be undone and punished.

But he did not stop here. He went into all the details of ruined trade and manufactures since the Union;—immensely increased drains in the shape of absentee rents and surplus taxation; frauds in subjecting Ireland to a charge for the *English* national debt; and even charging to Ireland's special account the very moneys expended in bribes and military expenses for carrying the Union—which, he said, was about as fair as "making Ireland pay for the knife with which Lord Castlereagh cut his throat;" injustice in giving Ireland but one hundred members in the House of Commons, while her population and revenue entitled her to one hundred and seventy-five; and, above all, the injustice of fixing the qualification of *electors* of these members much higher in Ireland, the poorer country, than in England.

This is a sketch only of the case for repeal of the Union; the necessity for some remedy or other was only too apparent in the poverty and wretchedness which moved and scandalized all Europe.

The petition for repeal was adopted by a vote of forty-one to fifteen in the Corporation; and a similar petition, shortly after, by the Corporation of Cork. Hitherto the English press, and Irish press in the English interest, looked on with affected or real indifference and contempt.

O'Connell then left Dublin for the provinces. Then began the series of vast open-air meetings, to which the peasantry, accompanied by their priests, repeal wardens, and "temperance bands," flocked in numbers varying from fifty thousand to two hundred and fifty thousand (we take the reduced and disparaging estimate of enemies, but the repeal newspapers put up the Tara meeting to four hundred thousand). Of course, the orator always addressed these multitudes, but though his voice was the most powerful of his day, he could not be heard by a tenth of them. Neither did they come to hear. They were all well indoctrinated by local repeal wardens; had their minds made up, and came to convince their leader that they were with him, and would be ready at any time when called upon.

But all was to be peaceable; they were to demand their rights imperatively; they were, he assured them, tall men and strong; at every monster meeting he had around him, as he often said, the materials of a greater army than both the armies combined that fought at Waterloo. "But take heed," he cried, "not to misconceive me. Is it by force or violence, bloodshed or turbulence, that I shall achieve this victory, dear above all earthly considerations to my heart? No! perish the thought for ever. I will do it by legal, peaceable, and constitutional means alone —by the electricity of public opinion, by the moral combination of good men, and by the enrolment of four millions of repealers. I am a disciple of that sect of politicians who believe that *the greatest of all sublunary blessings is too dearly purchased at the expense of a single drop of human blood.*"

Many persons did not understand this sort of language. The prevailing impression was, that while the Repeal Association was, indeed, a peaceable body, contemplating only "constitutional agitation," yet the parade of such immense masses of physical force had an ulterior meaning, and indicated that if the British Parliament remained absolutely insensible to the reasonable demands of the people, the Association must be dissolved; and the next question would be, How best and soonest to exterminate the British forces. Many who were close to O'Connell expected all along that the English Parliament and Government never would yield; and these would have taken small interest in the movement, if it was never to go beyond speeches and cheers.

Meanwhile, nothing could be more peaceful, orderly, and good-humoured than the meetings. Father Mathew's temperance reformation had lately been working its wonders, and all the people were sober and quiet; repeal wardens everywhere organized an "O'Connell Police," with wands; and any person of the whole immense multitude who was even noisy, was instantly and quietly removed. The Government, indeed, soon took alarm, or affected to do so, for the peace of the country; and they sent large forces of armed constabulary to bivouac on the ground; but there never was the slightest excuse for interference.

The movement of the people, throughout this whole summer, was profound and sweeping; it carried along with it the Catholic clergy, though in many cases against their will; but they were of the people, bound up with the people, dependent on the people, and found it their best policy to move not only with the people, but at their head. The Catholic bishops and archbishops gave in their adhesion, and began to take the chair at meetings; the French and German press began to notice the struggle, and eagerly watch how England would deal with it. At last, on April 27th, Mr. Lane Fox, a Tory member of Parliament, gave notice, "That it is the duty of Her Majesty's Government to take immediate steps to put an end to the agitation for repeal;" and on the same day, Lord Eliot, Chief Secretary for Ireland, gave notice of a bill "for the regulation of *arms* in Ireland." At the same moment the funds fell one and a half per cent.

The first threat of coercion brought important accessions to the ranks of the repealers; and the monster meetings became now more monstrous than ever; but, if possible, even gayer and more good-humoured.

Mr. O'Connell affected to treat very lightly all these menaces of violence. His sarcasm was bitter, his reason irrefragable, his array multitudinous in its peaceful might; but, in the meantime, Lord Eliot was preparing his Arms Bill; and, on the 9th of May, the Duke of Wellington in the Lords, and Sir Robert Peel in the Commons, declared that all the resources of the empire should be exerted to preserve the Union; and Sir Robert Peel added, quoting Lord Althorpe, that, deprecating civil war as he did, he should hold civil war preferable to the "dismemberment of the empire." Mr. Bernal [Osborne] instantly asked Sir Robert, as he cited Lord Althorpe's words, "whether he would abide by another declaration of that noble lord—namely, that if all the members for Ireland should be in favour of repeal, he would consider it his duty to grant it?" And Sir Robert replied: "I do not recollect that Lord Althorpe ever made any such declaration; but if he did, *I am not prepared to abide by it.*"

At this point, issue was joined. The majority of the Irish nation desired to undo the Union with England; but England declared that, if all Ireland demanded that measure, England would rather drown the demand in blood.

The new Association for Repeal contained many men of great ability and influence. Mr. Shiel, indeed, though he had publicly declared himself in favour of repealing the Union, had desisted from all active agitation after the Catholic Relief Bill. He never entered at all into this new repeal movement, perhaps because he knew it meant war, and knew O'Connell would never fight; perhaps because he chose to identify himself with the higher class of Catholics, who thought enough had been done, and "called it freedom when themselves were free;" perhaps because he was somewhat intolerant of O'Connell's autocratic sway—for, like every great leader of a democracy, the agitator was a most despotic disciplinarian in ruling the movement he had created. Up to the time of the Ministerial declaration against repeal in April, very few members of Parliament were actual members of the Association; but amongst them was Henry Grattan, member for Meath, who brought to its ranks an illustrious name, if nothing else of great value. O'Brien still stood aloof.

But within this same Association there was a certain smaller Association, composed of very different men. Its head and heart was Thomas Davis, a young Protestant lawyer of Cork County, who had been previously known only as a scholar and antiquarian—a zealous member of the Royal Irish Academy, and of the Archæological Society. In the autumn of '42, he and his friend Dillon had projected the publication of a weekly literary and political journal of the highest class, to sustain the cause of Irish nationhood, to give it a historic and literary interest which would win and inspire the youth of the country, and, above all, to conciliate Protestants by stripping the agitation of a certain suspicion of sectarianism, which, though disavowed by O'Connell, was naturally connected with it by reason of the antecedents of its chief.

So commenced the *Nation* newspaper; which, for several years, was, next to O'Connell, the strongest power on the national side. Its editor was Mr. Duffy, but Thomas Davis was its chief writer. By his ardent temperament, amiable character, and high accomplishments, he soon gathered around him a gifted circle of educated young men—both Protestant and Catholic—whose headquarters was the *Nation* office, and whose chief bond of union was their warm attachment to their friend. It was the one grand object of these men—and it was grand—to lift up the Irish cause high above both Catholic claims and Protestant pretensions, and unite all sects, in the one character of "Irishmen," to put an end to English domination. Their idea was precisely the idea of the United Irishmen; although their mode of action was very different. Mr. Davis and his friends soon received the nickname of "Young Ireland," which designation they never themselves assumed nor accepted.

O'Connell knew well, and could count, this small circle of literary privateer repealers; he felt that he was receiving, for the present, a powerful support from them—the *Nation* being by far the ablest organ of the movement; but he knew, also, that they were outside of his influence, and did not implicitly believe his confident promises that repeal would be yielded to "agitation;" that they were continually seeking by their writings to arouse a military spirit among the people; and had most diligently promoted the formation of temperance bands, with military uniforms, the practice of marching to monster meetings in ranks and squadrons, with banners, and the like; showing plainly, that while they helped the Repeal Association, they fully expected that the liberties of the country must be *fought* for at last. O'Connell, therefore, suspected and disliked them; but could not well quarrel with them. Apparently they worked in perfect harmony; and during all this "repeal year" few were aware how certainly that alliance must end. Personally they sought no notoriety; and the *Nation* was as careful to swell O'Connell's praise, and make him the sole figure to which all eyes should turn, as any of his own creatures could be. O'Connell accepted their services to convert the "gentry" and the Protestants: they could not dispense with O'Connell to stir and wield the multitudinous people.

It has been mentioned that on the same day when the Ministers declared, in the Queen's name, that the Union must, at all hazards, be maintained, Lord Eliot introduced a new "Arms Bill" for Ireland. This new bill was recommended by Lord Eliot, in the House of Commons, by the remark, "that it was substantially similar to what had been the law in Ireland for half a century" (June 15th); and again (June 26th), "He would ask the noble lord to compare it with the bill of 1838, and to point out the difference. In fact, this was milder." This mild Act, then, provided, That no man could keep arms of any sort, without first having a certificate from two householders, "rated to the poor" at above £20, and then producing that certificate to the justices at sessions (said justices being all appointed by the Crown, and all sure men); and then, if the justices permitted the applicant to keep arms at all, they were to be registered and *branded* by the police. After that they could not be removed, sold, or inherited without new registry. And every conversation respecting these arms in which a man should not tell truly whatever he might be asked by any policeman, subjected the delinquent to penalties. To have a pike or spear, "or instrument serving for a pike or spear," was an offence punishable by transportation for seven years. Domiciliary visits by the police might be ordered by any magistrate "on suspicion," whereupon any man's house might be broken into by day or night, and his very bed searched for concealed arms. Blacksmiths were required to take out licenses similar to those for keeping arms, and under the same penalties, in order that the workers in so dangerous a metal as iron might be known and approved persons. And, to crown the code, if any weapon should be found in any house, or out-house, or stack-yard, the occupier was to be convicted unless he could prove that it was there without his knowledge.

Such had been "substantially the law of Ireland for half a century." The idea of arms had come to be associated in the people's minds with handcuffs, jails, petty-sessions, and transportation; a good device for killing the manly spirit of a nation.

The Disarming Act passed into a law, of course by large majorities. It was in vain that some Irish members resisted. In vain Mr. Smith O'Brien, then member for Limerick, moved that instead of meeting the discontent of Ireland with a new Arms Bill, the House should resolve itself into a committee "to consider the cause of the discontent with a view to the redress of grievances." O'Brien, who was afterwards to play so conspicuous a part, was not yet a repealer. He had been for twenty years one of the most industrious members of Parliament, and was attached, on most questions, to the Whig party. His speech, however, on this motion showed that he regarded it as a last effort to obtain any approach to justice in a British Parliament, and that if they still resolutely adhered to the policy of coercion, and nothing but coercion, he would very shortly be found by O'Connell's side.

He pointed out the facts which justified discontent; that the Union made Ireland poor and kept her poor; that it encouraged the absenteeism of landlords, and so caused a great rental to be spent in England; that nearly a million sterling of "surplus revenue" over what was expended in the government of Ireland was annually remitted from the Irish to the English exchequer; that Irish manufactures had ceased, and the profits on all the manufactured articles consumed in that island came to England; that the tenantry had no permanent tenure or security that they would derive benefit by any improvements they might make; that Ireland had but one hundred and five members of Parliament, whereas her population and revenue together entitled her to one hundred and seventy-five; that the municipal laws of the two countries were not the same. Then the new "Poor Law" was a failure, and was increasing the wretchedness and hunger of the people; and the right honourable gentleman (Sir R. Peel) had now declared his *ultimatum;* he declared that "conciliation had reached its limits, and that the Irish should have an Arms Bill, and nothing but an Arms Bill" (speech of July 4th, 1843).

His facts were not disputed. Nobody in Parliament pretended to say that anything in this long catalogue was overstated; but the House refused the committee of inquiry, would discuss no grievances, and proceeded with their Arms Bill.

It has been said, indeed, that these excessive precautions to keep arms out of the hands of the Irish people testified the high esteem in which the military spirit of that people was held in England; and in this point of view the long series of Arms Acts may be regarded as a compliment. In truth, the English had some occasion to know that the Irish make good soldiers. In this very month of July, 1843, for example, a British general fought the decisive battle of Meeanee, by which the Ameers of Scinde were crushed. While the bill for disarming Ireland was pending, far off on the banks of the Indus Napier went into action with less than three thousand troops against twenty-five thousand, only four hundred of his men being "British" soldiers; but those four hundred were a Tipperary regiment—the Twenty-second—and they did their work in such style as made the gray old warrior shout aloud, "Magnificent Tipperary!"

Along with the new Arms Act several additional regiments, mostly of English and Scotch troops, were sent to Ireland; and several war-steamers, with a fleet of gun-brigs, were sent to cruise round the coast. Barracks began to be fortified and loop-holed, and police-stations were furnished with iron-grated windows. It was quite evident that the English Government intended, on the first pretext of provocation, to make a salutary slaughter.

In the meantime the vast monster meetings continued, with even intenser enthusiasm, but always with perfect peace and order. "Whom are they going to fight?" O'Connell would exclaim; "We are not going to fight them. We are unarmed, we meet peacefully to demand our country's freedom. There is no bloodshed, no drunkenness even, or ill-humour. Hurrah for the Queen, God bless her!"

The speeches of O'Connell at these meetings, though not heard by a fourth of the multitudes, were carefully reported, and flew over all Ireland, and England too, in hundreds of newspapers, so that probably no speeches ever delivered in the world had so wide an audience. The people began to neglect altogether the proceedings of Parliament, and felt that their cause was to be tried at home. More and more of the Irish members of Parliament discontinued their attendance in London and gathered round O'Connell. Many of those who still went to London were called on by their constituents to come home or resign.

Sir Edward Sugden was then Lord-Chancellor of Ireland, and he began offensive operations on the British side, by depriving of the commission of the peace all magistrates who joined the Repeal Association, or took the chair at a repeal meeting. He had dismissed in this way about twenty, including O'Connell and Lord French, usually accompanying the announcement of the *supersedeas* with an insolent letter, when Smith O'Brien wrote to him that *he* had been a magistrate for many years, that he was not a repealer, but could not consent to hold his commission on such humiliating terms. Instantly his example was followed by many gentlemen, who flung their commissions in the Chancellor's face, sometimes with letters as insulting as his own. And now O'Connell brought forward one of his grand schemes. It was to have all the dismissed magistrates appointed "arbitrators," who should hold regular courts of arbitration in their respective districts— all the people pledging themselves to make no resort to the Queen's magistrates, but to settle every dispute by the award of their arbitrators. This was put into operation in many places, and worked very well.

In reply to questions in Parliament as to what they were concentrating troops in Ireland for, Peel and Wellington had said they did not mean to make war or attack anybody, but only to maintain the peace of the country.

It was very obvious that all England, and men of all parties and creeds in England, were fully resolved to resist, at any cost of blood and havoc, the claim for a repeal of the Union; and it must be admitted to have been a strange weakness on the part of O'Connell, if he really believed that the same sort of "agitation" which had extorted the Relief Bill could now coerce the prosperous and greedy British nation to yield up its hold upon Ireland. That Relief Act, it must be remembered, was a measure for the *consolidation* of the "British Empire;" it opened high official position to the wealthier Catholics and educated Catholic gentlemen, and thus separated their interest from that of the peasantry. But it was of the peasantry mainly that the Government had any apprehension, and British Ministers felt that Catholic Emancipation would place this peasantry more completely in their power than ever.

Besides, Emancipation had a strong party in its favour, both amongst Irish Protestants and in England; and in yielding to it England made no sacrifice except of her ancient grudge. To her it was positive gain. O'Connell did not bethink him that when his agitation should be directly aimed at the "integrity of the empire," and the supremacy of the British in Ireland, it would be a different matter.

One fact showed very plainly that Englishmen of all sorts regarded this repeal movement as a mortal stab aimed at the heart of the empire—the English Catholics were as bitterly hostile to Ireland, on this question, as the highest "No-Popery" Tories. Thus Lord Beaumont, an English Catholic Peer, who owed his seat in the House to O'Connell, thought himself called upon to denounce the repeal agitation. "Do you know who this Beaumont is?" asked O'Connell at his next meeting. "Why, the man's name is Martin Bree, though he calls himself Stapleton. His grandfather married a Stapleton for her fortune, and then changed the name. He was a Stapleton when I emancipated him. I beg your pardon for having emancipated such a fellow."

For the last twenty years the English press has mocked at the whole repeal movement; and in Parliament it was never mentioned save with a jeer. In the summer of 1843 they neither laughed nor jeered. Sir James Graham, earnestly appealing to the House to refuse O'Brien's motion of inquiry, exclaimed:—

"*Any hesitation* now, *any delay* and *irresolution*, will multiply the danger a hundredfold. If Parliament expresses its sense in favour of the course pursued by Government, ministers have every *hope* that, with the confidence of the House, they will be enabled to triumph over all difficulties. I appeal, then, to both sides —not to one, but to both—I appeal to both sides, and say, if you falter now, if you hesitate now in repressing the rebellious spirit which is at work in the struggle of repeal, *the glory of the country is departed*—the days of its power are numbered; and England, this all-conquering England, must be classed with those countries *from whom power has dwindled away*, and present the melancholy aspect of a falling nation."

To refuse a committee of inquiry was reasonable enough; because Parliament, and all the people—men, women, and children — already knew all. The sole and avowed idea of the Government was, that to admit the idea of *anything* being wrong, would make the repeal movement altogether irresistible. The various projects now brought forward in England showed the perplexity of that country. Lord John Russell made an elaborate speech for conciliation; but the meaning of it seemed to be merely that it was no wonder Ireland was unquiet, seeing *he* was out of power. The grievance of Ireland, said he, in effect, is a Tory Ministry. Let her be ruled by us Whigs, and all will be well. Lord Brougham also gave it as his opinion that "you must purchase, not prosecute, repeal." The *Morning Chronicle* (Whig organ), in quite a friendly spirit, said, "Let us have a *perfect* Union; let us know each other; let the Irish judges come circuit in England, and let the English judges occasionally take the same round in Ireland," and so forth. "Is it absolutely certain," asked the *Westminster Review*, "that we can beat this people?" And the *Naval and Military Gazette*, a high military authority, thus expresses its apprehensions:—

"There are now stationed in Ireland thirty-five thousand men of all arms; but widely scattered over the island. In the event of a rebellion (and who can say that we are not on the eve of one?) we feel great solicitude for the numerous small detachments of our gallant soldiers. . . . It is time to be up and doing. We have heard that the order and regularity of movement displayed by the divisions which passed before Mr. O'Connell, in review order, *en route* to Donnybrook lately, surprised many veteran officers, and led them to think that some *personal* training, in private and in small parties, must be practised. The ready obedience to the word of command, the silence while moving, and the general combinations, all prove organization to have gone a considerable length. In these trained bands our soldiers, split up into detached parties, would find no ordinary opponents; and we, therefore, hope soon to learn that all small parties have been called in, and that our regiments in Ireland are kept together and complete. That day, we fear, is near when '*quite peaceably*' every repealer will come armed to a meeting, to be held simultaneously as to day and hour all over the island, and then try to cut off quite peaceably every detachment of Her Majesty's loyal army."

What contributed to disquiet the British exceedingly was, that great and excited repeal meetings were held every week in American cities—meetings not only of Irish-born citizens, but of natives also— and considerable funds were remitted from thence to O'Connell's repeal exchequer.

"If something is not done," said Colonel Thomson, in the *Westminster*, "a fleet of steamboats from the United States will, some fine morning, be the Euthanasia of the Irish struggle."

We might cite many extracts from the press of France, exhibiting a powerful interest in what the French conceived to be an impending military struggle. Take one from the Paris *Constitutional*:—

"When Ireland is agitated—when, at the sound of the powerful voice of O'Connell, four hundred thousand Irish assemble together in their meetings, and pronounce, as if it were by a single man, the same cry, and the same word—it is a grand spectacle which fills the soul, and which even at this distance moves the very strongest feelings of the heart. for it is the spectacle of an entire people who demand justice—of a people who have been despoiled of everything, even of the means of sustenance, and yet who require, with calmness and with firmness, the untrammelled exercise of their religion, and some of the privileges of their ancient nationality."

Now, nobody, either in France or in the United States, would have given himself the trouble to watch that movement with interest, if they had not all believed that O'Connell and the Irish people meant to fight. Neither in America nor in France had men learned to appreciate "the ethical experiment of moral force." Clearly, also, the English expected a fight, and were preparing for it, and greatly preferred that mode of settling the difficulty (having a powerful army and navy ready), to O'Brien's method—inquiry, discussion, and redress—seeing that they were wholly unprovided with argument, and had no idea of giving redress.

It is also quite as clear that the Irish people then expected, and longed, and burned for battle, and never believed that O'Connell would adhere to his "peace policy" even in the last extremity. Still, as he rose in apparent confidence, and became more defiant in his tone, the people rallied more ardently around him; and thousands of quiet, resolute men flocked into the repeal cause, who had hitherto held back from all the agitations merely because they had always believed O'Connell insincere. They thought that the mighty movement which now surged up around him had whirled him into its own tempest at last, and that "the time was come."

No speech he ever uttered roused such a stormy tumult of applause as when, at Mallow "monster meeting," referring to the threats of coercion, and to an anxious Cabinet Council which had just been held, he said:—

"They spent Thursday in consulting whether they would deprive us of our rights, and I know not what the result of that council may be; but this I know, there was not an Irishman in the council. I may be told that the Duke of Wellington was there. Who calls him an Irishman? If a tiger's cub was dropped in a fold, would it be a lamb? But, perhaps, I am wrong in anticipating; perhaps I am mistaken in warning you. But is there reason to caution you? The council sat for an entire day, and even then did not conclude its deliberations, but adjourned to the next day, while the business of the country was allowed to stand still. What had they to deliberate about? The repealers were peaceable, loyal, and attached—affectionately attached—to the Queen, and determined to stand between her and her enemies. If they assailed us to-morrow, and that we conquered them—as conquer them we will one day—the first use of that victory which we would make would be, to place the sceptre in the hands of her who has ever shown us favour, and whose conduct has ever been full of sympathy and emotion for our sufferings. Suppose, then, for a moment, that England found the Act of Union to operate not for her benefit; if, instead of decreasing her debt, it added to her taxation and liabilities, and made her burden more onerous; and if she felt herself entitled to call for a repeal of that Act, I ask Peel and Wellington, and let them deny it if they dare (and if they did they would be the scorn and by-word of the world), would she not have the right to call for a repeal of that Act? And what are Irishmen that they should be denied the same privilege? Have we not the ordinary courage of Englishmen? Are we to be trampled under foot? Oh, they shall never trample me, at least. I was wrong: they may trample me under foot—I say they may trample me, but it will be my dead body they will trample on, not the living man."

And a roar, two hundred thousand strong, rent the clouds. From that day the meetings went on increasingly in numbers, in regularity of training, and in highly-wrought excitement; until at Tara and at Mallaghmast the agitator shook with the passion of the scene, as the fiery eyes of three hundred thousand upturned faces seemed to crave *the word*.

Whig newspapers and politicians in England (the Whigs being then in opposition) began now to suggest various conciliatory measures—talked of the anomaly of the "Established Church"—and generally gave it to be understood that, if *they* were in power, they would know how to deal with the repeal agitation. At every meeting O'Connell turned these professions into ridicule. It was too late now, he said, to offer to buy up repeal by concessions or good measures. An Irish Parliament in College Green: this was his *ultimatum*.

We approach the end of the monster meetings. Neither England nor Ireland could bear this excitement much longer. The two grandest and most imposing of these parades were at Tara and Mullaghmast, both in the province of Leinster, within a short distance of Dublin; both conspicuous, the one in glory, the other in gloom, through past centuries, and haunted by ghosts of kings and chiefs.

On the great plain of Meath, not far from the Boyne river, rises a gentle eminence, in the midst of a luxuriant farming country. On and around its summit are still certain mouldering remains of earthen mounds and moats, the ruins of the "House of Cormac," and the "Mound of the Hostages," and the "Stone of Destiny." It is Temora of the Kings. On Tuesday morning, the 15th of August, most of the population of Meath, with many thousands from the four counties round, were pouring along every road leading to the hill. Numerous bands, banners, and green boughs enlivened their march, or divided their ordered squadrons. Vehicles of all descriptions, from the handsome private chariot to the Irish jaunting-car, were continually arriving, and by the wardens duly disposed around the hill. In Dublin, the "Liberator," after a public breakfast, set forth at the head of a *cortège*, and his progress to Tara was a procession and a triumph. Under triumphal arches, and amidst a storm of music and acclamations, his carriage passed through the several little towns that lay in his way. At Tara, the multitudes assembled were estimated in the *Nation* at seven hundred and fifty thousand—an exaggeration, certainly. But they were at least three hundred and fifty thousand. Their numbers were not so impressive as their order and discipline; nor these so wonderful as the stifled enthusiasm that uplifted them above the earth. They came, indeed, with naked hands; but the agitator knew well that if he had invited them, they would have come still more gladly with extemporaneous pikes or spears, "or instruments serving for pikes and spears." He had been proclaiming from every hill top in Ireland for six months that *something was coming*—that repeal was "on the wild winds of Heaven." Expectation had grown intense, painful, almost intolerable. He knew it; and those who were close to him as he mounted the platform, noticed that his lip and hand visibly trembled, as he gazed over the boundless human ocean, and heard its thundering roar of welcome. He knew that every soul in that host demanded its enfranchisement at *his* hand.

O'Connell called this meeting "an august and triumphant meeting;" and as if conscious that he must at least seem to make another step in advance, he brought up at the next meeting of the Repeal Association a detailed "plan for the renewed action of the Irish Parliament," which, he said, it only needed the Queen's writs to put in operation. The new House of Commons was to consist of three hundred members, quite fairly apportioned to the several constituencies; and, in the meantime, he announced that he would invite three hundred gentlemen to assemble in Dublin, early in December, who were to come from every part of Ireland, and virtually represent their respective localities. This was the "Council of Three Hundred," about which he had often talked before in a vague manner; but had evidently great difficulty in bringing to pass *legally*. For it would be a "Convention of Delegates,"—and such an assembly, though legal enough in England, is illegal in Ireland. Conventions (like arms and ammunition) are held to be unsuitable to the Irish character. For, in fact, it was a convention which proclaimed the independence of Ireland in Dungannon, and the arms and ammunition of the volunteer army that made it good in 1782.

Two weeks after this the London Parliament was prorogued; and the Queen's speech (composed by Sir Robert Peel) was occupied almost entirely by two subjects—the disturbances in Wales and the repeal agitation in Ireland. There had been some rioting and bloodshed in Wales, in resistance to oppressive turnpike dues and the like; there was a quiet and legal expression of opinion in Ireland, unattended by the slightest outrage, demanding back the Parliament of the country. The Queen first dealt with Wales. She had taken measures, she said, for the repression of violence, *and*, at the same time, directed an inquiry to be made into the circumstances which led to it. As to Ireland, Her Majesty said, there was discontent and disaffection, but uttered not a word about any inquiry into the causes of that. "It had ever been her earnest desire," Her Majesty said, "to administer the government of that country in a spirit of strict justice and impartiality,"—and "she was firmly determined, under the blessing of Divine Providence, to maintain the Union."

The little principality of Wales was in open revolt—*there* Ministers would institute inquiry. Ireland was quiet, and standing upon the law—*there* they would meet the case with horse, foot, and artillery; for all knew that was what the Queen meant by "the blessing of Divine Providence."

Again the agitator mustered all Connaught at three monster meetings—in Roscommon, Clifden, and Loughrea. Again he asked them if they were for the repeal; and again the mountains and the sea-cliffs resounded with their acclaim. Yes, they were for the repeal; they had said so before. What next?

Leinster, too, was summoned again to meet on the 1st of October, at Mullaghmast, in Kildare County, near the road from Dublin to Carlow, and close on the borders of the Wicklow highlands.

This was the most imposing and effective of all the meetings. The spot was noted as the scene of a massacre of some chiefs of Offaly and Leix, with hundreds of their clansmen, in 1577, by the English of the Pale, who had invited them to a great feast, but had troops silently drawn around the banqueting hall, who, at a signal, attacked the place and cut the throat of every wassailer. The hill of Mullaghmast, like that of Tara, is crowned by a rath, or ancient earthen rampart, inclosing about three acres.

The members of the town corporations repaired to the rath in their corporate robes. O'Connell took the chair in his scarlet cloak of alderman; and, amidst the breathless silence of the people, John Hogan, the first of Irish sculptors, came forward and placed on the Liberator's head a richly embroidered cap, modelled after the ancient Irish Crown, saying: "*Sir, I only regret this cap is not of gold.*" Then the deep roar of half a million voices, and the waving of at least a thousand banners, proclaimed the enthusiasm of the people. Again O'Connell assured them that England could not long resist these demonstrations of their peaceful resolve— that the Union was a nullity—that he had already arranged his plan for the new Irish Parliaments—and that this was the repeal year.

In truth, it was time for England either to yield with good grace, or to find or make some law applicable to this novel "political offence," or to provoke a fight and blow away repeal with cannon. Many of the Protestants were joining O'Connell; and even the troops in some Irish regiments had been known to throw up their caps with "hurrah for repeal!" It was high time to grapple with the "sedition."

Accordingly, the Government was all this time watching for an occasion on which it could come to issue with the agitation, and on which all advantages would be on its side. The next week that occasion arose. A great metropolitan meeting was appointed to be held on the historic shore of Clontarf, two miles from Dublin, along the bay, on Sunday the 8th of October. The garrison of Dublin amounted then to about four thousand men, besides the one thousand police; with abundance of field artillery.

Late in the afternoon on Saturday, when it was already almost dusk, a *proclamation* was posted on the walls of Dublin, signed by the Irish Secretary and Privy-Councillors, and the Commander of the Forces, forbidding the meeting; and charging all magistrates and officers, "and others whom it might concern, to be aiding and assisting in the execution of the law, in preventing said meeting."

"Let them not dare," O'Connell had often said, "to attack us!" The challenge was now to be accepted.

CHAPTER XXII.

1843—1844.

Why England could not Yield—Cost to Her of Repeal—Intention of Government at Clontarf—The "Projected Massacre"—Meeting Prevented— State Prosecution—O'Brien declares for Repeal —Packing of the Jury—Verdict of *Guilty*—Debate in Parliament—Russell and Macaulay on Packing of Juries—O'Connell in Parliament—Speculation of the Whigs—Sentence and Imprisonment of "Conspirators"—Effects on Repeal Association —Appeal to the House of Lords—Whig Law Lords—Reversal of the Sentence—Enthusiasm of the People—Their Patience and Self-denial— Decline of the Association.

BRITISH Government then closed with repeal; and one or the other, it was plain, must go down.

For this was, in truth, the alternative. The British empire, as it stands, looks vast and strong, but none know so well as the statesmen of that country how intrinsically feeble it is, and how entirely it depends for its existence upon *prestige*— that is, upon a superstitious belief in its power. England, in short, could by no means afford to part with her "sister island;" both in money and in credit the cost would be too much. In this repeal year, for example, there was an export of provisions from Ireland to England of the value of £16,000,000. And between surplus revenue remitted to England, and absentee rents spent in England, Mr. O'Connell's frequent statement that £9,000,000 of Irish *money* was annually spent in England, is not over the truth. These were substantial advantages, not to be yielded up lightly.

In point of national *prestige*, England could still less afford to repeal the Union, because all the world would know the concession had been wrung from her against her will. Whigs and Tories were of one mind upon *this;* and nothing can be more bitter than the language of all sections of the English press, after it was once determined to crush the agitation by force.

"A repeal," says the *Times,* "is not a matter to be argued on. It is a blow which despoils the Queen's domestic territory, splinters her crown, undermines and then crushes her throne, exposes her to insult and outrage from all quarters of the earth and ocean; a repeal of the Union leaves England stripped of her vitality. Whatever might be the inconvenience or disadvantage, therefore, or even unwholesome restraint upon Ireland—although the Union secures the reverse of all these—*but even were it gall to Ireland*, England must guard her own life's blood, and sternly tell the disaffected Irish : ' You shall have me for a sister or a subjugatrix; this is my *ultimatum.*' "

And the *Morning Chronicle*, speaking of the Act of " Union," says:—

" True, it was coarsely and badly done; but stand it must. A Cromwell's violence, with Machiavelli's perfidy, may have been at work; but the treaty, after all, is more than parchment."

The first bolt launched, then, was the proclamation to prevent the meeting at Clontarf. The proclamation was posted in Dublin only an hour before dusk on Saturday. But long before that time thousands of people from Meath, Kildare, and Dublin Counties were already on their way to Clontarf. They all had confidence in O'Connell's knowledge of law; and he had often told them (and it was true) that the meetings, and all the proceedings at them, were perfectly legal; and that a proclamation could not make them illegal. They would, therefore, have most certainly flocked to the rendezvous in the usual numbers, even if they had seen the proclamation.

Many persons did not at first understand the object of the Privy-Council in keeping back the proclamation to so late an hour on Saturday, seeing that the meeting had been many days announced ; and they might as well have issued their command earlier in the week. One may also be at a loss to understand why the proclamation called not only upon all magistrates, and civil and military officers, to assist in preventing the assembly, but also " all others whom it might concern."

But the thing was simple enough. They meant to take O'Connell by surprise—so that he might be unable to prevent the assembly entirely, or to organize it (if such were his policy) for defence—and thus they hoped to create confusion and a pretext for an onslaught, or " salutary lesson." Besides, they had already made up their minds to arrest O'Connell and several others, and subject them to a State prosecution ; and the Crown lawyers were already hard at work arranging a case against him. It is quite possible that they intended (should O'Connell go to Clontarf in the midst of such confusion and excitement) to arrest him then and there, which would have been certainly resisted by the people ; and so there would have been a riot, and everything would have been lawful then. As to the " others whom it might concern," that meant the Orange associations of Dublin, and everybody else who might take the invitation to himself. "Others whom it may concern!" exclaimed O'Connell. " Why, this is intended for, and addressed to Tresham Gregg and his auditory."*

Thus, the enemy had well provided for confusion, collision, and a salutary lesson. Lord Cloncurry made no scruple to term the whole of these Government arrangements " a projected massacre."

For O'Connell and the committee of the Repeal Association there were but two courses possible: one to prevent the meeting, and turn the people back from it, if there was still time ; the other was, for O'Connell to let the people of the country come to Clontarf—to meet them there himself as he had invited them, but, the troops being almost all drawn out of the city, to keep the Dublin repealers at home, and to give them a commission to take the Castle and all the barracks, and to break down the canal bridge, and barricade the streets leading to Clontarf. The whole garrison and police were five thousand. The city has a population of two hundred and fifty thousand. The multitudes coming in from the country would probably have amounted to almost as many ; and that handful of men between. There would have been a horrible slaughter of the unarmed people without if the troops would fire on them—a very doubtful matter—and O'Connell himself might have fallen. But those who have well considered the destinies of Ireland since that day may reasonably enough be of the opinion that the death of five or ten thousand men at Clontarf might have saved Ireland the slaughter by famine of a hundred times as many shortly afterwards.

The first course was the one adopted. The committee issued another proclamation, and sent it off by parties of gentlemen known to the people, and on whom they would rely, to turn back the crowds upon all the roads by which they were likely to come in. All that Saturday night their exertions were unremitting; and the good Father Tyrrell, whose parishioners, swarming in from Fingal, would have made a large part of the meeting, by his exertions and fatigue that night, fell sick and died. The meeting was prevented. The troops were marched out, and drawn up on the beach and on the hill; the artillery was placed in a position to rake the place of meeting, and the cavalry ready to sweep it ; but they met no enemy.

Within a week, O'Connell and eight

* Rev. Tresham Gregg was then the Orange agitator, on whom had fallen the mantle of Sir Harcourt Lees.

others were held to bail to take their trial for "conspiracy and other misdemeanours."

O'Connell, on his side, laughed both at the "Clontarf war" and at the State trials. He seemed well pleased with them both. The one proved how entirely under discipline were the virtuous, and sober, and loyal people, as he called them. The other would show how wisely he had steered the agitation through the rocks and shoals of law. In this he would have been perfectly right, his legal position would have been impregnable, but for two circumstances — *first*, "conspiracy" in Ireland means anything the Castle judges wish; *second*, the Castle Sheriff was quite sure to pack a Castle jury, so that, whatever the Castle might desire, the jury would affirm on oath, "so help them God!" The jury system in Ireland we shall have occasion, more than once, to explain hereafter.

For the next eight months—that is, until the end of May, 1844—the State prosecution was the grand concern around which all public interest in Ireland concentrated itself. The prosecuted "conspirators" were nine in number—Daniel O'Connell; his son, John O'Connell, M.P. for Kilkenny; Charles Gavan Duffy, Editor of the *Nation*; the Rev. Mr. Tyrrell, of Lusk, County Dublin (he died while the prosecution was pending); the Rev. Mr. Tierney, of Clontibret, County Monaghan; Richard Barrett, Editor of the *Pilot*, Dublin; Thomas Steele, "Head Pacificator of Ireland;" Thomas M. Ray, Secretary of the Repeal Association; and Dr. Gray, Editor of the *Freeman's Journal*, Dublin.

During all the eight months of these legal proceedings, the repeal agitation continued to gain strength and impetus. The open-air meetings, indeed, ceased (Clontarf was to have been the last of them), owing to the approach of winter. But the new hall, which had been built as a place of meeting for the Association, was just finished; and O'Connell, who had a peculiar taste in nomenclature, christened it "Conciliation Hall;" intending to indicate the necessity for uniting all classes and religions in Ireland in a common struggle for the independence of their common country.

On the 22d of October the new hall was opened in great form and amidst great enthusiasm. The chair was taken by John Augustus O'Neill, of Bunowen Castle, a Protestant gentleman, who had been early in life a cavalry officer, and member of Parliament for Hull, in England. Letters from Lord French, Sir Charles Wolesley, Sir Richard Musgrave, and Mr. Caleb Powell, one of the members for Limerick County, were read and placed on the minutes—all breathing vehement indignation against the "Government," and pledging the warmest support. But this first meeting in the new hall was specially notable for the adhesion of Mr. Smith O'Brien. Nothing encouraged the people, nothing provoked and perplexed the enemy, so much as this.

For O'Brien was not only a member of the great and ancient house of Thomond, but was further well known as a man both of calmness and resolution. The family had been Protestant for some generations; and Smith O'Brien, though always zealous in promoting everything which might be useful to Ireland in Parliament, had remained attached to the Whig party, and was hardly expected to throw himself into the national cause so warmly, and at so dangerous a time.

It has been already related how this excellent and gallant Irishman had flung to the Lord Chancellor his commission of the peace, when that functionary began to dismiss magistrates for attending peaceful meetings. He now saw that the British Government had commenced the deliberate task of crushing down a just national claim in the blood of the Irish people. The letter in which he announced his adhesion was extremely moderate; and it produced the deeper impression upon that account. One passage of it is highly characteristic of the writer. He says:—

"Lest I should be led to form a precipitate decision, I availed myself of the interval which followed the close of the session to examine whether, among the governments of central Europe, there are any so indifferent to the interests of their subjects as England has been to the welfare and happiness of our population. After visiting Belgium and all the principal capitals of Germany, I returned home impressed with the sad conviction that there is more human misery in one County in Ireland than throughout all the populous cities and districts which I had visited. On landing in England I learn that the Ministry, instead of applying themselves to remove the causes of complaint, have resolved to deprive us even of the liberty of discontent,—that public meetings are to be suppressed, and that State prosecutions are to be carried on against Mr. O'Connell and others, on some frivolous charges of sedition and conspiracy.

"I should be unworthy to belong to a nation which may claim, at least, as a characteristic virtue, that it exhibits increased fidelity in the hour of danger, if I were to delay any longer to dedicate myself to the cause of my country. Slowly, reluctantly convinced that Ireland has nothing to hope from the sagacity, the justice, or the generosity of the English Parliament, my reliance shall henceforth be placed upon our own native energy and patriotism."

This chivalrous example, set by a man so justly esteemed, of course induced many other Protestants to follow his example. The weekly contributions to the revenue of the Association became so great as to place in the hands of the committee a large treasury, to be used in spreading and organizing the movement; arbitration courts decided the people's complaints with general acceptation; and great meetings in American cities sent by every steamship their words of sympathy and bills of exchange.

It is not very certain that the "Government" was at first resolutely bent on pressing their prosecution to extremity. Probably they rather hoped that the show of a determination to put down the agitation somehow would cool the ardour both of demagogues and people. Plainly it had no such effect; and it was therefore resolved to pursue the "conspirators" to conviction and imprisonment at any cost and by any means.

The "State trials" then began on the 2d of November, 1843. These trials cannot be considered as really a legal proceeding, though invested with legal forms. It was a *de facto* government using its courts and tribunals and juries, and all the other apparatus of justice, to crush a political enemy, under the false and fraudulent pretence of a trial. Everybody understood from the first that there was here no question of pleading, or of evidence, or of forensic rhetoric; and that all depended upon the *vote* of the jury—which vote, however, was to be termed a "verdict."

A revisal of the special jury list took place before Mr. Shaw, Recorder of Dublin, with a special view to these trials. The names, when passed by the recorder from day to day, were then sent to the sheriff's office to be placed on his book. Counsel were employed before the recorder to oppose, by every means, the admission of every Catholic gentleman against whom any colour of objection could be thought of; yet, with all this care, a large number of Catholics were placed on the list. As the names were transferred to the sheriff's office, it happened that the slip which contained the largest proportion of Catholic names missed its way or was mislaid; and the sixty-seven names it contained never appeared on the sheriff's book. This became immediately notorious, and excited what one of the judges called "grave suspicion."

In striking a special jury in Ireland, forty-eight names are taken by ballot out of the juror's book in the Crown office. Then each party, the Crown and the traverser, has the privilege of striking off twelve—leaving twenty-four names. On the day of trial the first twelve out of these twenty-four, who answer when called, are sworn as jurors. Now, so well had the sheriff discharged his duty in this case, that of the forty-eight names there were eleven Catholics. They were all struck off by the Crown, together with a great number of Protestants whose British principles were not considered sure at the Castle, and a "jury" was secured on whose patriotic vote Her Majesty could fully rely.

These details respecting juries may not, perhaps, be very interesting to the general reader; yet the history of our country can by no means be understood without them. Ever since the days of Queen Elizabeth juries have been merely one of the arms of British domination in Ireland, just as the troops and police, the detectives and spies are. The jury may be said to be the one point at which the Government and the people touch one another; and if it be a real jury of the "neighbourhood," as described in the law books, then can be easily appreciated that profound saying—"that the only use of a government is to make sure that there shall be twelve impartial men in the jury box." But the English Government has never been able to sustain itself in Ireland without making sure of the very opposite arrangement. And it has been said, with truth, that the real *Palladium* of the British Constitution in that land is a packed jury and the suspension of the *Habeas Corpus*. If Ireland truly and effectively possessed those two institutions, as England possesses them, the British power would not exist in our island three months.

The details of the trials are of small interest. All knew how they would end. The Government, on this prosecution for "conspiracy," had not only its inevitable jury, but its post-office spies at work, by whose means the "authorities" had spread out before them every morning all the correspondence of all the traversers, and of all their counsel and attorneys—no small advantage in dealing with conspiracy, if there had been a conspiracy.

Early in February the trials ended; and when the Chief-Justice, in his charge to the jury, argued the case like one of the counsel for the prosecution, and so far forgot himself as to term the traversers' counsel "the gentlemen on the other side," there was more laughter than indignation throughout the country. The jury brought in their verdict of GUILTY, of course. O'Connell addressed a letter to the people of Ireland, informing them that "the repeal" was now sure; that all he wanted was peace, patience, and perseverance; and that if they would only "keep the peace for six, or at most for twelve months, repeal was certain." In the meantime, he and his friends were appointed to come before the Court on a certain day in May to receive sentence.

Immediately on the verdict being known in London, there arose in Parliament a violent debate on the state of Ireland. The Whig party being then out of place, and who saw in this whole repeal movement nothing but a machinery by which they might raise themselves to power, affected great zeal for justice to Ireland, and even indignation at the conduct of the trials. It is almost incredible, but remains on record, that Lord John Russell used these words:—

"Nominally, indeed, the two countries have the same laws. Trial by jury, for instance, exists in both countries; but is it administered alike in both? Sir, I remember on one occasion when an honourable gentleman, Mr. Brougham, on bringing forward a motion, in 1823, on the administration of the law in Ireland, made use of these words: 'The law of England esteemed all men equal. It was sufficient to be born within the King's allegiance to be entitled to all the rights the loftiest subject of the land enjoyed. None were disqualified; the only distinction was between natural-born subjects and aliens. Such, indeed, was the liberality of our system in the times which we called barbarous, but from which, in these enlightened days, it might be as well to take a hint, that if a man were even an alien born, he was not deprived of the protection of the law. In Ireland, however, the law held a directly opposite doctrine. The sect to which a man belonged, the cast of his religious opinions, the form in which he worshipped his Creator, were grounds on which the law separated him from his fellows, and bound him to the endurance of a system of the most cruel injustice.' Such was the statement of Mr. Brougham, when he was the advocate of the oppressed. But, sir, let me ask, Was what I have just now read the statement of a man who was ignorant of the country of which he spoke? No; the same language, or to the same effect, was used by Sir M. O'Loghlen, in his evidence before the House of Lords. That gentleman stated that he had been in the habit of going the Munster circuit for nineteen years, and on that circuit it was the general practice for the Crown, in criminal prosecutions, to set aside all Catholics and all the Liberal Protestants; and he added, that he had been informed that on other circuits the practice was carried on in a more strict manner. Sir M. O'Loghlen also mentioned one case of this kind which took place in 1834, during the Lord-Lieutenancy of the Marquis of Wellesley, and the Attorney-Generalship of Mr. Blackburne, the present Master of the Rolls, and in which, out of forty-three persons set aside (in a cause, too, which was not a political one), there were thirty-six Catholics and seven Protestants, and all of them respectable men. This practice is so well known, and carried out so generally, that men known to be Liberals, whether Catholics or Protestants, have ceased to attend assizes, that they might not be exposed to these public insults. Now, I would ask, are these proofs of equal laws, or laws equally administered? Could the same or similar cases have happened in Yorkshire, or Sussex, or Kent? Are these the fulfilment of the promise made and engagements entered into at the Union?"

This sounds extremely fair. *Who would think that Lord John Russell was Prime Minister afterwards in 1848?* Mr. Macaulay said, in the same debate, February 19th, 1844:—

"I do say that on this question it is of the greatest importance that the proceedings which the Government have taken should be beyond impeachment, and that they should have obtained a victory in such a way that that victory should not be to them a greater disaster than a defeat. Has that been the result? First, is it denied that Mr. O'Connell has suffered wrong? Is it denied, if the law had been carried into effect without those irregularities and that negligence which has attended the Irish trials, Mr. O'Connell's chance of acquittal would have been better. No person denied that. The affidavit which has been produced, and which has not been contradicted, states that twenty-seven Catholics were excluded from the jury list. I know that all the technicalities of the law were on the side of the Crown; but my great charge against the Government is, that they have merely regarded this question in a technical point of view. We know what the principle of the law is in cases where prejudice is likely to arise against an alien, and who is to be tried *de medietate linguæ.* Is he to be tried by twelve Englishmen? No. Our ancestors knew that that was not the way in which justice could be obtained—they knew that the only proper way was to have one half of the jurymen of the country in which the crime was committed, and the other half of the country to which the prisoner belonged. If any alien had been in the situation of Mr. O'Connell, that law would have been observed. You are ready enough to call the Catholics of Ireland 'aliens' when it suits your purpose; you are ready enough to treat them as aliens when it suits your purpose; but the first privilege, the only advantage of alienage, you practically deny them."

This orator, also, was a member of the Administration in 1848; and he did not utter any of his fine indignation at the gross packing of juries which was perpetrated then. In 1848, however, these "Liberals" were *in*, not out; had resting upon them the responsibility of maintaining the British empire; and, therefore, desired to hear no more of "justice to Ireland."

In the same debate, there was much ferocious language on the part of Tory members of the House. The infamous nature of the alleged conspiracy was dwelt upon, and the necessity of bringing to condign punishment that "Arch-agitator," that "hoary criminal," who was endeavouring to overthrow the British empire. In the midst of all this, O'Connell himself, the "hoary criminal," strode into the House. In a discussion upon the state of Ireland, *he* had had somewhat to say. First, he listened to the debate for a whole week, and then, amidst breathless silence, arose.

He did not confine himself to the narrow ground of the prosecution, but reviewed the whole career of British power in Ireland, with bitter and taunting comments. As to the prosecution, he treated it slightly and contemptuously.

"I have, at greater length than I intended, gone through the crimes of England since the Union—I will say the follies of England. I have but little more to say; but I have, in the name of the people of Ireland—and I do it in their name—to protest against the late prosecution. And I protest, *first*, against the nature of that prosecution. Forty-three public meetings were held, and every one of them was admitted to be legal; not one was impeached as being against the law, and every one of them making on the calendar of crime a cipher; but by multiplying ciphers, you come, by a species of legal witchcraft, to make it a number that shall be fatal. *One meeting is legal, another meeting is legal, a third is the same, and three legal meetings, you say, make one illegal meeting.* The people of Ireland understand that you may oppress them, but not laugh at them. That, sir, is my first objection. The *second* is the striking out all the Catholics from the jury panel. There is no doubt of the fact. Eleven Catholics were upon the jury panel, and every one of them was struck out."

All the world knew it. Nobody pretended to deny it, or publicly to excuse it; but what availed all this? The *ultimatum* of England was, that the Union must be maintained at any cost, and by all means. And O'Connell was to return to Dublin by a certain day for judgment and sentence. His taunts and invectives against the whole system of Irish government were very welcome and highly entertaining to English Whigs, who only looked to their own party chances. But no man in all England ever, for one moment, suffered the idea to enter his head that Ireland was to be in any case permitted to govern herself.

And British Whigs could well afford to let O'Connell have a legal triumph, to the damage of British Tories, so long as the real and substantial policy of England in Ireland was pursued without interruption. As to this point there must be no mistake. No British Whig or British Tory regarded the Irish question in any other point of view than as a question on which might occur a change of Ministry.

An army of fifty thousand men, including police, was all this while in full military occupation of the island. The Arms Bill had become law; and, in the registration of arms before magistrates under that Act, those who were in favour of their country's independence were refused the privilege of keeping so much as an old musket in their houses for purposes of self-defence.*

* Of the proceedings upon these applications for registry of arms at all the petty sessions of Ireland we have no record, but to the Cork *Southern Reporter* we are indebted for the minute report of a session at Marcroom, in that county, which may be taken as a kind of sample.

"Maurice Dullea, Glaun—Applicant for leave to keep one gun.

"Mr. Gillman, Magistrate—Are you a repeal warden? I am not.

"Would you answer the question on your oath, if it were put to you? I would.

"Mr. Warren—The question should not be asked, unless it was known he had so acted. Admitted.

"John M'Auliffe, Mill Street—One pistol.

"Captain Wallace—Are you a repeal warden? I am, sir.

The police barracks were still further strengthened; the detectives were multiplied; the regular troops were kept almost constantly under arms, and marched to and fro with a view of striking terror: improved codes of signals were furnished to the police for use by day and night—to give warning of everything they might conceive suspicious. With so firm a hold upon the island, the British Ministers might have thought themselves in a condition to abandon their questionable prosecution; but they had the idea that O'Connell's power lay very much in the received opinion of his legal infallibility, so they were resolved to imprison him, at any rate for a short time—even though he should finally trample on their prosecution and come forth in triumph—as, in fact, he did.

On the 30th May, the "conspirators" were called up for sentence, and were imprisoned in Richmond Penitentiary—a suburban prison at the south side of Dublin, with splendid gardens and handsome accommodations. Here they rusticated for three months, holding *levées* in an elegant *marquée* in the garden, receiving daily deputations, and visits from bishops, from Americans, and from ladies. O'Connell still wrote once a week to Conciliation Hall, that repeal never was so sure, never so imminent, as now, if only the people would keep the peace.

The great multitudinous people looked on in some amaze. "Peace" was still the order, and they obeyed; but they much marvelled what it meant, and when it would end.

Still it was doubtful whether the enemy's government had really gained much by their prosecution. Very considerable indignation had been excited, even amongst the reasonable Protestants, by the means which had been used to snatch this conviction. The agitation had rather gained than lost; and many gentlemen who had held back till now, sent in their names and subscriptions. Smith O'Brien was now a constant attendant at the Association, and by the boldness and purity of his character, and by his extensive knowledge of public affairs, gave it both impetus and steadiness.

Yet O'Connell and his friends were in prison, sentenced to an incarceration of one year; and it would be vain to deny that there was humiliation in the fact. True, the jury had been notoriously packed; the trial had been but a sham; and the sentence would probably be reversed by the House of Lords. Still, there was Ireland, represented by her chosen men, suffering the penalties of crime in a jail. The island was still fully and effectively occupied by troops, as a hostile country; and all its resources were in clear possession of the enemy. Many began to doubt whether the "moral force" principle of O'Connell would be found sufficient.

In truth, the repeal agitation, as a living and formidable power, was over from the day of imprisonment. The judgment of the Irish Court of Queen's Bench was brought up to the British House of Peers on Writ of Error; and on the 2d and 4th of September, the opinions of nine English judges were delivered, and the decision pronounced. Eight of the judges gave their opinion that the jury was a good jury, the verdict good, and the judgment good. It appeared, however, that Mr. Justice Coleridge dissented. Lord Lyndhurst, the Lord-Chancellor, then delivered his decision. He agreed with the majority of the judges, and thought the judgment should stand, the packing of the jury being immaterial. He was followed by Lord Brougham, and nobody could doubt what would be the decision of that learned person—the jury was a good enough jury: some of the counts in the indictment might be bad; but, bad or good, the judgment of the Irish Court was to stand, and O'Connell was to remain in prison.

Lord Denman, Chief-Justice of England, then rose. I have already told you that the whole Irish question was regarded in the British Parliament solely with reference to its affording a chance of turning out the Tory Ministry, and conducting the Whigs into power and place. We have seen, accordingly, the pretended indignation of Lord John Russell and of Mr. Macaulay against the packing of the juries. It may seem an atrocious charge to make upon judges and law lords—that they could be influenced by any other considerations than the plain law and justice of the case. But the mere matter of fact was, that the majority of the English judges were of the Tory party. Of the law lords, also, Lord-Chancellor Lyndhurst was a violent Tory, and, moreover, an avowed enemy to Ireland. Lord

---

"Mr. M'Carthy O'Leary, Attorney—The man bears a most unimpeachable character."

"Mr. Warren—We cannot reject one repeal warden and admit another. Rejected."

At the same sessions was made manifest the fact that the Protestant "gentry" of the country were providing themselves with a sufficient armament. For example, Mrs. Charlotte Stawell, of Kilbritton Castle, registers "six guns and six pistols," and Richard Quinn, of Skivanish, "nine guns, one pair pistols, two dirks, two bayonets, and one sword." No objection was offered against these persons keeping as many fire-arms as they chose. So worked the Disarming Act.

Brougham was at that time a Tory, and also a well-known personal foe to O'Connell, having been often stung by the vicious taunts and sarcasms of that gentleman. But Lord Denman, Lord Cottenham, and Lord Campbell were Whigs; and Denman, Cottenham, and Campbell gave it as their opinion that the jury had been unfair and fraudulent—that no fair trial had taken place—and, therefore, that the judgment against the repeal conspirators should be reversed.

Now, it is to be observed that the British Government, by openly and ostentatiously striking off from the jury panel all Catholics without exception, and all Protestants of moderate and liberal opinions, made proclamation that they knew the great mass of the people to be averse to them and their rule—avowed that they accounted that small remainder out of whom they selected their jurors to be the only "good and lawful men." These were the *vicinage* contemplated in the law books; and the repeal conspirators being arraigned, not before their countrymen, not even before one sect of their countrymen, but before chosen men carefully selected by the Crown out of one section of one sect, were told to consider themselves on their trial *per pais*. This, to be sure, amounted to an admission that nine-tenths of Irishmen desired the freedom of their country; but then it also amounted to a declaration that the English meant to hold the country, whether Irishmen would or not. On the reversal of the judgment, however, there was a show of high rejoicing in Dublin, and the prisoners were escorted from the jail through the city, by a vast and orderly procession, to O'Connell's house. The procession marched through College Green; and just as O'Connell's carriage came in front of the Irish Parliament House (the most superb building in Dublin), the carriage stopped — the whole procession stopped—and there was a deep silence as O'Connell rose to his full height and, pointing with his finger to the portico, turned slowly round and gazed into the faces of the people, without a word. Again and again he stretched forth his arm and pointed, and a succession of pealing cheers seemed to shake the city.

The State trials, then, were at an end; and all the country, friends and enemies, Ireland and England, were now looking eagerly and earnestly for O'Connell's first movement, as an indication of his future course. Never, at any moment in his life, did he hold the people so wholly in his hand. During the imprisonment, both clergy and repeal wardens had laboured diligently in extending and confirming the organization; and the poor people proved their faith and trust by sending greater and greater contributions to the repeal treasury. They kept the "peace," as their Liberator bade them; and the land was never so free from crime—lest they should give strength to the enemy.

It is impossible to record without profound admiration the steady faith, patient zeal, self-denial, and disciplined enthusiasm which the Irish people displayed for these two years. To many thousands of those peasants the struggle had been more severe than any war; for they were expected to set at nought potent landlords, who had over them and their children power of life and death—with troops of insolent bailiffs and ejecting attorneys, and the omnipresent police; and they did set them at nought. Every vote they gave at an election might cost them house and home, land and life. They were naturally ardent, impulsive, and impatient; but their attitude was now calm and steadfast. They were an essentially military people; but the great "Liberator" told them that "no political amelioration was worth one drop of human blood."

They did not believe the formula, and in assenting to it often winked their eyes; yet steadily and trustfully, this one good time, they sought to liberate their country peacefully, legally, under the advice of counsel. They loyally obeyed that man, and would obey no other. And when he walked in triumph out of his prison, at one word from his mouth they would have marched upon Dublin from all the five ends of Ireland, and made short work with police and military barracks.

But O'Connell was now old, approaching seventy; and the fatal disease of which he was then really dying had already begun to work upon his iron energies.* After his release he did not propose to hold the Clontarf meeting, as many hoped. He said nothing more about the "Council of Three Hundred," which the extreme section of nationalists were very desirous to see carried into effect; and the more desirous because it would be illegal, according to what passes for law in Ireland. Yet the Association all this time was becoming more powerful for good than ever. O'Brien had instituted a "Parliamentary Committee," and worked on it continually himself; which, at all events, furnished the nation with careful and authentic memoirs on all Irish questions and interests, filled with accurate statistical

---

* It was softening of the brain; and the physicians, after his death, pronounced that it had been in operation for two years at least.

details. Many Protestant gentlemen, also, of high rank, joined the Association in 1844 and 1845—being evidently unconscious how certainly and speedily that body was going to destruction.

In short, the history of Ireland must henceforth be sought for elsewhere than in the Repeal Association.

CHAPTER XXIII.

1844.

Decadence of Repeal Association—Land Tenure Commission—Necessity of exterminating "Surplus Population"—Report of the "Landlord and Tenant Commission"—Tenant Right to be *Disallowed*—Farms to be Consolidated—People to be Extirpated—Methods of the Minister to Divide Repealers—Grant to Maynooth—Queen's Colleges—Secret Agent at Rome—American Slavery—Distraction in Repeal Ranks—Bill for "Compensation to Tenants"—Defeated—Death of Thomas Davis—The Famine—Commission of Chemists to gain Time—Demands of Ireland—Of the Corporations—Of O'Connell and O'Brien—Repudiation of Alms—Coercion Bill—Repeal of Corn Laws—Irish Harvests go to England—"Repeal Measures"—Delays—Fraud—Havoc of the People—Peel's System of Famine Slaughter fully established—Peel resigns Office.

DURING the last two years of the existence of the Repeal Association it made no progress whatever towards the attainment of its great object; which is equivalent to saying that it was going back. One of the first things proposed by Mr. O'Connell after his release, in a secret meeting of the committee, was a dissolution of the body, in order to its reconstruction on a somewhat more safe and legal basis. This was his old policy, whenever his agitations had come in conflict with what the Government called "law," and it had generally answered its purpose whilst those agitations were directed against penal laws, or tithes and Church rates—against something, in short, which was not vital to the existence of the British empire. But he now found himself, at last, in front of a castle wall, armed and garrisoned, totally unassailable by any "agitation" yet invented. He could not make a single step in advance upon that line, and he seemed to feel it. Yet the whole country was earnestly expecting that step in advance. The proposal to dissolve was combated and was given up. He occupied his weekly speeches with collateral issues upon Parliamentary questions which were often arising—the "Bequests Act," the "Colleges Bill," the Papal Rescript Negotiation, and the like; all matters which would have been of moment in any self-governing nation, but were of next to no moment in the circumstances. Or he poured forth his fiery floods of eloquence in denunciation, not of the British Government, but of *American slavery*, with which he had nothing on earth to do. He praised too much, as many thought, the sublime integrity and justice of the three Whig law lords who had voted for reversing his judgment. But the most significant change in his behaviour was in the querulous captiousness he showed towards the *Nation*, and those connected with it, whom he now frequently rebuked as "rash young men," who would goad the country into a dangerous course.

In the meantime, the English press and people ceased, in a great degree, to speak of the repeal movement with alarm and horror—they seemed satisfied now that there was no danger in it, at least while O'Connell lived.

For, in fact, all this time, the steady policy of England towards her "sister island" was proceeding on the even tenor of its way quite undisturbed. Four millions sterling of the rental of Ireland was, as usual, carried over every year, to be spent in England; and the few remaining manufactures which our island had struggled to retain were growing gradually less and less. The very "frieze" (rough home-made woollen cloth) was driven out of the market by a far cheaper and far worse Yorkshire imitation of it. Some repeal artist had devised a "repeal button," displaying the ancient Irish crown. The very repeal button was mimicked in Birmingham, and hogsheads of ancient Irish crowns were poured into the market, to the utter ruin of the Dublin manufacturer. True, they were of the basest of metal and handiwork; but they lasted as long as "the repeal" lasted.

All great public expenditures were still confined to England; and in the year 1844 there was, quite as usual, Irish produce to the value of about fifteen millions sterling exported to England.

In 1843 the Government had sent forth the famous "Landlord and Tenant Commission," to travel through Ireland, collect evidence, and report on the relations of landlord and tenant in that country. The Commissioners were all, without exception, Irish landlords. In '44, it travelled and investigated; and the next year its report came out, in four great volumes. The true function and object of this commission was to devise the best means of getting rid of what Englishmen called "the surplus population" of Ireland. Ever since the year 1829, the year of Catholic Emancipation, British policy had been directing itself to this end.

About the time of emancipation, when the small farmers, by the abolition of their franchise, were left more absolutely at the mercy of their landlords, it happened that new theories of farming became fashionable. "High farming" was the word. There was to be more grazing, more green cropping; there were to be larger farms; and more labour was to be done by horses and by steam. But consolidation of many small farms into one large one could not be effected without clearing off the "surplus population;" and then, as there would be fewer mouths to be fed, so there would be more produce for export to England. The clearance system, then, had begun in 1829, and had proceeded with great activity ever after, but never with such remorseless fury as just after the year of the "monster meetings." The surplus population had appeared more than usually excessive and perilous in the form of those huge masses of powerful men, whom O'Connell's voice could call around him upon any hill in the island. Now, therefore, the "assistant barristers" were especially busy in decreeing ejectments, which they issued by whole sheaves. These formidable documents, once placed in the hands of sheriffs' officers, often came down upon the people with a more sweeping desolation than an enemy's sword and torch.

Whole neighbourhoods were often thrown out upon the highways in winter, and the homeless creatures lived for a while upon the charity of neighbours; but this was dangerous, for the neighbours were often themselves ejected for harbouring them. Some landlords contracted with emigration companies to carry them to America "for a lump sum," according to the advertisement cited before. Others did not care what became of them, and hundreds and thousands perished every year of mere hardship. The new Poor law was now in full operation; and workhouses, erected under that law, received many of the exterminated people; but it is a strangely significant fact that the *deaths by starvation* increased rapidly from the first year of the Poor law. The Report of the Census Commissioners, for 1851, declares that while in 1842 the deaths registered as deaths by famine amounted to one hundred and eighty-seven, they increased every year until the registered deaths in 1845 were five hundred and sixteen. The "registered" deaths were, perhaps, one-tenth of the unregistered deaths by mere hunger.

Such, then, was the condition of Ireland in 1844-45, and all this before the "Famine."

Now, the "Landlord and Tenant Commission" began its labours in '44. The people were told to expect great benefits from it. The commissioners, it was diligently given out, would inquire into the various acknowledged evils that were becoming proverbial throughout Europe and America; and there were to be Parliamentary "ameliorations." This "commission" looked liked a deliberate fraud from the first. It was composed entirely of landlords; the chairman, Lord Devon, being one of the Irish absentee landlords. It was at all times quite certain that they would see no evidence of any evils to be redressed on the part of the tenants; and that if they recommended any measures, those measures would be such as should promote and make more sweeping the depopulation of the country. "You might as well," said O'Connell, "consult butchers about keeping Lent, as consult these men about the rights of farmers."

The report of this set of commissioners would deserve no more especial notice than any of the other reports of innumerable commissions which the British Parliament was in the habit of issuing, when it pretended to inquire into any Irish "grievance," but that the report of this particular "Devon Commission" has become the very creed and gospel of British statesmen with regard to the Irish people from that day to this, and has often been cited by Secretaries for Ireland as affording the fullest and most conclusive authority upon the relations of landlord and tenant in that island. It is the programme and scheme upon which the last conquest of Ireland was undertaken, in a business-like manner, twenty-four years ago; and the completeness of that conquest is due to the exactitude with which the programme was observed.

The problem to be solved was how to get rid of the Irish people.

But one of the strongest demands and most urgent needs of these people had always been permanence of tenure in their lands. O'Connell called it "fixity of tenure," and presented it prominently in his speeches as one of the greatest benefits to be gained by repealing the Union. It was, indeed, the grand necessity of the nation that men should have some security that they who sowed should reap—that labour and capital expended in improving farms should, in part at least, profit those who expended it. This would at once abolish pauperism, put an end to the necessity of emigration, supersede Poor laws, and prevent the periodical famines which had desolated the island ever since the Union. It is a measure which would have been sure to be recommended as the first, or, indeed, the only measure for Ireland, by any other commission than a commission of Irish landlords.

In the northern province of Ulster there was, as before mentioned, a kind of unwritten law or established custom, which in some counties gave the tenant such needful security. The "tenant-right of Ulster" was the name of it. By virtue of that tenant-right a farmer, though his tenure might be nominally "at will," could not be ejected so long as he paid his rent; and if he desired to remove to another part of the country, he could sell his "good-will" in the farm to an incoming tenant. Of course, the greater had been his improvements, the larger price would his tenant-right command. In other words, the improvements created by his own or his father's industry were his own. The same custom prevented rents from being arbitrarily raised in proportion to the improved value; so that in many cases which came within the knowledge of all lawyers, lands held "at will" in Ulster, and subject to an ample rent, were sold by one tenant at will to another tenant at will at full half the fee simple value of the land. Conveyances were made of it. It was a valuable property, and any violent invasion of it, as a witness told Lord Devon's commission, would have "made Down another Tipperary."

The custom was almost confined to Ulster. It was by no means (though this has often been stated) created or commenced by the terms of the Plantation of Ulster in the time of King James I., but was a relic of the ancient free social polity of the nation,* and had continued in Ulster longer than in the other three provinces, simply because Ulster had been the last part of the island brought under British dominion, and forced to exchange the ancient system of tribe lands for feudal tenures. Neither is "tenant-right" by any means peculiar to Ireland, but prevails in all countries formerly embraced by the feudal system, except Ireland alone.

The people of Ireland are not *idle*. They anxiously sought opportunities of exertion on fields where their landlords could not sweep off all their earnings; and many thousands of small farmers annually went to England and Scotland to reap the harvest, lived all the time on food that would sustain no other working men, and hoarded their earnings for their wives and children. If they had had tenant-right, they would have laboured for themselves, and Tipperary would have been a peaceful and blooming garden.

In this stage of our narrative a difficulty arises. It is hard to conceive it possible that noble lords and gentlemen, the landlords and legislators of an ancient and noble people, should deliberately conspire to slay one out of every eight—men, women, and little children; to strip the remainder barer than they were, to uproot them from the soil where their mothers bore them, to force them to flee to all the ends of the earth, to destroy that tenant-right of Ulster where it was, and to cut off all chance and hope of it where it was not. There is nothing but a patient examination of the facts and documents which can make this credible to mankind.

First, then, for the Report of the Devon Commission. As first printed, it fills four stupendous Blue Books. But it contained too much valuable matter to be buried, like other reports, in the catacombs which yawn for that species of literature. The secretary of the commission, therefore, was employed to abstract and condense, and present the cream of it in an abridgement. This had the advantage not only of condensation, but of selection. The commissioners could then give the pieces of evidence which they liked the best, together with their own recommendations.

This portentous abstract is called a "Digest of the Evidence," &c., is published by authority, and has a preface signed "Devon."

Much of the volume is occupied with dissertations and evidence respecting "tenant-right," which the North had, and the South demanded. The commissioners are clearly against it in every shape. They term it "unphilosophical," and in the preface they state that the Ulster landlords and tenants look upon it in the light of a life insurance—that is, the landlord allows the sale of the tenant-right, and the incoming tenant buys it, lest they should both be murdered by the outgoing tenant. The following passage treats this tenant-right as injurious to the tenant himself:—

"It is even questionable whether this growing practice of tenant-right, which would *at the first view* appear to be a *valuable assumption* on the part of the tenant, be so in reality; as it gives to him, without any exertion on his own part, an *apparent property* or security, by means of

---
* See an article on the "True Origin of Tenant-right," written by Samuel Ferguson, in the *Dublin University Magazine* for May, 1848.

which he is enabled to incur future incumbrance, in order to avoid present inconvenience—a practice which frequently terminates in the utter destitution of his family, and in the sale of his farm, when the debts thus created at usurious interests amount to what its sale would produce."

It appears, then, that in the opinion of these landlords it is injurious to the tenant to let him have anything on the security of which he can borrow money—a theory which the landlords would not relish if applied to themselves. Further, the commissioners declare that this tenant-right is enjoyed without any exertion on the part of tenants. Yet they have, in all cases, either created the whole value of it by the sweat of their brows, or bought it from those who did so create it.

The commissioners " foresee some danger to the *just rights of property* from the unlimited allowance of this tenant-right."

But they suggest a substitute—"compensation for future improvements;" surrounding, however, that suggestion with difficulties which have prevented it from ever being realized.

Speaking of the *consolidation* of farms, they say:—

"When it is seen in the evidence, and in the return of the size of the farms, how small those holdings are, it cannot be denied that such a step is absolutely *necessary.*"

And then, as to the people whom it is thus "necessary" to eject, they say:—

"*Emigration* is considered by the committee to be peculiarly applicable as a remedial measure."

They refer to one of their tables (No. 95, p. 564), where—

"The calculation is put forward showing that the consolidation of the small holdings up to eight acres would require the removal of about one hundred and ninety-two thousand three hundred and sixty-eight families." That is, the removal of about one million of persons.

Such was the Devon programme. Tenant-right to be disallowed; one million of people to be *removed*—that is, swept out on the highways, where their choice would be America, the poor house, or the grave. We shall see with what accuracy the details were carried out in practice.

In affirming that there was a conspiracy of landlords and legislators to destroy the people, it would be unjust, as it is unnecessary, to charge all members of the Queen's Government, or all of the Devon Commissioners, with a privity to that design. Sir Robert Peel knew how Irish landlords would inquire—and what report they would make—just as well as he knew what verdict a jury of Dublin Orangemen would give. Sir Robert Peel had been Irish Secretary. He knew Ireland well; he had been Prime Minister at the time of Catholic Emancipation; and he had taken care to accompany that measure with another, *disfranchising* all the small farmers in Ireland. This disfranchisement, as before explained, had given a stimulus and impetus to the clearance system. He had helped it by Cheap Ejectment Acts. It had not worked fast enough.

The same Sir Robert Peel was now again Prime Minister in 1855, when the first of the reports was published by the Land Tenure Commission; and it at once opened to him a plan for the faster clearing off of the "Irish enemy," under the pretext of "ameliorations."

In the meantime, as the repeal movement was still considered formidable, and as Davis and the younger nationalists were earnestly labouring to give it more of a military organization, it became necessary to take some measures for the purpose of dividing and distracting the repealers.

Danger was then threatening from the side of America, on the question of Oregon. True Irish nationalists, of course, hoped that this would end in a war; and the *Nation* gave unmistakeable notification that in case of war about Oregon, the Americans might count upon a diversion in Ireland.

Suddenly Sir Robert Peel's ministerial organs announced that there were "good measures," or what the English call "amelioration," in store for Ireland. And, in truth, three measures, having much show of liberality, were soon brought forward. They were all cunningly calculated to the great end—the breaking up of the Repeal organization. On the 2d of April, then, Sir Robert Peel "sent a message of peace to Ireland:" it was a proposed bill to give some additional thousands *per annum* to the Catholic College of Maynooth; and in the House of Commons the Premier thus urged his measures:—

"I say this without hesitation, and recollect that we have been responsible for the peace of Ireland; you must, in some way or other, break up that formidable confederacy which exists against the British Government and British connection. I do not believe you can break it up by force. You can do much to break it up by acting in a spirit of kindness, and forbearance, and generosity."

It was novel to hear these good words; and all knew they meant fraud. But the Premier continued:—

"There rises in the far western horizon a cloud [Oregon], small, indeed, but threatening future storms. It became my duty, on the part of the Government, on that day, in temperate but significant language, to depart so far from the caution which is usually observed by a minister, as to declare publicly, that, while we were most anxious for the amicable adjustment of the differences—while we would leave nothing undone to effect that amicable adjustment—yet, if our rights were invaded, we were prepared and determined to maintain them. I own to you, that when I was called upon to make that declaration, I did recollect with satisfaction and consolation, that the day before *I had sent a message of peace to Ireland.*"

The object of the bill was to provide more largely for the endowment of Catholic professors, and the education of young men for the Catholic Church; and the minister prudently calculated that it would cool the ardour of a portion of the Catholic clergy for repeal of the Union. It was forced through both Lords and Commons as a party question, though vehemently opposed by the intense bigotry and ignorance of the English nation. But the Premier put it to them in that irresistible form—vote for our measure, or we will not answer for the Union!

Another of the Premier's ameliorations was the College bill, for creating and endowing three purely secular colleges in Ireland, to give a good course of education without reference to religious belief. This also was sure to be regarded as a great boon by a portion of the Catholic clergy, while another portion was just as sure to object violently to the whole scheme; some, because it would place education too much under the control of the English Government; and others, because the education was to be "mixed,"—strict Catholics being much in favour of educating Catholic youth separately. Here, then, was a fruitful source of quarrel amongst repealers; and, in fact, it arrayed bishop against bishop, and O'Connell against "Young Ireland." The walls of Conciliation Hall rung with denunciations, not of the Union, but of "godless Colleges," and of the "young infidel party."

But the Premier had another plot in operation. Protestant England had for ages refused to recognize the Pope as a Sovereign, or to send a minister to the Vatican. It was still illegal to send an avowed minister; but Sir Robert Peel sent a secret one. He was to induce His Holiness to take some order with the Catholic bishops and priests of Ireland, to draw them off in some degree from the repeal agitation. By what motives and inducements that agent operated upon the Pope, we can only conjecture; and one conjecture is this—Italy was then, as now, in continual danger of revolution. Within the year that had passed, England had demonstrated that she held in her hand the clue to all those Republican conspiracies by her post-office *espionage;* and it was evident that the same Sir James Graham, who had copied the private correspondence of Mazzini and the Bandieras, and laid it before the King of Naples, could as easily have kept it all to himself. Highly desirable, surely, that "peace, law, and order" in Italy should secure so useful a friend.

In short, the Sacred College sent a rescript to the Irish clergy, declaring that, whereas it had been reported to His Holiness that many of them devoted themselves too much to politics, and spoke too rashly in public concerning affairs of state, they were thereafter to attend to their religious duties. It was carefully given out in the English press that the Pope had denounced Repeal: if he had done so, nobody would have minded it, because Catholics do not admit his jurisdiction in temporal affairs; and Quarantotti's interference about the *veto* had been a significant warning. It was soon settled that the rescript had no such power, and presumed it had no such intention, on the part of the Pope; yet a certain prudent reserve began to be observable in the repeal speeches of the clergy. So far, the Premier's Roman policy had succeeded.

The distraction in the repeal ranks was much aided at the same time by a certain well-meaning James Haughton, a repealer himself, but one who concerned himself more about the wrongs and rights of American negroes than about those of his own countrymen. In O'Connell's perplexity as to his course, in the necessity which was upon him to appear to do something, he took hold of this slavery question, made some vehement speeches upon it, and sent back, with contumelious words, some money remitted from a Southern State, in aid of his repeal exchequer.

So far the Premier's plans were successful in breaking up the repeal movement. Religious disputes were introduced by the Colleges Bill; and this held the Protestants aloof, and produced bitter altercation throughout the country. By the discussion on slavery American alliance and co-operation were checked (a great gain to the Premier), for the Americans, and the Irish in America, all looked forward to something stronger than moral force.

The Minister thought he might proceed, under cover of this tumult of senseless debate, to take the first step in his plan for the depopulation of Ireland, in pursuance of the "Devon Commission" report. Accordingly, his third measure for the "amelioration" of Ireland was a bill, ostensibly providing for "Compensation of Tenants in Ireland," but really calculated for the destruction of the last relics of tenant-right. We need not to go through the details of the proposed measure; it is enough to observe that Lord Stanley admitted that he contemplated the "removal of a vast mass of labour" from its present field. "In justice to the colonies," he would not recommend, as the Devon Commissioners did, merely that the whole of this vast mass should be shot out naked and destitute upon their shores; and his bill proposed the employment of a part of it on the *waste lands* of Ireland—of which waste lands there were four millions of acres, capable of improvement. A portion of the "vast mass of labour" removed from other places was to be set to work, under certain conditions, to reclaim these lands for the landlords.

The bill, though framed entirely for the landlords, did yet propose to interfere in some degree with their absolute rights of property. They did not choose that tenants should be presumed to have any right to "compensation," even nominally, or any other right whatever; and as for the waste lands, they wanted them for snipe-shooting. Accordingly, they resisted the bill with all their power; and English landlords, on principle, supported them in that resistance. On the other hand, the Irish tenants, with one consent, exclaimed against the bill, as a bill for open robbery and slaughter, A meeting of County Down tenants resolved that it would rob their class (in one province, Ulster alone) of £1,500,000 sterling. The *Nation* commented upon it under the title of "Robbery of Tenants (Ireland) Bill." The opposition of the tenant class, and of the repeal newspapers, would have been of small avail, but for the resistance, upon other grounds, of the landlords. The bill was defeated; Sir Robert Peel had to devise some other method of getting rid of the "surplus population."

He was soon to be aided by a most efficient ally—the famine; and to tell how the famine helped Sir Robert Peel, and how Sir Robert Peel helped the famine, forms the whole history of the island for the next five years.

In the meantime, Thomas Davis died in September, 1845, full of sad foreboding despondency, as he witnessed the gradual disintegration and discomfiture of that repeal movement, which had so many elements of power at first. The loss of this rare and noble Irishman has never been repaired, neither to his country nor to his friends. Before the grave had yet closed on Thomas Davis, began to spread awful rumours of approaching famine. Within the next month, from all the counties of Ireland came one cry of mortal terror. Blight had fallen on the crop of potatoes, the food on which five millions of the Irish people had been reduced to depend for subsistence; three millions of them wholly and exclusively. That winter of 1845-46 was the first season of Ireland's last and greatest agony of famine.

Lord Brougham, in his high-flown classical way, described the horrors of the famine in Ireland as "surpassing anything in the page of Thucydides, on the canvas of Poussin, in the dismal chant of Dante." Such a visitation falling suddenly upon any land, certainly imposes onerous duties upon its *de facto* government; and the very novelty of the circumstances, driving everything out of its routine course, might well excuse serious mistakes in applying a remedy to so monstrous a calamity. *First*, however, we are to bear in mind that all the powers, revenues, and resources of Ireland had been transferred to London. The Imperial Parliament had dealt at its pleasure with the "sister island" for forty-six years, and had brought us to this. *Second*, a great majority of the Irish people had been earnestly demanding back those powers, revenues, and resources; and the English people, through their executive, Parliament, and press, had unanimously vowed this must never be. They would govern us in spite of us, "under the blessing of Divine Providence," as the Queen said. "Were the Union *gall*," said the *Times*, "swallow it you must."

Well, then, whatsoever duties may be supposed to fall upon a government, in case of such a national calamity, rested on the English Government. We had no Legislature at home; in the Imperial Legislature we had but a delusive semblance of representation; and so totally useless was it, that *national* Irish members of Parliament preferred to stay at home. We had no authoritative mode of even suggesting what measures might (in mere Irish opinion) meet the case.

But we will see what was proposed by such public bodies in Ireland as still had power of meeting together in any capacity—the city corporations, for example, and especially the Repeal Association. It has been carefully inculcated upon the world by the British press, that the moment Ireland fell into distress, she became an abject beggar at England's gate—nay, that she even craved alms from all mankind. Many will, perhaps, be surprised to learn that *neither Ireland, nor anybody in Ireland, ever asked alms or favours of any kind, either from England or from any other nation or people.* On the contrary, it was England herself that begged for us, asking a penny, for the love of God, to relieve the poor Irish. And further, constituting herself the almoner and agent of all that charity, *she*, England, took all the profit of it.

Before describing the actual process of the "relief measures," it is well to consider what would be the natural, obvious, and inevitable course of conduct in a nation which was, indeed, one undivided nation—France, for example. If blight and famine fell upon the South of France, the whole common revenue of the kingdom would certainly be largely employed in setting the people to labour upon works of public utility; in purchasing and storing for sale, at a cheap rate, such quantities of foreign corn as might be needed, until the reason of distress should pass over, and another harvest should come. If Yorkshire and Lancashire had sustained a like calamity in England, there is no doubt such measures as these would have been taken promptly and liberally. And we know that the English Government is not slow to borrow money for great public objects, when it suits British policy so to do. They borrowed twenty million sterling to give away to their slaveholding colonists for a mischievous whim.

In truth, they are always glad of any occasion or excuse for borrowing money and adding it to the national debt; because, as they never intended to pay that debt, and as the stock and debentures of it are, in the meantime, their main safeguard against revolution, they would be well pleased to incur a debt of a hundred millions more at any moment. But the object must be popular in England; it must subserve some purpose of British policy, as in the case of the twenty millions borrowed to free negroes, or the loans freely taken to crush the people of India, and preserve and extend the opium trade with China.

To make an addition to the national debt in order to preserve the lives of a million or two of Celts, would have seemed in England a singular application of money. To *kill* so many would have been well worth a war that would cost forty millions.

On the first appearance of the blight, the Government sent over two learned commissioners, Playfair and Lindley, to Ireland, who, in conjunction with Doctor (now Sir Robert) Kane, were to examine and report upon potatoes generally, their diseases, habits, &c. This passed over the time for some weeks. Parliament was prorogued, and did not meet again till January.

In the meantime, the Corporation of Dublin sent a memorial to the Queen, praying her to call Parliament together at an early day, and to recommend the appropriation of some public money for public works, especially railways, in Ireland. A deputation from the citizens of Dublin, including the Duke of Leinster, the Lord Mayor, Lord Cloncurry, and Daniel O'Connell, waited on the Lord-Lieutenant (Lord Heytesbury), to offer suggestions as to opening the ports to foreign corn, at least for a time, stopping distillation from grain, providing public works, and the like; and to urge that there was not a moment to be lost, as millions of people would shortly be without a morsel of food. The reply of Lord Heyterbury is a model in that kind. He told them they were premature; told them not to be alarmed; that learned men had been sent over *from England* to inquire into all those matters; that, in the meantime, the inspectors of constabulary and stipendiary magistrates were charged with making constant reports from their several districts; that, in the meantime, there was "no immediate pressure on the market;" finally, that the case was a very important one, and it was evident "no decision could be taken without a previous reference to the responsible advisers of the Crown." In truth, no other answer was possible, because the Viceroy knew nothing of Sir Robert Peel's intentions. To wait for the report of learned men—to wait for Parliament—in short, *to wait;* that was the sole policy of the enemy for the present. He could wait; but he knew that hunger could not wait.

The Town Council of Belfast met and made suggestions similar to those of the Dublin Corporation, *but neither body asked charity.* They demanded that if Ireland was indeed an integral part of the realm, the common exchequer of both islands should be used—not to give alms, but to provide employment on public works of general utility.

The plea of the enemy for not being ready with any remedy, was the suddenness of the calamity. Now, it happened that nearly eleven years before, a certain "select committee," composed principally of Irish members of Parliament, had been appointed by the House of Commons to inquire into the condition of the Irish poor. They had reported, even then, in favour of promoting the reclamation of waste lands; had given their opinion decidedly (being Irish) that there was no real surplus of population, seeing that the island could easily sustain much more than its actual population, and export immensely besides. Nevertheless, they warn the Government that, "if the potato crop were a failure, its produce would be consumed long before they could acquire new means of subsistence; and then a famine ensues."*

Yet, when the famine did ensue, it took "the Government" as much by surprise (or they pretended that it did) as if they had never been warned.

Not only the citizens of Cork and Belfast, but the Repeal Association also, had suggestions to make. Indeed, this last-named body was the only one that could pretend especially to represent the very class of people whose lives were endangered by the dearth. Let us see what *they* had to propose.

On the 8th of December, O'Connell, in the Repeal Association, said: "If they ask me what are my propositions for relief of the distress, I answer, first, *tenant-right*. I would propose a law giving to every man his own. I would give the landlord his land, and a fair rent for it; but I would give the tenant compensation for every shilling he might have laid out on the land in permanent improvements. And what next do I propose? *Repeal of the Union.*" In the latter part of his speech, after detailing the means used by the Belgian Legislature during the same season—shutting the ports against exports of provisions, but opening them to import, and the like—he goes on:—

"If we had a domestic Parliament, would not the ports be thrown open—would not the abundant crops with which heaven has blessed her be kept for the people of Ireland—and would not the Irish Parliament be more active even than the Belgian Parliament to provide for the people food and employment? The blessings that would result from repeal—the necessity for repeal—the impossibility of the country enduring the want of repeal—and the utter hopelessness of any other remedy—all those things powerfully urge you to join with me, and hurrah for the repeal!"

* Report of the "Select Committee," 1836.

Still earlier, in November, O'Brien had used these words:—

"I congratulate you, that *the universal sentiment hitherto exhibited upon this subject has been that we will accept no English charity*. The resources of this country are still abundantly adequate to maintain our population, and until those resources shall have been utterly exhausted, I hope there is no man in Ireland who will so degrade himself as to ask the aid of a subscription from England."

And the sentiment was received with "loud cheers." O'Brien's speech is an earnest and vehement adjuration not to suffer promises of "relief," or vague hopes of English boons, to divert the country one moment from the great business of putting an end to the Union. Take one other extract from a speech of O'Connell's:—

"If we had a paternal government, I should be first to counsel the appropriation of a portion of the revenues of Ireland to the wants of the people, and this, too, without very strictly considering whether the whole should be repaid or not. We have an abstract claim to such application of the Irish revenues; but were we to advocate such an arrangement now, we should be mocked and insulted. Therefore, I approach the Government of England on equal terms. I say to the English people: You are the greatest money-lenders in Europe, and I will suppose you to be as determined as Shylock in the play. During the last session of Parliament, an Act was passed for the encouragement of drainage in England and Ireland. According to the provisions of that Act, any money advanced for the purpose of draining estates takes priority over the other charges affecting those estates; so that whatever amount of money may be so applied becomes the first charge on the estate of the proprietors of Ireland, and thus its repayment secured beyond all hazard. The Government can borrow as much money as they please on Exchequer bills, at not more than three per cent. If they lend it out for the purposes of drainage, they can charge such proprietors as may choose to borrow, interest at the rate of four per cent. They, therefore, will have a clear gain of one per cent., and we shall owe them nothing, but they will stand indebted to us for affording them an opportunity of obtaining an advantageous investment of the capital at their disposal."

All this while, until after the meeting of Parliament, there was no hint as to the intentions of Government; and all this while the new Irish harvest of 1845 (which was particularly abundant), with immense herds of cattle, sheep, and hogs, quite as usual, was floating off on every tide, out of every one of our thirteen sea-ports, bound for England; and the landlords were receiving their rents, and going to England to spend them; and many hundreds of poor people had lain down and died on the road sides for want of food, even before Christmas; and the famine not yet begun, but expected shortly."*

All eyes were turned to Parliament. The commission of learned naturalists; the inquiries and reports made by means of the constabulary; and various mysterious intimations in the Government newspapers;—all tended to produce the belief that the Imperial "Government" was about to charge itself with the whole care and administration of the famine. And so it was, with a vengeance.

Late in January, Parliament assembled. From the Queen's (that is, Sir Robert Peel's) speech one thing only was clear—that Ireland was to have a new "Coercion Bill." Extermination of tenantry had been of late more extensive than ever, and, therefore, there had been a few murders of landlords and agents—the most natural and inevitable thing in the world. The Queen says:—

"*My Lords and Gentlemen*,—I have observed with deep regret the very frequent instances in which the crime of deliberate assassination has been of late committed in Ireland.

"It will be your duty to consider whether any measure can be devised, calculated to give increased protection to life, and to bring to justice the perpetrators of so dreadful a crime."

This meant more police, more police taxes, police surveillance, and a law that every one should keep at home after dark. The speech goes on to refer to the approaching famine, and declares that Her Majesty had "adopted precautions" for its alleviation. This intimation served still further to make our people turn to "Government" for counsel and for aid. Who can blame them? "Government" had seized upon all our means and resources. It was confidently believed they intended to let us have the use of some part of our own money in this deadly emergency. It was even fondly imagined, by some sanguine persons, that the Government had it in contemplation to stop the export of provisions from Ireland—as the Belgian Legislature had done from Belgium, and the Portugese from Portugal — until our own people should first be fed. It was not known, in short, what "Government" intended to do, or how far they would go; all was mystery; and this very mystery paralyzed such private and local efforts, by charitable persons, as might otherwise have been attempted in Ireland.

The two great leading measures proposed in this Parliament by the administration were, *first*, a Coercion Bill for Ireland, and, *second*, Repeal of the Corn Laws. This repeal of the duties on foreign corn had long been demanded by the manufacturing and trading interests of England, and had been steadily opposed by the great landed proprietors. Sir Robert Peel, as a Conservative statesman, had always hitherto vigorously opposed the measure; but early in this Parliament he suddenly announced himself a convert to free-trade in corn; and even used the *pretext* of the famine in Ireland to justify himself and carry his measure. He further proposed to abolish the duties on foreign beef, and mutton, and bacon. Shall we exclude any kind of meat from our ports, he said, while the Irish are starving?

That is to say, the Premier proposed to cheapen those products which England bought, and which Ireland had to sell. Ireland imported no corn or beef—she exported those commodities. Hitherto she had an advantage over American and other corn growers in the English market, because there was a duty on foreign but not on Irish provisions. Henceforth, the agricultural produce of all the world was to be admitted on the same terms, duty-free; and precisely to the extent that this would cheapen provisions to the English consumer, it would impoverish the Irish producer. The great mass of the Irish people were almost unacquainted with the taste of bread and meat; they raised those articles, not to eat, but to sell and pay their rents with. Yet many of the Irish people, stupefied by the desolation they saw around them, had cried out for "opening the ports," instead of closing them. The Irish ports were open enough; much too open; and an Irish Parliament, if there had been one, would instantly have closed them in this emergency.

In looking over the melancholy records of those famine years, we find that usually the right view was seized, and

---

* The Census Commissioners admit only five hundred and sixteen "registered deaths" by starvation alone, up to January 1st. There was, at that time, no *registry* for them at all; and thousands perished, registered by none but the Recording Angel. Besides, the commissioners do not count the much greater numbers who died of typhus fever, the consequence of insufficient nourishment.

the right word said, by William Smith O'Brien. He said in the Repeal Association:—

"With respect to the proposal before us, I have to remark that it professes to abrogate all protection. It is, in my opinion, a proposal manifestly framed with a view to English rather than Irish interests. About two-thirds of the population of England (that, I believe, is the proportion) are dependent on manufactures and commerce, directly or indirectly. In this country about nine-tenths of the population are dependent on agriculture, directly or indirectly. It is clearly the object of the English minister to obtain the agricultural produce which the people of this country send to England at the lowest possible price—that is to say, to give as little as possible of English manufactures and of foreign commodities in return for the agricultural produce of Ireland."

If this *was* the minister's design, we may appreciate the spirit in which he addressed himself to the "relief measures" for Ireland.

The other measure was the *Coercion Bill*. It authorized the Viceroy to *proclaim* any district in Ireland he might think proper, commanding the people to remain within doors (whether they had houses or not) from sunset to sunrise; authorized him to quarter on such district any additional police force he might think needful; to pay rewards to informers and detectives; to pay compensation to the relatives of murdered or injured persons; and to levy the amount of all by *distress* upon the goods of the occupiers, as under the Poor law—with this difference, that whereas under the Poor law the occupier could deduct a portion of the rate from his rent, under the new law he could not; and with this further difference, that whereas under the Poor law householders whose cabins were valued under £4 per annum were exempt from the rate, under this law they were not exempt. Thus, every man who had a house, no matter how wretched, was to pay the new tax; and every man was bound to *have* a house; for if found out of doors after sunset, and convicted of that offence, he was to be transported for fifteen years, or imprisoned for three—the court to have the discretion of adding hard labour or solitary confinement.

Now, the first of these two laws, which abolished the preference of Irish grain in the English markets, would, as the Premier well knew, give a great additional stimulus to the consolidation of farms—that is, the ejectment of tenantry; because "high farming"—farming on a large scale, with the aid of horses, and steam, and all the modern agricultural improvements—was what alone would enable Irish agriculture to compete with all mankind.

The second law would drive the survivors of the ejected people (those who did not die of hunger) into the poor houses or to America; because, being bound to be at *home* after sunset, and having neither house nor home, they would be all in the absolute power of the police, and in continual peril of transportation to the colonies.

By another Act of this Parliament the police force was increased, and taken more immediately into the service of the Crown; the Irish counties were in part relieved from their pay; and they became, in all senses, a portion of the regular army. They amounted to twelve thousand chosen men, well armed and drilled.*

The police were always at the command of sheriffs for executing ejectments; and if they were not in sufficient force, troops of the line could be had from the nearest garrison. No wonder that the London *Times*, within less than three years after, was enabled to say: "Law has ridden roughshod through Ireland—it has been taught with bayonets, and interpreted with ruin. Townships levelled with the ground, straggling columns of exiles workhouses multiplied and still crowded, express the determination of

---

* No population was ever more peaceable than the Irish at this time; but they were assumed to be in an unusually dangerous temper, and to require the especial vigilance of this terrible police force. To show the pains taken by the authorities for repressing all disturbance, we may give a few sentences out of a manual published in this same year, 1846, by David Duff, Esq., an active police magistrate. It is entitled *The Constable's Guide.*

"The great point towards efficiency is, that every man should know his duty and do it, and should have a thorough and perfect knowledge of the neighbourhood of his station; and men should make themselves not only acquainted with roads and passes, but the *character of all*, which, with a little trouble, could be easily accomplished. A policeman cannot be considered *perfect* in his civil duty as a constable, who could not, when required, march direct to any house at night.

* * * *

"Independent of regular night patrols, whose hours should vary, men should by day take post on hills commanding the houses *of persons having registered arms*, or supposed to be obnoxious. The men so posted will be within view of other parties, so as to co-operate in pursuit of offenders.

* * * *

"Patrols hanging about ditches, plantations, and, above all, visiting the houses of suspicious characters, are most essential.

"The telescope to be taken always on day patrol, and rockets and blue-lights used, as pointed out in the *confidential* memorandum."

The "confidential memorandum" we have not been privileged to see.

the Legislature to rescue Ireland from its slovenly old barbarism, and to plant the institutions of this more civilized land "— *meaning England.*

These were the two principal measures for the prudent administration of the famine; but there was also another, purporting to aim more directly at *relief*.

Mr. Secretary Labouchere, making his ministerial statement in Parliament this session, estimated the total money-loss accruing by the potato blight at sixteen millions sterling. It was about the value of the Irish provisions consumed every year in England. The people likely to be affected by this dearth were always, in ordinary years, on the brink of destruction by famine, and many were every year starved to death. Now, to replace in some measure this *absolutely necessary* food by foreign corn, and to pay the higher price of grain over roots (besides freight), would have required an appropriation of twenty millions sterling —the same amount which had been devoted without scruple to turning of West India negroes wild.

England had for so many years drawn so vast a tribute from Ireland (probably eight millions *per annum* for forty years), that now, when the consequence of our intercourse with the sister island turned out to be that she grew richer every year, while Ireland, on her side of the account, had accumulated a famine, we claimed that there was something surely *due* to us. It is out of the question to enter here into these multifarious accounts. England beats all mankind in book-keeping by double entry; and as she has had the keeping of the books as well as everything else, it has been very difficult even to approximate to the truth. But to those who have followed the course of this narrative, and who call to mind the immense drain—first of provisions, and then of the money paid for those provisions—steadily going on from Ireland to England since the Union, it will seem quite within bounds to affirm that the value of *one year's* plunder, or the loan of that amount (if Ireland had had a Legislature to effect such a loan), would have amounted to the needful twenty millions sterling; would have saved Ireland the first year's famine, and made the succeeding famines impossible.

Considering all these things, it was believed not unreasonable that the common exchequer of the "three kingdoms" (so liberal when it was a question of turning negroes wild) ought to devote at least as great a sum to the mitigation of so dreadful a calamity as the famine. Accordingly, our people demanded such an appropriation, not as alms, but as a right. The Committee of the Repeal Association, for example, said:—

"Your committee beg distinctly to disclaim any participation in appeals to the bounty of England or of Englishmen. They demand as a right that a portion of the revenue which Ireland contributes to the State may be rendered available for the mitigation of a great public calamity."

Up to the meeting of Parliament, the enemy concealed their intentions in mystery; they consulted nobody in Ireland about this Irish emergency, but prepared their plans in silence.

In the meantime, the abundant and magnificent crops of grain and herds of cattle were going over to England, both earlier in the season and in greater quantities than ever before, for speculators were anxious to realize, and the landlords were pressing for their rents, and agents and bailiffs were down upon the farmers' crops before they could even get them stacked. So the farmers sold them at a disadvantage in a glutted market, or they were sold for them by auction, and with costs. The great point was to put the English Channel between the people and the food which Providence had sent them, at the earliest possible moment.

By New-Year's day it was almost swept off. Up to that date Ireland sent away, and England received, of grain alone, of the crop of 1845, three millions two hundred and fifty thousand *quarters*, besides innumerable cattle, making a value of at least seventeen millions sterling.*

Now, when Parliament met in January, the sole "remedial measure" proposed by Sir Robert Peel (besides the Coercion Bill, and the Corn Bill, to cheapen bread in England) was a grant of £50,000 for public works, and another grant of as much for drainage of estates; both these being grants *not* to Ireland, but to the "Commissioners of Public Works;" and to be administered, not as Irishmen might suggest, but as to the said Commissioners might seem good.†

It was the two-hundredth part of what might probably have sufficed to stay the famine. It might have given sensible

* Thom's *Official Directory*. It appears even in that Government publication that the export of grain from Ireland to England was considerably *greater* in this first famine year (1845) than it had been in any year before. So that the famine is not at all a mysterious dispensation of Providence.

† O'Connell pointed out that the Quit and Crown rents drawn from Ireland last year, and spent at that time in beautifying Trafalgar Square and Windsor Castle, amounted to more than £60,000.

relief, if honestly administered, to the smallest of the thirty-two counties. How it *was* used, not for relief, but for aggravation of the misery, we shall see hereafter. For that season's famine it was at any rate too late, and before any part of it became available many thousands had died of hunger. The London newspapers complacently stated that the impression "in political circles" was, that two millions of the people must perish before the next harvest.

January, February, and part of March passed away. Nothing was done for relief; but much preparation was made in the way of appointing hosts of commissioners and commissioners' clerks, and preparing the voluminous stationery, schedules, specifications, and red-tape to tie them up neatly, which so greatly embarrass all British official action—a very injurious sort of embarrassment in such a case as the Crimean war, but the very thing that did best service (to the Government) on the present occasion.*

O'Connell, O'Brien, and some other repeal members, proceeded to London in March, to endeavour to stir up ministers, or at least discover what they were intending. In answer to Mr. O'Brien, Sir James Graham enumerated the grants and loans I have above mentioned, and added something about other public moneys, which, he said, were also available for relief of distress, adding:—

"Instructions have been given, on the responsibility of the Government, to meet every emergency. It would not be expedient for me to detail those instructions; but I may state, generally, there is no portion of this distress, however widespread or lamentable, on which Government have not endeavoured, on their own responsibility, to take the best precautions to give the best directions of which circumstances could admit."

O'Brien had just come from Ireland, where he had anxiously watched the progress of the "relief measures," and of the famine. He had seen that while the latter was quick, the former were slow; in fact, they had not then appeared in Ireland at all. But the very announcement that Government intended to interpose in some decisive manner had greatly hastened collection of rents and ejectment of tenants, and both hunger and its sure attendant, the typhus, were sweeping them off rapidly. British ministers listened to all he could say with a calm, incredulous smile. "Have we not told you," they said, "we have sent persons—Englishmen, reliable men—to inquire into all those matters? Are we not going to meet every emergency?"

"Mr. W. S. O'Brien was bound to say, with regard to the sums of money mentioned by the right honourable baronet, as having been, on a former occasion, voted by the House for the relief of Ireland, that as far as his own information went, not one single guinea had ever been expended from those sources. He was also bound to tell the right honourable baronet that one hundred thousand of his fellow-creatures in Ireland were famishing."

And here the report adds: "The honourable gentleman, who appeared to labour under deep emotion, paused for a short time." Doubtless it was bitter to that haughty spirit to plead for his plundered people, as it were, *in forma pauperis*, before the plunderers; and their vulgar pride was soothed; but soon it was wounded again, for he added:—

"Under such circumstances, did it not become the House to consider of the way in which they could deal with the crisis? He would tell them frankly—and it was a feeling participated in by the majority of Irishmen—that he was not disposed to appeal to their generosity in the matter. They had taken and they had tied the purse-strings of the Irish purse!"

Whereupon the report records that there were cries of *Oh! oh!* They were scandalized at the idea of Ireland having a purse.

Notwithstanding this repeated repudiation of alms, all the appropriations of Parliament purporting to be for relief, but really calculated for aggravation of the Irish famine, were persistently called alms by the English press. These Irish, they said, are never done craving alms. It is true they did not *answer* our statement that we only demanded a small part of what was due; they chose to assume that the exchequer was *their* exchequer; neither did they think it fit to remember that Mr. O'Brien, and such as he, were by no means suffering from famine themselves, but were retrenching the expenses of their households at home to relieve those who were suffering. To the common English intellect it was enough to present this one idea—here are these starving Irish coming over to beg from *you*.

Thus it will be easy to appreciate the feelings which then prevailed in the two islands,—in Ireland, a vague and dim sense that we were somehow robbed; in

---

* In April of next year (1846), Jones, Twisleton, &c., were enabled to report that they had sent to Ireland "ten thousand books, besides fourteen tons of paper."

England, a still more vague and blundering idea, that an impudent beggar was demanding their money, with a scowl in his eye and a threat upon his tongue.

In truth, only a few, either in England or in Ireland, fully understood the bloody game on the board. The two cardinal principles of the British policy in this business seem to have been these :— *First*, strict adherence to the principles of "political economy;" and, *second*, making the whole administration of the famine a Government concern. "Political economy" became, about the time of the repeal of the Corn Laws, a favourite study, or rather, indeed, the creed and gospel of England. Women and young boys were learned in its saving doctrines; one of the most fundamental of which was, "there must be no interference with the natural course of trade." It was seen that this maxim would insure the transfer of the Irish wheat and beef to England; for that was what they called the natural course of trade. Moreover, this maxim would forbid the Government, or relief committees, to sell provisions in Ireland any lower than the market price—for this is an interference with the enterprise of private speculators; it would forbid the employment of Government ships—for this troubles individual shipowners; and further, and lastly, it was found (this invaluable maxim) to require that the public works, to be executed by labourers employed with borrowed public money, should be unproductive works—that is, works which would create no fund to pay their own expenses. There were many railroad companies at that time in Ireland that had got their charters—their roads have been made since; but it was in vain they asked them for Government advances, which they could have well secured, and soon paid off. The thing could not be done. Lending money to Irish railroad companies would be a discrimination against English companies —flat interference with private enterprise.

The other great leading idea completed Sir Robert's policy. It was to make the famine a strictly Government concern. The famine was to be administered strictly through officers of the Government, from high commissioners down to policemen. Even the Irish General Relief Committee, and other local committees of charitable persons, who were exerting themselves to raise funds to give employment, were either induced to act in subordination to a Government Relief Committee, which sat in Dublin Castle, or else were deterred from importation of food by the announcement in Parliament that the *Government* had given orders somewhere for the purchase of foreign corn. For instance, the Mayor of Cork, and some principal inhabitants of that city, hurried to Dublin, and waited on the Lord-Lieutenant, representing that the local committee had applied for some portion of the Parliamentary loans, but "were refused assistance on some points of official form : that the people of that county were already famishing, and both food and labour were urgently needed. Lord Heytesbury simply recommended that they should communicate at once with the *Government* Relief Committee"— as for the rest, that they should consult the Board of Works. Thus every possible delay and official difficulty was interposed against the efforts of local bodies—Government was to do all. These things, together with the new measure for an increase in the police force (who were the main administrative agents throughout the country), led many persons to the conclusion that the enemy had resolved to avail themselves of the famine in order to increase Governmental supervision and *espionage*, so that every man, woman, and child in Ireland, with all their goings out and comings in, might be thoroughly known and registered; that when the mass of the people began to starve, their sole resource might be the police barracks; that Government might be all in all— omnipotent to give food or withhold it, to relieve or to starve, according to their own ideas of policy, and of good behaviour in the people.

It is needless to point out that Government patronage also was much extended by this system; and by the middle of the next year, 1847, there were ten thousand men salaried out of Parliamentary loans and grants for relief of the poor—as commissioners, inspectors, clerks, and so forth; and some of them with salaries equal to that of an American Secretary of State. So many of the middle classes had been dragged down almost to insolvency by the ruin of the country, that they began to be eager for the smaller places, as clerks and inspectors. For those ten thousand officers, then, it was estimated there were one hundred thousand applicants and canvassers—so much clear gain from "Repeal."

The Repeal Association continued its regular meetings, and never ceased to represent that the true remedies for Irish famine were tenant-right, the stoppage of export, and repeal of the Union; and as those were really the true and only remedies, it was clear they were the only expedients which an English Parliament would *not* try. The repeal members gained a kind of Parliamentary victory, however, this spring. They caused the defeat of the Coercion bill, with the aid of the Whigs. Sir Robert Peel had very cunningly, as he thought, made this bill precede the Corn Law Repeal bill; and as the English public was all now most eager for the cheapening of bread, he believed that all parties would make haste to pass his favourite measure first. The Irish members went to London; and knowing they could not influence legislation otherwise, organized a sort of mere mechanical resistance against the Coercion bill—that is, they opposed first reading, second reading, third reading, opposed its being referred to committee, moved endless amendments, made endless speeches, and insisted upon dividing the House on every clause. In vain it was represented to them that this was only delaying the Corn Law Repeal, which would "cheapen bread." O'Brien replied that it would only cheapen bread to Englishmen, and enable them to devour more and more of the Irish bread, and give less for it. In vain ministers told them that they were stopping public business. They answered that English business was no business of theirs. In vain their courtesy was invoked. They could not afford to be courteous in such a case, and their sole errand in London was to resist an atrocious and torturing tyranny threatened against their poor countrymen.

Just before this famous debate, there had been very extensive clearing of tenantry in Connaught; and, in particular, one case in which a Mrs. Gerard had, with the aid of the troops and police, destroyed a whole village, and thrown out two hundred and seventy persons on the highroad. The *Nation* thus improved the circumstances with reference to the "Coercion bill":—

"Some Irish member, for instance, may point to the two hundred and seventy persons thrown out of house and home the other day in Galway, and in due form of law (for it was all perfectly legal) turned adrift in their desperation upon the wide world, and may ask the minister, If any of these two hundred and seventy commit a robbery on the highway—if any of them murder the bailiff who (in exercise of his duty) flung out their naked children to perish in the winter's sleet—if any of them, maddened by wolfish famine, break into a dwelling-house, and forcibly take food to keep body and soul together, or arms for vengeance—what will you do? How will you treat that district? Will you, indeed, *proclaim* it? Will you mulct the householders (not yet ejected) in a heavy fine to compound for the crimes of those miserable outcasts, to afford food and shelter to whom they wrong their own children in this hard season? Besides sharing with those wretches his last potato, is the poor cottier to be told that he is to *pay* for policemen to watch them day and night—that he is to make atonement in money (though his spade and poor bedding should be auctioned to make it up) for any outrage that may be done in the neighbourhood?—but that these GERRARDS are not to pay one farthing for all this—for perhaps their property is encumbered, and, it may be, they find it hard enough to pay their interest, and keep up such establishments in town and country as befit their rank? And will you, indeed, issue your commands that those houseless and famishing two hundred and seventy—after their roof-trees were torn down, and the ploughshare run through the foundations of their miserable hovels—are to be *at home* from sunset to sunrise?—that if found straying, the jails and the penal colonies are ready for their reception?"

It was precisely with a view to meet such cases that the Coercion bill had been devised. The English Whigs, and, at length, the indignant Protectionists, too, joined the repealers in this resistance—not to spare Ireland, but to defeat Sir Robert Peel, and get into his place. And they did defeat Sir Robert Peel, and get into his place. Whereupon, it was not long before Lord John Russell and the Whigs devised a new and more murderous Coercion bill for Ireland themselves.

It was on the 25th of May, that the Coercion bill for Ireland was defeated—the first Coercion bill for Ireland that was ever refused by a British Parliament; and it was rejected, not by the exertions of Ireland's friends, but by political combinations of her enemies.

Sir Robert Peel immediately resigned office, and left the responsibility of dealing with the Irish affair to the Whigs. He knew he might do so safely. His system was inaugurated. His two great ideas—free trade and police administration—were fully recognized by the Whigs; and Lord John Russell was even a blind bigot about what he imagined to be political economy. This "Liberal" statesman never had an idea of his own; and as the system of Sir Robert Peel was really the true and only English method of dealing with the Irish difficulty, it was quite certain that the Whigs would not only adopt it, but improve upon it.

CHAPTER XXIV.

1846—1847.

Progress of the Famine Carnage—Pretended Relief Measures—Imprisonment of O'Brien—Dissensions in Repeal Association—Break-up of that Body—Ravages of Famine—"Labour Rate Act"—Useless Public Works—Extermination—Famine of 1847—How they Lived in England—Advances from the Treasury—Attempts of Foreign Countries to Relieve the Famine—Defeated by British Government—Vagrancy Act—Parish Coffins—Constant Repudiation of Alms—An Englishman's Petition for Alms to Ireland—"Ingratitude" of the Irish—Death of O'Connell—Preparations to Insure the Next Year's Famine—Emigration—British Famine Policy—New Coercion Act called for—Famine in Ireland.

In the first year of the Famine, then, we find that the measures proposed by the English Government were, *first*, repeal of the Corn laws, which depreciated Ireland's only article of export; *second*, a new Coercion law, to torture and transport the people; and, *third*, a grant of £100,000 to certain clerks or commissioners, chiefly for their own profit, and from which the starving people derived no benefit whatever. Yet Ireland was taunted with this grant, as if it were *alms* granted to her. Double the sum (£200,000) was, *in the same session*, appropriated for Battersea Park, a suburban place of recreation much resorted to by Londoners.

It is to be observed that all the employment to be provided for the poor under this first "Relief Act," was to be given under the order and control of English officials; further, the professions of "Government"—that *they* had taken all needful measures to guard against famine—had made people rely upon them for everything, and thus turned the minds of thousands upon thousands from work of their own, which they might have attempted if left to themselves. This sort of government spoon-feeding is highly demoralizing; and for *one* who derived any relief from it, one thousand neglected their own industry in the pursuit of it.

In truth, the amount of relief offered by these grants was infinitesimally small, when we consider the magnitude of the calamity, and had no other effect than to unsettle the minds of the peasantry, and make them more careless about holding on to their farms.

It is true, also, that the Government did, to a certain small extent, speculate in Indian corn, and did send a good many cargoes of it to Ireland, and form depots of it at several points; but as to this, also, their mysterious intimations had led all the world to believe they would provide very large quantities, whereas, in fact, the quantity imported by them was inadequate to supply the loss of the grain *exported* from any one county; and a Government ship, sailing into any harbour with Indian corn, was sure to meet half a dozen sailing out with Irish wheat and cattle. The effect of this, therefore, was only to blind the people to the fact that England was exacting her tribute as usual, famine or no famine. The effect of both combined was to engender a dependent and pauper spirit, and to free England from all anxiety about "repeal." A landless hungry *pauper* cannot afford to think of the honour of his country, and cares nothing about a national flag.

How powerfully the whole of this system and procedure contributed to accomplish the great end of uprooting the people from the soil, one can readily understand. The exhibition and profession of public "relief" for the destitute, stifled compunction in the landlords; and agents, bailiffs, and police swept whole districts with the besom of destruction.

Another act had been done by Sir Robert Peel's Ministry, just before retiring, with a view of breaking up the Repeal Association. This was the imprisonment of Mr. Smith O'Brien several weeks in the cellar of the House of Commons. It grievously irritated the enemy that O'Connell, O'Brien, and the repeal members, still continued to absent themselves from Parliament. The House of Commons tried various methods of persuading or coercing them to London. Mr. Hume had written them a friendly letter imploring them to come over to their legislative duties, and *he* would aid them in obtaining justice for Ireland. A "call of the House" was proposed; but they declared beforehand, that if there were a call of the House they would not obey it, and the Sergeant-at-Arms must come to Ireland for them—he would find them in Conciliation Hall. They were nominated on English railroad committees, and the proper officer had intimated to them the fact. They replied that they were attending to more important business. Now, when they went over to oppose the Coercion bill, it was understood that this was to be their sole errand, and they were not to engage themselves in the ordinary details of legislation. But they were not long in London before the opportunity was seized to place their names on railway committees. O'Connell and his son both obeyed the call. O'Brien, of course, refused, and was imprisoned in the cellar for "contempt."

London and all England were highly pleased and entertained. The press was brilliant upon the great "Brian Boru" in a cellar; and Mr. O'Brien was usually afterwards termed (with that fine sarcasm so characteristic of English genius) the "martyr of the cellar."

Instantly arose dissension in the Repeal Association. To approve and fully sustain O'Brien's action in refusing to serve, would be to censure O'Connell for serving. In that body a sort of unsatisfactory compromise was made, but the "Eighty-two Club," where the *young* party was stronger, voted a warm address of full approval to O'Brien (who was a member of the club), and dispatched several members to present it to him in his dungeon.

The divisions in O'Connell's Association were soon brought to a crisis when the Whigs came in. O'Connell instantly gave up all agitation of the Repeal question, and took measures to separate himself from those "juvenile members" who, as he declared Lord John Russell had asserted, were plotting not only to repeal the Union, but to sever the connection with England ("the golden link of the Crown"), and that by *physical force*. All this famous controversy seems now of marvellously small moment; but a very concise narrative of it may be found in Mr. O'Brien's words, which will be enough :—

"Negotiations were opened between Mr. O'Connell and the Whigs at Chesham Place. 'Young Ireland' protested in the strongest terms against an alliance with the Whigs. Mr. O'Connell took offence at the language used by Mr. Meagher and others. When I arrived in Dublin, after the resignation of Sir Robert Peel, I learned that he contemplated a rupture with the writers of the *Nation*. Before I went to the County of Clare, I communicated, through Mr. Ray, a special message to Mr. O'Connell, who was then absent from Dublin, to the effect, that though I was most anxious to preserve a neutral position, I could not silently acquiesce in any attempt to expel the *Nation* or its party from the Association. Next came the Dungarvan election, and the new "moral force" resolutions. I felt it my duty to protest against both at the Kilrush dinner. Upon my return to Dublin, I found a public letter from Mr. O'Connell, formally denouncing the *Nation;* and no alternative was left me but to declare, that if that letter were acted upon, I could not co-operate any longer with the Repeal Association. The celebrated two-day debate then took place. Mr. J. O'Connell opened an attack upon the *Nation* and upon its adherents. Mr. Mitchel and Mr. Meagher defended themselves in language which, it seemed to me, did not transgress the bounds of decorum or of legal safety. Mr. John O'Connell interrupted Mr. Meagher in his speech, and declared that he could not allow him to proceed with the line of argument necessary to sustain the principles which had been arraigned. I protested against this interruption. Mr. J. O'Connell then gave us to understand that unless Mr. Meagher desisted, he must leave the hall. I could not acquiesce in this attempt to stifle a fair discussion, and sooner than witness the departure of Mr. J. O'Connell from an association founded by his father, I preferred to leave the assembly."*

When O'Brien left the assembly, he was accompanied by his friends, and there was an end of the Repeal Association, save as a machinery of securing offices for O'Connell's dependents. Even for that purpose it was not efficient, because it had too clearly become impotent and hollow; there was no danger in it, and ministers would not buy a patriot in that market, unless at a very low figure.

In the meantime, the famine and the fever raged; many landlords regained possession without so much as an ejectment, because the tenant died of hunger; and the county coroners, before the end of this year, were beginning to strike work—they were so often called to sit upon famine-slain corpses. The verdict, "Death by starvation," became so familiar that the county newspapers sometimes omitted to record it; and travellers were often appalled when they came upon some lonely village by the western coast, with the people all skeletons upon their own hearths. Irish landlords are not all monsters of cruelty. Thousands of them, indeed, kept far away from the scene, collected their rents through agents and bailiffs, and spent them in England or in Paris. But the resident landlords and their families did, in many cases, devote themselves to the task of saving their poor people alive. Many remitted their rents, or half their rents; and ladies kept their servants busy and their kitchens smoking with continual preparation of food for the poor. Local committees soon purchased all the corn in the Government depôts (at market price, however), and distributed it gratuitously. Clergymen, both Protestant and Catholic, generally did their duty; except those absentee clergymen, bishops, and wealthy rectors, who usually reside in England, their services being not needed in the places from whence they draw their wealth. But

* Mr. O'Brien's letter to Dr. Miley, December, 1846.

many a poor rector and his curate shared their crust with their suffering neighbours; and priests, after going round all day administering extreme unction to whole villages at once, all dying of mere starvation, often themselves went supperless to bed.

The details of this frightful famine, as it ravaged those Western districts, need not be narrated. It is enough to say, that in this year, 1846, not less than three hundred thousand perished, either of mere hunger or of typhus fever caused by hunger. But, as it has ever since been the main object of the British Government to conceal the amount of the carnage (which, indeed, they ought to do if they can), we find that the Census Commissioners, in their report for 1851, admit only two thousand and forty-one "registered" deaths by famine alone.

A Whig ministry, however, was now in power; and the people were led to expect great efforts on the part of Government to stay the progress of ruin. In August, it became manifest that the potato crop of '46 was also a total failure; but the products otherwise were most abundant—much more than sufficient to feed all the people. Again, therefore, it became the urgent business of British policy to promise large "relief," so as to insure that the splendid harvest should be allowed peacefully to be shipped to England as before; and the first important measure of the Whigs was to propose a renewal of the *Disarming Act*, and a further increase in the police force. Apparently, the outcry raised against this had the effect of shaming ministers, for they suddenly dropped the bill for this time. But the famine could not be correctly administered without a Coercion bill of some sort; so the next year they devised a machinery of this kind, the most stringent and destructive that had yet been prescribed for Ireland. In the meantime, for "relief" of the famine, they brought forward their famous *Labour Rate Act.*

This was, in few words, an additional Poor rate, payable by the same persons liable to the other Poor rates; the proceeds to be applied to the execution of such public works as *the Government* might choose; the control and superintendence to be intrusted to *Government officers*. Money was to be, in the meantime, advanced from the Treasury, in order to set the people immediately to work; and that advance was to be repaid in ten years by means of the increased rate. There was to be an *appearance* of local control, inasmuch as barony sessions of landlords and justices were to have power to meet (under the Lord-Lieutenant's order), and suggest any works they might think needful, provided these were strictly unproductive works; but the control of all was to be in the Government alone.

Now, the class which suffered most from the potato blight consisted of those small farmers who were barely able, in ordinary years, to keep themselves above starvation after paying their rents. These people, by the Labour Rate Act, had an additional tax laid on them; and not being able to pay it, could but quit their holdings, sink to the class of able-bodied paupers, and enrol themselves in a gang of Government *navvies;* thus throwing themselves for support upon those who still strove to maintain themselves by their own labour on their own land.

In addition to the proceeds of the new Poor rate, Parliament appropriated a further sum of £50,000, to be applied in giving work in some absolutely pauper districts where there was no hope of ever raising rates to repay it. £50,000 was just the sum which was that same year voted out of the English and Irish revenue to improve the buildings of the British Museum.

So there was to be *more* Poor law, more commissioners (this time under the title of Additional Public Works Commissioners), innumerable officials in the public works, commissariat and constabulary departments, and no end of stationery and red-tape, *all* to be paid out of the rates. On the whole, it was hoped that provision was made for stopping the "Irish howl" this one season.

Irishmen of all classes had almost universally condemned the Poor law at first; so, as they did not like Poor law, they were to have *more* Poor law. Society in Ireland was to be reconstructed on the basis of Poor rates, and a broad foundation of able-bodied pauperism. It did not occur to the English, and it never will occur to them, that the way to stop Irish destitution is to repeal the Union, so that Irishmen might make their own laws, use their own resources, regulate their own industry. It was in vain, however, that anybody in Ireland remonstrated. In vain that such journals as were of the popular party condemned the whole scheme. The *Nation* of that date treats it thus:—

"Unproductive work to be executed with borrowed money; a ten years' mortgage of a new tax, to pay for cutting down hills and filling them up again; a direct impost upon landed proprietors, in the most offensive form, to feed all the rest of the population; impoverishing the rich without benefiting the poor; not creating, not developing, but merely transferring, and in the transfer wasting, the means of all; perhaps human ingenuity, sharpened by intensest malignity, could contrive no more deadly and unerring method of arraying class against class in diabolical hatred, making them look on one another with wolfish eyes, as if to prepare the way for "*aristocrates à la lanterne!*" killing individual enterprise, discouraging private improvement, dragging down employers and employed, proprietors, farmers, mechanics, and cottiers, to one common and irretrievable ruin."

It may seem astonishing that the gentry of Ireland did not rouse themselves at this frightful prospect, and universally demand the repeal of the Union. They were the same class, sons of the same men who had, in 1782, wrested the independence of Ireland from the English Government, and enjoyed the fruits of that independence in honour, wealth, and prosperity for eighteen years. Why not now? It is because, in 1782, the Catholics of Ireland counted as nothing; now they are numerous, enfranchised, exasperated; and the Irish landlords dare not trust themselves in Ireland without British support. They looked on tamely, therefore, and saw this deliberate scheme for the pauperization of a nation. They knew it would injure themselves; but they took the injury, took insult along with it, and submitted to be reproached for begging *alms*, when they demanded restitution of a part of their own means.

Over the whole island, for the next few months, was a scene of confused and wasteful attempts at relief—bewildered barony sessions striving to understand the voluminous directions, schedules, and specifications under which alone they could vote their own money to relieve the poor at their own doors; but generally making mistakes, for the unassisted human faculties never could comprehend those ten thousand books and fourteen tons of paper; insolent commissioners, and inspectors, and clerks snubbing them at every turn, and ordering them to study the documents; efforts on the part of the proprietors to expend some of the rates at least on useful works, reclaiming land or the like, which efforts were always met with flat refusal and a lecture on political economy (for political economy, it seems, declared that the works must be strictly useless—as cutting down a road where there was no hill, or building a bridge where there was no water—until many good roads became impassable on account of pits and trenches); plenty of jobbing and peculation all this while; and the labourers, having the example of a great public fraud before their eyes, themselves defrauding their fraudulent employers—quitting agricultural pursuits and crowding to the public works, where they pretended to be cutting down hills and filling up hollows, and with tongue in cheek received half wages for doing nothing. So the labour was wasted, the labourers were demoralized, and the *next* year's famine was insured.

Now began to be a rage for extermination beyond any former time; and many thousands of the peasants who could still scrape up the means fled to the sea, as if pursued by wild beasts, and betook themselves to America. The British army, also, received numberless recruits this year (for it is sound English policy to keep our people so low that a shilling a day would tempt them to fight for the devil, not to say the Queen); and insane mothers began to eat their young children who died of famine before them; and still fleets of ships were sailing with every tide, carrying Irish cattle and corn to England. There was also a large importation of grain from England into Ireland, especially of Indian corn; and the speculators and shipowners had a good time. Much of the grain thus brought to Ireland had been previously exported *from* Ireland, and came back laden with merchants' profits, and double freights, and insurance, to the helpless people who had sowed and reaped it. This is what commerce and free trade did for Ireland in those days.

Two facts, however, are essential to be borne in mind—*first*, that the net result of this importation, exportation, and re-importation (though many a ship-load was carried four times across the Irish Sea, as prices "invited" it) was, that England finally received the harvests to the same amount as before; and *second*, that she gave Ireland, under free trade in corn, less for it than ever. In other words, it took more of the Irish produce to buy a piece of cloth from a Leeds manufacturer, or to buy a rent receipt from an absentee proprietor.

Farmers could do without the cloth, but as for the rent receipts, these they must absolutely buy; for the bailiff, with his police, was usually at the door even before the fields were reaped; and he, and the Poor rate collector, and the additional Poor rate collector, and the county cess collector, and the process-server with decrees, were all to be paid out of the first proceeds. If it took the farmer's whole crop to pay them, which it usually did, he had, at least, a pocketful of receipts, and might see lying in the next harbour the very ship that was to carry his entire harvest and his last cow to England.

What wonder that so many farmers gave up the effort in despair, and sunk to paupers? Many Celts were cleared off this year, and the campaign was so far successful.

The winter of 1846-47, and succeeding spring, were employed in a series of utterly unavailing attempts to use the "Labour Rate Act," so as to afford some sensible relief to the famishing people. Sessions were held, as provided by the Act, and the landed proprietors liberally imposed rates to repay such Government advances as they thought needful; but the unintelligible directions constantly interrupted them, and, in the meantime, the peasantry, in the wild blind hope of public relief, were abandoning their farms, and letting the land lie idle.

Even the Tory or British party in Ireland furnish ample testimony to this deplorable state of things. From Limerick we learn, through the Dublin *Evening Mail*:—

"There is not a labourer employed in the county except on public works; and there is every prospect of the lands remaining untilled and unsown for the next year."

In Cork, writes the *Cork Constitution*:— "The good intentions of the Government are frustrated by the worst regulations—regulations which, diverting labour from its legitimate channels, left the fields without hands to prepare them for the harvest."

At a Presentment Session in Shanagolden, after a hopeless discussion as to what possible meaning could be latent in the Castle "instructions," and "supplemental instructions," the Knight of Glin, a landlord of those parts, said that, "while on the subject of mistakes," he might as well mention, "on the Glin Road some people are filling up the original cutting of a hill with the stuff they had taken out of it. That's another slice out of our £450"—

Which he and the other proprietors of that barony had *to pay*. For you must bear in mind that all the advances under this Act were to be strictly *loans*, repayable by the rates secured by the whole value of the land, and at higher interest than the Government borrowed the money so advanced.

The innocent Knight of Glin ascribed the perversions of labour to "mistake." But there was no mistake at all. Digging holes and filling them up again was precisely the kind of work prescribed in such case by the principles of political economy; and then there were innumerable regulations to be attended to before even this kind of work could be given. The Board of Works would have the roads torn up with such tools as they approved of, and none other—that is, with picks and short shovels; and picks and short shovels were manufactured in England, and sent over by ship-loads for that purpose, to the great profit of the hardware merchants in Birmingham. Often there were no adequate supply of these on the spot; then the work was to be *task-work*, and the poor people, delving macadamized roads with spades and turf-cutters, could not earn as much as would keep them alive, though luckily they were thereby disabled from destroying so much good road.

That all interests in the country were swiftly rushing to ruin was apparent to all. A committee of lords and gentlemen was formed, called "Reproductive Committee," to urge upon the Government that, if the country was to tax itself to supply public work, the labour ought, in some cases at least, to be employed upon tasks that might be of use. This movement was so far successful that it elicited a letter from the Castle, authorizing such application, but with supplemental instructions so intricate and occult that this also was fruitless.

And the people perished more rapidly than ever. The famine of 1847 was far more terrible and universal than that of the previous year. The Whig Government, bound by political economy, absolutely refused to interfere with market prices, and the merchants and speculators were never so busy on both sides of the Channel. In this year it was that the Irish famine began to be a world's wonder, and men's hearts were moved in the uttermost ends of the earth by the recital of its horrors. The London *Illustrated News* began to be adorned with engravings of tottering windowless hovels in Skibbereen, and elsewhere, with naked wretches dying on a truss of wet straw; and the constant language of English ministers and members of Parliament created the impression abroad that Ireland was in need of *alms*, and nothing but alms; whereas Irishmen themselves uniformly protested that what they required was a repeal of the Union, so that the English might cease to devour their substance.

It may be interesting to know how the English people were faring all this while;

and whether "that portion of the United Kingdom," as it is called, suffered much by the famine in Ireland and in Europe. Authentic *data* upon this point are to be found in the financial statement of Sir Charles Wood, Chancellor of the Exchequer, in February, 1847. In that statement he declares, and he tells it, he says, with great satisfaction, that "the English people and working classes" were steadily growing more comfortable, nay, more luxurious in their style of living. He goes into particulars even, to show how rapidly a taste for good things spreads amongst English labourers, and bids his hearers "recollect that consumption could not be accounted for by attributing it to the higher and wealthier classes, but must have arisen from the consumption of the large body of the people and the working classes."

In the matter of *coffee*, they had used nearly seven million pounds of it more than they did in 1843. Of *butter* and *cheese* they devoured double as much within the year as they had done three years before within the same period. "I will next," says the Chancellor of the Exchequer, "take *currants*" (for currants are one of the necessaries of life to an English labourer, who must have his pudding on Sunday at least); and we find that the quantity of currants used by the "body of the people and working classes" had increased in three years, from two hundred and fifty-four thousand hundredweight to three hundred and fifty-nine thousand hundredweight by the year. Omitting other things, we come to the Chancellor's statement, that since 1843 the consumption of *tea* had increased by five million four hundred thousand pounds. It is unnecessary to say they had as much beef and bacon as they could eat, and bread *à discrétion*, and beer!

This statement was read by Sir Charles Wood at the end of a long speech, in which he announced the necessity of raising an additional loan to keep life in some of the surviving Irish; and he read it expressly in order "to dispel some portion of the gloom which had been cast over the minds of members," by being told that a portion of the surplus revenue must go to pay interest on a slight addition to the national debt. And the gloom *was* dispelled; and honourable members comforted themselves with the reflection, that whatever be the nominal debt of the country, after all, a man of the working classes can ask no more than a good dinner every day, and a pudding on Sundays.

One would not grudge the English labourer his dinner or his tea. And we refer to his excellent table only to bid the reader remark that during those same three years, exactly as fast as the English people and working classes advanced to luxury, the Irish people and working classes sank to starvation; and further, that the Irish people were still sowing and reaping what they of the sister island so contentedly devoured, to the value of at least £17,000,000 sterling.

As an English farmer, artizan, or labourer began to insist on tea in the morning as well as in the evening, an Irish farmer, artizan, or labourer, found it necessary to live on one meal a day; for every Englishman who added to his domestic expenditure by a pudding thrice a week, an Irishman had to retrench *his* to cabbage leaves and turnip tops; as dyspepsia creeps into England, dysentery ravages Ireland; "and the exact correlative of a Sunday dinner in England is a coroner's inquest in Ireland."

Ireland, however, was to have "alms." The English would not see their useful drudges perish at their very door for want of a trifle of alms. So the ministry announced in this month of February a new loan of ten millions, to be used from time to time for relief of Irish famine—the half of the advances to be repaid by rates, the other half to be a grant from the Treasury to feed able-bodied paupers for doing useless work, or no work at all. As to this latter half of the ten millions, English newspapers and members of Parliament said that it was so much English money granted to Ireland. This of course was a falsehood. It was a loan raised by the Imperial Treasury on a mortgage of the taxation of the three kingdoms; and the principal of it, like the rest of the "national debt," was not intended to be ever repaid; and as for the interest, Ireland would have to pay her proportion of it, as a matter of course.

This last Act was the *third* of the "relief measures" contrived by the British Parliament, and the most destructive of all. It was to be put in operation as a system of out-door relief; and the various local boards of Poor law guardians, if they could only understand the documents, were to have some apparent part in its administration, but all, as usual, under the absolute control of the Poor Law Commissioners, and of a new Board—namely, Sir John Burgoyne, an engineer; Sir Randolph Routh, Commissary-General; Mr. Twisleton, a Poor Law Commissioner; two Colonels, called Jones and M'Gregor, police inspectors; and Mr. Redington, Under-Secretary.

In the administration of this system there were to be many thousands of officials, great and small. The largest salaries were for Englishmen, but the smaller were held up as an object of ambition to Irishmen; and it is very humiliating to remember what eager and greedy multitudes were always canvassing and petitioning for these.

In the new Act of the out-door relief there was one significant clause. It was, that if any farmer who held land should be forced to apply for aid under this Act, for himself and his family, he should not have it until he had first given up all his land to the landlord—except one quarter of an acre. It was called the quarter-acre clause, and was found the most efficient and the cheapest of all the Ejectment Acts. Farms were thereafter daily given up, without the formality of a notice to quit, or summons before quarter sessions.

On the 6th of March, there were seven hundred and thirty thousand *heads* of families on the public works. Provision was made by the last-recited Act for dismissing these in batches. On the 10th of April, the number was reduced to five thousand seven hundred and twenty-three. Afterwards, batches of a hundred thousand or so were in like manner dismissed. Most of these had now neither house nor home; and their only resource was in the out-door relief. For this they were ineligible, if they held but one rood of land. Under the new law it was able-bodied idlers only who were to be fed—to attempt to till even a rood of ground was death.

Steadily, but surely, the "Government" was working out its calculation; and the product anticipated by "political circles" was likely to come out about September, in round numbers—*two millions of Irish corpses.*

That "Government" had at length got into its own hands all the means and materials for working this problem, is now plain. There was no longer any danger of the elements of the account being disturbed by external interference of any kind. At one time, indeed, there were odds against the Government sum coming out right; for charitable people in England and America, indignant at the thought of a nation perishing of political economy, did contribute generously, and did full surely believe that every pound they subscribed would give Irish famine twenty shillings worth of bread; they thought so, and poured in their contributions, and their prayers and blessings with them.

In vain! "Government" and political economy got hold of the contributions, and disposed of them in such fashion as to prevent their deranging the calculations of political circles.

For example, the vast supplies of food purchased by the "British Relief Association," with the money of charitable Christians in England, were everywhere locked up in Government stores. Government, it seems, contrived to influence or control the managers of that fund; and thus there were thousands of tons of food rotting within the stores of Haulbowline, at Cork Harbour; and tens of thousands rotting without. For the market must be followed, not led (to the prejudice of Liverpool merchants!)—private speculation must not be disappointed, nor the calculations of political circles falsified!

All the nations of the earth might be defied to feed or relieve Ireland, beset by such a Government as this. America tried another plan. The ship *Jamestown* sailed into Cork Harbour, and discharged a large cargo, which actually began to come into consumption; when lo! Free Trade—another familiar demon of Government—Free Trade, that carried off our own harvests of the year before—comes in, freights another ship, and carries off from Cork to Liverpool a cargo *against* the American cargo. For the private speculators must be compensated; the markets must not be *led;* if these Americans will not give England their corn to lock up, then she defeats them by "the natural laws of trade!" So many Briarean hands has Government—so surely do official persons work their account.

Private charity, one might think, in a country like Ireland, would put out the calculating Government sadly; but that, too, was brought in great measure under control. The "Temporary Relief Act," *talking* of eight millions of money (*to be used if needed*)—distributing, like Cumæan Sybil, its mystic leaves by the myriad and the million—setting charitable people everywhere to con its pamphlets, and compare clause with clause—putting everybody in terror of its rates, and in horror of its inspectors—was likely to pass the summer bravely. It would begin to be partly understood about August, would expire in September;—and in September the "persons connected with Government" expected their round two millions of carcases.

A further piece of the machinery, all working to the same great end, was the "Vagrancy Act," for the punishment of vagrants—that is, of about four millions of the inhabitants—by hard labour, "for any time not exceeding one month."

Many poor people were escaping to England, as deck passengers, on board the numerous steamers, hoping to earn their living by labour there; but "Government" took alarm about typhus fever—a disease not intended for England. Orders in Council were suddenly issued, subjecting all vessels having *deck passengers* to troublesome examination and quarantine, thereby quite stopping up that way of escape; and, six days afterwards, four steamship companies, between England and Ireland, on request of the Government, raised the rate of passage for deck passengers. Cabin passengers were not interfered with in any way; for, in fact, it is the cabin passengers from Ireland who spend in England five millions sterling *per annum*.

Whither now were the people to fly? Where to hide themselves? They had no money to emigrate, no food, no land, no roof over them, no hope before them. They began to envy the lot of those who had died in the first year's famine. The poor houses were all full, and much more than full. Each of them was an hospital for typhus fever; and it was very common for three fever patients to be in one bed, some dead, and others not yet dead. Parishes all over the country being exhausted by rates, refused to provide coffins for the dead paupers, and they were thrown coffinless into holes; but in some parishes (in order to have, at least, the look of decent interment), a coffin was made with its bottom hinged at one side, and closed at the other by a latch—the uses of which are obvious.

It would be easy to horrify the reader with details of this misery; but let it be enough to give the results in round numbers. Great efforts were this year made to give relief by private charity; and sums contributed in that way by Irishmen themselves far exceeded all that was sent from all other parts of the world besides. As for the ship-loads of corn generously sent over by Americans, it has been already shown how the benevolent object was defeated. The moment it appeared in any port, prices became a shade lower; and so much the more grain was carried off from Ireland by "free trade." It was not foreign corn that Ireland wanted—it was the use of her own; that is to say, it was repeal of the Union.

The arrangements and operations of the Union had been such that Ireland was bleeding at every vein; her life was rushing out at every pore; so that the money sent to her for charity was only so much added to landlords' rents and Englishmen's profits. The American corn was only so much given as a handsome present to the merchants and speculators—that is, the English got it.

But no Irishman begged the world for alms. The benevolence of Americans, and Australians, and Turks, and Negro slaves, was excited by the appeals of the English press and English members of Parliament; and in Ireland many a cheek burned with shame and indignation at our country being thus held up to the world, by the people who were feeding on our vitals, as abject beggars of broken victuals. The Repeal Association, low as it had fallen, never sanctioned this mendicancy. The true nationalists of Ireland, who had been forced to leave that Association, and had formed another society, the "Irish Confederation," never ceased to expose the real nature of these British dealings—never ceased to repudiate and disavow the British beggarly appeals; although they took care to express warm gratitude for the well-meant charity of foreign nations; and never ceased to proclaim that the sole and all-sufficient "relief measure" for the country would be, that the English should let us alone.

On the 16th of March, for example, a meeting of the citizens of Dublin assembled, by public requisition, at the Music Hall, presided over by the Lord Mayor, expressly to consider the peril of the country, and petition Parliament for proper remedies. It was known that the conveners of the meeting contemplated nothing more than suggestions as to importing grain in ships of war, stopping distillation from grain, and other trifles. Richard O'Gorman was then a prominent member of the Irish Confederation; and being a citizen of Dublin, he resolved to attend this meeting, and if nobody else should say the right word, say it himself. After some helpless talk about the "mistakes" and "infatuation" of Parliament, and suggestions for change in various details, O'Gorman rose, and in a powerful and indignant speech moved this resolution:—

"That for purposes of temporary relief, as well as permanent improvement, the one great want and demand of Ireland is, that foreign legislators and foreign ministers shall no longer interfere in the management of her affairs."

In this speech he charged the Government with being the "murderers of the people," and said:—

"Mr. Fitzgibbon has suggested that the measures of Government may have been adopted under an infatuation. I believe there is no infatuation. I hold a very different opinion on the subject. I think the

British Government are *doing what they intend to do.*"

Another citizen of Dublin seconded Mr. O'Gorman's resolution, and the report of his observations has these sentences:—

"I have listened with pain and disappointment to the proceedings of a meeting purporting to be a meeting of the citizens of Dublin, called at such a crisis, and to deliberate upon so grave a subject, yet at which the resolutions and speakers, as with one consent, have carefully avoided speaking out what nine-tenths of us feel to be the plain truth in this matter. But the truth, my lord, must be told—and the truth is, that Ireland starves and perishes, simply because the English have eaten us out of house and home. Moreover, that all the legislation of their Parliament is, and will be, directed to this one end—to enable them hereafter to eat us out of house and home as heretofore. It is for that sole end they have laid their grasp upon Ireland, and it is for that, and that alone, they will try to keep her."

Greatly to the consternation of the quiet and submissive gentlemen who had convened the meeting, O'Gorman's resolution was adopted by overwhelming acclamation.

Take another illustration of the spirit in which British charity was received by the Irish people. The harvest of Ireland was abundant and superabundant in 1847, as it had been the year before. The problem was, as before, to get it quietly and peacefully over to England. First, the Archbishop of Canterbury issued a form of thanksgiving for an "abundant harvest," to be read in all churches on Sunday, the 17th of October. One Trevelyan, a Treasury clerk, had been sent over to Ireland on some pretence of business, and the first thing he did when he landed was to transmit to England a humble intreaty that the Queen would deign to issue a Royal "Letter," asking alms in all the churches on the day of thanksgiving. The petition was complied with; the *Times* grumbled against those eternal Irish beggars; and the affair was thus treated in the *Nation*, which certainly spoke *for the people* more authentically than any other journal:—

"Cordially, eagerly, thankfully, we agree with the English *Times*, in this one respect—*there ought to be no alms for Ireland*.

"It is an impudent proposal, and ought to be rejected with scorn and contumely. We are sick of this eternal begging. If but one voice in Ireland should be raised against it, that voice shall be ours. To-morrow, to-morrow, over broad England, Scotland, and Wales, the people who devour our substance from year to year are to offer up their canting thanksgivings for our 'abundant harvest,' and fling us certain crumbs and crusts of it for charity. Now, if any church-going Englishman will hearken to us, if we may be supposed in any degree to speak for our countrymen, we put up our petition *thus:* 'Keep your alms, ye canting robbers—button your pockets upon the Irish plunder that is in them—and let the begging-box pass on. Neither as *loans* nor as *alms* will we take that which is our own. We spit upon the benevolence that robs us of a pound, and flings back a penny in *charity*. Contribute now if you will—these will be your thanks!'

"But who has craved this charity? Why, the Queen of England, and her Privy-Council, and two officers of her Government, named Trevelyan and Burgoyne! No Irishman, that we know of, has begged alms from England.

"But the English insist on our remaining beggars. Charitable souls that they are! they like better to give us charity than let us earn our bread. And consider the time when this talk of almsgiving begins: our 'abundant harvest,' for which they are to thank God to-morrow, is still here; and there has been talk of keeping it here. So they say to one another: 'Go to; let us promise them charity and church subscriptions—they are a nation of beggars—they would rather have alms than honest earnings—let us talk of *alms*, and they will send us the bread from their tables, the cattle from their pastures, and the coats from their backs.'

"We charge the 'Government,' we charge the Cabinet Council at Osborne House, with this base plot. We tell our countrymen that a man named Trevelyan, a Treasury clerk—the man who advised and administered the Labour-Rate Act—that this Trevelyan has been sent to Ireland, that he, an Englishman, may send over from this side the Channel a petition to the charitable in England. We are to be made to beg, whether we will or no. The Queen begs for us; the Archbishop of Canterbury begs for us; and they actually send a man to Ireland that a veritable *Irish* begging petition may not be awanting.

"From Salt Hill Hotel, at Kingstown, this piteous cry goes forth to England. 'In justice,' Trevelyan says, 'to those who have appointed a general collection in the churches on the 17th, and still more in pity to the unhappy people in the Western districts of Ireland,' he implores his countrymen to have mercy; and gets his letter published in the London papers (along with another from Sir John Burgoyne), to stimulate the charity of those good and well-fed Christians who will enjoy the luxury of benevolence to-morrow.

"Once more, then, we scorn, we repulse, we curse, all English alms; and only wish these sentiments of ours could reach, before noon to-morrow, every sanctimonious thanksgiver in England, Scotland, Wales, and Berwick-upon-Tweed."

In the same number the *Nation* took the pains to collect and present statistics by which it appeared that *every day*, one day with another, twenty large steamships, not counting sailing vessels, left Ireland for England, all laden with that "abundant harvest," for which the English, indeed, might well give thanks in their churches.

It must be acknowledged that if the English Government and people really and truly did endeavour to relieve the famine in their sister country, that generosity met a most ungrateful return—from a people, too, who are proverbially warm-hearted.

For the famine of 1847, it is only needful to add that, during this year, coroners' juries in several counties repeatedly, on inquests over famine-slain corpses, found, upon their oaths, verdicts of "Wilful Murder against John Russell, commonly called Lord John Russell," he being then the Queen's Prime Minister.

The verdict was perfectly justifiable, and the crime quite manifest; but as there was no power to bring the criminal over to Ireland for trial, and as there would have been no use in arraigning him before an English jury, he was never brought to justice.

It is essential that foreign nations should never believe, for the future, (what the English press has diligently inculcated), that our people, when smitten by famine, fell a-begging from England or from America. Let them never hereafter wonder when they meet with Irishmen ungrateful for the "relief measures"—and, above all, if Ireland should again starve (as she is most likely to do), and should still be under British dominion, let them never send her a bushel of corn or a dollar of money. Neither bushel nor dollar will ever reach her.

In February, 1847, and amidst the deepest gloom and horror of the famine, O'Connell, old, sick, and heavy-laden, left Ireland, and left it for ever. Physicians in London recommended a journey to the south of Europe, and O'Connell himself desired to see the Pope before he died, and to breathe out his soul at Rome, in the choicest odour of sanctity. By slow and painful stages he proceeded only as far as Genoa, and there died on the 15th of May.

For those who were not close witnesses of Irish politics in that day—who did not see how vast this giant figure loomed in Ireland and in England for a generation and a half—it is not easy to understand the strong emotion caused by his death, both in friends and enemies. Yet, for a whole year before, he had sunk low indeed. His power had departed from him; and in presence of the terrible apparition of his perishing country, he had seemed to shrink and wither. Nothing can be conceived more helpless than his speeches in Conciliation Hall, and his appeals to the British Parliament during that time; yet, as I before said, he never begged *alms* for Ireland—he never fell so low as that; and the last sentences of the very last letter he ever penned to the Association still proclaim the true doctrine:—

"It will not be until after the deaths of hundreds of thousands that the regret will arise that more was not done to save a sinking nation.

"How different would the scene be if we had our own Parliament—taking care of our own people—of our own resources. But, alas! alas! it is scarcely permitted to think of these, the only sure preventatives of misery, and the only sure instruments of Irish prosperity."

To no Irishman can the wonderful life of O'Connell fail to be impressive—from the day when, a fiery and thoughtful boy, he sought the cloisters of St. Omers for the education which penal laws denied him in his own land, on through the manifold struggles and victories of his earlier career, as he broke and flung off, with a kind of haughty impatience, link after link of the social and political chain that six hundred years of steady British policy had woven around every limb and muscle of his country, down to that supreme moment of the blackness of darkness for himself and for Ireland, when he laid down his burden and closed his eyes. Beyond a doubt his death was hastened by the misery of seeing his proud hopes dashed to the earth, and his well-beloved people perishing; for there dwelt in that brawny frame tenderness and pity soft as a woman's. To the last he laboured on the "Relief Committees" of Dublin, and thought every hour lost unless employed in rescuing some of the doomed.

O'Connell's body rests in Ireland, but without his heart. He gave orders that the heart should be removed from his body and sent to Rome. The funeral was a great and mournful procession through the streets of Dublin; and it will show how wide was the alienation which divided him from his former confederates, that, when O'Brien signified a wish to attend the obsequies, a public letter from John O'Connell sullenly forbade him.

In the year 1847 great and successful exertions were used to make sure that the next year should be a year of famine too. This was effected mainly by holding out the prospect of "out-door relief"—to obtain which tenants must abandon their lands and leave them untilled. A paragraph from a letter of Mr. Fitzpatrick, parish priest of Skibbereen, contains within it an epitome of the history of that year. It was published in the *Freeman*, March 12th:—

"The ground continues unsown and uncultivated. There is a mutual distrust between the landlord and the tenant. The landlord would wish, if possible, to *get up his land;* and the unfortunate tenant is anxious to stick to it as long as he can. A good many, however, are giving it up, and preparing for America; and these are the substantial farmers who have still a little means left."

"A gentleman travelling from Borris-in-Ossory to Kilkenny, one bright spring morning, counts at both sides of the road, in a distance of twenty-four miles, 'nine men and four ploughs' occupied in the fields; but sees multitudes of wan labourers, 'beyond the power of computation by a mail-car passenger,' labouring to destroy the road he was travelling upon. It was a 'public work.'"—*Dublin Evening Mail.*

In the same month of March, "the land," says the Mayo *Constitution*, "is one vast waste: a soul is not to be seen working on the holdings of the poor farmers throughout the country, and those who have had the prudence to plough or dig the ground, are *in fear* of throwing in the seed."

When the new "Out-door Relief Act" began to be applied, with its memorable quarter-acre clause, all this process went on with wonderful velocity, and millions of people were soon left landless and homeless. That they should be left landless and homeless was strictly in accordance with British policy; but then there was danger of the millions of outcasts becoming robbers and murderers. Accordingly, the next point was to clear the country of them, and diminish the poor rates, by *emigration.*

For, though they were perishing fast of hunger and typhus, they were not perishing fast enough. It was inculcated by the English press that the temperament and disposition of the Irish people fitted them peculiarly for some remote country in the East, or in the West—in fact, for any country but their own—that Providence had committed some mistake in causing them to be born in Ireland. As usual, the *Times* was foremost in finding out this singular freak of nature. Says the *Times* (February 22, 1847):—

"Remove Irishmen to the banks of the Ganges or the Indus—to Delhi, Benares, or Trincomalee—and they would be far more in their element there than *in a country to which an inexorable fate has confined them.*"

Again, a Mr. Murray, a Scotch banker, writes a pamphlet upon the proper measures for Ireland. "The surplus population of Ireland," says Mr. Murray, "have been trained *precisely* for those pursuits which the unoccupied regions of North America require." Which might appear strange—a population expressly trained, and that *precisely*, to suit any country except their own!

But these are comparatively private and individual suggestions. In April of this year, however, six peers and twelve commoners, who call themselves Irish, but who include among them such "Irishmen" as Dr. Whately and Mr. Godley, laid a scheme before Lord John Russell, for the transportation of one million and a half of Irishmen to Canada, at a cost of nine millions sterling, to be charged on "Irish property," and to be paid by an income-tax.

Again, within the same year, a few months later, a "Select Committee" (and a very select one) of the House of Lords brings up a report "On Colonization from Ireland." Their lordships report that all former committees on the state of Ireland (with one exception) had agreed, at least on this point, that it was necessary to remove the "excess of labour." They say:—

"They have taken evidence respecting the state of Ireland, of the British North American Colonies (including Canada, New Brunswick, Nova Scotia, Newfoundland), the West India Islands, New South Wales, Port Philip, South Australia, Van Diemen's Land, and New Zealand. On some of these points it will be found that their inquiries have little more than commenced; on others, that those inquiries have been carried somewhat nearer to completion; but in no case can it be considered that the subject is yet exhausted. . . . The committee are fully aware that they have as yet examined into many points but superficially, and that some—as, for example, the state of the British possessions in *Southern Africa*, and in the Territory of *Natal*—have not yet been considered at all. Neither have they obtained adequate information respecting what we sincerely hope may hereafter be considered as the prospering settlement of *New Zealand*. The important discoveries of Sir T. Mitchell in Australia have also been but slightly noticed."

It appears that any inquiry into the state of Ireland naturally called their lordships to a consideration distant of latitudes and longitudes.

Their lordships further declare that the emigration which they recommend must be "voluntary"—and, also, that "there was a deep and pervading anxiety for emigration exhibited by the people themselves."

A deep and pervading anxiety to fly—to escape any whither! From whom? Men pursued by wild beasts will show a pervading anxiety to go *anywhere* out of reach. If a country be made too hot to hold its inhabitants, they will be willing even to throw themselves into the sea.

All this while, that there were from four to five millions of acres of improvable waste lands in Ireland—and even from the land in cultivation Ireland was exporting food enough every year to sustain eight millions of people in England.

None of the vast public schemes of emigration was adopted by Parliament in its full extent; though aid was, from time to time, given to minor projects for that end; and landlords continued very busy all this year and the next, shipping all their "surplus tenantry" by their own private resources, thinking it cheaper than to maintain them by rates. The Poor law guardians, also, were authorized to transport paupers, and to appropriate part of the rates to that purpose.

There has now been laid before the reader a complete sketch, at least in outline, of the British famine policy—expectation of Government spoon-feeding at the point of police bayonets—shaking the farmers loose from their lands, employing them for a time on strictly public useless works, then disgorging them in crowds of one hundred thousand at a time, to beg, or rob, or perish—then "out-door relief," administered in quantities altogether infinitesimal in proportion to the need—then that universal ejectment, the quarter-acre law—then the corruption of the middle class by holding out the prize of ten thousand new Government situations—then the Vagrancy Act, to make criminals of all houseless wanderers—then the "voluntary" emigration schemes—then the omnipresent police, hanging like a cloud over the houses of all "suspected persons"—that is, all persons who still kept a house over their heads—then the quarantine regulations, and increased fare for *deck* passengers to England, thus debarring the doomed race from all escape at that side, and leaving them the sole alternative—America or the grave. This gives something like a map or plan of the field as laid out and surveyed for the final conquest of the island.

The Irish landlords were now in dire perplexity. Many of them were good and just men; but the vast majority were fully identified in interest with the British Government, and desired nothing so much as to destroy the population. They would not consent to tenant-right; they dared not trust themselves in Ireland without a British army. They may have felt, indeed, that they were themselves both injured and insulted by the whole system of English legislation; but they would submit to anything rather than fraternize with the injured Catholic Celts. A few landlords and other gentlemen met and formed an "Irish Council;" but these were soon frightened into private life again by certain revolutionary proposals of some members, and especially by the very name of tenant-right. At last, about the end of this year, seeing that *another* season's famine was approaching, and knowing that violent counsels began to prevail amongst the extreme section of the national party, the landlords, in guilty and cowardly rage and fear, called on Parliament for a new Coercion Act.

From this moment all hope that the landed gentry would stand on the side of Ireland against England utterly vanished. This deadly alliance between the landlords and the Government brought Irish affairs to a crisis, broke up the "Irish Confederation," (composed of the extreme nationalists, who could no longer exist in the Repeal Association), and provoked an attempt at insurrection.

Before going further, however, three facts should be mentioned: *First*, That by a careful census of the agricultural produce of Ireland for this year, 1847, made by Captain Larcom, as a Government Commissioner, the total value of that produce was £44,958,120 sterling; which would have amply sustained *double* the entire people of the island.* This return is given in detail, and agrees generally with another estimate of the same, prepared by

* In Thom's *Official Almanac and Directory*, the Government has taken care to suppress the statement of gross amount.

John Martin, of Loughorn, in the County Down—a gentleman whose name will be mentioned again in this narrative. Second, That at least five hundred thousand human beings perished this year of famine, and of famine-typhus;* and two hundred thousand more fled beyond the sea to escape famine and fever. Third, That the loans for relief given to the Public Works and Public Commissariat Departments to be laid out as they should think proper, and to be repaid by rates on Irish property, went in the first place to maintain ten thousand greedy officials; and that the greater part of these funds never reached the people at all, or reached them in such a way as to ruin and exterminate them.

A kind of sacred wrath took possession of a few Irishmen at this period. They could endure the horrible scene no longer, and resolved to cross the path of the British car of conquest, though it should crush them to atoms.

CHAPTER XXV.

1847—1848.

Lord Clarendon Viceroy—His Means of Insuring the Shipment to England of the Usual Tribute—Bribes the Baser Sort of Editors—Patronage for Catholic Lawyers—Another Coercion Act—Projects for Stopping Export of Grain—Arming—Alarm of Government—Whigs Active in Coercion—French Revolution of February—Confederate Clubs—Deputation from Dublin to Paris—O'Brien's Last Appearance in Parliament—Trials of O'Brien and Meagher—Trial of Mitchel—Packing of the Jury—Reign of Terror in Dublin.

In the summer of this year, 1847, Lord Clarendon was sent over as Lord-Lieutenant to finish the conquest of Ireland—just as Lord Mountjoy had been sent to bring to an end the wars of Queen Elizabeth's reign; and by the same means substantially—that is, by corruption of the rich and starvation of the poor. The form of procedure, indeed, was somewhat different; for English statesmen of the sixteenth century had not learned to use the weapons of "amelioration" and "political economy;" neither had they yet established the policy of keeping Ireland as a store-farm to raise wealth for England. Lord Mountjoy's system, then, had somewhat of a rude character; and he could think of nothing better than sending large bodies of troops to cut down the green corn, and burn the houses. In one expedition into Leinster, his biographer, Moryson, estimates that he destroyed "ten thousand pounds worth of corn," that is, wheat; an amount which might now be stated at £200,000 worth. In O'Cahan's country, in Ulster, as the same Moryson tells us, after a *razzia* of Mountjoy: "We have none left to give us opposition, nor of late have seen any but dead carcases, merely starved for want of meat." So that Mountjoy could boast he had given Ireland to Elizabeth "nothing but carcases and ashes."

Lord Clarendon's method was more in the spirit of the nineteenth century, though his slaughters were more terrible in the end than Mountjoy's. Again there was growing upon Irish soil a noble harvest; but it had been more economical to carry it over to England by help of free trade than to burn it on the ground. The problem then was, as it had been the last year, and the year before, how to insure its speedy and peaceful transmission. Accordingly, Lord Clarendon came over with conciliatory speeches, and large professions of the desire of "Government" now, at last, to stay the famine. Sullen murmurs had been heard, and even open threats and urgent recommendations that the Irish harvest must not be suffered to go another year; and there were rumours of risings in the harvest to break up the roads, to pull down the bridges, in every way to stop the tracks of this fatal "commerce;" rumours, in short, of an insurrection. Some new method, then, had to be adopted, to turn the thoughts and hopes of that too credulous people once more towards the "Government." Lord Clarendon recommended a tour of agricultural "lectures," the expense to be provided for by the Royal Agricultural Society, aided by public money. The lecturers were to go upon every estate, call the people together, talk to them of the benevolent intentions of his Excellency, and give them good advice.

The poor people listened respectfully, but usually told the lecturers that there was no use in following that excellent agricultural advice, as they were all going to be *turned out* the next spring. These lecturers published their report—a most amazing picture of patient suffering on the one hand, and of official insolence on the other. One Fitzgerald, a most energetic lecturer, full of Liebig's *Agricultural Chemistry*, tells us: "They all agreed that what I said was just; but they always had *some excuse*, that they could not get seed, or had nothing to live on in the meantime."

---

* The deaths by famine of the year *before*, we may set down at three hundred thousand. There is no possibility of ascertaining the numbers: and when the Government Commissioners pretend to do so, they intend deception.

And a Mr. Goode, who was also instructing the West, says:—

"The poor people here appeared to be in a most desponding state: they always met me with the argument that there was no use in their working there, for they were going to be turned out in spring, and would have their houses pulled down over them. I used to tell them that I had nothing to do with that; that I was sent among them by some kind, intelligent gentlemen, barely to tell them *what course to pursue.*"

That was all. Lord Clarendon had not sent down Mr. Goode to lecture on *tenant-right;* and the people had no business to obtrude their Jacobin principles upon a Government "instructor." They might as well have prated to him about repeal of the Union.

Another measure of Lord Clarendon was to buy support at the press with secret-service money. To the honour of the Dublin press, this was a somewhat difficult matter. The Government had, at that time, only one leading journal in the metropolis on which it could surely rely—the *Evening Post.* Lord Clarendon wanted another organ, and of lower species; for he had work to do which the comparatively respectable *Post* might shrink from. He sought out a creature named Birch, editor of the *World*, a paper which was never named nor alluded to by any reputable journal in the city. This Birch lived by *hush-money,* or black-mail of the most infamous kind—that is, extorting money from private persons, men and women, by threats of inventing and publishing scandalous stories of their domestic circles. He had been tried more than once and convicted of this species of swindling. "I then offered him £100, if I remember rightly," says Lord Clarendon,* "for it did not make any great impression on me at the time. He said that would not be sufficient for his purpose, and I think it was then extended to about £350." On further examination, his lordship confessed that he had paid Birch "further sums" —in short, kept him regularly in pay; and, finally, on Birch bringing suit against him for the balance due for "work and labour," had paid him in one sum £2000, at the same time taking up all the papers and letters (as he thought) which might bring the transaction to light. Everybody can guess the nature of Birch's work and labour, and *quantum meruit.* His duty was to make weekly attacks of a private and revolting nature upon Smith O'Brien, upon Mr. Meagher, upon Mr. Mitchel, and every one else who was prominent in resisting and exposing the Government measures. Further, the public money was employed in the gratuitous distribution of the *World;* for, otherwise, decent persons would never have seen it.

It was long afterwards that the public learned how all this subterranean agency had come to light, on the trial of one of the suits which Birch was forced to institute for recovery of his wages.

A third measure of the Viceroy was—extreme liberality towards Catholic lawyers and gentlemen in the distribution of patronage; that so they might be the more effectually bought off from all common interest and sympathy with the "lower orders," and might stand patiently by and see their people slain or banished. Amongst others, Mr. Monahan, an industrious and successful Catholic barrister, was made Attorney-General for Ireland, from which the next step was to the bench. Mr. Monahan became a grateful and useful servant to the enemies of his country.

The summer of '47 had worn through wearily and hopelessly. All endeavours to rouse the landlord class to exertion entirely failed, through their coward fear of an outraged and plundered people; and, at last, when out of the vast multitudes of men thrown from public works, houseless and famishing, a few committed murders and robberies, or shot a bailiff or an incoming tenant, the landlords in several counties besought for a new Coercion and Arms Act, so as to make that code more stringent and inevitable. Lord John Russell was but too happy to comply with the demand; but the landlords were to give something in exchange for this security.

Addresses of confidence were voted by Grand Juries and county meetings of landlords. The Irish gentry almost unanimously volunteered addresses denouncing repeal and repealers, and pledging themselves to maintain the Union. At the same time ejectment was more active than ever; and it is not to be denied that, amongst the myriads of desperate men who then wandered houseless, there were some who would not die tamely. Before taking their last look at the sun, they could, at least, lie in wait for the agent who had pulled down their houses and turned their weeping children adrift; him, at least, they could send to perdition before them.

The crisis was come. The people no longer trusted the ameliorative professions of their enemies; and there were some who zealously strove to rouse them now, at last, to stand up for their own lives, to keep

---

* See evidence on the trial, Birch against Sir T. Redington.

the harvest of '47 within the four seas of Ireland, and by this one blow to prostrate Irish landlordism and the British empire along with it.

This was a perilous, and, perhaps, an utterly desperate enterprise, while England was at peace with all the world, and at full liberty to hurl the whole mass of her military power upon a small island which she already held with so firm a grasp. Even those who counselled armed resistance were fully conscious of the desperation of that course, but honestly thought that any death—especially death in just war—was better than the death of a dog, by hunger.

In the meantime, the beautiful metropolis of Ireland was extremely gay and brilliant. After two years' frightful famine—and when it was already apparent that the *next* famine, of 1847-48, would be even more desolating—you may imagine that Dublin city would show some effect or symptom of such a national calamity. Singular to relate, that city had never before been so gay and luxurious; splendid equipages had never before so crowded the streets; and the theatres and concert-rooms had never been filled with such brilliant throngs. In truth, the rural gentry resorted in greater numbers to the metropolis at this time: some to avoid the sight and sound of the misery which surrounded their country seats, and which British laws almost expressly enacted they should *not* relieve; some to get out of reach of an exasperated and houseless peasantry. Any stranger arriving in those days, guided by judicious friends only through fashionable streets and squares, introduced only to proper circles, would have said that Dublin must be the prosperous capital of some wealthy and happy country.

The new Poor law was now on all hands admitted to be a failure—that is, a failure as to its ostensible purpose. For its real purpose—reducing the body of the people to "able-bodied pauperism"—it had been no failure at all, but a complete success. Nearly ten millions sterling had now been expended under the several Relief Acts—expended mostly in salaries to officials; the rest laid out in useless work, or in providing rations, for a short time, to induce small farmers to give up their land, which was the condition of such relief. Instead of ten millions in three years, if twenty millions had been advanced in the first year, and expended on useful labour (that being the sum which had been devoted promptly to turning wild the West India negroes), the whole famine slaughter might have been averted, and the whole advance would have been easily repaid to the Treasury.*

Long before the Government Commissioners had proclaimed their law a failure, the writers in the *Nation* had been endeavouring to turn the minds of the people towards the only real remedy for all their evils—that is, a combined movement to prevent the export of provisions, and to resist process of ejectment. This involved a denial of rent and refusal of rates; involved, in other words, a root-and-branch revolution, socially and politically.

Such revolutionary ideas could only be justified by a desperate necessity, and by the unnatural and fatal sort of connection between Irish landlords and Irish tenants. The peasantry of England, of Scotland, and of Ireland, stand in three several relations towards the lords of their soil. In England they are simply the emancipated serfs and *villeins* of the feudal system; never knew any other form of social polity, nor any other lords of the soil, since the Norman conquest. As England, however, prosecuted her conquests by degrees in the other two kingdoms, she found the free Celtic system of clanship; and as rebellion after rebellion was crushed, her statesmen insisted upon regarding the chiefs of clans as feudal lords, and their clansmen as their vassals or tenants. In Scotland the chiefs gladly assented to this view of the case, and the MacCallum More became, nothing loath, Duke of Argyle, and owner of the territory which had been the tribe lands of his clan. Owing mainly to the fact that estates in Scotland were not so tempting a prey as the rich tracts of Ireland, and partly owing also to the Scottish people having generally become Protestants on the change of religion, there was but little change in the ruling families; and the Scottish clansmen, now become "tenantry," paid their duties to the heads of their own kindred as before. So it has happened that to this day there is no alienation of feeling or distinction of race to exasperate the lot of the poor cultivators of the soil.

In Ireland, wherever the chiefs turned Protestant, and chose to accept "grants" of their tribe lands at the hands of British kings (as the De Burghs and O'Briens), much the same state of things took place for a while. But Ireland never submitted to English dominion as Scotland has done;

* Of the £10,000,000 advanced by the Treasury, three millions had been repaid by rates in 1854. What may have been refunded since, it is not easy to learn with any accuracy. The accounts between Ireland and the Imperial Treasury are kept in England.

and there were continual "rebellions" (so the English termed our national resistance), followed by extensive confiscations. Many hundreds of great estates in Ireland have thus been confiscated twice and three times; and the new proprietors were Englishmen, and, in a portion of Ulster, Scotchmen. These, of course, had no common interest or sympathy with the people, whom they considered and called "the Irish enemy." Still, while Ireland had her own Parliament, and the landlords resided at home, the state of affairs was tolerable; but when the Act of "Union," in 1800, concentrated the pride and splendour of the empire at London, and made England the great field of ambition and distinction, most of our grandees resided out of Ireland, kept agents and bailiffs there, wrung the utmost farthing out of the defenceless people, and spent it elsewhere.

Now, it never would have entered the mind of any rational or just man, at this late date, to call in question the title to long ago confiscated estates; nor, supposing those titles proved bad, would it have been possible to find the right owners. But when the system was found to work so fatally—when hundreds of thousands of people were lying down and perishing in the midst of abundance, and superabundance, which their own hands had created—society itself stood dissolved. That form of society was not only a failure, but an intolerable oppression, and cried aloud to be cut up by the roots and swept away.

Those who thought thus, had reconciled their minds to the needful means—that is, a revolution as fundamental as the French revolution, and to the wars and horrors incident to that. The horrors of war, they knew, were by no means so terrible as the horrors of peace which their own eyes had seen; they were ashamed to see their kinsmen patiently submitting to be starved to death, and longed to see blood flow, if it were only to show that blood still flowed in Irish veins.

The enemy began to take genuine alarm at these violent doctrines—especially as they found that the people were taking them to heart; and already, in Clare County, mobs were stopping the transport of grain towards the seaports. If rents should cease to be levied, it was clear that not only would England lose her five millions sterling *per annum* of absentee rents, but mortgagees, fundholders, insurance companies, and the like, would lose dividends, interests, bonus, and profits. There was then in England a gentleman who was in the habit of writing able but sanguinary exhortations to ministers, with the signature "S. G. O." His addresses appeared in the *Times*, and were believed to influence considerably the counsels of Government. In November, 1847, this "S. G. O." raised the alarm, and called for prompt coercion in Ireland. Here is one sentence from a letter of his reverence —for "S. G. O." was a clergyman:—

"Lord John may safely believe me when I say that the prosperity, nay, almost the very existence of many insurance societies, the positive salvation from utter ruin of many, very many *mortgagees*, depends on some instant steps to make life ordinarily secure in Ireland; of course, I only mean life in that class of it in which individuals effect insurances and give mortgages."

In short, his reverence meant high life. Lord Clarendon, as Parliament was not then sitting, issued an admonitory address, wherein he announced that—

"The constabulary will be increased in all disturbed districts (whereby an additional burden will be thrown upon the rates), military detachments will be stationed wherever necessary, and efficient patrols maintained; liberal rewards will be given for information," &c.

In the meantime, large forces were concentrated at points where the spirit of resistance showed itself; for a sample of which we take a paragraph from the Tipperary *Free Press*:—

"A large military force, under the civil authority, has seized upon the produce of such farms in Boytonrath as owed rent and arrears to the late landlord, Mr. Roe, and the same will be removed to Dublin, and sold there, if not redeemed within fourteen days. There are two hundred soldiers and their officers garrisoned in the mansion house at Rockwell."

Whereupon, the *Nation* urged the people to begin calculating whether ten times the whole British army would be enough to act as bailiffs and drivers everywhere at once; or, whether, if they did, the proceeds of the distress might answer expectation. In fact, it was obvious that if the enemy should be forced to employ their forces in this way over the island— to lift and carry the whole harvests of Ireland, and that over roads broken up and bridges broken down to obstruct them, and with the daily risk of meeting bands of able-bodied paupers to dispute their passage—the service would soon have been wholly demoralized, and after three months of such employment, the remnant of the army might have been destroyed.

Parliament was called hastily together. Her Majesty told the Houses that there were atrocious crimes in Ireland—a spirit of insubordination, an organized resistance to "legal rights;" and, of course, that she required "additional power" for the protection of life—that is, high life.

The meaning of this was a new Coercion bill. It was carried without delay, and with unusual unanimity; and it is instructive here to note the difference between a Whig in power and a Whig out. When Sir Robert Peel had proposed his Coercion bill *the year before*, it had been vehemently opposed by Lord John Russell and Lord Grey. It was time to have done with coercion, they had said; Ireland had been "misgoverned:" there had been too many Arms Acts; it was "justice" that was wanted now; and they, the Whigs, were the men to dispense it. Earl Grey, speaking of the *last* Coercion bill (it was brought in by the other party), said, emphatically (*see debate in the Lords, March* 23, 1846), "that measures of severity had been tried long enough;" and repeated with abhorrence the list of coercive measures passed since 1800, all without effect; how, in 1800, the *Habeas Corpus* Act was suspended, the Act for the Suppression of the Rebellion being still in force; how coercion was renewed in 1801; continued again in 1804; how the Insurrection Act was passed in 1807, which gave the Lord-Lieutenant full and legal power to place any district under martial law, to suspend trial by jury, and make it a transportable offence to be out of doors from sunset to sunrise; how this Act remained in force till 1810; how it was renewed in 1814—continued in '15, '16, '17—revived in '22, and continued through '23, '24, and '25; how another Insurrection Act was needed in 1833, was renewed in '34, and expired but five years ago. "And again," continued this Whig, "again in 1846, we are called on to renew it!" Horrible!—revolting to a Liberal out of place! "We must look further," continued Earl Grey—vociferating from the opposition bench—"we must look to the root of the evil; the state of law and the habits of the people, *in respect to the occupation of land*, are almost at the roots of the disorder;—it was undeniable that the *clearance system* prevailed to a great extent in Ireland; and that such things could take place, he cared not how large a population might be suffered to grow up in a particular district, was *a disgrace to a civilized country.*"

And Lord John Russell in the Commons had said, on the same occasion : "If they were to deal with the question of the crimes, they were bound to consider also whether there were not measures that might be introduced which would reach *the causes of those crimes*"—and he horrified the House by an account he gave them of "a whole village, containing two hundred and seventy persons, razed to the ground, and the entire of that large number of individuals sent adrift on the highroad, to sleep under the hedges, without even being permitted the privilege of boiling their potatoes, or obtaining shelter among the walls of the houses." Disgusting!—to a Whig statesman in opposition!

Now, these very same men had had the entire control and government of Ireland for a year and a half. Not a single measure had been proposed by them in that time to reach "the cause of those crimes;" not a single security had been given "in respect of the occupation of land;" not one check to that terrible "clearance system," which was "a disgrace to a civilized country." On the contrary, every measure was carefully calculated to accelerate the clearance system; and the Government had helped that system ruthlessly by the employment of their troops and police. They had literally swept the people off the land by myriads upon myriads; and now, when their Relief Acts were admittedly a *failure*, and when multitudes of homeless peasants, transformed into paupers, were at length making the landed men, and mortgagees, and Jews, and insurance officers, tremble for their gains—the Liberal Whig Ministry had nothing to propose but more jails, more handcuffs, more transportation.

The new Coercion bill was in every respect like the rest of the series ; in Ireland, these bills are all as much like one another as one policeman's carabine is like another. Disturbed districts were to be proclaimed by the Lord-Lieutenant. He might proclaim a whole county, or the whole thirty-two counties. Once proclaimed, everybody in that district was to be within doors (whether he had a house or not) from dusk till morning. Any one found not at home, to be arrested and transported. If arms were found about any man's premises, and he could not *prove* that they were put there without his knowledge—arrest, imprisonment, and transportation. All the arms in the district to be brought in on proclamation to that effect, and piled in the police offices. Lord-Lieutenant to quarter on the district as many additional police, inspectors, detectives, and sub-inspectors, as he might think fit ; offer such rewards to informers as he might think fit; and charge all the expense upon the tenantry, to be levied by rates—*no part* of these rates to be charged to the landlords—constabulary to collect them at the point of the bayonet; and these rates to be in addition to poor rates, cess, tithe (*rent charge*), rent, and imperial taxes.

The passage of the Coercion bill at the instance of the landlords, and the break-up of the Irish Confederation, occasioned the establishment of the *United Irishman*, an avowed organ of insurrection. Events for a time moved rapidly. Soon there burst in upon us news of the February revolution in Paris, and the flight of King Louis Philippe, for between the French people and the Irish there has always been an electric telegraph whose signals never fail; and British statesmen had not forgotten that it was the first great French revolution which cost them the war of '98. The February revolution, also, at once obliterated the feuds of the Irish Confederation. Nobody would now be listened to there who proposed any other mode of redress for Irish grievances than the sword. A resolution was brought up, with the sanction of the committee, and passed with enthusiastic acclamation, that the confederate clubs should become armed and officered, so that each man should know his right-hand and his left-hand comrade, and the man whose word he should obey. All the second-rate cities, as well as Dublin, and all the country towns, were now full of clubs, which assumed military and revolutionary names—the "Sarsfield Club," the "Emmet Club," and so forth; and the business of arming proceeded with commendable activity. Such young men as could afford it, provided themselves with rifles and bayonets; those who had not the means for this, got pike-heads made, and there was much request for ash poles. What was still more alarming to the enemy, the soldiers in several garrisons were giving unmistakable symptoms of sharing in the general excitement; not Irish soldiers alone, but English and Scottish, who had Chartist ideas. A large part of the circulation of the *United Irishman*, in spite of all the exertions of the officers, was in military barracks.

Undoubtedly it behoved the British Government, if it intended to hold Ireland, to adopt some energetic measures; and, as it certainly did so intend, these measures were not wanting.

New regiments were poured into Ireland of course, and Dublin held an army of ten thousand men—infantry, cavalry, artillery, and engineers. The barrack accommodations being insufficient, many large buildings were taken as temporary barracks; the deserted palaces of the Irish aristocracy—as Aldborough House on the north-east—the deserted halls of manufactures and trade in the "Liberty," and the Linen Hall, were occupied by detachments. The Bank of Ireland—our old Parliament House—had cannon mounted over the entablatures of its stately Ionic colonnades; and the vast and splendid Custom House, not being now needed for trade (our imports being all from the "sister country," and our exports all to the same), was quite commodious as a barrack and arsenal. The quiet quadrangles of Trinity College were the scene of daily parades, and the loyal Board of that institution gave up the wing which commands Westmoreland Street, College Street, and Dame Street, to be occupied by troops. Superb squadrons of hussars, of lancers, and of dragoons, rode continually through and around the city; infantry practised platoon firing in the squares; heavy guns, strongly guarded, were for ever rolling along the pavement; and parties of horse artillery showed all mankind how quickly and dexterously they could wheel and aim, and load and fire, at the crossings of the streets. These military demonstrations, and the courts of "Law," constituted the open and avowed powers and agencies of the Government.

But there was a secret and subterranean machinery. The editor of the *World* was now on full pay, and on terms of close intimacy at the Castle and Viceregal Lodge. His paper was gratuitously furnished to all hotels and public-houses by means of secret service money. Dublin swarmed with detectives. They went at night to get their instructions at the Castle from Colonel Brown, head of the police department; and it was one of their regular duties to gain admittance to the clubs of the Confederation, where it afterwards appeared that they had been the most daring counsellors of treason and riot.

Frankly, and at once, the Confederation accepted the only policy thereafter possible, and acknowledged the meaning of the European revolutions. On the 15th of March, O'Brien moved an address of congratulation to the victorious French people; and ended his speech with these words:—

"It would be recollected that a short time ago he thought it his duty to deprecate all attempts to turn the attention of the people to military affairs, because it seemed to him that, in the then condition of the country, the only effect of leading the people's mind to what was called 'a guerrilla warfare,' would be to encourage some of the misguided peasantry to the commission of murder. Therefore it was that he declared he should not be a party to giving such a recommendation. But the state of affairs was totally different now; and he had no hesitation in declaring that he thought the minds of intelligent young men should be turned to the consideration of such questions as, how strong places can be captured, and weak ones defended—how supplies of food and ammunition can be cut off from an enemy —and how they can be secured to a friendly force. The time was also come when every lover of his country should come forward openly, and proclaim his willingness to be enrolled as a member of a national guard. No man, however, should tender his name as a member of that national guard unless he was prepared to do two things: one, to preserve the State from anarchy; the other, to be ready to die for the defence of his country."

Two days after this meeting was Saint Patrick's Day. A meeting of the citizens of Dublin was announced for that anniversary, to adopt an address, from Dublin to Paris, but was adjourned for two or three days to allow time for negotiations to unite all repealers of the two parties in the demonstration. Lord Clarendon, doubtless under the advice of his Privy-Councillor of the *World*, thought it would be a good opportunity to strike terror by a military display. He pretended to apprehend that Saint Patrick's Day would be selected for the first day of Dublin barricades; and the troops were kept under arms—the cavalry, with horses ready saddled in all the barracks, waiting for the moment to crush the first movement in the blood of our citizens.

The meeting was adjourned; but there was no intention of abandoning it. O'Brien had offered, even in case of a *Proclamation* forbidding it, to attend and take the chair; and what he promised, the enemy well knew he would perform.

The meeting was held without interruption; but it was well known that the public buildings, and some private houses, were filled with detachments under arms. These addresses, both from the Confederation and from the city, were to be presented in Paris to the President of the Provisional Government, M. de Lamartine; and O'Brien, Meagher, and an intelligent tradesman, of high character and independence of mind, named Hollywood, were appointed a deputation to Paris.

All this, it was evident, could not go on long. The clubs were, in the meantime, rapidly arming themselves with rifles; and blacksmiths' forges were prolific of pike-heads. The Confederates hoped, and the Government feared, that no armed collision would be made necessary until September, when the harvest would be all cut, and when the commissariat of the people's war, the cause of the war, and the prize of the war, would be all bound up in a sheaf together. But the foe to be dealt with was no weak fool. The Government understood these views thoroughly, and resolved to precipitate the issue somehow or other. One morning, after that meeting of Dublin citizens, three men, Smith O'Brien, Mr. Meagher, and Mr. Mitchel, were waited on by a police-magistrate, and requested to give bail that they would stand their trial on a charge of sedition. The ground of prosecution in the two former cases was the language held at the meeting of the Irish Confederation (quoted above in part). In the third case, there were two distinct indictments, for two articles in the *United Irishman*.

Before the trials, O'Brien and Meagher went to France and presented their address to the Provisional Government.*

On their return, O'Brien walked into the British Parliament, and found that august body engaged in discussing a new bill "for the further security of Her Majesty's Crown." Ministers, in fact, had determined to meet the difficulty by a new "law," the Treason-felony law, by which the writing and printing, or open and advised speaking, of incitements to insurrection in Ireland, should be deemed "felony," punishable by transportation. The bill was introduced by the Whigs, and was warmly supported by the Tories; Sir Robert Peel declaring that what Ireland needed was to make her national aspirations not only a crime, but an ignominious crime; so as to put this species of offence on a footing with arson, or forgery, or waylaying with intent to murder. O'Brien rose to address the House, and never, since first Parliament met in Westminster, was heard such a chorus of frantic and obscene outcries.

He persisted, however, and made himself

* These were mere addresses of congratulation and of sympathy. De Lamartine made a highly poetic, but rather unmeaning reply to them. He has since, in his history, violently misrepresented them; being, in fact, a mere Anglo-Frenchman. Mr. O'Brien has already convicted him of these misrepresentations. We content ourselves here with pronouncing the two following sentences poetic fictions: "Les Irlandais, unis aux chartistes Anglais, se precipitaient sur le continent et cherchaient des complicités insurrectionnelles en France, à la fois parmi les demagogues au nom de la liberté, et parmi les chefs du parti Catholique au nom du Catholicisme." And again: "L'Angleterre n'attendait pas avec moins de sollicitude la reception que ferait Lamartine aux insurgés Irlandais, partis de Dublin pour venir demander *des encouragements et des armes* à la Republique française."

heard; and those to whom the name and fame of that good Irishman are dear, will always remember with pride that his last utterance in the London Parliament was one of haughty defiance, in the name of his oppressed and plundered country. He avowed that he had advised his countrymen to arm, and fight for their right to live upon their own soil; and he added, amidst the horrible yells of the House:—

"I conceive that it is the peculiar duty of the Irish people to obtain the possession of arms at a time when you tell them you are prepared to crush their expression of opinion, not by argument, but by brute force."

The bill was passed into "law" by immense majorities; and, thereafter, an Irish repealer of the Union was to be a "felon." O'Brien returned to Dublin. The deputies were received by a multitudinous and enthusiastic meeting in the Dublin Music Hall, and Meagher presented to the citizens of Dublin, with glowing words, a magnificent flag, the Irish tricolor, of green, white, and orange, surmounted by a pike head.

The trials came on. They were to be before special juries, struck by the process before described. O'Brien and Meagher were first tried, and as their "sedition" had been so open and avowed —and as the Whig ministers were extremely reluctant to pack juries *if they could help it*—the Crown officers left on each of the two juries *one* repealer. It was enough. A true repealer knew that no Irishman *could* commit any offence against a foreign Queen; and in each case the one repealer stood out, refused to convict, though he should be starved to death; and the traversers, amidst cheering multitudes, were escorted triumphantly from the four courts to the Confederate Committee Rooms, where they addressed the people, and promised to repeat and improve upon all their seditions. The excitement of the country was intense. The defeat of the "Government" was celebrated all over the country by bonfires and illuminations, and the clubs became more diligent in arming themselves; but Mr. Monahan, the Attorney-General, foamed and raged.

Next came the two trials of Mr. Mitchel; and it was very evident to the Government that there must be no possibility of mistake or miscarriage here. The time, indeed, was become exceedingly dangerous, and the people rapidly rising into that state of high excitement in which ordinary motives and calculations fail, and a single act of desperation may precipitate a revolution. As usual in such cases, the British Government had recourse to brutality, in order to strike terror. Police magistrates were ordered to arrest parties of young men practising at targets in the neighbourhood of country towns, and march them in custody through the streets. Men in Dublin were seized upon and dragged to jail on the charge of saying "halt" to the clubmen marching to a public meeting—it was "training in military evolutions," under the Act; and one young man was actually brought to trial, and transported for seven years, on an indictment charging him, for that he had, in a private room in Dublin, said to thirteen other young men, then and there ranged in line, these fatal words, "Right shoulders forward," contrary to the peace of our lady the Queen, and so forth.

On the two juries being struck for the trial of Mr. Mitchel, it was at once evident that upon each of them would be one or two men who desired the independence of their country; and, perhaps, one or two others of whom the Castle could not be perfectly sure. But, as the new "Treason-felony" Act had now become law, the Government suddenly abandoned the two prosecutions already commenced, and arrested Mr. Mitchel on a charge of treason under the new Act.

On this occasion it was determined to proceed, not by a special, but by a common jury; which latter method, as was supposed, gave the sheriff more clear and unquestioned power of fraudulently packing the jury. For the jury was to be closely packed, of course. Lord John Russell and Mr. Macaulay, who had been in opposition in 1844, and who had then so earnestly denounced the packing of juries in Ireland, were now in office; were responsible for the Government of the country, and understood perfectly that upon the careful packing of this jury depended the Queen's Government in Ireland. The judges had already appointed the day for holding the commission to try cases in Dublin; and the sheriff had summoned his select hundred and fifty jurors to try the cases; but after the arrest of this new prisoner, and when the sheriff knew that important business was to be done, he altered his list, and summoned a new set, so that all was ready for the trial.

In the meantime Lord Clarendon was busily getting up, through the Grand Masters of the Orangemen, loyal addresses, and declarations against "rebels" and "traitors." In fact, the Orange farmers and burghers of the North were fast becoming diligent students of the *United*

Irishman, and although they and their order had been treated with some neglect of late both by England and by the Irish aristocracy, they were now taken into high favour, and arms were very secretly issued to some of their lodges from Dublin Castle.*

But this needed prudence; for Protestant Repeal Associations had been formed in Dublin, in Drogheda, and even in Lurgan, a great centre of Orangeism. To counteract the progress we had made in this direction, the aristocracy and the clergy were incessant in their efforts, and the Protestants were assured that if Ireland should throw off the dominion of Queen Victoria, we would all instantly become vassals to the woman who sitteth upon seven hills.

The Viceroy, at the same time, took care to frighten the moneyed citizens of Dublin and other towns by placards warning them against the atrocious designs of "Communists" and "Jacobins," whose only object, his lordship intimated, was plunder.†

Whether the Whigs and "Liberals" who then ruled the English councils were really desirous to give a fair trial to their political enemy, or whether they only pretended this desire, or what communications took place on the subject between Downing Street and the Castle, we cannot certainly know; but we find that only two days before this most foul pretence of a trial, Lord John Russell, in answer to questions in the House of Commons, declared that he had written to "his noble friend" (Lord Clarendon) that "he trusted there would not arise any charge of any kind of unfairness as to the composition of the juries; as for his own part, he would rather see those parties acquitted, than that there should be any such unfairness."‡

Lord Clarendon, however, informed him that for this once he could not adhere to the Whig maxims—that a conviction must be had, *per fas et nefas.*

The venerable Robert Holmes, brother-in-law of the Emmets, defended the prisoner; but no defence could avail there.

* This was quite unknown to the public at the time: one case of it only ever came clearly to light. It was a shipment of five hundred stand of arms to the Belfast Orangemen.
† These placards may be attributed to Lord Clarendon, without scruple. They were printed by the Government printer, and paid for out of our taxes. But it is quite possible that the Viceroy, if charged with these things, would deny them, because they were done through a third party—perhaps Birch. In like manner, he denied all knowledge of the shipment of muskets to the Belfast Orangemen. They were sent, however, from his Castle, and through a subordinate official of his household.
‡ Debate of 23d May.

Of course, he challenged the array of jurors, on the ground of fraud; but the Attorney-General's brother, Stephen Monahan, clerk in the Attorney-General's office, and also one Wheeler, clerk in the Sheriff's office, had been carefully sent out of the city to a distant part of Ireland; and Baron Lefroy was most happy to avail himself of the defect of evidence to give his opinion that the panel was a good and honest panel. The Crown used its privilege of peremptory challenge to the very uttermost; *every* Catholic, and *most* Protestants, who answered to their names, were ordered to "stand by." There were thirty-nine challenges, and of these but nineteen were Catholics; all the Catholics who answered to their names were promptly set aside, and twenty other gentlemen, who, although Protestants, were suspected of national feeling—that is to say, the Crown dared not go to trial before the people, Catholic or Protestant. The twelve men finally obtained by this sifting process had amongst them two or three Englishmen; the rest were faithful slaves of the Castle, and all Protestants of the most Orange dye.

Of course, there was a "verdict" of guilty; and a sentence of fourteen years' transportation. The facts charged were easily proved; they were patent, notorious, often repeated, and perfectly deliberate; insomuch, that jurymen who felt themselves to be subjects of the Queen of England, could not do otherwise than convict. On the other hand, any Irish nationalist must acquit. Never before or since have the Government of the foreign enemy and the Irish people met on so plain an issue. Never before was it made so manifest that the enemy's Government maintains its supremacy over Ireland by systematically breaking the "law," even its own law, defiling its temples of justice, and turning the judges of the land into solemn actors in a most immoral kind of play.

An armed steamer waited in the river, on the day of Mr. Mitchel's sentence; the whole garrison of Dublin was under arms, on pretence of a review in the Park; a place was secretly designated for the prisoner's embarkation below the city, where bridges over a canal, and over the entrance to the Custom House docks, could be raised, in order to prevent any concourse of the people in that direction; and, two or three hours after the sentence, Mr. Mitchel was carried off, and never saw his country any more.

The enemy were themselves somewhat surprised at the ease with which they had borne him out of the heart of Dublin, at noon-day, in chains; and evidently thought they would have but small trouble in crushing any attempt at insurrection afterwards. The confederates waited until "the time" should come; and some of them, indeed, were fully resolved to make an insurrection in the harvest. Yet, as might have been expected, "the time" never came. The individual desperation of Dillon, Meagher, O'Gorman, Leyne, Reilly, could achieve nothing while the people were dispirited both by famine and by long submission to insolent oppression. "When will *the time* come?" exclaimed Martin, "the time about which your orators so boldly vaunt, amid the fierce shouts of your applause? If it come not when one of you, selected by your enemies as your champion, is sent to perish among thieves and murderers, for the crime of loving and defending his native land—then it will never come—*never.*"

During the trial, Dublin was under a complete reign of terror. Reilly was arrested on the charge of saying to men of his club, when turning into their place of meeting, "left wheel." It was a term of military drilling, though the clubmen were without weapons. He was kept in a station-house all night; and bail was refused in the morning. In the course of the day he was fully committed for trial, and bail was taken. During the whole week, the whole large force of the city police had orders to stop all processions, to arrest citizens, on any or no charge; and generally to "strike terror." In the meantime, every day was bringing in more terrible news of the devastation of the famine, and evictions of the tenantry. "On Friday," says the Tipperary *Vindicator* (describing one of these scenes), "the landlord appeared upon the ground, attended by the sheriff and a body of policemen, and commenced the process of ejectment," &c. On that morning, and at that spot, thirty persons were dragged out of their houses, and the houses pulled down. One of the evicted tenants was a widow. "A solvent tenant comes and offers to pay the arrears due by the widow; but a desire on Mr. Scully's part to *consolidate*, prevented the arrangement."

The same week, a writer in the Cork *Examiner*, writing from Skibbereen, says:—

"Our town presents nothing but a moving mass of military and police, conveying to and from the court house crowds of famine culprits. I attended the court for a few hours this day. The dock was crowded with the prisoners, not one of whom, when called up for trial, was able to support himself in front of the dock. The sentence of the court was received by each prisoner with apparent satisfaction. Even transportation appeared to many to be a relaxation from their sufferings."

On Tuesday, of the same week — it being then well known that the Crown would pack their jury—a meeting of the citizens of Dublin was held at the Royal Exchange, to protest; and Mr. John O'Connell went so far as to move this resolution: "*Resolved*, That we consider the right of trial by a jury as a most sacred inheritance, in the security of person, property, and character." The meeting then proceeded to protest against "the practice of arranging juries to obtain convictions." During the same week the poor houses, hospitals, jails, and many buildings taken temporarily for the purpose, were overflowing with starving wretches; and fevered patients were occupying the same bed with famished corpses;—but on every day of the same week large cargoes of grain and cattle were leaving every port for England. The Orangemen of the North were holding meetings to avow hostility to repealers and to "Jezebel," and eagerly crying "To hell with the Pope!" Thus British policy was in full and successful operation at every point on the day when the Government seized on its first victim, under a new law specially made for his case, and carried him off in fetters under the false pretence of a trial and conviction.

CHAPTER XXVI.

1848—1849.

Reconstitution of the Irish Confederation—New National Journals Established—The *Tribune*—The *Felon*—New Suspension of *Habeas Corpus*—Numerous Arrests—O'Brien Attempts Insurrection—Ballingarry—Arrest and Trial of O'Brien and others—Conquest of the Island—Destruction of the People—Encumbered Estates Act—Its Effects — No Tenant-Right — "Rate-in-Aid"— Queen's Visit to Ireland—Places given to Catholics—Catholic Judges—Their Office and Duty—Ireland "Prosperous"—Statistics of the Famine Slaughter — Destruction of Three Millions of Souls—Flying from "Prosperity."

THE fierce enthusiasm of the Irish Confederates appeared to be redoubled after the removal of the first convicted "felon." They hoped, at least, that if they were restrained from action *then*, it was to some good end, with some sure and well-defined purpose; and, assuredly, there were many thousands of men then in Ireland who longed and burned for that end and that purpose, to earn an honourable death. How the British system disappointed them, even of an honourable death, remains still to be told. A man may die in Ireland of hunger, or of famine-typhus, or of a broken heart; but to die for your country—the death *dulce et decorum*—to die on a fair field fighting for freedom and honour—to die the death even of a defeated soldier, as Hofer died; or so much as to mount the gallows, like Robert Emmet, to pay the penalty of a glorious "treason"—even this was an *euthanasia* which British policy could no longer afford to an Irish nationalist.

Yet with all odds against them—with the Irish gentry thoroughly corrupted or frightened out of their senses, and with the "Government" enemy obviously bent on treating our national aspiration as an ignominious crime worthy to be ranked only with the offences of burglars or pickpockets—still, there were men resolved to dare the worst and uttermost for but one chance of rousing that down-trodden people to one manful effort of resistance against so grievous a tyranny. The Irish Confederation reconstituted its council, and set itself more diligently than ever to the task of inducing the people to procure arms, with a view to a final struggle in the harvest. And as it was clear there was nothing the enemy dreaded so much as a bold and honest newspaper which would expose their plots of slaughter, and turn their liberal professions inside out, it was, before all things, necessary to establish a newspaper to take the place of the *United Irishman.*

It was a breach as deadly and imminent as ever yawned in a beleaguered wall; but men were found prompt to stand in it. Within two weeks after Mitchel's trial the *Irish Tribune* was issued, edited by O'Dogherty and Williams, with Antisell and Savage as contributors. In two weeks more, on the 24th of June, came forth another, and, perhaps, the ablest of our revolutionary organs—the *Irish Felon.* Its editor and proprietor was John Martin, a quiet country gentleman of the County Down, who had been for years connected with all national movements in Ireland,— the Repeal Association, the Irish Confederation,—but who had never been roused to the pitch of desperate resistance till he saw the bold and dashing atrocity of the enemy on the occasion of Mitchel's pretended trial and conviction. He came at last, along with many other quiet men, to the conclusion that the nation must now set its back to the wall. James Fintan Lalor, one of the most powerful writers of his day, came up from Kildare County to aid in conducting the *Felon*, and for five weeks thereafter "Treason-felony" continued to be taught and enforced with great boldness and ability. But *six* weeks would have been too much for the patience of the Government. The police were ordered to forcibly stop the sale of papers by vendors in the streets; and warrants were issued for the arrest of all the editors—Martin, Duffy, O'Dogherty, and Williams. The country was beginning to bristle with pikes; men were praying for the whitening of the harvest; and it was plain that, before the reign of "law and order" should begin, other terrible examples must be made; other juries must be packed; then, after *that*, a Whig "Government" would surely begin to deal with Ireland in a conciliatory spirit!

Throughout all these scenes the horrible famine was raging as it had never raged before—the police and military, both in towns and in the country, were busily employed in the service of ejecting tenants—pulling down their houses—searching out and seizing hidden weapons—and escorting convoys of grain and provisions to the sea-side, as through an enemy's country. Yet rumours began to grow and spread (much-exaggerated rumours) of a very general arming amongst the peasantry and the clubmen of the towns, and the police had but small success in their searches for arms; for, in fact, these were carefully built into stone walls, or carried to the graveyards with a mourning funeral escort, and buried in coffins, shrouded in well-oiled flannel, "in hope of a happy resurrection."

The enemy thought it wisest not to wait for the harvest, and resolved to bring matters to a head at once. Accordingly, they asked Parliament to suspend the *Habeas Corpus* Act in Ireland, so as to enable them to seize upon any person or number of persons whom they might think dangerous, and throw them into prison without any charge against them. Parliament passed the bill at once; and, in truth, it is an ordinary procedure in Ireland.

Instantly numerous warrants were placed in the hands of the omnipresent police; and in every town and village in Ireland sudden arrests were made. The enemy had taken care to inform themselves who were the leading and active confederates all over the island, the presidents and secretaries of clubs, and zealous organizers of drilling and pike exercise. These were seized from day to day, sometimes with circumstances of brutality (which was useful to the enemy in "striking terror"), and thrust into dungeons, or paraded before their fellow-citizens in chains. Martin and the other editors were in Newgate prison awaiting transportation as felons. Warrants were out against O'Brien and Meagher.

Well, *the time* had come at last. If Ireland had one blow to strike, now was her day. Queen Victoria would not wait till the autumn should place in the people's hands the ample commissariat of their war, and decreed that if they *would* fight, they should, at least, fight fasting. O'Brien was at the house of a friend in Wexford County when he heard of the suspension of the *Habeas Corpus*, and that a warrant had been issued for his own arrest. He was quickly joined by Dillon and Meagher. Doheny and MacManus, with some others, betook themselves to the Tipperary hills, and "put themselves upon the country." O'Gorman hurried to Limerick and Clare to see what preparation existed there for the struggle, and to give it a direction. Reilly and Smith ranged over Kilkenny and Tipperary, eagerly seeking for insurrectionary fuel ready to be kindled, and sometimes in communication with O'Brien and his party, at other times alone. To O'Brien, on account of his character, his services, and his value to the cause, the leadership seemed to be assigned by common consent.

It is very easy for those who sat at home in those days to criticise the proceedings of O'Brien, and the brave men who sought, in his company, for an honourable chance of throwing their lives away. But it must be obvious, from the narrative of the three years' previous famine, what a hopeless sort of material for spirited national resistance was then to be found in the rural districts of Ireland. Bands of exterminated peasants, trooping to the already too full poor houses; straggling columns of hunted wretches, with their old people, wives, and little ones, wending their way to Cork or Waterford to take shipping for America; the people not yet ejected frightened and desponding, with no interest in the land they tilled, no property in the house above their heads, no food, no arms, with the slavish habits bred by long ages of oppression ground into their souls, and that momentary proud flush of passionate hope kindled by O'Connell's agitation, long since dimmed and darkened by bitter hunger and hardship. It was no easy task to rouse such a people as this. But there is in the Irish nature a wonderful spring and an intense vitality, insomuch that the chances of a successful insurrection in '48 may have been by no means desperate. At any rate, O'Brien and his comrades were resolute to give the people a chance, knowing full well that though they should be mown down in myriads by shot and steel, it would be a better lot than poor houses and famine graves.

It is needful, here, to speak of the Irish priesthood, and the part which they took in that last agony of our country. Hitherto, there has not been occasion to say much of the Catholic Church, though it makes so potent an element in Irish life, for the reason that in all vehement popular movements it always follows the people, and never leads. Unless the movement be strong and sweeping enough to command and coerce the clergy, the clergy keep aloof from it altogether. Instinctively the Church adheres to what is established, and opposes violent action. Thus, in O'Connell's Repeal agitation, several bishops held themselves neutral; and hundreds of priests, as was well known, were zealous repealers against their will—only because the popular passion was too strong for them to resist. Afterwards, however, many of the Catholic clergy had come over to the "Young Ireland" party. Some of them, indeed, being more Irishmen than Romans, did from the *first* fully sympathize with the national aspirations of their island—did profoundly feel her wrongs, and burn to redress or avenge them. When the final scene opened, however, and the whole might of the empire was gathering itself to crush us, the clergy, as a body, were found on the side of the Government, and cannot be severely blamed for it, as they were convinced of the utter hopelessness of the struggle at that time.

O'Brien, Dillon, and Meagher, with some few followers, and without arms or stores, taking the field against the potent monarchy of England, were, indeed, but a forlorn hope. They can scarcely be said to have had a plan. O'Brien resolutely refused to commence a struggle, which he felt to be for man's dearest rights, by attacking and plundering the estates and mansions of the gentry, who, however, were then generally fortified and barricaded in their own houses, to hold the country for the enemy.

For several days he went from place to place, attended by his friends, followed sometimes by two or three hundred people, half armed, always expecting to meet a party with a warrant for his arrest; in which case it would be *war*, both defensive and offensive, to the last extremity. All round him were country mansions of nobles and gentlemen who had openly avowed themselves (in their "Addresses of Confidence") for the English, and against their own people; who had publicly branded *him* as a rebel, and offered their lives and fortunes for the work of crushing him; and he, an outlaw, declined to exact contributions from them to feed his followers and hold them together. All this was resolved and done from the purest and most conscientious motives, undoubtedly; but it was, perhaps, not the best mode of commencing a revolution.

All this while, from day to day, crowds of stout men, many of them armed, flocked to O'Brien's company; but they uniformly melted off, as usual, partly compelled by want of provisions, partly under the influence of the clergy. The last time he had any considerable party together was at Ballingarry, where forty-five armed police had barricaded themselves in a strong stone house, under the command of a certain Captain Trant, who certainly had the long-expected warrant to arrest O'Brien, but who was afraid to execute it until after the arrival of some further reinforcement. O'Brien went to one of the front windows, and called on Captain Trant to surrender. Trant demanded half an hour to consider. During this half hour some of the crowd had thrown a few stones through the windows; and Captain Trant, seeing that the people could not be controlled much longer by O'Brien, gave orders to fire. O'Brien rushed between the people and the window, climbed on the window, and once more called upon the police to surrender. At the first volley from the house two men fell dead, and others were wounded, and the crowd on that side fell back, leaving O'Brien almost alone in the garden before the house.

Trant was shortly afterwards reinforced by the force he expected. Mr. O'Brien's followers were by this time scattered and gone. He scarce made an effort even to provide for his own safety, and was soon arrested.

In fact, there was no insurrection. The people in those two or three counties did not believe that he meant to fight; and nothing would persuade them of that but some desperate enterprise. Yet they were all ready and willing; and, indeed, are at all times ready and willing to fight against a dominion, which represents to them nearly all that they know of evil in this world.

From the first moment that the repeal of the *Habeas Corpus* Act placed the liberties of Irishmen at the disposal of Lord Clarendon, the police received secret orders to arrest all leading confederates, both in town and country. A return was in the beginning of the next year, 1849, made to Parliament of the number of persons, and their names, who were imprisoned under that law. There were one hundred and eighteen of them; including most of the very men on whom O'Brien might reasonably have relied to sustain his movement. They were all imprisoned in various jails, without any charge, or one word of explanation; removed in batches from one prison to some other, in a distant part of the island, with no other object, apparently, but to exhibit them in chains, and strike a wholesome terror into all spectators.

To arrive at an accurate list and due selection of leading confederates, Lord Clarendon employed without scruple both post-office spying* and the regular service of detectives.

Certain "trials" ensued in the usual style. First, the editors were brought to trial under the new "Treason-felony" Act; and O'Brien and his immediate comrades, under the Common Law, for the crime of "high treason," having appeared in arms against the "Government." The Government would gladly have dispensed with these trials, and removed their captives out of the way by a more summary process. But they must not forget that they were a "Liberal" Government, and had a reputation to support before the world. Ireland was not Naples, but, indeed, a far more miserable country, and political offenders could by no means be suffered to perish by long confinement in subterranean dungeons without trial. But, then, arose the question of juries; and the "Government" knew full well that no jury in Ireland impartially empaneled according to law, and really representing the nation, would convict one of those men for any offence whatsoever.

They could not refuse a trial; but one thing they could do, which the King of Naples had not yet learned—they could pack the juries. No doubt it was painful to have to pack juries *again.* Whig reputation could ill endure it. But they hoped this would be the last time. They knew that in the eyes of Englishmen, the extreme urgency of the occasion would justify this one last tremendous fraud. When we say, "in the eyes of Englishmen," the reader will understand that we

* The return on this subject laid before Parliament only brings down the letter-spies as far as Lord De Grey, in 1843. But as the report on the occasion declared the post-office *espionage* a needful branch of administration in Ireland, it may be assumed without scruple that it was resorted to not only by Lord Clarendon, but by every Viceroy since.

mean the ruling classes of Englishmen—namely, the landed interests, and the monied and mercantile interests; in short, those Englishmen whose opinions and interests are alone consulted in the government of that country. To *them* it was an absolute necessity of their existence that Irish national movements should be crushed down by any means and all means.

The Whig Government, in fact, felt that if they satisfied the men of rank and money in England, they did the whole duty of Whigs; and the men of rank and money were eagerly crying out to have the last embers of that long national struggle stamped out.

O'Brien, Meagher, MacManus, and O'Donohoe were to have their trial before a special commission in Clonmel, the capital of Tipperary. On the details of these trials we need not dwell, because they were on the same pattern with other scenes of this same kind already narrated. The officials of the Crown showed a stern, dogged determination to disregard every remonstrance, to refuse every application, and to do the work intrusted to them in the most coarse, insolent, and thorough-going style. For example, Mr. Whiteside, O'Brien's counsel, reminded the Court "that, *in England*, persons charged with high treason are allowed a copy of the jurors' panel, and a list of the witnesses to be examined on the part of the Crown." Here is one extract from the report of the "trial":—

"The learned counsel put it to the Court, whether Mr. O'Brien, under trial in a country said to be under the same Government and laws as England, should not have the same privilege which he would enjoy, as a matter of right, if he happened to be tried on the other side of the channel.

"The Court decided that the prisoner was not entitled to the privilege."

When the clerk read the names of the jury-panel, Mr. O'Brien, of course, challenged the array, on the ground of fraud; and, of course, the Court ruled against him.

"Mr. Whiteside stated that it made little difference whether his client were tried by a jury selected from a panel thus constituted, or taken and shot through the head on the high-road. No less than one hundred Catholics had been struck off the panel, and so few left on, that Mr. O'Brien's right to challenge was now little better than a farce. This objection was also overruled—Chief-Justice Blackburne having decided that the panel was properly made out."

O'Brien, whose mind was made up to meet any fate, stood in the dock during this nine days' trial with a haughty calmness. What thoughts passed through that proud heart as the odious game proceeded, no human eye will ever read; but of one thing we may be sure—his grief, shame, and indignation were not for himself, but for the down-trodden country where such a scene could be enacted in the open day, and against the will of nine-tenths of its inhabitants.

There followed, in due course, the usual barbarous death sentence :—

"That sentence is, that you, William Smith O'Brien, be taken from hence to the place from whence you came, and be thence drawn on a hurdle to the place of execution, and be there hanged by the neck until you are dead; and that afterwards your head shall be severed from your body, and your body divided into four quarters, to be disposed of as Her Majesty shall think fit. And may the Lord have mercy on your soul."

He hears it unmoved as a statue, inclines his head in a stately bow, politely takes leave of his counsel, and returns to his prison.

Again, and again, and again, the same process was performed in all its parts. MacManus was next tried, then O'Donohoe, then Meagher; their juries were all carefully packed; they were all sentenced to be hanged; and they all met the announcement of their fate as men ought. For more than a month these trials went on from day to day; and it was the 23d of October when the last sentence was pronounced. A strong garrison of cavalry, infantry, and artillery, occupied the town, and inclosed the scene with a hedge of steel. Outside, the people muttered deep curses, and chafed with impotent rage. A few daring spirits, headed by O'Mahony, once contemplated an attack and rescue; but the people had been too grievously frightened, and too effectually starved by the Government, to be equal to so dashing an exploit; and so that solemn and elaborate insult was once more put upon our name and nation, and the four men who had sought to save their people from so abject a condition lay undisturbed in Clonmel jail, sentenced to death. And whosoever has studied even the imperfect sketch given in these pages of the potent and minutely elaborated system of oppression that pressed upon that nation at every point, and tied down every limb, watching over every man, woman, and child, at their uprising and downlying, so as to be enabled to foresee and to baffle even the slightest approach to combination for a national purpose,* will assuredly not wonder at the utter and abject helplessness of the nation in presence of so cruel an outrage.

The newspaper editors were still to be "tried." In the months of October and November, 1848, Duffy, of the *Nation*, Williams and O'Doherty, of the *Tribune*, and Martin, of the *Felon*, were successively brought up for trial in the City Court House, of Green Street. Their newspapers had been suppressed weeks before, their offices broken up, their types, and presses, and books seized. O'Doherty and Martin were "convicted" by well-packed juries, containing not a single Catholic. In the cases of Duffy and Williams, the enemy ventured to leave one or two Catholics on the juries. Williams was acquitted; Duffy's jury disagreed, and he was retained in prison till a more tractable jury could be manufactured. Again he was brought to trial, and again the jury disagreed. Still he was kept in custody, though his health was rapidly failing; and at last, when all apprehension of trouble seemed to be over, and the more dangerous conspirators were disposed of, the "Government" yielded to a memorial on his behalf, and abandoned the prosecution.

In the matter of those sentenced to death, ministers, after much deliberation, decided on sparing their lives, and commuting their punishment to transportation for life. This was done under the false pretence of clemency; but it was, in truth, the most refined cruelty. It was, moreover, illegal—there being no law to authorize such a commutation. The prisoners, therefore, objected through their counsel; they had no use for life under such circumstances, and demanded to have the extreme benefit of the law. Ministers, however, were resolved to be merciful—introduced an Act into Parliament, empowering the Queen to transport them, had it passed at once, and immediately shipped them off to herd with felons in the penal colony of Van Diemen's Land. O'Doherty and Martin, having been originally sentenced to ten years' transportation, were sent away at the same time, but in another ship; and for more than five years, in the most degrading bondage, they expiated the crime of "not having sold their country."

A few unconcerted and desperate attempts were made in Munster, by O'Mahony and Savage, by Brennan and Gray, to draw the people together, and achieve some one daring act which might awaken the insurrectionary spirit. They all failed, or were easily suppressed. The clergy were now decidedly and actively in the interest of "law and order"—that is, in the interest of England; and the more regular police were on the alert by day and night, and the island bristled with forty thousand bayonets. "Tranquillity reigned in Warsaw." John O'Connell, in Conciliation Hall, pointed to the sad fate of those who had disregarded the counsels of the "Liberator;" intreated the people to sustain him in his moral and peaceful appeals to Parliament; and promised that Ireland should be, at some early day, "first flower of the earth and first gem of the sea."

What to do now with this Ireland, thus fallen under the full and peaceful possession of her "sister island," was the subject of serious thought in England. The famine was still slaying its tens of thousands, and the Government emigration scheme was drawing away many thousands more, and shooting them out naked and destitute on the shores of the St. Lawrence, so that it was hoped the "Celts" would soon be thinned out to the proper point. The very danger so lately escaped, however, brought home to the British Government, and to the Irish landlords, the stern necessity of continued extermination. It was better, they felt, to have too few hands to till the ground, than too many for the security of law and order.

A plan for a new "Plantation of Ireland" was promulgated by Sir Robert Peel—that is, for replacing the Irish with good Anglo-Saxons. This project for a new plantation in Ireland was anxiously revolved in the councils of the Government. It began to be believed that the peasant class, being now almost sufficiently thinned out, and the claim of tenants to some sort of right or title to the land they tilled having been successfully resisted and defeated—that the structure of society in Ireland having been well and firmly planted upon a basis of able-bodied pauperism (which the English, however, called "independent labour")— the time was come to effect a transfer of the real estate of the island from Irish to English hands. This grand idea afterwards elaborated itself into the famous "Encumbered Estates Act."

The conquest of the island was now regarded in England as effectually consummated. England, great, populous, and wealthy, with all the resources and vast

---

* We may once more refer to the memorable words of an English Attorney-General's description of the British *régime* in Ireland: "Notice is taken of every person that is able to do either good or hurt. It is known not only how they live, and what they do, but it is foreseen what they purpose or intend to do."

patronage of an existing Government in her hands; with a magnificent army and navy; with the established course and current of commerce steadily flowing in the precise direction that suited her interests; with a powerful party on her side in Ireland itself, bound to her by lineage and by interest; and above all, with her vast brute mass lying between us and the rest of Europe, enabling her to intercept the natural sympathies of other struggling nations, to interpret between us and the rest of mankind, and represent the troublesome sister island exactly in the light in which she wished to be regarded. England, prosperous, potent, and at peace with all the earth besides, had succeeded (to her immortal honour and glory) in anticipating and crushing out of sight the last agonies of resistance in a small, poor, and divided island, which she had herself made poor and divided, carefully disarmed, almost totally disfranchised, and almost totally deprived of the benefits of that very British "law" against which we revolted with such loathing and horror. England had done this; and whatsoever credit and prestige, whatsoever profit and power could be gained by such a feat, she has them all. "Now, for the first time these six hundred years," said the London *Times,* "England has Ireland at her mercy, and can deal with her as she pleases."

It was an opportunity not to be lost, for the interests of British civilization. Parliament met late in January, 1849. The Queen, in her "speech," lamented that "*another* failure of the potato crop had caused severe distress in Ireland," and thereupon asked Parliament to continue, "for a limited period," the extraordinary powers—that is, the power of proclaiming any district under martial law, and of throwing suspected persons into prison, without any charge against them. The Act was passed, of course.

Then, as the famine of 1848 was fully as grievous and destructive as any of the previous famines—as the rate-payers were impoverished, and in most of the unions could not pay the rates already due, and were thus rapidly sinking into the condition of paupers, giving up the hopeless effort to maintain themselves by honest industry, and throwing themselves on the earnings of others—as the poor houses were all filled to overflowing, and the exterminated people were either lying down to die or crowding into the emigrant ships—in short, the Poor law and the New Poor law, and the Improved Poor law, and the Supplementary Poor law, had all manifestly proved a "failure," Lord John Russell's next step was to give Ireland *more* Poor laws.

The expression *failure* must, however, be qualified as before. They were a failure for their professed purpose, that of relieving the famine, but were a complete success for their real purpose, that of uprooting the people from the land, and casting them forth to perish. Irishmen have not much faith in the "Government" statistics of their country; but as it is well to see how much the enemy was willing to admit, we give some details from a report furnished in '48 by Captain Larcom, under the orders of Government, and founded on local reports of police inspectors. The main facts are epitomized thus, for one year:—

"In the number of farms, of from *one to five* acres, the decrease has been twenty-four thousand one hundred and forty-seven; from *five* to *fifteen* acres, twenty-seven thousand three hundred and seventy-nine; from *fifteen* to *thirty* acres, four thousand two hundred and seventy-four; whilst of farms *above* thirty acres, the *increase* has been three thousand six hundred and seventy. Seventy thousand occupiers, with their families, numbering about three hundred thousand, were rooted out of the land.

"In Leinster, the decrease in the number of holdings not exceeding one acre, as compared with the decrease of '47, was three thousand seven hundred and forty-nine; above one, and not exceeding five, was four thousand and twenty-six; of five, and not exceeding fifteen, was two thousand five hundred and forty-six; of fifteen to thirty, three hundred and ninety-one; making a total of ten thousand six hundred and seventeen.

"In Munster, the decrease in the holdings under thirty acres is stated at eighteen thousand eight hundred and fourteen; the increase over thirty acres, one thousand three hundred and ninety-nine.

"In Ulster, the decrease was one thousand five hundred and two; the increase one thousand one hundred and thirty-four.

"In Connaught, where the labour of extermination was least, the clearance has been most extensive. There, in particular, the roots of holders of the soil were never planted deep beneath the surface, and consequently were exposed to every exterminator's hand. There were, in 1847, thirty-five thousand six hundred and thirty-four holders of from one to five acres; in the following year there were less by nine thousand seven hundred and three. There were seventy-six thousand seven hundred and seven holders of from five to fifteen acres; less in one year by twelve thousand eight hundred and ninety-one. Those of from fifteen to thirty acres were reduced by two thousand one hundred and twenty-one. A total depopulation of twenty-six thousand four hundred and ninety-nine holders of land, exclusive of their families, was effected in Connaught in one year."

On this report it may be remarked that it was a list of killed and wounded in one year of carnage only—and of one class of people only. It takes no account of the dead in that multitudinous class thinned the most by famine, who had no land at all, but lived by the labour of their hands, and who were exposed before the others as having nothing but life to lose. As for the landlords, already encumbered by debt, the pressure of the poor rates was fast breaking them down. In most cases they were not so much as the receivers of their own rents, and had no more control over the bailiffs, sheriffs, and police, who plundered and chased away the people, than one of the pillars of their own grand entrance gates.

The slaughter by famine was enormous this season. Here is one paragraph from amongst the commercial reports of the Irish papers, which will suggest more than any laboured narrative could inculcate :—

"Upwards of one hundred and fifty ass hides have been delivered in Dublin from the County Mayo, for exportation to Liverpool. The carcases, owing to the scarcity of provisions, had been used as food!"

But those who could afford to dine upon famished jackasses were few indeed. During this winter of 1848-49, hundreds of thousands perished of hunger. During this same winter the herds and harvests raised on Irish ground were floating off to England on every tide; and during this same winter almost every steamship *from* England daily carried Irish paupers, men, women, and children, away from Liverpool and Bristol, to share the good cheer of their kinsmen at home.

It was in this state of things that Lord John Russell, having first secured a continued suspension of the *Habeas Corpus* Act, proposed an additional and novel sort of poor rate for Ireland. It was called the "Rate in Aid." That to say, Poor Law Unions which were still solvent, and could still in some measure maintain their own local poor, were to be rated for relief of such unions as had sunk under the pressure. Assuming that Ireland and England are two integral parts of a "United Kingdom" (as we are assured they are), it seems hard to understand why a district in Leinster should be rated to relieve a pauper territory in Mayo, and a district in Yorkshire not; or to comprehend why old and spent Irish labourers, who had given the best of their health and strength to the service of England, should be shipped off to Ireland to increase and intensify the pauperism and despair. But so it was. The maxim was that "the property of Ireland must support the poverty of Ireland," without consideration of the fact that the property of Ireland was all this time supporting the luxury of England.

The next measure passed in the same session of Parliament was the "Encumbered Estates Act"—the Act of Twelfth and Thirteenth Victoria, chap. 77. Under this a royal commission was issued constituting a new court "for the sale of Encumbered Estates;" and the scope and intent of it were to give a short and summary method of bringing such estates to sale, on petition either of creditors or of owners. Before that time the only mode of doing this was through the slow and expensive proceedings of the Court of Chancery; and the number of encumbered landlords had grown so very large since the famine began, their debts so overwhelming, and their rental so curtailed, that the London Jews, money-brokers, and insurance offices required a speedier and cheaper method of bringing their property to the hammer. What ought to be fully understood is, that this Act was not intended to relieve, and did not relieve, anybody in Ireland; but that, under pretence of facilitating legal proceedings, it contemplated a sweeping confiscation and new plantation of the island. The English press was already complacently anticipating a peaceable transfer of Irish land to English and Scotch capitalists, and took pains to encourage them to invest their money under the new Act. Ireland, it was now declared, had become tranquil; "the Celts were gone;" and if any trouble should arise, there was the *Habeas Corpus* Suspension Act, and the horse, foot, and artillery, and the juries. Singular to relate, however, the new Act did not operate satisfactorily in that direction. English capitalists had a wholesome terror of Tipperary, and of the precarious tenure by which an Irish landlord holds his life; insomuch that the great bulk of the sales made by the commissioners were made to Irishmen; and in the official return of the operations of the court up to October, 1851, it appears that, while the gross amount produced by the sales had been more than three and a half millions sterling, there had only been fifty-two English and Scottish purchasers, to the amount of £319,486.*

Seeing this imperfect progress in the new plantation of Ireland, Ministers, in March, 1850, introduced a supplemental bill. The Solicitor-General, who moved it, was even so incautious as to admit the motive. "They had devised a plan," he said, "which, it was hoped, would induce *capitalists from England* to take an interest in these sales." The plan was a mere financial operation, creating a species of debentures chargeable on the land, and passing current like any other stock or scrip; but it need not be described in detail, for the plan was abandoned, and it is only mentioned here to exhibit the policy of England, as indicated by the Solicitor-General.

Down to the 25th May, 1857, there had been given orders for sale to the number of three thousand one hundred and ninety-seven; the property had been sold to seven thousand two hundred and sixteen purchasers, of whom six thousand nine hundred and two were Irish, the rest English, Scotch, or other foreigners. The estates already sold brought upwards of twenty millions sterling, which was almost all distributed to creditors and other parties interested. The result to Ireland was simply this: about one-fifteenth part of the island had changed hands, had gone from one landlord and come to another landlord; the result to the great tenant class was simply *nil*. The new landlord came over them armed with the power of life and death, like his predecessor, but he had no local or personal attachment, which in some cases used to mitigate the severity of landlord rule, and he was bound to make interest on his investment. The estates, therefore, have been broken up, on an average, into one-half their former size, and this has been much dwelt upon as an "amelioration;" but we have yet to learn that small landlords are more mild and merciful than great ones. On the whole, the "Encumbered Estates Act" has benefited only the money-lenders of England.

As to "tenant-right," the salutary custom explained before, and which did once practically secure to the tenantry in some portions of Ulster a permanency of tenure on payment of their rent, our Parliamentary patriots have been agitating for it, begging for it, conferring with ministers about it, eating public dinners,

* *Almanac and Directory*, 1852.

making speeches, and soliciting votes on account of it; but they have never made, and are never like to make, an approach by one hair's breadth to its attainment. It is absolutely essential to the existence of the British empire that the Irish peasant class be kept in a condition which will make them entirely manageable, easy to be thinned out when they grow too numerous, and an available *matériel* for armies. It is a necessity for the British commercial, social, and governmental system; but this is not said by way of complaint. Those who are of opinion that British civilization is a blessing, and a light to lighten the world, will easily reconcile themselves to the needful condition. Those who deem it the most base and horrible tyranny that has ever scandalized the earth, will probably wish that its indispensable prop, Ireland, were knocked from under it.

In the meantime, neither the Encumbered Estates Act, nor any other Act made or to be made by an English Parliament, has done or aimed to do anything towards giving the Irish tenant at will the smallest interest in the land he tills; but, on the contrary, the whole course of the famine legislation was directed to the one end of shaking small lease holders loose from the soil, and converting them into tenants at will, or into "independent labourers," or able-bodied paupers, or lean corpses. Understand, further, that the condition of an Irish "tenant at will" is unique on the face of the globe,* is utterly unintelligible to most civilized Europeans, and is only to be found within the sway of that Constitution which is the envy of surrounding nations. The German, Von Raumer, making a tour in Ireland, thus tries to explain the thing:—

"How shall I translate *tenants at will? Weggjagbare?* Expellable? Serfs? But, in the ancient days of vassalage, it consisted rather in keeping the vassals attached to the soil, and by no means in driving them away. An ancient vassal is a lord compared with the present tenant at will, to whom the law affords no defence. Why not call them *Jagabare (chaseable)*? But this difference lessens the analogy; that for hares, stags, and deer, there is a season during which no one is allowed to hunt them, whereas tenants at will are hunted all the year round. And if any one would defend his farm (as badgers and foxes are allowed to do), it is here denominated *rebellion.*"

* Paralleled in some sort only by the *ryots* of India —another people privileged to enjoy the blessings of British rule.

In 1849 it was still believed that the depopulation had not proceeded far enough; and the English Government was fully determined, having so gracious an opportunity, to make a clean sweep. One of the provisions of Lord John Russell's *Rate in Aid* bill was for imposing an additional rate of two shillings and sixpence in the pound to promote *emigration*. During the two years 1848-49, the Government Census Commissioners admit nine thousand three hundred and ninety-five deaths by famine alone; a number which would be about true if multiplied by twenty-five. In 1850 they were nearly seven thousand; as admitted by the same authorities; and in the first quarter of 1851, six hundred and fifty-two deaths by hunger, they say, "are recorded."

In the very midst of all this havoc, in August, 1849, Her Majesty's Ministers thought the coast was clear for a royal visit. The Queen had long wished, it was said, to visit her people of Ireland, and the great army of persons who, in Ireland, are paid to be loyal, were expected to get up the appearance of rejoicing. Of course, there were crowds in the streets, and the natural courtesy of the people prevented almost everything which could grate upon the lady's ear, or offend her eye. One Mr. O'Reilly, indeed, of South Great George's Street, hoisted on the top of his house a large *black* banner, displaying the crownless harp, and draped his windows with black curtains, showing the words *famine* and *pestilence;* but the police burst into his house, tore down the flag and the curtains, and thrust the proprietor into jail.

On the whole, the Viceroy's precautions against any show of disaffection were complete and successful. Nine out of ten citizens of Dublin eagerly hoped that Her Majesty would make this visit the occasion of a "pardon" to O'Brien and his comrades. Lord Clarendon's organs, therefore, and his thousand placemen, and agents of every grade, diligently whispered into the public ear that the Queen would certainly pardon the State prisoners if she were not insulted by repeal demonstrations—in short, if there was not one word said about those individuals. The consequence was that no whisper was heard about repeal nor about the State prisoners.

Although there was no chance of tenant-right, no chance of Ireland being allowed to manage her own affairs—yet, towards Catholics of the educated classes, there was much liberality. Mr. Wyse was sent as an ambassador to Greece; Mr. More O'Ferrall was made Governor of Malta; many barristers, once loud in their patriotic devotion at Conciliation Hall, were appointed to commissionerships and other offices, * and Ireland became "tranquil" enough. For result of the whole long struggle, England was left, for a time, more securely in possession than ever of the property, lives, and industry of the Irish nation. She had not parted with a single atom of her plunder, nor in the slightest degree weakened any of her garrisons, either military, civil, or ecclesiastical. Her "Established Church" remained in full force—the wealthiest Church in the world, quartered upon the poorest people, who abhor its doctrine, and regard its pastors as ravening wolves. It had, indeed, often been denounced in the London Parliament by Whigs out of place. Mr. Roebuck had called it "the greatest ecclesiastical enormity in Europe." Mr. Macaulay had termed it "the most utterly absurd and indefensible of all the institutions now existing in the civilized world." But we have already learned what value there is in the liberal declarations of Whigs out of place. Once in place and power, they felt that the "enormity" of the Established Church, absurd and indefensible as it was, constituted one of their greatest and surest holds upon the Irish aristocracy, to whose younger sons and dependents it affords a handsome and not too laborious livelihood.

* By degrees, considerable numbers of Catholic barristers have been admitted to the judicial bench (although never to the rank of Chancellor). They usually earned this promotion by political services; and they have proved, in fact, the most useful servants to the English Government in carrying on the infamous transactions which pass for trials of "political offenders" in Ireland. They sit by gravely and complacently, and see juries packed for the destruction of better and braver men than those judges ever were. They know that the object of the odious fraud over which they preside is to perpetuate British dominion over their unhappy country—unhappy in nothing more than in having given birth to *them*. They know, further, that the operation and intent of that British domination are to plunder and to exterminate their countrymen, their kinsmen, their own flesh and blood. And they have deliberately elected their side—against their countrymen and kinsmen, and with the mortal enemies of their countrymen. In other words, they have sold their country and themselves; and the special service which *they* are expected to do, the job which they sit on that bench to put through, is precisely to countenance this very fraud and villany of jury-packing,—to grace it with their robes and ermine—to preside with dignified gravity while the Sheriff and Attorney-General do their wicked business—looking all the while as if it were a solemn inquest they are holding—and then, with feeling voice, and in a high moral tone, and with the solemn prate usual on such occasions, to sentence to death or exile a man who has *not been tried;* a man, too, whom they are forced to respect, even in their own depraved hearts, while they hypocritically lecture him upon his own enormous iniquities.

The Orangemen, also, were still maintained in full force. They are all armed; for no bench of magistrates will refuse a good Protestant the liberty of keeping a gun; and, lest they might not have enough, the Government sometimes supplies arms for distribution among the lodges. The police and detective system continued to be more highly organized than ever; and the Government Board of "National" Education more diligently than ever inculcated the folly and vice of national aspirations.

Yet Ireland, we are told, has been, since the famine, improving and prosperous. Yes; it cannot be denied that, two millions and a half of the people having been slain or driven to seek safety by flight, the survivors began to live better for a time. There was a smaller supply of labour, with the same demand for it—therefore wages were higher. There was more cattle and grain to export to England, because there were fewer mouths to be fed; and England (in whose hands are the issues of life and death for Ireland) can afford to let *so* many live. Upper classes, and lower classes, merchants, lawyers, state officials, civil and military, are indebted for all that they have, for all that they are, or hope for, to the sufferance and forbearance of a foreign and hostile nation. This being the case, the prosperity of Ireland, even such ignominious prosperity as it is, has no guarantee or security.

A few statistics may fitly conclude this part of the subject.

The census of Ireland in 1841 gave a population of eight millions one hundred and seventy-five thousand one hundred and twenty-five. At the usual rate of increase, there must have been, in 1846, when the famine commenced, at least eight millions seven hundred and fifty thousand; at the same rate of increase, there ought to have been, in 1851 (according to the estimate of the Census Commissioners), nine millions eighteen thousand seven hundred and ninety-nine. But in that year, after five seasons of artificial famine, there were found alive only six millions five hundred and fifty-two thousand three hundred and eighty-five—a *deficit* of about two millions and a half. Now, what became of those two millions and a half?

The "Government" Census Commissioners, and compilers of returns of all sorts, whose principal duty it has been, since that fatal time, to conceal the amount of the havoc, attempt to account for nearly the whole deficiency by emigration. In Thom's *Official Almanac*, we find set down on one side the actual decrease from 1841 to 1851 (that is, without taking into account the increase by births in that period), one million six hundred and twenty-three thousand one hundred and fifty-four. Against this, they place their own estimate of the emigration during those same ten years, which they put down at one million five hundred and eighty-nine thousand one hundred and thirty-three. But, in the first place, the decrease did not *begin* till 1846—there had been till then a rapid increase in the population; the Government returns, then, not only ignore the increase, but set the emigration of *ten* years against the depopulation of *five*. This will not do. We must reduce their emigrants by one-half, say to six hundred thousand, and add to the depopulation the estimated increase *up* to 1846, say half a million. This will give upwards of two millions, whose disappearance is to be accounted for, and six hundred thousand emigrants in the other column. Balance unaccounted for, *a million and a half*.

This is without computing those who were born in the five famine years; whom we may leave to be balanced by the deaths from *natural* causes in the same period.

Now, that million and a half of men, women, and children, were carefully, prudently, and peacefully *slain* by the English Government. They died of hunger, in the midst of abundance which their own hands created; and it is quite immaterial to distinguish those who perished in the agonies of famine itself from those who died of typhus fever, which in Ireland is always caused by famine.

Further, this was strictly an *artificial* famine—that is to say, it was a famine which desolated a rich and fertile island, that produced every year abundance and superabundance to sustain all her people and many more. The English, indeed, call that famine a dispensation of Providence; and ascribe it entirely to the blight of the potatoes. But potatoes failed in like manner all over Europe, yet there was no famine save in Ireland. The British account of the matter, then, is, first, a fraud; second, a blasphemy. The Almighty, indeed, sent the potato blight, but the English created the famine.

And, lastly, it has been shown, in the course of this narrative, that the depopulation of the country was not only encouraged by artificial means, namely, the Out-door Relief Act, the Labour Rate Act, and the emigration schemes; but that extreme care and diligence were used to prevent relief coming to the doomed island from abroad; and that the benevolent contributions of Americans and other foreigners were turned aside from their desired objects—not, let us say, in order that none should be saved alive, but that no interference should be made with the principles of political economy.

The Census Commissioners close one of their late reports with these words:—

"In conclusion, we feel it will be gratifying to your Excellency to find that, although the population had been diminished in so remarkable a manner, by famine, disease, and emigration, and has been since decreasing, the results of the Irish census are, *on the whole, satisfactory.*"

The commissioners mean to say that, although there are fewer men and women, there are more cattle and hogs for the English markets.

But the depopulation of the country by no means ended with the famine. Between 1851 and 1861, during which period of ten years there was no officially declared famine, but, on the contrary, Ireland was continually felicitated by English Viceroys and statesmen upon her returning prosperity, we find that the diminution of the people steadily proceeded, so that, in 1861, the Census Commissioners found alive upon the Irish soil only five millions seven hundred and sixty-four thousand five hundred and forty-three individuals—less by three millions of souls than the population in 1845. This destruction of people is to be accounted for only in part by emigration, although emigration was very large in all those years. But there is no fact better established in social and economic science than that emigration never does thin the people of any country to anything like its apparent amount; because, in a healthy condition of society, the loss from this cause is compensated by the greater increase of people at home. But the cruel truth is, that society in Ireland is in ruins; it has no longer any recuperative energy. British civilization has taken so powerful and deadly a hold of it, that not only do the people fly in multitudes from the terrible "prosperity" of their country, but those who remain and strive to hold their ground are perishing where they stand.

CHAPTER XXVII.
1850—1851.

Depopulation—Emigration—"Plea for the Celtic Race"—Decay of the Irish Electoral Body—Act to amend Representation—"Papal Aggression"—Rage in England—Ecclesiastical Titles Bill—Never Enforced—And Why?—Orange Outrage in Down County—"Dolly's Brae"—Style of Orange Processions—Condition of the Country—Further Emigration—Still more Extermination—Crime and Outrage—Plenty and Prosperity in England—Conclusion.

In 1851 the island of Ireland still contained six and a half millions of people; which was much too large a population to be compatible with English policy. It has been seen, in an earlier page of this narrative, that the British Government and Parliament had been long anxiously occupied, even before the first symptom of the "famine," in devising the best, cheapest, and readiest mode of getting rid of what was constantly called the "surplus population" of Ireland. In fact and practice, the migration of the poorer people had been proceeding on a considerable and still increasing scale for many years. No season passed in which thousands of Irishmen, wearied and worn out by the struggle against remediless misery and hopeless aggression, did not bid adieu to their dear native country, to seek a happier future in some distant land. The general use of steam in ocean navigation had also greatly facilitated the movement of emigration, by shortening distances and bringing continents nearer to one another. The whole amount of the emigration from Great Britain and Ireland, for the year 1815, was but two thousand and eighty-one persons; but in 1852 it amounted to one hundred and seventy-six times that number — namely, three hundred and sixty-eight thousand seven hundred and sixty-four.*

In 1835 a Parliamentary Commission reported that there were in Ireland two millions three hundred and eighty thousand persons always in danger of perishing by hunger; and the island (although the most fertile country in all the earth) being even then periodically visited by terrible dearths and famine. It may have been natural to conclude that it would be doing Ireland a signal service to multiply the means of emigration; but in carrying out this idea, the Government was resolved to bring the whole movement of emigration, as well as everything else that was *Irish*, under its own control as far as possible. During the fifteen years which preceded the famine (1831-46), Ireland alone had furnished more than eight hundred thousand emigrants out of the total emigration from the three kingdoms. The exact numbers are eight hundred and nine thousand two hundred and forty-four, making an annual average of fifty-three thousand nine hundred and forty-nine; and the number for all the three kingdoms during the same period was one million one hundred and seventy-one thousand four hundred and eighty-five.†

* General Report of the Emigration Commissioners, 1861. Appendix.
† Reports of Commissioners of Emigration, in Thom's *Official Directory*. We often cite this sta-

Yet the excess of births, over both deaths and emigration, continued to make a sensible increase in the population; and in the very same year (1841), in which had occurred the largest *exodus* during that period, the census showed that the population of the island was greater than it had ever been before, and greater than it has ever been since officially declared— namely, eight millions one hundred and seventy-five thousand one hundred and twenty-four.*

This result, showing the nullity of emigration as an agency of depleting a population, might have been more surprising if it had not been long foreseen. Far from deranging the calculations of economic science, it confirmed the conclusions of the best economists. No writer, native or foreign, who has treated of Irish affairs, has estimated with more sagacity the actual condition and necessities of our country than the illustrious French publicist, M. Gustave de Beaumont. Studying, in 1839, the condition of Ireland, and considering whether the favourite British prescription of emigration could in any great measure cure the miseries which he had witnessed in the country, M. de Beaumont applied himself to the solution of these questions:—1st. What should be the proportions of the emigration if it were to materially affect the situation of the people? 2nd. Would emigration upon such a scale be possible? 3rd. Supposing it possible, would it be a radical solution of the difficulty? The advocates of wholesale emigration (all of them Englishmen) answered the first question by estimating at two millions—or from two to four millions—the number of persons who must quit Ireland, in order to create at once so sensible a void in the population as should leave the rest at ease. The second question, then, was easy to answer —that on so vast a scale the project was simply impossible, for want of sufficient means of transport. For supposing that each emigrant vessel carried a thousand passengers, there must be employed in the operation two thousand ships. This would put in requisition the whole British merchant navy, and withdraw it from the commerce of the world, for a project in itself chimerical; for it would have been impossible to provide funds for the needful expenses; and no country, not even the United States, could be expected to receive such an invasion *en masse*, and provide the unhappy invaders with the means and opportunity of earning their bread by their labour. But, assuming all these difficulties overcome, then arose M. de Beaumont's third question: Was it certain that, the system of land tenure remaining the same, emigration would cure the evils of the country, and effect a social transformation? On this point our very intelligent foreign visitor found it easy to demonstrate that the removal of one-third, or even half, of the population would be no radical remedy. The difficulty for Ireland, as he plainly saw, was not to make the land produce a sufficiency of food for all its people, but lay altogether in the system of land tenure. "For," says the author, "if it be one of the settled principles of land proprietors that the farmer should have no other profit out of his cultivation but just what is strictly necessary for his subsistence; and if it be the general custom to apply this system rigorously, so that every improvement in the farmer's way of living brings with it necessarily a rise in his rent, on this hypothesis, which, for those who know Ireland, is a sad reality, what would be the advantage of a diminution of the population?"*
"Thus," he continues, "after many thousands of the Irish shall have disappeared, the lot of the remainder will probably be no way altered—they still may remain as miserable as they were before. It has been seen, in the preceding inquiry, that with but one-third of its present inhabitants, Ireland was a century ago as indigent as in our own day, being subjected then, as at present, to the same causes of misery, independent of numbers." M. de Beaumont here refers to the authority of Swift and of Berkeley, which sufficiently establishes the misery of Ireland in their days.

In all this investigation the singularity is, that M. de Beaumont, knowing the wealth and fertility of Ireland, and how she not only produced every year more than her people could consume, but also exported immense quantities of her produce, did not come at once to the conclusion, and proclaim his conclusion, that Ireland and the Irish are under the control of mortal enemies, whose single policy is to abolish the Irish race off the face of the earth.

Another calm and diligent inquirer,† after giving an account of the immense

---

tistical annual, prepared by authority of the British Government. But (on that very account) it is untrustworthy, unless when it bears necessarily or unintentionally *against* the Government, and it is only for such evidence that we have recourse to it.

* But in 1845 (when no census was taken) the population must have amounted almost to nine millions. This fact is too often overlooked, and by the enemy's Government purposely ignored, for obvious reasons.

* M. de Beaumont, II., 108.
† The Abbé Perraud. *Etudes sur l'Irlande contemporaine.*

schemes of wholesale emigration, remarks:—"It is in view of these sad teachings of the past that the most sincere and intelligent friends of Ireland counselled the British Government rather to expend in vast works of drainage and cultivation the sums estimated as required for the transport of emigrants. Lord Devon's Commission calculated that the emigration of one hundred thousand persons *per annum*, if effected at the public expense, and putting the cost at the moderate amount of six pounds sterling for each person, would cost £600,000 a year—a sum which, annually applied to the purchase and improvement of unproductive lands, would undoubtedly permit the Irish to live at home, and rescue them from the necessity of going into exile to save their lives." Here the Abbé Perraud also seems to misapprehend, or else shrinks from uttering the horrible fact, that the object of all British policy in Ireland is now, and ever has been, to make it impossible for the Irish to live at home. In the writings of foreigners, even the most acute and most friendly to Ireland, there is a steady, almost stolid, persistence in assuming that British statesmen, if they only knew how, would hasten to redress the ills of Ireland. For this reason, and for this alone, has the real history of Ireland remained a puzzle and a secret even to the most intelligent inquirers from other countries. They may as well understand at once that the key of the whole mystery is this one fundamental truth—The single policy of England towards Ireland is, as it always has been, to extirpate the Irish nation. This maxim, well borne in mind, everything becomes simple enough.

In 1841 the number of inhabited houses in all Ireland, according to the official census,* was one million three hundred and twenty-eight thousand eight hundred and thirty-nine. In 1851 it was one million forty-six thousand two hundred and ninety-four. But this decrease between those two periods of the census does not by any means represent the actual amount of destruction, because from 1841 (the census year) till 1845 the population had been rapidly increasing (as has been observed in a former chapter). When the "famine" commenced, in 1846, we may fairly assume that the inhabited houses amounted to one million and a half; the decrease, then, in 1851, must be set down at almost *half a million* of houses or cabins, giving shelter on an average to five human beings each. These figures are in themselves sufficient to give a ghastly idea of the agony of Ireland, and of the too cruel efficiency of the methods so steadily pursued for the extirpation of its native inhabitants. "The Celts were gone," or rapidly going; and this not the result of emigration, as we have seen, but of mere hunger and hardship. The system, and the motives and operation of the system, became at length so clear and plain that Mr. Isaac Butt, a Protestant barrister (O'Connell's opponent in the famous Corporation Debate upon Repeal), published some years later (1866) a work entitled, *A Plea for the Celtic Race*, urging the impolicy, even in the interest of England, of entirely abolishing the whole breed.*

It is no way surprising, then, to find that the number of persons in all Ireland qualified to vote for county representatives in Parliament, had dwindled down, on January 1, 1850, to considerably less than one thousand for each county, or twenty-seven thousand one hundred and eighty for the thirty-two counties. The great County of Mayo had but two hundred electors, and these almost all landed proprietors. This cannot be surprising to those who have followed the narrative of that long, wasting war, systematically made on the race of small farmers, first by the abolition of the forty-shilling franchise, then by the "consolidation" of farms; by the frequent ejectment Acts; by the stimulus given to extermination

* See Thom's *Official Almanac and Directory*, 1861.

* We give two suggestive passages from this performance:—"Whatever may be the difficulties that attend the discussion of the question, any man who can contribute ever so little to its investigation, does some service to his country. To say that the land question is the most important part of all Irish public questions, but feebly expresses its magnitude. It would be nearer the truth to say that it forms the whole. While the 'unsatisfactory relations' between the owners and occupiers of the soil continue, there can never be peace or prosperity in the land. Let these relations be placed on a satisfactory basis, and all other questions will very soon adjust themselves. The question, however, is not exclusively of Irish interest. It is true that, so far as Ireland is concerned, it involves nothing less than the continued existence in their own land of the old Irish race. But in the face of troubles which are gathering and darkening over Europe, it is not too much to say that the continuance of England's greatness may depend upon her being able to satisfy and conciliate that race in their native land.

"English statesmen must ask themselves whether the British Empire can afford to lose the hardy and bold population, a portion of which every month is now transferring itself to the other side of the Atlantic. They must seriously reflect on the danger which arises from sending a hostile and embittered Irish colony to the American continent. All the emigrants who are now leaving the country carry with them the most determined hatred of British power. Those whom they leave behind sympathize in their feelings, and whenever the opportunity occurs, the Irish abroad and a large portion of the Irish at home will be ready to aid any attempt that can strike a blow at that power."

and emigration; finally, by the Poor laws and the famine.

The condition of the county representation, therefore, had become so scandalous that Ministers in 1850 judged it needful to extend, somehow or other, the numbers qualified to vote. But here arose a difficulty, there were no more freeholders. That class had been too effectually shaken loose from the soil, impoverished, and extirpated. Many thousands of them who had escaped death were by this time digging canals and railways in America. It was evident that nothing like an apparently adequate representation could be looked for, based upon the old and respectable condition of a freehold estate in land. But it occurred to Lord John Russell to found the franchise upon the *poor rates;* thus connecting this ancient privilege of freemen with the odious and destructive system of public pauperism which had been forced upon the island against its will, and had been corroding its people so fatally ever since.

Accordingly, a bill was introduced to "amend" the representation both in counties and in boroughs. The Irish *Official Directory* thus shortly states the facts:—

"The number of electors under the Reform Act was, in 1832, ninety-eight thousand eight hundred and fifty-seven; on January 1, 1850, the constituency had diminished to sixty-one thousand and thirty-six; twenty-seven thousand one hundred and eighty in the counties, and thirty-three thousand eight hundred and fifty-six in the cities and boroughs. The Act 13th and 14th Vic., chap. 69, was passed in 1850, to amend the representation; and in addition to those persons previously qualified to register and vote in county elections, occupiers of tenements *rated in the last poor rate* at a net annual value of £12 and upwards, are entitled to vote in elections for counties, subject to registration, in accordance with the Act, and to certain limitations therein; also owners of certain estates of the rated net annual value of £5. But no persons are to be entitled to vote in counties in respect of tenements in virtue of which they may be entitled to vote in boroughs. In boroughs, occupiers rated in the last poor rate at £8 and upwards are entitled to vote, subject to registration and certain limitations in the Act. By the 13th and 14th Vic., chap. 68, the polling at contested elections is to continue in counties for two days only, and in cities and boroughs for one day only; the returning officer is to provide booths, so that not more than six hundred voters shall poll at each booth for a county, and two hundred for a city or borough. The number of electors registered under the new Act, on January 1, 1851, was one hundred and sixty-three thousand five hundred and forty-six, being one hundred and thirty-five thousand two hundred and forty-five in the counties, and twenty-eight thousand three hundred and one in the cities and boroughs.

This enlargement of the electoral basis was undoubtedly a seeming advantage, assuming that the Irish representation in a British Parliament is a thing desirable. But it was not in the nature of the Whigs, nor, indeed, of the Tories, to concede to Ireland even an apparent advantage, and not accompany the "boon" with an outrage. Lord John Russell flung us the Franchise Act with one hand, and with the other a new Coercion law and the "Ecclesiastical Titles Act." As for the former, it was only the usual atrocity, this time under the title of an "Act for the better Prevention of Crime and Outrage in Ireland;" with the customary power to proclaim districts, to quarter police on them, to search for arms, to keep everybody at home after sunset, and to transport delinquents. There was nothing uncommon in this, and the uncommon and exceptional thing for Irishmen would have been to find themselves living under the civil laws of the land. But the other measure (Ecclesiastical Titles bill) needs further notice.

In the summer of this year, 1850, arrived in England a most startling document; nothing less than a Papal Brief, direct from Rome, directing the English Catholic "Vicars Apostolic"—who were bishops, in fact, possessing all episcopal jurisdiction—to assume the true titles of their Sees, as Bishop of Hexham, Bishop of Birmingham, and so forth; and further appointing the illustrious Doctor Wiseman a Cardinal and first Archbishop of Westminster. The soil of Protestant England was thus mapped out by a foreign prince into separate governments (dioceses), and placed under the control of certain Popish priests, in utter disdain of the exclusive rights of the Anglican Church, and of the Queen as its Pope and head. Here was papal aggression! Immediately arose a vehement "No-Popery" excitement throughout England. It is true that the Pope herein exercised the undoubted jurisdiction which he possessed in things spiritual over his Church, and which he had long notoriously exercised under other names and forms.

Still, it was against the "law"—that is, against some of the old penal laws yet unrepealed, but always violated—to introduce into Great Britain or Ireland any Papal Bull, Brief, Rescript, or writing whatsoever. And then the high tone assumed (necessarily) by the Pope in his Brief, and by Cardinal Wiseman in promulgating it, appeared to the enlightened mind of Protestant England to amount to nothing less than Jezebel herself, formally entering in and taking possession.

At once there was a shout of alarm and wrath, from all the ends of England and Scotland, to which the Irish Orangemen, of course, contributed their best vociferation. County meetings were held all over England, to denounce this audacious "Papal aggression;" and platforms, pulpits, and press rung for months with the old and well-worn denunciations against Jezebel, the Sacrifice of the Mass, and the whole mystery of iniquity generally. Lord John Russell—a statesman who hated Catholics and their religion with all the venom of his small, shrivelled, and spiteful soul, and who was distressed, besides, by the late concession of franchise to certain Catholics in Ireland—Lord John Russell, though Prime Minister of the Queen, was not above the paltry task of stimulating this ignoble rage. He selected the 4th of November, the day before the anniversary of the "Gunpowder Plot," to publish in the newspapers a letter to the Bishop of Durham, expressing alarm and indignation, "but less alarm than indignation," at the daring invasion of England by the Pope of Rome; enlarging upon the enormity of Catholic doctrines, and terming Catholic worship "superstitious mummery." His lordship, however, though he saw great cause for apprehension, assured the bishop that the noble Protestant State of England should never, never be yielded up into the hands of a foreign priest. Next day was the fifth, when Guy Fawkes is always burned in effigy. This time there was in many towns of England, and especially in London, an astonishing uproar of "No-Popery" zeal. Multitudinous processions celebrated the occasion, orators spouted out of *Fox's Martyrs* (taking care to say nothing of the martyrs that Protestants had made), and the ignorant masses were inflamed to madness by pictures of the racks and pincers which they were assured were shortly to be introduced into England, under the new Papal Bull. Instead of Guy Fawkes, they burned effigies of the Pope, of the Virgin, of Cardinal Wiseman, and swore deep oaths, under the influence of deep potations, that they would all die, with the Bible on their bosoms, before they would submit to the tyranny of the Propaganda and the pincers of the Inquisition. It would have been an insane action, on the part of any Catholic priest, to allow himself to be seen in the streets upon that evening.

The conclusion of this affair of "Papal aggression" belongs to the following year, 1851; but we may here anticipate a little. Lord John Russell lost no time in availing himself of the stupid fanaticism of his countrymen. Parliament met again in February, 1851. He made the chief feature in the Queen's speech this very affair of the Pope's Bull, and made her earnestly recommend to Parliament efficient action upon so important a subject. A bill was at once introduced by his lordship, absolutely prohibiting the assumption of the title of any existing See, or of any title whatsoever, from *any place* in the United Kingdom, under a penalty of £100 for each such offence. This was an extension of the provisions of the Catholic Relief Act of 1829, which imposed the same penalty on the assumption of the title to any *existing See* only. That prohibition in Ireland, and the penalty attached to it, had been always entirely neglected and ignored by the Catholic hierarchy, and the Catholic Archbishop of Armagh signed himself Archbishop of Armagh and Primate of all Ireland, just as the other one did. In the new ecclesiastical division of England, however, care had been taken to avoid giving to Catholic bishops the precise titles of Protestant Sees—except in one instance—and therefore it became necessary for the legislators against Papal aggression to extend the prohibition and penalty to all territorial titles whatsoever, derived from any place in the three kingdoms.

The new bill, which was intended to be highly stringent and menacing—a new and formidable bulwark to the Reformation in England—was only on its passage when Lord John Russell's Government went out, and the Tories, under Lord Derby, came in. It made no difference in this case. The bill to repress "Papal aggression" was not only taken up by the new administration, but was eventually passed with amendments extending the penalty to the introduction of *any* document or rescript from Rome, as well as the one lately arrived, and further empowering and inviting any common informer to prosecute. The bill was carried through all its stages by immense majorities, English Whigs and English

Tories being once more an unit on this vital matter; and thereafter it was not only to be illegal for the Archbishop of Westminster to sign himself Archbishop of Westminster, but for the Archbishop of Armagh to take the title of his undoubted office, under the penalty of £100 for each offence.

On the passage of this bill it was really believed by ignorant Protestants that a new and mighty bulwark had been set up against the Pope, and that the "Reformation" was at length secured. Much to the surprise of these ignorant Protestants, no notice whatever was taken of the new law by English bishops or by Irish bishops. Indeed, Doctor MacHale, the bold Archbishop of Tuam, who has the spirit of a patriot and, if need be, of a martyr, took an early occasion of publicly violating the new law, by reading in his cathedral the actual rescript of the Pope, and inviting any informer or priest-hunter, who might wish to earn a hundred pounds, to institute a prosecution against him. The law was never executed in a single instance. Doctor Newman signed his name in public documents as Cardinal Archbishop of Westminster, and the Archbishop of Armagh continued to style himself Primate of all Ireland. The "Law" stands on record upon the scandalous chronicle of English legislation as a mere impotent example of No-Popery spite.

Why was this law, passed by immense majorities, and with every appearance of determination, never enforced in a single case? Why were not the Catholic bishops prosecuted under its provisions? The answer is too obvious—the Irish Catholic bishops have been so useful to the British Government, ever since the Union, in preserving the "peace of the country"— that is, its perpetual subjugation to England—that it was not safe to make enemies of them. On this subject we may trust the Rev. Father Perraud, who thus expresses himself in his able work on Ireland.* "It is useless to conceal the fact : it is not the regiments encamped in Ireland ; it is not the militia of twelve thousand *peelers* distributed over the whole of the surface of the land, which prevents revolt and preserves the peace. During a long period, especially in the last century, the excess of misery to which Ireland was reduced had multiplied, even in the most Catholic counties, the *secret societies* of the peasantry. At this very moment, it is said, America is making great efforts to entice patriotic young men into those obscure Associations in which men *swear hatred to governments*, in which are prepared the conspiracies against *public institutions*, in which are silently organized social wars. . . . But who have ever been so energetic in resistance to secret societies as the Irish episcopacy ? Who have denounced these *illegal* Associations with the most persevering, powerful, and formidable condemnation ? On more than one occasion the bishops have even hazarded their popularity in this way. They could at a signal have armed a million combatants against a persecuting government; *and that signal they refused to give*."

Passing over the various singular misstatements of the reverend writer—that secret societies in Ireland swear hatred to governments in general, instead of the English Government *alone* — that they conspire against "public institutions" generally, instead of the institutions of famine and packed juries, and the rest of our British institutions—and that they organize "social war," instead of war against the English troops,—passing over these errors, one thing is, at least, evident from the pages of the *Père* Perraud—that the Catholic bishops take credit to themselves for preserving British institutions and British government in Ireland.* It is possible that they are entitled to this credit, such as it is. And herein lies the reason why they were never prosecuted under the "Ecclesiastical Titles Bill." The English Government did not enforce its own law, because it dared not.†

The Parliamentary session of 1850 is further notable as the occasion of a discussion upon the Orange outrage at Dolly's Brae, near Castlewellan, in the County Down. The transaction had taken place in the July of the year before, at the usual celebration of the Orange anniversary. It happened in this manner: —The Orangemen of various districts of that region had assembled, marching by various routes, at the splendid demesne called Tollymore Park, the seat of the Earl of Roden, one of the highest dignitaries of their order. One of the parties had marched through an exclusively Catholic district, and in the true spirit of

---

* *Etudes sur l'Irlande contemporaine.* Par le R. P. Adolphe Perraud. Paris, 1862.

* M. Perraud had made two visits to Ireland in order to collect material for his valuable work; had communicated freely with the Catholic bishops; and must be supposed to speak *for them* in claiming merit for them on account of their loyal efforts.

† It is observable that Father Perraud speaks of the bishops as denouncing "illegal Associations." But there is no society in Ireland so *illegal* as the Catholic Episcopacy. No White-Boy, Young Irelander, or "Fenian," ever more deliberately broke the law than those bishops habitually do in taking the title of their Sees, and in reading rescripts from Rome.

the anniversary had insulted the peaceable people with the flaunting of their Orange banners and lilies, and by playing before the poor cabins the tune of "Croppies Lie Down."* After the muster at Tollymore Park, a dinner, and some drink, and a speech from Lord Roden concerning the Mystery of Iniquity and the duty of all good Protestants—if they were to be martyred for their faith—at least to die with their Bibles clasped to their bosoms, it was determined to march back by way of Dolly's Brae. One Beers, a very ignorant Orange magistrate, accompanied them. Violent proceedings were expected to occur upon the passage by Dolly's Brae, and might have been prevented by Lord Roden and other magistrates present at the banquet, if they had used their influence to prevent the march by that particular road; but it was thought advisable to give the Papists a lesson, and the Lodges started for Dolly's Brae. It appeared, on the subsequent investigation, that so strong was the reason to apprehend disturbance as to induce some magistrates to send forward a strong force of police. On the arrival of the Orangemen in the townland, it was found that most of the inhabitants were gathered near the roadside, whether from mutual protection or for active resistance to the Orange march in that direction, did not clearly appear; but the latter motive was unlikely, as the Catholics were quite unarmed, save with a few scythes and hayforks. An immediate collision took place, of course. The chief of police led his men at once into the scene of disorder; ascertaining to his own satisfaction, as usual, that the Catholics were solely to blame, and were the atrocious aggressors, he directed all the efforts of his force against them. In short, by the joint operations of the armed Orangemen and the armed police, the unarmed Papists were victoriously defeated; several corpses were left upon the field, and most of the houses were burned or wrecked.

Such was the day of Dolly's Brae. A lawyer was sent down from Dublin as a "Commissioner," on the usual pretence of examining into the facts and collecting the evidence; and it appears that his report was not so grossly partial as had been expected; for Lord Clarendon could not avoid the plain necessity of dismissing from the Commission of the Peace both Lord Roden and Beers. It was on this report that the debate arose in Parliament, and many severe judgments were expressed of the conduct of the Irish Government in encouraging and arming such a banditti as the Orangemen. Lord Clarendon, who attended in his place in the House of Peers upon this occasion, defended his proceedings as he best could; and, in particular, he most emphatically denied that, in 1848, he had furnished arms to Orange Lodges. He said that, in fact, a certain Captain Kennedy (at the time of the debate serving in India) had given money out of his own pocket to provide arms for Lodges; but he (Lord Clarendon) was quite innocent of any such proceedings. It is scarcely necessary to say that nobody believed his lordship. What had been charged was, that not money, but *arms*, had been sent from Dublin Castle to Belfast for distribution

* The usual Orange style is thus described by one who knew the North of Ireland well:—"In some districts of that country Protestants are the majority of the people; the old policy of the "Government" has been to arm the Protestants and disarm the Catholics. The magistrates at all sessions are Orangemen or high British loyalists. In those districts, therefore, Catholics lead the lives of dogs—lie down in fear and rise up with foreboding; their worship is insulted, and their very funerals are made an occasion of riot. One of the July anniversaries comes round—the days of Aughrim and the Boyne; the pious Evangelicals must celebrate those disastrous but hard fought battles where William of Nassau, with his army of French Huguenots, Danes, and Dutchmen, overthrew the power of Ireland, and made the noble old Celtic race hewers of wood and drawers of water even unto this day. Lodges assemble at some central point, with drums and fifes playing the 'Protestant Boys.' At the rendezvous are the Grand Masters with their sashes and aprons—a beautiful show. Procession formed, they walk in Lodges, each with its banner of orange or purple and garlands of orange lilies borne high on poles. Most have arms, yeomanry muskets or pistols, or ancient swords whetted for the occasion. They arrive at some other town or village, dine in the public-houses, drink the 'glorious, pious, and immortal memory of King William,' and 'To Hell with the Pope;' re-form their procession after dinner, and *then* comes the time for Protestant action. They march through a Papist townland: at every house they stop and play 'Croppies lie down!' and the 'Boyne Water,' firing a few shots over the house at the same time. The doors are shut—the family in terror—the father standing on the floor with knitted brows and teeth clenched through the nether lip, grasping a pitchfork (for the police long since found out and took away his gun). Bitter memories of the feuds of ages darken his soul. Outside, with taunting music and brutal jests and laughter, stand in their ranks the Protestant communicants. The old grandmother can endure no longer: she rushes out, with gray hair streaming, and kneels on the road before them, she clasps her old thin hands and curses them in the name of God and his Holy Mother. Loud laughs are the answer, and a shot or two over the house or in through the window. The old crone, in frantic exasperation, takes up a stone and hurls it with feeble hand against the insulting crew. There; the first assault is committed; everything is lawful now: smash go the unglazed windows and their frames; zealous Protestants rush into the house raging; the man is shot down at his own threshold, the cabin is wrecked, and the procession, playing 'Croppies lie down,' proceeds to another Popish den.

"So the Reformation is vindicated. The names of Ballyvarly and Tullyorier will rise to the lips of many a man who reads this description."

amongst Orangemen; and, besides, if the money given by Captain Kennedy came, in fact, out of the Secret Service Fund, Lord Clarendon, as the distributor of that fund in Ireland, would have felt it his right and his duty to deny the fact when charged. It is an official necessity; because, otherwise, there would be nothing secret nor sacred in secret service money.

It only remains to be mentioned, that no person was ever brought to justice for the predetermined massacre of Dolly's Brae.

At this point—the middle of the current century—the present history closes. It leaves in full operation the whole system of British rule in Ireland. Every department of Irish life was brought under complete subordination to English interests; and the arrangements seemed to be perfect for preventing national aspirations or national interests in Ireland from ever again becoming a disturbing element in the course of imperial policy. The Celtic population was securely put in the way of steady diminution.* The famine was past, and the people were continually called on by the smooth-spoken Viceroy to rejoice in the return of prosperity; yet there was still a multitudinous rush to the sea, in order to escape from such prosperity. The emigration from Ireland in 1851 amounted to two hundred and fifty-seven thousand three hundred and seventy-two. The number of paupers relieved in the poorhouses in 1850 was eight hundred and five thousand seven hundred and two, without counting nearly four hundred thousand who were receiving "outdoor relief." No attempt had been made to secure to the tenant, by just laws, any right whatsoever in the improvements he might make on his farm. Extermination of peasantry was not only the practice but the fashion; and ruthless consolidation of farms had come to be thought the criterion of high intelligence, and even philanthropy, in an Irish proprietor, because it proved that he had studied the "Devon Commission" report, and appreciated the conclusions of the Commissioners.

In the same year, 1850, the Government was holding in its own hands, by means of the savings banks, the earnings and savings of poor Irish people, to the amount of £1,291,798; so that every industrious artizan and careful maid-servant who had made a deposit, was directly interested, to the amount of such a deposit, in maintaining what is called "the peace of the country"—that is to say, submitting implicitly to the British system, and influencing others to submit.

The Established Church and the police were flourishing; the Orangemen were as insolent and ferocious as they had ever been; and the Coercion Act (for suppression of "crime and outrage") was always ready in the Castle, to be launched at a moment's warning against any barony or county in the land. Yet the truth is, that Ireland was at that time remarkably free from crimes and outrages (except those perpetrated against her people); and it is instructive to remark, that crimes and outrages were at the same time steadily on the increase in England and Scotland. A speech in Parliament, of Lord John Russell, contains a wonderful revelation upon this point.* His lordship stated, that in one year (1857) the *convictions* in Great Britain were, for "shooting, stabbing, and wounding," two hundred and eight; for highway robbery, three hundred and seventy-eight; for burglary and housebreaking, one thousand and thirty-four; for forgery, one hundred and eighty-four; a catalogue which could by no means be matched in Ireland. However, those English and Scotch crimes and outrages were not done in assertion of public right or resistance of public wrong; that is to say, they were real crimes and outrages; they did not alarm the higher classes; and had seldom any social, political, or religious character. Therefore, it never entered into the mind of Government or Parliament to apply their "Crime and Outrage Act" to England or Scotland. In other words, the series of coercion laws for Ireland have always been proposed and passed under a false pretence; they are not to prevent crime, but to keep the people for ever helpless in the hands of their mortal enemies. They are not measures for reformation of society, but engines and arms for perpetuation of British rule in Ireland.

While our country was so rapidly sinking to beggary, and diminishing in population, it may be useful to cast a glance at the progress of the other island. This cannot be done better than by quoting a passage from Alison (chap. 56), in which he gives a general view of English affairs during a period of four years: "From 1848," he says, "to 1853, the effects of free-trade were displayed, undisturbed by any other or counteracting influences. *Plenty had again returned*, and spread its sunshine over the land. The harvest of 1847 had been so favourable that, at Lord John Russell's suggestion, a public thanks-

---

* It is now (1868) considerably under six millions.

* It is cited by Sir Archibald Alison, in chapter 56 of his *History*.

giving was offered up for it;* and this blessing continued unabated in a sensible degree throughout the period." The same historian proceeds to give statements exhibiting the enormous development of English commerce and wealth during the same period of four years, by reason of the gold discoveries in California and in Australia. But nothing of all that prosperity is for Ireland. Having scarcely any manufactures, she has no commerce, except her fatal commerce with England, under that "free-trade" which cheapens all which she has to sell, and makes dearer to that precise amount everything which she is forced to buy.

It may, therefore, be affirmed that in or about the year 1850, Ireland became thoroughly subjugated, without almost a hope of escape. Everything was fitted to the hand of her enemy, and that enemy made most unrelenting use of the advantage.

The Catholic bishops counselled obedience and submission; the formidable kind of "agitation" devised by O'Connell had become altogether impossible; because in the first place the very material for it (the "surplus population") had been swept off the face of the earth, and besides, the English Government had now so firm a hold of the poor, through "Crime and Outrage Acts," police and poor-laws, that it was more difficult than formerly to move the masses.

Parliamentary efforts, or rather pretences of effort, were made from time to time, to obtain ameliorations of some grievance or other. These pretences of effort, if they really tended to any good for Ireland, were always defeated, or rather, indeed, spurned by Parliament with disdain and insult, as it was always known they would be: and the total result of those Parliamentary movements may be defined as consisting of a few places distributed to rhetorical patriots. Thus, far from the Irish representation in Parliament serving as means of asserting Irish rights or interests, it helps to rivet the chains of our unhappy island, by opening a market overt, where patriots may be purchased (while still vociferating for justice to Ireland), and so silenced for ever.

Whatever has been effected for the good of the Irish people, whether to promote their moral and intellectual culture, or even to aid them in saving their lives, has been done exclusively by themselves. Two wonderful examples of this nature must be mentioned: *first*, the establishment of the Catholic University; and *second*, the immense fund which has been systematically contributed for some years by Irish people settled in the United States to aid their friends in escaping from British government.

It has already been seen, in the course of this history, what rigorous means were used during the last century to prevent the Catholic people, under the heaviest penalties, from being educated at all; and how the extraordinary eagerness for education on the part of those people had impelled them to seek in foreign schools and universities the instruction which none dared to give them at home—although there were both great risk and enormous expense incurred in these efforts to obtain contraband learning. It was the true English horror of "French principles," about the time of the great French revolution, which caused the penal laws against education to be relaxed; but no measures were taken by the enemy's Government to supply the place of that continental education for many years after; and when at last the "National Schools" were established, and, later still, when the three "Queen's Colleges" were built and endowed, it was found that the National Schools were so constituted as to be extremely un-national, or anti-national, and that the Queen's Colleges were still more adroitly arranged to wean Catholic students both from national sentiment, and from the faith and morals of their Church. Such, at least, was the judgment of the majority of the Irish bishops and clergy; and when we reflect upon the two chairs of history and moral philosophy, which must exist in every university, and on the effect of training up Catholic youth in the British principles upon these subjects, and causing them to regard human life and history from a strictly British point of view, it cannot be matter of wonder if the Catholic hierarchy lifted its voice against the new plans of education imposed on us by a London Parliament. In short, there was a necessity to provide some other and better system for the collegiate education of Catholic youth, and therefore, in the year 1854, pursuant to a recommendation coming from Rome, the Irish bishops formally instituted a free Catholic University, destined, like the Church (whose offspring it was) to subsist only upon the charity of the faithful, and to be completely independent of the State. Yet all this while the wealthy Protestant Corporation of Trinity College was maintained in splendour by estates plundered from

---

* The harvest of 1847 was also very abundant in Ireland, and it was one of the deadliest years of famine. The English offered thanksgivings to God for the Irish harvests, and then devoured them.

Catholic monasteries, and the "Queen's Colleges" were kept up at the public cost, to which the Catholics, as tax-payers, of course, had to contribute their full share. There was nothing, indeed, new in all this: they had been long used to maintain schools and churches for others, and to find the means of providing for their own religious services, and instruction also, as best they could.

The Board of the Catholic University of Dublin consists of the four archbishops, and two other prelates for each province. The institution comprises five faculties: those of theology, law, medicine, belles-lettres, and science. Its government is carried on by a committee of archbishops and bishops, meeting once a year. The immediate and ordinary administration is conducted by the "Senate" of the university, consisting of the rector and vice-rector, the secretary, the professors, the superiors of certain institutions dependent on the university, and the Fellows.* A yearly collection, made in every diocese, provides for the expenses of the foundation. The spirit and zeal with which this great national enterprise has been sustained, form an admirable illustration of the unselfish devotedness of the Irish people to an object which they believe to be good, or, in other words, anti-English. In the year 1859 they had already bestowed freely—and given their blessing along with it—the considerable sum of £80,000 sterling, for promotion of this noble object; and every year, even in the poorest chapels among the mountains of remote parishes, the appeal of the parish priest in favour of an institution blessed by the Pope and the bishops brings forth an offering even from the poorest.

All this great work has been done, it is true, in contravention of the views and policy of the British Government, not only without its help, but under the frown of its displeasure. The Catholic University has no charter of incorporation, and no legal right to confer degrees in arts or laws. In the eyes of the Government, it is but a private Association, tolerated but not recognized, as indeed the Catholic Church itself is.

Another strange and admirable example of the generous zeal of the Irish people in resisting the utter destruction of their race, is seen in the regular and systemized aid furnished by Irish citizens of the United States, to assist their friends and relatives in withdrawing themselves from the domination of England, and establishing themselves in a free country. The emigration of what is called the "surplus population" of Ireland has been aided and furthered in several ways. The landed proprietors, with a view to facilitate the consolidation of farms, and also to reduce the burden of poor rates in their respective "Unions," have largely contributed to help the emigration of the poor people whom they themselves exterminate; but this is a matter of private arrangement, and no *data* exist for even approximating to the amount supplied from this source. In 1848 the Poor-Law Unions were invited by the Government to co-operate in the movement of deportation, in order to furnish a gratuitous passage to such poor persons as had no other resource than expatriation. But this was to be at the expense of the Irish ratepayers, and was, moreover, to be in strict accordance with the views of the British Government itself. The emigration thus promoted was, therefore, to be almost entirely to the British Colonies, especially Australia. From 1847 to 1859 inclusive, the Unions contributed about £100,000 to the cost of emigration, removing from Ireland about 25,000 persons. But this was a trifle. The great rush of emigrants was to the United States, and the cost of the immense exodus was mainly provided for by the savings of Irish citizens already settled in that republic.

The Colonial Land and Emigration Commissioners, in their twelfth report, state that they do not believe that "The emigration will be arrested by anything short of a great improvement in the position of the labouring population in Ireland; all those obstacles which in ordinary cases would be opposed to so wholesale an emigration appear, in the case of the Irish, to be smoothed away. The misery which they have for many years endured has destroyed the attachment to their native soil, the numbers who have already emigrated and prospered remove the apprehension of going to a strange and untried country, while the want of means is remedied by the liberal contributions of their relations and friends who have preceded them. The contributions so made, either in the form of prepaid passages or of money sent home, and which are almost exclusively provided by the Irish, were returned to us, as in

1848, upwards of.................£460,000
1849,   "   540,000
1850,   "   957,000
1851.   "   990,000

And although it is probable that all the money included in these returns is not expended in emigration, yet, as we have reason to know that much is sent home of which these returns show no trace, it seems not unfair to assume that of the

---

* *Rules and Regulations.* § 7. The institutions dependent on the Catholic University are those of St. Patrick, St. Lawrence (Harcourt Street), Carmel, and Corpus Christi.

money expended in Irish emigration in each of the last four years a very large proportion was provided from the other side of the Atlantic."

The Abbé Perraud, in his *Etudes sur l' Irlande contemporaine*, says: "From the returns furnished by American bankers, the Emigration Commissioners give the precise amount of these remittances of money; but for North America only. The total for thirteen years (1848-1861) is £11,674,596 sterling. These statistics apply, indeed, to the emigrants from the three kingdoms; but as the Irish are in the immense majority, so it is the Irish who remit the far larger proportion of the money." It must be added, that the reports made up by American bankers can represent only a portion of the remittances from Irish citizens to their friends at home, because much money is sent through other channels, which cannot enter into those returns. On the whole, however, it is evident that the strong natural affection of the Irish for their parents and relatives, and their constant and ardent desire to deliver them from an odious bondage, have in this instance materially served the policy of the British Government, which is, to get rid of the Celtic enemy by any and by all means.

And, for the present, the policy of that Government seems to be eminently successful. The Celtic Irish in Ireland have greatly diminished in numbers, and are still diminishing. Yet there is another aspect of this affair. A vast mass of Irish power and Irish passion has been gathering and growing in the United States, all of it cherishing a mortal hatred of the British Empire, and a fierce thirst of vengeance on their enemies, as well as a loving and generous desire to emancipate their native country from the bitter thraldom of so many ages. From the Celtic Irish on the American continent arises one universal cry of execration against English dominion and English ideas. With independent means, a fair career for industry, and an increased and still increasing acquaintance with the story of their native country, there has grown up in their hearts an intense desire to right the wrongs of centuries, to lift up their kinsfolk and ancient clansmen out of the abject misery in which British policy requires them to be kept, and to see their countrymen in fair and full possession of the lovely land where Providence has placed them. This is a dangerous matter for the British Empire.

For the present, indeed, it may seem that, by the operation of all the well-devised arrangements for getting rid of the Irish people, what used to be called the "Irish difficulty" has become more manageable; the "Irish enemy," if not wholly destroyed, is at least disarmed and bound. No way of redress is left open except a violent revolution; and for this the people of Ireland and their kinsmen in America only await the opportunity of a war which shall tax the strength of their enemy.

A tabular summary of the financial condition of the country (as furnished by her enemy), up to the year 1852, may fitly close this story. It is to be observed upon these official returns, that we have no means of checking them, because our books are kept in England. Yet one or two remarks are obvious.

Most Irishmen are of opinion that they do not receive value for the charge on account of "Army, Navy, and Ordnance," believing, in fact, that the money would be much better spent in destroying those British services. [*Tabular Summary, see next page.*]

CONCLUSION.

THE compiler of this continuation of the Abbé MacGeoghegan's *History of Ireland* purposely stops short of the most recent events which have agitated that country, and disquieted and exasperated England. The time for relating the history of those events has not yet arrived. It may be said, however, that a powerful illustration has been thereby given to the fact, that while England is at peace with other powerful nations, it is extremely difficult, if not impossible, to make so much as a serious attempt at a national insurrection, in the face of a government so vigilant and so well prepared.

The high patriotic enthusiasm that impelled many brave Irishmen in America to fly across the Atlantic and devote to the rescue of their country that art of war which they had learned chiefly to that end, their experience in training men, the gallantry of the peasants, their extensive secret organizations—all seemed to break and dissolve away in the very hour of highest hope and resolve. All honour be to the men who made the daring effort, and staked their lives upon it. Whatever judgment may be formed of others, *they*, at least, "stood the cast their rashness played," and the best of them are expiating in dungeons the crime of loving their country and striving to serve her—just as Irishmen have generally expiated that offence for many ages. Yet no cause is utterly lost so long as it can inspire heroic devotion. No country is hopelessly vanquished whose sons love her better than their lives.

ACCOUNT of the INCOME and EXPENDITURE of IRELAND, in the Years ending 5th January, from 1847 to 1852, inclusive; showing the whole of the Ways and Means provided within the same period, together with the application thereof.—[*House of Commons Papers*, No. 528, 1849; No. 600, 1850; No. 477, 1851; No. 504, 1852.]

INCOME.	1847.			1848.			1849.			1850.			1851.			1852.		
	£	s.	d.	£	s.	d.	£	s.	d.	£	s.	d.	£	s.	d.	£	s.	d.
Net Payments into the Exchequer of the following several Duties or Revenues, viz.:—																		
Customs,	2,258,043	7	9	2,009,132	10	5	2,069,772	16	11	1,941,122	1	5	1,827,289	9	10	1,854,268	5	7
Excise,	1,467,060	4	5	1,152,931	12	1	1,321,914	19	9	1,231,548	8	3	1,312,122	15	10	1,348,911	6	5
Stamps,	573,766	10	4	567,996	9	1	532,924	8	6	504,072	19	1	462,691	1	11	451,534	5	11
Postage,	29,000	0	0	59,000	0	0	39,000	0	0	26,000	0	0	—			5,000	0	0
Crown Lands,	—			—			—			—			—			—		
Poundage Fee, Pells Fee, Treasury Fees, Hospital Fees, and Casualties,	6,062	5	4	5,698	18	4	4,835	1	6	6,632	17	1	5,744	2	7	8,999	11	10
Total Ordinary Revenue,	4,333,932	7	10	3,794,759	9	11	3,968,447	6	8	3,707,376	5	10	3,607,847	19	2	3,668,713	9	9
Moneys remaining in the Exchequer at the commencement of the year,	791,504	8	$7\frac{3}{4}$	702,151	3	$10\frac{3}{4}$	834,453	7	$11\frac{3}{4}$	815,371	13	$9\frac{3}{4}$	1,026,990	8	$10\frac{3}{4}$	621,891	8	$3\frac{3}{4}$
Other Receipts:—																		
Repayment of Money advanced for Public Works and other Public objects,	352,641	17	2	484,924	5	1	304,927	9	0	621,155	6	11	480,741	16	3	327,498	11	$1\frac{1}{4}$
Moneys Repaid by Public Accountants, and other Miscellaneous Payments,	5,887	19	0	46,160	5	0	2,000	16	9	3,928	3	3	6,063	5	5	4,469	16	6
Total Income,	5,483,966	12	$7\frac{3}{4}$	5,027,995	3	$10\frac{3}{4}$	5,109,829	0	$4\frac{3}{4}$	5,147,831	9	$9\frac{3}{4}$	5,121,643	9	$8\frac{3}{4}$	4,622,573	5	8
EXPENDITURE.																		
Dividends, Interest, and Management of Public Funded Debt, payable in Ireland,	1,315,550	3	10	1,347,611	17	2	1,391,586	14	7	1,386,101	1	2	1,373,222	4	0	1,394,097	17	1
Other Payments out of the Consolidated Fund,	902,855	15	0	849,082	4	8	949,957	12	4	939,321	18	10	909,836	1	0	854,272	7	2
Total Payments out of the Consolidated Fund,	2,218,405	18	10	2,196,694	1	10	2,341,544	6	11	2,325,423	0	0	2,283,058	5	0	2,248,370	4	3
Payments on account of Grants of Parliaments, viz.:—																		
Army,	1,143,980	0	0	910,000	0	0	625,000	0	0	626,000	0	0	785,000	0	0	585,000	0	0
Navy,	3,940	0	0	—			—			—			—			—		
Ordnance,	105,000	0	0	91,850	0	0	31,400	0	0	—			—			—		
Miscellaneous,	463,463	13	6	642,640	12	3	554,216	13	9	565,903	11	7	664,019	3	1	611,382	4	8
Other Payments:—																		
Money Advanced out of the Consolidated Fund for Public objects,	790,214	3	5	302,022	17	6	695,738	9	7	554,336	14	6	728,272	1	2	300,493	7	2
Total Expenditure,	4,730,003	15	9	4,143,207	11	7	4,247,899	10	3	4,071,663	6	1	4,460,379	9	3	3,715,245	16	1
Application of the Ways and Means provided:—																		
Applied to the Redemption of Exchequer Bills, per Act 57 Geo. III., cap. 48 (Deficiency Bills),	—			—			—			—			—			—		
Sums remitted through the Excise in Ireland to the Exchequer in England,	51,811	13	0	50,334	4	4	46,557	16	4	49,177	14	10	39,372	12	2	101,888	11	6
	4,781,815	8	9	4,193,541	15	11	4,294,457	6	7	4,120,841	0	11	4,499,752	1	5	3,847,134	7	7
Money remaining in Exchequer at end of year,	702,151	3	$10\frac{3}{4}$	834,453	7	$11\frac{3}{4}$	815,371	13	$9\frac{3}{4}$	1,026,990	8	$10\frac{3}{4}$	621,891	8	$3\frac{3}{4}$	775,438	18	1
TOTAL,	5,483,966	12	$7\frac{3}{4}$	5,027,995	3	$10\frac{3}{4}$	5,109,829	0	$4\frac{3}{4}$	5,147,831	9	$9\frac{3}{4}$	5,121,643	9	$8\frac{3}{4}$	4,622,573	5	8

APPENDIX No. I.

THE ARTICLES OF UNION.

RESOLVED, 1. That in order to promote and secure the essential interests of Great Britain and Ireland, and consolidate the strength, power, and resources of the British Empire, it will be advisable to concur in such measures as may best tend to unite the two kingdoms of Great Britain and Ireland into one kingdom, in such manner, and on such terms and conditions, as may be established by the Acts of the respective Parliaments of Great Britain and Ireland.

Resolved, 2. That for the purpose of establishing an Union upon the basis stated in the resolution of the two Houses of Parliament of Great Britain, communicated by His Majesty's command in the message sent to this House by his Excellency the Lord-Lieutenant, it would be fit to propose as the first article of Union, that the kingdoms of Great Britain and Ireland shall upon the first day of January, which shall be in the year of Our Lord, one thousand eight hundred and one, and for ever after, be united in one kingdom, by the name of the United Kingdom of Great Britain and Ireland, and that the royal style and titles appertaining to the Imperial Crown of the said United Kingdom and its dependencies, and also the ensigns, armorial flags, and banners thereof, shall be such as His Majesty by his royal proclamation, under the Great Seal of the United Kingdom, shall be pleased to appoint.

Resolved, 3. That for the same purpose it would be fit to propose, that the succession to the Imperial Crown of the said United Kingdom, and of the dominions thereunto belonging, shall continue limited and settled in the same manner as the succession to the Imperial Crown of the said kingdoms of Great Britain and Ireland now stands limited and settled, according to the existing laws, and to the terms of the Union between England and Scotland.

Resolved, 4. That for the same purpose it would be fit to propose, that the said United Kingdom be represented in one and the same Parliament, to be styled the Parliament of the United Kingdom of Great Britain and Ireland.

Resolved, 5. That for the same purpose it would be fit to propose, that the charge arising from the payment of the interest and sinking fund, for the reduction of the principal of the debt incurred in either kingdom before the Union, shall continue to be separately defrayed by Great Britain and Ireland respectively.

That for the space of twenty years after the Union shall take place, the contribution of Great Britain and Ireland respectively, towards the expenditure of the United Kingdom in each year, shall be defrayed in the proportion of fifteen parts for Great Britain and two parts for Ireland, that at the expiration of the said twenty years the future expenditure of the United Kingdom, other than the interest and charges of the debt to which either country shall be separately liable, shall be defrayed in such proportion as the said United Parliament shall deem just and reasonable, upon a comparison of the real value of the exports and imports of the respective countries, upon an average of the three years next preceding the period of revision, or on a comparison of the value of the quantities of the following articles consumed within the respective countries, on a similar average, viz., beer, spirits, sugar, wine, tea, tobacco, and malt; or according to the aggregate proportion resulting from both these considerations combined, or on a comparison of the amount of income in each country, estimated from the produce for the same periods of a general tax, if such shall have been imposed on the same descriptions of income in both countries, and that the Parliament of the United Kingdoms shall afterwards proceed in like manner, to revise and fix the said proportions according to the same rules or any of them, at periods not more distant than twenty years, nor less than seven years from each other, unless previous to any such period the United Parliament shall have declared, as hereinafter provided, that the general expenses of the empire shall be defrayed indiscriminately by equal taxes, imposed on the like articles in both countries.

Resolved, 6. That for defraying the said expenses, according to the rules above laid down, the revenues of Ireland shall hereafter constitute a consolidated fund, upon which charges equal to the interest of the debt and sinking fund shall, in the first instance, be charged, and the remainder shall be applied towards defraying the proportion of the general expense of the United Kingdom to which Ireland may be liable in each year.

That the proportion of contribution to which Great Britain and Ireland will by these articles be liable, shall be raised by such taxes in each kingdom respectively as the Parliament of the United Kingdom shall from time to time deem fit, provided always, that in regulating the taxes in each country by which their respective proportion shall be levied, no article in Ireland shall be liable to be taxed to any amount exceeding that which will be thereafter payable in England on the like articles.

Resolved, 7. That if at the end of any year any surplus shall accrue from the revenues of Ireland, after defraying the interest, sinking fund, and proportioned contribution and separate charges to which the said country is liable, either taxes shall be taken off to the amount of such surplus, or the surplus shall be applied by the United Parliament to local purposes in Ireland, or to make good any deficiency which may arise in her revenues in time of peace, or invested by the commissioners of the national debt of Ireland in the funds, to accumulate for the benefit of Ireland, at compound interest, in case of contribution in time of war. *Provided*, The surplus so to accumulate shall at no future period be suffered to exceed the sum of five millions.

Resolved, 8. That all monies hereafter to be raised by loan, in peace or war, for the service of the United Kingdom by the Parliament thereof, shall be considered to be a joint debt, and the charges thereof shall be borne by the respective countries in the proportion of their respective contributions. *Provided*, That if at any time in raising the respective contributions hereby fixed for each kingdom, the Parliament of the United Kingdom shall judge it fit to raise a greater proportion of such respective contributions in one kingdom within the year than in the other, or to set apart a greater proportion of sinking fund for the liquidation of the whole, or any part of the loan raised on account of the one country than that raised on account of the other country, then such part of the said loan for the liquidation of which different provisions have been made for the respective countries, shall be kept distinct, and shall be borne by each separately, and only that part of the said loan be deemed joint and common, for the reduction of which the respective countries shall have made provision in the proportion of their respective contributions.

Resolved, 9. That if at any future day the separate debt of each kingdom respectively shall have been liquidated, or the values of their respective debts (estimated according to the amount of the interest and annuities attending the same, of the sinking fund applicable to the reduction thereof, and the period within which the whole capital of such debt shall appear to be redeemable by such sinking fund), shall be to each other in the same proportion with the respective contributions of each kingdom respectively, or where the amount by which the value of the larger of such debts shall vary from such proportion, shall not exceed one hundredth part of the said value; and if it shall appear to the United Parliament, that the respective circumstances of the two countries will thenceforth admit of their contributing indiscriminately, by equal taxes imposed on the same articles in each, to the future general expense of the United Kingdom, it shall be competent to the said United Parliament to declare, that all future expense thenceforth to be incurred, together with the interest and charges of all joint debts contracted previous to such declaration, shall be defrayed indiscriminately by equal taxes imposed on the same articles in each country, and thenceforth from time to time, as circumstances may require, to impose and apply such taxes accordingly, subject only to such particular exemptions or abatements in Ireland, and that part of Great Britain called Scotland, as circumstances may appear from time to time to demand, that from the period of such declaration, it shall no longer be necessary to regulate the contribution of the two countries towards the future general expenses, according to any of the rules hereinbefore provided.

Provided, nevertheless, That the interest or charges which may remain on account of any part of the separate debt with which either country is chargeable, and which shall not be liquidated or consolidated proportionately as above, shall, until extinguished, continue to be defrayed by separate taxes in each country.

Resolved, 10. That a sum not less than the sum which has been granted by the Parliament of Ireland, on the average of six years, as premiums for the internal encouragement of agriculture or manufacture, or for the maintaining institutions for pious and charitable purposes, shall be applied for the period of twenty years after the Union to such local purposes, in such manner as the Parliament of the United Kingdom shall direct.

Resolved, 11. That from and after the first day of January, one thousand eight hundred and one, all public revenue arising from the territorial dependencies of the United Kingdom shall be applied to the general expenditure of the empire, in the proportions of the respective contributions of the two countries.

Resolved, 12. That for the same purpose it would be fit to propose that . . . . . Lords spiritual of Ireland, and . . . . Lords temporal of Ireland, shall be the number to sit and vote on the part of Ireland in the House of Lords of the Parliament of the United Kingdom, and one hundred commoners (two for each county of Ireland, two for the City of Cork, one for the University of Trinity College, and one for each of the thirty-one most considerable cities, towns, and boroughs), be the number to sit and vote on the part of Ireland in the House of Commons in the Parliament of the United Kingdom.

Resolved, 13. That such Acts as shall be passed in the Parliament of Ireland previous to the Union to regulate the mode by which the Lords spiritual and temporal and the Commons to serve in the Parliament of the United Kingdom on the part of Ireland, shall be summoned or returned to the said Parliament, shall be considered as forming part of the Treaty of Union, and shall be incorporated in the Act of the respective Parliaments, by which the said Union shall be ratified and established.

Resolved, 14. That all questions touching the election of members to sit on the part of Ireland in the House of Commons of the United Kingdom, shall be heard and decided in the same manner as questions touching such elections in Great Britain now are, or at any time hereafter shall by law be, heard and decided, subject nevertheless to such particular regulations in respect of Ireland, as from local circumstances the Parliament of the said United Kingdom may from time to time deem expedient.

Resolved, 15. That the qualifications in respect of property of the members elected on the part of Ireland to sit in the House of Commons of the United Kingdom, shall be respectively the same as are now provided by law, in cases of elections for counties, and cities, and boroughs respectively, in that part of Great Britain called England, unless any other provision shall hereafter be made in that respect by Act of the Parliament of the United Kingdom.

Resolved, 16. That when His Majesty, his heirs, or successors, shall declare his, her, or their pleasure, for holding the first or any subsequent Parliament of the United Kingdom, a proclamation shall issue under the Great Seal of the United Kingdom, to cause the Lords spiritual and temporal and Commons who are to serve in the Parliament thereof on the part of Ireland, to be returned in such manner as by any Act of this present session of the Parliament of Ireland shall be provided; and that the Lords spiritual and temporal and Commons of Great Britain shall together with the Lords spiritual and temporal and Commons so returned as aforesaid, on the part of Ireland, constitute the two Houses of Parliament of the United Kingdom.

Resolved, 17. That if His Majesty on or before the first day of January, one thousand eight hundred and one, on which day the Union is to take place, shall declare, under the Great Seal of Great Britain, that it is expedient that the Lords and Commons of the present Parliament of Great Britain should be members of the respective Houses of the first Parliament of the United Kingdom on the part of Great Britain, then the said Lords and Commons of the present Parliament of Great Britain shall accordingly be the members of the respective Houses of the first Parliament of the United Kingdom on the part of Great Britain, and they, together with the Lords spiritual and temporal and Commons so summoned and returned as above on the part of Ireland, shall be the Lords spiritual and temporal and Commons of the first Parliament of the United Kingdom; and such first Parliament may (in that case), if not sooner dissolved, continue to sit so long as the present Parliament of Great Britain may now by law continue to sit, and that every one of the Lords of Parliament of the United Kingdom, and every member of the House of Commons of the United Kingdom, in the first and all succeeding Parliaments, shall, until the Parliament of the United Kingdom shall otherwise provide, take the oaths, and make and subscribe the declaration, which are at present by law enjoined to be taken, made, and subscribed by the Lords and Commons of the Parliament of Great Britain.

Resolved, 18. That for the same purpose it would be fit to propose that the churches of that part of Great Britain called England, and of Ireland, should be united into one Church, and the archbishops, bishops, deans and clergy of the churches of England and Ireland shall, from time to time, be summoned to and entitled to sit in convocation of the United Church in the like manner, and subject to the same regulations as are at present by law established, with respect to the like orders of the Church of England, and the doctrine, worship, discipline, and government of the United Church shall be preserved as now by law established for the Church of England; and the doctrine, worship, discipline, and government of the Church of Scotland shall likewise be preserved as now by law established for the Church of Scotland And that the continuance and preservation for ever of the said United Church, as the Established Church of that part of the United Kingdom called England and Ireland, shall be deemed and taken to be an essential and fundamental condition of the treaty of Union.

Resolved, 19. That for the same purpose all laws in force at the time of the Union, and all courts of civil and ecclesiastical jurisdiction within the respective kingdoms, shall remain as now by law established, subject only to such alterations and regulations, from time to time, as circumstances may appear to the Parliament of the United Kingdom to require, provided that all writs of error and appeals depending at the time of the Union, or hereafter to be brought, and which might now be finally decided by the House of Lords of either kingdom, shall from and after the Union be finally decided by the House of Lords of the United Kingdom; and provided that, from and after the Union there shall remain in Ireland an instance Court of Admiralty, for the determination of causes, civil and maritime only; and that all laws at present in force in either kingdom, which shall be contrary to any of the provisions which may be enacted by any Act for carrying this article into effect, be from and after the Union repealed.

Resolved, 20. That for the same purpose it would be fit to propose that His Majesty's subjects of Great Britain and Ireland shall, from and after the first day of January, one thousand eight hundred and one, be entitled to the same privileges, and be on the same footing as to encouragement and bounties on the like articles, being the growth, produce, or manufacture of either kingdom respectively, and generally in respect of trade and navigation in all ports and places in the United Kingdom and its dependencies; and that in all treaties made by His Majesty, his heirs and successors, with any foreign power, His Majesty's subjects of Ireland shall have the same privileges, and be on the same footing as His Majesty's subjects of Great Britain.

Resolved, 21. That from the first day of January, one thousand eight hundred and one, all prohibitions and bounties on the export of articles, the growth or manufacture of either country, to the other shall cease and determine; and that the said articles shall thenceforth be exported from one country to the other without duty or bounty on such export.

Resolved, 22. That all articles, the growth, produce, or manufacture of either Kingdom, not hereinafter enumerated as subject to specific duties, shall from henceforth be imported into each country from the other free from duty, other than such countervailing duty as shall be annexed to the several articles contained in the Schedule No. I;* and that the articles hereinafter enumerated shall be subject for the period of twenty years from the Union, on importation into each country from the other, to the duties specified in the Schedule No. II.,* annexed to this article, viz.:—

Apparel.	Millinery.
Brass, wrought.	Paper, stained.
Cabinet ware.	Pottery.
Coaches and carriages.	Saddlery.
Copper, wrought.	Silk, manufactured.
Cottons.	Stockings.
Glass.	Thread, bullion for lace, pearl, and spangles.
Haberdashery.	
Hats.	Tin plates, wrought iron, and hardware.
Lace, gold and silver; gold and silver threads.	

And that the woollen manufacture shall pay on importation into each country the duties now payable on importation into Ireland; salt and hops on importation into Ireland, duties not exceeding

* This refers to Schedules annexed to the resolutions, as originally introduced.

those which are now paid in Ireland; and coals on importation to be subject to burdens not exceeding those to which they are now subject.

That calicoes and muslins be subject and liable to the duties now payable on the same, until the fifth day of January, one thousand eight hundred and eight; and from and after the said day, the said duties shall be annually reduced in such proportion, and at such periods as shall hereafter be enacted, so as that the said duties shall stand at ten per cent. from and after the fifth day of January, one thousand eight hundred and sixteen, until the fifth day of January, which shall be in the year one thousand eight hundred and twenty-one; and that cotton, yarn, and cotton twist, shall also be subject and liable to the duties now payable upon the same, until the fifth day of January, one thousand eight hundred and eight, and from and after the said day the said duties shall be annually reduced at such times, and in such proportions, as shall be hereafter enacted, so as that all duties shall cease on the said articles from and after the fifth day of January, one thousand eight hundred and sixteen.

Resolved, 23. That any articles of the growth, produce, or manufacture of either country, which are or may be subject to internal duty, or to duty on the materials of which they are composed, may be made subject on their importation into each country respectively from the other, to such countervailing duty as shall appear to be just and reasonable in respect to such internal duty or duties on the materials; and that for the said purposes the articles specified in the said Schedule No. I. should, upon importation into Ireland, be subject to the duty which shall be set forth therein, liable to be taken off, diminished, or increased in the manner herein specified; and that upon the like export of the like articles from each country to the other respectively, a drawback shall be given, equal in amount to the countervailing duty, payable on the articles hereinbefore specified, on the import into the same country with the other; and that in like manner, in future, it shall be competent to the United Parliament to impose any new or additional countervailing duties, or to take off or diminish such existing countervailing duties as may appear on like principles to be just and reasonable, in respect of any future or additional internal duty on any article of the growth or manufacture of either country, or of any new additional duty on any materials of which such article may be composed, or any abatement of the same; and that when any such new or additional countervailing duty shall be so imposed on the import of any article into either country from the other, a drawback equal in amount to such countervailing duty, shall be given in like manner on the export of every such article respectively from the same country.

Resolved, 24. That all articles, the growth, produce, or manufacture of either kingdom, when exported through the other, shall in all cases be exported subject to the same charges as if they had been exported directly from the country of which they were the growth, produce, or manufacture.

Resolved, 25. That all duty charged on the import of foreign or colonial goods into either country, shall, on their export to the other, be either drawn back, or the amount, if any be retained, shall be placed to the credit of the country to which they shall be so exported, so long as the general expenses of the empire shall be defrayed by proportional contributions. *Provided*, Nothing herein shall extend to take away any duty, bounty, or prohibition which exists with respect to corn, meal, malt, flour, and biscuit, but that the same may be regulated, varied, or repeated, from time to time, as the United Parliament shall deem expedient.

APPENDIX No. II.

AN ACT FOR THE UNION OF GREAT BRITAIN AND IRELAND.

2d JULY, 1800.

WHEREAS, In pursuance of His Majesty's most gracious recommendation to the two Houses of Parliament in Great Britain and Ireland respectively, to consider of such measures as might best tend to strengthen and consolidate the connection between the two kingdoms, the two Houses of the Parliament of Great Britain and the two Houses of the Parliament of Ireland have severally agreed and resolved that, in order to promote and secure the essential interests of Great Britain and Ireland, and to consolidate the strength, power, and resources of the British empire, it will be advisable to concur in such measures as may best tend to unite the two kingdoms of Great Britain and Ireland into one kingdom, in such manner, and on such terms and conditions, as may be established by the Acts of the respective Parliaments of Great Britain and Ireland.

And whereas, in furtherance of the said resolution, both Houses of the said two Parliaments respectively have likewise agreed upon certain articles, for effectuating and establishing the said purposes, in the tenor following:—

ARTICLE I. That it be the first article of the Union of the kingdoms of Great Britain and Ireland, that the said kingdoms of Great Britain and Ireland shall, upon the first day of January, which shall be in the year of Our Lord one thousand eight hundred and one, and for ever after, be united into one kingdom, by the name of The United Kingdom of Great Britain and Ireland; and that the royal style and titles appertaining to the imperial crown of the said United Kingdom and its dependencies; and also the ensigns, armourial flags, and banners thereof shall be such as His Majesty, by his royal proclamation under the Great Seal of the United Kingdom, shall be pleased to appoint.

ARTICLE II. That it be the second article of Union, that the succession to the imperial crown of the said United Kingdom, and of the dominions thereunto belonging, shall continue limited and settled in the same manner as the succession to the imperial crown of the said kingdoms of Great Britain and Ireland now stands limited and settled, according to the existing laws, and to the terms of Union between England and Scotland.

ARTICLE III. That it be the third article of Union, that the said United Kingdom be represented in one and the same Parliament, to be styled "The Parliament of the United Kingdom of Great Britain and Ireland."

ARTICLE IV. That it be the fourth article of Union, that four lords spiritual of Ireland by rotation of sessions, and twenty-eight lords temporal of Ireland elected for life by the peers of Ireland, shall be the number to sit and vote on the part of Ireland in the House of Lords of the Parliament of the United Kingdom; and one hundred commoners (two for each county of Ireland, two for the city of Dublin, two for the city of Cork, one for the University of Trinity College, and one for each of the thirty-one most considerable cities, towns, and boroughs) be the number to sit and vote on the part of Ireland in the House of Commons of the Parliament of the United Kingdom.

That such Act as shall be passed in the Parliament of Ireland previous to the Union, to regulate the mode by which the lords spiritual and temporal and the commons, to serve in the Parliament of the United Kingdom on the part of Ireland, shall be summoned and returned to the said Parliament shall be considered as forming part of the treaty of Union, and shall be incorporated in the Acts of the respective Parliaments by which the said Union shall be ratified and established.

That all questions touching the rotation or election of lords spiritual or temporal of Ireland to sit in the Parliament of the United Kingdom, shall be decided by the House of Lords thereof; and whenever, by reason of an equality of votes in the election of any such lords temporal, a complete election shall not be made according to the true intent of this article, the names of those peers for whom such equality of votes shall be so given, shall be written on pieces of paper of a similar form, and shall be put into a glass, by the clerk of the Parliaments at the table of the House of Lords whilst the House is sitting; and the peer or peers whose name or names shall be first drawn out by the clerk of the Parliaments shall be deemed the peer or peers elected, as the case may be.

That any person holding any peerage of Ireland now subsisting, or hereafter to be created, shall not thereby be disqualified from being elected to serve, if he shall so think fit, or from serving or continuing to serve, if he shall so think fit, for any county, city, or borough of Great Britain, in the House of Commons of the United Kingdom, unless he shall have been previously elected as above, to sit in the House of Lords of the United Kingdom; but that so long as such peer of Ireland shall so continue to be a member of the House of Commons, he shall not be entitled to the privilege of peerage, nor be capable of being elected to serve as a peer on the part of Ireland, or of voting at any such election; and that he shall be liable to be sued, indicted, proceeded against, and tried as a commoner, for any offence with which he may be charged.

That it shall be lawful for His Majesty, his heirs and successors, to create peers of that part of the United Kingdom called Ireland, and to make promotions in the peerage thereof, after the Union; *Provided*, That no new creation of any such peers shall take place after the Union until three of the peerages of Ireland, which shall have been existing at the time of the Union, shall have become extinct; and upon such extinction of three peerages, that it shall be lawful for His Majesty, his heirs and successors, to create one peer of that part of the United Kingdom called Ireland; and in like manner so often as three peerages of that part of the United Kingdom called Ireland; and in like manner so often as three peerages of that part of the United Kingdom called Ireland shall become extinct, it shall be lawful for His Majesty, his heirs and successors, to create one other peer of the said part of the United Kingdom; and if it shall happen that the peers of that part of the United Kingdom called Ireland shall, by extinction of peerages or otherwise, be reduced to the number of one hundred, exclusive of all such peers as shall hold any peerage of Great Britain subsisting at the time of the Union, or of the United Kingdom created since the Union, by which such peers shall be entitled to an hereditary seat in the House of Lords of the United Kingdom, then and in that case it shall and may be lawful for His Majesty, his heirs and successors, to create one peer of that part of the United Kingdom called Ireland as often as any one of such one hundred peerages shall fail by extinction, or as often as any one peer of that part of the United Kingdom called Ireland shall become entitled, by descent or creation, to an hereditary seat in the House of Lords of the United Kingdom; it being the true intent and meaning of this article, that at all times after the Union it shall and may be lawful for His Majesty, his heirs and successors, to keep up the peerage of that part of the United Kingdom called Ireland to the number of one hundred, over and above the number of such of the said peers as shall be entitled by descent or creation to an hereditary seat in the House of Lords of the United Kingdom.

That if any peerage shall at any time be in abeyance, such peerage shall be deemed and taken as an existing peerage; and no peerage shall be deemed extinct, unless on default of claimants to the inheritance of such peerage for the space of one year from the death of the person who shall have been last possessed thereof; and if no claim shall be made to the inheritance of such peerage, in such form and manner as may from time to time be prescribed by the House of Lords of the United Kingdom, before the expiration of the said period of a year, then and in that case such peerage shall be deemed extinct; *Provided*, That nothing herein shall exclude any person from afterwards putting in a claim to the peerage so deemed extinct; and if such claim shall be allowed as valid, by judgment of the House of Lords of the United Kingdom reported to His Majesty, such peerage shall be considered as revived; and in case any new creation of a peerage of that part of the United Kingdom called Ireland shall have taken place in the interval, in consequence of the supposed extinction of such peerage, then no new right of creation shall accrue to His Majesty, his heirs or successors, in consequence of the next extinction which shall take place of any peerage of that part of the United Kingdom called Ireland.

That all questions touching the election of members to sit on the part of Ireland in the House of Commons of the United Kingdom shall be heard and decided in the same manner as questions touching such elections in Great Britain now are or at any time hereafter shall by law be heard and decided; subject nevertheless to such particular regulations in respect to Ireland as, from local circumstances, the Parliament of the United Kingdom may from time to time deem expedient.

That the qualifications in respect of property of the members elected on the part of Ireland to sit in the House of Commons of the United Kingdom, shall be respectively the same as are now provided by law in the cases of elections for counties and cities, and boroughs respectively in that part of Great Britain called England, unless any other provision shall hereafter be made in that respect by Act of Parliament of the United Kingdom.

That when His Majesty, his heirs or successors, shall declare his, her, or their pleasure for holding a first or any subsequent Parliament of the United Kingdom, a proclamation shall issue, under the Great Seal of the United Kingdom, to cause the Lords spiritual and temporal, and Commons, who are to serve in the Parliament thereof on the part of Ireland, to be returned in such manner as by any Act of this present session of the Parliament of Ireland shall be provided; and that the Lords spiritual and temporal and Commons of Great Britain shall together with the Lords spiritual and temporal and Commons so returned as aforesaid on the part of Ireland, constitute the two Houses of the Parliament of the United Kingdom.

That if His Majesty, on or before the first day of January, one thousand eight hundred and one, on which day the Union is to take place, shall declare, under the Great Seal of Great Britain, that it is expedient that the Lords and Commons of the present Parliament of Great Britain should be the members of the respective Houses of the first Parliament of the United Kingdom on the part of Great Britain; then the said Lords and Commons of the present Parliament of Great Britain shall accordingly be the members of the respective Houses of the first Parliament of the United Kingdom on the part of Great Britain; and they, together with the Lords spiritual and temporal and Commons, so summoned and returned as above on the part of Ireland, shall be the Lords spiritual and temporal and Commons of the first Parliament of the United Kingdom; and such first Parliament may (in that case), if not sooner dissolved, continue to sit so long as the present Parliament of Great Britain may by law now continue to sit, if not sooner dissolved: *Provided always*, That until an Act shall have passed in the Parliament of the United Kingdom, providing in what cases persons holding offices or places of profit under the Crown of Ireland, shall be incapable of being members of the House of Commons of the Parliament of the United Kingdom, no greater number of members than twenty, holding such offices or places as aforesaid, shall be capable of sitting in the said House of Commons of the Parliament of the United Kingdom; and if such a number of members shall be returned to serve in the said House, as to make the whole number of members of the said house holding such offices or places as aforesaid more than twenty, then and in such case the seats or places of such members as shall have last accepted such offices or places shall be vacated, at the option of such members, so as to reduce the number of members holding such offices or places to the number of twenty; and no person holding any such office or place shall be capable of being elected or of sitting in the said House, while there are twenty persons holding such offices or places sitting in the said House; and that every one of the Lords of Parliament of the United Kingdom, and every member of the House of Commons in the United Kingdom, in the first and all succeeding Parliaments, shall, until the Parliament of the United Kingdom shall otherwise provide, take the oaths, and make and subscribe the declaration, and take and subscribe the oath now by law enjoined to be taken, made, and subscribed by the Lords and Commons of the Parliament of Great Britain.

That the Lords of Parliament on the part of Ireland, in the House of Lords of the United Kingdom, shall at all times have the same privileges of Parliament which shall belong to the Lords of Parliament on the part of Great Britain; and the Lords spiritual and temporal respectively on the part of Ireland shall at all times have the same rights in respect of their sitting and voting upon the trial of peers, as the Lords spiritual and temporal respectively on the part of Great Britain; and that all Lords spiritual of Ireland shall have rank and precedency next and immediately after the Lords spiritual of the same rank and degree of Great Britain, and shall enjoy all privileges as fully as the Lords spiritual of Great Britain do now or may hereafter enjoy the same (the right and privilege of sitting in the House of Lords, and the privileges depending thereon, and particularly the right of sitting on the trial of peers, excepted); and that the persons holding any temporal peerages of Ireland, existing at the time of the Union, shall, from and after the Union, have rank and precedency next and immediately after all the persons holding peerages of the like orders and degrees in Great Britain, subsisting at the time of the Union; and that all peerages of Ireland created after the Union shall have rank and precedency with the peerages of the United Kingdom so created, according to the dates of their creations; and that all peerages both of Great Britain and Ireland, now subsisting or hereafter to be created, shall in all other respects, from the date of the Union, be considered as peerages of the United Kingdom; and that the peers of Ireland shall, as peers of the United Kingdom, be sued and tried as peers, except as aforesaid, and shall enjoy all privileges of peers as fully as the peers of Great Britain; the right and privilege of sitting in the House of Lords, and the privileges depending thereon, and the right of sitting on the trial of peers, only excepted.

ARTICLE V. That it be the fifth article of Union, that the Churches of England and Ireland, as now by law established, be united into one Protestant Episcopal Church, to be called *The United Church of England and Ireland*; and that the doctrine, worship, discipline, and government of the said United Church shall be and shall remain in full force for ever, as the same are now by law established for the Church of England; and that the continuance and preservation of the said United Church as the Established Church of England and Ireland, shall be deemed and taken to be an essential and fundamental part of the Union; and that in like manner the doctrine, worship, discipline, and government of the Church of Scotland shall remain and be preserved, as the same are now established by law, and by the Acts for the Union of the two kingdoms of England and Scotland.

ARTICLE VI. That it be the sixth article of Union, that His Majesty's subjects of Great Britain and Ireland shall, from and after the first day of January, one thousand eight hundred and one, be entitled to the same privileges, and be on the same footing, as to encouragements and bounties, on the like articles, being the growth, produce, or manufacture of either country respectively, and generally in respect of trade and navigation in all ports and places in the United Kingdom and its dependencies; and that in all treaties made by His Majesty, his heirs and successors, with any foreign power, His Majesty's subjects of Ireland shall have the same privileges, and be on the same footing, as His Majesty's subjects of Great Britain.

That, from the first day of January, one thousand eight hundred and one, all prohibitions and bounties on the export of articles, the growth, produce, or manufacture of either country, to the other, shall cease and determine; and that the said articles shall henceforth be exported from one country to the other without duty or bounty on such export.

That all articles, the growth, produce, or manufacture of either country (not hereinafter enumerated as subject to specific duties), shall from thenceforth be imported into each country from the other free from duty, other than such countervailing duties on the several articles enumerated in the Schedule Number One, A. and B., hereunto annexed, as are therein specified, or to such other countervailing duties as shall hereafter be imposed by the Parliament of the United Kingdom, in the manner hereinafter provided; and that, for the period of twenty years from the Union, the articles enumerated in the Schedule Number Two, hereunto annexed, shall be subject, on importation into each country from the other, to the duties specified in the said Schedule Number Two; and the woollen manufactures, known by the names of *Old* and *New Drapery*, shall pay, on importation into each country from the other, the duties now payable on importation into Ireland; salt and hops, on importation into Ireland from Great Britain, duties not exceeding those which are now paid on importation into Ireland; and coals, on importation into Ireland from Great Britain, shall be subject to burdens not exceeding those to which they are now subject.

That calicos and muslins shall, on their importation into either country from the other, be subject and liable to the duties now payable on the same, on the importation thereof from Great Britain into Ireland, until the fifth day of January, one thousand eight hundred and eight; and from and after the said day the said duties shall be annually reduced, by equal proportions, as near as may be in each year, so as that the said duties shall stand at ten per centum from and after the fifth day of January, one thousand eight hundred and sixteen, until the fifth day of January, one thousand eight hundred and twenty-one; and that cotton yarn and cotton twist shall, on their importation into either country from the other, be subject and liable to the duties now payable upon the same on the importation thereof from Great Britain into Ireland, until the fifth day of January, one thousand eight hundred and eight, and from and after the said day the said duties shall be annually reduced by equal proportions as near as may be in each year, so as that all duties shall cease on the said articles from and after the fifth day of January, one thousand eight hundred and sixteen.

That any articles of the growth, produce, or manufacture of either country, which are or may be subject to internal duty, or to duty on the materials of which they are composed, may be made subject, on their importation into each country respectively from the other, to such countervailing duty as shall appear to be just and reasonable in respect of such internal duty or duties on the materials; and that for the said purposes the articles specified in the said Schedule Number One A. and B. shall be subject to the duties set forth therein, liable to be taken off, diminished, or increased in the manner herein specified; and that upon the export of the said articles from each country to the other respectively, a drawback shall be given equal in amount to the countervailing duty payable on such articles on the import thereof into the same country from the other; and that in like manner in future it shall be competent to the United Parliament to impose any new or additional countervailing duties, or to take off or diminish such existing countervailing duties as may appear, on like principles, to be just and reasonable in respect of any future or additional internal duty on any article of the growth, produce, or manufacture of either country, or of any new or additional duty on any materials of which such article may be composed, or of any abatement of duty on the same; and that when any such new or additional countervailing duty shall be so imposed on the import of any article into either country from the other, a drawback, equal in amount to such countervailing duty, shall be given in like manner on the export of every such article respectively from the same country to the other.

That all articles, the growth, produce, or manufacture of either country, when exported through the other, shall in all cases be exported subject to the same charges as if they had been exported directly from the country of which they were the growth, produce, or manufacture.

That all duty charged on the import of foreign or colonial goods into either country shall, on their export to the other, be either drawn back, or the amount, if any be retained, shall be placed to the credit of the country to which they shall be so exported, so long as the expenditure of the United Kingdom shall be defrayed by proportional contributions: *Provided always*, That nothing herein shall extend to take away any duty, bounty, or prohibition, which exists with respect to corn, meal, malt, flour, or biscuit; but that all duties, bounties, or prohibitions, on the said articles, may be regulated, varied, or repealed, from time to time, as the United Parliament shall deem expedient.

ARTICLE VII. That it be the seventh article of Union that the charge arising from the payment of the interest, and the sinking fund for the reduction of the principal, of the debt incurred in either kingdom before the Union, shall continue to be separately defrayed by Great Britain and Ireland respectively, except as hereinafter provided.

That for the space of twenty years after the Union shall take place, the contribution of Great Britain and Ireland respectively, towards the expenditure of the United Kingdom in each year, shall be defrayed in the proportion of fifteen parts for Great Britain and two parts for Ireland; and that at the expiration of the said twenty years, the future expenditure of the United Kingdom (other than the interest and charges of the debt to which either country shall be separately liable) shall be defrayed in such proportion as the Parliament of the United Kingdom shall deem just and reasonable, upon a comparison of the real value of the exports and imports of the respective countries, upon an average of the three years next preceding the period of revision; or on a comparison of the value of the quantities of the following articles consumed within the respective countries, on a similar average; viz., beer, spirits, sugar, wine, tea, tobacco, and malt; or according to the aggregate proportion resulting from both these considerations combined; or on a comparison of the amount of income in each country, estimated from the produce for the same period of a general tax, if such shall have been imposed on the same descriptions of income in both countries; and that the Parliament of the United Kingdom shall afterwards proceed in like manner to revise and fix the said proportions according to the same rules, or any of them, at periods not more distant than twenty years, nor less than seven years from each other; unless, previous to any such period, the Parliament of the United Kingdom shall have declared, as hereinafter provided, that the expenditure of the United Kingdom shall be defrayed indiscriminately, by equal taxes imposed on the like articles in both countries: that, for the defraying the said expenditure according to the rules above laid down, the revenues of Ireland shall hereafter constitute a consolidated fund, which shall be charged in the first instance with the interest of the debt of Ireland, and with the sinking fund applicable to the reduction of the said debt, and the remainder shall be applied towards defraying the proportion of the expenditure of the United Kingdom to which Ireland may be liable in each year; that the proportion of contribution to which Great Britain and Ireland will be liable shall be raised by such taxes in each country respectively as the Parliament of the United Kingdom shall from time to time deem fit: *Provided always*, That in regulating the taxes in each country, by which their respective proportions shall be levied, no article in Ireland shall be made liable to any new or additional duty, by which the whole amount of duty payable thereon would exceed the amount which will be thereafter payable in England on the like article; that if, at the end of any year, any surplus shall accrue from the revenues of Ireland, after defraying the interest, sinking fund, and proportional contribution and separate charges to which the said country shall then be liable, taxes shall be taken off to the amount of such surplus, or the surplus shall be applied by the Parliament of the United Kingdom to local purposes in Ireland, or to make good any deficiency which may arise in the revenues of Ireland in time of peace, or be invested, by the commissioners of the national debt of Ireland, in the funds, to accumulate for the benefit of Ireland at compound interest, in case of the contribution of Ireland in time of war: *Provided*, That the surplus so to accumulate shall at no future period be suffered to exceed the sum of five Millions: that all moneys to be raised after the Union, by loan, in peace or war, for the service of the United Kingdom by the Parliament thereof, shall be considered to be a joint debt, and the charges thereof shall be borne by the respective countries in the proportion of their respective contributions: *Provided*, That if at any time, in raising their respective contributions hereby fixed for each country, the Parliament of the United Kingdom shall judge it fit to raise a greater proportion of such respective contributions in one country within the year than in the other, or to set apart a greater proportion of sinking fund for the liquidation of the whole or any part of the loan raised on account of the one country than that raised on account of the other country, then such part of the said loan, for the liquidation of which different provisions shall have been made for the respective countries, shall be kept distinct, and shall be borne by each separately, and only that part of the said loan be deemed joint and common, for the reduction of which the respective countries shall have made provision in the proportion of their respective contributions: that if at any future day the separate debt of each country respectively shall have been liquidated, or if the values of their respective debts (estimated according to the amount of the interest and annuities attending the same, and of the sinking fund applicable to the reduction thereof, and to the period within which the whole capital of such debt shall appear to be redeemable by such sinking fund) shall be to each other in the same proportion with the respective contributions of each country respectively; or if the amount by which the value of the larger of such debts shall vary from such proportion, shall not exceed one-hundredth part of the said value; and if it shall appear to the Parliament of the United Kingdom that the respective circumstances of the two countries will thenceforth admit of their contributing indiscriminately, by equal taxes imposed on the same articles in each, to the future expenditure of the United Kingdom, it shall be competent to the Parliament of the United Kingdom to declare that all future expense thenceforth to be incurred, together with the interest and charges of all joint debts contracted previous to such declaration, shall be so defrayed indiscriminately by equal taxes imposed on the same articles in each country, and thenceforth from time to time, as circumstances may require, to impose and apply such taxes accordingly, subject only to such particular exemptions or abatements in Ireland, and in that part of Great Britain called Scotland, as circumstances may appear from time to time to demand; that, from the period of such declaration, it shall no longer be necessary to regulate the contribution of the two countries towards the future expenditure of the United Kingdom according to any specific proportion, or according to any of the rules herein before described: *Provided nevertheless*, That the interest or charges which may remain on account of any part of the separate debt with which either country shall be chargeable, and which shall not be liquidated or consolidated proportionally as above, shall, until extinguished, continue to be defrayed by separate taxes in each country; that a sum, not less than the sum which has been granted by the Parliament of Ireland on the average of six years immediately preceding the first day of January, in the year one thousand eight hundred, in premiums for the internal encouragement of agriculture or manufactures, or for the maintaining institutions for pious and charitable purposes, shall be applied, for the period of twenty years after the Union, to such local purposes in Ireland, in such manner as the Parliament of the United Kingdom shall direct; that, from and after the first day of January, one thousand eight hundred and one, all public revenue arising to the United Kingdom from the territorial dependencies thereof, and applied to the general expenditure of the United Kingdom, shall be so applied in the proportions of the respective contributions of the two countries.

ARTICLE VIII. That it be the eighth article of the Union, that all laws in force at the time of the Union, and all the courts of civil and ecclesiastical jurisdiction within the respective kingdoms, shall remain as now by law established within the same, subject only to such alterations and regulations from time to time as circumstances may appear to the Parliament of the United Kingdom to require. *Provided*, That all writs of error and appeals depending at the time of the Union or hereafter to be brought, and which might now be finally decided by the House of Lords of either kingdom, shall, from and after the Union, be finally decided by the House of Lords of the United Kingdom: *And provided*, That from and after the Union there shall remain in Ireland an instance Court of Admiralty, for the determination of causes, civil and maritime only, and that the appeal from sentences of the said court shall be to His Majesty's delegates in his Court of Chancery in that part of the United Kingdom called Ireland: and that all laws at present in force in either kingdom, which shall be contrary to any of the provisions which may be enacted by any Act for carrying these articles into effect, be from and after the Union repealed.

And whereas, the said articles having, by address of the respective Houses of Parliament in Great Britain and Ireland, been humbly laid before His Majesty, His Majesty has been graciously pleased to approve the same; and to recommend it to his two Houses of Parliament in Great Britain and Ireland, to consider of such measures as may be necessary for giving effect to the said articles; in order, therefore, to give full effect and validity to the same, be it enacted by the King's Most Excellent Majesty, by and with the advice and consent of the Lords spiritual and temporal, and Commons, in this present Parliament assembled, and by the authority of the same, that the said foregoing recited articles, each and every one of them, according to the true import and tenor thereof, be ratified, confirmed, and approved. and be and they are hereby declared to be the articles of the Union of Great Britain and Ireland; and the same shall be in force and have effect forever, from the first day of January, which shall be in the year of our Lord, one thousand eight hundred and one. *Provided*, That before that period an Act shall have been passed by the Parliament of Ireland, for carrying into effect, in the like manner, the said foregoing recited articles.

[Here follows the supplementary enactment for regulating the mode of summoning the Irish Lords and Commons to sit in the then current United Parliament. This enactment is sufficiently described in the text.]

APPENDIX No. III.

PROCLAMATIONS FOUND IN EMMET'S ARMS-DEPOTS, INTENDED TO BE ISSUED ON THE DAY OF THE OUTBREAK.

The Provisional Government to the People of Ireland:

"You are now called upon to show to the world that you are competent to take your place among nations, that you have a right to claim their recognizance of you as an independent country, by the only satisfactory proof you can furnish of your capability of maintaining your independence, your wresting it from England with your own hands.

"In the development of this system, which has been organized within the last eight months, at the close of internal defeat, and without the hope of external assistance—which has been conducted with a tranquillity mistaken for obedience, which neither the failure of a similar attempt in England has retarded, nor the renewal of hostilities has accelerated—in the development of this system you will show to the people of England that there is a spirit of perseverance in this country beyond their power to calculate or repress. You will show them that as long as they think to hold unjust dominion over Ireland, under no change of circumstances can they count upon its obedience; under no aspect of affairs can they judge of its intentions; you will show to them that the question which it now behooves them to take into serious and instant consideration is not, whether they will resist a separation, which it is our fixed determination to effect, but whether or not they will *drive us beyond separation*—whether they will, by a sanguinary resistance, create a deadly national antipathy between the two countries, or whether they will take the only means still left of driving such a sentiment from our minds—a prompt, manly, and sagacious acquiescence in our just and unalterable determination.

"If the secrecy with which the present effort has been conducted shall have led our enemies to suppose that its extent must have been partial, a few days will undeceive them. That confidence which was once lost by trusting to external support, and suffering our own means to be gradually undermined, has been again restored. We have been mutually pledged to each other, to look only at our own strength, and that the first introduction of a system of terror, the first attempt to execute an individual in one county should be a signal for insurrection in all. We have now, without the loss of a man, with our means of communication untouched, brought our plans to the moment when they are ripe for execution, and in the promptitude with which nineteen counties will come forward at once to execute them, it will be found that neither confidence nor communication are wanting to the people of Ireland.

"In calling on our countrymen to come forward, we feel ourselves bound at the same time to justify our claim to their confidence by a precise declaration of our views. We therefore solemnly declare that our object is to establish a free and independent Republic in Ireland; that the pursuit of this object we will relinquish only with our lives; that we will never, but at the express call of our country, abandon our post till the acknowledgment of its independence is obtained from England; and that we will enter into no negotiation (but for exchange of prisoners) with the Government of that country while a British army remains in Ireland. Such is the declaration which we call on the people of Ireland to support. And we call first on that part of Ireland which was once paralyzed by the want of intelligence to show that to that cause only was its inaction to be attributed; on that part of Ireland which was once foremost by its fortitude in suffering; on that part of Ireland which once offered to take the salvation of the country on itself; on that part of Ireland where the flame of liberty first glowed; we call upon the North to stand up and shake off their slumber and oppressions.

"Citizens of Dublin:

"A band of patriots, mindful of their oath, and faithful to their engagement as united Irishmen, have determined to give freedom to their country, and a period to the long career of English oppression.

"In this endeavour they are now successfully engaged, and their efforts are seconded by complete and universal co-operation from the country, every part of which, from the extremity of the North to that of the South, pours forth its warriors in support of our hallowed cause. Citizens of Dublin, we require your aid. Necessary secrecy has prevented, to many of you, notice of our plan, but the erection of our national standard, the sacred, though long degraded, green, will be sufficient to call to arms and rally round it every man in whose breast exists a spark of patriotism or sense of duty. Avail yourselves of your local advantages—in a city each street becomes a defile, and each house a battery. Impede the march of your oppressors; charge them with the arms of the brave—the pike; and from your windows and roofs hurl stones, bricks, bottles, and all other convenient implements, on the head of the satellites of your tyrant, the mercenary, the sanguinary soldiery of England.

"Orangemen! add not to the catalogue of your follies and crimes. Already have you been duped to the ruin of your country, in the legislative union with its tyrant; attempt not an opposition which will carry with it your inevitable destruction. Return from your paths of delusion—return to the arms of your countrymen, who will receive and hail your repentance.

"Countrymen of all descriptions, let us act with union and concert. All sects, Catholic, Protestant, Presbyterian, are equally and indiscriminately embraced in the benevolence of your object. Repress, prevent, and discourage excesses, pillage, and intoxication. Let each man do his duty, and remember that during public agitation inaction becomes a crime. Be no other competition known than that of doing good. Remember against whom you fight—your oppressors for six hundred years; remember their massacres, their tortures; remember your murdered friends, your burned houses, your violated females; keep in mind your country, to whom we are now giving her high rank among nations, and in the honest terror of feeling let us exclaim, that as in the hour of trial we serve this country, so may God serve us in that, which will be last of all."

CAMERON & FERGUSON'S
POPULAR PUBLICATIONS.

⁎* *Any of the Books mentioned in this List, as well as the other Publications of* CAMERON & FERGUSON, *may be had of the Booksellers, or will be sent, post free, to any person who forwards to the Publishers, at their address, 88 West Nile Street, Glasgow, the required number of postage stamps.*

MUSIC BOOKS.

FOR THE PIANOFORTE.

The Excelsior Collection of Pianoforte Music: the Cheapest and most Comprehensive Work for this Instrument ever issued; containing over 600 MELODIES OF ALL NATIONS, and a Selection of DANCE MUSIC. By C. H. MORINE. This handsome volume, which is full music size, may be had bound in Extra Fancy Cloth, price 16s.; or half-bound in Morocco, price 18s.; and is an elegant and appropriate Gift for a lady. The Publishers will forward a copy, free to any address in the United Kingdom, on receipt of any of the prices named. The above work comprises the following Twelve separate Books, each complete in itself, and done up in Coloured Pictorial Cover. Any of the Series, price 1s., or free by post for 14 stamps.

1. SIXTY SCOTTISH AIRS.
2. FIFTY CHRISTY'S MINSTRELS' AIRS.
3. FIFTY-EIGHT ENGLISH AND NATIONAL AIRS.
4. FIFTY-EIGHT IRISH AIRS.
5. FIFTY-FOUR AIRS OF ALL NATIONS.
6. FORTY-SIX FAVOURITE OPERATIC AIRS.
7. FIFTY AMERICAN AND NEGRO MELODIES.
8. FIFTY-FOUR SCOTTISH MELODIES. *Second Series.*
9. FIFTY-SIX MOORE'S AND OTHER IRISH MELODIES.
10. SCOTTISH DANCE MUSIC, consisting of REELS and STRATHSPEYS.
11. QUADRILLES AND COUNTRY DANCES.
12. WALTZES, POLKAS, SCHOTTISCHES, MAZURKAS, JIGS, HORNPIPES, MARCHES, AND MISCELLANEOUS DANCES.

Morine's Pianoforte Tutor: a complete Course of Instructions, arranged on a simple, novel, and progressive plan, by which the usually dry details of the Elementary Lessons are rendered easy of acquirement and pleasing to the Pupil. The Work consists of a *Selection of Tunes* in graduated succession, from the most simple melody performed with one hand to the more perfect composition requiring facility with both: advancement in the art of playing being thus simultaneous with the acquisition of the Rudiments, the labour of both Teacher and Pupil is greatly lessened. Full music size, in beautifully Illustrated Cover, price 1s., or free by post for 14 stamps.

88 and 94 WEST NILE STREET, GLASGOW.

FOR THE HARMONIUM.

The Alexandre Tutor for the Harmonium: a complete Course of Lessons, with Progressive Exercises, and Selection of Favourite Airs, Sacred and Secular. Full music size. Price 1s., free by post for 14 stamps.

FOR THE CORNETTE AND TROMBONETTE.

Bain's Selection of Airs for the Cornette and Trombonette, with Instructions and Scales, being a complete Self-instructor for these Instruments. Price 6d., free by post for 7 stamps.

FOR THE CONCERTINA.

SONGS SERIES.

Containing the Words and Music of all the Songs, and admirably adapted for Vocal Accompaniment to this popular Instrument. Each book done up in handsome Illustrated Cover, printed in Colours.

The Treasury of Songs for the Concertina; containing One Hundred and Twenty of the most Popular Songs of the Day, with the Words and Music, arranged for Singing and Playing. Price 1s., free by post for 14 stamps.

Sixty Christy's Minstrels' Songs for the Concertina, with the Words and Music. Price 6d., free by post for 7 stamps.

Sixty English and National Songs for the Concertina, with the Words and Music. Price 6d., free by post for 7 stamps.

Sixty Scottish Songs for the Concertina, with the Words and Music. Price 6d., free by post for 7 stamps.

Sixty Irish Songs for the Concertina, with the Words and Music. Price 6d., free by post for 7 stamps.

Sixty American and Negro Songs for the Concertina, with the Words and Music. Price 6d., free by post for 7 stamps.

Sixty Sacred Songs—Psalms and Hymns—for the Concertina, with the Words and Music. Price 6d., free by post for 7 stamps.

Sixty Comic and Burlesque Songs for the Concertina, with the Words and Music. Price 6d., free by post for 7 stamps.

The Green Flag of Ireland National Songs for the Concertina, with the Words and Music. Price 6d., free by post for 7 stamps.

FOR THE CONCERTINA.

ADAMS'S NEW AND POPULAR SERIES.

The Complete Tutor for the Concertina: a concise Course of Lessons in Music, simple Instructions for Playing, and a varied Selection of the most Popular Airs of the day, marked and figured for playing. Price 1s., post free for 14 stamps.

The Art of Playing the Concertina without a Master: an improved and complete Tutor for the Instrument. With Lessons on Music, Scales, and a Selection of Favourite Airs marked and figured. Price 6d., post free for 7 stamps.

100 Christy's Minstrels' Airs, marked and figured for the 10, 20, 22, and 28 keyed Concertina. With complete Instructions and Scales. Price 6d., post free for 7 stamps.

100 English and National Airs, marked and figured for the 10, 20, 22, and 28 keyed Concertina. With complete Instructions and Scales. Price 6d., post free for 7 stamps.

100 Scottish Airs, marked and figured for the 10, 20, 22, and 28 keyed Concertina. With complete Instructions and Scales. Price 6d., post free for 7 stamps.

100 Irish Airs, marked and figured for the 10, 20, and 22 keyed Concertina. With complete Instructions and Scales. Price 6d., post free for 7 stamps.

100 Favourite Airs, Dances, Songs, &c., marked and figured for the 10, 20, 22, and 28 keyed Concertina. With complete Instructions and Scales. Price 6d., post free for 7 stamps.

100 Moore's Irish Melodies, marked and figured for the 10, 20, 22, and 28 keyed Concertina; containing the most popular of those exquisite National Airs. Price 6d., post free for 7 stamps.

Adams's Dancing Tunes; containing a variety of Quadrilles, Waltzes, Polkas, Schottisches, Country Dances, Jigs, Reels, &c., &c., marked and figured for playing. Price 6d., post free for 7 stamps.

Scottish Dance Music; containing Reels, Strathspeys, Jigs, Country Dances, &c., marked and figured. Price 6d., post free for 7 stamps.

100 American and Negro Melodies: a Second Series of the Popular Airs performed by Christy's Minstrels, Buckley's Serenaders, and Ethiopian Companies, marked and figured. Price 6d., post free for 7 stamps.

120 Sacred Airs, marked and figured for the 10, 20, 22, and 28 keyed Concertina. With complete Instructions and Scales. Price 6d., post free for 7 stamps.

Adams's Selection of Airs for the 20 keyed Concertina, marked and figured. Price 6d., post free for 7 stamps.

230 Airs of All Nations: a varied and popular Collection of Tunes, marked and figured. Price 1s., post free for 14 stamps.

Adams's Miscellany of Popular Airs for the Concertina; containing the best Collection of Tunes for the Instrument yet published. With Instructions, Scales, &c. Price 1s., post free for 14 stamps.

FOR THE FLUTE.

ADAMS'S POPULAR SERIES.

The Art of Playing the Flute without a Master: an improved and complete Tutor for the Instrument; with Instructions, Scales, and 66 Popular Airs. Price 6d., post free for 7 stamps.

100 Scottish Airs for the Flute; with Instructions and Scales for the Instrument. Price 6d., post free for 7 stamps.

100 English and National Airs for the Flute; with Instructions and Scales for the Instrument. Price 6d., post free for 7 stamps.

100 Irish Airs for the Flute; with Instructions and Scales for the Instrument. Price 6d., post free for 7 stamps.

100 Christy's Minstrels' Airs for the Flute; with Instructions and Scales for the Instrument. Price 6d., post free for 7 stamps.

215 Airs of All Nations for the Flute; containing a great variety of Popular Airs; with Instructions, Scales, &c. Price 1s., post free for 13 stamps.

FOR THE VIOLIN.

ADAMS'S POPULAR SERIES.

The Art of Playing the Violin without a Master: an improved and complete Tutor for the Instrument; with Instructions, Scales, and 65 Popular Airs. Price 6d., post free for 7 stamps.

100 Scottish Airs for the Violin; with Instructions and Scales for the Instrument. Price 6d., post free for 7 stamps.

100 English and National Airs for the Violin; with Instructions and Scales for the Instrument. Price 6d., post free for 7 stamps.

100 Irish Airs for the Violin; with Instructions and Scales for the Instrument. Price 6d., post free for 7 stamps.

100 Christy's Minstrels' Airs for the Violin; with Instructions and Scales for the Instrument. Price 6d., post free for 7 stamps.

228 Airs of All Nations for the Violin; containing a varied Selection of Popular Airs; with Instructions, Scales, &c. Price 1s., post free for 13 stamps.

SENSATION SHILLING VOLUMES,

CONSISTING OF

NOVELS AND ROMANCES,

Now Ready, Price One Shilling, or Free by Post for 14 Stamps.

1. **Five Sea Novels, Complete. 512 pages, Crown 8vo,** Illustrated Cover.
2. **Romances of the American War; containing Eight** Exciting Tales of Love and Battle. Royal 8vo, 336 pages, with Pictorial Cover, and Eight full-page Illustrations printed on Toned Paper.
3. **Tales of the Far West, abounding in Excitement and** Adventure. Crown 8vo, 512 pages, Illustrated Cover.
4. **The Story Teller; or, Romances of the Land and the** Sea. Royal 4to, with Large Illustrations.
5. **Round the Camp-Fire; or, Tales of the Bivouac and** Battle-Field. Foolscap 8vo, Enamelled Boards, Pictorial Cover.
6. **Adventures on the Prairies; and Life among the** Indians: abounding in thrilling Interest and Romance. Royal 8vo, with full-page Illustrations.
7. **Romances of Crime; or, The Disclosures of a Detec-**tive. By James M'Levy. Foolscap 8vo, Illustrated Pictorial Boards.

N.B.—Other Volumes in Preparation.

*** *The extraordinary value and bulk for the money offered in the above List is quite unprecedented, each volume being in itself a treasury of interesting reading.*

SIXPENNY LIBRARY

OF

ROMANCE AND ADVENTURE.

*** Containing first-class Reprints and Original Works of an interesting character. Each Volume is complete in itself, contains 128 or 160 pages Crown 8vo, or 240 pages Foolscap 8vo, printed on good Paper, done up in handsome Illustrated Coloured Cover.

Price 6d. each, or Free by Post for 7 Stamps.

1. **The Scottish Chiefs. By Miss Jane Porter.**
2. **St. Clair of the Isles; or, The Outlaws' Revenge.**

3. Thaddeus of Warsaw. By Miss Jane Porter.
4. The Warrior Brothers: a Romance of Love and Crime.
5. The Insurgent Chief: a Romance of the Irish Rebellion.
6. The Chamber Mystery; or, A Father's Crime.
7. The Pirate of the Slave Coast.
8. The Shawnee Fiend; or, Nick of the Woods.
9. Ripperda the Renegade; or, The Siege of Ceuta.
10. The Arkansas Ranger; or, Dingle the Backwoodsman.
11. Neverfail; or, The Children of the Border.
12. The White Queen and the Mohawk Chief.
13. Paul the Rover; or, The Scourge of the Antilles.
14. The Witch of the Wave; or, The Rover's Captive.
15. The Heir and the Usurper.
16. The Mystic Tie: a Tale of the Camp and Court of Buonaparte.
17. The Turkish Slave; or, The Dumb Dwarf of Constantinople.
18. Disinherited; or, The Heir of Motcombe.
19. The Silver Hand: a Story of Land and Sea.
20. The King's Talisman: an Eastern Romance.
21. The Child of the Sea; or, The Pirate's Adopted.
22. Hearts of Steel; or, The Celt and the Saxon.
23. Galloping O'Hogan; a Romance of Sarsfield.
24. Fitzhern; or, The Rover of the Irish Seas.
25. Michael Dwyer: the Insurgent Captain of the Wicklow Mountains.
26. The Virginian Hunter; or, The Mystery of the Backwoods.
27. The Lover's Revenge; or, The Brothers of the Prairie.
28. Romances of Love, War, and Mystery.
29. Too Late; and other Tales.
30. Alley Sheridan, by W. Carleton, and Other Tales.

New Volumes at Press.